DATE DUE

NOV 0 9 1993	
SEP 0 9 1996	
NOV - 5 1997	

BRODART   Cat. No. 23-221

Columbian Consequences

A Contribution from the Society for American Archaeology
in Recognition of the Columbian Quincentenary
1492–1992

Columbian Consequences

Volume 3

The Spanish Borderlands in Pan-American Perspective

Edited by David Hurst Thomas

Smithsonian Institution Press, Washington and London

Copyright © 1991 by Smithsonian Institution
All rights reserved
Editor: Vicky Macintyre
Designer: Janice Wheeler

Library of Congress Cataloging-in-Publication Data

The Spanish borderlands in Pan-American perspective / edited by David
  Hurst Thomas.
        p.   cm. — (Columbian consequences ; v. 3)
    Includes bibliographical references and index.
    ISBN 0–87474–388–5 (alk. paper)
    1. Spaniards—Southwest, New—History.   2. Spaniards—Southern
States—History.   3. Columbus, Christopher—Influence.   4. Indians
of North America—Southwest, New—First contact with Occidental
civilization.   5. Indians of North America—Southern States—First
contact with Occidental civilization.   6. Southwest, New—History—
to 1848.   7. Southern States—History—Colonial period, ca.
1600–1775.   8. United States—Civilization—Spanish influences.
9. Latin America—Civilization—Spanish influences.   I. Thomas,
David Hurst.   II. Series.
F799.C66   1989 vol. 3
979 s—dc20   91-7111
[970.01′6]   CIP

British Library Cataloguing-in-Publication Data available

Manufactured in the United States of America

10   9   8   7   6   5   4   3   2   1
98   97   96   95   94   93   92   91   90
⊗The paper used in this publication meets the minimum requirements of the American
National Standard for Permanence of Paper for Printed Library Materials Z39.48–1984.

Columbian Consequences

Volume 1   Archaeological and Historical Perspectives on the Spanish Borderlands West
(previously published)

Volume 2   Archaeological and Historical Perspectives on the Spanish Borderlands East
(previously published)

Volume 3   The Spanish Borderlands in Pan-American Perspective

Vicky Macintyre edited each of the manuscripts in these three volumes, worked with the individual contributors, collaborated with the volume editor, organized and proofed all the art, and monitored corrections on final copy of the whole. Her editing skill, professional expertise, and resolute intelligence, gratefully acknowledged, are imprinted upon these pages.

Contents

List of Illustrations

David Hurst Thomas

Cubist Perspectives on the Spanish Borderlands: Past, Present, and Future

In the *Columbian Consequences* seminars, we attempt to explore the range of contemporary thought about New World encounters and to provide an interested public with an accurate and factual assessment of what did—and what did not—transpire as a result of the Columbian encounter. Specifically, we have probed the social, demographic, ecological, ideological, and human repercussions of European-Native American encounters across the Spanish Borderlands. Although initiated and cosponsored by the Society of American Archaeology, this inquiry moves far beyond the traditional scope of archaeological investigation, drawing together a diverse assortment of perspectives. Nine symposia, involving 107 scholars, have been held, and the results are presented in this three-volume series.

The format of *Columbian Consequences* has been engineered to bring the fruits of this inquiry to both the scholarly community and the public at large. Overviews prepared by leading scholars in the field synthesize current thinking about the specific geographical setting, the Native American context, the history of European involvement, and the history of scholarly research. Each overview also contains a concise chronological table of salient events and extensive suggestions for additional reading.

The first installment addresses the European-Native American interface along the western Spanish Borderlands—from the Pacific Slope across the southwestern heartland to East Texas, from Russian Fort Ross to southern Baja California (Thomas 1989a). The participants brought to the project a wide range of backgrounds that enabled them to inspect the Spanish Borderlands from numerous angles. Many are practicing archaeologists; their essays treat the surviving material evidence relating to the sociopolitics, economics, iconography, and the physical environment of the Contact period in the Spanish Borderlands West. Other participants provide a critical balance from the disciplines of American history, art history, ethnohistory, physical anthropology, geography, and Native American studies.

The second contribution in the *Columbian Consequences* series (Thomas 1990) takes up a similar agenda for the Spanish Borderlands East, concentrating on La Florida (modern Florida, Georgia, and South Carolina), the greater Southeast, and the Caribbean. In that volume, 45 scholars dissect the Hispanic-Native American interactions that resulted from the militant entradas into the eastern borderlands, the stubborn colonies, and the durable missions that held sway over the southeastern landscape for more than a century. Archaeologists present fresh (if at times conflicting) evidence that is reshaping our perception of where early explorers like de Soto went and whom they encountered along the way. Other archaeologists present up-to-date interpretations, fleshing out our knowledge of the demography, economics, architecture, and social dynamics of the frontier towns and missions that sprang up in the second wave of interaction. Several borderlands historians contribute insights derived from documents handed down by the Spaniards themselves. A Franciscan scholar tells us why contemporary Catholics are keeping up with the fast-breaking archaeological news from Spanish Florida.

Columbian Consequences in Cubist Perspective

In the initial chapter of the *Columbian Consequences* series, I argued for a *cubist* perspective to Spanish Borderlands scholarship (Thomas 1989b). The early twentieth-century cubist movement seemed to me an appropriate analogy because it was the cubists who invalidated the restrictive conventions that had characterized Western art since the Renaissance. For centuries, artists had labored to perfect various illusionary devices for abbreviating three-dimensional visual reality onto a synthetic two-dimensional medium. In effect, such art tried to convince the viewer that reality was best seen from a single, conventional perspective. In place of this decorous, Renaissance vantage point, the cubists felt that one's perspective could—and should—be shifted at will. Picasso and his cubist colleagues thus broke with the European illusionistic tradition and rejected as self-delusion any pretense at absolute visual truth. Rather than rendering a snapshot of objects as they momentarily appeared to the eye, the cubists reordered and rendered the images conceptually, attempting to register previously unspoken states of mind. Rejecting classical norms for the human figure, they reduced anatomical parts to geometrical lozenges and triangles, abandoning normal anatomical proportions altogether.

Here, we compare traditional Spanish Borderlands scholarship to the work of the Renaissance masters, both of which endeavored to capture reality from a single perspective—the snapshot of the past approach. We argue instead that a more thorough understanding of the Columbian encounters is possible only through a cubist approach. Just as Renaissance painters believed that they were depicting reality, some borderlands scholars and special interest groups persist even today in pursuing and promoting their single-point version of the "truth"—the way it *really* was. But the only truth is the artificiality of our perspectives because, to one degree or another, all views of the human past are created by those telling the story.

In *Columbian Consequences*, we approach the past from multiple directions simultaneously. While we do not reject most conventional borderlands scholarship, we, like the cubists, think that the past is best addressed by considering fresh, even conflicting perspectives as well. Accordingly, we search the borderlands for both traditional and novel approaches, augmenting the positive aspects of Boltonian scholarship with newer insights from other directions, including historical archaeology, Native American studies, historical demography, and ethnohistory. The *Columbian Consequences* seminars attempt to provide an overarching mechanism of balance, criticism, and synthesis—stressing throughout the importance of recognizing multiple pasts, and the necessity of decoupling intellectual inquiry from its associated mythologies. We have been more successful in some places than in others.

In this, the final *Columbian Consequences* volume, we apply our cubist strategy to seek an understanding of the Pan-American processes behind the borderlands experience: past, present, and future.

Learning from Scholarship Past

In Part 1, we shift the temporal perspective to the past, to see how late nineteenth-century America viewed the Columbian encounter. The inquiry is basically epistemological, a longitudinal look at a century of scholarship and public opinion that conditioned contemporary perceptions about Native American–European interactions across the 4,000-mile expanse of the Spanish Borderlands.

The cubists employed their art to simulate their perceptions of the basic learning process. They drew upon the philosophy of Henri Bergson and others who emphasized the role of duration in human experience. Cubist epistemology recognized that with the passage of time, an observer accumulates in the memory a store of perceptual information about a given object from the external, visible world. It is this accumulated experience that becomes the basis of one's conceptual knowledge of that object. Because human perception evolves not from the single, all-encompassing glance, but rather from an infinite number of momentary glimpses, cubist painters attempted to depict objects as one knows them to be, rather than as one sees them at any given point in time—from several angles at once.

We explore accumulated experience in the cubist's sense by taking a retrospective look at the impact of previous Columbus-related "celebrations," especially the Columbian Quatrocentenary held at the Chicago World's Fair of 1893. Such international encounters conditioned the direction of scholarly research for a century, and the chapters by Raymond Fogelson and Ira Jacknis explore the implications of the World Columbian Exposition. Other chapters place the Chicago fair in a broader intellectual framework. David Weber examines the history and evolution of the Spanish Borderlands as a conceptual device. Dora Crouch describes how the sixteenth-century Spanish colonists turned to the Romans for guidance in constructing their ambitious New World utopia. Catherine Fowler and Don Fowler search the evidence from the late nineteenth- and early twentieth-century world's fairs to clarify the roots of anthropology's critical concept of "the ethnographic present"; they also explain how American Indian people eventually became lumped with the rest of so-called natural history. My own contribution explores California's elaborate nineteenth-century mission myth and its influence on western perceptions, not only of bygone Indian and Hispanic pasts, but of contemporary America's Far West.

Learning from the Mesoamerican and Central American Experience

The cubists insisted on enlarging the spectator's vision to include multiple, simultaneous views of a subject. In the second set of papers, we introduce considerable spatial variability to the *Columbian Consequences*. Several scholars investigate the Hispanic colonial strategies employed in the Mesoamerican and Central American heartland; lessons learned in these early encounters were ultimately taken northward to the borderlands. These chapters also attempt to define the range of Native American counterstrategies for coping with the Hispanic conquest. Although some indigenous groups were overwhelmed almost overnight, others retain their distinctive cultural identity even today.

This look southward both complements and contrasts with the survival strategies played out along the Spanish Borderlands proper. These chapters highlight a little-known but rapidly growing inquiry into the native context of colonialism. Although many of the contributions remain at the descriptive, empirical level, this is truly trail-blazing research. These dozen chapters, addressing the Native American–Hispanic interactions in this pivotal arena, provide a compelling contrast to the colonial experience on the northern borderlands.

Looking toward the Horizon of Borderlands Research

The final part of *Columbian Consequences* looks to the future of borderlands scholarship. Prediction is always a precarious exercise, but this is precisely what we attempt. We feel strongly that, if properly conducted, our pre-1992 stocktaking stands to condition the direction and strategies of scholarly research and the public perception of the borderlands past for decades to come.

Having assayed the nature of borderlands research over the past century, we conclude that the most significant, potentially most revolutionary horizons involve new perceptions of the demographic consequences of European-Native American contacts. Although still in the developmental stages, the emerging demographic synthesis suggests a radically transfigured view of 1492 America.

These chapters assess the consequences of catastrophic depopulation in the early years of the Columbian encounter. As in Part 1, the contributions are epistemological; as Ann Ramenofsky points out, this unlikely consortium of scholars shares the belief that the full impact of disease on Native American populations has yet to be acknowledged.

The absolute degree of depopulations is hotly debated, and settling upon precise population figures is not the issue. Rather, these chapters call into question all assumptions deriving from the so-called *ethnographic present* in Native America. These contributions suggest the strong possibility that epidemic diseases could have—some would say must have—swept across parts of Native America with such velocity that assumptions of cultural continuity between prehistoric and protohistoric populations must be closely scrutinized. Robert Dunnell suggests that the destruction of indigenous cultural systems and the resulting founders' effects were so extensive that the validity of the extant ethnographic record must be questioned. And without solid ethnographic underpinning, whither American archaeology and history?

If research into the radically changing picture of Native American demographics lives up to its present potential—and the issues raised are by no means resolved—then archaeologists, ethnologists, historians, and geographers, and perhaps even some Indians, will soon be required to rethink current assumptions, and to reassess prevailing opinions about the very nature of Precolumbian Native America. We feel that understanding the nature and impact of the demographic collapse may be the primary Columbian consequence yet to be fully explored.

Cubist Perspectives: How Are We Doing?

Like the cubist paintings themselves, the results of the *Columbian Consequences* seminars will not be uniformly pleasing nor universally accepted by the public. Without question, the Renaissance masters produced artwork more pleasing to many eyes than were those of the cubists, more comfortable views of a conventional reality. Similarly, we will surely disappoint any readers looking for "the definitive history" of Hispanic–Native American interactions in the Spanish Borderlands. Other readers, those personally more comfortable with conventional face-front perspectives, will resent the intrusion of collateral, sometimes contradictory viewpoints. But, as we have repeatedly emphasized, several distinct histories were played out on the borderlands. Some of these are well-known, but others are only now being discovered. We have chosen to emphasize diversity at the expense, perhaps, of harmony.

So, the closing concern is this: How well have our cubist perspectives served us?

While I do not anticipate consensus, I feel that, in general, we rather successfully approximated our ambition—to move away from the quest for absolute truth, seeking instead to view past events from multifold directions concurrently. We broke ranks with traditional borderlands historians by relying heavily on the non-Hispanic, nonwritten records of the past. We looked not only at the diversity and evolution of Hispanic objectives, but also encountered numerous Native American counterstrategies for coping with the European intrusions.

Accordingly, the 93 chapters of *Columbian Consequences* have enlisted a broad sweep of scholarly opinions from an equally diverse range of disciplines. In all, we involved 64 archaeologists, 11 historians, 9 physical anthropologists, 9 ethnohistorians, 6 cultural anthropologists, 5 art historians, and 3 geographers. Included in the dialogue were 4 archaeologists who hail from Latin America, two Native American scholars, one Franciscan historian, and one Jesuit ethnohistorian. It is not my intention to synthesize this multifarious concoction, but I think it fair to conclude that we have looked to a broad community of scholars representing widely different intellectual persuasions. Thus, in one sense, we accomplished our mission.

But, viewed from a slightly different—perhaps more appropriately cubist—vantage point, the results remain somewhat frustrating and dissatisfying. Any objective assessment of the Columbian Consequences inquiry (if there is such a thing) would point out that not only are the Native American, Latin American, and Hispanic perspectives seriously underrepresented, but less than a third of the participants are women.

In other words, despite our best efforts to elicit an extended suite of opinion and perspective, the final result remains biased toward white, Anglo, male scholarship.

Some of this lingering bias doubtless reflects my own parochialism in drawing together the seminar participants. In other cases, we encountered well-qualified, if contentious, cliques and individuals who refused our invitation to participate. Clear-cut peer pressure removed a couple of highly desirable collaborators. To these select few, we seemed to personify an only slightly warmed-over conventional wisdom. So it goes.

But provincialism and factualism are not the complete story. It remains painfully clear that significant obstacles still remain for minorities and women who wish to pursue careers in any kind of scholarship, borderlands or otherwise. As a direct result, not enough do.

This is why the proceeds from all three volumes of *Columbian Consequences* have been specifically earmarked to address this situation, if only in a small way. The *Columbian Consequences* royalties will establish a series of scholarships to assist qualified American Indians aspiring to become professional archaeologists. As discussed in Chapter 6, the Native American Scholarship Fund (sponsored by the Society for American Archaeology) will show that professional scholars recognize—and wish to do something about—the acute difficulties still facing Indians who seek higher education. In this program, we are actively soliciting private donations and matching revenues to assist and encourage qualified

American Indians in pursuing graduate education in the field of American archaeology.

The Native American Scholarship Fund is a bounded, and very limited beginning. But we hope that it sends a message to upcoming generations that those of us in the existing scholarly community are indeed serious about encouraging a diversity of opinion from a wide range of constituent groups. The meaningful involvement of scholars who happen to be minority or women will be the final step in implementing a thoroughly cubist perspective.

Acknowledgments

I am especially grateful to the officers of the Society for American Archaeology (SAA) for their interest in and support of the *Columbian Consequences* enterprise: Presidents Dena Dincauze, Don Fowler, Prudence Rice, and Jerry Sabloff; James A. Moore, program chair of the 1990 annual meetings in Las Vegas; and SAA Executive Committee members Robert Bettinger, Kathleen Deagan, and Bruce Smith.

The Advisory Board for this final volume consisted of Don Fowler, Grant Jones, David Pendergast, and Ann Ramenofsky. Each provided unparalleled support in helping to organize the various symposia, helping to chair the sessions, reviewing draft manuscripts, and, where appropriate, preparing the topical overviews that introduce each subdivision.

I am likewise grateful to the staff of the Smithsonian Institution Press for their perseverance through this extensive ambitious project, particularly Daniel Goodwin, Vicky Macintyre, and Ruth Spiegel.

Dennis O'Brien prepared the graphics throughout the volume, and I also thank Margot Dembo and Lorann S. A. Pendleton of the American Museum of Natural History for helping out in so many useful ways.

References

Thomas, David Hurst (editor)
    1989a *Columbian Consequences*, vol. 1, *Archaeological and Historical Perspectives on the Spanish Borderlands West*. Smithsonian Institution Press, Washington D.C.
    1989b Columbian Consequences, The Spanish Borderlands in Cubist Perspective. In *Columbian Consequences*, vol. 1, *Archaeological and Historical Perspectives on the Spanish Borderlands West*, pp. 1–14. Smithsonian Institution Press, Washington D.C.
    1990 *Columbian Consequences*, vol. 2, *Archaeological and Historical Perspectives on the Spanish Borderlands East*. Smithsonian Institution Press, Washington D.C.

CALVIN AND HOBBES COPYRIGHT 1990. UNIVERSAL PRESS SYNDICATE.
(Reprinted with permission. All rights reserved)

Columbian Consequences

Part 1 ■

Restrospective on a Century of Borderlands Scholarship

Chapter 1 ■

David J. Weber

The Idea of the Spanish Borderlands

In 1921, historian Herbert Eugene Bolton introduced the term "Spanish Border-lands" to American scholarship when he included it in the title of a small book, *The Spanish Borderlands: A Chronicle of Old Florida and the Southwest*.[1] Bolton defined the borderlands as "the regions between Florida and California, now belonging to the United States, over which Spain held sway for centuries." Bolton believed that throughout this area, which corresponds roughly to the present Sunbelt, "the imprint of Spain's sway is still deep and clear." He pointed to Spanish influence on place names, language, food, architecture, law, and literature (1921:vii). Bolton's idea was, quite simply, to expand the scope of American history, which had previously emphasized English, Dutch, and French antecedents, to include an appreciative awareness of the nation's long-neglected Hispanic origins in the borderlands.[2]

Herbert Bolton's slender volume gave an enduring name to the Spanish Borderlands, but it contained no elaboration of the idea. Bolton explained it more fully in subsequent works, particularly in an essay entitled "Defensive Spanish Expansion and the Significance of the Borderlands" (1930). That essay reveals several features of the Spanish Borderlands as Bolton imagined them. First, he saw the borderlands as both a place and a process—"the meeting place and fusing place of two streams of European civilization, one coming from the south, the other from the north" (p. 36). Second, he exhibited unabashed affection for his subject, describing the history of the borderlands as "picturesque" and "romantic" (p. 1). Third, he defined the borderlands as existing within the framework of the present-day United States, even as he recognized that it occupied one of the fringes of Spain's colonial American empire.

The Hispanic "imprint" that Bolton perceived has grown more apparent than it was in his day. Not only have the numbers of Hispanics in the Sunbelt grown astonishingly in the twentieth century, but reminders of the Hispanic past have become more visible. Preservationists have lovingly restored or reconstructed landmarks from the Spanish era, and developers have created new structures and even entire communities in "Spanish" styles. The number of books and articles that examine North America's Hispanic heritage has also proliferated, with much of the fresh research originating from the so-called Bolton or Spanish Borderlands school of American historiography.[3] Indeed, since Bolton introduced it and popularized it, the idea of the "Spanish Borderlands" as a distinctive and important American region has won currency among humanists and social scientists, although they do not always agree about its meaning or significance. Bolton himself still enjoys a reputation as one of America's preeminent historians of the frontier, along with Frederick Jackson Turner and Walter Prescott Webb.[4]

Earliest Histories

By asserting that the history of the Spanish Borderlands represented a distinctive, significant, and appealing part of the larger history of the United States, Herbert Bolton implicitly rejected the views of those Englishmen and Anglo-Americans who first wrote about Spain's North American provinces.[5] Initially, foreigners did not see Spain's provinces as a single region or as a place with a history worth recording. Indeed, to some of the earliest travelers and writers, the area seemed to have no written past. Of all the borderlands provinces, the isolated interior of the continent seemed most obscure to outsiders.[6] In late 1853, for example, William Watts Hart Davis, a Massachusetts lawyer and distinguished volunteer in the recent war with Mexico, came to New Mexico as the new U.S. district attorney. Curious about this region that the United States had recently wrested from Mexico, Davis later recalled: "I made inquiries . . . about the history of the country but I scarcely met an individual who could give me any reliable information, nor were books on the subject to be had" (1869:vi).

Like visitors to the Southwest both before and after him, Davis had the impression that he had entered a historiographical void—a place without a remembered or recorded history. He was wrong. By the early seventeenth century, Spaniards had already written histories of their own explorations and initial settlement of what is today southwestern America.[7] They had also recorded their activities along the Gulf of Mexico and the Atlantic.[8] Most of Spain's chroniclers and historians had known the Spanish Borderlands by its parts rather than imagining it as a whole (although some of the earliest chroniclers imagined the parts to be the whole). They had written about Florida, where Spain planted its first permanent settlement in North America at St. Augustine in 1565. They had written about New Mexico, where permanent Spanish settlement began in 1598; about Arizona, where Jesuits first proselytized about 1700; about Texas, whose first enduring missions, run by Franciscans, had their beginnings in 1716; about Louisiana, held by Spain from 1763 to 1800; and about California, where Spanish colonization got under way in 1769.

Each of these areas, then, had its own historical literature before Anglo-Americans arrived on the scene, but learning about the early history of the Spanish Borderlands proved difficult for Davis and other early Anglo-American visitors, just as it had for Spanish chroniclers who preceded them.[9] Much of the literature had remained unpublished or obscure. A half-century before Davis came to Santa Fe, a Spanish mining engineer, José Cortés, noted in a report to his king: "In Mexico . . . the people speak with as much ignorance about the regions immediately to the north as they might about Constantinople" (1989:17 –18). Scanty information about the past resulted in remarkable misunderstandings, as in the case of one writer (Williams 1976:91–92) who was mystified by the presence of Spanish artifacts in the interior of Florida. In a book published in 1827, he explained that they had been left by lost survivors of Hernando de Soto's expedition who had built a civilization in Florida that lasted for over a hundred years until it became "effeminate" and collapsed.

Nonetheless, when William Davis and other early American visitors to the borderlands persisted in their inquiries, they discovered that some of the history of the old Spanish provinces had been published. Moreover, vast quantities of documents remained from which scholars could reconstruct still more of the region's past. Utilizing these archival sources and early Spanish imprints, Anglophones began to rewrite the histories of each of the old Spanish provinces, from California to Florida.

In contrast to Bolton's appreciative view of borderlands history as "picturesque" and "romantic," most of the early works by English-speaking foreigners took a decidedly negative tone. The first book that William Davis published as a result of his labors in New Mexico, *El Gringo; or, New Mexico and Her People* (1857), proved no exception. Certain of the inferiority of Hispanic institutions, particularly the Catholic Church and the Spanish monarchy, and convinced of profound defects in the Spanish character, including laziness, untrustworthiness, cowardliness, and superstition, writers such as Davis made little effort to conceal their prejudices.

The anti-Hispanic sentiment that characterized the earliest English-language writing on the borderlands reflected deeper prejudices that distorted understanding of Spain's colonizing activities throughout the western hemisphere (Powell 1971:118–122; Williams 1955:1:157–160). The anti-Mexican prejudices of writers such as Davis had their roots in the Hispanophobia of Anglo Americans' English forebears. Together with other Europeans, Englishmen elaborated what Spaniards would come to call the *leyenda negra*—the Black Legend. In addition to Hispanophobia, anti-Mexican sentiment in the southwestern United States was reinforced by Anglo-Americans' historic disdain for Indian culture, xenophobia, abhorrence of miscegenation, and racism (De León 1983:1–13; Paredes 1977). Writers such as Thomas Jefferson Farnham deplored "the mingling of the Indian and white races in California and Mexico," who were, he said, condemned by the laws of nature to "a constitution less robust than that of either race from which [they] sprang. . . . They must fade away" (1844, quoted in Weber 1979:295).

In the southeastern borderlands, virulent racism toward mestizos did not become an important source of Hispanophobia, for miscegenation was not a conspicuous feature of Hispanic life in places like Mobile, Pensacola, or St. Augustine. Nonetheless, Hispanophobia also characterized some of the early English and Anglo-American descriptions of Florida. Among the more notable examples was the Reverend Rufus King Sewall. Apparently a descendant of the seventeenth-century Puritan and Hispanophobe Samuel Sewall, Rufus Sewall settled in St. Augustine in 1845, where he became pastor of the Presbyterian church. Three years later he published a small book, *Sketches of St. Augustine*, in which he characterized one segment of the town's Hispanic residents as being "of servile extraction" and lacking "enterprise." The target of his criticism, descendants of immigrants from Minorca, drove Sewall from town and tore the offensive pages from all available copies of his book (Sewall 1976:xvii–xix).[10]

The Romantic View

In the last decades of the nineteenth century, Anglo-Americans' critical stance toward Hispanics and their history in North America began to soften. In some areas, vilification gave way to sentimentality, and Hispanophilia supplanted Hispanophobia. This shift took place at different rates in different areas of the borderlands depending on local circumstances, but a necessary precondition seemed to be the decline of Hispanic economic and political power.

As the Anglo-American population grew in proportion to the number of Hispanics across the southern rim of America, and as Hispanics became assimilated or marginalized, they ceased to threaten Anglo-American hegemony (large-scale immigration from Mexico and the Caribbean has been a twentieth-century phenomenon). Thus, it became safe for Anglo Americans to legitimize the past of this vanquished people—to render their history respectable.

In the Far Southwest, from New Mexico to California, a romanticized version of the Hispanic past had special utility for Anglo-American newcomers. It permitted rootless English-speaking immigrants to identify with the region's earliest European settlers, and it provided continuity, tradition, regional identity, and pride. Indeed, in the rapidly industrializing and increasingly urban America of the late 1800s, alienated historians were among those who sentimentalized the Hispanic past as a bucolic era.[11]

In southwestern America, the shift from vilification to romanticization was accompanied in the Anglo-American consciousness[12] by the idea of an Anglo-Hispanic borderland as a place where, in the words of historian Burl Noggle, writers and scholars began "to recognize and to value the peculiar blending of cultures that characterized the region" (Noggle 1959:131). Noggle has argued that the idea of the "borderlands" emerged in the late nineteenth century, well before the publication in 1921 of Bolton's *Spanish Borderlands*: "When Professor Bolton gave the borderlands a name, he brought to fruition a concept that had been slowly maturing" (p. 131). Noggle seems to have had in mind just part of Bolton's idea—that of the borderlands as a meeting place of two European cultures.

Some of the most vivid examples of the late-nineteenth-century romanticization of borderlands history are to be found in Charles F. Lummis's popular writings on the Southwest. "The Spanish pioneering of America was the largest and most marvelous feat of memory in all history," Lummis (1889:12) enthused in the opening pages of *The Spanish Pioneers*. He lamented the absence of information on Spanish colonization in American textbooks, noting that "it was not possible for a Saxon boy to learn that truth in my boyhood" (1889:12). Attempting to counter the Hispanophobia that he saw as characteristic of previous writing, Lummis applauded the "humane and progressive spirit" of the Spaniards in America (1889:23).[13] Lummis's unabashedly pro-Spanish viewpoint and his charge that American history was unbalanced soon dominated the literature on the Spanish Borderlands and became a major motif of the Bolton school.[14]

Together with the development of a Hispanophilic counterweight to the American Hispanophobia came a growing professionalization of historical work along the Spanish rim in the 1880s. No one better exemplified this, or had produced a more substantial oeuvre, than Hubert Howe Bancroft. Working in San Francisco, Bancroft applied the techniques of an American businessman to the writing of history and produced 39 massive volumes based on a stunning foundation of archival sources, and on oral interviews that he had commissioned.[15]

Bancroft's *Works*, which included the two-volume *The North Mexican States and Texas* (1889), the one-volume *History of Arizona and New Mexico, 1530–1888* (1889), the *History of California* (1884–90) in seven volumes, and the single-volume *California Pastoral, 1769–1848* (1888), devoted considerable attention to Spain in North America. Looking back at California's Hispanic past, Bancroft expressed the new romanticism of his era succinctly: "Never before or since was there a spot in America where life was a long happy holiday, where there was less labor, less care or trouble" (Bancroft 1888:179).[16] One Spanish writer (Romera-Novarro 1917:325) credits Bancroft with "breaking the traditional legend of our disgraceful and barbarous conquest and colonization of America, and reestablishing, in part, the true history and initiating the new orientation so favorable to the Spanish cause."[17] That, however, may be giving Bancroft more credit than he deserves, for he had a substantial number of accomplices among the California literati.

Bancroft had the advantage of being at the right place at the right time. His work, and Bolton's as well, had been anticipated in the Southeast a generation before by Buckingham Smith, whose aspirations had exceeded his achievements. Smith, who was born on Cumberland Island, Georgia, and had spent his childhood in St. Augustine, was a generation ahead of his time when he issued a call in midcentury for a multivolume "Documentary History of that part of the

United States once under Spanish domination."[18] Had it succeeded, Smith would have launched the first effort to document comprehensively the Spanish past in North America, but Smith did not enjoy Bancroft's good fortune. Only one volume appeared.[19] The number of subscribers remained insufficient to publish subsequent titles, and Smith lacked personal resources to continue the project.

It may be that in the Southeast, as one historian has noted, Smith met "sharp hostility . . . [because] the vigorous old Elizabethan and 'leyenda negra' conception of Spain, Mexicans, and those of Hispanic race was very alive" (Bernstein 1961:152). Hispanics, however, had posed no political, economic, or cultural threat to Anglo-Americans in the Southeast after 1821. There, too, historians and other writers romanticized the Spanish era, especially in the decades following the Civil War, but the idea of the Spanish Borderlands failed to win the popular currency in the Southeast that it enjoyed in the Southwest.[20] In the case of Georgia, for example, one historian (Coulter 1937:v) has noted that until the mid–1920s "it was not generally known that Spaniards had occupied Georgia."

Explanations other than Hispanophobia suggest themselves for the indifference of Southerners to the idea of the Spanish Borderlands. First, relatively few Hispanic residents remained in the region to remind Anglo-Americans of Spanish antecedents. Then, too, crumbling missions that served as powerful symbols of the Spanish past across much of the Southwest had vanished almost entirely in the Southeast (Thomas 1988:78–81). Bolton's observation that "scattered all the way from Georgia to San Francisco are the ruins of Spanish missions" proved to be false (1921:vii; see Floyd 1937:161–189). Moreover, Anglo-Americans in the Deep South did not have to reach back to the Spanish era to find a usable past; their own regional traditions stretched into the seventeenth and eighteenth centuries and provided a strong sense of continuity. In Louisiana, where Anglo-Americans' roots ran only to the nineteenth century, French language and culture had remained preeminent even during the years that the Spanish flag flew over Louisiana, from 1763 to 1800. As one writer (Williams 1955:1:311) has noted, over forty years of Spanish rule seemed "to solidify French characteristics rather than to establish . . . a quality basically Spanish" (see also Lachance 1982:47–81).

The idea of the Spanish Borderlands, then, fell on more fertile soil in the Far Southwest. There, especially in California and New Mexico, the views of Lummis, Bancroft, Bolton, and others flourished exuberantly. Those writers drew inspiration from popular culture even as they, in turn, inspired popular culture and gave the romantic view scholarly respectability. Nonetheless, Hispanophilia did not completely replace the Hispanophobia that had dominated historical writing in southwestern America up to the 1880s. Bancroft himself displayed a deep ambivalence toward Hispanic culture, and other writers, such as Frank Blackmar and Elliott Coues, seemed ill-disposed toward Spain and Spaniards even as they studied them.[21] Texas historians in particular, shaped perhaps by what some writers have termed an "Alamo complex," were slow to embrace the new appreciation of *lo español* (De León 1983; Stagner 1981).[22]

The Bolton School and Its Critics

In contrast to Frederick Jackson Turner, who is remembered primarily for a single seminal idea, Herbert Eugene Bolton not only articulated and popularized an idea, but added prodigiously to the historiography of his field. As Bolton once explained to Turner, "a field so new and so foreign to most American students" required writing that was sometimes "fearfully heavy with details" (June 4, 1915, quoted in Bannon 1978:151). Much of the detail that Bolton gathered came from the bedrock of archival sources. He was fond of translating and editing previously unpublished documents and did so extravagantly. His most significant edited works included *Athanase de Mézières and the Louisiana-Texas Frontier, 1768–1780* (2 vols., 1914), *Kino's Historical Memoir of Pimería Alta* (2 vols., 1919), *Arredondo's Historical Proof of Spain's Title to Georgia* (1925), *Historical Memoirs of New California, by Fray Francisco Palóu* (4 vols., 1926), *Anza's California Expeditions* (5 vols., 1930), and *Pageant in the Wilderness: The Story of the Escalante Expedition to the Interior Basin, 1776* (1950). Bolton also wrote original works, many of which appeared in book-length studies, including: *Texas in the Middle Eighteenth Century* (1915), *The Colonization of North America, 1491–1783* (1920), *The Spanish Borderlands* (1921), *Rim of Christendom: A Biography of Eusebio Francisco Kino* (1936), and *Coronado: Knight of Pueblos and Plains* (1949). Several of Bolton's articles proved as influential as his books, most notably "The Mission as a Frontier Institution in the Spanish American Colonies" (1917), and "The Epic of Greater America" (1933).[23]

Attracted by his enthusiasm, encouragement, accessibility, and his example of extraordinary achievement, students flocked to Bolton like iron filings to a magnet. Over the course of his long professorial career, which began at the University of Texas, Austin, in 1901 and ended with his retirement from the University of California, Berkeley, in 1944, Bolton directed 104 doctoral dissertations and 323 master's theses. Many of his students went on to follow their mentor's example, occupying positions in Latin American history at universities across the nation and publishing widely on the history of the borderlands, the United States, Latin America, and Spain. A roll call of some of the most illustrious of Bolton-trained doctors would include Thomas Maitland Marshall, Charles Chapman, Herbert Ingram Priestley, Charles Wilson Hackett, James Fred Rippy, J. Lloyd Mecham, Arthur Aiton, William Binkley, LeRoy Hafen, George P. Hammond, Abraham Nasatir, John Caughey, Lawrence Kinnaird, John Tate Lanning, Irving Leonard, Alfred Barnaby Thomas, Charles Nowell, Philip Brooks, Peter Masten Dunne, Russell Ewing, Theodore Treutlein, John Haskell Kemble, Engel Sluiter, Adele Ogden, John Francis Bannon, Woodrow Borah, Gregory Crampton, and Max Moorhead.[24]

Bolton, then, had succeeded brilliantly in not only giving voice to the idea of the Spanish Borderlands, but in nurturing its growth into a field with a substantial scholarly literature (Cutter 1983). As he had once explained to Frederick Jackson Turner, "until the field is covered by monographs . . . we shall have no basis for a clear understanding of the work of the Spaniards in the American

West" (June 4, 1915, quoted in Bannon 1978:151). There could be no doubt that Bolton had done his share to see that the field was "covered by monographs."

Nonetheless, when Bolton died in 1953, an important part of his agenda remained unfilled. Although Bolton and his students had opened new horizons in American history, the story of the Spanish Borderlands had not yet been integrated into the larger story of American history. Meanwhile, Latin American historians began to see the borderlands as a field apart from their own—a curious development in light of the fact that Bolton and many of his successors regarded the borderlands as an integral if peripheral area of colonial Spanish America. One of Bolton's former students, John Caughey, articulated the frustration that many Boltonians apparently felt by the 1960s.

> His Spanish borderlands are rejected by Latin Americans and neglected by historians of the West. The general histories and bibliographies of Latin America often are constructed as though these outlying provinces were never Spanish. Western writers tend to treat them as though they were an exotic prior figuration extraneous to all that developed later [Caughey 1965:66].

In arguing that Bolton's borderlands had been "rebuffed," Caughey may have overstated the case, but without question Bolton's ideas and his methodology had come under severe attack. Bolton's narrative verve and skill as a "literary craftsman," which some historians admired (Ewing 1947:79), came to be regarded as rhetorical excess and a symptom of his romanticism.[25] Bolton's emphasis on narrative, drama, and heroic individuals seemed quaint to a generation of historians who had turned to the more impersonal forces of social, economic, and intellectual history. To some scholars, the borderlands idea had become irrelevant and the subject of sharp critiques. In an influential essay, Earl Pomeroy had argued that the roles of Hispanics and other "local foreign groups" had been exaggerated. "Actually," Pomeroy wrote, "the native Spanish and Mexican elements in many parts of the West—particularly California where they are revered today —were small and uninfluential" (Pomeroy 1955:590).[26] Echoing Pomeroy's argument, historian Moses Rischin dismissed the idea of the Spanish Borderlands in California as "eccentric and escapist." "Bolton," Rischin wrote, "contributed little that has enlarged the historical understanding of the United States" (Rischin 1968:51, 50).[27]

Although many historians implicitly defended Bolton's borderlands by reiterating his arguments (Bannon 1970:1–7; Jones 1974:1–10), few historians explicitly defended the Bolton school in print. One exception was France V. Scholes. Harvard-trained, Scholes was not a Bolton student, but in an essay, "Historiography of the Spanish Southwest: Retrospect and Prospect" (1962), Scholes responded vigorously to Bolton's critics, arguing that the field was not "washed up." But he acknowledged that its future health required historians "to enlarge traditional areas of research" and to move into new ones (p. 21). Scholes suggested social, economic, and ethnohistory in particular.

A number of historians followed Scholes's prescription, but in the 1980s some scholars continued to maintain that the field remained underdeveloped. "Borderlands history," José Cuello wrote in an essay that focused on the southwestern borderlands, "has mysteriously lagged behind the thematic and methodological advances that have characterized the study of colonial Mexico's central regions since the end of World War II" (1982:2). Similarly, Michael Scardaville criticized borderlands scholars in the Southeast for concentrating on "traditional and romantic Borderlands themes," and he urged them to "strike out in new directions of scholarship" (1985:188, 190).

One new direction urged upon borderlands scholars was to increase the geographical scope of their inquiry. Howard F. Cline had advanced such an argument in a provocative article, "Imperial Perspectives on the Borderlands" (1962). Like Scholes, Cline was a Harvard-trained historian whose roots were not in the Bolton tradition. Cline agreed with critics that borderlands historians had become obsessed with "pathfinders' trails, or the date a particular mission or town was founded, or the genealogy of a particular local hero or martyr" (p. 174). Beyond that, however, he identified still another problem. From Cline's viewpoint, the study of the borderlands suffered from excessive parochialism. Cline urged historians of the borderlands to place their work in the larger perspective of the Spanish colonial empire, and he suggested the study of "the Greater Borderlands, including the Central American, Caribbean, and Gulf peripheries, together with the vast area of Aridamérica" (p. 173). Comparison with other peripheral areas, he argued, would clarify what was unique to Spanish North America and what was common to borderlands areas in general.

Cline's call for a broader definition of the borderlands was never fully heeded by borderlands specialists. If anything, the field seemed to contract, as some borderlands scholars came to regard the southwestern borderlands as synonymous with the borderlands and to ignore the southeastern borderlands, the region from Louisiana to Florida.[28] Meanwhile, the tendency of many historians of the southwestern borderlands to cross over the present border to pursue themes in northern Mexico led José Cuello (1982) to call for a still more restricted definition of the borderlands. Cuello urged a return to Bolton's original paradigm of the borderlands as existing largely within the boundaries of the present United States. Whereas some historians of the borderlands had lamented that Latin Americanists ignored the borderlands, Cuello found that by the 1980s Latin American historians had embraced it so thoroughly that they had come to confuse it with the study of colonial Mexico. "We are mistaken in our assumption that borderlands history is a natural and logical part of the Latin American field," Cuello wrote. "Rather, it is an exotic subset of United States history that has risen to treat the pre-Anglo, yet European, past of the United States Southwest and Southeast" (p. 2).

Chicano Perspectives

Borderlands historiography vigorously took on new dimensions in American history in the early 1970s as the long-neglected stories of Hispanic peoples in contemporary America—most of them residents of the old Spanish Borderlands —began to be told. Mexican-Americans, the most numerous of the nation's Hispanic minorities, became the special subject of scholarly scrutiny. Some who worked in this new field of Mexican-American history identified themselves as Chicano historians and turned their backs on borderlands scholars whom they regarded as elitist (i.e., interested in the "Spanish" past), antiquarian, and irrelevant. Other historians saw Chicano history as a logical extension of borderlands history—a continuation of Bolton's idea that the borderlands represented "the meeting place and fusing place of two streams of European civilization, one coming from the south, the other from the north" (1921:36).[29] From the perspective of historian Ralph Vigil, Chicano history was "New Borderlands History." But Vigil argued that most writers of Mexican-American history either gave short shrift to the colonial antecedents in the region or handled the subject poorly (Vigil 1973).

Just as many historians of the Mexican-American experience ignored the Spanish Borderlands, many borderlands historians displayed little enthusiasm for studying Mexican Americans. There were, however, important exceptions, among them one of the field's most eminent practitioners, Donald Worcester. In an article entitled "The Significance of the Spanish Borderlands to the United States" (1976), Worcester reminded his readers of the enduring legacy of Spain's long tenure in the region and urged that the field be expanded into the nineteenth and twentieth centuries to include the histories of Hispanic immigrants who continue to settle in North America.

Worcester's expansive definition of the borderlands promised to bring the field up to date and make it more relevant to modern Americans. At the same time, Chicano scholars invigorated the study of the Spanish era with fresh perspectives and methodologies that began to change the way in which scholars told the story of the borderlands (Chávez 1984; Cortés 1983; Weber 1987). While some traditional borderlands historians worried about the distorting effects of presentism on our understanding of the past, one Chicano scholar, Antonio José Ríos Bustamante, wrote a suggestive critique of the method and theory of borderlands historiography, arguing that the Bolton school itself had fallen into the historical fallacy of anachronism by adopting what he termed a "developmentalist" model based on the idea of the rise and fall of civilizations (Ríos Bustamante 1976).

New Directions

By the 1980s, then, the idea of the Spanish Borderlands that seemed so clear in Bolton's day had become murky. Borderlands historians fended off criticism from outside their ranks and wrestled with their own identity. In an essay published in 1987 and prompted by the death of John Francis Bannon, one of Bolton's most vigorous disciples, I explored the field's current malaise as well as its extraordinary vitality as measured by the number and variety of recent publications (Weber 1987). My survey of the literature through the mid–1980s suggested that some of the most interesting new work in the field had come from scholars who had heeded France Scholes's advice to "enlarge traditional areas of research." By the 1980s many borderlands historians had embraced new methodologies, welcomed interdisciplinary approaches, expanded their definition of the border-lands, and become more interested in theory (Dobyns 1980; Swagerty 1984; Weber 1986). In addition, aspects of borderlands history had been illuminated by an extraordinary outpouring of books and articles from specialists in a vari-ety of disciplines, and some historians had expanded the field to include the nineteenth and the twentieth centuries.

Nonetheless, in history departments with a Ph.D. program, the number of fac-ulty with expertise in the study of North America's Spanish colonial era had fallen sharply, and the future of the field had become uncertain. The paucity of historians with expertise in the borderlands as Bolton defined them remains particularly acute in the Southeast. Historian Amy Bushnell recently noted that "there are only four or . . . five historians presently publishing on the first 250 years of Florida history. We are outnumbered by archaeologists at least five to one" (1989:4). Although Bolton had interdisciplinary interests, his idea of the Spanish Borderlands was essentially a historical construction. If present trends continue, however, the history of the borderlands seems likely to be studied without a coterie of sophisticated, university-trained historians.

Specialists have also continued to express dismay that the field has failed to achieve one of Bolton's main goals—to weave the borderlands story into the larger fabric of American history (Axtell 1987). Writing from the perspective of the southeastern borderlands, Michael Scardaville placed much of the responsi-bility for this failure on borderlands historians themselves, who, he argued, had overemphasized the initial exploration and settlement of the borderlands and military and diplomatic themes. In so doing, Scardaville argued, historians "re-inforced the long-held stereotypes of Spanish cruelty, greediness, bigotry, and depravity" (1985:188).

In another recent essay, "Spanish Texas and Borderlands Historiography in Transition: Implications for United States History," Gerald E. Poyo and Gilberto M. Hinojosa (1988) echoed Scardaville's disquiet from a Texas perspective. Like Scardaville, they viewed borderlands historians themselves as partly responsible for the failure of the field to become better integrated into American history. The work of borderlands scholars, they argued, "focused on themes and utilized methodologies that made such integration difficult" (p. 393). Moreover, Poyo and Hinojosa found in the work of borderlands scholars the implication "that the Spanish era was a failure and could thus be dismissed as an integral part of this nation's history" (p. 397). They maintained that the story of the borderlands could be more effectively integrated into the national story if historians would place greater emphasis on socioeconomic history, particularly that of communi-ties and regions, and if historians would avoid the teleological trap of explaining the Spanish Borderlands in terms of its ultimate absorption into the United States. Thus, Poyo and Hinojosa concluded somewhat paradoxically by wonder-ing if "the conventional framework [of U.S. history] is perhaps no longer the most effective conceptual tool for understanding the Spanish Borderlands" (p. 415).

Their question strikes at an apparent contradiction in the borderlands idea as Bolton defined it. Could the borderlands be a place within the "conventional framework" of United States history and yet still transcend national boundaries as "the meeting place and fusing place of two streams of European civilization" (Bolton 1930:36). Apparently Bolton never regarded these aspects of his idea as contradictory. His own writing did focus on what would become the continental United States,[30] but he occasionally worked in what is now northern Mexico and he encouraged his students to examine both sides of the border. Although Bolton's primary purpose was to broaden the scope of the study of U.S. history, he consistently saw himself as a Latin American specialist contributing to the larger history of the hemisphere. Bolton's scholarship, as he once put it, rested "on the borders rather than within the field of most other students" (June 4, 1915, quoted in Bannon 1978:151).

Marginal by definition, as Bolton suggested, the borderlands will certainly remain peripheral to the core areas of both U.S. history and Latin American history. Moreover, if present trends continue, it seems unlikely that the idea of the Spanish Borderlands, as Bolton understood it, will ever regain the vitality that it once enjoyed as a field of historical inquiry. Nonetheless, the idea of the Spanish Borderlands has continued to evolve, just as it has over the last century. Invigorated by the the stunning growth of population in America's Sunbelt (both Hispanic and Anglo) and in Mexico's northern border states, scholars continue to reinvent the borderlands to fit their current multidisciplinary and comparative interests (Hall 1989; Maier 1985; Thomas 1989, 1990).

Notes

This chapter, meant to be suggestive rather than exhaustive, is adapted from my introduction to *The Idea of the Spanish Borderlands: A Sourcebook* (1991). The essay has benefited from comments by Amy Bushnell, of the University of South Alabama, my colleague, John Chávez, and Light Cummins of Austin College. I am also grateful to David Hurst Thomas, at whose urging I wrote this piece.

1. Bolton apparently did not coin the phrase. As he told his editor, "For the main title I prefer *The Spanish Borderlands*. . . . I took the phrase from one of your suggested subtitles." Bolton to Allen Johnson, November 26, 1917, quoted in Bannon (1978:129). Woodbury Lowery (1901 & 1905:1:vii), who, like Bolton, had a transcontinental vision, used the term "Border colonies" to describe the borderlands.

2. See, in particular, Bolton's "Need for the Publication of a Comprehensive Body of Documents Relating to the History of Spanish Activities within the Present Limits of the United States," in Bannon (1964:23–31).

3. As Charles Gibson (1966:189) once noted, "It is probable that no other part of colonial Spanish America has stimulated so extensive a program of research." Bannon (1970) remains the best single-volume introduction to this subject.

4. For a recent appraisal of Bolton's work within the larger context of American historiography, see Kraus and Joyce (1985:277–281).

5. North America in this essay refers to the area north of present-day Mexico.

6. The more accessible coastal provinces of California and Florida seem to have been more visited and written about at early stages of Europeanization than the much more populous province of New Mexico.

7. For a detailed guide to the early chroniclers of southwestern North America, see Wagner (1937). For a lively discussion of their work, see Simmons (1976).

8. Brinton (1859) constitutes one of the earliest English-language guides to the Span-

ish chronicles of southeastern America, and the most complete for its day (some of the manuscripts that Brinton mentions have since been published; some have been translated into English). There is no equivalent of Wagner (1937) for the Southeast.

9. Davis was not the only American writer interested in this subject. The U.S. conquest of New Mexico and California had promoted scholarly inquiry. For a sense of the literature available to an American scholar in northeastern libraries, see Squier (1848). Perhaps the most extensive account of New Mexico's pre–1821 history written in English prior to the Mexican-American War was in Gregg ([1844] 1954:81–91).

10. The immigrants from Minorca, an island that has generally belonged to Spain, included Greeks, Italians, and Corsicans. Residents of Florida in the late eighteenth century usually distinguished Minorcans from "Floridians" (those settled in Florida before the British occupation of 1763) and"Spaniards" (those who immigrated from the Spanish peninsula after Spain regained Florida in 1783). See Corbett (1978:54).

11. There is a considerable literature on this subject in California. For a guide to that literature and a summary of the arguments, see Langum (1983).

12. Hispanic Americans themselves were not immune from the tendency to romanticize. See, for example, Vallejo ([1890] 1973).

13. For an appreciative biography and a guide to other sources, see Fiske and Lummis (1974).

14. See, for example, Lowery (1901 & 1905:1:vii), whose work antedates the Bolton School and who noted in his initial volume that "to arouse the interest of the student in . . . the Spanish history of *our own country* the present work has been undertaken" (italics added).

15. For a full-length biography of Bancroft, see Caughey (1946).

16. Bancroft is quoted in Langum (1983:284). Like many writers of his day, Bancroft conflated the Spanish and Mexican eras of California into a single "golden age."

17. Romera-Novarro is quoted in Williams (1955:1:369). The translation is mine.

18. From the prospectus, quoted in Bernstein (1961:153). The prospectus is not dated, but Bernstein places it at about 1850. Bernstein includes a brief discussion of Smith's life and work, based on unpublished sources.

19. *Colección de varios documentos para la historia de Florida y tierras adyacentes* (1857), issued in 500 copies. Smith's "lands adjacent" to Florida extended as far west as California.

20. There is no study of this subject for the Southwest, but my comments derive in part from a work in progress, "The Spanish Frontier in North America, 1513–1821," in addition to sources cited here.

21. For Bancroft's Hispanophobia, see Vigil (1973); for Blackmar, see Noggle (1959); for Coues, see Ewing (1947).

22. Although Bolton taught at the University of Texas, from 1901 to 1909, his intellectual formation was not in Texas, and it does not seem appropriate to consider him a Texas writer.

23. Lists of Bolton's publications, arranged chronologically, appear in Bannon (1964:333–341; 1978:275–82). For appreciative appraisals of Bolton, see Ewing (1947) and Caughey (1965), in addition to Bannon (1978).

24. A complete list of "Bolton's Academic Progeny" is in Bannon (1978:283–90). The range of their work and their enthusiasm for their teacher is suggested in the two Festchriften they prepared for him (Hammond 1932; Ogden 1945).

25. For a detailed discussion of the rise, partial repudiation, yet continuing vitality of the romanticized image of Mexicans and Mexican Americans in literature, see Robinson (1963).

26. For one of the most devastating commentaries on the romanticization of the Spanish era, see McWilliams ([1948] 1968:35–47).

27. Rischin subsequently extended this argument (1970), accurately quoting John Higham's dismissive evaluation of Bolton ("he gave a specious appearance of significance

to a program of fragmentary research"). But Higham, as I read him, directed that barb at Bolton's famous thesis that the Americas had a common history, not at Bolton's program of borderlands studies. See Higham (1965:41) and also Keen (1985:662), who articulated a view held by some historians well before the 1980s.

28. In his *Spanish Borderlands: A First Reader*, for example, Jones (1974) acknowledged the scholarship on the Southeast, but the title of his book coupled with his decision to omit articles from that area gave the impression that the borderlands extended no farther east than Texas. See, too, Stoddard (1983).

29. For the gulf between Chicano and borderlands history, see Lotchin and Weber (1983) and De León (1989).

30. "In 1921 Bolton probably limited the scope of his Spanish Borderlands to the United States in order to fit the requirements of the series in which it appeared" (Weber 1987:342).

References

Axtell, James
    1987   Europeans, Indians, and the Age of Discovery in American History Textbooks. *American Historical Review* 92:621–632.

Bancroft, Hubert Howe
    1888   *California Pastoral, 1769–1848*. History Co., San Francisco.

Bannon, John Francis
    1970   *The Spanish Borderlands Frontier, 1513–1821*. Holt, Rinehart and Winston, New York.
    1978   *Herbert Eugene Bolton: The Historian and the Man*. University of Arizona Press, Tucson.

Bannon, John Francis (editor)
    1964   *Bolton and the Spanish Borderlands*. University of Oklahoma Press, Norman.

Bernstein, Harry
    1961   *Making an Inter-American Mind*. University of Florida Press, Gainesville.

Bolton, Herbert Eugene
    1921   *The Spanish Borderlands: A Chronicle of Old Florida and the Southwest*. Yale University Press, New Haven, Conn.
    1930   Defensive Spanish Expansion and the Significance of the Borderlands. In *The Trans-Mississippi West*, edited by James F. Willard and Colin B. Goodykoontz, pp. 1–42. University of Colorado, Boulder.

Brinton, Daniel G.
    1859   *Notes on the Floridian Peninsula, Its Literary History, Indian Tribes and Antiquities*. Joseph Sabin, Philadelphia.

Bushnell, Amy Turner
    1989   "Commentary" on "New Approaches to American Indian History in the Colonial South." Presented at Southern Historical Association Annual Meeting, Lexington, Ky.

Caughey, John W.
    1946   *Hubert Howe Bancroft: Historian of the West*. University of California Press, Berkeley.
    1965   Herbert Eugene Bolton. In *Turner, Bolton, and Webb: Three Historians of the American Frontier*, edited by Wilbur R. Jacobs et al., pp. 41–73. University of Washington Press, Seattle.

Chávez, John R.
    1984   *The Lost Land: The Chicano Image of the Southwest*. University of New Mexico Press, Albuquerque.

Cline, Howard, F.
1962 Imperial Perspectives on the Borderlands. In *Probing the American West: Papers from the Santa Fe Conference*, edited by K. Ross Toole et al., pp. 168–174. Museum of New Mexico, Santa Fe.

Corbett, Theodore G.
1978 The Problem of the Household in the Second Spanish Period. In *Eighteenth-Century Florida: The Impact of the American Revolution*, edited by Samuel Proctor, pp. 49–75. University Presses of Florida, Gainesville.

Cortés, Carlos E.
1983 The New Chicano Historiography. In *Borderlands Sourcebook: A Guide to the Literature on Northern Mexico and the American Southwest*, edited by Ellwyn R. Stoddard, Richard L. Nostrand, and Jonathan P. West, pp. 60–63. University of Oklahoma Press, Norman.

Cortés, José
1989 *Views from the Apache Frontier: Report on the Northern Provinces of New Spain by José Cortés, Lieutenant in the Royal Corps of Engineers, 1799*. Edited by Elizabeth A. H. John. Translated by John Wheat. University of Oklahoma Press, Norman.

Coulter, E. Merton, ed.
1937 *Georgia's Disputed Ruins*. University of North Carolina Press, Chapel Hill.

Cuello, José
1982 Beyond the "Borderlands" Is the North of Colonial Mexico: A Latin-Americanist Perspective to the Study of the Mexican North and the United States Southwest. In *Proceedings of the Pacific Coast Council on Latin American Studies*, edited by Kristyna P. Demaree, 9:1–34.

Cutter, Donald C.
1983 The Western Spanish Borderlands. In *Historians and the American West*, edited by Michael P. Malone, pp. 39–56. University of Nebraska Press, Lincoln.

Davis, W. W. H.
1857 *El Gringo; or, New Mexico and Her People*. Harper and Bros., New York.
1869 *The Spanish Conquest of New Mexico*. Harper and Bros., Doylestown, Pa.

De León, Arnoldo
1983 *They Called Them Greasers: Anglo Attitudes toward Mexicans in Texas 1821–1900*. University of Texas Press, Austin.
1989 Whither Borderlands History? A Review Essay. *New Mexico Historical Review* 64:349–360.

Dobyns, Henry F.
1980 The Study of Spanish Colonial Frontier Institutions. In *Spanish Borderlands Research*, edited by Henry F. Dobyns, pp. 5–26. Center for Anthropological Studies, Albuquerque.

Ewing, Russell C.
1947 Modern Histories and Historians of the Spanish Southwest. *Arizona Quarterly* 50:71–82.

Fiske, Turbesé Lummis, and Keith Lummis
1974 *Charles F. Lummis: The Man and his West*. University of Oklahoma Press, Norman.

Floyd, Marmaduke
1937 Certain Tabby Ruins on the Georgia Coast. In *Georgia's Disputed Ruins*, edited by E. Merton Coulter. University of North Carolina Press, Chapel Hill.

Gibson, Charles
1966 *Spain in America*. Harper and Row, New York.

Gregg, Josiah
1954 *Commerce of the Prairies*. Edited by Max L. Moorhead. University of Oklahoma Press, Norman. Originally published 1844.

Hall, Thomas D.
1989 *Social Change in the Southwest, 1350–1880*. University Press of Kansas, Lawrence.

Hammond, George P. (editor)
1932   *New Spain and the Anglo-American West: Historical Contributions Presented to Herbert Eugene Bolton.* 2 vols. Privately Printed, Los Angeles.

Higham, John
1965   *History: The Development of Historical Studies in the United States.* Prentice-Hall, Englewood Cliffs, N.J.

Jones, Oakah L., Jr. (editor)
1974   *The Spanish Borderlands: A First Reader.* Lorrin L. Morrison, Los Angeles.

Keen, Benjamin
1985   Main Currents in United States Writings on Colonial Spanish America, 1884–1984. *Hispanic American Historical Review* 65:657–682.

Kraus, Michael, and Davis D. Joyce
1985   *The Writing of American History.* Rev. ed. University of Oklahoma Press, Norman.

Lachance, Paul
1982   Intermarriage and French Cultural Persistence in Late Spanish and Early American New Orleans. *Histoire sociale—Social History* 15:47–81.

Langum, David J.
1983   From Condemnation to Praise: Shifting Perspectives on Hispanic California. *California History* 61:282–291.

Lotchin, Roger, and David J. Weber
1983   The New Chicano Urban History. *History Teacher* 16:219–247.

Lowery, Woodbury
1901 & 1905   *The Spanish Settlements within the Present Limits of the United States, 1513–1561 and the Spanish Settlements within the Present Limits of the United States: Florida, 1562–1574.* G. P. Putnam's, New York.

Lummis, Charles
1889   *The Spanish Pioneers.* A. C. McClurg, Chicago.

McWilliams, Carey
1968   The Fantasy Heritage. In *North from Mexico: The Spanish-Speaking People of the United States.* Greenwood Press, New York. Originally published 1948.

Maier, Pauline
1985   Colonial History: Is It All Mined Out? *Reviews in American History* 13 (March 1985):6.

Noggle, Burl
1959   Anglo Observers of the Southwest Borderlands, 1825–1890: The Rise of a Concept. *Arizona and the West* 1:105–141.

Ogden, Adele (editor)
1945   *Greater America: Essays in Honor of Herbert Eugene Bolton.* University of California Press, Berkeley.

Paredes, Raymund A.
1977   The Origins of Anti-Mexican Sentiment in the United States. *New Scholar* 6:139–165.

Pomeroy, Earl
1955   Toward a Reorientation of Western History: Continuity and Environment. *Mississippi Valley Historical Review* 41:579–600.

Powell, Philip Wayne
1971   *Tree of Hate: Propaganda and Prejudices Affecting United States Relations with the Hispanic World.* Basic Books, New York.

Poyo, Gerald E., and Gilberto M. Hinojosa
1988   Spanish Texas and Borderlands Historiography in Transition: Implications for United States History. *Journal of American History* 75:393–416.

Ríos Bustamante, Antonio José
1976   A Contribution to the Historiography of the Greater Mexican North in the Eighteenth Century. *Aztlán* 7:347–356.

Rischin, Moses
  1968 Beyond the Great Divide: Immigration and the Last Frontier. *Journal of American History* 55:42–53.
  1970 Continuities and Discontinuities in Spanish-Speaking California. In *Ethnic Conflict in California History*, edited by Charles Wollenberg, pp. 45–60. Tinnon-Brown, Los Angeles.
Robinson, Cecil
  1963 *With the Ears of Strangers: The Mexican in American Literature*. University of Arizona Press, Tucson.
Romera-Novarro, Miguel
  1917 *El hispanismo en Norte-América*. Renacimiento, Madrid.
Scardaville, Michael C.
  1985 Approaches to the Study of the Southeastern Borderlands. In *Alabama and the Borderlands*, edited by R. Reid Badger and Lawrence A. Clayton, pp. 184–196. University of Alabama Press, University.
Scholes, France V.
  1962 Historiography of the Spanish Southwest: Retrospect and Prospect. In *Probing the American West: Papers from the Santa Fe Conference*, edited by K. Ross Toole, et al., pp. 17–25. Museum of New Mexico, Santa Fe.
Sewall, R. K.
  1976 *Sketches of St. Augustine*. Facsimile reprint of 1st ed. 1848. Introduction by Thomas Graham. University Presses of Florida, Gainesville.
Simmons, Marc
  1976 Authors and Books in Colonial New Mexico. In *Voices from the Southwest: A Gathering in Honor of Lawrence Clark Powell*, edited by Donald C. Dickinson, et al., pp. 13–32. Northland Press, Flagstaff, Ariz.
Smith, Buckingham
  1857 *Colección de varios documentos para la historia de Florida y tierras adyacentes*. Trübner y Companía. London.
Squier, E. G.
  1848 New Mexico and California: The Ancient Monuments, . . . with an Abstract of the Early Spanish Explorations and Conquests in those Regions. Reprinted from *American Review*, November 1848.
Stagner, Stephen
  1981 Epics, Sciences, and the Lost Frontier: Texas Historical Writing, 1836–1936. *Western Historical Quarterly* 12:165–181.
Stoddard, Ellwyn R., Richard L. Nostrand, and Jonathan P. West (editors)
  1983 *Borderlands Sourcebook: A Guide to the Literature on Northern Mexico and the American Southwest*. University of Oklahoma Press, Norman.
Swagerty, W. R.
  1984 Spanish-Indian Relations, 1513–1821. In *Scholars and the Indian Experience*, edited by W. R. Swagerty, pp. 36–78. Indiana University Press, Bloomington.
Thomas, David Hurst
  1988 Saints and Soldiers at Santa Catalina: Hispanic Designs for Colonial America. In *The Recovery of Meaning: Historical Archaeology in the Eastern United States*, edited by Mark P. Leone and Parker B. Potter, Jr., pp. 73–140. Smithsonian Institution Press, Washington, D.C.
Thomas, David Hurst (editor)
  1989 *Columbian Consequences: Archaeological and Historical Perspectives on the Spanish Borderlands West*. Vol. 1. Smithsonian Institution Press, Washington, D.C.
  1990 *Columbian Consequences. Archaeological and Historical Perspectives on the Spanish Borderlands East*. Vol. 2. Smithsonian Institution Press, Washington, D.C.
Vallejo, Guadalupe
  1973 Ranch and Mission Days in Alta California. In *Foreigners in Their Native Land:*

Historical Roots of the Mexican Americans, edited by David J. Weber, University of New Mexico Press. Originally published in 1890, *Century Magazine*, 41.

Vigil, Ralph H.
1973   The New Borderlands History: A Critique. *New Mexico Historical Review* 48:189–208.

Wagner, Henry R.
1937   *The Spanish Southwest, 1542–1794: An Annotated Bibliography.* 2 vols. The Quivira Society, Albuquerque.

Weber, David J.
1979   "Scarce More than Apes": Historical Roots of Anglo-American Stereotypes of Mexicans. In New Spain's Far Northern Frontier: Essays on Spain in the American West, edited by David J. Weber, pp. 295–311. University of New Mexico Press, Albuquerque.
1986   Turner, the Boltonians, and the Borderlands. *American Historical Review* 91:66–81.
1987   John Francis Bannon and the Historiography of the Spanish Borderlands: Retrospect and Prospect. *Journal of the Southwest* 29:331–363.
1991   *The Idea of the Spanish Borderlands: A Sourcebook.* Garland Press, New York.

Williams, John Lee
1976   *View of West Florida: Embracing Its Geography, Topography, &c. . . . , Facsimile.* Reprint of 1st ed., 1827. Introduction by Herbert J. Doherty, Jr. University Presses of Florida, Gainesville.

Williams, Stanley T.
1955   *The Spanish Background of American Literature,* 2 vols. Yale University Press, New Haven, Conn.

Worcester, Donald E.
1976   The Significance of the Spanish Borderlands to the United States. *Western Historical Quarterly* 7:5–18.

Chapter 2 ■

Dora P. Crouch

Roman Models for Spanish Colonization

Spanish colonization of the new world during the sixteenth to nineteenth centuries was based on Roman colonization in the Mediterranean area during the republican and early imperial times, the Roman laws governing the process, and the literature derived from it. Parallels between the two histories are the subject of this chapter. Important linkages between the two can be found in the manuscripts of Vitruvius and Alberti, two architectural writers of the first century B.C. and the fifteenth century A.D., respectively. As a graduate student, I had studied the parallels between Vitruvius and Alberti, and then for *Spanish City Planning in North America* (Crouch et al. 1981) examined the correspondence between the Spanish new world cities as built and the provisions of the Laws of the Indies that were intended to control that building process. Later, when I read *Roman Colonization under the Republic* (Salomon 1970) and critically compared the sets of data, I began to sense a pattern for colonization per se. I hope that this discussion induces others to explore these parallels further.

Interrelationships among the factors affecting Roman and Spanish colonization practice are shown in the chart of Figure 2–1. Influence flows from the top down, each factor affecting the one below directly and those below cumulatively.

Thus, Roman practice was summed by Vitruvius, studied by Alberti as expressed in Vitruvius, and influential on Italian Renaissance practice both through the two writers and directly through inspection of ancient cities. In Spain, Roman practice was known from firsthand inspection of the fabric of such cities as Leon and Barcelona, indirectly from the books of Vitruvius and Alberti, and at third hand from Italian Renaissance practice as exported to Spain in books from Italy. Spanish visitors to Italy visited both ancient Roman cities and new Renaissance towns or city centers and brought these ideas back to Spain. All of these influences on Spanish practice both in Spain and in the New World became codified in the Laws of the Indies. New World experience rebounded to the Council of the Indies, where it not only modified the Laws but also affected urban theory and practice in Europe. The linkages are complicated, convoluted, and many faceted.

Similarities of language between Vitruvius and the Laws of the Indies were first noted by Dan Stanislawski (1947:101–104). Mundigo, Garr, and I expanded on that insight in our *Spanish City Planning*. This chapter incorporates additional information from Salomon about ancient Roman laws and practice, as well as data from excavations of Roman cities in Spain.

Roman Colonization

Roman builders of colonial cities during the Republic and the first century of the empire followed a standard pattern of activities. As new territory was conquered, until at least the early second century A.D., the usual way to secure it was to plant colonies there, either of veteran Roman soldiers or other citizens or allies. The new land and nascent city served as pension for the veterans who normally retired at the age of 36–40 and thus were still vigorous enough to secure the area for the central government.

Once the Roman Senate decided to found a colony, it passed enabling legislation (*les coloniae*) delegating responsibility for the site to a group of commissioners, usually three. They were empowered to conscript, enroll, or assign settlers and to nominate the first priests and officials, according to customary Roman municipal and religious arrangements.

The selected settlers then marched to the territory assigned to them, and a city site was selected within the territory. In this, as in so many matters, Roman practice built on what the Greeks had learned and done (Crouch 1987). The priests and commissioners performed the necessary rituals (see the next section on Vitruvius). The first order of business was to build defenses. Once secure, the settlers had time to survey the territory and town site, laying out fields and dividing the urban land. They planted crops that would make the new settlement self-sustaining. While the first crops were growing, the settlers could build an agricultural drainage/irrigation system and begin to construct the water and drainage system for the town.

Without waiting for the surveying to be completed, they began to build the town according to the standard pattern. Ramparts were a primary concern, first in the form of a stockade, and then as permanent enclosure for the new town.

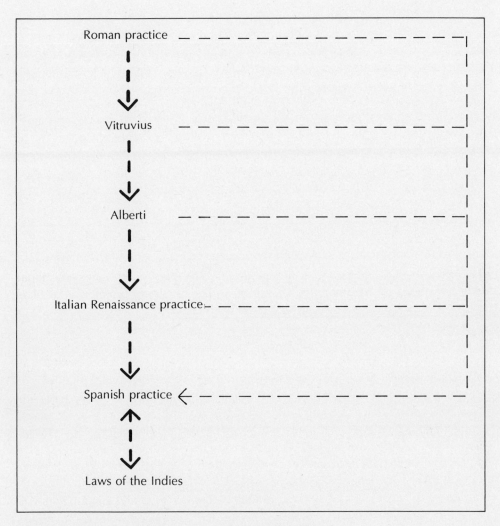

Figure 2–1. Flow chart of influences on Spanish colonial cities.

A *pomerium* (a streetlike strip of empty space) was placed just inside the defensive walls to make it easy for the defenders to rush to any part of the wall where they were needed. From the main gates ran the main streets, crossing at right angles at the center of the town. The forum (religious, commercial, municipal, and social center of the town) was placed adjacent to the main intersection. Public buildings were located along the streets near the forum. After about 100 B.C., porticoes enhanced the forum and the main streets (Downey 1961:173–174; and Crouch 1976). The buildings of the town, set on rectangular or square blocks, consisted of a mixture of large, small, and medium-size houses with and without shops and small factories. House lots were assigned to the settlers according to their status.

The expansion of the Latin people from their home city of Rome, first into

Etruscan territory to the north and eventually into all of Italy (Scullard 1967) was not without cost in money, lives, and abiding animosity. Even though the subject peoples in the early days of conquest of the Italian peninsula were closely related ethnically, the Romans did not treat them as equals, but neither did they go as far as Greeks, who characterized all others as "barbarians." Relations with these others did not become easier as the Romans expanded into Gaul (modern France), Spain, and even farther afield. The non-Latins were sometimes "hostile and bitterly resentful," and thus difficult to incorporate into the Roman state. To alleviate this problem, the Romans often used non-Latin and noncitizen colonists as go-betweens and as carriers of Roman culture.

To allow for changes in the settlement, the law provided that underutilized land could be reallocated and that additional land could be surveyed or subdivided for new settlers. No attempt was made to build all of the city at once; rather, the process of building went on for years, adding arches, baths, a theater near the forum, and an amphitheater outside the town, as well as more temples, houses and shops, and the necessary fountains and drains.

When enough of the city had been constructed so that it could be called complete, a plan of the city and a copy of the foundation decree were set up in the forum. These were either cast in bronze or carved in stone. Such a decree on stone can be found in the old forum at Leptis Magna (in modern Libya), the lettering in both Latin and Neo-Punic.

In general, this pattern of Roman expansion by colonies applied in Italy, Gaul, and North Africa during the Republican era. Quite a different process went on during the second century A.D. when existing cities were formally declared "colonies" so as to achieve desirable legal status within the Roman empire. A notable example is Palmyra, Syria, which became a colony under Hadrian about A.D. 130, when it was already about 500 years old (Crouch 1969).

Vitruvius

In a treatise about Roman cities written in the late first century B.C., Vitruvius summarized several centuries of Greco-Roman experience of colonization. Of primary importance was a healthy site:

> For fortified towns the following general principles are to be observed. First comes the choice of a very healthy site. Such a site will be high, neither misty nor frosty and in a climate neither hot nor cold, but temperate; further, without marshes in the neighborhood. For when the morning breezes blow toward the town at sunrise, if they bring with them mists from marshes and, mingled with the mist, the poisonous breath of the creatures of the marshes to be wafted into the bodies of the inhabitants, they will make the site unhealthy. Again if the town is on the coast with a southern or western exposure, it will not be healthy, because in summer the southern sky grows hot at sunrise and is fiery at noon, while a western exposure grows warm after sunrise, is hot at noon, and at evening all aglow. . . . These variations in heat and the subsequent cooling off are harmful to the people living on such sites [bk. 1, chap. 4].[1]

After tentatively selecting the site, the people must observe the necessary rituals. Vitruvius writes:

> I cannot too strongly insist upon the need of a return to the method of old times. Our ancestors, when about to build a town or an army post, sacrificed some of the cattle that were wont to feed on the site proposed and examined their livers. If the livers of the first victims were dark-colored or abnormal, they sacrificed others, to see whether the fault was due to disease or their food. They never began to build defensive works in a place until after they had made many such trials and satisfied themselves that good water and food made the liver sound and firm [bk. 1, chap. 4].

When a particular city site was chosen, the next task was defense. The walls were to be built on a deep foundation, with towers close enough to give enfilading fire (Vitruvius, bk. 1, chap. 5).

However, Vitruvius writes nothing about the political problem of relations with allied and subjugated peoples, because this was not an interesting problem to him as a professional architect. Lacking such advice, the Spanish colonizers took more than a century to realize that go-betweens were more effective than military force in establishing good relations. We shall come back to this point at the end of the chapter.

Alberti

Alberti was instrumental in bringing the manuscript of Vitruvius before a wide new audience in the last half of the fifteenth century. Since the Vitruvius manuscript contained both Greek and Latin terms whose meaning had been lost, Alberti undertook to elucidate and expand the ancient text in his own work, *De re aedificatoria* (On architecture), written between 1440 and 1472 and printed in 1485. Although both manuscripts were influential in written form, their accessibility in print increased that influence. By the first quarter of the sixteenth century, both works were known in Spain in printed versions (Carol Krinsky, personal communication, 1985) where they made a strong impact on those responsible for Spain's colonization efforts in the New World.

Not surprisingly, one finds in Vitruvius and Alberti not only some similar attitudes and information but also similar wording. Alberti argues like Vitruvius that a city should be sited in a territory that can provide all the necessities of life. The selected site should be easy to fortify and be located in the middle of its territory (bk. 4, chap. 2). Alberti admits with Vitruvius that some seaside locations are unhealthy—"If the town is on the coast with a southern or western exposure, it will not be healthy" (bk. 1, chap. 4), but Alberti qualifies this:

> A prospect of the sea from the shore is wonderfully pleasant, and generally is attended with wholesome air . . . but then the sea there . . . must be . . . deep, with a high, bold shore of living craggy rock. The placing a city upon the proud shoulders of a mountain . . . contributes greatly not only to dignity and pleasure, but yet more to healthy [bk. 4, chap. 2].

Throughout Alberti, the mind of the humanist is evident, expanding and refining Vitruvius's more purely architectural concerns.

Spanish Practice in Spain

Alberti's writings and Columbus's discoveries at the end of the fifteenth century inaugurated a period of great expansion of opportunity. To take advantage of the opportunities that presented themselves in settling the New World and to guide the process of conquest, the Spanish imperial court developed a policy of colonization by urbanization. The Spaniards had successfully reconquered the Iberian peninsula from the Moors, city by city. As they moved inexorably southward, each city became the base for the successful assault on the city, and for the expansion of Spanish Christian culture into areas occupied for many centuries by the Moors—a people different in race, religion, and culture. Having just completed the reconquest of Iberia at the end of the fifteenth century, the Spaniards from the sixteenth century on used the same process in the New World. They conquered existing cities such as Cuzco and Mexico City and then created many new settlements.

Many cities based on Roman settlements such as Barcelona and Leon (Figure 2–2; Crouch et al. 1982:Figures 3 and 5) survived in the Iberian peninsula. In spite of reuse and rebuilding for more than 1,200 years, these cities retained then and still reveal their basic Roman pattern: a wall enclosing a rectangular plat, crossed by a pair of main streets leading from the gates to meet at right angles at the center of the town, with a public plaza (the forum) occupying one angle of the intersection. Lesser streets paralleled the main ones, setting up a grid pattern. Already in Roman times the cities had begun to expand along the roads leading to the town, just outside the main gates. In medieval times, regular markets took place adjacent to the gates, eventually (as in the case of Leon) being enclosed within another circuit of walls. Sometimes these extramural quarters received their own porticoes surrounding their market areas.

A third element of Spanish urban practice ca. 1500 affected the form and process of city building in the New World. That was their experience in making new military cities such as Santa Fe de Granada and Puerto Real. These little cities were modeled on bastide towns (Crouch et al. 1982:39), being like them in having a simple grid form with an open square at the center, at the edge of which stood the church and the government building. Like the bastides and the Roman veterans' colonies before them, these military towns were foolproof in their simplicity of form. As practical urban models, easily built by amateurs, and by coincidence finished just as the need for new towns in the American wilderness became apparent, Santa Fe de Granada and Puerto Real were highly successful urban models.

Spain's reconquest experience, appreciation of Roman remnants, and grid-platted military towns explain why the Spanish planners were relatively indifferent to theoretical Renaissance innovations such as the ideal cities of Vignola and others. Spain was embarked on a colonial venture for which there were no precedents but the ancient Roman experience and the recent reconquest experi-

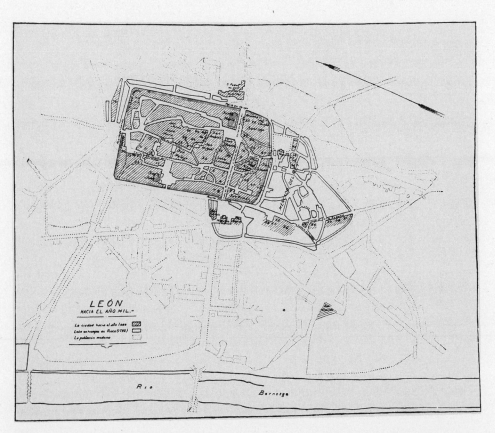

Figure 2–2. Leon, Spain. The Roman city, with the church of Santa Maria replacing the ancient temple on the main plaza, is shaded. Medieval extensions are also walled (Gutkind 1967:267). (Reprinted by permission from The Free Press, Macmillan)

ence. The Roman formula for imperial expansion—cities in the form of a grid with a central open space—provided a suitable model. As the urban centers of Spain were rebuilt, the rational and obvious grid plan served to distinguish the Christian cities form their "organic" Moslem predecessors on the same sites (Gutkind 1967). One may postulate that the necessity for this differentiation reinforced the utilization of Roman rather than medieval Islamic models (see Crouch et al. 1982:xvii).

Spanish Colonization in the New World

Spanish colonial policy was strikingly similar to the Roman approach we have already examined. This practice was codified in the Laws of the Indies and in the subsequent editions of the laws governing the Spanish empire. It can be inspected in the physical features of many extant cities of the new world, and in the ruins of others. It is evident in the documents and maps sent back to the Council of the Indies by the many governors and their assistants during approximately three and a half centuries, not to mention the records that still survive in many of those localities. (For further details on this policy, see Crouch et al. 1982: section I, and p. 75.)

After Columbus discovered the New World in 1492, the Spanish and Portuguese spent the next century exploring the lands of the Western Hemisphere, from Kansas to Tierra del Fuego. The inhabitants they found there—unlike the Moors, for whom the Spaniards had a grudging respect—were so vastly different from themselves that they considered the natives "without culture." Appalled by the human sacrifice intrinsic to Aztec religion, the Spaniards felt justified in stamping out this "devil worship." Aided by guns, horses, and a series of European diseases to which the natives had no immunity, the Spanish had no difficulty in conquering Central and South America, wiping out much of the population, which was replaced by Europeans and those of mixed blood.

Cities were being reorganized and newly founded and information on them sent back to the governing Council of the Indies in Seville. For the first 80 years, laws to govern these new domains were passed ad hoc, but by the 1570s it was apparent that a coherent body of law was needed, and in 1573 the king issued those documents known since as the Laws of the Indies. Every aspect of the control of these vast territories was detailed here. (*Spanish City Planning* translated and commented on only those ordinances relevant to its topic of urbanization.)

To ensure that settlement benefited the Crown, the council did not permit the founding of towns without a royal license. This license assigned territory and allowed the founder to enroll settlers. Typically, a group of settlers would consist of 1 or 2 priests, 4 to 6 soldiers, and 10 to 30 families. The group of settlers gathered, then sailed or marched to the assigned territory. The long walk of Fra Junípero Serra's settlers from Baja California, to Monterey, California, over 600 miles, has become part of the myth of the state's foundation. Arrived at the area assigned, the founder selected a city site. If he were fortunate enough to have the help of the architect that the Laws mandated, "to assure the beauty of the town," then that professional would choose a healthy and beautiful site and see that the settlement was properly laid out. Often, however, the group was too small and the government too impoverished to provide professional assistance at the new site, though even in those instances plans were usually sent from Mexico City for the major church and possibly for other important buildings.

The necessary rituals of dedication were the responsibility of the priest or priests. Usually the first ritual was a mass, held on a hilltop or under a tree, to celebrate the safe arrival of the settlers and their dedication to God and the king. By the beginning of the seventeenth century, the Spaniards were well aware that religious conversion was both a surer and a cheaper means of subduing native populations than military conquest (Crouch et al. 1982:86–87).

The first construction at a new site was a presidio (a fortified residence with a chapel) in which all the settlers could live safely. Then they laid out and allotted the fields, by lots, and planted crops. Building an irrigation system was an important priority, as was providing water supply for the town and the necessary drainage. Mexican settlers coming to Arizona, California, and New Mexico were comfortable with the arid climate and soil conditions, since they were similar to those in northern Mexico. Anglos from Missouri or New York, however, were initially repulsed by the aridity of the Southwest, greatly different from the green and lush settings they had left behind (Tuan 1974). The license given to the founder specified what size the town would be. Once the immediate question of security had been handled, the founder designated the proper number of government officials for the town, depending on its projected size, and the process of building the actual town as distinguished from the presidio was begun. If the threat of attack were great, the town might be walled. St. Louis, for instance, was walled against the British and their Indian allies, but it is one of only eleven cities in the United States to be so enclosed (Musick 1941). It was more common to locate forts at strategic places, like Fort Point at the entrance to San Francisco Bay.

A standard pattern of buildings and spaces was followed for the new town. The center was occupied by the four-sided plaza, from the corners of which ran the main streets. Public buildings faced onto the main plaza. Porticoes, which in Renaissance iconography signified public space, surrounded the main plaza and extended along the main streets, such as the one connecting the most important church to the central plaza. Residential blocks were rectangular or square and were divided into house plots that were selected by lot, although in very small settlements the houses of the leading citizens were found facing on the plaza, not distributed at random. In these Spanish colonial towns, the houses usually included corrals for animals, but rarely included shops.

The town itself, and especially its biggest church, were intended to impress the neighboring Indians just as the Roman town had impressed the non-Latin tribes, and make them want to live there. Subjection and conversion of the Indians was seen as an important goal of colonization. To create a bridge between the Spanish settlers and the surrounding population, "domesticated Indians" were used as models, go-betweens, and carriers of Christian culture.

Since each town hoped to attract additional settlers from Mexico and Spain, one-fourth of the land was to be held in reserve for new colonists. As the town grew, subsidiary plazas, streets, and house lots were laid out. A large church standing next to its own plaza replaced the simple military chapel of the presidio.

Records were to be kept of assignments of land. Reports with maps were sent back usually annually to Mexico City or Seville. A photocopy of an early map of St. Louis that I found in the Library of Congress, with no record of the whereabouts of the original or of how the copy had gotten into this collection, bears a note on the map that the original had been sent to the governor at New Orleans. Following proper procedure, that governor should have sent the report on to the Council of the Indies in Seville, where it should have been placed in the Archives of the Indies. When I wrote to the Archives to request a photographic print, sending a photocopy of the photocopy, the photo came by return mail, showing that the bureaucrats of the late eighteenth century had done their work correctly.

Thus the legal pattern and the actual practice of Spanish colonization were very similar to Roman practice. The two empires had the same motives—efficient conquest—and many of the same constraints. The physical process of building one city after another was paralleled by the legal and administrative one of reporting to the central government and receiving directives form it. During the sixteenth century, as Renaissance enthusiasm for the Roman past flourished, Spanish law and colonization came to rely more and more on Roman principles, from the writings of Alberti and of Vitruvius as mediated through Alberti, and from physical remains.

Alberti and the Laws of the Indies

A few examples of parallelism between Alberti's dicta and the ordinances of the Laws of the Indies will have to suffice as clues to a vast subject. For instance, Alberti cites with approval the practice of the ancients, who placed the "Senate-house in the Middle of the City, with the Place for the Administration of Justice and the Temple near adjoining" (bk. 5, chap. 9) and he wants the chief church to be well situated:

> The Place where you intend to fix a Temple, ought to be noted, famous, and indeed stately, clear from all Contagion of secular Things, and, in order thereunto, it should have a spacious handsome area in its Front, and be surrounded on every Side with great Streets, or rather with noble Squares, that you may have a beautiful View of it on every Side [bk. 7, chap. 3].

These precepts may be compared with Ordinance 124 of the Laws of the Indies:

> The temple in inland places shall not be placed on the square but at a distance and shall be separated from any other nearby building, or from adjoining buildings, and ought to be seen from all sides so that it can be decorated better, thus acquiring more authority; efforts should be made that it be somewhat raised from ground level in order that it be approached by steps, and near it, next to the main plaza, the royal council and cabildo and customs houses shall be built. [These shall be built] in a manner that would not embarrass the temple but add to its prestige [See Crouch et al. 1982:15].[2]

Both the Laws of the Indies and Alberti are concerned with aesthetics. Alberti says the attractiveness of the city can be enhanced:

> The principal Ornament of the City will arise from the disposition of the Streets, squares and public Edifices, and their being all laid out and contrived beautifully and conveniently, according to their several Uses [bk. 7, chap. 1]. . . . The Streets within the City, besides being handsomely paved and cleanly kept, will be rendered much more noble, if the Doors are built all after the same Model, and the Houses on each Side stand in an even Line, and none higher than another [bk. 8, chap. 6].

The laws, more generally, require that all buildings shall be "of one type for the sake of the beauty of the town" (Ord. 134, p. 17).

Both documents call for a sort of zoning to separate noxious activities, such as hospitals, from the rest of town. Alberti says: "The hospital for the poor who are not affected by contagious diseases shall be built near the temple and near its cloister, and the (hospital) for contagious diseases shall be built in an area where the cold north wind blows, but arranged in such a way that it may enjoy the south wind" (bk. 5, chap. 8). The laws again went further, demanding that such hospitals be placed downwind from the town (Ord. 121, p. 15). Tanneries were another problem. Alberti wanted them placed to the north of town and out of the path of winds that blow toward the town (bk. 7, chap. 1). The laws again specify further that they must be located where their filth could easily be disposed of (Ord. 122, p. 15).

Vitruvius and the Laws

Interestingly, the Laws of the Indies in some cases follow Vitruvius more closely than they do Alberti. It seems that the Spanish Crown like the Portuguese Crown (Roberta Delson, personal communication, 1985) called upon architects to study ancient sources directly, with greater concern for orderliness and imperial expansion than for Renaissance refinements, as can be seen in the question of proportions of the main plaza. Vitruvius writes that the best proportions are three to two (bk. 5, chap. 1). Alberti seems to follow Vitruvius initially, but ends by calling for a plaza with proportions of two to one (bk. 8, chap. 6). Under the Laws of the Indies, the plaza could be square—many are, especially in the late eighteenth and early nineteenth centuries—or rectangular with proportions of three to two. The minimum size was to be 200 by 300 feet, and the maximum 532 by 800 feet (Ord. 113, p. 13).

Vitruvius's criteria for site selection in addition to defensibility are particularly health, abundance, and good access. The Laws of the Indies agree heartily:

> And they should be in fertile areas with an abundance of fruits and fields, of good land to plant and harvest, of grasslands to grow livestock, of mountains and forests for wood and building materials for homes and edifices, and of good and plentiful water supply for drinking and irrigation [Ord. 35, p. 8].

> And they should have good access and outlet by sea and by land, and also good roads and passage by water, in order that they may be entered and departed easily with commerce, while bringing relief and establishing defenses [Ord. 37, pp. 8–9].

The laws, however, neglect Alberti's admonition, "Earth and water can be improved, but not air" (bk. 10, chap. 1). If this rule had been heeded, Los Angeles would never have been sited in a valley where the smoke from Indian campfires interacting with the strong sunlight already made smog in the sixteenth century!

A notable difference between the mandates of the Laws of the Indies and Vitruvius's ideas is the street pattern. Neither ancient Roman nor actual Renaissance cities (with very few exceptions) followed his ideal of streets radiating from a central plaza and generating wedge-shaped blocks. That may be because a radiating plan was too difficult for amateur surveyors (Crouch et al. 1982). The Laws of the Indies, after all, were not a theoretical treatise but a do-it-yourself manual for beginners. Even on this point, however, Vitruvius's ideas were not completely ignored because Ordinance 114 does call for the plaza to have its *angles* oriented to the four points of the compass so that the streets leaving the plaza from those corners will run northeast, southeast, southwest, and northwest, thus not into the full force of any of the winds blowing from the four cardinal directions (Ord. 114, p. 14).

Roman and Spanish Colonization: Two Comparisons

A great deal of work on the setting up of colonial cities remains to be done. One particularly interesting topic that needs to be explored is the way in which Roman and Spanish societies utilized intermediary peoples as their agents in the process of conquest and expansion. These mediators shared ethnic and cultural traits with both conquerors and subjects, facilitating communication in both directions.

As an example, Ordinances 135 and 138 required that "persons designated for this purpose" attempt to win the friendship of the wild Indians. At Santa Fe, New Mexico, about 50 "domesticated Indians" from Mexico, probably Tlascans, lived in a separate "Indian town" south of the Santa Fe River. During the seventeenth century, they made their living growing wheat and maize by irrigation, and they set an example of civilized and Christian living for the local Indians (Figure 2–3; Crouch et al. 1982:70–73, 80, and Figure 25).

In a similar fashion, the Romans used non-Latin Groups to extend Rome's rule via intermediary cultural interface. The Romans took advantage of their ongoing struggle against the Carthaginians of North Africa to expand into any and all contested areas lying between the two peoples. One such area was Sicily, which the Romans conquered in 212 B.C. To dominate the interior of the island, they entrusted the hill-town of Morgantina to a group of retired legionnaires, the Hispani, presumably from Spain (Erim 1958). Just as earlier colonists had made Italy securely Roman, so now these veterans held central Sicily for Rome against the indigenous Greco-Sicilian peoples and any Carthaginians who might have had designs on the territory. Morgantina was abandoned 200 years later, in the late first century B.C., but by then the whole population of Sicily was securely Roman.

Another example of the striking similarity between Roman and Spanish practices of urbanization can be found in their similar concepts of the city as a package of standard functional-cum-architectural elements in which an attractive mode of life could be lived out. The mode of life was to be so attractive and the architectural containers so dazzling (at least in concept) that the barbarians would be won over to both urban life and allegiance to the expanding power (Crouch 1976; Crouch et al. 1982:32, 44–47). The Greco-Roman attitude is reflected in the work of Pausanius, the second century A.D. Roman travel writer, who defines a city as having "government offices, gymnasium, theater, marketplace, water conducted to a fountain, and [decent] houses"(x.4.1) (see also Hassall 1970). The Spanish colonists wanted their town to be awe-inspiring. Ord. 137 required that the Indians be kept out of the town until it was complete, and then "when the Indians see the [completed defenses and houses of the

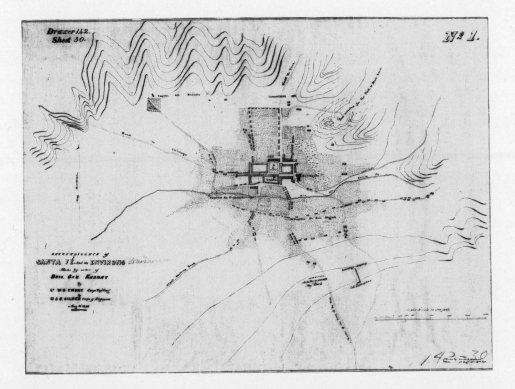

Figure 2–3. Map of Santa Fe, New Mexico, August 10, 1846. Made by Lieutenants Emory and Gilner and filed at the National Archives in Washington, D.C., drawer 142, sheet 30. The city focuses on the regular colonnaded plaza with its new American flag. South of the Rio Santa Fe, a second village for the Indians stretches out along the road leading to their Capilla de San Miguel, the oldest church in the state.

town] they will be struck with admiration." For both societies, cities were major instruments of conquest and control, as well as major collectors of wealth.

Conclusion

The histories of two peoples widely separated in both time and space—the Romans and the Spanish—reveal in their approach to urbanization an unmistakable similarity. Under central control, both required the building of complete new cities, planned as unities according to prescribed specifications and patterns. Even though central control was intended, in actual experience many local decisions escaped that control. As Daniel Garr has written to me, "No matter how explicit the 1573 laws, or their successors in the editions of the recopilacion, no matter how bureaucratically centralized the Spanish empire may have been, town-foundings were highly *decentralized* and given the heterogeneity of the colonial empire in terms of time (300–year era of settlement), geography, historical circumstance, etc., generalizations are risky." Yet there is a recognizable Spanish quality to these towns, the product of consensus if not of effective coercion. The city building activities and the manuscripts revealing their theoretical and legal base were products of rationalization fostered in both the Roman and the Spanish cases by a government extending its rule into hitherto unknown lands. The surprising similarities between Roman and Spanish methods of colonization are to be construed as the results of both deliberate imitation and expediency. We are now better able to understand how Roman ideas were transmitted to the Spaniards and thus to the 350 cities of the new world that were laid out according to the evergreen principles of the Laws of the Indies. We are also in a position to begin to understand colonization itself.

Notes

1. All quotations from Vitruvius are taken from the Dover edition, translated by M. H. Morgan. These citations are from Book 1, Chapter 4.
2. All translations of the ordinances cited here are from this translation; hereafter, Ord.____, p. ____.

References

Alberti
  1725 & 1755   (Ten Books) *On Architecture*. Leoni edition. Reissued in 1955 by Joseph Rykwert.
Crouch, Dora P.
  1969   *Palmyra*. Unpublished Ph.D. dissertation, Department of Art, University of California at Los Angeles.
  1976   Urban Design in Cities of the Roman Empire. *Ekistics* 42:253, 343–346.
  1987   Water System Evidence for Greek Civilization. In *Water for the Future*, edited by W. O. Wunderlich and J. E. Prins. Proceedings of the IAHR and IAHS symposium. Rome, Italy, 125–138.
Crouch, Dora P., Daniel J. Garr, and Axel I. Mundigo
  1982   *Spanish City Planning in North America*. MIT Press, Cambridge, Mass. This book includes a translation of and commentary on the ordinances of the Laws of the Indies that pertain to urbanization.
Delson, Roberta
  1975   *Town Planning in Colonial Brazil*. Ph.D. Dissertation. Columbia University, New York. Published by Geography Department, Syracuse University, Albany, N.Y.
Downey, G.
  1961   *Antioch in Syria*. Princeton University Press, Princeton, N.J.
Erim, K.
  1958   Morgantina. 62:85–87.
Garr, Daniel J. (editor)
  1991   *Hispanic Urban Planning in North America: A Sourcebook*. In *Hispanic Borderlands Sourcebooks*. Garland Press, New York.
Gutkind, E.
  1967   *International History of City Development*, vol. 3. Free Press, New York.
Hassall, M. W. C.
  1970   Roman Urbanization in Western Europe. In *Man, Settlement and Urbanism*, edited by P. J. Ucko, R. Tringham, and G. W. Dimblely, pp. 857–861. Schenkman, Cambridge, Mass.
Krinsky, Carol
  1965   *Cesasre Cesarino and the Como Vitruvius Edition of 1521*. Unpublished Ph.D. dissertation, Department of Art History, New York University.

Musick, James B.
   1941   *St. Louis as a Fortified Town*. St Louis, Mo.
Pausanias
   1965   *Pausanias's Description of Greece*. Translated by J. G. Frazer. Biblo and Tannen, New
       York.
Salomon, E. T.
   1970   *Roman Colonization under the Republic*. Cornell University Press, Ithaca, N.Y.
Scullard, H. H.
   1967   *The Etruscan Cities and Rome*. Cornell University Press, Ithaca, N.Y.
Stanislawski, D.
   1947   Early Spanish Town Planning in the New World. *Geographical Review* 37:101–104.
Tuan, I-Fu
   1974   *Topophilia*. Prentice-Hall, Englewood Cliffs, N.J.
Vitruvius, Pollio
   1960   *The Ten Books on Architecture*. ca. 11 B.C. Translated by Morris H. Morgan. Dover
       Press, New York. Originally published 1914, Harvard University Press.

Chapter 3 ■

Don D. Fowler and Catherine S. Fowler

The Uses of Natural Man in Natural History

The World Columbian Exposition, popularly called the Chicago World's Fair, was held in 1893. The fair exuberantly celebrated the Quatrocentenary of Columbus's "Discovery" of the New World and the subsequent domination of much of both the Old and New World by European culture and capitalism. The previous year, a smaller exposition was held in Madrid to celebrate the discovery of, and Spain's role in "civilizing," the New World. In 1992 at Seville, Spain will again celebrate the discovery, as well as its own place in the postmodern world. There will be no world's fair in the United States, although various celebrations are planned. The Quincentenary theme in the United States, at least among scholars, is "Encounter," which signifies not celebration but a mood of ambiguous stocktaking and rethinking of Columbian consequences.

The Quincentenary comes during a time of reflexive reappraisal in anthropology and archaeology that began in the 1960s (Hymes 1969). A particular focus of this rethinking is the complex problem of "the Other"—that is, the derivation and meanings of anthropological, and more generally, Western conceptions, or images, of non-European-derived peoples and cultures.[1] A reflexive view is that the conceptions reflect much more about Western political ideology than they do about the sociocultural realities of the Others. Stocking (1987), however, has reminded us that political ideology is only one of many complex sociocultural factors that influence the development of anthropological theory and images of the Other. Hanke (1959) provides a similar demonstration for sixteenth-century Spain.

Anthropology's Other has traditionally been *natural man*, glossed as *native*, *savage*, or *primitive*. His principal use is that of exemplar in investigations of the origins and "simpler" characteristics of society and culture. Archaeology has traditionally used anthropology's *natural man* as an *analog* in constructing accounts of prehistoric pasts, be they idiographic, processual, or hermeneutic in approach. The purpose of this chapter is to place such "uses" of natural man in historical perspective as a contribution to ongoing discussions of the Other. We first review changing images and stereotypes of natural man in Western thought from about A.D. 1492 to 1892; the focus is on the New World, but there is necessarily some consideration of images and stereotypes of black Africans, although these constructs are treated more fully elsewhere (e.g., Hammond and Jablow 1970). We then discuss how both anthropological and popular images of natural man, and the derived conceptions "native," "savage," and "primitive," were used in nineteenth-century museum and international exposition exhibitions. In many ways, these images continue to influence both anthropological discourse and popular beliefs about "primitive" Others.

Nature, Natural Law, and Natural Man

The racial and ethnic stereotypes of the nineteenth century have deep roots. These various Others were derived from four centuries and more of complex definition and redefinition of the concept of natural man. The shifting definitions were both influenced and used by apologists for colonialism, slavery, and capitalism; by social philosophers attempting to reconstruct European society; by natural historians; and finally by ethnologists.

To begin, we need to review how *nature*, *natural man*, *natural law*, and *natural history* were defined in the nineteenth century and before. The *Oxford English Dictionary* (*OED*) defines *nature* as: "1. The creative and regulative physical power which is conceived of as operating in the material world and as the immediate cause of all its phenomena; 2. The material world, or its collective objects and phenomena, especially those with which man is most directly in contact; *frequently the features and products of the earth itself as contrasted with those of human civilization.*" *State of nature* is defined as: "The condition of man before the formation of organized society" (emphasis added).

"Nature" then, is both the noncultural material world and a *force* that is ontological and regulative, causally "governing" the operation of natural phenomena by "natural law." And, *prior to* the emergence of "organized society," humans were "in nature," or were "natural beings."

Natural history, a term in use by 1585, is defined by the *OED* as "originally, the systematic study of all natural objects, animal, vegetable and mineral; now [twentieth century] restricted to the study of animal life and frequently implying a popular rather than a strictly scientific treatment of the subject."

The Invention of Natural Law

The concepts of nature and natural man and their study through natural history must be seen in relation to the idea of natural law. Western science assumes that natural laws "govern" the workings of the universe. The task of science is to discover and elucidate those laws. Barrow (1988:27–85) and Milton (1981) argue that the concept of the "laws of nature" derives ultimately from the idea of God as lawgiver or legislator, an ancient belief in Near Eastern and Judeo-Christian religions. Milton (1981) argues that the idea became central in a syncretism of Catholic canon law and Roman legal procedure in medieval theology, especially in the nominalism of William of Occam and others. In medieval society, "law" meant the *will* of the sovereign—God, Pope, or King. Thus, law was whatever the sovereign "ordained." The basic nominalist assumption was that God ordained laws for the regulation of nature. That is, God *willed* the universe into existence and made it go by *issuing*, imposing *on* it, or infusing *in* it, general operating rules: "laws" that "govern the most fundamental processes of nature" (Milton 1981:185–186). The result was that, "men were thinking of nature as governed by laws long before they were in a position to state any of the laws themselves" (Milton 1981:183).

"Natural law" that "governs" is a *legal* metaphor. In human society, laws, whether customary or codified, define the *forms and regularities* of human interaction. If the universe is a "lawful" place, then it operates according to metaphorically similar regularities. Durkheim (1915) argued that religion is society projected onto the universe. Like Barrow and Milton, we argue that natural law is a legal metaphor projected onto the universe to account for the observed, as well as the assumed, regularities of the universe. In Western thought, the assumption of a universe infused with, or governed by, "law" was carried down *as axiomatic* into seventeenth-century science. In the eighteenth century and later, as science progressively shed its supernatural frame of reference, the concept of natural law remained as a given. Indeed, the purpose of natural history was to seek and to understand natural laws and how they governed.

"Place" and the Great Chain of Being

Natural man must also be considered in relation to his place in the natural world. Medieval, Renaissance, and Enlightenment classifications of the natural world all derived from, or assumed the existence of, "the great ordered chain or hierarchy of being stretching from the archangels at the foot of God's throne to the meanest of inanimate objects" (Hodgen 1964:396). The chain-of-being metaphor is of great antiquity in Western thought (Lovejoy 1936). In medieval times the metaphor was sometimes represented as a stairway or ladder, sometimes as a tree—*arbor naturalis et logicalis*—but most commonly as a chain (Hodgen

1964:399–401). Each *link* ("type," "species") in the chain was said to differ from the link below and the link above it by the smallest *possible* degree of difference. The chain was "so scaled that the more remote it might be from its original source [God], the lower its grade of perfection" (Hodgen 1964:397). Humanity forms a crucial link between the animal (natural) series below, and the angelic (spiritual, intellectual) series above.

Until their encounters with the New World and sub-Saharan Africa, most Europeans thought that all humans constituted essentially *one* link in the chain. However, the new peoples posed a problem. By Papal Bull they were declared fully human, although perhaps bestial in behavior and insufficient in spiritual endowment, lacking as they did the Christian faith. But those in charge of colonization and slavery wished them defined as less than fully human, as one means of justifying slavery, genocide, and the expropriation of lands (Hanke 1959). Some approached this problem by exaggerating the physical differences between Europeans, on the one hand, and Africans and Indians, on the other (Vaughan 1982). Others used *negative ethnography* to claim the absence or the rudeness of languages and customs (Greenblatt 1976; Hodgen 1964).

The most serious of these claims were the oft-repeated charges that Indians and Africans were cannibals and committed incest, the ultimate acts of bestiality and improper behavior. The implication, of course, is that people who indulge in such practices are morally beyond the pale and "ought to be" killed or civilized, slavery being the preferred alternative in the latter case. Although actual evidence of cannibalism was quite uncertain, this did not stop the attribution of anthropophagy to New World, nor later, to African or South Seas, native peoples.[2]

Many tried to resolve the problem by determining the *place* of Indians and Africans along the great chain of being. All the "monstrous races" of classical and medieval legend—Amazons, Troglodytes, Blemmayae, Sciopods, Cynocephali, Wild Men, etc.—reported but never seen by various writers (Bernheimer 1952; Rackham 1947:2:bks. 3–7; Selincourt 1954), were intellectually dusted off, trotted out, and transported to the New World and southern Africa (Mason 1987:581–586). No one actually saw them there either, but they were *said* to exist, just as were the cannibals. The monstrous races were thought to be protohuman at best, and possibly linked to the seemingly exotic Indians and Hottentots.

The idea that humans make up more than one link in the chain of being began to appear in the seventeenth century, for example, in William Petty's ([1677] 1967) *Scale of Nature*. Petty thought that humans, monstrous and otherwise, comprised a *series* of links, culminating in white northwestern Europeans. The anatomist Edward Tyson's (Ashley Montagu [1709] 1943:225–345) essays carried this idea forward into biology, and it became embedded in Karl Linnaeus's (1735) *System of Nature*. To Petty, Tyson, Linnaeus, and others, there appeared to be gross differences between the various human "links," including the monstrous ones, and between them and the rest of the animal world. The task of the systematist was to place the links in "proper" hierarchical sequence.[3] The result was predictable: Hottentots, other Africans, American Indians, and Laplanders formed "inferior links"; Chinese and Malaysians were usually in the middle, and northern

Europeans at the top. Thus, by the time of Linneaus, the issue of "the savage's place in nature" was generally resolved. There was an indeterminate number of human and protohuman links in the chain of being. The links extended from the apes *up to* white Europeans, then beyond to the hierarchies of angels. An obvious implication was that the *further down* its position in the chain, the less spiritual, the more bestial, and the *closer to nature* was the group.

Natural Man in Nature

The long and complex articulation of natural man and nature in Western historical and sociopolitical thought has been termed *primitivism* (Lovejoy 1948; Lovejoy and Boas 1935). This belief is said to have emerged among the discontented members of "highly evolved complex" societies who held that the optimal human condition—the "good, simple life"—existed either in the distant past or among contemporary "savage" peoples. Underlying this view is one of the "most potent and most persistent" beliefs in Western thought, that "nature" is the standard of human values—that is, the good equals that which is "natural" or "according to nature," since natural man, living in a state of nature, is *ipso facto* "good" (Lovejoy and Boas 1935:8–13, 447).[4]

Natural Man in the New World

With these considerations as background, we turn next to the images of American Indians formulated by Europeans between 1500 and 1700. Columbus's "Indians" raised numerous disturbing questions in the minds of European savants, jurisprudes, and philosophers, not only about the origins of these peoples (Allen 1963:113–137; Huddleston 1967), but also about their "nature" and their status as human beings—in short, about their *place* in the cosmological scheme of things (Hodgen 1964:207–353; Keen 1971:49–410; Pagden 1982). The debates over these issues were vital. They affected the conquest and colonization of the New World by Spain, and later by France and Britain. Many verbal "images" of Indian people arose from these debates (Chiappelli 1976). These, coupled with numerous pictorial images (Honour 1975; Hulton 1984; Lehner and Lehner 1966; Lorant 1965; Sturtevant 1976), gave rise to often conflicting conceptions of New World peoples.

From Natural Man to Analogical Savage

By 1550, the term *savage* was in general use in French and English, primarily to refer to the Indians of the New World, particularly of North America. *Savage* is a complex term; like *nature*, it carries much semantic baggage. The *OED* takes two full pages to define its various uses in English. Robert's *Dictionnaire* devotes a full page to the French *sauvage*. At its simplest, in both English and French, the term is defined as "human in a state of nature." But it came to have numerous other connotations.

In general, sixteenth-century French and British descriptions of Indians, as well as derived literary images, were neutral or slightly derogatory. Wildness, fierceness, and occasionally cruelty were characteristics sometimes attributed to Indians along the northern coasts of North America, but there was no pervasive stereotype. The meaning of "savage" was still fluid. The French, British, and Dutch began settling northeastern North America in earnest early in the seventeenth century. They pursued different economic strategies. These, together with deep ideological differences, gave different meanings to the term"savage" and how they viewed the Indian people with whom they were in contact.

The British and the Dutch came primarily as farmers. To them the natural landscape, the forest, was a feared "wilderness" that was to be cleared, planted, dominated, and civilized as soon as possible. The Indian inhabitants of this wilderness were to be removed, or, if necessary, controlled and civilized. In general, the British and the Dutch attached a pejorative meaning to "natural man *in* nature." The images derived from this view became pervasively negative (Jennings 1975; Vaughan 1982).

The French in the St. Lawrence Valley, concerned principally with the fur trade, pursued a strategy of learning native languages and marrying Indian women as a means of controlling trade. When, in 1632, the Jesuits came to New France (Dickason 1984), they too learned the local languages and, where they could, gathered converts into villages similar to the theocratic *reductions* their cohorts later established in Bolivia and Paraguay (Fulop-Miller 1963:227–302). Between 1632 and 1674, the Jesuits issued annual reports from Paris concerning their missionary activities in New France. These *Jesuit Relations* (Thwaites 1896–1901) were primarily "truthful propaganda," designed to put the missionary work in the best light in order to solicit financial support. The constant theme of the reports was *Le Bon Sauvage*: Hurons, Iroquois, and others living good and just lives in an idyllic natural world. All those in France and elsewhere who attended Jesuit schools, and those who knew of the work in New France, heard the phrase often. The image of the *noble savage* that figured so prominently in eighteenth-century social philosophy was largely formed in the widely circulated seventeenth-century *Relations*, and in the numerous contemporary propagandistic travel descriptions and histories of New France that drew upon them (Dickason 1984:251–278).

The verbal image of the good savage was strengthened by graphic images. Although Indians were often drawn in a variety of ways concordant with the negative ethnography of the time (Colin 1987), equally often they were given the features of the idealized Classical Greeks and Romans known from extant statuary and from Renaissance painting. However Indians may have been described in the texts, they often looked like Greek gods and goddesses in the illustrations (Bucher 1981; Honour 1975; Lehner and Lehner 1966; Lorant 1965).

By the late seventeenth century, other similarities were being drawn between Indians, ancient Greeks and Romans, and the "nobler" Old World "barbarians." Filled with the enthusiasm of Enlightenment science, many thinkers hoped to create a "science of human society": If humans are part of the natural world, and if the natural world is governed by natural law, then the laws governing human behavior ought to be ascertainable. Giambattista Vico proposed such a "new science" in the 1730s (Bergin and Fisch 1970). In attempting to develop this science, philosophers and historians revived an idea from Classical times: that living "savage" societies are *analogs* of the past stages of development of civilized peoples. In effect, "as they are now, so our ancestors once were." Together with the assumption of psychic unity, that all human minds in all times and places are largely the same, the concept of the analogical savage made possible the so-called comparative method. The method was first applied by Joseph Francois Lafitau (Fenton and Moore [1724] 1974–1977), a Jesuit missionary to New France. Lafitau systematically compared the customs of the Iroquois with those of Old World ancients, using the former as analogs to account for the customs and institutions of the latter.

But analogical savages had more uses than simply explaining the origins of obscure past customs. For Jean Jacques Rousseau and other eighteenth-century social reformers, they provided useful standards against which to urge the reconstitution of European society (Mason 1987:586–596). The use of savages or "simpler peoples" as a means of showing up the decadence of civilized society is an ancient practice (Lovejoy and Boas 1935:8–9). Cicero (106–43 B.C.) and Tacitus (ca. A.D. 55–117) glorified the Scythians and the Germanic tribes, respectively, as examples against which to judge the corruption and immorality of Imperial Rome (Latham 1851; Shackleton 1915). But Rousseau and others attempted to go beyond comment to action.

Rousseau, like Vico, distinguished several stages in the development of humanity. The first is the "state of nature," in which protohumans are bestial but "naturally good." Competition for food and attacks from other animals lead protohumans to exercise their inherent intelligence and to begin making tools. It is this *transition* from animality to humanity, from nature to culture, and *the awareness of the transition*, that marked the *true* beginning of *human* nature. Humans then continued to develop toward an idealized hunter-gatherer stage:

> This period of the development of the human faculties, holding a just mean between the indolence of the primitive state and the petulant activity of our self-esteem, *must have been the happiest and the most lasting epoch. . . . The example of savages, almost all of whom have been found in this state, seems to confirm that the human race has been made to remain in it always; that this state is the veritable youth of the world;* and that all the subsequent progress has been in appearance so many steps toward the perfection of the individual, *and in fact toward the decay of the species* [Rousseau 1950:200, emphasis added].

The Jesuits' *le bon sauvages* thus became, for Rousseau, exemplars of the peak of human existence. Subsequent civilization was a matter of degeneration, not development.

Rousseau and his intellectual peers were deeply concerned that a way should be found to reverse the perceived degeneracy of civilization, particularly that of the French *ancien régime*. Their approach was to use the comparative method to seek what David Hume (cited by Becker 1932:100) referred to as the "constant and universal principles of human nature." They sought that which is *naturally good* in human society and expected to find it in the institutions and mores of analogical savages. Once found, the principles would somehow be used to *reconstruct* a rational and just society. Sadly, this did not happen.

The important point is that the "good" of humanity sought by the philosophers was found in the image of the good savages, an image manufactured principally in the *Jesuit Relations* (Dickason 1984). The image glossed as the "noble savage" was carried into the nineteenth century in Romantic literature and art, in the form of natural man living *freely*, "at one with nature." In the words of the playwright John Dryden ([1762] 1946), who coined the phrase:

> I am free as nature first made man,
> Ere the base laws of servitude began,
> When wild in the woods the noble savage ran.

Vanishing Savages

While the Jesuits' good savage was metamorphosed into the noble savage by the savants of Europe, quite another image emerged in the British colonies of North America and the succeeding United States: that of the *vanishing savage*. As we saw, the British view was that Indians should be removed or moved aside—and the reservation system was instituted soon after the Puritans reached Massachusetts (Vaughan 1965:260–308). By the time of American Independence, it was generally assumed that the Indians would vanish, literally or culturally, along with the wilderness they inhabited (Mitchell 1981), before the inevitable onslaught of white civilization. During the 1779 Sullivan campaign against the Iroquois, American army officers reportedly drank a toast (the tenth of an evening) to "Civilization or death to all American Savages" (cited by Pearce 1965:55). As Pearce notes, the toast expressed a great frontier truth and theme throughout the nineteenth century. Thomas Jefferson (1944:220–227), who also thought that Indians would vanish, tried to see that their languages and cultures would be recorded beforehand (Greene 1984:376–408). As an Enlightenment philosopher, he held that to properly know humanity, we must know it in all its variability. These two conceptions—that all human cultures should be recorded, if the commonalities, possibly the "laws," of human behavior are to be known, and that Indians and their cultures were vanishing—structured and drove anthropological research in the United States from Jefferson's time (Fowler 1975:20–22) until at least 1930. We will return to this point below.

Ethnology and Natural Man

When ethnology coalesced as a distinct field of study in 1840–1842 (Fowler 1975:19), its principal concern was natural man, by then glossed as "savage" or "primitive." The *OED* defines *ethnology* as "the science which treats of races and peoples, and their relations to one another, their distinctive physical and other characteristics." However, a definition closer to the way ethnology was used in the nineteenth century for political and colonial purposes, but justified as "science" (Stocking 1987:46–109), was offered in 1854 by J. C. Nott and George

Gliddon (1854:49) in their famed panegyric to white superiority, *Types of Mankind*:

> Ethnology includes the whole mental and physical history of the various types of mankind, as well as their social relations and adaptations. . . . Ethnology demands to know what was the primitive organic structure of each race?—what such race's *moral and psychical character?*—how far a race may have been, or may become, modified by the combined action of time and moral and physical causes? —*and what position in the social scale Providence has assigned to each type of man* [emphasis added].

Providentially, the "Higher Caucasians" were *assigned*, "in all ages, the largest brains and the most powerful intellect," and gave them

> the *mission* of extending and perfecting civilization—they are *by nature* ambitious, daring, domineering and reckless of danger. . . . The Creator has implanted in this group of races an *instinct* that, *in spite of themselves*, drives them through all difficulties, to carry out their great mission of civilizing the earth. It is not reason, or philanthropy, which urge them on; but it is *destiny* . . . [Higher caucasians are] born to be rulers; . . . It is written in *man's nature* by the hand of the Creator [Nott and Gliddon 1854:221, emphasis added].

The authors conclude that their studies "seem to render fugacious all probability of a brighter future for the *organically-inferior* types [the "lower races"], however sad the thought may be" (Nott and Gliddon 1854:278, emphasis added).

To sum up, between the time of the Columbian Encounter and its Tricentenary in 1792, the idea of *natural man* had gone through a number of iterations. Natural man had been both vilified and glorified. He was firmly placed in an *inferior* position in the natural world, vis-à-vis white northern Europeans. As part of the natural world, he should properly be studied by natural historians. But also as part of the natural world he should be dominated. According to Nott and Gliddon, it was the white man's *duty* to do so.

Soon after 1792, natural man, as savage or primitive, became synonymous with "native"—which meant any person subjugated by colonialism or slavery, particularly one who was an American Indian, African, or a South Sea Islander. These conceptions were carried into, and amplified during, the nineteenth century, to which we now turn.

The Heyday of Natural History

The popular acceptance of, and broad support for, natural history museums, as well as zoos and botanic gardens, in the nineteenth century was part of a popular natural history "craze" that swept Britain, and to a lesser but significant extent, northern Europe and North America.[5] Victorians studied natural history not for its own sake, but for the lessons it provided in *natural theology*. The archetype of the religious natural history treatise was William Paley's ([1802] 1828) *Natural Theology or Evidences of the Existence and Attributes of the Deity Collected from the Appearance of Nature*. Therein, Paley set forth his famous metaphor of the watch as a means of "arguing from design" the existence of God. A watch has such intricacy and precision of design that it must have had a maker. Just as any-one contemplating a watch must infer a maker, so either atheist or pious believer must infer a maker when contemplating nature, for "every indication of contriv-ance, every manifestation of design, exists in the works of nature; with the dif-ference, on the side of nature, of being greater or more, and that in a degree which exceeds all computation" (Paley 1828:12, cited by Dawkins 1965:5).

Paley urged the *active* contemplation of nature—as the lesson book of God's design of the world. As Barber (1980:13–26) shows, studying natural history as natural theology was a socially acceptable, morally uplifting, hence very popu-lar activity. The pious flocked to the countryside in droves to net butterflies, pick and press flowers, impale insects, frighten frogs, and participate in numerous archaeological digs to study the remains of natural man. In Britain, the home of the amateur enthusiast, there were dozens of specialized local and regional natural history societies, devoted to everything from algology to zoology. Hun-dreds of natural history treatises were published; many were best sellers, and remained so for years. It mattered little that the scientific information therein was often dreadfully inaccurate (Barber 1980:13–26), for it served a "higher pur-pose."[6]

In the United States, there was a similar interest in natural history, and in "In-dian relics," particularly the "mysterious Mound Builders" (Silverberg 1968; see Dunnell, this volume). Many towns had natural history societies, which were often focal points for both research and education. This intense interest in natu-ral history as natural theology in European countries and the United States, and their colonies, supported the development or expansion of zoos, botanic gar-dens, and natural history museums.

Anthropology and "The Imperial Synthesis"

Trigger (1989:84–147), in a cogent analysis of the political and economic forces that shaped the development of early nineteenth-century archaeology, notes that the growing capitalist middle class increasingly saw itself as the leading force in bettering life on a worldwide scale. The emergence of laissez-faire capitalism was seen as preordained; progress was merged with morality. "By identifying moral and social progress as concomitants of technological developments and the latter as a fundamental characteristic of human history, . . . the middle classes [reassured themselves] . . . of the cosmic significance and hence of the inevitable success of their role in history" (Trigger 1989:85). Since their roles as purveyors of progress were cosmically ordained, it was unseemly to question the idea of the inherent superiority of the "white races." And, it would have been unchari-table not to assume the noblesse oblige of the white man's burden, to bring Christian civilization to the rest of the benighted world, as that world "inevita-bly" came under the white man's influence or domination.

The nineteenth century was also a time of intensifying nationalism, reflected particularly in ideas of national, or ethnic superiority, the Aryan myth in its vari-ous manifestations among them (Poliakov 1974). There was also a great expan-sion of European colonialism into Africa, Asia, and the Pacific and the internal colonialism within the United States and Canada. Finally, the battles over slavery reached their peak in 1861, with the outbreak of the American Civil War. All these factors fueled the racism reflected in Nott and Gliddon (1854), a racism that intensified in subsequent decades (Frederickson 1971; Haller 1971; Stanton 1960; Takaki 1979).

These developments were reflected in the nascent fields of ethnology and anthropology (the latter term gained acceptance after about 1870). Ethnology was not a dispassionate scientific inquiry, despite considerable mystification to make it seem so. In the 1840s–1860s, ethnology provided a "scientific" framework within which slavery and colonialism could be justified. "Race" became the main preoccupation of ethnological research. Many papers read before various ethnological societies discoursed effusively on the "place" of Negroes, or American Indians, or other colonized peoples, in the *natural and sociocultural* scheme of things. "Science" was invoked at every turn to "prove" the assertions (Haller 1971; Stanton 1960).

After the publication of Darwin's *On the Origin of Species* and Herbert Spencer's ([1850–1870] 1971) writings on social evolution, ethnological and anthropological discourse was cast in an evolutionary framework (Greene 1959). Morgan's (1878) *Ancient Society* revivified the eighteenth-century comparative method and the role of the analogical savage in it. Tylor's (1865, 1871; see Hodgen 1936) doctrine of survivals seemed to provide proof of sociocultural evolution from savagery to civilization. Morgan (1878), Tylor (1865), Lubbock (1870), and others provided what Trigger (1989:110–147) calls the "Imperial Synthesis," that is, a scheme of sociocultural evolution making nineteenth-century Western civilization the culmination of human history. The analogical savage and Tylor's survivals provided the "evidence." A plethora of "racial" studies clearly evinced the "inferior place" of the "lower races" (Haller 1971; Stanton 1960). Thus, all peoples were assigned their "place" in the scheme of things, just as in Petty's great chain of being. Savages or primitives were assigned a "lower" place, one "closer to nature." It was perhaps "only natural" that such folk and their cultures should be exhibited in natural history museums.

The Age of Museums and World's Fairs

The period 1850 to 1920 is often called the Age of Museums. The intense popular interest in natural history early in the nineteenth century helped existing institutions such as the British Museum metamorphose into modern forms and stimulated the creation of new ones. But the second half of the century was the true Age of Museums, particularly of natural history and anthropology museums in Europe and North America (Farrington 1899; Hovey 1898). Twenty-three museums with anthropology components were established between 1875 and 1905 in western and central Europe, seventeen in United States and Canada, and another dozen or more in colonial countries (Frese 1960:10 and Figure 1; Sheets-Pyenson 1988). A few were ethnographic museums only, but most were natural history museums with"ethnological" exhibits. Many of the great art museums, as well as museums of industry and technology, were founded, or greatly expanded in the same period to celebrate the artistic, as well as the scientific and technological achievements of Western societies. The natural and cultural phenomena of the subordinate colonies, or tribes in the United States and Canada, were placed in the natural history museums.

Such an arrangement had in fact been made at the beginning of the nineteenth century by Charles Willson Peale, proprietor of the famed Peale's Philadelphia Museum, founded in 1786. In many ways, Peale's museum was a prototype for later and larger natural history museums, in terms of the arrangement of exhibits and what properly belongs in a natural history museum (Appel 1980; Sellers 1969, 1980). In 1800, Peale envisioned an ideal museum in which specimens of all the links in the chain of being would be displayed, including "the animal man." With the latter should be displayed "every curious article of dress; arms and utensils of the aborigines of this, and of other new discovered countries." Such a museum would reflect "the fundamental laws of nature" and the "great harmony of life . . . from the lowliest worm to the human" (cited by Sellers 1969:332, 337).

Many natural history museums founded during the nineteenth century utilized an exhibit scheme similar to Peale's and, after about 1870, gave it an evolutionary interpretation. For example, W. A. Herdman (1887), a professor of natural history in University College, Liverpool, presented an elaborate plan in 1887 for *his* ideal natural history museum. Herdman envisioned a long rectangular floor plan on which was superimposed a tree diagram of evolutionary development. A visitor would begin at the "base" of the tree with the earliest and simplest fossils, then follow along the "trunk" and out along "evolutionary limbs and branches" as they occurred. At the far end of the hall, the mammal limb divided into appropriate branches, the last two being apes and humans (Herdman 1887:Plate 1).

The Age of Museums was synchronous with the Age of World's Fairs. In various forms, fairs are ancient and venerable institutions in many societies. They provide a setting for large numbers of people to congregate for purposes of transacting business, being entertained, seeing new and different people, and exchanging information and sometimes genes. Modern large-scale fairs, "International Exhibitions" (later called "Expositions," and popularly, after 1893, "World's Fairs") began in 1851 with the Crystal Palace Exhibition in London. The principal purpose was to show off the wonders of the Industrial Revolution and stimulate commerce, but there were also cultural displays and exhibitions of exotica drawn from Britain's rapidly expanding empire. Other countries scrambled to imitate Britain's success. In the following 70 years, at least three dozen fairs large enough to claim the title "International Exposition" were held in Europe or the United States.

Existing museum collections and exhibits were displayed at fairs, and the practice of funding large-scale ethnographic collecting for display materials added many new collections. Fairs were the stimulus for the expansion of existing museums or the creation of new ones, for example, the Smithsonian's National Museum (1876), the Trocadero complex in Paris (1878), the Field Columbian (Chicago Natural History) Museum (1893), the St. Louis Public Museum

(1904), and the San Diego Museum of Man (1915) (Collier 1969; Collier and Tschopik 1954; Dorsey 1901; Goode 1882; Rydell 1980; Williams 1985). This intertwining of anthropological museum and exposition exhibits provided the context within which images of the Other—images shaped by four centuries of colonialism, and a variety of philosophical, political, and anthropological uses—were conveyed to tens of millions of people. Herein we focus primarily on U.S. museums and fairs between 1876 and 1916.

Museums and Exhibitions of Natural Man

Neil Harris (1962, 1981) points out that nineteenth-century libraries, museums, and universities were bastions of conservatism and guardians of "traditional" values—the values held by the wealthy and the power brokers who founded, supported, and governed the institutions. Several writers who have mused reflexively on the roles of natural history and anthropological museums (Ames 1986; Ave 1980; Frese 1960; Durrans 1988; Stocking 1985) echo Harris's point, noting in particular that nineteenth-century natural history and ethnographic museums generally reflected the values of the larger society and attitudes about "the Other" derived from them. And, they assert, many still do.

It is useful to examine the general assertions of Ames and others and to track the uses of natural man in exhibitions by reviewing some specific exhibition philosophies of anthropology curators and museum directors in the late nineteenth century. This will also provide a context for examining anthropological exhibitions at world's fairs.

The epitome of evolution-oriented exhibits was in the museum at Oxford University founded in 1884 by the redoubtable Gen. A. H. L. F. Pitt Rivers (Chapman 1985). Pitt Rivers's metaphor for human evolution was a tree on which extant races were "'taken to represent the budding twigs and foliage' and European man the main stem" (cited by Chapman 1985:31). In this museum, case upon case contained thousands of artifacts arranged to demonstrate Pitt Rivers's assumption that artifacts evolved from rude to sophisticated forms by a process of "unconscious selection." Given the assumptions of psychic unity and the inevitable linear development of human culture, typologically similar artifacts from widely separated tribes were placed together, as long as they fit the assumed developmental sequence of the type.

Otis T. Mason had developed a similar evolutionary philosophy at the Smithsonian Institution. His anthropology exhibition at the Philadelphia Centennial Exposition in 1876 (see below) was arranged strictly according to the "typological method." He continued to use the approach for more than two decades in some Smithsonian exhibitions. A general evolutionary display philosophy was formulated by George Brown Goode, first director of the Smithsonian's National Museum, which opened in 1881. He visualized the entire museum as

> showing, arranged according to one consistent plan, the resources of the earth
> and the results of human activity in either direction [i.e., from savagery to civili-
> zation, and vice-versa]. . . . The collections should form a museum of anthropol-

ogy, the word anthropology being used in its most comprehensive sense. It should exhibit the physical characteristics, the history, the manners, past and present, *of all peoples, civilized and savage,* and should illustrate human culture and industry in all their phases; the earth, its physical structure and its products is to be exhibited *with special reference to its adaptation for use by man and its resources for future needs* [Goode 1882:5, emphasis added].

(Goode, in the last phrase, is properly mindful of the natural resources needs of modern industrial capitalism.)

As Jacknis (1985:77) and others have pointed out, Franz Boas (1887) began a discussion of alternative approaches to anthropology displays in 1887. In a letter to *Science,* Boas (1887) strongly criticized Mason's evolutionary displays in the U.S. National Museum. Soon Mason, William Henry Holmes, John Wesley Powell, and others were involved in the discussion. There were, of course, larger theoretical issues, and these were debated vigorously by Boas and his opponents over the next two decades and more (Stocking 1974:1–41). By questioning the assumptions of unilinear cultural evolution, by making psychic unity a research issue and not a truism, and by insisting on a holistic approach to exhibitions, stressing the integrity of a culture and its environmental setting, Boas helped force a change in exhibition design, behind which ultimately lay a reorientation of anthropological theory. The reorientation was toward the culture historical method, centered on the concept of culture areas.

By the time of the Chicago World's Fair in 1893, Mason had reoriented his own thinking, apparently influenced by the "living exhibits" he saw at the 1889 International Exposition in Paris (see below). In the Smithsonian anthropology exhibition, the focal point was a 12-x-16-foot reproduction of the map of Powell's (1891) linguistic classification of North American Indian tribes. Mason selected "typical" tribes from the map and placed them on another map of North American "biogeographic areas" to show a correlation between environment and material culture. Reference to the linguistic map, however, made the point that there is no necessary correlation between language family, material culture, and environment (Mason 1894). Mason used "lay-figure groups"—mannequins with the proper dress and implements of the proper tribes, placed in an environmentally appropriate setting (Fagin 1984:255). This exhibition seemingly was the first to use life-groups and the first to be based on the principles of what would later be called culture areas (Jacknis 1985:81).

Over the next two decades, Mason and Holmes at the Smithsonian, Putnam and Boas at the American Museum of Natural History, George Dorsey at the Field Columbian Museum, and others (Dorsey 1907; Holmes 1900, 1903; Mason 1896) continued to refine the culture area concept and exhibitions based thereon.

However, deep theoretical differences remained, as Jacknis (1985) demonstrates. Mason and Holmes in effect synthesized the older evolutionary view with the newer geographical orientation. For example, Holmes (1900:22–23) described two [types of exhibition methods] of primary importance, . . . the *geographical or ethnographical* assemblage, and . . . the *developmental or genetic* assemblage . . . [each] adapted to the presentation of the general truths of anthropology. [The former shows] the peoples themselves in more or less well-defined geographical divisions. [The latter illustrates] not that of tribes or nations and their connection with particular environments, but that of the development of the race along the various lines of culture progress, each series beginning with the inceptive or lowest stages and extending to the highest.

In subsequent decades, as the historical particularist orientation of Boas gained ascendancy, "the older" cultural evolutionism was cast aside, until the 1940s when Leslie White (1949) began to recycle it. But particularism itself was shaped by older ideas about natural man. The claim of anthropology to be the "Science of Man" derived from the Enlightenment requirement that to know humanity we must know all humans. Preferably, we should know them as untainted as possible by the evils (or in modern parlance, "acculturative forces") of Western civilization. This view in turn underlay particularist attempts to establish an *ethnographic present* for every tribe: "how it was," culturally, the day before Western influence arrived. Myopically, this often was defined as *white American* influence, more or less ignoring the direct and indirect processes of acculturation prior to about 1800. In an important statement about exhibition philosophy, Holmes (1903:270) says exhibitions should show "native ethnology" set in "natural areas." Native peoples were to be shown in costumes and settings of the appropriate ethnographic present. Their close adaptation to their environments should be stressed. In translation, this is another version of the old image of natural man living in harmony with nature.[7]

Another image that drove anthropological research in the United States throughout the nineteenth century and was a significant factor in world's fairs exhibitions as well as the popular imagination was the vanishing savage, noted previously. In some European colonies, some ethnic populations did indeed vanish as a result of disease or genocide, as in the case of the Tasmanian aborigines. In others, colonial populations, while affected to varying degrees, did not vanish; they became the labor force that produced the raw materials to be shipped to the controlling countries. In the United States, the Puritan philosophy prevailed: Either kill the Indians or push them out of the way onto reservations. Once the Indians were there, attempts were made to make them vanish culturally through policies of enforced acculturation and assimilation (Kelly 1983:3–162).

By 1879, the vanishing savage was considered to be an eventual certainty in the United States. It was a constant theme used by John Wesley Powell and Spencer F. Baird before congressional appropriations committees as they sought funds to support the Bureau of Ethnology and the Anthropology Division of the U.S. National Museum, respectively (Fowler and Fowler 1969:160; Hinsley 1981:81–189). They hoped to impress their countrymen of the urgent need to collect languages, kin terms, rituals and artifacts "before it's too late"—that is, before the knowledgeable old people died, the younger ones were assimilated, and the material culture swamped by modern manufactured goods. This theme of "urgent anthropology" continued into the late twentieth century on a world-wide scale.

An observation by Kenneth Hudson (1975:157) is appropriate as a final note on the uses of natural man in natural history museums. The South African Museum in Capetown, South Africa, has state-of-the-art museology and displays. But the displays are a source of

> racial antagonism since they have been devoted to showing the primitive way of life of non-White people in South Africa. To a coloured person, there is no essential difference between presenting a butterfly and a bushman to the world in this fashion. Both are the white man's specimens, symbols of his power and freedom to collect what pleases him. There are, in South African museums, no dioramas which illustrate the life and habits of white men and women. To present the master-race in this way would be politically explosive [Hudson 1975:157].

Similar feelings were voiced in December 1989 at hearings to establish a new Museum of the American Indian on the National Mall in Washington, D.C., as part of the Smithsonian Institution. Indian people were quoted as saying that exhibitions about them, placed next to the dinosaurs and other extinct creatures in the Natural History Museum, made it appear that they, too, are extinct and no longer a part of American society (National Native News, National Public Radio, December 8, 1989). According to Durrans (1988:145), echoing Ames (1986), Frese (1960), and others, museums should make it very clear

> that every contemporary community, whatever its way of life, and whether dominant or dominated, inherits a stake in the whole of human evolution. Whether fractured or continuous, exclusive or interwoven with that of other groups, the past development of all surviving societies has the same time-depth. Within that time, their responses to different cultural and environmental opportunities are as interesting for their unique qualities as for what they share in common. This does not mean that they meet the needs of their members equally well or are equally prepared to cope with current and future pressures; but it does mean they cannot be evaluated according to the idea of intrinsic "primitiveness." This is an important challenge to which many ethnographic museums have responded as well as they can by stressing the complexity and sophistication of traditional ways of life. In a world where the "primitive" other has long been the victim of imperial domination, this is one way of attacking the ideology that supports it.

Savages and Imperialism at the World's Fairs

Exhibiting subservient or conquered peoples at public gatherings is at least as old as city-states. From Sumeria and Old Kingdom Egypt to the staged triumphal entries of the Roman emperors and beyond, captives were paraded and exhibited as evidence of conquest and hegemony. Thus, Christopher Columbus was simply following a very old tradition. The seven Taino Indians he brought back in 1493 were of great interest in Lisbon, Seville, and Barcelona. Several hundred American Indians were in Europe by 1502, primarily as slaves, but were also exhibited from time to time in various cities (Hodgen 1964:111–112). In 1550, a contingent of some 50 Brazilian Indians were part of "un spectacle magnifique" staged in Rouen, France, to celebrate a visit by Henry II. Much of the time, the Indians were presented naked, engaged in mock fights and hunts (Honour 1975:63 and Figure 52). In 1565, a village of several hundred Brazilian Indians, complete with an imitation tropical landscape, was established at Bordeaux as part of a gala to celebrate a state visit by Charles IX. There was also a display of captives from other countries (Hodgen 1964:112; Honour 1975:64). There was thus considerable precedence for the "ethnological zoos" of the world's fairs.

A few fairs held in Europe and the United States between 1876 and 1916—Philadelphia (1876), Paris (1889), Chicago (1893), Omaha (1898), St. Louis (1904), and San Diego (1915–1916)—can serve as examples.

Ethnological Exhibits at World's Fairs

The first official exhibitions to include native peoples were those at the 1876 Philadelphia Centennial Exposition, although various kinds of concession exhibitions before and after this event often included native peoples. Concession exhibitions occupied space, paid for with a percentage of gross income, in the "pleasure" areas of fairs, usually outside, or adjacent to, the "official" exhibit spaces or buildings. Concessions were vital to the economics of fairs; usually the income therefrom made the difference between a profit and a loss for the fair sponsors. For example, at Chicago in 1893, on the Midway, the famed "Streets of Egypt," one of three concessions where fairgoers ogled women belly dancers, grossed $790,000, the most successful concession at the fair. The fair took 20 percent of gross (Higinbotham 1898:482–491).

At the 1876 Philadelphia Centennial, the official Indian exhibitions were in the charge of the Smithsonian Institution and the Bureau of Indian Affairs. Spencer F. Baird, assistant secretary of the Smithsonian, John Wesley Powell, and others proposed a series of "living exhibits"—ethnological exhibits in which Indians would live in traditional houses, wear traditional clothing, and carry out traditional activities for the edification of the visitors (Baird 1876:61). But Congress balked at the $115,000 price tag, so papier-maché mannequins dressed in traditional costumes were substituted (Trennert 1974:122). In the unofficial pleasure area outside the fair grounds, however, there was "an Indian encampment with three hundred native Americans from fifty tribes in charge of George Anderson, the famous Texas scout." The encampment was located next to a "magnificent soda-fountain equipped with seventy-six syrup tubes" (McCullough 1966:35). There is little information on the encampment, but the Indians were there to be gaped at, for a fee. We suspect there was much gaping when the news of General Custer's tête-à-tête with Sitting Bull and his allies at the Little Big Horn reached Philadelphia in July 1876.

The Paris Universal Exposition of 1889

The 1889 Paris Exposition set the tone and the standard for anthropological exhibitions at all subsequent world's fairs. In addition to the controversial Eiffel

Tower, built for the exposition, there was a great panoply of exhibits. Among them was a large ethnological exhibit. According to Otis T. Mason (1890:31),

> On the Esplanade des Invalides *side by side with the latest inventions and with the whole civilized world as spectators* . . . [there were] twelve types of Africans, besides Javanese, Tonkinese, Chinese, Japanese, and other oriental peoples, living in native houses, wearing native costumes, eating native foods, practicing native arts and rites [emphasis added].

There was also an official

> exhibition of Africans and Franco-Indian natives at their characteristic occupations, chief among which . . . were the Javanese theatre and the Annamite Buddhist temple. The members of the [anthropological] Congress . . . spent many hours in these *savage enclosures and houses* studying the people and their arts and listening to their *rude music* [Mason 1890:35, emphasis added].

A week-long session of the International Congress of Anthropological and Prehistoric Sciences considered numerous questions, including "ethnographic survivals which throw light upon the social condition of primitive populations in Central and Western Europe" (Mason 1890:33).

We see here a pattern repeated in numerous subsequent world's fairs over the next three decades. That is, "savage, rude natives" on display next to the "latest inventions . . . for all the civilized world to see." What better affirmation of the assumptions of unilinear evolution, the ideology of capitalist progress and the expanding European and Euroamerican domination of the world?

Chicago World Columbian Exposition, 1893

The 1893 World's Columbian Exposition was the largest, most expensive world's fair held in the nineteenth century (Burg 1976). Despite the financial panic of 1893, more than 27,000,000 people flocked to the "Great White City" alongside Lake Michigan. Amidst all the wonders and hoopla, there were three anthropology exhibitions, two on the exposition grounds, the third on the famous Midway Plaisance, a 600–foot-wide, mile-long strip filled with concessions. The numerous "living villages" on the Midway were nominally under the Ethnology Division of the fair, which was directed by Frederic Ward Putnam. These ethnic or national exhibitions were occupied by over 3,000 people from 48 nations or dependent colonies worldwide. Prominent among the living villages was the Dahomey settlement, where fairgoers could ogle "Cannibal men and their Amazon wives" (Buell 1894:*passim*; Flinn 1893:47). Outside the fair grounds, Buffalo Bill Cody's Wild West Show had a six-month, 618–performance run and reputedly netted a million dollars. The Indians lost the battles in the show every time.

As noted, the official anthropology exhibitions of the fair were under the direction of Frederic Ward Putnam, assisted by Franz Boas. The Anthropology Building had 161,000 square feet of exhibition space. Funds for collecting and installing exhibits totaled $140,450 (Higinbotham 1898:350–352, 482–491). The exhibitions therein were eclectic, because Putnam was obligated to display collections donated by states and individuals (Fagin 1984).

Northwest of the Anthropology Building was the ethnographical exhibition, designed and directed by the Bureau of Indian Affairs. Here, Cree, Haida, Kwakiutl, Iroquois, Sioux, Apaches, Navajos, Coahuillas, Papagos, and Yaquis lived in traditional houses and "made trinkets for sale" (Flinn 1893:70). These "living exhibits" were carefully interpreted to show the Indians "in transition"—from the "wild" savages of the very recent past (the incident at Wounded Knee had occurred only three years earlier) through the "semicivilized" groups and on to those who, when fully assimilated, would take their "proper place" in American society—as trained lower-class workers. Next door, there was a model Indian School to show how Indians were being "civilized" under the beneficent tutelage of the Bureau and Christian missionaries. But in the meantime they could still exhibit their "quaint" and "savage" ways for the amusement of the fairgoers.[8]

We have already noted that the Smithsonian anthropology exhibition was housed in the Government Building. Many of the faces on the mannequins in Mason's life-groups were of prominent Indian leaders, the faces modeled from "plaster casts from life." One commentator rhapsodized, "They have reproduced these chiefs exact in stature, features, complexion, dress. It is a work of the utmost value, *the last true records of a dying race of men*" (Truman 1893:404, emphasis added).

Soon after his appointment as head of the Ethnology Division, Putnam had proposed that a permanent natural history museum be established to house collections made for the fair. At first, the idea was met with considerable opposition from the fair organizers and the Chicago authorities. But the idea prevailed. Edward Ayer, a prominent Chicago collector of Indian artifacts, persuaded Marshall Field to build the museum (Collier 1969). The Field Columbian Museum ultimately became one of the great natural history museums with anthropology as a prominent feature. As the Chicago Natural History Museum, it will stand in 1992 as a monument to the Columbian Quatrocentenary and its vision of the Other.

The Trans-Mississippi and International Exposition, 1898

In 1898 Omaha, Nebraska, made its bid for international exposition fame and fairgoer dollars. On a site overlooking the Missouri River, progress was celebrated in a smaller version of Chicago's Great White City (Rydell 1980:207–248). A large feature of the Omaha extravaganza was an Indian Congress of 400 to 550 prominent Indian leaders, elders, and their families from 20 tribes who had been "recruited" by the Bureau of Indian Affairs. Among the Indians were Geronimo, then imprisoned at Fort Sill, Oklahoma Territory, and members of his band. The Indian encampment on the fairgrounds could be visited for twenty-five cents, and fairgoers could watch the Indians doing "traditional" tasks and ceremonies, acting out their "aboriginality," as the Omaha *Bee*, put it (cited by Rydell 1980:221). There were also daily pageant/sham battles involving Indians from the Congress and Indians and cowboys from a wild west show at the fair (Rydell 1980:221–224). James Mooney, hired to direct Indian exhibitions but largely shunted aside by the fair managers, put on stage performances of the Ghost Dance, using Indian Congress volunteers (Mooney 1899:128). Much of the publicity for the fair trumpeted the Indian Congress as "the last gathering" of the "Vanishing Red Man." When President William McKinley visited the fair, the Indians put on a special pageant in which they massacred each other, not whites. The Omaha *Bee* reported:

> Yesterday morning President McKinley received the homage of a hundred thousand representatives of a race that stands at the pinnacle of the greatest civilization of the world's history. . . . In the afternoon the president was rendered honor by a thousand representatives of a passing civilization that was in its way great and of a dying nation that acted within its limitations as magnificent (cited by Rydell 1980:235).

In Omaha, Indian people were officially defined as vanishing savages. They also became actors, performing their daily life activities and ceremonies before live audiences. In the daily pageants and sham battles with the cowboys of the wild west show, they helped incorporate themselves into the growing myth of cowboys and Indians in the Wild West (Taylor 1983), soon to be magnified into *The American Epic* by the nascent motion picture industry (Stedman 1982). In Mooney's (1899:127) view, "the general result was such—particularly from the practical standpoint of the ticket seller—that we may expect to see ethnology as a principal feature at future expositions so long as our aboriginal material holds out." He was indeed correct.

St. Louis, Louisiana Purchase Exposition, 1904

The Louisiana Purchase Exposition, known in song and story as the St. Louis World's Fair, like its predecessors, celebrated progress and American capitalism. It also celebrated American imperialism by its extensive use of ethnological exhibits. A summary history of the St. Louis fair (Francis 1913:1:522–532) provides a clear picture of how the living ethnological exhibitions were interpreted:

> At the Exposition were assembled numerous types of many of the primitive races of the earth. . . . Groups of various tribes from different parts of the earth and of varying degrees of development were presented as in actual life. Some of the tribes were of the lowest existing types, others were fairly advanced in more primitive arts of civilization. . . . The Philippine exhibit furnished a complete exposition of the slow evolution of civilization among tribes comparatively adjacent to but isolated from each other when left to their own resources, though in the region of the oldest civilization; also of the effect of contact and mixture of certain races with Caucasian blood and western civilization. A group of African pygmies, some of them of man-eating tribes [sic], brought the collection of primitive races down to the lowest known human stage; the Ainus and Patagonians represented the semi-civilized savages still existing like our Indians in countries dominated by highly civilized races and like the Indians rapidly disappearing.

This is, in fact, an excellent summary of the ethnology at the fair. W J McGee,[9] recently forced out of the Bureau of American Ethnology at the Smithsonian, was the director of anthropology. Together with the fair directors and the federal government, McGee created several "living displays" totaling between 5,000 and 6,000 "natives" (fair publicity estimates vary). One of them was a 37–acre compound occupied by Filipinos, brought by the federal government to demonstrate the beneficence of its colonial policy, after the United States took the Philippines from Spain in 1898. Another was an encampment around a Bureau of Indian Affairs school. The school was designed so that visitors could walk down the hallway and observe elderly Indian people, including Geronimo, once again, doing traditional craft work. Across the hall were young Indian men and women, dressed in white man's clothes, learning white man's jobs, such as printing, harness making, and home making . The lesson was clear. Under the benevolent guidance of bureau teachers, young Indian people were being taught to vanish, culturally. The young people would not be allowed to grow up to be like their elders across the hall.

The vanishing savage theme was made more explicit by two colossal statues on the main concourse of the fair. One, by Solon Borglum, titled "A Step toward Civilization" (Figure 3–1), showed an Indian man, clutching a book and pointing his son toward the "White Man's Way." Behind him on the ground were his traditional tools, which he had cast away, and his wife, weeping for her son. The second, "The Destiny of the Red Man" (Figure 3–2), by Adolph Weinman, had a robed and hooded Indian skeleton of death pointing Indian people and the buffalo toward extinction. A vulture sat menacingly on a Northwest Coast totem pole on the side (McCue 1988:58–62).

San Diego Panama-California Exposition, 1915

In 1915, both San Francisco and San Diego staged expositions to celebrate the opening of the Panama Canal. San Francisco had the "official" exposition, which meant access to considerable government funding. San Diego, with less than 80,000 people, nonetheless presented an event of "world's fair" class. It lasted two years. The San Diego sponsors hired Edgar Lee Hewett as exhibits director. Hewett decided to make the main theme "The Science of Man." The sponsors put up $100,000 for the exhibition. Hewett gained the cooperation of William Henry Holmes and Ales Hrdlicka, of the U.S. National Museum. Hrdlicka spent three years traveling to European museums to get duplicate artifacts as well as to Siberia, Mongolia, Alaska, Africa, and the Philippines to obtain life masks from which busts were made (Hrdlicka 1917).

According to the San Diego *Union*, Hrdlicka arranged for copies of busts of "Primal Man" from European museums. These included Java Man, Sussex Man [the Piltdown hoax], Heidelberg Man, La Quina Woman, Neanderthal Man, Galley Hill Man, Man of Spy, Grenelle Man, Chapelle Man and Cro-Magnon. In the illustration accompanying the article, the first six are considerably more simian in appearance than more recent reconstructions of *Homo erectus* and *H. neanderthalensis*. There were also 15 male and 15 female busts, modeled from life

Figure 3–1. *A Step toward Civilization*, by Solon H. Borglum. Exhibited at Louisiana Purchase Exposition, St. Louis, 1904. Statue subsequently destroyed. (Photo WF939, Missouri Historical Society)

masks, of each of the "three main races—the white, the yellow-brown and the black." These were arranged in a sequence—Negritos, Pygmies, Bushmen, Zulus, Asians, American Indians, and whites—making it quite clear that the "darker" races were lower in the "scale of evolution" than the whites. "The series of the white race include casts of living representatives of eminent American

Figure 3–2. *Destiny of the Red Man*, by Adolph A. Weinmann. Exhibited at Louisiana Purchase Exposition, St. Louis, 1904. Statue subsequently destroyed. (Photo 941, Missouri Historical Society)

families" (San Diego *Union* 1915). The full exhibition treated "man's natural history, growth and development, varieties or races, and pathology" (Raymenton 1962:1).

In the California Building next door, a cast-concrete "Renaissance Spanish" melange designed by Bertram Goodhue, Hewett placed the famous molds of stelae and large sculptures from Quirigua and other Mayan centers, together with Carlos Vierra's spectacular murals of Maya cities. These remain to the present time. During the fair, Hewett and San Diego's city authorities initiated a plan for a permanent museum in the California Building. Hewett was appointed director of what ultimately became the San Diego Museum of Man (Wright 1980).[10]

At the far end of the "Isthmus," San Diego's version of the Midway, lay the Painted Desert exhibition. The several-acre compound was funded by the Santa Fe Railway and was designed and built by Jesse Nusbaum and a crew of San Ildefonso Indian workers, led by Julian Martinez. It contained replicas of Taos Pueblo and "cliff dwellings," occupied by Indians pretending to be "cliff dwellers," as well as a San Ildefonso kiva. There were also various hogans, wickiups, corrals, and sheep and goat pens. Living cacti, yuccas, and juniper trees, transplanted from Arizona, dotted the grounds. Here lived Hopis, Zunis, Rio Grande

Puebloans, Navajos, Apaches, and Havasupais. They daily performed ceremonies and dances, did chores, wove blankets, and made baskets and pots. One of the potters was Maria Martinez. By 1915, the Santa Fe Railway and the related Fred Harvey Company had fully developed their program of emphasizing the "romantic" southwestern Indians (Thomas 1978) to attract tourists to New Mexico, Arizona, and southern California. The Painted Desert was a great advertisement, visited by hundreds of thousands of fairgoers. Thus, at San Diego, as at St. Louis, "native" peoples became actors mimicking their own cultures for the benefit of a large capitalist enterprise.

San Francisco Panama-Pacific Exposition

The San Francisco exposition, which ran for several months in 1915, did not have an official ethnological exhibit, although there were the usual ethnic exhibitions in the "Joy Zone" (Benedict 1983). It did have the famous "End of the Trail" statue (Figure 3–3) by the sculptor James Earl Fraser, designer of the Indianhead nickel. According to an exposition catalog, "The drooping, storm-beaten figure of the Indian on the spent pony symbolizes the end of the race which was once a mighty people. The sorrowful story is so simply told it grips and haunts the beholder" (Burness 1915:n.p.).[11]

After 1915, ethnological exhibits waned at world's fairs, at least as official exhibitions. However, there was a last imperialist gasp at the World Exhibition at Brussels in 1958. Belgium, nearly the last of the old-time colonial powers (by then neocolonialism was well under way), exhibited a native village from the Congo. "However, the public response partly consisted of throwing peanuts and bananas to the inhabitants and treating them as if they were caged-in wild animals. [This] was not appreciated by the Congolese, who consequently left the exhibition and returned indignantly to their home country" (Frese 1960:11). *Sic transit gloria mundi.*

Conclusion

Natural man has had many uses in natural history, generally in anthropology as part of natural history, and has played many roles in the justifications of colonialism and imperialism. In his role of savage, he has been vilified and glorified, accused of heinous crimes, and defined as bad, good, lowly, exhalted, noble, and analogical. He has been thought ready to vanish since at least 1784. As analog, he has played prominent roles in social criticism and anthropological theory for two centuries and more. He and his cultures have been exhibited and variously interpreted in natural history museums, while the founders of those museums exhibited themselves and their cultures in museums of high art and science and technology. As colonialized native, natural man was placed in ethnological exhibits at world's fairs as a curiosity for the amusement of "civilized" fairgoers and as a symbol of "lowly" subservience. Obviously natural man, as one manifestation of the Other, is a very complex persona in the eyes of his creators, and his uses are many. What he may be in "reality" seems yet to be understood.

Figure 3–3. *End of the Trail*, by James Earl Fraser. Exhibited at the San Francisco Panama-Pacific Exposition, 1915. Original statue now in the National Cowboy Hall of Fame and Western Heritage Center, Oklahoma City. The statue, and print imitations of it, were widely reproduced for over 50 years in the United States and Europe. (Photograph courtesy of the National Cowboy Hall of Fame and Western Heritage Center)

Acknowledgments

Some of the ideas herein are explored in another form in Fowler (1990) and are used with the permission of the University of Nevada Press. Our thanks to the able staffs of the Missouri Historical Society, St. Louis, the San Diego Historical Society, and the San Diego Museum of Man for assistance with archival materials and illustrations.

Notes

1. Current anthropological discourse on the Other is beyond the scope of this chapter. Guidepost works include Asad (1973), Clifford and Marcus (1986), Diamond (1974), Douglas (1989), Fabian (1983), Marcus and Fischer (1986), and Said (1979).

2. For the complex problems of the existence and interpretation of cannibalism, see Arens (1979), Green (1972), and Sanday (1986).

3. Given the principle of the "least degree of difference" between links in the chain, it seemed probable that "missing links" must exist. Within the burgeoning scientific program of inventorying and describing the natural world, searches for such missing links proceeded apace. In modern dress, the search continues, in paleoanthropology.

4. Western conceptions of nature as the standard of value and human relationships to nature are examined in detail by Glacken (1967) and Thomas (1983). A central aspect is how human interaction with nature has been conceived. On the one hand, there is the Stoic idea that "the law of living [is] to act in harmony with nature" (Matheson 1968:56). On the other hand, there is the notion of subjugating and dominating nature. Certainly this idea was a driving force in European expansion after 1492, and it accelerated with the advent of the Industrial Revolution (Glacken 1967:623–705). In the dichotomy of harmony versus subjugation, *natural man* was usually seen on the harmonic side.

5. The complex histories of botanic gardens and zoos, together with the earlier history of museums, cannot be detailed here. See especially Alexander (1983), Braunsholtz (1970), Brockway (1979), Duval (1982), Miller (1974), Pieters (1980), Prest (1981), and Zuckerman (1980). The key role played by Henry A. Ward, founder of the still-extant Ward's Scientific Establishment, in nineteenth-century natural history museum design and development in the United States should be further examined (Kohlstedt 1980; Ward 1948).

6. The intense popular interest in natural history qua natural theology, especially in nineteenth-century Britain, accounts for much of the furor surrounding the publication of Robert Chambers's ([1844] 1969) *Vestiges of Creation* and Darwin's (1859) *Origin of Species*. Both deeply threatened to replace Paley's omniscient creator of the providential watch with Dawkins's (1965) "blind watchmaker"—the seemingly random process of evolution.

7. As a final note on the updating of natural man in harmony with nature, in the view of most late nineteenth- and early twentieth-century romantics, artists and anthropologists alike, natural man in North America not only lived in harmony with nature, he sanctified it, because he was part of it. According to Alice Fletcher (1916:293), "Finding himself to be one of a wide-reaching cosmic family, the Indian considered it imperative for him to conform to what he conceived to be nature's order." The plethora of anthropological studies of American Indian religion that stress the harmonic worship of nature may tell us more, yet again, about anthropologists and the Other than about Indian religion.

8. Very little is known about how the participants in the world's fair ethnological exhibitions reacted to the fairs and to being on display. Julian and Maria Martinez, the famed potters from San Ildefonso Pueblo, New Mexico, honeymooned at the 1904 St. Louis fair and were at San Diego in 1915. They pretended not to understand English, "and then they had something to laugh about when the white people had gone home" (Marriott 1948:119). Geronimo, a prisoner at Fort Sill, Oklahoma Territory, was exhibited, despite his objections, at Omaha in 1898, Buffalo in 1899, and St. Louis in 1904 (Debo 1976:400–427). His autobiographical reactions to the St. Louis fair (Barrett 1915:197–206)

are rather like those of most other fairgoers—a sense of wonder at the buildings, the displays, the fairgoers, and the other native peoples he met.

9. One of McGee's many pompous affectations was not using periods after the initials of his name.

10. Hewett was then and remained a director of the Museum of New Mexico and the School of American Research in Santa Fe, in addition to directing the Museum of Man. In 1920 he also became professor of anthropology at San Diego State College (Chauvenet 1983:97–109).

11. Both the Borglum and Weinmann statues were destroyed after the St. Louis fair. Fraser's statue is preserved in the National Cowboy Hall of Fame, Oklahoma City, Oklahoma (Samuels and Samuels 1976).

References

Alexander, Edward P.
    1983 *Museum Masters. Their Museums and Their Influence*. American Association for State and Local History, Nashville, Tenn.
Allen, Don C.
    1963 *The Legend of Noah. Renaissance Rationalism in Arts, Science and Letters*. University of Illinois Press, Urbana.
Ames, Michael
    1986 *Museums, the Public and Anthropology. A Study in the Anthropology of Anthropology*. University of British Columbia Press, Vancouver and Concept Publishing, New Delhi.
Appel, Toby A.
    1980 Science, Popular Culture and Profit: Peale's Philadelphia Museum. *Journal of the Society for the Bibliography of Natural History* 9:619–634.
Arens, W.
    1979 *The Man-Eating Myth: Anthropology and Anthropophagy*. Oxford University Press, New York.
Asad, Talal (editor)
    1973 *Anthropology and the Colonial Encounter*. Humanities Press, New York.
Ashley Montagu, M. F.
    1943 Edward Tyson, M.D., F.R.S. 1650–1708 and the Rise of Human and Comparative Anatomy in England. *American Philosophical Society Memoirs* 20. Originally published 1709.
Ave, J. B.
    1980 Ethnographic Museums in a Changing World. In *From Field-Case to Show-Case. Research, Acquisition and Presentation in the RijksMuseum voor Volkenkunde (National Museum of Ethnology), Leiden*, edited by W. R. van Gulik, H. S. Van der Straaten, and G. D. Van Wengen, pp. 11–28. J. C. Gieben, Amsterdam.
Baird, Spencer F.
    1876 International Centennial Exhibition. *Smithsonian Institution Annual Report for 1875*, pp. 58–71. Washington, D.C.
Barber, Lynn
    1980 *The Heyday of Natural History, 1820–1870*. Doubleday, Garden City.
Barrett, S. M. (editor)
    1915 *Geronimo's Story of His Life*. Duffield, New York.
Barrow, John D.
    1988 *The World within the World*. Clarendon Press, Oxford.
Becker, Carl
    1932 *The Heavenly City of the Eighteenth Century Philosophers*. Yale University Press, New Haven, Conn.

Benedict, Burton
    1983 *The Anthropology of World's Fairs: San Francisco's Panama Pacific International Exposition of 1915*. Lowie Museum of Anthropology, Berkeley, Calif., and Scolar Press, London.
Bergin, Thomas G., and Max H. Fisch (editors and translators)
    1970 *The New Science of Giambattista Vico*. Cornell University Press, Ithaca, N.Y.
Bernheimer, Richard
    1952 *Wild Men in the Middle Ages: A Study in Art, Sentiment and Demonology*. Harvard Univerity Press, Cambridge, Mass.
Boas, Franz
    1887 Museums of Ethnology and Their Classification. *Science* 9:587–589.
Braunsholtz, Hermann
    1970 *Sir Hans Sloane and Ethnography*. British Museum, London.
Brockway, Lucile H.
    1979 *Science and Colonial Expansion. The Role of the British Botanic Gardens*. Academic Press, New York.
Bucher, Bernadette
    1981 *Icon and Conquest. A Structural Analysis of the Illustrations of de Bry's Great Voyages*. University of Chicago Press, Chicago.
Buell, J. W.
    1894 *The Magic City. A Massive Portfolio of Original Photographic Views of the Great World's Fair*. Historical Publishing, St. Louis.
Burg, David F.
    1976 *Chicago's White City of 1893*. University Press of Kentucky, Lexington.
Burness, Jessie N.
    1915 *Sculpture and Mural Paintings in the Beautiful Courts, Colonnades and Avenues of the Panama-Pacific International Exposition at San Francisco, 1915*. Robert A. Reid, San Francisco.
Chambers, Robert
    1969 *Vestiges of the Natural History of Creation*. Humanities Press, New York. Originally published 1844.
Chapman, William R.
    1985 Arranging Ethnology: A. H. L. F. Pitt Rivers and the Typological Tradition. In *Objects and Others. Essays on Museums and Material Culture*, edited by George W. Stocking, Jr., pp. 15–48. History of Anthropology, vol. 3. University of Wisconsin Press, Madison.
Chauvenet, Beatrice
    1983 *Hewett and Friends. A Biography of Santa Fe's Vibrant Era*. Museum of New Mexico Press, Santa Fe.
Chiappelli, Fredi (editor)
    1976 *First Images of America. The Impact of the New World on the Old*. 2 vols. University of California Press, Berkeley.
Clifford, James, and George E. Marcus (editors)
    1986 *Writing Cultures: the Poetics and Politics of Ethnography*. University of California Press, Berkeley.
Colin, Susi
    1987 The Wild Man and the Indian in Early 16th Century Book Illustration. In *Indians and Europe. An Interdisciplinary Collection of Essays*, edited by C. W. Feest, pp. 5–36. Rader Verlag, Aachen.
Collier, Donald
    1969 Chicago Comes of Age: the World's Columbian Exposition and the Birth of the Field Museum. *Field Museum Bulletin* 40(5):2–7.
Collier, Donald, and Harry Tschopik
    1954 The Role of Museums in American Anthropology. *American Anthropologist* 56:768–799.

Darwin, Charles
  1859 *On the Origin of Species by Means of Natural Selection, or the Preservation of Favored Races in the Struggle for Life.* John Murray, London.
Dawkins, Richard
  1965 *The Blind Watchmaker.* W. W. Norton, New York.
Debo, Angie
  1976 *Geronimo. The Man, His Time, His Place.* University of Oklahoma Press, Norman.
Diamond, Stanley
  1974 *In Search of the Primitive. A Critique of Civilization.* Transaction Books, New Brunswick, N.J.
Dickason, Olive P.
  1984 *The Myth of the Savage and the Beginnings of French Colonialism in the Americas.* University of Alberta Press, Edmonton.
Dorsey, George A.
  1901 Recent Progress in Anthropology at the Field Columbian Museum. *American Anthropologist* 3:247–265.
  1907 The Anthropological Exhibits at the American Museum of Natural History. *Science* 25:584–589.
Douglas, Mary
  1989 The Hotel Kwilu—a Model of Models. *American Anthropologist* 91:885–865.
Dryden, John
  1946 The Conquest of Granada by the Spaniards [1672]. In *The Works of John Dryden,* vol. 11, *Plays,* edited by J. Loftus and D. S. Rodes, pp. 102–199. University of California Press, Berkeley. Originally published 1762.
Durkheim, Emile
  1915 *The Elementary Forms of the Religious Life.* George Allen and Unwin, London.
Durrans, Brian
  1988 The Future of the Other:Changing Cultures on Display in Ethnographic Museums. In *The Museum Time-Machine: Putting Cultures on Display,* edited by R. Lumley, pp. 144–169. Routledge, London.
Duval, Marguerite
  1982 *The King's Garden.* University Press of Virginia, Charlottesville.
Fabian, Johannes
  1983 *Time and the Other: How Anthropology Makes Its Object.* Columbia University Press, New York.
Fagin, Nancy L.
  1984 Closed Collections and Open Appeals: The Two Anthropology Exhibits at the Chicago World's Columbian Exposition of 1893. *Curator* 27:249–264.
Farrington, Oliver C.
  1899 Notes on European Museums. *American Naturalist* 33:763–781.
Fenton, William N., and Elizabeth L. Moore (editors and translators)
  1974 Customs of the American Indians Compared with the Customs of Primitive Times, 2 vols. *Publications of the Champlain Society* 48. Toronto. Originally published 1724.
Fletcher, Alice C.
  1916 Nature and the Indian Tribe. *Art and Archaeology* 4:291–296.
Flinn, John J.
  1893 *The Best Things to Be Seen at the World's Fair.* Columbian Guide Company, Chicago.
Fowler, Don D.
  1975 Notes on Inquiries in Anthropology—a Bibliographic Essay. In *Toward a Science of Man. Essays in the History of Anthropology,* edited by T. H. H. Thoresen, pp. 15–32. Mouton, The Hague.
  1990 Images of American Indians, 1492–1892. *Halcyon 1990. A Journal of the Humanities* 11:75–100.

Fowler, Don D., and Catherine S. Fowler
  1969 John Wesley Powell, Anthropologist. *Utah Historical Quarterly* 37:152–172.
Francis, David R.
  1913 *The Universal Exposition of 1904.* 2 vols. Louisiana Purchase Exposition Co., St. Louis.
Frederickson, George M.
  1971 *The Black Image in the White Mind. The Debate on Afro-American Character and Destiny, 1817–1914.* Harper & Row, New York.
Frese, H. H.
  1960 Anthropology and the Public: the Role of Museums. *Mededelingen van vet Rijksmuseum voor Volkenkunde, Leiden* no. 14.
Fulop-Miller, Rene
  1963 *The Jesuits. A History of the Society of Jesus.* Capricorn Books, New York.
Glacken, Clarence J.
  1967 *Traces on the Rhodian Shore. Nature and Culture in Western Thought from Ancient Times to the End of the Eighteenth Century.* University of California Press, Berkeley.
Goode, G. Brown
  1882 Outline of a Scheme of Museum Classification. *Anthropological Society of Washington Transactions* 2:5–7.
Green, Andre
  1972 Le Cannibalisme: réalité ou fantasme agi? In *Destins du cannibalisme,* edited by J-B Pootalis, pp. 27–54, Nouvelle Revue de Psychanalyse no. 6.
Greenblatt, Stephen J.
  1976 Learning to Curse: Aspects of Linguistic Colonialism in the Sixteenth Century. In *First Images of America* II, edited by F. Chiappelli, pp. 561–580. University of California Press, Berkeley.
Greene, John C.
  1959 *The Death of Adam. Evolution and Its Impact on Western Thought.* Iowa State University Press, Ames.
  1984 *American Science in the Age of Jefferson.* Iowa State University Press, Ames.
Haller, John S., Jr.
  1971 *Outcasts from Evolution. Scientific Attitudes of Racial Inferiority, 1850–1900.* University of Illinois Press, Urbana.
Hammond, Dorothy, and Alta Jablow
  1970 *The Africa That Never Was.* Twayne, New York.
Hanke, Lewis
  1959 *Aristotle and the American Indian. A Study in Race Prejudice in the Modern World.* Indiana University Press, Bloomington.
Harris, Neil
  1962 The Gilded Age Revisited: Boston and the Museum Movement. *American Quarterly* 14:546–566.
  1981 Cultural Institutions and American Modernization. *Journal of Library History* 16:28–47.
Herdman, W. A.
  1887 An Ideal Natural History Museum. *Proceedings of the Literary and Philosophical Society of Liverpool* 12:61–81.
Higinbotham, Harlow
  1898 *Report of the President to the Board of Directors of the World's Columbian Exposition.* Rand, McNally, Chicago.
Hinsley, Curtis.
  1981 *Savages and Scientists. The Smithsonian Institution and the Development of American Anthropology, 1846–1910.* Smithsonian Institution Press, Washington, D.C.
Hodgen, Margaret T.
  1936 *The Doctrine of Survivals.* Allenson, London.

1964 *Early Anthropology in the Sixteenth and Seventeenth Centuries*. University of Pennsylvania Press, Philadelphia.

Holmes, William H.

1900 Report of the Department of Anthropology for the Year 1897–98. *Annual Report of the Smithsonian Institution, Report of the U.S. National Museum, 1897–98*, pp. 19–26. Washington, D.C.

1903 Classification and Arrangement of the Exhibits of an Anthropological Museum. *Annual Report of the Smithsonian Institution, Report of the U.S. National Museum, 1900–01*, pp. 253–278. Washington, D.C.

Honour, Hugh

1975 *The New Golden Land. European Images of America from the Discoveries to the Present Time*. Random House, New York.

Hovey, Edmund O.

1898 Notes on Some European Museums. *American Naturalist* 32:697–715.

Hrdlicka, Ales

1917 The Most Ancient Skeletal Remains of Man. *Smithsonian Institution Annual Report for 1916*, pp. 491–552. Washington, D.C.

Huddleston, Lee E.

1967 *Origins of the American Indians. European Concepts, 1492–1729*. University of Texas Press, Austin.

Hudson, Kenneth

1975 *Social History of Museums: What the Visitors Thought*. Macmillan, London.

Hulton, Paul

1984 *America 1585, The Complete Drawings of John White*. University of North Carolina Press, Chapel Hill, and British Museum, London.

Hymes, Dell (editor)

1969 *Reinventing Anthropology*. Pantheon Books, New York.

Jacknis, Ira

1985 Franz Boas and Exhibits: On the Limitations of the Museum Method of Anthropology. In *Objects and Others. Essays on Museums and Material Culture*, edited by George W. Stocking, Jr., pp. 75–111. History of Anthropology vol. 3. University of Wisconsin Press, Madison.

Jefferson, Thomas

1944 Notes on Virginia [1784]. In *The Life and Selected Writings of Thomas Jefferson*, edited by A. Koch and W. Peden, pp. 185–288. Modern Library, New York.

Jennings, Francis

1975 *The Invasion of America. Indians, Colonialism, and the Cant of Conquest*. W. W. Norton, New York.

Keen, Benjamin

1971 *The Aztec Image in Western Thought*. Rutgers University Press, New Brunswick, N.J.

Kelly, Lawrence C.

1983 *The Assault on Assimilation*. University of New Mexico Press, Albuquerque.

Kohlstedt, Sally G.

1980 Henry A. Ward: the Merchant Naturalist and American Museum Developer. *Journal of the Society for the Bibliography of Natural History* 9:647–661.

Latham, R. G.

1851 *The Germania of Tacitus, with Ethnological Dissertations and Notes*. Taylor, Walton and Maberly, London.

Lehner, Ernst, and Johanna Lehner

1966 *How They Saw the New World*. Tudor, New York.

Linneaus, Carl

1735 *Systema Naturae, sive Regna tria naturae systematice proposita classes, ordines, genera and species*. Lugduni Batarorum, Stockholm.

Lorant, Stephan

1965 *The New World. The First Pictures of America.* Rev. ed. Duell, Sloan and Pearce, New York.

Lovejoy, Arthur O.

1936 *The Great Chain of Being.* Harvard University Press, Cambridge, Mass.

1948 *Essays in the History of Ideas.* Johns Hopkins Press, Baltimore, Md.

Lovejoy, Arthur O., and George Boas

1935 *Primitivism and Related Ideas in Antiquity.* Johns Hopkins Press, Baltimore, Md.

Lubbock, John (Lord Avebury)

1865 *Pre-historic Times, as Illustrated by Ancient Remains, and the Manners and Customs of Modern Savages.* Williams and Norgate, London.

1870 *The Origins of Civilisation and the Primitive Condition of Man.* Longmans, Green, London.

McCue, George

1988 *Sculpture City. St. Louis Public Sculptures in the "Gateway to the West."* Hudson Hills Press, New York.

McCullough, Edo

1966 *World's Fair Midways.* Arno Press, New York.

Marcus, George E., and Michael M. J. Fischer

1986 *Anthropology as Cultural Critique.* University of Chicago Press, Chicago.

Marriott, Alice

1948 *Maria: the Potter of San Ildefonso.* University of Oklahoma Press, Norman.

Mason, O. T.

1890 Anthropology in Paris during the Exposition of 1889. *American Anthropologist* o.s. 3:27–36.

1894 Ethnological Exhibits of the Smithsonian Institution at the World Columbian Exposition. In *Memoirs of the International Congress of Anthropology,* edited by C. S. Wake, pp. 206–216. Schulte Publishing, Chicago.

1896 Influence of Environment upon Human Industries or Arts. *Annual Report of the Smithsonian Institution, Report of the U.S. National Museum, 1894–95,* pp. 639–665. Washington, D.C.

Mason, Peter

1987 Seduction from Afar. Europe's Inner Indians. *Anthropos* 82:581–601.

Matheson, P. E. (editor and translator)

1968 *The Discourses of Epictetus.* Heritage Press, New York.

Miller, Edward

1974 *That Noble Cabinet: a History of the British Museum.* Ohio University Press, Athens.

Milton, John R.

1981 The Origin and Development of the Concept of the "Laws of Nature." *Archives of European Sociology* 22:173–195.

Mitchell, Lee C.

1981 *Witnesses to a Vanishing America. The Nineteenth Century Response.* Princeton University Press, Princeton, N.J.

Mooney, James A.

1899 The Indian Congress at Omaha. *American Anthropologist* 1:126–149.

Morgan, Lewis H.

1878 *Ancient Society.* Henry Holt, New York.

Nott, J. C., and George R. Gliddon

1854 *Types of Mankind; or Ethnological Researches Based upon the Ancient Monuments, Paintings, Sculpture, and Crania of Races, and upon Their Natural, Geographical, Philological and Biblical History.* Lippincott, Grambo, Philadelphia.

Pagden, Anthony

1982 *The Fall of Natural Man. The American Indian and the Origins of Comparative Ethnology.* Cambridge University Press, Cambridge.

Paley, William
  1828 *Natural Theology*. 2d ed. J. Vincent, Oxford. Originally published 1802.
Pearce, Roy H.
  1965 *Savagism and Civilization. A Study of the Indian and the American Mind*. Johns Hopkins University Press, Baltimore, Md.
Petty, Willam
  1967 The Scale of Creatures. In *The Petty Papers. Some Unpublished Writings of Sir William Petty*, edited by the Marquis of Landsdowne, pp. 21–34. Augustus M. Kelley, New York. Originally published 1677.
Pieters, Florence F.
  1980 Notes on the Menagerie and Zoological Cabinet of Stadholder William V of Holland. *Journal of the Society for the Bibliography of Natural History* 9:539–563.
Poliakov, Leon
  1974 *The Aryan Myth. A History of Racist and Nationalist Ideas in Europe*. Basic Books, New York.
Powell, John W.
  1891 Indian Linguistic Families North of Mexico. *Seventh Annual Report of the Bureau of Ethnology, 1885–86*, pp. 1–142. Washington, D.C.
Prest, John
  1981 *The Garden of Eden. The Botanic Garden and the Recreation of Paradise*. Yale University Press, New Haven, Conn.
Rackham, Horace (editor and translator)
  1947 *Pliny, Natural History*. 10 vols. Harvard University Press, Cambridge, Mass.
Raymenton, H. K.
  1962 *History of the San Diego Museum Association*. San Diego Museum of Man, San Diego, Calif.
Rousseau, Jean J.
  1950 *The Social Contract and Discourses*. E. P. Dutton, New York. Originally published 1750–1762.
Rydell, Robert W. II
  1980 *All the World's a Fair: America's International Expositions, 1876–1916*. Unpublished Ph.D. dissertation, University of California, Los Angeles. University Microfilms, Ann Arbor.
Said, Edward
  1979 *Orientalism*. Vintage Books, New York.
Samuels, Peggy, and Harold Samuels
  1976 *The Illustrated Biographical Encyclopedia of the Artists of the American West*. Doubleday, New York.
Sanday, Peggy R.
  1986 *Divine Hunger. Cannibalism as a Cultural System*. Cambridge University Press, Cambridge.
San Diego *Union*
  1915 Priceless Busts of Primal Man at Fair. San Diego *Union*, 31 January 1915, n.p. Clipping in archives of San Diego Historical Society, San Diego.
Sellers, Charles C.
  1969 *Charles Willson Peale*. Charles Scribner's Sons, New York.
  1980 *Mr. Peale's Museum*. W. W. Norton, New York.
Selincourt, A. de (editor and translator)
  1954 *Herodotus. The Histories*. Penguin Books, Baltimore, Md.
Shackleton, D. B. (editor)
  1915 *Cicero's Letters to Atticus*. 6 vols. Cambridge University Press, Cambridge.
Sheets-Pyenson, Susan
  1988 *Cathedrals of Science. The Development of Colonial Natural History Museums during the*

Late Nineteenth Century. McGill-Queen's University Press, Kingston and Montreal.

Silverberg, Robert
1968 *Mound Builders of Ancient America. The Archaeology of a Myth*. New York Graphic Society, Greenwich.

Spencer, Herbert
1971 *Herbert Spencer: Structure, Function and Evolution*. Edited by S. Andreski. Charles Scribner's Sons, New York. Originally published 1850–1870.

Stanton, William
1960 *The Leopard's Spots. Scientific Attitudes toward Race in America, 1815–59*. University of Chicago Press, Chicago.

Stedman, Raymond W.
1982 *Shadows of the Indians. Stereotypes in American Culture*. University of Oklahoma Press, Norman.

Stocking, George W., Jr.
1987 *Victorian Anthropology*. Free Press, New York. Stocking, George W., Jr. (editor)
1974 *The Shaping of American Anthropology 1883–1911. A Franz Boas Reader*. Basic Books, New York.
1985 Objects and Others, Essays on Museums and Material Culture. *History of Anthropology*, vol. 3. University of Wisconsin Press, Madison.

Sturtevant, William C.
1976 First Visual Images of Native America. In *First Images of America. The Impact of the New World on the Old*, edited by F. Chiappelli, pp. 417–454. University of California Press, Berkeley.

Takaki, Ronald T.
1979 *Iron Cages. Race and Culture in 19th-Century America*. University of Washington Press, Seattle.

Taylor, Lonn
1983 The Cowboy Hero: an American Myth Examined. *The American Cowboy*, edited by L. Taylor and I. Maar, pp. 62–176. American Folklife Center, Library of Congress, Washington, D.C.

Thomas, D. H.
1978 *The Southwestern Indian Detours*. Hunter Publishing, Phoenix, Ariz.

Thomas, Keith
1983 *Man and the Natural World. A History of the Modern Sensibility*. Pantheon Books, New York.

Thwaites, Reuben C. (editor)
1896–1901 *The Jesuit Relations and Allied Documents*. 73 vols. Burrow Brothers, Cleveland, Ohio.

Trennert, Robert A., Jr.
1974 A Grand Failure: the Centennial Indian Exhibition of 1876. *Prologue: The Journal of the National Archives* 6:118–129.

Trigger, Bruce G.
1989 *A History of Archaeological Thought*. Cambridge University Press, Cambridge.

Truman, Benjamin C.
1893 *History of the World's Fair*. Mammoth Publishing, Philadelphia and Chicago.

Tylor, Edward B.
1865 *Researches into the Early History of Mankind and the Development of Civilization*. J. Murray, London.
1871 *Primitive Culture*, 2 vols. J. Murray, London.

Vaughan, Alden T.
1965 *New England Frontier. Puritans and Indians, 1620–1675*. Little, Brown, Boston.
1982 From White Man to Redskin: Changing Anglo-American Perceptions of the American Indian. *American Historical Review* 87:917–953.

Ward, Roswell
  1948 Henry A. Ward. Museum Builder to America. *Rochester Historical Society Publications*, vol. 24.
White, Leslie A.
  1949 *The Science of Culture*. Farrar, Strauss, New York.
Williams, Elizabeth A.
  1985 Art and Artifact at the Trocadero: Ars Americana and the Primitivist Revolution. In *Objects and Others. Essays on Museum and Material Culture*, edited by George W. Stocking, Jr., pp. 146–166. History of Anthropology vol. 3. University of Wisconsin Press, Madison.
Wright, Barton
  1980 San Diego Museum of Man. *American Indian Art* 5(4):48–53.
Zuckerman, Lord
  1980 The Rise of Zoos and Zoological Gardens. In *Great Zoos of the World. Their Origins and Significance*, edited by Lord Zuckerman, pp. 3–26. Westview Press, Boulder, Colo.

Chapter 4 ■

Raymond D. Fogelson

The Red Man in the White City

Perhaps, after all, America has never been discovered.
I myself would say that it had merely been detected.
—Oscar Wilde, *The Picture of Dorian Gray*

On May 1, 1893, a restive crowd of about 350,000–500,000 had gathered in front of the Administration Building to witness the opening ceremonies of Chicago's long-awaited World Columbian Exposition. At 11:15 a.m., recently elected President Grover Cleveland and an entourage of fair officials and visiting dignitaries—including the Duke of Veragua, a lineal descendant of Columbus—took their places on the podium. Amid rousing cheers, a near panic ensued as the mob surged forward to get a better view of the proceedings.[1] Meanwhile, "high up on the portico of the Administration Building several Oglala Sioux braves in full ceremonial dress watched with detached curiosity the chaos below" (Badger 1979:xii). This chapter examines the representation of Native North Americans at the Chicago Fair and some of the apparent moral ambiguities surrounding their participation in this international spectacular.

Hosting the World Columbian Exposition fulfilled a conscious desire by the emergent Chicago business and social elite to change their city's image from that of a boisterous, corrupt porkopolis to a world-class center of commerce and culture. Chicago had recently recovered from the disastrous fire of 1871 and had experienced dynamic growth. However, behind the facade of prosperity and civic boosterism lurked serious social problems. The country as a whole was suffering a severe economic recession that had local repercussions in the form of abject poverty, chronic labor strife, a high crime rate, and a repressive and corrupt city government. Winning the competition to host the World's Fair provided a great boon for troubled Chicago. Jobs for laborers and artisans and anticipated tourist dollars temporarily eased the crisis and galvanized city morale. Out of the swampy lakeside lagoons of Jackson Park emerged monumental structures of impressive impermanence—the fabulous White City, clusters of enormous Neoclassical and Renaissance buildings built of "staff," a combination of plaster of paris and concrete bound together with jute or other fibers.[2]

World's fairs were evolving institutions, each of which attempted to surpass or improve upon its predecessors.[3] Most official reports and many popular accounts of particular fairs usually begin with a history of previous fairs. This historicity implied a teleological theory of cultural development. While fairs of some sort may be a generic feature of historic human culture, international world's fairs are products of the Industrial Revolution, usually thought to have begun with the 1851 Crystal Palace Exhibition in London.[4] Although many world's fairs occurred between those held in Hyde Park, London, and Hyde Park, Chicago, two such events had a special influence on the World Columbian Exposition.

The 1876 Centennial Celebration in Philadelphia was the first American fair of international scope. Government support played a role in the success of the Philadelphia Fair, even though the Centennial Celebration lost money. The Smithsonian Institution was represented in many capacities, including exhibitions documenting the history and present conditions of the American Indian (McCabe 1975:205–206). Philadelphia also featured a separate Woman's Pavilion administered and financed by a national Woman's Centennial Commission. While the Philadelphia Fair was long on machinery and fine arts, including a model of Sleeping Iolanthe sculpted in butter by Caroline Brooks of Arkansas (Ingram 1876:705–706), it was short on amusement.[5] Outside the fairgrounds arose an unofficial "Shantyville" devoted to less austere pleasures.

The immediately preceding Paris World's Fair of 1889 had set new standards of excellence. With the dominating symbol of the Eiffel Tower and the unquestioned elegance of Paris, the exposition exuded an unmistakable joie de vivre. One significant innovation that impressed American visitors was the native villages from far-flung French colonies. These villages provided a living ethnographic presence and complemented the usual museum-case displays of artifacts.

The ostensible theme of the Chicago Fair was, of course, Columbus's discoveries, and Columbian imagery was ubiquitous in everything from numismatics and postage stamps to heroic statuary. A replica of the monastery of La Rabida, where Columbus retreated after his initial failure to secure support for his proposed voyage, was built on the fairgrounds and filled with historical manuscripts, artifacts, and other Columbian memorabilia, 890 items in all. These relics, assembled by William Curtis of the State Department, were lent by the Pope, the Spanish government, West Indian sources, and by the Duke of Veragua and other descendants of Columbus (Smith and Graham 1893:1:9). The collection was curated by Col. J. G. Bourke, an important early anthropologist and folklorist who published extensively on southwestern ethnology and who had authored a notorious volume entitled *The Scatological Rites of All Nations* (1891).[6]

However, the fundamental ethos pervading the World Columbian exhibitions and their organization was the idea of progress, especially as manifested in the assumed triumph of civilization on the North American continent. In this self-congratulatory orgy of ethnocentrism, the world's uncivilized races and cultures were taken as markers to measure the distance that separated "them" from "us." As our predecessors on this continent, Native Americans played a special role in this evolutionary docudrama. Indians were judged to be a disappearing species doomed either to physical extinction or cultural assimilation. Their presence at the fair was justified for their historical, educational, and scientific value.

At Chicago, the fledgling discipline of anthropology flapped its wings to propel and popularize these dogmas. The prominence of anthropology was greater in Chicago than at any previous or subsequent world's fair.

Ideas of civilizational progress are implicit in the spatial arrangements of world's fairs. The central core of most fairs was heavy industry, marvels of modern science, commercial products, fine art, and the arts of refinement. Generally outside the central core were ethnic displays and performances of popular arts by colorfully dressed peasants and national minorities. At the extreme periphery were the exotic primitives and their supposed affines, the freaks and atavistic throwbacks, who constituted not the main show but the sideshow.

The correlation is not perfect, but the arrangement of center and periphery, resembling a kind of pre-Wisslerian age-area hypothesis, seems to hold at the Chicago Fair (Figure 4–1). The center was the majestic White City whose architectural splendor took on an almost sacred or utopian quality. Its mission was enlightenment and elevation of the spirit. For Chicago, as Miller (1990) suggests, the White City represented the culmination of a redemptive apocalypse set in motion by the purifying fire of 1871.

The Midway was a narrow strip of land extending almost a mile westward, away from the lake, appended to the White City. Its name derives from the fact that it originally served as a landscaped passage connecting Jackson Park with Washington Park. In the early planning for the fair, consideration was given to locating some exhibits in Washington Park.[7] The Midway was intended to control the excesses that had taken place outside the fairground at Philadelphia, to accommodate native villages, to serve as a bazaar, and to be the center of popular entertainment. The exhibits on the Midway were expected to have redeeming cultural, historical, or educational value and to be displayed in a dignified and decorous manner. Oversight of the Midway was entrusted to Department M, "Ethnology, Archaeology, Progress of Labor and Invention, and Collective Exhibits," under the overburdened directorship of Professor Frederic Ward Put-

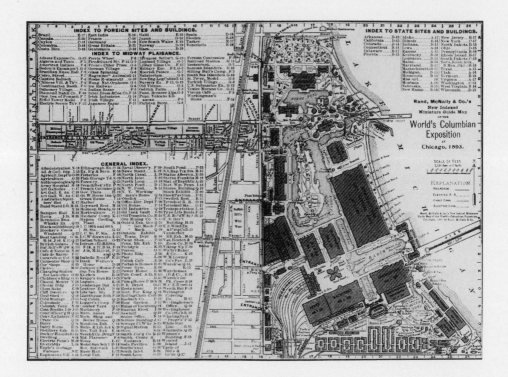

Figure 4–1. Guide map to the World's Columbian Exposition.

nam of Harvard (Dexter 1966).[8] Putnam's rein was loose, and entertainment soon overwhelmed education on the Midway. In contrast to the serenity of the White City, the Midway became a cacophony of barker spiels, runaway donkey carts, and jostling tourists. Although the sleaze factor on the Midway has been exaggerated—Little Egypt may never have performed there nor was there any hootchy-cootchy dancing, according to entrepreneur Sol Bloom (1948)—the *Danse du Ventre*, more colloquially known as "belly dancing," of Middle Eastern maidens aroused male libidos and compromised their superegos.[9] A subtitle on a contemporary photograph of a belly-dance performance states:

> The *danse du ventre*, . . . which was executed by girls not only in the Egyptian theater, but also in the Persian, Turkish, and with some modification, in the Moorish Theatres, on the Plaisance, is a suggestively lascivious contorting of the abdominal muscles, which is extremely ungraceful and almost shockingly disgusting. Curiosity prompted many to view the performance, but very few remained more than five minutes before this was fully satisfied [Smith and Graham 1893:1:13].

Professor Putnam rides to the relativistic rescue of the redeeming educational value of this popular Midway attraction:

> The national *dans* [*sic*] *du ventre* which not being understood was by many regarded as low and repulsive. What wonderful muscular movements did those

dancers make, and how strange did this dance seem to us; but is it not probable that our waltz would seem equally strange to these dusky women of Egypt. What is a dance, is a question one was forced to ask after a trip through the Midway. Every nation had its own form. With some it was rhythmic movement of the hands and arms; with others of the feet and legs; and with others of the body; some were ceremonial, others for amusement, according to the national traditions and customs [1894:2].

Comparative choreography proved to be a lucrative enterprise.

One can perceive a primitive-civilized gradient in the locations on the Midway. Near the western gate was a Bedouin encampment, where "Wild East" shows were enacted; Sitting Bull's grounds featured daily war dances by various Indian troupes; nearby was a village of languid Lapplanders, an ostrich farm, and a settlement of 100 recently pacified Dahomeans, popularly believed to be cannibals. Toward the center of the Midway could be found Old Vienna, Algerian and Tunisian exhibitions, a Chinese theater, Cairo Street, Persian and Turkish concessions, a German beer hall, and an extensive Javanese village with a theater for puppet plays. Further on were large Irish concessions, a small settlement of Malays, a popular exhibition of South Sea Islanders, and a diorama of a Hawaiian volcano. Closer to the entrance to the White City were corporate displays by such firms as the Diamond Match Company and Libby Glass. The Midway also featured ascents in a captive balloon and rides on the gigantic, original ferris wheel, which rotated to a height of 265 feet and became, for many, the fair's central symbol.[10]

Buffalo Bill's Wild West and Congress of Rough Riders of the World may have reached its theatrical apex at the Columbian Exposition (Figure 4–2). Unable to be accommodated within the fairgrounds proper, the show leased over 15 acres between 62nd and 63rd Street outside the southwest confines of the fair. A horseshoe-shaped covered arena seating 18,000 spectators was hastily erected, surrounded by an open campground. Two hundred Indians, mostly Oglala Sioux (but falsely advertised to include large contingents of Blackfeet, Comanches, and Pawnees), along with spectacular equestrian groups from Russia, Arabia, France, Germany, and England, plus many cowboys, a troop of American soldiers, and various auxiliary personnel swelled the campground population to over 500 people. The show opened on April 3, 1893, four weeks before the official opening of the fair, and had two performances daily, including Sunday, until the close of the fair on October 29.[11] It is estimated that over four million people attended the Buffalo Bill Show, and the event netted more than a million dollars.

The Indians from the Wild West Show were a conspicuous presence on the fairgrounds. Chief Rain-in-the Face, Red Cloud, Kicking Bear, Two Strike, Young Bull, Young Man Afraid-of-Horses, Rocky Bear, and No Neck regularly made the rounds and frequently became the subjects of photographic portraits (Sell and Weybright 1955:194–195). They spent much time on the beach observing the vast expanse of Lake Michigan and occasionally riding the boats. They were also fascinated by the merry-go-round, which they would ride for hours at a time. One account tells of a night

Figure 4–2. Buffalo Bill's Encampment. Behind is the back of the covered arena. W. F. Cody stands under the buffalo head trophy on the right. In front of him, holding a cat, is Annie Oakley.

when fifteen painted, blanketed chiefs marched up, bought tickets and solemnly mounted the painted ponies. When the machine started and the big calliope began to play "Maggie Murphy's Home," Chief No Neck held on to the bridle with both hands as his blanket floated out behind him. Then as the horses whirled more swiftly, he let go a full-throated war cry, "Yip, yip, yi, yi, yip!" The others at once took it up and the tent walls billowed to the breeze [Yost 1979:240].

The Indians developed a taste for buttered popcorn, peanuts, and chewing gum and also indulged their fancy by purchasing buttonhole posies, glass canes, and coconut-fiber hats (Yost 1979:240). Much has been written on Buffalo Bill as an Indian fighter and perpetrator of negative Indian stereotypes. However, no less an authority than Vine Deloria, Jr., argues that Buffalo Bill generally treated the Indians fairly, gave them an opportunity to escape reservation persecution, and allowed them to demonstrate their equestrian skills on a par with horsemen of other nationalities (1981:52–56).

Surviving guide maps reveal that the center-periphery hypothesis also holds up well with respect to the White City, proper. A village of Eskimos from southern Labrador was situated in the extreme northwest corner of the fair near the

57th Street entrance. There was snow on the ground when the Eskimos arrived in March 1893, but they grew increasingly uncomfortable as the summer heat arrived. Unfortunately, several of the people and six dogs perished. Little Prince Pommiuk gained celebrity with his dexterity in whip-snapping. The Eskimo contingent were housed in dark, bark-shingled huts with framed windows, and they brought with them stone lamps, supplies of seal oil and whale blubber, and stone carvings. Anthropologist Harlan Smith (1901) collected texts from some of the elders, as well as valuable ethnographic material on shamanism, although most of his informants professed Christianity, having been converted by the Moravians. The Eskimos displayed their proverbial ingenuity by adapting their heavy sledges to wheels after the snow disappeared (Jenks 1893:96).

The Anthropology Building was located in the extreme southeast corner of the fairgrounds (Figures 4–3, 4–4). Originally, Putnam planned to display the extensive collections that had been assembled for the fair from all over the world in the centrally located Manufactures and Liberal Arts Building, but he soon discovered that he needed more space. The Anthropology Building was hastily constructed and fully operational two months after the fair opened, although, as Appelbaum notes (1980:95), it had little architectural merit.

Putnam also reserved some land immediately south of the Anthropology

Figure 4–3. Anthropology Building at the 1893 Exposition.

Figure 4–4. Interior of the Anthropology Building, showing mode of display.

Building where an artificial mountain of Cliff Dwellers was built, and fabricated monuments from Yucatan were installed.[12] Also located in this area was a small Penobscot village with three birchbark tepees and a square dwelling occupied by four families from Old Town, Maine; an Iroquois settlement, sponsored by New York State, featured four traditional dwellings and a longhouse accompanied by 12 Tuscaroras and Senecas (Figure 4–5); the spectacular Kwakiutl exhibit was also installed here (see Jacknis, this volume), as well as individual house structures from other tribes. Some of the themes, variations, and overriding progressivist ideology are captured in a misplaced caption for a Canadian Indian exhibit in the Manufactures and Liberal Arts Building:

> This is one of the most popular features of the World's Fair at the south end, and is associated with outdoor exhibits of decidedly living interest. . . . Here they have their canoes, fishing and hunting tackle, costumes and all the appurtenances of Indian life. They carry on their industries, cook their meals, perform their songs and dances, and go through all the routine of daily life as in their own villages. Those who employ themselves in making trinkets, beaded necklaces and moccasins, pipes and other souvenirs, do a thriving business with the visitors. The tribes and their habitations are various. The Esquimaux dwell in a tent of skins. Skin and bark wigwams form the lodging of the Crees and Chippewas of North-

Figure 4–5. An Iroquois Longhouse in the New York State Iroquois exhibition. The sides are covered with several kinds of bark, while the roof is primarily elm bark.

western Canada. The Winnebagoes from Wisconsin live in a house of bark and mat; the Penobscots of Maine have used birch-bark, and there are skin tepees, hogans and other dwellings belonging to the various Western tribes. They are all in amazing contrast to the white palaces stretching away to the north, that evidence the skill and prosperity of their successors in this western domain [Anonymous n.d.].

Indeed, from the perspective of the nameless caption writer, the domestic achievements of the Red Man pale in comparison with the edifice complexes of the White City.

Putnam's staff numbered over 100 people (Dexter 1966:315). His chief assistants were Franz Boas, who handled much of the ethnology and physical anthropology, and Joseph Jastrow, who was in charge of the psychological laboratories and exhibits and also advised on religious studies. Zelia Nuttall consulted on the Middle American displays, and George Dorsey handled South America. C. C. Abbot and Ernest Volk helped with the extensive archaeological materials from New Jersey, while Midwestern archaeological exhibits were in the hands of Charles Metz, G. Frederick Wright, Harland Smith, and Warren K. Moorehead, fresh from his important work at Hopewell (Collier 1969:4). The librarian duties were assumed by the British anthropologist, C. Staniland Wake, who later edited the papers of the International Congress of Anthropology (1894) that convened at the fair in late August 1893. In addition to housing the huge collection of New World artifacts, a sample of materials from elsewhere, and the active laboratories, the Anthropology Building highlighted archaeologi-

Figure 4–6. Interior of the U.S. Government Building, Smithsonian exhibition. Note John Wesley Powell's Linguistic Map (upper right), used to help delimit cultural areas. Each area is faced with a bust or full figure of a famous leader or typical representative of the group. In the cubicles are photographs, drawings and prints, representative artifacts, and life figures.

cal materials from Greece, Assyria, Egypt, and Rome; collections of fossils, shells, and corals; mounted skins and skeletons of mammals, birds, reptiles, and fish; and human anatomical and skeletal specimens. Stewart Culin's comparative exhibition of games drew much attention, as did special displays on religious symbols and folklore.

The Smithsonian's Indian Exhibits enjoyed a central location in the Government Building (Figure 4–6). Primarily the responsibility of Otis T. Mason and W. H. Holmes, with the assistance of such Smithsonian stalwarts as James Mooney and Frank Hamilton Cushing, the Smithsonian exhibits did not feature living Indians. Archaeological materials were displayed in glass cases, while ethnological information was conveyed innovatively through Mason's pioneering effort to delineate culture areas. Taking J. W. Powell's recently published classification of linguistic families as his cue, Mason tried to depict major cultural types through photographs, drawings, representative artifacts, and life-size models engaged in characteristic industries. Each major area was allotted a separate alcove fronted by a pedestal-mounted bust of a famous chief or life-size manne-

Figure 4-7. Life figures of California Indians in the Smithsonian exhibition.

quin (Figure 4-7). Although incompletely realized, these exhibitions, conceived by Mason and executed by Homes, set new museological standards.[13]

Mason was also prevailed upon to set up an exhibition on primitive feminine industries for the Women's Building. Mary Lockwood, supported by the head of the Woman's Commission, Mrs. Potter Palmer, wanted to represent the role of woman as inventor of such domestic products as dressed skins, sewing, weaving, basket-making, and pottery, all of which were considered vital in human cultural development. An official statement by one of the women managers bears an uncanny resemblance to contemporary gender controversies: "It will be shown that women, among all the primitive peoples, were the originators of most of the industrial arts, and that it was not until these became lucrative that they were appropriated by men, and women pushed aside" (quoted in Bancroft [1894]:267). A basic collection of relevant materials from the National Museum was assembled and supplemented by newer acquisitions from Colorado, New Mexico, South Dakota, and Alaska. "Woman's Work in Savagery" comprised many cases that filled a large suite of rooms and displayed embroidery, bodkins, beadwork, needle cases, work bag fasteners, baskets, pots, dishes, spoons, dolls, weaving implements, and Navajo blankets. A Navajo weaver was even imported from Arizona to demonstrate her skills (Weimann 1981:393–404). Involvement in this project doubtless inspired Otis Mason to publish *Woman's Share in Primitive Culture* in 1897.

Native American materials also found their way into many of the state buildings. Although most of these edifices were used as clubhouses and meeting places, many housed exhibits. The Utah Building displayed mummies of Cliff Dwellers along with supporting photographs and descriptions; Minnesota was reported to have exhibited historical Indian relics; the combined Arizona, Oklahoma, New Mexico Building contained such Indian handicrafts as Navajo blankets, Moqui water baskets, and Apache whips; the Washington State Building featured a fine collection of Northwest Coast artifacts; and the Michigan Building proudly displayed a poem, "Red Man's Rebuke," written on birchbark by the last chief of the Pottawatomies. Ambitious exhibitions were mounted by the host state of Illinois: These included a comprehensive review of Illinois archaeology based upon the researches of Professor William McAdams of Alton. McAdams (1895) surveyed private collections, borrowed objects, made photographs, engaged in new mound explorations, and produced an interesting, 77-page illustrated report for the Illinois Board of World's Fair Commissioners.

An Alaskan exhibition, sponsored by the Bureau of the Interior, was located in the Government Building. Naval Lt. George T. Emmons assembled a large collection of Tlingit and Alaskan Eskimo materials that ultimately was acquired by the American Museum of Natural History, where it survives today along with his valuable ethnographic notes. The collection included a war canoe, sleds, totem poles, an extensive collection of furs, ceremonial pipes, headdresses, robes, blankets, weapons, household and fishing implements, clothing, and various charms and ornaments (Bancroft[1894]:123).

A model Indian school building, located north of Putnam's outdoor villages, was a source of contention. Originally, the Indian school was to be administered by Putnam in collaboration with the Bureau of Indian Affairs (BIA). However, Putnam had come under attack from many quarters. Many felt the decision to locate some Indians on the Midway was degrading. Richard Henry Pratt, the heavy-handed founder of the Carlisle Indian School, was particularly vocal in his criticism of the fair's emphasis on traditional Indian culture at the expense of showcasing Indian progress. He refused an invitation to direct a proposed Indian Exhibition in the government Building, jointly sponsored by the Bureau of Indian Affairs and the Bureau of American Ethnology. This exhibition was to contrast "the red man as a savage wrapped in a blanket, and his child in the dress of civilization endeavoring to master benignant mysteries" (quoted in Badger 1979:105). In Pratt's view, such exhibitions were deterimental to educating Indians for the modern world.

The model BIA School, located north of the living Indian villages and between the Agricultural Building and the Krupp Gun Exhibit, contained workshops, classrooms, sitting rooms, a dining room, kitchen, dormitories, and apartments for employees. The walls were decorated with pictures of famous chiefs and objects of native industry; the windows were covered with transparencies illustrating Indian culture (Bancroft [1894]:122). After the Pratt falling-out, BIA Commissioner T. J. Morgan recruited delegations of Indian students from government and religious schools to attend the fair. Over a thousand tourists a week witnessed Indian students studying, reciting, working at trades, preparing meals, and displaying products of their industry (Hoxie 1984:88–89).[14]

Pratt relocated his Carlisle School in the East Gallery of the Manufactures and Liberal Arts Building. Displayed here in glass cases were examples of penmanship, map-drawing, uniforms, and fancy work made by students (Bancroft [1894]:256). Pratt arranged to bring 10 platoons of Carlisle students to Chicago to march in the October 1892 dedication celebrations. Each platoon paraded in sharp military precision, bearing icons of their academic and industrial training (Bancroft [1894]:87; Hoxie 1984:89). Over the summer, more than 500 Carlisle students visited the fair, where they presented marching and musical performances and trooped under the banner "Into Civilization and Citizenship" (Badger 1979:161).

An anonymous subtext to a photograph of a small Canadian Indian exhibit in the Manufactures and Liberal Arts Building, showing a tepee, snowshoes, nets, and canoes, reiterates a similar refrain regarding Indian progress:

> In Canada, no less than in this country the aboriginal American seems doomed to extinction. . . . Nor has Canada been much more successful in teaching him civilization, though it is apparent that very humane and enlightened efforts are put forth in this direction. . . . [One] learns with interest that in older provinces of Canada the Indians have long since been gathered into settlements, under the care of proper government offices, and in some cases with industrial schools and other helps for hastening their progress to an equalty [sic] in all respects with the white settler. Missions under the care of different Christian bodies have also undertaken the work of their religious training and supervision of their schools. An interesting contrast is seen in the above exhibit between the products of these settlements, both of handicraft and intelligence, and the rude appliances of war and the chase from the tribes that still roam free by the Saskatchewan and Red River [Anonymous n.d.].

The civilized-primitive dilemma of public presentation was confronted directly by Rev. John W. Sanborn who supervised the New York Iroquois delegation to the fair:

> The Indians are emerging from their former state of semi-barbarism and awakening to the better condition which is before them; the question, therefore, whether the New York Iroquois should represent at Chicago their ancient savagery, and go back to what they were 400 years ago, or show the progress which they have made and the civilization which they have attained, was difficult to determine; but as director-in-chief of this exhibit, my conclusion was that it would be an injustice to our high-minded and self-respecting chiefs to require them to lapse into barbarism even for one summer for the sake of showing their past history. It did seem proper, however, that the most ancient bark houses should be erected, and that the people should dress in deer-skin suits of the genuine Iroquois pattern, while at the same time, they gave daily exhibition of their progress in education, religion and the arts of peace. The thousands of visitors were, for the most part, astonished to learn that our Indians were capable of such improvement as was shown [1894:498].

The moral conflict surrounding how living Indians were to be presented at the fair—whether to have them portray their traditional cultures as staged authenticity (see MacCannell 1976:91–107) in the name of science and popular entertainment or to have them demonstrate the degree to which they embraced civilization and had assimilated into late nineteenth-century American life— was, to be sure, more a problem for whites than it appears to have been for Indians. What is lacking in this supposed moral drama is sufficient Indian voices. The few soundings we can record reverberate positively. As Deloria maintains (1981), few, if any, Sioux felt demeaned by their participation in Buffalo Bill's Wild West Show. The hundreds of Indian students who attended the fair probably found it an exciting adventure and enlightening experience for the most part. Many Kwakiutls who participated in the Columbian Exposition were eager for a return engagement 11 years later in St. Louis, despite the fact that the media were not very kind to them (see also Jacknis, this volume). Seneca Chief Solomon O'Bail, a direct descendant of Cornplanter and an outspoken traditionalist, expressed his feelings about the fair in the following fashion: "Had good time all summer; no mad words; good time" (Sanborn 1894:501).

Indian feelings about the fair notwithstanding, the person who took the most fire in this controversy was Frederic Ward Putnam, who occupied a hot seat as director of Section M. Part of Putnam's problem was his inability to control the activities on the Midway, where the educational and scientific ideals rapidly eroded into tawdry amusement and the feverish quest for a fast buck. It soon became apparent that the Midway was the money pump that would guarantee the financial fluidity of the fair. Putnam never gave up his belief in the positive virtues of the Midway, but soon surrendered his authority to the enterprising Sol Bloom, who later became a real estate tycoon and national politician who helped draft the United Nations charter (Rydell 1984:62). In his autobiography, Bloom wryly comments that "to have made this unhappy gentleman [Professor Putnam] responsible for the establishment of a successful venture in the field of entertainment was about as intelligent a decision as it would be today to make Albert Einstein manager of the Ringling Brothers and Barnum and Bailey Circus" (quoted in Badger 1979:81).

But Putnam was also threatened from within his ranks. One of his staff members, an outspoken woman named Emma Sickles, objected to the degradation of Indians at the fair, particularly those located on the Midway. Ms. Sickles was summarily fired and complained in a letter to the *New York Times* that the exhibitions had "been used to work up sentiments against the Indian by showing that he is either savage or can be educated only by Government agencies. . . . Every means was used to keep the self-civilized Indians out of the Fair" (quoted in Rydell 1984:63). Indeed, representatives from the Five Civilized Tribes in Oklahoma were scarce in Chicago. Perhaps their conservative members seemed less civilized in the light of their ongoing struggle against the allotment of their lands and the dissolution of their tribal governments.

It is easy in retrospect to brand Putnam as a racist and as a person lacking in cultural sensitivity. However, he must be judged in the context of his times, and he deserves credit for his efforts to promote anthropology as a scientific discipline, to popularize its research, and to leave Chicago with a permanent legacy in the form of the collections that later became the nucleus of the Field Museum.

The World Columbian Exposition ended on a tragic note with the assassination of popular Mayor Carter Harrison by a deranged office-seeker. Like the city he led, Mayor Harrison experienced something of a spiritual and social rebirth during the fair and was even anticipating a third marriage. The elaborately planned closing ceremonies were sharply curtailed. The angry crowds on the Midway grew ugly. Soon the exhibitions were slowly dismantled and the buildings deserted. Economic and labor woes continued to beset Chicago in the winter of 1893–1894, and the fairgrounds were vandalized by unemployed vagrants and roving street gangs. The desecration of the White City was completed on July 5, 1894, when the great structures were torched by striking railway workers. The White City was reduced to skeletal girders and burned-out rubble. Only the Palace of Art survived this holocaust because of its brick construction and marginal location. Today it houses the Museum of Science and Industry.[15] Time has obliterated even faint traces of the momentous events that took place in Hyde Park almost a century ago. The nameless Oglala Sioux warriors who witnessed the opening day ceremonies are long gone, but the circumstantial moral issues posed by Indian presence at the fair remain with us today. Such is progress.

Notes

1. A full account of the dedicatory ceremonies held on October 21, 1892, and the opening day ceremonies of May 1, 1893, can be found in the official *Memorial of the World's Columbian Exposition* (Joint Committee on Ceremonies 1893).

2. "Staff" was invented in Paris about 1876 and was used in the Exposition Universelle de Paris of 1878. It was essentially composed of powdered gypsum, with additives of alumina and glycerine, as well as fibrous material as binder. Mixed with water, "staff" could be molded or applied directly on a wood lath. When hardened, it had an ivory cast, but could easily become discolored. As a result, to obtain a uniform, durable color for the "White City" and to make the structures more waterproof, the "staff" had to be painted. In the deadline "crunch," necessity again mothered invention, as Frank D. Millet, an artist in charge of the Decoration Department, devised a means to discharge a mist of paint using an air-pump driven by electric power (Bancroft [1894]:67–68). This was the first, large-scale use of spray-painting.

3. See Burton Benedict (1983) for a provocative and timely review of "The Anthropology of World's Fairs."

4. The significance of the Crystal Palace Exhibition as a collective representation for the Industrial Revolution and the emergence of sociocultural evolutionary theory is highlighted in Stocking (1987:1–6).

5. Mrs. Brooks repeated her butter performance at the Arkansas Pavilion in the Chicago Fair 17 years later. Some of her more "serious" and enduring work was also displayed in the Woman's Building at Chicago.

6. Princess Eulalia, the *Infanta* of Spain, visited La Rabida on June 12, 1893, in an intoxicated state and behaved rudely. Bourke derisively comments in his diary,

> The Bourbons of Spain who have not been strumpets have been lunatics back to Crazy Jane of Naples, daughter of Ferdinand and Isabella, who remained bereft of reason for 54 years, after she had given birth to Charles V in a water closet of a nunnery in Ghent. . . . Altogether the Bourbon line, especially the Spanish

branch, has been consistently contemptible. . . . I showed my indifference to it, by walking in front of the *Infanta*, with my back to her [quoted in Porter 1986:296–297].

Despite the honors bestowed on Spanish dignitaries during the Columbian celebration, Bourke's antipathies appear to anticipate the Spanish-American War that arose five years later.

7. Miller (1990:212–216) comments on the symbolic separation of the fair from the city as something resembling the distinction between the sacred and the profane. The discontinuities were especially marked by architectural choice with the fair opting for Romanesque Neoclassicism, while an ongoing architectural revolution was going on downtown with the recently completed Adler/Sullivan Auditorium Theater and the prototypical skyscrapers. Unlike the 1933 Century of Progress, which made practical use of existing cultural resources, the World Columbian Exposition did not link itself to the new Art Institute (built ironically on the previous site of the Interstate Exposition Building erected in 1873), the Auditorium Theater, the Newberry Library, the Chicago Historical Society, or other cultural centers of the "new" Chicago.

8. The classification into lettered departments was constructed by G. Brown Goodes, assistant secretary of the Smithsonian and a noted museum administrator and ichthyologist. Goode continually stressed that exhibitions should primarily be concerned with systematic ideas rather than objects and that visual arts were increasingly important in presenting the living thoughts of civilization (Rydell 1984:43–46).

9. There were probably many "Little Egypts," but it is impossible to be sure that whoever bore the name at the Chicago Fair was identical to the belly-dancer who later gained fame at Coney Island. Appelbaum (1980:97, 102) presents evidence that "hootchy-cootchy" dancing did, indeed, take place on the Midway, probably performed by Algerian women.

10. Perhaps it is symbolic that in the shadow of the ferris wheel at a French concession was a miniature Eiffel Tower, the central icon of the 1889 Paris Fair. Unlike the Eiffel Tower, the ferris wheel did not become a permanent landmark. It was dismantled and later installed in north Chicago. The ferris wheel made a final appearance at the St. Louis Fair in 1904 before being scrapped.

11. The fair agreements contracted for Sunday closings to observe the Sabbath. However, after the first month the fair stayed open seven days a week. The early Sunday closings had a positive effect in increasing attendance at the Wild West Show.

12. The imposing Cliff Dweller exhibit was a fairly accurate reproduction of an archaeological site from southern Colorado, supposedly ancestral to contemporary Moquees (Hopis). Lieutenant Schwatka was in charge of the restoration. The exhibit failed to attract public interest and met with some scientific scorn, particularly from the illustrious Frank Hamilton Cushing of the Smithsonian. The Yucatan ruins were from the Labna group and from Uxmal and included the celebrated "House of the Nuns." Papier-maché molds were taken from the original ruins by Mr. E. H. Thompson, U.S. consul at Yucatan, under instructions from Professor Putnam, and cast in staff by artisans at the fair. Their installation was enhanced by native flora (Anonymous 1893c:97).

13. W. H. Holmes, an illustrator cum geologist and archaeologist, stayed on in Chicago after the fair to become the director of the Field Columbian Museum, a post he relinquished in 1897 to return to the U.S. National Museum in Washington. It is interesting to note the little-known fact that Holmes was listed as an original faculty member of the newly established University of Chicago for 1892–1893. His title was "Non-Resident Professor of Archaeologic Geology" (Goodspeed 1916:487); there is no record of his ever having taught classes at the University of Chicago.

14. Another demonstration of Indian education was presented in the Children's Building, where methods of teaching native children were displayed with a class of

young girls from the Ramona Indian School of Santa Fe, New Mexico (Bancroft [1894]: 293).

15. The building was refurbished and made permanent by a generous gift from philanthropist Julius Rosenwald of Sears-Roebuck before the Century of Progress in 1933–1934.

References

Anonymous
  1893a *Das Columbische Weltausstellungs-Album*. Rand McNally, Chicago.
  1893b *Glimpses of the World's Fair*. Laird and Lee, Chicago.
  1893c *The Columbian Exposition Album*. Rand McNally, Chicago.
  n.d. *The Vanished City*. Werner, Chicago.
Appelbaum, Stanley
  1980 *The Chicago World's Fair of 1893: A Photographic Record*. Dover, New York.
Badger, R. Reid
  1979 *The Great American Fair*. Nelson Hall, Chicago.
Bancroft, Hubert Howe
  [1894] *The Book of the Fair*. Reprint. Bounty Books, New York. Originally published 1894.
Benedict, Burton
  1983 The Autobiography of World's Fairs. In *The Anthropology of World's Fairs: San Francisco's Panama Pacific International Exposition of 1915*, edited by Burton Benedict et al., pp. 1–65. The Lowie Museum of Anthropology, Berkeley, Calif., in association with Scolar Press.
Bloom, Sol
  1948 *The Autobiography of Sol Bloom*. G. P. Putnam's Sons, New York.
Bourke, John G.
  1891 *Scatologic Rites of All Nations: A Dissertation upon the Employment of Excrementious Remedial Agents in Religion, Therapeutics, Divination, Love Philters, etc. in All Parts of the Globe*. W. H. Lowdermilk, Washington, D.C.
Collier, Donald
  1969 Chicago Comes of Age: The World's Columbian Exposition and the Birth of the Field Museum. *Bulletin, Field Museum of Natural History* 40(5):2–7.
Deloria, Vine, Jr.
  1981 The Indians. In *Buffalo Bill and the Wild West*, edited by George Weisman et al. University of Pittsburgh Press, Pittsburgh.
Dexter, Ralph W.
  1966 Putnam's Problems Popularizing Anthropology. *American Scientist* 54:315–332.
Goodspeed, Thomas Wakefield
  1916 *A History of the University of Chicago: The First Quarter-Century*. University of Chicago Press, Chicago.
Hoxie, Frederick E.
  1984 *A Final Promise: The Campaign to Assimilate the Indians, 1880–1920*. Cambridge University Press, New York.
Ingram, J. S.
  1876 *The Centennial Exposition Described and Illustrated*. Hubbard Bros., Philadelphia.
Jenks, Tudor
  1893 *The Century World's Fair Book for Boys and Girls*. Century, New York.
Joint Committee on Ceremonies
  1893 *Memorial of the World's Columbian Exposition*. Stone, Kastler, and Painter, Chicago.

McAdams, William
  1895 Archaeology. In *Report of the Illinois Board of World's Fair Commissioners at the World's Columbian Exposition*. H. W. Rokker, Springfield, Ill.
McCabe, James D.
  1975 *The Illustrated History of the Centennial Exhibition*. Reprint. National Publishing Company, Philadelphia. Originally published 1876.
MacCannell, Dean
  1976 *The Tourist:A New Theory of the Leisure Class*. Schocken Books, New York.
Mason, Otis Tufton
  1897 *Woman's Share in Primitive Culture*. D. Appleton, New York.
Miller, Ross
  1990 *American Apocalypse: The Great Fire and the Myth of Chicago*. University of Chicago Press, Chicago.
Porter, Joseph C.
  1986 *Paper Medicine Man: John Gregory Bourke and His American West*. University of Oklahoma Press, Norman.
Putnam, F. W.
  1894 Introduction. *Portrait Types of the Midway Plaisance*. N. D. Thompson, St. Louis.
Rydell, Robert W.
  1984 *All the World's A Fair*. University of Chicago Press, Chicago.
Sanborn, Rev. John W.
  1894 Report on the New York Indian Exhibit. In *Report of the Board of General Managers of the Exhibit of the State of New York at the World's Columbian Exposition*. James B. Lyon, Albany.
Sell, Henry Blackman, and Victor Weibright
  1955 *Buffalo Bill and the Wild West*. Oxford University Press, New York.
Smith, Harlan I.
  1901 Notes on Eskimo Traditions. In *Report of the Committee on Awards of the World's Columbian Commission*. House of Representatives Document no. 410, vol. 1, pp. 347–354. Government Printing Office, Washington, D.C.
Smith, H. S., and C. R. Graham
  1893 *The Magic City: A Portfolio of Original Photographic Views of the Great World's Fair*. Historical, Philadelphia.
Stocking, George W., Jr.
  1987 *Victorian Anthropology*. Free Press, New York and London.
Todd, F. Dundas
  1893 *World's Fair through a Camera*. Woodward and Tiernan, St. Louis.
Wake, C. Staniland
  1894 *Memoirs of the International Congress of Anthropology*. Schulte, Chicago.
Weimann, Jeanne Madeline
  1981 *The Fair Women: The Story of the Woman's Building, World's Columbian Exposition, Chicago 1893*. Academy Chicago, Chicago.
Yost, Nellie Snyder
  1979 *Buffalo Bill: His Family, Friends, Fame, Failures, and Fortunes*. Swallow Press, Chicago.

Chapter 5 ■

Ira Jacknis

Northwest Coast Indian Culture and the World's Columbian Exposition

Before the World's Columbian Exposition of 1893 the study of Northwest Coast Indian culture was still in its infancy. This single event was so influential that almost all subsequent work was related to it in some way. Northwest Coast Indian culture was represented at Chicago in two main forms: exhibitions of artifacts and performances by a visiting troupe of Kwakiutl. This essay examines the role the exposition played in ethnological research, artifact collection, exhibition, ethnic performance, photography, and music recording; its personal significance in the lives of Franz Boas and George Hunt; and its impact on the Kwakiutl Indians who demonstrated crafts and dance at the fair, as well as its continuing legacy for their culture.[1] Whereas most recent discussions of the World's Columbian Exposition have emphasized the very real issues of race and imperialism embedded in the fair, this essay stresses other important concerns it raised—semiotic issues of ethnographic representation, context, and authenticity.

Preparations

In Europe and America, the period spanning the late nineteenth and early twentieth century was the great age of international expositions—celebrations of material and technological progress, supported and made possible by colonial empires (Benedict 1983; Rydell 1984). Striving to demonstrate its civic glory, Chicago won the honor of hosting an international exposition to celebrate the quadricentennial of Columbus's first voyage (Badger 1979; Burg 1976). The presence of anthropology displays at the Columbian Exposition was due directly to the efforts of Frederic Ward Putnam, professor of anthropology at Harvard University and director of its Peabody Museum of American Archaeology and Ethnology. An institutional entrepreneur, Putnam played a role in founding anthropology departments in Cambridge, Chicago, and San Francisco museums (Mark 1980:14–61). As he outlined his plans in May 1890, he expressed the hope that Chicago would be able to "secure and place in the Exposition a perfect ethnographical exhibition of the past and present peoples of America and thus make an important contribution to science, which at the same time will be appropriate, as it will be the first bringing together on a grand scale representatives of the peoples who were living on the continent when it was discovered by Columbus" (cited in Dexter 1966:316).

Putnam also hoped to see a great museum established in Chicago after the fair: "Such a collection would form a grand beginning for a permanent ethnological museum which would grow in importance and value as time goes on and the present American tribes are absorbed by the peoples of the several republics, an absorption which is taking place quite rapidly" (Dexter 1966:316). These passages demonstrate the evolutionary and imperialist rhetoric that Putnam shared with many other nineteenth-century anthropologists. Like the great museums that would grow out of them (see Harris 1978), these expositions were to bring together in one metropolitan center representatives from the colonial hinterlands. As one of Putnam's assistants noted: "From the first to the last the exhibits of this department will be arranged and grouped to teach a lesson; to show the advancement or evolution of man" (Smith 1893:117).

Despite some initial criticism, Putnam's proposals were accepted, and in February 1891 he became chief of the fair's Department of Ethnology and Archaeology, the first such office to be included in an international exposition. Putnam set in motion a massive collecting effort that involved almost one hundred paid and volunteer assistants. In accepting the position, Putnam made it a condition that "the Directory should appropriate sufficient money for original research and exploration to enable him to bring together as much new scientific material as the time would permit" (Johnson 1898:316).

The presence of Northwest Coast Indian culture was given a great boost in early 1891 when Putnam hired Franz Boas as his chief assistant. Assuming responsibility for Northwest Coast ethnology and the division of physical anthropology, Boas devoted his full time to the fair after leaving his position at Clark University in June 1892 (Hinsley and Holm 1976:311). Boas had been researching Northwest Coast native cultures since his first expedition to British Columbia in 1886, returning to the region yearly between 1888 and 1891.[2] Ironically, in view of the personal significance of the region to Boas, he himself neither collected nor did field research for the fair.[3] Instead he organized an extensive collecting operation.

Boas outlined his aims for North Pacific Coast research in his final report:

> The general plan of this exhibit was to illustrate the culture of one of the tribes of this region most fully, and to bring together supplementary collections from neighboring tribes, in order to bring out the local differences of culture as clearly and as strongly as possible. It was decided to make the tribes of northern Vancouver Island the central point of interest, and to group all the other collections round them [cited in Johnson 1898:344].

The Kwakiutl were Boas's featured group, "because they have exerted an influence over all the tribes on the North Pacific coast. It is my belief that the peculiar culture of the whole region has had its origin among the tribes of Fort Rupert, the Kwakiutl" (Johnson 1898:344). Franz Boas was responsible for the largest representation of Northwest Coast cultures at the fair, but a number of other Coastal displays were brought in through the efforts of others.

What was the state of Northwest Coast Indian studies on the eve of the fair? Although some artifact collections from the region had accumulated since contact in the late eighteenth century, systematic collection had only begun about 1875 (Cole 1985:1–101). In that year the Smithsonian Institution sent James G. Swan to collect Northwest Coast material for the U.S. Centennial Exposition of 1876, held in Philadelphia. After the fair, Swan's material was accessioned by the U.S. National Museum. The National Museum also sponsored the collecting and research of numerous government personnel, among them biologist William H. Dall and U.S. Navy Ensign Albert P. Niblack. The most active Northwest Coast collector, Naval Lt. George T. Emmons, had been collecting Tlingit artifacts in Alaska since 1882. In 1887 he sold a large Tlingit collection to the American Museum of Natural History, which already had a strength in the region. There was also activity in Canada, though on a smaller scale. George M. Dawson, of the Geological Survey, gathered Haida and Kwakiutl collections in 1878–1879 and 1885, respectively, and Indian Commissioner Israel Wood Powell made one collection for the Department of Indian Affairs in 1879 and another for the American Museum in 1881.

Europe, especially Germany, also possessed important Northwest Coast collections. In 1881–1882, the Bremen Geographical Society sent to Alaska Aurel and Arthur Krause, who returned with a relatively small but important Tlingit collection. At the same time, Johan Adrian Jacobsen journeyed to Alaska and British Columbia, sponsored by Berlin's Royal Ethnographic Museum. In 1885–1886 he and his brother B. Fillip brought a troupe of nine Bella Coola to Germany, sparking Boas's interest in the region. However, the Krause and Jacobsen collections were the last major collections to go to Continental Europe (Cole 1985:73); thereafter, the scene shifted to America. These early collections varied greatly in size and documentation. Although Swan, Dall, Niblack, Dawson, Krause, and Jacobsen all published important accounts of their travels, none were ethnologists, and little of their collecting was tied to research. The stage was thus set for Boas's ambitious plans.

Artifact Collections and Display

The World's Columbian Exposition was held on 553 acres of Jackson Park on Chicago's south side, near Lake Michigan. The exhibitions of Putnam's department were housed in the Anthropological Building, the first time the discipline was given its own pavilion at a fair. These displays were originally to be housed in the Manufactures and Liberal Arts Building, whose size of 1,687 by 787 feet made it the largest structure in the world (Collier 1969:5). Because of a shortage of space, however, plans were made in September 1892 to give Anthropology its own building. As a result of this last-minute shift and an unending series of delays, the Anthropological Building did not open until July 4, more than two months after the opening of the fair. In contrast to the fair's generally grandiose Beaux-Arts architecture, the style of Anthropology was simple and unadorned, and in contrast to its planned home, it now measured a modest 255 by 415 feet. Furthermore, it had moved to a poorer location—at the southeast corner near the railroad tracks and the lake beyond (Cole 1985:126). Here its neighbors were the dairy and agriculture pavilions and the Leather and Shoe Trades Building.

Northwest Coast Indian artifacts were exhibited in a wide diversity of venues. As one scholar has noted, "Little attempt was made to consolidate exhibits, and the result was repetition and duplication" (Fagin 1984:249). The most important Northwest collections were presented by the Anthropology Department. Four of them came from British Columbia: George Hunt collected from the Kwakiutl of Fort Rupert and Vancouver Island, Fillip Jacobsen from Bella Coola, James Deans from the Haida of the Queen Charlotte Islands, and Mrs. E. O. Morison from the Tsimshian of the Skeena River. Three collectors gathered material from Washington State: James G. Swan among the Makah of Cape Flattery, Myron E. Eells among the Salish of Puget Sound and western Washington, and Mr. L. L. Bush among the Salish of Shoalwater Bay, on the Pacific Coast. Boas sent no one to Alaska because he knew that large collections were being assembled from the territory by Lieutenant Emmons and others. Gathered during 1892, the collections began arriving in Chicago later that fall.

These Anthropology assistants were a diverse group (Cole 1985:123). Two were natives: Mrs. Morison was a Tsimshian who had married a merchant, and George Hunt had been raised in Fort Rupert as a Kwakiutl. The son of an English merchant and a Tlingit noblewoman, Hunt had earlier assisted I. W. Powell and Adrian Jacobsen, but this was his first opportunity to make a collection on his own (Jacknis 1991b). Boas met with Hunt in Victoria in August, 1891 and commissioned him to "obtain a large house and the model of a whole village, buy canoes and a complete outfit to show the daily life of the Indians, and everything that is necessary to the performance of their religious ceremonies."[4] After a delay of several months due to stormy weather, a shipment of 365 pieces arrived to form the largest collection from the Northwest Coast in the Anthropology Department.

For the rest of the collection Boas relied on a group of experienced local residents. One was the Scotsman James Deans, "widely known as a geologist, ethnologist, archaeologist and magazine writer" (Anonymous 1893a:185), who had worked for the Hudson's Bay Company and had assisted numerous collectors. Judge Swan, a New Englander by birth, had many professions during his years on the coast, principally in Washington State. Of these, he was most interested in collecting natural and artificial curios for the Smithsonian, which he had been doing since 1860. From 1874 to 1907, the Reverend Eells served as a Congregationalist missionary in the Puget Sound area (especially among the Twana of Hood Canal). After bringing the Bella Coola to Germany, Fillip Jacobsen had settled in the area. These Anthropology assistants generally received no salary, but their collection and travel expenses were covered.

In response to Putnam's open appeals, several miscellaneous Northwest Coast collections also came to the Anthropology Building, although they were not directly part of Boas's presentation. A collection from British Columbia and Baffinland was listed under Marie Boas's name, although undoubtedly it had been collected by her husband. Explorer and guide Captain Newton H. Chittenden presented his Haida collection made in 1884. Several displays came from Alaska: one made in the Territory and Siberia by missionary Sheldon Jackson, and a Tlingit collection from Edward E. Ayer, a wealthy Chicago collector who had gathered most of his Northwest Coast material on a trip to Alaska in 1887. There were several other minor Alaskan assemblages as well, along with a display in the Physical Anthropology gallery upstairs of the skulls Boas had collected on Vancouver Island during previous research trips.

The ethnological material in the Anthropological Building was arranged geographically, by tribe, but the display was somewhat confused and unsystematic owing to the lack of time, money, and personnel (Fagin 1984:255–262). A special feature of the Northwest Coast display was a scale model of the Haida village of Skidegate, as it appeared in 1864 (Figure 5–1). Haida artists under the supervision of James Deans constructed models of 25 houses, 10 memorial columns, 6 grave posts, and 2 burial houses. These were mounted on a 50–foot platform behind which stood a painted screen representing a forested panorama.

Northwest Coast Indian artifacts were also presented in the federal buildings of the United States and Canada and in the state pavilion of Washington. In the U.S. Government Building, the Smithsonian Institution exhibition combined efforts of the Bureau of American Ethnology and the U.S. National Museum, under the guidance of William H. Holmes and Otis T. Mason, respectively (Mason 1894, 1895; cf. Ewers 1959; Fagin 1984:250–255). Consulting with Putnam to avoid duplication in the ethnology exhibits, the team decided on a systematic display of Native American culture. While Boas's Northwest Coast displays revealed few innovations in exhibition technique, the Smithsonian introduced several novel styles to America (Jacknis 1985:80–83).

One innovation was the culture-area approach. In trying to associate artifacts with linguistic groups, Mason discovered that native material culture could be

Figure 5–1. Model of the Haida village of Skidegate, Queen Charlotte Islands, British Columbia, collected by James Deans, Anthropological Building, Chicago World's Fair, 1893. (Peabody Museum, Harvard University, N 28375 A,B)

more satisfactorily related to local environments (Ewers 1959:520–521). Mason was able to divide the Northwest Coast into the Black Slate and the Giant Cedar groups on the basis of material; but from the standpoint of food, all groups fell into the fish region (1894:213). Although Mason was not specific, Black Slate must have meant argillite, a black shale used by the Haida. Ironically, although it was a distinctive material in the area, argillite was not an important part of traditional technology, but was exploited principally for sale to whites. As Mason noted, both slate and cedar were worked by carving tools, thus unifying this culture area.

The life-group, the other display innovation, was primarily associated with Holmes, an artist-turned-archaeologist, although it was a collaborative effort. Instead of exhibiting isolated mannequins, which had been used for years, the fair introduced to America groups of costumed figures acting out a dramatic scene. Although Mason planned a life-group for each of the language groups in the region—Koluschan (Tlingit), Skidegetan (Haida), Wakashan (Kwakiutl, Nootka, Makah), Salishan (Salish, Bella Coola)—the display had to be curtailed owing to the lack of space (Mason 1895:127). A contributing factor may have been the fact that although the Smithsonian had ample collections from the Northwest Coast, at the time it had no staff members interested in the region. Presumably some Northwest Coast artifacts were shown in the Smithsonian exhibition, but the surviving evidence indicates no life-groups from the region.[5]

As the Territory of Alaska did not have its own building, its displays were included with those of the Interior Department in the U.S. Government Building. Like most state and national exhibitions, the Alaska section combined natural and human displays in order to advertise its bounty and development potential. It housed "a full collection showing the resources of that great territory. There [were] minerals, fish, furs, oils, timber, etc. There [was] also a great collection of curios manufactured by the native Alaskans" (Handy 1893:157). Here was a predominantly Tlingit collection that George T. Emmons had been gathering since 1888 (Jonaitis 1988:108–110). Comprising 2,700 pieces, this exhibition reportedly took three months to arrange. Emmons had initially offered his collection for display as part of Boas's Anthropology exhibitions, but Boas and Putnam had refused it on the grounds that it was being offered for sale to a museum, and that the government should have some control over the objects secured by naval officers (Cole 1985:142). As Cole suggests, they may actually have been pressuring the fair's administration to fund their own collecting in the Territory. Even more likely, their refusal probably stems from their skepticism of the lieutenant's scientific abilities.

The fair held still other Northwest Coast Indian presentations. Like many state buildings, the one dedicated to Washington included Indian artifacts. In addition to their work for Boas, both Judge Swan and the Reverend Eells supplied collections to the State Fair Commission (Holm 1987:12).[6] Within the Canadian Pavilion, the British Columbia room displayed a relatively small, but "handsome collection of curios" (see Cole 1985:132). These had been gathered in the province by Indian agents under the direction of Indian Commissioner A. W. Vowell, who carried out his mandate reluctantly, complaining about the great sums being spent by Boas and his agents and the consequent competition for artifacts. In addition, Northwest Coast artifacts were included in private, commercial displays. Carl Hagenbeck, German impresario and developer of a famous zoo in Hamburg, exhibited material collected in British Columbia in 1885–1886 by the Jacobsen brothers.

The largest Northwest Coast artifacts on display were part of the Anthropology Department's "out-of-doors exhibits." During their time in Chicago, the Kwakiutl lived in a simulated Coastal village, situated on the edge of the South Pond, near the Anthropological Building and the adjacent Midway (Figure 5–2). According to the official history, "Here the groups of native American peoples were to be arranged geographically, and to live under normal conditions in their natural habitations during the six months of the Exposition" (Johnson 1898: 315).[7] Although these were hardly "normal conditions" or "natural habitations," the Kwakiutl party occupied a cedar-plank house that George Hunt had acquired in the village of Nuwitti. Covered with a frontal painting of a thunderbird and moon crests, the house measured 45 feet square.[8] Next to it stood the smaller Haida house (nearly 29 feet square) that Deans had brought from

Skidegate. In addition to a 40–foot totem pole outside the Haida house, the Northwest Coast village included a Tsimshian heraldic column, Bella Coola memorial columns, Salish house posts, and two Tlingit poles loaned by E. E. Ayer. To complete the scene, several canoes were drawn up on the pond's edge. Despite this impressive array, these native structures paled beside the immense Manufactures and Liberal Arts Building.

The Northwest Coast artifacts on display evoked mixed reactions among the general public. One newspaper found the Haida house models "decorated in front with the curiously and hideously carved and painted totem poles peculiar to the Heidah tribe," and noted, "One peculiarity of the ornamentation is the frightful carvings of dragon heads protruding from the eaves."[9] Yet there was also appreciative commentary. The official directory praised Emmons's display: "The handiwork of the Alaskan natives showed a degree of skill with which they were not generally credited, especially the carvings on ivory, horn, and wood, and the samples of ingenious metal work" (Handy 1893:506). A journalist recommended this "interesting" exhibit as one "worth seeing," noting that the "intelligent system of labeling draws one into sympathy and friendship with the wild children of the glaciers as no monograph, however well written, could do" (Kate Field 1893, cited in Jonaitis 1988:110).

After the fair, almost all of these collections became the foundation of important museum holdings. The Anthropology Department collections went to the

Figure 5–2. Kwakiutl and Haida houses (center and left, respectively), Chicago World's Fair, 1893. (American Museum of Natural History, Department of Library Services, 322897)

Field Columbian Museum, founded at the close of the fair (Collier 1969; Weber and Crane 1982). The Field Museum also purchased the Jacobsen-Hagenbeck material and was given the Ayer collection. The artifacts that Swan and Eells had gathered for Washington State appropriately went to the State Museum. In 1894, the massive Emmons collection was purchased for $25,000 by the American Museum of Natural History (Jonaitis 1988:112). Several collections went to the B.C. Provincial Museum (now the Royal B.C. Museum). Captain Chittenden had promised his Haida collection to British Columbia in 1891, and after its appearance in Chicago and other expositions, it finally entered the museum in 1894 (Cole 1985:133, 225–226). The Provincial Museum also purchased collections of Deans and Fillip Jacobsen. The exhibition of the Canadian Department of Indian Affairs was eventually taken in by the Geological Survey, whose collections were later incorporated into the National Museum (Cole 1985:133).

The World's Columbian Exposition presented two visions of Native American culture. On the one hand, there was the salvage paradigm of Putnam and Boas, shared by almost all ethnologists of the time (see Gruber 1970). As Putnam instructed his ethnographic collectors:

> The most important things to be collected are those of genuine native manufacture, and especially those objects connected with olden times. Objects traded to the native by whites are of no importance, and are not desired; the plan being to secure such a complete collection from each tribe as will illustrate the condition and mode of life of the tribe before contact with Europeans [cited in Johnson 1898:319].

Putnam believed that it was possible, and indeed desirable, to strip away acculturated elements and present native culture in its pre-Columbian state, a task made all the more urgent by the "rapid absorption" of these peoples by industrial civilization.

The opposing image was presented by the U.S. Bureau of Indian Affairs, which used a model boarding school to demonstrate "the civilized side of the Indian, portraying the educational work which the government is doing" (Handy 1893:156; cf. Hoxie 1979:331–335).[10] Along with objects in traditional media, the operating boarding school exhibited penmanship, drawing, composition, and mechanical shop work. Although it included no Northwest Coast content, the Indian school was the ever-present counterpoise to Putnam's exhibitions of "ethnographic purity." In fact, the Kwakiutl village was located precisely between the demonstration school house and the replica of Mayan ruins in front of the Anthropological Building, caught in a kind of temporal framing of their putative evolutionary stage.

Although these Northwest Coast artifacts were scrupulously authentic in one sense, in that they were all native-made, they were fictional in another, their selection. Paradoxically, as Boas advocated comprehensive, systematic collections, the actual collecting was a creative act of omission, for Putnam's instructions to his agents amounted to the falsification of a truly representative record of native cultures as they found them, by then heavily acculturated. Coastal natives were making extensive use of western trade materials—paints, copper, beads, flannel, pearl buttons—and had been carving wood with iron-tipped tools for over a century. Beyond these western-influenced artifacts, Coastal Indians were using many objects—such as guns, metal and porcelain containers, cotton clothing, and blankets—that were completely Euro-American in origin. Yet none of these were collected, nor was any serious description or research devoted to their use.

The displays that followed compounded the transformation of native culture. To a great extent, the meaning of objects in a museum exhibition is determined through juxtaposition, and in Chicago the Northwest Coast artifacts were presented in several radically different surroundings. The pavilions of political entities (nation, state, and territory) demonstrated civic pride and encouraged commercial development. In most of these buildings, for example, the Alaska section, Northwest Coast artifacts were juxtaposed with raw materials, on the one hand, or with the glories of manufactured goods and fine arts, on the other. Hagenbeck's presentation harked back to an earlier exhibit style, as Coastal Indian artifacts were linked to exotic animals and were something of a miscellaneous sideline.

The outdoor village was intended to suggest, if not duplicate, native "natural habitations," and this contextual approach was an important innovation in the display of Northwest Coast art. There was a Tsimshian housefront at the Centennial Exposition, but this was the first time that a group of houses and poles were combined (even more so along a shore) to invoke a Northwest Coast environment, the model for many more totem pole parks to follow in British Columbia and Alaska. Yet this assemblage displayed a great deal of anthropoetic license, combining poles with diverse functions from different tribes, before a village of only two houses, also with distinct styles and structures. In any case, it is unlikely that the average visitor was in a position to grasp the extent of the creative recombination involved. The Skidegate house models represented an interesting and different attempt at recreating a village plan context. Paradoxically, while they were native-made displays, they were a kind of tourist art. Like argillite sculpture, they were a portable reduction of Haida culture commissioned by a white man (Wyatt 1984:46–52).

Both of the more "scientific" displays—Anthropology and the Smithsonian—innovatively attempted to invoke a native context, a context that lay in far-off Alaska and British Columbia. Both employed a culture-area approach, placing objects together with others of the same tribe or geographic region. This was the position advocated by Boas in his 1887 debate with Mason over the principles of museum classification and display (Boas 1887a, 1887b; Mason 1887). By 1893, Mason seemed to have rejected his earlier use of cross-cultural, typological, and evolutionary case displays and adopted Boas's position. However, this surface convergence masked underlying theoretical differences, as Mason continued to espouse evolutionary sequences and argued for a more materialist conception of geographical influence (see Jacknis 1985:77–83). Moreover, both displays were compromised by practical problems: The exhibits in Anthropology were somewhat jumbled and poorly documented, while the Smithsonian ran out of time and space to devote to its material (especially that from the Northwest Coast).

It was perhaps not coincidental that the life-group made its debut in America along with the display of living peoples. As Holmes noted, "for exposition purposes," these live groups were superior to mannequins: "The real family, clothed in its own costumes, engaged in its own occupations, and surrounded by its actual belongings, would form the best possible illustration of a people" (1903:201). However, besides the great trouble and expense, the real people would have to scatter at the close of the fair. On the other hand, "the creation of a set of adequate and artistic lay-figure groups forms a permanent exhibit, which, set up in a museum, continues to please and instruct for generations" (1903:201). While the life-group appeared to be more realistic and contextual than older exhibit styles, it still involved a great deal of anthropological and artistic construction.

Despite the lack of a Northwest Coast life-group at the Columbian Exposition, the fair led to important displays in this genre. Franz Boas first witnessed the return of the Kwakiutl *hamatsa* (or cannibal dancer) initiate in a dramatized version at the fair (Figure 5–3). He then reproduced this scene in a diorama he arranged for the U.S. National Museum in 1895 (Jacknis 1985:76, 82). Moreover, though varying in some details, the cedar-plank screen at the Smithsonian was clearly modeled after the one used in Chicago (Hinsley and Holm 1976:306–307). Boas's display, in turn, was copied by George Dorsey and Charles Newcombe at the Field Columbian Museum in 1901. The Field Museum exhibit was renovated in 1982 and remains on view to this day (Jacknis 1991a). Thus, a performance at Chicago in the summer of 1893 has continued to serve as a key image of Kwakiutl culture.[11]

Performance

The Kwakiutl were only one of many groups of living peoples displayed at the Chicago World's Fair. The plans for Indian participation at the Centennial Exposition fell through, and thus the great model for such displays in the minds of American ethnologists was the gathering of colonial Africans and Asians at the Paris International Exposition of 1889 (Rydell 1984:55–56). At all such events, visitors could watch the natives work at their distinctive crafts, and experience their ceremonial dance, music, and song. Little serious communication took place, however; the audiences simply observed and, more often than not, came away with the prejudices they had brought with them. The Kwakiutl were under the direct supervision of the Anthropology Department, unlike most of the groups of visiting ethnics, which were part of the commercial Midway Plaisance. The Midway, a mile-long strip under the shadow of the first Ferris wheel, was only nominally under Putnam's control (Rydell 1984:61–63). Here visitors could marvel at an international spectacle of ethnic villages—from Irish to Dahomean; Egyptian to Samoan. Patrons could refresh themselves at exotic restaurants, coffeehouses, taverns, and pubs. In addition to overseeing the Kwakiutl, the An-

Figure 5–3. Kwakiutl hamatsa dancer (with David Hunt on the left), Chicago World's Fair, 1893. (Photographed by John H. Grabill, Peabody Museum, Harvard University, N 29640)

thropology Department presented several other Native American groups—Penobscot, Iroquois, Sioux, Winnebago, and Navajo. Commercial operations presented still other Indian groups—Laguna Pueblos and Labrador Eskimos.

Popular attitudes toward these foreign visitors are apparent in the imperialistic summary of the fair's official history:

> Here was an opportunity to see these people of every hue, clad in outlandish garb, living in curious habitations, and plying their unfamiliar trades and arts with incomprehensible dexterity; to listen to their barbaric music and witness their heathenish dances, their acrobatic feats, and curious theatrical spectacles. There were three thousand of these denizens of the Midway gathered from all quarters of the earth, many of them led thither by the hope of gain, and many influenced still more by the desire to visit this wondrous land of general well-being, of universal intelligence, more modern than Europe, more transformed by steam and electricity, teeming with a livelier commerce and a busier industry [Johnson 1897:433–434].

Twice before, attempts had been made to bring a troupe of visiting Kwakiutl to Europe. In 1882, under instructions from Carl Hagenbeck, J. Adrian Jacobsen had convinced a group of Kwakiutl from Koskimo to come with him, only to have them take fright and desert. Although he tried again in 1885 with another party (and with George Hunt as interpreter), the same thing happened. In their place, he persuaded a group of Bella Coola, who had successfully toured Germany in 1885–1886 (Cole 1985:67–72). The Kwakiutl were finally encouraged to come to Chicago by favorable reports from the neighboring Bella Coola.

This time, under the direction of George Hunt and James Deans, the Kwakiutl troupe arrived in Chicago on April 12, after traveling for almost two weeks. In addition to George Hunt as manager and interpreter, the Kwakiutl party totaled sixteen: nine men, five women, and two children (a 5–year old girl and an 18–month-old boy).[12] Included in the number were Hunt's son David and his brother William (and his wife).[13] Upon their arrival, they were housed in the stock pavilion until their quarters could be completed.

Native performance at the fairs, as in many interethnic settings, included both work and ceremony (see Kirshenblatt-Gimblett 1991). An important part of the natives' daily activities was craft production, partly as a demonstration, but also as a much-needed source of income. In applying for permission from the exposition administration, Putnam argued, "There is no doubt that this sale of native manufactures by the natives themselves, dressed in native costume and living in their habitations and largely negotiating by sign language, will form a special attraction to visitors."[14] However, he went on to ask that the natives be allowed to bring duplicates of such crafts to sell, "as in many cases (as for instance the Navajo blanket-weavers) it would take nearly the whole time of the Fair to complete one specimen of their handiwork and they would thus be unable to realize anything toward their support or to accommodate visitors who after watching the process of manufacture should wish to purchase a finished article."

Putnam needed to reassure the director-general that these sales would not compete with the commercial concessions, and he thus promised that all sales would be "within or at the doors of their respective habitations and that nothing of the character of a booth or shop shall be allowed, nor shall white men be permitted to make the sales." For the natives, of course, this *was* an operation like a "booth or shop," but Putnam was striving for an illusion of exoticism: "My object is simply to allow the sale of native manufactures by the natives in the same way that a traveller going to their respective countries would purchase a few articles from their wigwams or teepees." Any profits made were to be split between the Indians (one-half), George Hunt (one-fourth), and the Ethnology Department (one-fourth).[15] Supplies for the Kwakiutl also included craft materials: paints, brushes, and tools for wood-working; red and blue flannel and pearl buttons for button blankets.[16] Despite these arrangements, one finds relatively little mention of craftwork at the fair, perhaps because the Kwakiutl were paid $20 per month, for seven and a half months, in addition to their living and traveling expenses.

The performances of the Kwakiutl, a people known for their drama and stagecraft, attracted a great deal of attention. Yet these very talents for illusion and spectacle were not always appreciated. The Chicago troupe began their series of regular performances (often for invited guests) with a festive housewarming. On the afternoon of May 6, shortly after the opening of the fair, the Kwakiutl marched in procession from their temporary quarters to their plank house, where they dedicated the house and totem poles with dancing. A Kwakiutl "princess" sponsored a formal feast, complete with orators for the host and guests.[17] A week later they danced for a party that included Prince Roland Bonaparte (noted by the newspaper as "an ethnologist of international fame"). There were selections from the repertoire of the winter ceremonials, including the dances of the hamatsa (or cannibal dance), the *tokwit* (a woman's dance), and one with a raven mask. "Professor [Frederick] Starr had to move out of the way of the big beak as it whirled around and Prince Bonaparte looked a trifle scared as the warrior pranced toward him," reported the *Chicago Herald*.[18] George Hunt and James Deans acted as masters of ceremonies.

As the summer wore on, the Kwakiutl drew greater crowds, but press reaction, probably an accurate mirror of popular sentiment, was not sympathetic. On June 12, for instance, the natives danced for the Infanta Eulalia of Spain, who claimed to have enjoyed the performance. According to the *Chicago Times*, however,

> A band of Quoc Queth Indians, gorgeous in red and blue blankets and gayly bedizened head dresses, burst into the cave singing one of their atrocious melodies. One detachment of them pounded away at the tam-tams, while the rest, bucks, squaws, and papooses, danced and howled. It seemed to please the Spaniards. The Quoc Queths screeched, rolled in the sand, and fought imaginary insects. That was the mosquito dance and the mosquitoes seemed to have all the best of it. They hopped and cavorted around, clawed at each other, and squealed like hyenas. That was the laughing dance to celebrate a victory over foes of the tribe.[19]

Such racist misunderstanding of Kwakiutl performances was quite similar to the reactions to their artifacts.

These performances proved to be a privileged forum for displaying the complex mixture of religious fact and dramatic illusion in Kwakiutl ceremonialism. However, these distinctions were not always appreciated by the general public. One perceptive and sympathetic observer, New York journalist Henry Krehbiel, described an evening's performance in the Kwakiutl big house:

> All the dances performed were dramatic in character, and required what it is no verbal impropriety to speak of as theatrical "properties." This fact, and the obvious intellectual attitude of the Indians toward the performances, as betrayed by the nature of the pantomimes and their reception, showed plainly as possible that however the Indians may once have thought of these dances, they are now chiefly performed for the sake of diversion. Dr. Boas described them as semi-religious in character, and explained that though the performers have become sceptical about their efficacy, they are yet believers in the spiritual agencies that are supposed to play a part in them. . . . [HK describes the exorcism of a disease spirit.] It was all play-acting, clever mimicry, performed and witnessed in a spirit of amusement. Back of it, of course, was some ancient superstition, possibly some mythological occurrence, which is now forgotten, or but half remembered.[20]

The ceremonial use of violence, or the illusion of violence, had caused problems for the Kwakiutl back in Canada, and it continued to create controversy in Chicago. Shocked news correspondents reported bites into living flesh, ropes being pulled through slits on dancers' backs, and what appeared to be cannibalism. Most notable among the complainants were the Reverend A. J. Hall, an Anglican missionary from Alert Bay, British Columbia, and Emma Sickles, a self-styled "friend of the Indian" (Cole 1985:129–131; Dexter 1966:326–328).

As he had done earlier with the Kwakiutl party invited to Germany, the reverend did his utmost to persuade his Indians not to go, and in fact, only two of the Kwakiutl came from Alert Bay. On his way to London, Hall stopped in Chicago, where he was so upset at this "display of paganism" that he wrote to several Canadian officials, asking them to cancel further performances. While they all concurred with him, there was little that could be done, as "the Indians, like white men, are free to make arrangements with whomsoever they please, and the Department [of Indian Affairs] cannot prevent their doing so. And, as you are aware, the law prohibiting Potlatch feasts or Tamanawas dances in Canada cannot be enforced in the United States."[21]

Miss Sickles criticized the performances on much the same grounds as Reverend Hall, saying that they portrayed the worst in the Indian and gave no indication of the great progress he was making in acquiring the benefits of civilization.[22] As she complained to the *New York Times*, "The exhibit of Indian life now given at the fair is an exhibit of savagery in its most repulsive form, participated in by only the lowest specimens of the Indian race or by those noted for bloodthirsty deeds."[23]

In his defense of the Kwakiutl performances, Putnam explained the illusionistic stagecraft habitually employed. When they appeared to bleed from a blow on the head, in fact, the "blood" was red paint contained in a hollow kelp tube. "But even this exhibition, which is pure jugglery and of the same class as the jugglery of Hindoos and others, is in itself of considerable scientific importance and interest as illustrating a custom which has been in existence with these people from time immemorial."[24] Still worried about public reaction, Putnam went on to claim that this display had been given without the knowledge of the Ethnology Department, had only been performed once, and would not be repeated.

Although it is impossible to determine precisely, some of this violence might have been real. Clearly, newspaper accounts exaggerated what occurred, but some contemporary Kwakiutl ceremonials did involve bloodshed. One Kwakiutl reported taking part in rites in Alert Bay around the turn of the century where dancers were hung by ropes (Ford 1941:115–117), a ritual Boas described as the *Hawi'nalaL* or war dance (Boas 1897:495–497). On the other hand, similar bloody acts were performed at the St. Louis Exposition in 1904, and one of the participants, Charles Nowell, recounted some of the illusionistic tricks involved (Ford 1941:186–190). Kwakiutl acts of ritual violence are well-documented in the ethnohistorical literature, but this violence was increasingly replaced with theatrical illusion, especially as the Indians were subjected to British colonial pressure during the nineteenth century (Holm 1977:15, 19). Whatever their status, such seemingly grisly shows were prime evidence for those who viewed Indians as savages (and whose principal experience with American Indian performance

was the Wild West Show). As far as one can tell, these—the first Kwakiutl performances in an intercultural setting—generated more disgust than appreciation.

One journalist noted the incongruity of a roaring fire in the Kwakiutl big
house on a sweltering Chicago summer's evening, reportedly used for illumina-
tion and as a "ceremonial agent" for the winter dances. He felt that the hamatsa
dance he had seen was "evidently much abridged and modified."[25] Citing Boas's
publications, he concluded that "it is manifest that the Chicago performance was
but a feeble imitation of the real dance, in which corpses are used, not effigies."
For this observer, authenticity lay in Fort Rupert, not Chicago. However, if he
had been present in Fort Rupert, he would not have seen winter dances in the
summer, but he very well might have seen effigies and other forms of "jugglery"
used. The line between ritual and theater was not rigid among the Kwakiutl,
particularly at the turn of the century.[26]

Despite the degree of ritual illusion, these exposition performances did represent a fundamental shift in context, for this was the first known instance in
which the Kwakiutl had performed their sacred winter ceremonials during the
secular summer season and for a nonnative audience. It would not be the last,
nor would the Kwakiutl be the only Native American group to theatricalize their
rituals (Sweet 1983). The displays of the Midway and the related anthropological
exhibitions amounted to a simulated tourist site (Hinsley 1991), as suggested by
Putnam's reference to the "special attraction to visitors" of buying crafts from
costumed natives living in their native habitations. One can only speculate on
the modifications the Kwakiutl made in their dances. Certainly, they changed
the time of year and undoubtedly shortened the entire proceeding. Without access to their stores of food and wealth, the feasting and potlatch gift-giving was
probably nonexistent. And with such a small group—many of whom may have
lacked the requisite ceremonial knowledge—and a primarily non-Kwakwala-
speaking audience, the full range of dances must have been curtailed and con-
densed. However, as Krehbiel has suggested, these dances were, on the whole,
less ritual action and more secular demonstrations of inherited privilege. So, in
the end, the question of authenticity must be moot; some things changed, others
did not. What was actually happening was that an altogether new cultural form
was being created.

Photography and Sound Recording

These Kwakiutl performances were also recorded mechanically by the camera
and phonograph. The World's Columbian Exposition was captured in thousands
of photographs that spread the experience of the fair to the masses who could
not visit it (Rydell 1989:198–199). In planning for the participation of the Kwakiutl and other natives, Putnam suggested to the fair's administration that the
"sale . . . of photographs of the natives and their habitations . . . will be a considerable revenue."[27] While a handful documented the artifact exhibits, most of the
Northwest Coast pictures captured the exotic appearances of the Kw kiutl
troupe. Several of these were included in the often racist photo albums issued
to commemorate the fair (Anonymous 1893b; Todd 1893). Many were anony-

mous, but an important series was taken by John H. Grabill, a commercial photographer from the frontier Dakotas (Jacknis 1984:6). Franz Boas promised the Kwakiutl copies of their portraits (a promise he fulfilled on his next field trip in 1894), and he used several of Grabill's images to illustrate his 1897 monograph on Kwakiutl ceremonialism (Jacknis 1984:36–39). However, at least four (and probably another) of these were retouched so that the setting of the fair was removed. For instance, in the photograph of a dancer with a ceremonial bow (Figure 5–4), not only were the pavilion in the rear and the blanket backdrop removed, but also the line of singers behind him (Boas 1897:Plate 15). Because the retouched photos were juxtaposed with images taken in Fort Rupert in 1894, the implication was that they had also been exposed in the field. This, plus the blank background, served to decontextualize the Kwakiutl, literally placing them in a timeless and spaceless "ethnographic present."

The Chicago Fair was also the scene of the first mechanical records of Kwakiutl music. This was a very early date, as Jesse Walter Fewkes had made the first recordings of American Indian music only in 1890 (Densmore 1927:80).[28] The actual recording of the 116 cylinders was executed in late September and early October by musicologist John C. Fillmore, who worked with Boas's assistance.[29]

Figure 5–4. Kwakiutl dancer with ceremonial bow, Chicago World's Fair, 1893. (Photographed by by John H. Grabill, Peabody Museum, Harvard University, N 28011. Published in retouched version, Boas 1897:Plate 15)

George Hunt was one of the three principal singers, along with MalEte and Tom Hemasilaq. Boas transcribed many of the melodies and published them in his 1897 monograph.

At the same time, Benjamin Ives Gilman recorded 18 cylinders of the Kwakiutl, sponsored by Mary Hemenway, Fewkes's patron. These were part of a series of 100 cylinders that he made of various groups from the Midway (Javanese, Fijian, Samoan, Turkish theater music, and European classical music).[30] And there was yet another recording session that we know of: That summer, Henry E. Krehbiel, music critic for the New York Tribune, recorded Kwakiutl songs for his own study purposes.[31] For many years these were the only recordings of Kwakiutl music. There was nothing comparable until Boas's own field recordings of 1931 in Fort Rupert.[32]

These cylinder recordings of Kwakiutl music, and Fillmore's articles based on them, played an important role in the early ethnomusicological debate in the 1890s on the nature of "primitive music" (Mark 1988:216–237). The general issue was the relationship between primitive and Western styles of music, especially the tonal scale. A more specific question was the relationship between the mechanical recording of a given performance and cultural norms. As performances varied, could one take the individual cylinder as an adequate sample of the song? This was made even more problematic when the recording was not made in the field. Concerning his experience, Gilman noted:

> A Kwakiutl Indian, whose performance before a phonograph I once heard through Dr. Boas's kindness, sheepish as was his air before beginning, when once buried in his song crooned away as simply and unhesitatingly as if he had been squatting on damp stones in a circle of his mates by a British Columbia river, instead of being seated in an office amid inquisitive Americans [Gilman 1908:66].[33]

From this, and evidently other occasions, Gilman concluded that self-consciousness was generally not a factor, and this suggested to him that the fair's setting did not seriously affect the song's authenticity.

Franz Boas, on the other hand, was generally skeptical of a single ethnographic inscription (Jacknis 1984:45), and on his 1894 field trip re-elicited the Kwakiutl songs recorded at the fair. Writing to his wife, he noted: "Either the Indians sang very differently into the phonograph, or [Fillmore] could not hear them well. I am positive that I have written them down correctly now, and the difference between my rendering and his is immense" (Boas 1969:179). Evidently Boas was not comparing Fillmore's transcriptions to the cylinders, but he could have. One point that Fewkes, Fillmore, and Gilman all perceived was that the phonograph could make "a permanent record which can be consulted over and over again by many students," as Fillmore put it.[34] As Fewkes also argued, this meant that the original transcription could be separated from the analysis of native music (1890:268). The phonograph, like the camera, removed the cultural object from the intercultural and intersocial dialogue that originally surrounded the inscription. Given the extensive uses made of the various ethnographic objects created at the Columbian Exposition, ethnologists needed to be all the more sensitive to their behavioral and symbolic status.

Conclusion

By the close of the fair's six-month run on October 30, over 27,000,000 people had witnessed its marvels (Rydell 1978:254). For these visitors, the displays of the Kwakiutl and other ethnic groups all contrasted—implicitly and explicitly— with the glories of Euro-American industrial civilization presented in the "White City." This central portion of the exposition received its name from the painted surfaces of its Beaux-Arts pavilions, but it could have just as easily re- ferred to the racial dominance that lay behind it. Frederic Putnam worked stren- uously to defend the scientific and educational value of the Anthropology exhibi- tions in the face of the fair's overwhelming commercial and national interests (Dexter 1966:219–220), but despite this high-mindedness, the common reactions were thoroughly racist, evolutionary, and imperialistic (Rydell 1978, 1984:38–71).

Legacy

According to one historian, "The fair's anthropology exhibit was something of a failure. It was significant enough in its own right," but "it became marginal to the exposition. Moreover, the sheer size and diversity of the fair overwhelmed the department" (Cole 1985:127). "Even the Kwakiutl made very little impres- sion," as they had to share the ethnological grounds with other native groups, and "the exoticism of these official exhibitions could not match the enormous color and panache of the ethnological exhibition 'run riot' on the Midway Plaisance" (Cole 1985:127–128). Strictly speaking, this view is correct, as it stresses the place of anthropology within the fair; yet when the place of the fair within anthropology is considered, the occasion becomes much more important. The event involved most of the leading anthropologists of the time. In addition to Putnam and Boas, Mason and Holmes, they included Stewart Culin, Frank Cushing, George Dorsey, Alice Fletcher, James Mooney, and Zelia Nuttall. A di- rect result of the fair was the founding of the Field Museum, initially made up of collections that had been gathered for it. Perhaps more significant than re- search were the innovations in exhibit techniques: the culture area and life- group.

The World's Columbian Exposition played an even more critical role for North- west Coast Indian culture. In this, the fair's most significant legacy was undoubt- edly the gathering of raw data, not research or analysis, per se. These artifact collections contributed to the beginning of major Northwest Coast holdings at the Field Museum, the Royal British Columbia Museum, and the Canadian Mu- seum of Civilization. The case is even stronger for the study of Northwest Coast Indian music, as the fair was the locus for the first and for many years the only such recordings. Franz Boas made great claims for the scientific results of the fair: "The collection illustrating the life of the Indian tribes of the North Pacific coast which was brought together in this manner was the most systematic one that ever has been presented; and the results of the systematic collection in the regions mentioned above have materially increased our knowledge of the ethnology of the whole Pacific coast" (cited in Johnson 1898:344). Boas's claims were somewhat exaggerated, as historian Douglas Cole correctly notes, citing the thin documentation and often poorly labeled displays (1985:124–125). However, the collections were fairly comprehensive, and this large-scale effort was undoubtedly the model for Boas's Jesup North Pacific Expedition for the American Museum of Natural History from 1897 to 1902.

The Chicago fair's slighting of research is reflected in the few publications that resulted from it. Of the two Northwest Coast addresses that Boas delivered at the Congress of Anthropology—"Classification of Languages of the North Pacific Coast" and "Ritual of the Kwakiutl Indians," coauthored with Hunt—only the former appeared in print (1894).[35] Boas's final report was only partly published in the official fair history (Johnson 1898:344–355).[36] What was published dealt almost entirely with the iconography of Deans's Skidegate models. Upon hearing that the fair's administration would not pay for the complete publication of the research, Boas complained to Putnam:

> The specimens from the North Pacific Coast are interesting, but their vital interest lies in their interpretation. Nobody can give this interpretation besides myself, because no one else understands the native languages from that region, and the collections will remain dead letters until the interpretation which is indicated on the labels is substantiated in a report.[37]

Boas believed that the collections would remain "unauthentic documents until we shall be able to submit to the judgment of science our methods and our material." To some extent, Boas's 1897 monograph on Kwakiutl ceremonialism was this final report, at least for the Kwakiutl.

Direct publications, however, were not the only form of public presentation. Perhaps equally important, though often in a negative fashion, was the fair's forum for popularization and intercultural presentation. Although some Northwest Coast material had been exhibited at the Philadelphia Centennial and was included in several museums, the Columbian Exposition was the largest public display of it to date, and many visitors were seeing it for the first time. Moreover, compared to later expositions (except those at Portland in 1905 and Seattle in 1909), which featured nearby Indian cultures and other regions, the display of Northwest Coast artifacts at Chicago was relatively large. Boas's presence, while important, can only be part of the reason. Alaska and British Columbia were undergoing rapid development. The fair came at an opportune moment for collecting and studying Northwest Coast culture—after several decades of serious interest in the region's native cultures, but before major American museums had taken the lead away from the exposition.

The Chicago Fair had great personal significance for Franz Boas and George Hunt. Boas saw his first Kwakiutl winter ceremonials in Chicago; it was not until his trip to Fort Rupert in the fall of 1894 that he was able to see them in their natural habitat. The exposition led to a job at the Field Museum and soon after with Putnam at the American Museum of Natural History (Hinsley and Holm 1976). This allowed Boas to firmly establish a position in American anthropology, one that was somewhat apart from the then-dominant center at the Smithsonian. Although Hunt had assisted earlier collectors, the fair represented his first opportunity to make an artifact collection on his own. During the six months they were able to spend together, Boas taught him an orthography with which to transcribe Kwakwala, allowing him to send thousands of pages of native texts to Boas in New York. For Hunt, the Chicago Fair was the single most important event in his transformation into a native ethnographer.

It is harder to judge the impact of the fair on the other Kwakiutl who traveled to Chicago. According to one scholar, "the Native Americans who participated in the exhibits did not benefit from the Exposition" (Rydell 1984:63). Most of the Kwakiutl probably had little sense of the racist scorn addressed to them in the popular press and photo albums. Whatever their abilities in English, Boas and Hunt would have insulated them.[38] However, the Kwakiutl, at least, did not do too poorly financially. When Johnny Drabble returned home to Alert Bay with his wife, he gave a potlatch with his earnings.[39] Despite the initial reluctance of some of their people to venture to Germany, by 1893 many Kwakiutl were widely traveled. For several decades they had been journeying down to Victoria and Washington State for work in the city and fields, and quite a few men had gone to Hawaii and Japan on whaling and sealing trips (Knight 1978:44–49). One can imagine that the Kwakiutl troupe enjoyed their trip to the Windy City. In any case, their evidently good experiences encouraged several Kwakiutl to come to the St. Louis Fair in 1904.

The Role of the Kwakiutl

The Columbian Exposition gave a special place to the Kwakiutl relative to other Northwest Coast groups. First, the presence of the Kwakiutl, Hunt, and Boas at the Chicago Fair was no accident. To some extent, the precursor for the display of Northwest Coast Indian culture at the fair was the 1881–1882 expedition to the region by J. Adrian Jacobsen. Boas had worked with the Bella Coola when they were in Berlin in 1886, and one of his aims in going to British Columbia later that year was to document the Jacobsen collection. George Hunt had worked intimately with Jacobsen as a collecting assistant in 1881, and the favorable reports of the Bella Coola had encouraged the Kwakiutl to finally make the trip. The Columbian Exposition was a reunion, as both the Jacobsen brothers came with collections they had made. Finally, "Boas discovered that almost all the Kwakiutl material in Berlin had been bought from members of the Chicago troupe" (Cole 1985:131). This strong connection was a prime factor in limiting scholarly sources of Northwest Coast culture to the Kwakiutl, and within Kwakiutl culture to George Hunt, his family, and Fort Rupert. The subsequent history of intercultural contact has only deepened this concentration (Jacknis 1991a).

On the scholarly front, Boas was wrong about the pervasive influence of the Kwakiutl on Northwest Coast culture. He reasoned that "the names of all the ceremonies which play so important a part in the customs of these tribes are borrowed from the Kwakiutl language" (cited in Johnson 1898:344). While these terms and the ceremonial complex of which they were a part had diffused from a Kwakiutl group, actually they spread to Coastal peoples—including the Southern Kwakiutl groups living in Fort Rupert—from the Northern Kwakiutl Haisla-speakers. Moreover, other traits central to the cultural area, like monumental, free-standing totem poles and the form-line graphic style, were borrowed by the Kwakiutl from more northern groups. Boas's misunderstandings can be explained by the fact that in 1893 he was still near the beginning of his more than four decades of Kwakiutl research.

Despite some ambivalence toward the Kwakiutl, the public's perception of them was on the whole, negative, as we have seen from the reactions to their art and performances. The apparent strangeness of Kwakiutl culture is evident from an advance notice written by the young Harlan Smith (who would later work with Boas on the Jesup expedition): "Here will be seen the natives of Vancouver's Island, in their queer long boats drawn up ashore, or in and about their curious plank houses, performing their feats of jugglery and going through their peculiar ceremonies" (1892:290). On the other hand, the Kwakiutl were seen as less depraved than some other Native American groups. According to one journalist, "There is nothing about them that suggests the Indian of the plains save their copper color. Simple in their modes of life, farmers as well as hunters, religious in their tendencies, and trustful of all men as they are themselves honest, they are a strong contrast to the treacherous and wily Sioux and bloodthirsty Apaches."[40] Journalists obtained some of their material from Boas, Hunt, and Deans. Deans was responsible for much of the faulty information, saying, for instance, that the Kwakiutl were "probably the result of an ancient mixture of the Japanese and the Eskimos" (Anonymous 1893a:185).

Like the fair itself, the World's Columbian Exposition proved more significant to the Kwakiutl for its role in displaying and popularizing their culture than for its scholarship. The Chicago Fair was the first major exhibition of Kwakiutl Indian artifacts (eclipsing in scale and audience the mid–1880s Jacobsen display in Berlin). Until then, large American museums like the Smithsonian and American Museum had focused their Northwest Coast collections on the Haida and Tlingit. There was a persisting general interest in the northern, "classical" styles of Haida and Tlingit art, to which the more theatrical and flamboyant Kwakiutl styles were a great contrast. The fair also led to a long tradition of Kwakiutl self-presentations. Following their participation at the St. Louis Fair in 1904, there was a gap of several decades. Beginning in 1949, the tradition was reinvigorated by carver Mungo Martin and his family. With his son-in-law and grandson, Henry and Tony Hunt, Martin demonstrated crafts and ceremonial dances at the Anthropology Museum of the University of British Columbia, Vancouver, and the B.C. Provincial Museum, Victoria. The work of these relatives and descendants of George Hunt has since become the best-known variety of Kwakiutl art. While Boas's concentration on the group dated back to his first trip in 1886, his work with Hunt in 1893 greatly intensified it. The Kwakiutl were on their way to becoming better known through the work of Boas and Hunt, but the fair gave them a vastly increased audience.

Objects, Context, and the Other

In the Chicago of 1893, the cultures of the Kwakiutl, other Northwest Coast groups, and, in fact, all participating non-Western peoples were displaced, their representation controlled by whites. It was the representation of a culture that was out of its cultural, spatial, and temporal context, or more precisely, a culture that had been placed in a new context (Halpin 1983). This estrangement resulted in a process of cultural objectification. The transformation from living subject to ethnographic object is borne out by some of Putnam's comments. Writing at the close of the fair to the Canadian Pacific Railroad, which had agreed to pay for the return shipping of all exhibits, Putnam argued that they should accordingly cover the cost of sending the Kwakiutl troupe back to British Columbia. As he complained, they should "be returned free like other exhibits, as they were exhibits in every sense of the term" (Dexter 1966:328).[41] One scholar has noted that the White City was a city without residences (Trachtenberg 1982:209), but, of course, the Kwakiutl and other visiting ethnic groups *did* live on the fairgrounds, always on view.

The World's Columbian Exposition is an excellent case study of the interethnic relations that surround and run through anthropology. In 1893, the Kwakiutl did not control their own representations. Increasingly over the twentieth century, they asserted their autonomy, until now they have their own anthropologists and two native-run museums. Although they still do not frame the anthropological argument, their views can now be ignored only with difficulty, especially in the arenas of artifact collection, performance, photography, and sound recording, which were featured at the fair. It is ironic that the production of these representations took place in a displaced setting. Emblematic of this irony were the repeated shifts in context involved in Boas's hamatsa diorama: from Fort Rupert to Chicago to Fort Rupert to Washington to Chicago, and beyond. While the fair presented Northwest Coast Indian culture in an often radically different and rearranged form, in many ways it also marked the beginning of a new tradition of the serious presentation of those cultures to the Other.

Notes

For help in formulating my ideas on the Chicago Fair, I would like to thank Curtis Hinsley (who commented on an earlier draft) and Barbara Kirshenblatt-Gimblett. The following abbreviations have been used in the notes: World's Columbian Exposition (WCE); Frederic Ward Putnam Papers, Harvard University Archives, Harvard University (FWPP).

1. Cole (1985:122–134) contains an excellent review of Northwest Coast Indian culture at the Chicago Fair, which should be consulted for supplementary details on a number of points.

2. Sponsored primarily by the British Association for the Advancement of Science, but also by the Bureau of American Ethnology.

3. However, on his 1891 trip to Oregon, Washington, and Victoria, B.C., Boas made arrangements with several collectors in the region (Cole 1985:122).

4. Frederic W. Putnam to George R. Davis, Monthly Report for October 1891, p. 13, WCE Correspondence, FWPP.

5. According to Ewers (1959:519), there were life-groups for only the Powhatan, Sioux, Kiowa, Zuni, Navajo, Hupa, and Kutchin.

6. The Swan collection also included material he had gathered in British Columbia.

7. In addition to the Northwest Coast village, Native American architectural forms in the area included skin tents of the Greenland and Labrador Eskimos, a Sioux tepee, a Winnebago mat house, a Navajo hogan, and bark lodges of the Penobscot and Iroquois.

8. Like all Kwakiutl domiciles, it had a name (in this case, two): "Qua-Qua-Kyum-Le-Las" ("The House So Large That You Cannot See the People on the Other Side") and "Na Gagith" ("House of the Waves"). The former is given in the *Chicago Record*, 14 April 1893, and the latter in the *Chicago Tribune*, 6 May 1893, and the *Chicago Times*, 7 May 1893; WCE Scrapbooks, vol. 2, FWPP.

9. *Chicago Tribune*, 2 July 1893, Professional Activities Scrapbook, 1887–1894, Stewart Culin Archival Collection, The Brooklyn Museum.

10. The Canadian pavilion had a similar display.

11. Working with Lieutenant Emmons, William Holmes created a life-group of a Tlingit family for the Pan-American Exposition at Buffalo in 1901. It was subsequently installed in the U.S. National Museum, where the figure of a woman weaving a Chilkat blanket is still on display.

12. Among the Kwakiutl subgroups represented were the Kwaguł and Gwetela, the Nimpkish, the Koskimo, and Nuwitti, all tribes at or close to Hunt's home in Fort Rupert.

13. The press accounts were ambiguous regarding Hunt's membership in the party of Kwakiutl; usually he was not counted. Although he was the de facto guide and had signed a contract with Putnam, James Deans was often referred to as the official guide.

14. Frederic W. Putnam to George R. Davis, 27 March 1893, WCE Correspondence, FWPP. The following quotations are also taken from this letter.

15. Contract between Frederic W. Putnam and George Hunt, 29 September 1892, WCE Miscellaneous Papers, FWPP.

16. Frederic W. Putnam to George R. Davis, 29 April 1893, WCE Correspondence, FWPP.

17. *Chicago Tribune*, 6 May 1893, WCE Scrapbooks, vol. 2, FWPP.

18. *Chicago Herald*, 13 May 1893, WCE Scrapbooks, vol. 2, FWPP.

19. *Chicago Times*, 13 June 1893, WCE Scrapbooks, vol. 2, FWPP.

20. Henry E. Krehbiel, 6 August 1893, "Folk-Music in Chicago, II: Cannibal Songs of the Indians," *New York Tribune*, WCE Scrapbooks, vol. 2, FWPP.

21. L. Vankoughnet to Rev. Alfred J. Hall, [September?] 1893, "Request to put together an Indian exhibit at the Columbian World's Fair, 1892–1894," Canadian Department of Indian Affairs, RG 10, vol. 3865, file 85,529, National Archives of Canada, Ottawa. See also Cole (1985:129–130) for further details.

22. Emma Sickles had long been a thorn in the side of Professor Putnam (see Dexter 1966:326–128). Owing to political connections she was given an appointment in the Ethnology Department over Putnam's objections. After several spats, she was dismissed, but returned in the guise of the chairman of the Indian Committee of the Universal Peace Union.

23. *New York Times*, 8 October 1893, WCE Scrapbooks, vol. 2, FWPP.

24. Putnam's statement was widely reproduced in contemporary papers, e.g., *San Francisco Chronicle*, 7 October 1893, WCE Scrapbooks, vol. 2, FWPP.

25. Henry E. Krehbiel, 6 August 1893, "Folk-Music in Chicago, II: Cannibal Songs of the Indians," *New York Tribune*, WCE Scrapbooks, vol. 2, FWPP.

26. However, citing Boas, Holm (1990:378) notes that it was possible to hold these ceremonies "at any time, given the proper circumstances," although it was "formerly very unusual." In more recent times, Kwakiutl winter ceremonials have been given in the summer, especially around June.

27. Frederic W. Putnam to George R. Davis, 27 March 1893, WCE Correspondence, FWPP.

28. Fewkes made his first recordings in March, among the Passamaquoddy of Maine, and his second in June-July among the Zuni of New Mexico.

29. In 1897, Boas deposited 114 of these cylinders in the Anthropology Department of the American Museum of Natural History. They have subsequently been transferred to the Archives of Traditional Music, Indiana University.

30. In 1970 these were transferred from Harvard's Peabody Museum to the Archive of Folk Culture, Library of Congress.

31. Henry E. Krehbiel, 6 August 1893, "Folk-Music in Chicago, II: Cannibal Songs of the Indians," *New York Tribune*, WCE scrapbooks, FWPP.

32. George Dorsey recorded seven cylinders in 1899 (probably in Victoria), and Edward Curtis made several in July 1910. Boas later made a series of 156 cylinders in January 1931 on his last field trip to Fort Rupert, and another series on aluminum disks in 1938 and/or 1941 when Daniel Cranmer, Hunt's son-in-law, visited New York. Major Kwakiutl recordings since the late forties include those by Ida Halpern, Wilson Duff, and Bill Holm.

33. The unself-consciousness singer in this example may well have been George Hunt. According to Mark, this session was held in Boas's office (1988:235).

34. John C. Fillmore, "Preliminary Report on the Kwakiutl Songs," p. 2, WCE Miscellaneous Papers, FWPP. See also Fillmore (1893).

35. Fillip Jacobsen was scheduled to offer "Legends of the Bella Coola Indians," but evidently did not give it.

36. For the entire 50–page report, see WCE Miscellaneous Papers, FWPP.

37. Franz Boas to Frederic W. Putnam, 11 December 1893, General Correspondence, FWPP, cf. Jacknis (1985:104).

38. However, one paper claimed that "the younger men and women understand English and some of them write it with ease." *Chicago Record*, 14 April 1893, WCE Scrapbooks, vol. 2, FWPP.

39. Wilson Duff, 1955, Notebook no. 10, "Kwakiutl Totem Survey," miscellaneous notes at back, KWA-W–007, Anthropological Collections Section, Royal British Columbia Museum, Victoria.

40. *Chicago Times*, 16 April 1893, WCE scrapbooks, vol. 2, FWPP.

41. However, it should be noted that this argument may have been less an indication of his true feelings, and more an attempt to save money.

References

Anonymous
1893a James Deans and his Company of Indians. *American Antiquarian and Oriental Journal* 15:185–186.
1893b *Glimpses of the World's Fair: A Selection of Gems of the White City Seen Through a Camera*. Laird and Lee, Chicago.
Badger, R. Reid
1979 *The Great American Fair: The World's Columbian Exposition and American Culture*. Nelson-Hall, Chicago.
Benedict, Burton
1983 The Anthropology of World's Fairs. In *The Anthropology of World's Fairs: San Francisco's Panama Pacific International Exposition of 1915*, Burton Benedict et al., pp. 1–65. Lowie Museum of Anthropology, Berkeley, Calif., in association with Scolar Press, London.
Boas, Franz
1887a The Occurrence of Similar Inventions in Areas Widely Apart. *Science* 9:485–486.
1887b Museums of Ethnology and Their Classification. *Science* 9:587–589.
1894 Classification of the Languages of the North Pacific Coast. In *Memoirs of the Interna-*

tional Congress of Anthropology, edited by C. S. Wake, pp. 339–346. Schulte, Chicago.

1897 *The Social Organization and the Secret Societies of the Kwakiutl Indians.* Report of the U.S. National Museum for 1895, pp. 311–738. Washington, D.C.

1969 *The Ethnography of Franz Boas: Letters and Diaries of Franz Boas Written on the Northwest Coast from 1886 to 1931.* Compiled and edited by Ronald P. Rohner. University of Chicago Press, Chicago.

Burg, David F.
1976 *Chicago's White City of 1893.* University of Kentucky Press, Lexington.

Cole, Douglas
1985 *Captured Heritage: The Scramble for Northwest Coast Artifacts.* University of Washington Press, Seattle.

Collier, Donald
1969 Chicago Comes of Age: The World's Columbian Exposition and the Birth of Field Museum. *Field Museum Bulletin* 40(5):2–7.

Densmore, Frances
1927 The Study of Indian Music in the Nineteenth Century. *American Anthropologist* 29:77–86.

Dexter, Ralph W.
1966 Putnam's Problems Popularizing Anthropology. *American Scientist* 54(3):315—332.

Ewers, John C.
1959 A Century of American Indian Exhibits in the Smithsonian Institution. *Annual Report of the Smithsonian Institution for 1958*, pp. 513–525. Washington, D.C.

Fagin, Nancy
1984 Closed Collections and Open Appeals: The Two Anthropology Exhibits at the Chicago World's Columbian Exposition of 1893. *Curator* 27(4):249–264.

Fewkes, Jesse Walter
1890 On the Use of the Phonograph in the Study of the Languages of American Indians. *Science* 15:267–269.

Fillmore, John C.
1893 A Woman's Song of the Kwakiutl Indians. *Journal of American Folklore* 6(23): 285–290.

Ford, Clellan S.
1941 *Smoke from Their Fires: The Life of a Kwakiutl Chief.* Yale University Press, New Haven, Conn.

Gilman, Benjamin Ives
1908 Hopi Songs. *Journal of American Archaeology and Ethnology* 5. Houghton Mifflin, Boston.

Gruber, Jacob W.
1970 Ethnographic Salvage and the Shaping of Anthropology. *American Anthropologist* 72:1289–1299.

Halpin, Marjorie M.
1983 Anthropology as Artifact. In *Consciousness and Inquiry: Ethnology and Canadian Realities*, edited by Frank Manning, pp. 262–275. Canadian Ethnology Service, Mercury Series, paper no. 89E. National Museum of Man, Ottawa.

Harris, Neil
1978 Museums, Merchandising, and Popular Taste: The Struggle for Influence. In *Material Culture and the Study of American Life*, edited by Ian M. G. Quimby, pp. 140–174. W. W. Norton, New York, published for The Henry Francis du Pont Winterthur Museum.

Handy, Moses
1893 *The Official Directory of the World's Columbian Exposition.* W. B. Conkey, Chicago.

Hinsley, Curtis M., Jr.
1991 The World as Marketplace: Commodification of the Exotic at the World's Columbian Exposition in Chicago, 1893. In *Exhibiting Cultures: The Poetics and Politics of Mu-*

seum Display, edited by Ivan Karp and Steven D. Lavine. Smithsonian Institution Press, Washington, D.C.

Hinsley, Curtis M., Jr., and Bill Holm
1976 A Cannibal in the National Museum: The Early Career of Franz Boas in America. *American Anthropologist* 78:306–316.

Holm, Bill
1977 Traditional and Contemporary Kwakiutl Winter Dance. *Arctic Anthropology* 14(1):5–24.
1987 *Spirit and Ancestor: A Century of Northwest Coast Indian Art at the Burke Museum*. University of Washington Press, Seattle.
1990 Kwakiutl: Winter Ceremonies. In *Northwest Coast*, edited by Wayne Suttles, pp. 378–386. Handbook of North American Indians, vol. 7, William C. Sturtevant, general editor. Smithsonian Institution, Washington, D.C.

Holmes, William H.
1903 The Exhibit of the Department of Anthropology, Report on the Exhibits of the U.S. National Museum at the Pan-American Exposition, Buffalo, New York, 1901. *Annual Report of the U.S. National Museum for 1901*, pp. 200–218. Washington, D.C.

Hoxie, Frederick E.
1979 Red Man's Burden. *The Antioch Review* 37(3):326–342.

Jacknis, Ira
1984 Franz Boas and Photography. *Studies in Visual Communication* 10(1):2–60.
1985 Franz Boas and Exhibits: On the Limitations of the Museum Method of Anthropology. In *Objects and Others: Essays on Museums and Material Culture*, edited by George W. Stocking, Jr., pp. 75–111. History of Anthropology, 3. University of Wisconsin Press, Madison.
1991a *The Storage Box of Tradition: Museums, Anthropologists, and Kwakiutl Art, 1881–1981*. Smithsonian Institution Press, Washington, D.C., in press.
1991b George Hunt, Collector of Indian Specimens. In *Chiefly Feasts: The History and Art of the Kwakiutl Potlatch*, edited by Aldona Jonaitis. American Museum of Natural History, New York; University of Washington Press, Seattle.

Johnson, Rossiter (editor)
1897 *A History of the World's Columbian Exposition, held in Chicago in 1893*, vol. 3, *Exhibits*. D. Appleton, New York.
1898 *A History of the World's Columbian Exposition, held in Chicago in 1893*, vol. 2, *Departments*. D. Appleton, New York.

Jonaitis, Aldona
1988 *From the Land of the Totem Poles: The Northwest Coast Indian Art Collection at the American Museum of Natural History*. American Museum of Natural History, New York; University of Washington Press, Seattle.

Knight, Rolf
1978 *Indians at Work: An Informal History of Native Indian Labour in British Columbia, 1858–1930*. New Star Books, Vancouver.

Kirshenblatt-Gimblett, Barbara
1991 Objects of Ethnography. In *Exhibiting Cultures: The Poetics and Politics of Museum Display*, edited by Ivan Karp and Steven D. Lavine. Smithsonian Institution Press, Washington, D.C.

Mark, Joan
1980 *Four Anthropologists: An American Science in its Early Years*. Science History Publications, New York.
1988 *A Stranger in Her Native Land: Alice Fletcher and the American Indians*. University of Nebraska Press, Lincoln.

Mason, Otis T.
1887 The Occurrence of Similar Inventions in Areas Widely Apart. *Science* 9:534–535.
1894 Ethnological Exhibit of the Smithsonian Institution at the World's Columbian Ex-

position. In *Memoirs of the International Congress of Anthropology*, edited by C. S. Wake, pp. 208–216. Schulte, Chicago.

1895 Department of Ethnology. *Annual Report of the U.S. National Museum for 1893*, pp. 125–132. Washington, D.C.

Rydell, Robert W.

1978 The World's Columbian Exposition of 1893: Racist Underpinnings of a Utopian Artifact. *Journal of American Culture* 1(2):253–275.

1984 *All the World's a Fair: Visions of Empire at American International Expositions, 1876–1916.* University of Chicago Press, Chicago.

1989 The Culture of Imperial Abundance: World's Fairs in the Making of American Culture. In *Consuming Visions: Accumulation and Display of Goods in America, 1880–1920*, edited by Simon J. Bronner, pp. 191–216. W. W. Norton, New York, published for The Henry Francis du Pont Winterthur Museum.

Smith, Harlan I.

1892 Antiquity at the World's Fair. *American Antiquarian and Oriental Journal* 14:289–292.

1893 "Man and his Works": The Anthropological Building at the World's Columbian Exposition. *American Antiquarian and Oriental Journal* 15:115–117.

Sweet, Jill Drayson

1983 Ritual and Theatre in Tewa Ceremonial Performances. *Ethnomusicology* 27(2): 253–269.

Todd, F. Dundas

1893 *World's Fair through a Camera: Snap Shots by an Artist.* Woodward and Tiernan, St. Louis, Mo.

Trachtenberg, Alan

1982 White City. In *The Incorporation of America: Culture and Society in the Gilded Age*, pp. 208–234. Hill and Wang, New York.

Weber, Ronald L., and Constance Crane

1982 Those Who Dwell beside the Sea. *Alaska Journal* 12(2):20–27.

Wyatt, Victoria

1984 *Shapes of Their Thoughts: Reflections of Culture Contact in Northwest Coast Indian Art.* University of Oklahoma Press, Norman; Peabody Museum of Natural History, Yale University, New Haven, Conn.

Chapter 6 ■

David Hurst Thomas

Harvesting Ramona's Garden: Life in California's Mythical Mission Past

Plymouth Rock was a state of mind.
So were the California Missions.
    —Charles Fletcher Lummis

A century ago, Californians spun for themselves a romanticized mission past. Drawing heavily from Helen Hunt Jackson's Victorian novel *Ramona* (1884), rootless Anglo immigrants began to identify with the region's earliest European settlers, deriving from them a sense of continuity, tradition, pride, and regional identity. The architectural manifestations of the *Ramona* myth—the imaginatively "restored" missions and the assorted buildings in the copycat Mission Revival style—underscore the truism that an appropriate past springs from a present need and interpretation. For several decades, the serious archaeological investigation of California's missions was handicapped by the public infatuation with Ramona.

The genesis of *Ramona* and the overnight acceptance of such romanticism provide an eye-opening example of a past made appropriate. To mid-nineteenth-century observers, these mission ruins were quaint or melancholy or simply timeworn. But Californians distilled a different past. Through diverse literary, artistic, preservationist, and promotional devices, they arrived at a past rooted in romantic protest, which ultimately succeeded because of the potential for hard cash that Franciscan ruins held for tourism and tract development. The Mission Revival style stated and restated this myth thousands of times—in hotels, railroad stations, business blocks, schools, and bungalows strewn across a rapidly urbanizing landscape, far beyond the original reach of the California Mission system (Figure 6–1).

This mythical past began as well-meaning artistic license, was reinforced by an architectural cliché, and underwritten by exploding land values. This chapter examines the evolution of the myth, the reasons behind its success, and the legacy of this myth as it influences the practice of mission archaeology even today.

Defining a Mythical Mission Past

Each of the California missions has a unique history, but the basic pattern is similar at each: the initial founding and struggle to establish itself, the years of "busi-

Figure 6–1. The Las Vegas & Tonopah railroad depot in Rhyolite, Nevada (1909), a classic example of Mission Revival architecture. Although Rhyolite became a ghost town by 1920, the structure still stands, having served variously as a saloon and casino. This building is today a crumbling remembrance of the neo-Franciscan architectural style that once swept the American West. (Photograph courtesy of the Nevada Historical Society, Nye County negative 74)

ness as usual," secularization, recycling, deterioration, rediscovery, veneration, and, too commonly, fanciful reconstruction.[1] Mission San Gabriel Arcángel, located nine miles from today's downtown Los Angeles, is typical. Founded as California's fourth mission in 1771 by Frs. Angel Fernandez de la Somera and Pedro Benito Cambón, the earliest San Gabriel Arcángel was constructed on a site personally chosen by Fray Junípero Serra. But persistent flooding of the fields forced the padres to move the mission to its present location in 1775. The earthquake of 1812 badly damaged the monastery and toppled the church tower; by 1828, the church had been completely rebuilt. Mission records, complete through 1832, claim more than 7,800 baptisms, nearly 2,000 marriages, and about 5,600 deaths. The mission was secularized in 1834. Then in 1862, the United States returned it to the Catholic Church and the buildings served as the parish church for the city of San Gabriel until 1908, when the Missionary Order of the Sons of the Immaculate Heart of Mary took charge. These Claretian Missionary Fathers have conducted extensive restorations to the church and mission quadrangle. A small museum, several restored buildings, the mission gardens, and a gift shop serve a devoted public.

Over their two-century life span, the California missions evolved as institutions, as architectural statements, and as archaeological sites. By looking closely at these transformations, one can monitor the development of California's distinctive regional identity.

Changing Literary Reflections

Prior to the Anglo conquest of California in 1846, American writers were generally critical of the *Californio* lifeway. The cumulative effect of benign climate, unusually fertile soil, and an abundance of Indian labor was perceived as dulling initiative and producing a stagnant lifeway. Hispanic institutions, particularly the Catholic Church and the Spanish monarchy were deprecated, and American writers decried the grave defects in the *Californio* character, alleging slothfulness, disloyalty, and spinelessness. During this period, Anglos derived what Starr (1973:21) terms a "California expectation": a sense of mismanagement awaiting correction, of luxuriance awaiting improvement.[2]

But not long after California was absorbed into the Union, the attitude toward the Hispanic past softened considerably. Whereas the first Anglo travelers carped about the retrograde tendencies of the old order, new writers vaunted the virtues of graciousness and tranquility. Bret Harte, one of California's earliest romanticizers, imbued the now-subordinated Hispanic lifeway with a retrospective sense of charm, animation, and color. Harte extolled those "happy, tranquil days. The proprietors of the old ranchos ruled in a patriarchal style, and lived to a patriarchal age. On a soil half tropical in its character . . . a soft-handed Latin race slept and smoked the half year's sunshine away. . . . They awoke from their dreams only to find themselves strangers on their own soil, foreigners in their own country, ignorant even of the treasure they had been sent to guard" (quoted in Williams 1955:216).

This shifting viewpoint, from criticism to sympathy and even admiration for the pre-Anglo *Californios*, had distinctive ramifications for the missions. The first Anglos in the new state of California scarcely noticed the missions. The infrequent traveler's account during this period tended to be perfunctory, graphic, and somewhat disparaging. When geologist William H. Brewer visited Mission San Carlos Borromeo (Carmel) in 1861, his observations were expressed in characteristically candid, forthright language: "About half of the roof had fallen in, the rest was good. The paintings and inscriptions on the walls were mostly obliterated. . . . A dead pig lay beneath the finely carved font for holy water. . . . The number of ground squirrels burrowing in the old mounds made by the crumbling adobe walls and the deserted adobe houses was incredible" (Farquhar 1930:106–107).

But when Bret Harte visited Mission San Francisco de Asís in 1863, he enriched the raw present with his romantic sense of a sadly vanishing past: "Its ragged senility contrasting with the smart spring sunshine, its two gouty pillars with the plaster dropping away like tattered bandages, its rayless windows, its crumbling entrances, and the leper spots on its whitewashed wall eating through the dark adobe. . . ." (cited in Walker 1939:128–129).

Although still tinged here and there with remnants of the Black Legend, this increasingly romantic literature was soon to result in an exalted perception of the missions and their place in California's past, romanticizing "the other" when it was no longer a threat. These same derelict structures—becoming each year more delapidated—began to assume an aura of dignity, honor, antiquity, and mystery.[3] It was not long until the crumbling sacristy at Mission San Carlos Borromeo had become "a picturesque mass of ruins, with wild birds flitting in and out through its arches . . . with all nature in a mood of serenity . . . an owl sits in an empty window, contemplating the decay about him" (Manning 1884).

By the time Robert Louis Stevenson attended San Carlos Day Mass in 1879, the dingy, dusty ruins of the mission at Carmel-by-the-Sea had become the very symbols of perseverance and fortitude:

> The church is roofless and ruinous, sea-breezes and sea-fogs, and the alteration of the rain and sunshine, daily widening the breaches and casting the crockets from the wall. . . . Only one day in the year, . . . the "padre" drives over the hill from Monterey; the little sacristy, which is the only covered portion of the church, is filled with seats and decorated for the service; the Indians troop together, their bright dresses contrasting with their dark and melancholy faces. . . . I have never seen faces more vividly lit up with joy than the faces of these Indian singers. It was to them not only the worship of God, nor an act by which they recalled and commemorated better days, but was besides an exercise of culture, where all they knew of art and letters was united and expressed [Stevenson 1895:167–168].

As literary interest and economic speculation heightened, so did the stature of the relic missions. Although mission architecture might have been bare, unpolished, and primitive, allusion to "olden days" was about to eclipse reality.[4]

Enter *Ramona*

Helen Hunt Jackson—hailed by Ralph Waldo Emerson as "America's greatest woman poet"—made the first of three visits to California in the winter of 1881. That year, she had published her well-known *A Century of Dishonor*, an eloquent and impassioned 500–page plea for better treatment of American Indians. Jackson went to California in part because the Department of the Interior had appointed her to investigate the plight of the Mission Indians. She was also on assignment for *Century* magazine, which commissioned stories on the same topic. While in California, Jackson interviewed scores of old-timers who had lived in and about the missions, pueblos, and rancherías.

What began as fact-finding soon evolved into an obsession with pre-Yankee *Californio* culture. A child of rigid Calvinists—raised to regard the Pope as the Anti-Christ—Jackson became enthralled with the elusive mission mystique. Finding such sleepy southern California charm a welcome contrast to her own eastern, provincial society, she came to believe that the Anglo-American invasion had done a great wrong to both the Hispanic and Indian populations.

But beneath this veneer of sentimentality, Jackson's passion was honest and deep-seated, reflecting her concern for the plight of the surviving Indian population. The more she learned about California, the more alarmed she became with continued treaty violations and usurpation of Indian lands that legally should have remained inviolate. She filed her detailed report with the Department of the Interior, but although legislation was passed by the Senate, her recommendations died in the House of Representatives.

Realizing that *A Century of Dishonor* and her California report had fallen upon deaf ears, Jackson changed strategies, deciding to cloak her message in the guise of a romantic novel. Chronic bronchitis forced her to leave California, and she rushed to New York and sequestered herself in the Berkeley Hotel. Surrounded by Indian baskets and Spanish embroideries—to evoke memories of the warmth and color of the Golden State—she churned out her epic novel in a phenomenal four-month period.[5]

In a book she named *Ramona*, Jackson detailed the historical predicament of Franciscan missionaries in their heyday, Mexican dons in their decline, and Mission Indians in a state verging on deterioration. Clearly intended as a defense of California Indians, Jackson set out to awaken an entire nation, employing fictional characters, mystery, poetry, and romance to soften the hard truth.

Ramona ranks with Margaret Mitchell's *Gone with the Wind* among America's all-time best-sellers. Jackson's plot chronicles the plight of Ramona Ortegna, a young half-breed orphan raised to think of herself as Spanish, who falls in love with Alessandro Assis, an Indian captain of a sheep-shearing band from Temecula. Through the simple, homespun character of Aunt Ri, Jackson outlined her case and pointed up the injustices of federal policy toward the American Indian. The California mission ruins were "proofs of a spiritual enthusiasm and exaltation of self-sacrifice . . . rarely paralleled in the world's history" (Jackson 1883a:211–212).

Ramona has often been compared to *Uncle Tom's Cabin*, Harriet Beecher Stowe's landmark novel of three decades earlier, and there are some parallels (see e.g., Mathes 1983, 1990; Nevins 1941). These two New England women poured their moral and religious indignation into parables of tragedy and heroism. The popularity of both books was enhanced by dramatic stage productions. Both authors have been faulted for stylistic and literary lapses, and both were accused of excessive sentimentality. Eulogizing Jackson after her death in 1885, the New York-based *Nation* declared that—second only to Harriet Beecher Stowe—Helen Hunt Jackson was the most admired woman writer in America. This parallel was also obvious to Jackson, who wrote, "If I could write a story that would do for the Indians a thousandth part that Uncle Tom's Cabin did for the Negro, I would be thankful for the rest of my life" (cited in Mathes 1990:77).

But in the final analysis, *Ramona* was not *Uncle Tom's Cabin*. Harriet Beecher Stowe had produced one of the world's most potent pieces of propaganda, in part because of its timing. The issue of human slavery had been a festering American sore for a century, and ready-made public sentiment existed in large sectors of the United States. America was prepared to hear about the sordid details of slavery and, after serialization in the *National Era*, the first edition of *Uncle Tom's Cabin* was greeted with instant success, selling an unprecedented 300,000 copies within the first year. By any account, *Uncle Tom's Cabin* became a factor to be reckoned when summing up the causes of the Civil War.

A different fate awaited *Ramona*. As reform, *Ramona* fizzled. "It was unlooked for and unwanted" (Davis and Alderson 1914:79). *Ramona* sparked a firestorm of criticism from westerners when it first appeared. Not a single local newspaper, politician, or public figure joined Jackson's Indian cause. Civic groups and local critics denounced the novel as "a tissue of falsehoods, a travesty on history, and a damnable libel on Southern California" (McWilliams 1973:73).

But as regional romance, *Ramona* triumphed. Somewhere along the line, rather than indicting present injustices, *Ramona* turned into wistful memory of pastoral days. While Aunt Ri made trenchant observations about present injustices to the Indians, it was clearly the ancient Franciscan Padre Salvierderra's recollection of bygone days that had captured Jackson's imagination.[6]

Rushed into print with Christmas sales in mind, *Ramona* coincided perfectly with the great invasion of the American West by homeseekers and tourists. In its very first year of publication, *Ramona* became one of America's three most popular novels. The *Ramona* promotion soon reached epic proportions, with thousands of *Ramona*-style mission postcards flooding the nation. Seeing the flocks of winter tourists on pilgrimages to view Ramonaland firsthand, western antipathy vanished overnight, and southern Californians themselves became passionately *Ramona*-conscious.

From the pages of *Ramona* arose the myth of California's missions.[7] *Ramona* created (rather than recreated) a romantic time and place that came eventually to be accepted without question.

RAMONA'S MYTH: The kindhearted industrious Franciscans, led by the saintly Serra, had brought civilization and temporary affluence to the docile and grateful

California Indians. The great ranchos soon covered the land; they were lavish in their hospitality and were peopled with brightly dressed caballeros and beautiful, fine-tempered senoritas. Everyone took it easy in that Arcadia, and there was nothing of the push and shove of modern commercial life. The adobe houses were cool and comfortable; the tinkling guitars and the lovely mission bells brought music to a quiet land; and everywhere courtesy, generosity, and lightheartedness reigned supreme [Walker 1950:121–123].

This new folklore was tailor-made for the Anglo-Protestant population that flooded southern California in the late nineteenth century. The Franciscan fantasy overlaid the Protestant virtues of hard work, order, and productivity. It was a utopian vision of progress free of labor problems, sweatshops, and Anglo workaholics (Langum 1983; see also McWilliams 1973:21; Starr 1985:62, 89).[8]

For the first time, the romantic image of California's bygone, golden past permeated America. Rather than focus on what was, an Anglo readership became fascinated with what might have been. In a few short years, the facts of mission imagery became inextricably merged with allegory, setting the stage for the architectural revival that froze the myth in a million neo-Franciscan buildings.

Ramona as Mission Revival Architect

This new, utopian view of missions was soon reflected in the developing California life-style. When Senator Leland Stanford began planning his new university, he drew an explicit parallel with California's Franciscan missions. In 1892, Stanford wrote: "I think we should keep steadily before the students the fact that our aim is to fit men to realize the possibilities of humanity, in order that our graduates may in a measure become missionaries to spread correct ideas of civilization" (quoted in Weitze 1984:23).

Stanford, like many of his contemporaries, strove to wrap this visionary notion in a distinctive architectural style appropriate to the climate and "newness" of the American West, and he boldly seized on the missions for inspiration. A Stanford University publicity brochure, published in 1888, explained that "in adopting this peculiar style of grouping and construction, it was the desire of Senator Stanford to preserve as a local characteristic the style of architecture given to California in the churches and the mission buildings of the early missionary fathers" (quoted in Weitze 1984:22). This design melded a distinctive combination of fenestration, arches, curved capitals, and polychrome ornamentation. Although the resulting architecture is most properly classified as late Richardsonian Romanesque, Stanford considered these structures to be generally compatible with some kind of universal Franciscan style.

The California World's Fair Commission soon authorized a distinctive state building for the upcoming 1893 Columbian Exposition in Chicago. Although selecting the actual plan proved difficult, the commission ultimately adopted a proposal by A. Page Brown from among 30 competing entries (Figure 6–2). Brown's 1893 California pavilion was second only to the Illinois State Building in size, no mean feat, given that the Columbian Exposition abounded in heroic public spaces (Starr 1985:190; see also Fogelson, this volume). Brown's design featured three different mission facades, each distinguished by alternative tower forms. The long primary access was highlighted by a stepped gable, buttressed by solid mission piers; unusual quatrefoil windows accentuated the design.

Discussing Brown's achievement, *World's Fair Magazine* initiated a trend by confusing this eclectic hodgepodge with historical reality: "The visitor will stand face to face with the California of yesterday. . . . We will have a building whose architecture is all our own, which will take the beholder back to the days when the Fathers, with their old Missions, started the march of civilization into the Golden West" (Anonymous 1892). The official exposition handbook further reinforced the fiction, noting that the California building was "a reproduction of the typical mission that was once common in that state" (Anonymous 1893:183).

The design competition drew a generation of architects into California's developing dialogue, and in the first post-*Ramona* decade, Mission Revival architecture took off in earnest.[9] In the flood of state expositions to follow, the 1893 California pavilion was variously emulated and reinterpreted a year later in the

Figure 6–2. A. Page Brown's California Building at the Columbian Exposition in Chicago (1893). This eclectic assemblage of mission elements single-handedly kicked off the explosion of Mission Revival buildings throughout the American West. The Roman-style facade of Mission Santa Bárbara appears at the left; the main entrance is a heavily modified version of that of Mission San Carlos Borromeo, as are the quatrefoil windows along the long axis. A third stylized mission facade appears on the far end. (Photograph courtesy of Raymond Fogelson)

Cotton Palace in Waco (Texas), the California Midwinter International Exposition (San Francisco), and a "Fiesta" hosted by the Merchant's Association of Los Angeles, in which parade floats reflected mission themes. California mission style pavilions cropped up in Buffalo (1901), St. Louis (1904), Portland (1905), and Seattle (1909).

For Californians, Mission Revival became the logical culmination of a wish for a simpler, indigenous architecture (Gebhard et al. 1985:19). With each successive exposition, Californians increasingly felt they were creating America's first architectural style rooted in strictly native precedents. Capitalizing upon America's love affair with *Ramona*, the California pavilions also established a unique public image. Symmetrical towers, garden courtyards, red tile, and white stucco soon adorned train stations, hotels, libraries, schools, and private dwellings. In so doing, architectural forms of the old Hispanic social order were appropriated, translated, and simplified into a regional style disconnected from the values and institutions that had originally produced them.

As the Mission Revival spread, it diversified into other forms, such as the Bungalow Court style, creating housing for the workers, retirees, aspiring actors, and others who streamed into southern California between 1890 and 1920. Responding to popular taste rather than academic tradition, the Hispanic flavor was expressed in a low-rise, multifamily courtyard complex that came to dominate Los Angeles. More than one million Mission Revival residences graced southern California by 1939, and the state's pavilion for that year's New York World's Fair was yet another elaboration on the cliché.

A Curious Revival Indeed

According to the actual physical remnants, Alta California architecture was among the least appealing of possible models for post-Victorian imitation. Legitimate Spanish architecture in California was rare, confined to the mission complexes and Spanish homesteads that had been constructed in a vernacular Spanish tradition (Gowans 1986). After the successful Anglo conquest of California, Americans had done their best to ignore and even eradicate the vestiges of Hispanic dwellings, civic buildings, and urban structure. How curious, then, that Hispanic architectural forms were so revered only five decades later.

The Mission Revival movement is also ironic in the light of nineteenth-century global politics. Spain was incorrectly perceived by many as an enemy in the Mexican-American War of the 1840s (although independent by that time, Mexicans were still commonly confused with Spaniards). Then, in the 1890s, the United States went to war with Spain itself. Anti-Spanish feelings ran high in both confrontations, and politicians fanned the flames by pointing to corruption and degeneracy in all things Spanish.

The triumph of *Ramona*-style architecture is likewise remarkable, given the nineteenth-century frontier mentality in America (see also Weber, this volume). *Ramona* drew instant criticism from that archenemy of sentimentalism, Teddy Roosevelt—like Jackson, a nonwestern, self-styled expert on western America.

Whereas Helen Hunt Jackson espoused the Indian and Hispanic cause, Roosevelt argued the case of the Anglo-American pioneer and settler.

Let sentimentalists remember, Roosevelt declared in the first volume of *Winning of the West* (1889), that the Indians had no real title to the lands over which they rode, since Indians never effectively occupied this land. It was unthinkable that these grasslands and forests should be withheld from civilized homesteaders by the claims of a few squalid savages. Let Helen Hunt Jackson and the other sentimentalists also recall, he continued, that Indians were responsible for countless appalling crimes. For Roosevelt, Indians were a treacherous, brutal, degraded race, and he told chilling tales of "the hideous, unnameable, unthinkable tortures practiced by the red men on their captured foes." It was the American frontiersman, Roosevelt argued, who was the long-suffering and wronged person, "a stern race of freemen who toiled hard, endured greatly, and fronted adversity bravely, who prized strength and courage and good faith, whose wives were chaste and who were generous and loyal to their friends." How doubly curious, then, that Teddy Roosevelt himself became such an ardent booster of Hispanic Mission Revival architecture (Starr 1985:87).

Why, Then, Did the Ramona Myth Prevail?

Despite Jackson's sensibilities, *Ramona* contributed little toward improving the lot of California's Indian population. Rather, from the passionate pages of *Ramona* arose a fictive contrast between the dreamy, romantic Latins and disciplined, business-minded Yankees. All the major actors took the stage together —literally. Breathtakingly lovely Ramona and courageous Alessandro, fleeing hand in hand into the foothills to escape the encroaching Anglo menace, defined Hispanic and Indian stereotypes that were to survive into the next century. The compassionate Franciscan father, praying in his mission garden, and the Old Spanish Don, dreaming away in the courtyard of his rancho, also contributed their share toward this mythical mission past, replete with instantaneous traditions, counterfeit legends, and racial stereotypes.

As America embraced *Ramona*, Jackson's best-selling novel became a metaphor for California's mythical past. But by itself, no single romantic novel could have had such a dramatic impact on Californians and other westward-looking Americans. That *Ramona* prevailed in such bully times reflects the dynamics of late nineteenth-century California—the unbridled commercialism, the need to make sense of a confusing century of cultural pluralism. By enthusiastically embracing all things Spanish, southern California set out to establish local cultural traditions as rapidly as possible.

Promoting *Ramona*

RAMONA'S MYTH: The mission myth baptized boosterism. The new Franciscans were the members of the chamber of commerce; the workers of Southern California were the Indians—needing tutelage and occasional chastisement, but capable of productivity when carefully supervised. As in the mission days, Southern California was being put to use in the Lord's name. A better order—productive, stable, conservative, pious—was in the making [Starr 1985:89].

Ramona was born during the Far West's great land boom of the 1880s, sparked in part by the expanding railroads, the end of the Civil War, the construction of waterworks necessary to make California bloom, and the replacement of ranching by agriculture. By 1869, the railroads were bringing 70,000 passengers each year to California, and many of the old missions had become nuclei for rapidly expanding settlements. *Ramona* and its architectural reification imbued California with a charming, romantic flavor. Despite the war propaganda emanating from the Spanish-American conflict, adroit real estate promoters were able to associate "Spanish" with the easygoing, relaxed, fun-loving life-style of a semitropical people, a fantasy attainable by any hardworking Anglo willing to settle in sunny California.

Private concerns pitched *Ramona* with a vengeance, and the missions, as well as legendary sites from the pages of *Ramona*, became prime tourist attractions. The *Los Angeles Times* ran a large advertisement for the townsite of "Ramona" in 1886: "RAMONA! The Greatest Attraction Yet Offered. In the Way of Desirable Real Estate Investment and for Beautiful Villa Homes" (quoted in Weitze 1984:13–14). The Southern Pacific and Santa Fe railroads instituted countless "Ramona tours" to the missions, to the "House of Ramona," and virtually anywhere else sporting a Hispanic place-name (Figure 6–3). The Southern Pacific Railroad purchased *Sunset* magazine and cranked out endless local color pieces to lure restless easterners to the Far West.

One of the chief architects of this hoopla and hyperbole was another enterprising New Englander, Charles Fletcher Lummis. Drawn by the "sun, silence and adobe," this nineteenth-century polymath instantly grasped the full possibilities of mission romanticism. Lummis repeated the *Uncle Tom's Cabin* comparison, boasting that Helen Hunt Jackson's pen "has made all these crumbling piles dearer and more beautiful," and six years later, he astutely recognized the missions as the "best capital Southern California has" (Lummis 1895:43–44). Interviewing Frank Miller, the owner of Riverside's legendary Mission Inn, Lummis inquired what *Ramona* had been worth to California, to which Miller reportedly replied: "I figure that book has brought at least fifty million dollars into this region" (Lummis 1927).[10]

Ramona as Regional Identity

The Mission Revival style reflected the development of a larger, more pervasive "Mediterranean analogy" that swept across late nineteenth-century southern California. Whereas there was an initial comparison with the flowering of ancient Greek culture, southern Californians quickly shifted to the not-so-remote Hispanic past. In culture, literature, and architecture, Anglo Californians were increasingly drawn to what they regarded as the aristocratic life of leisure lived in preconquest California. Forgetting the extent to which earlier Anglo settlers had derided the Hispanic lifeways they encountered, the new wave of late

Figure 6–3. The Pasear Tour of 1912 visited several California missions, the "Home of Ramona," and Riverside's renowned Mission Inn. This caravan of Studebakers from Inyo Good Roads Club stops at Mission San Diego de Alcalá. (Photograph courtesy of California Department of Transportation, McCurry Glassplate Negative 3881)

nineteenth-century Yankee newcomers recognized the potential of a distinctive, homegrown tradition. An anticommercial, anti-Anglo attitude arose, encouraged by endless sympathetic descriptions of Hispanic California, contrasting it with the rude nature of contemporary America (Langum 1983:2).[11]

Turn-of-the-century California proclaimed its special identity in buildings derived from the missions and Hispanic residences, and civic-minded groups began erasing all evidence to the contrary. Local architects and town councils were encouraged to oppose the "Anglo-ization" of their cities, buildings, and street names. Figure 6–4 was photographed in 1915, when San Diego's Victorian railroad station was demolished to make room for a Mission Revival structure, considered a more appropriate Hispanic-style introduction to visitors arriving for the nearby Panama-California Exhibition.

These countless Mission Revival buildings created the misleading impression that California had been long settled by Europeans—an important assurance for the Anglo-American immigrant. One critic, Frenchman Jules Huret, visiting in 1905, was amused and amazed by the veneration Californians displayed toward "these walls without history and without architecture, near-secular; the same respect which we experience before our cathedrals of the Middle Ages or the ruins of the Parthenon" (translated in Gowans 1986:114).

Ramona Returns to the Fair

Mission Revival architecture began and ended at the fair. California's State Building at the 1893 Chicago Exposition put the Mission Revival before the world as the Golden State's official style. Then, at the 1915 Panama-California Exposition, held in San Diego's Balboa Park to celebrate completion of the Panama Canal and promote the city's harbor, the Mission style bid farewell. "Here in California we are tired, very tired, not of the Missions, but of the sort of thing which has so long masqueraded in their name" (John Galen Howard, cited in Starr 1973:412). Recognizing this, the primary architect for the Panama-California Exposition, Bertram Grosvenor Goodhue, employed occasional reminiscences of California missions, but blended these architectural details with those of Mexico, Spain, and Italy (Amero 1990). California's Mediterranean analogy continued long after the San Diego Fair, but it was expressed not in imagi-

Figure 6–4. California helped obliterate its Anglo-American past by expunging the architectural record. Here, San Diego's Victorian railroad station is demolished to make room for the Mission Revival style depot in 1915, just in time for the Panama California Exposition. (Photograph courtesy of the San Diego Historical Society—Ticor Collection, photograph no. 6717)

nary Mission Revival terms, but through a more authentic, more literal Spanish Colonial style.

Robert Rydell has argued that fairs such as that in San Diego, the combined effects of science, religion, art, and architecture tendered a powerful and highly visible justification for long-standing racial and cultural parochialism. Once inside the fair, "dark-eyed Spanish girls" and "gaily-clad caballeros" could be seen strolling alongside "somber-clad monks," and visitors discovered California's history mingled within a limitless future, arranged to reflect a logical progression from the remote past into a utopian tomorrow. Such gatherings, Rydell (1984:4) suggests, reinforced nationalistic ideals in a pluralistic society: "World's fairs performed a hegemonic function precisely because they propagated the ideas and values of the country's political, financial, corporate, and intellectual leaders and offered these ideas as the proper interpretation of social and political reality."

Constructed by the country's most prominent anthropologists, the San Diego exhibits demonstrated how progress and the resulting inequities were the inevitable outcome of the process of natural selection, presenting California's recent history as a consistent, coherent, and directional story of cultural achievement. "The exhibits afforded fairgoers a scientific explanation for evolutionary racial progress that could easily encompass events in the not-so-distant past when one group of whites, Anglo-Americans, wrenched land titles away from another group of whites, the Californios" (Rydell 1984:226; see also Fowler and Fowler, this volume).

The popular press fortified the message. As the *San Diego Union* spelled it out, twentieth-century California was created by the Darwinian struggle between the races:

> The old world conquered the new until the restless hordes met and mingled on the California coast—here in San Diego in the beginning of this later and latest history of the moving ideas of men. And the weaker was absorbed by the stronger; but with the passing of the weaker they left a legacy of their art and culture, which the survivor has gladly possessed to beautify and decorate his own. They left us their tradition, their romance, and their musical nomenclature. . . . We have received this tradition gladly; we have made of this romance the background of our own history . . . in this fair port of San Diego and on this golden coast of California [quoted in Rydell 1984:209, 211].[12]

Reconstructing the Mission Past

> As the cult matured, it was only natural that they should move to protect their shrines.
>
> —John Kessell

Ramona was an antiquarian odyssey, a sentimental passage through the relics and ruins of a dimly remembered past. Both real and imaginary, the sites of *Ramona* became places of pilgrimage and, for some, bait to lure easterners to California.

But the sanctified sites were falling apart. And hordes of tourists to Ramonaland expedited matters by chipping away tons of adobe remembrances. Only those missions still in use—San Gabriel Arcángel, San Buenaventura, and Santa Bárbara—remained in repair. The movement to rescue the California missions began in the late 1880s, when Tessa L. Kelso of the Los Angeles Public Library organized the Association for the Preservation of the Missions. In 1893, she approached Lummis for assistance, and within a year he had characteristically jumped headlong into the project (Butz 1985). Despite considerable anti-Catholic sentiments, Lummis argued on humanitarian grounds that the missions had significance beyond religious affiliation. In 1895, the Landmarks Club was formally incorporated (with Lummis as president) under the club's official logo—"To Conserve the Missions and Other Historic Landmarks of Southern California." Lummis penned almost monthly columns in *Land of Sunshine* (and later, *Out West*) exhorting potential members to pay their dues and join the fight. Under the watchful guidance of Lummis, the Landmarks Club became a stellar example of what historical preservation should be.

Yet Lummis harbored mixed feelings about the growing mission mania that had swept over Southern California. On the one hand, he admired and respected Helen Hunt Jackson's stand against the injustices to Mission Indians (e.g., Lummis 1903b). But he abhorred the mission fallacies that *Ramona* had engendered.[13] Lummis repeatedly stated the objectives of the Landmarks Club in the pages of *Land of Sunshine* and *Out West*: "There is no 'restoring' and no botching. All work is done under the supervision of recognized experts. The result thus far attained is that the most important structures at these three Missions will now stand as they are for another full century" (Lummis 1902:185). He captioned one of his photographs of Mission San Luis Obispo: "The mission . . . before it was 'restored' out of semblance of beauty'" (Lummis 1903a:291).[14]

The Landmarks Club survived until 1917. Unlike Jackson and Lummis, many California boosters felt that the mission ruins, no matter how romantic, were too remote and confusing for an everyday audience. If California was to eulogize a glorious pre-Anglo Hispanic past—and in the process, chisel out its unique regional identity—then the missions must perforce be restored "so that they could be read more easily by a popular audience" (Gebhard 1980:138).

And restore them they did. From here on, the emphasis shifted from preservation to restoration. As Gebhard and Winter (1985:27) note, "The old Landmarks Club concern for the missions [went] somewhat astray. At San Gabriel and San Fernando the efforts at preservation, particularly at the latter, have resulted in elaborate misinterpretations of history." As the missions were variously restored, a highly romantic conception of the Spanish period was cultivated, primarily for the benefit of the incoming tides of tourists (McWilliams 1973:77).[15]

Today's mission visitor, after elbowing past gift shops stocked with typical mission mementos—my personal favorite is the "Just a Swallow from Capistrano" shotglass—cannot escape *Ramona*-derived revelations of what the missions "must have looked like." Many of the earlier reconstructions were poorly researched and conducted with little understanding of the archaeological reality. The best were well-meaning fabrications, conducted with great enthusiasm and widespread support; the worst were revisionist muddling. An early attempt to restore the stone church at San Juan Capistrano resulted in further destruction when gunpowder charges brought down more of the church. After the earthquake of 1906 toppled the initial stabilization at Mission San Antonio de Padua, the California Landmarks League rebuilt the church with adobes from the surrounding ruins, and added a new roof to the church. When the Hearst Foundation re-restored Mission San Antonio in 1948, it leveled almost everything in sight; the only standing remains were the front facade of the church and the front colonnade. Bulldozers stripped away both archaeological deposits and sterile dissolved adobe until floor tiles were exposed, and room outlines could be charted.

The sweeping restorations at Mission San Carlos Borromeo were the handiwork of Sir Henry Downie. A cabinetmaker by profession, Downie turned a temporary job of repairing Carmel statuary in 1931 into a lifetime position as restorer/curator. To his credit, Downie doggedly tracked down many of the mission's original furnishings and installed them permanently. He also distinguished himself through his conscientious effort to ensure that historical reconstructions were accurate (Barton 1980; Costello and Hornbeck 1989). Throwing himself into his work, Downie cheerfully guided tourists through the church often—for the sake of atmosphere—donning a Franciscan cassock. When the visitors would address him as "Brother Harry" or "Father Downie," he never bothered to correct them, feeling that his vestments aroused interest in the mission and stimulated the visitors' desire to contribute money for the rebuilding (Temple 1980:135).

However well-intentioned, in three decades Downie single-handedly reconfigured Carmel and several other mission churches and *conventos*, rendering future archaeological examinations problematic. Such a well-meaning, if theatrical approach to restoration will always remain a mixed blessing for serious students of history because without appropriate archaeological input, the integrity of both buried deposits and above-ground architecture is inevitably destroyed. In California, fanciful enhancements were all too common, and that problem persists today.

> I did it the way they would have done it if they'd had a little money.
> —Henry John Downie

Restoring Life in Ramona's Garden

> RAMONA'S MYTH: And the delicious, languid, semi-tropic summer came hovering over the valley. The apricots turned golden, the peaches glowed, the grapes filled and hardened, like opaque emeralds hung thick under the canopied vines. The garden was a shade brown, and the roses had fallen; but there were lilies, and orange-blossoms, and poppies, and carnations, and geraniums in the pots, and musk,—oh, yes, ever and always musk [Jackson (1884) 1912:125].

Landscape gardening was an integral part of the Mission Revival architectural message. Berkeley poet Charles August Keeler was instrumental in codifying and promoting California's garden ideology. "Let us have gardens wherein we can assemble for play or where we may sit for seclusion at work; gardens that will exhilarate our souls by the harmony and glory of pure and brilliant color, that will nourish our fancy with suggestions of romance as we sit in the shadow of the palm and listen to the whisper of rustling bamboo; gardens that will bring nature to our homes and chasten our lives with the purity of great Earth Mother" (1904:16). Although Keeler's synthetic ideal drew upon both Oriental and Mediterranean models, the California mission garden was considered to be the most appropriate model, serving both to order the innate vigor of the California landscape and to confer historicity. Thousands of tourists flock annually to California's restored missions, luxuriant amidst the jasmine and ever-blooming lantana. Today's California mission, with rare exception, hosts luxurious gardens of "stately palms mixed with colorful bougainvillea, banana and pepper trees, [recalling] the days when mission fathers and wealthy landowners planted gardens as a reminder of their native soil" (Eddy 1983:276–277).

The unfortunate truth is that these cornucopian mission gardens are pure *Ramona*-derived hyperbole. Period paintings, textual descriptions, photographs, and archaeology amply demonstrate that such flowery enchantment never existed in the original missions (Brown 1987; see also Neuerburg 1987: 3). The great plaza garden at Mission Carmel, with its majestic fountain, was barren dirt during mission times. The plaza at Santa Bárbara—Queen of the Missions—was also vacant of vegetation. The patio gardens—to many, the most striking features of contemporary missions—are counterfeit, planted only in this century.[16]

The unvarnished truth is this: There were no pleasure gardens of any kind at the original California missions—no cloisters, no bird-of-paradise plants, no flower-bedecked cemeteries, no ornamental gardens, only hardscrabble reality. The magnificent mission gardens, hallmark of today's restorations, are Anglo-Germanic interpretations, not historically accurate originals.

The Problems with Reconstruction

> For future archaeologists, these reconstructions will likely provide more information on the restorers than on the past they were trying to depict.
> —Leo Barker and Julia Costello

No visit to Mission San Carlos Borromeo is complete without a stopover at the personal bedroom (the "cell") of the venerable Father Junípero Serra, patriarch of California's mission chain (Figure 6–5). In this very room, on Saturday, August 28, 1784, a devoted Father Francisco Palóu brought the weary Serra a cup of broth. As he later recorded in his diary (Morgado 1987:97), Father Palóu heard Serra whisper: "Now, let us go to rest." It was siesta time and when Palóu returned, he found Serra "asleep in the Lord . . . his body showing no other sign of death than the cessation of breathing." Each day, dozens of weary tourists pause for a few moments in Serra's cell, reflecting perhaps upon kinder, gentler mission days.

But Serra's cell is a simulated reality, completely reconstructed during the Depression (Figure 6–6). Downie did his best: the floor tiles were scavenged from elsewhere at Carmel, the replica bed and table constructed from original mission timbers. Serra practiced private self-mortification in this room, and, hanging on a nail, is his iron-and-braided wire "discipline" (his penitential scourge). His eighteenth-century Bible lies on the reconstructed bench. Serra's cell looks just like the real thing, yet virtually everything you see is fake. And it takes an expert to tell the difference.

The distortions involved in retrofitting the past extend far beyond the missions of California, and the scholarly community has been slow to appreciate the hazards of overzealous reconstruction.[17] Schuyler (1976), for instance, has chronicled the rather shabby circumstances surrounding restoration of the Hugo Reid adobe, located in the Los Angeles County Arboretum in Arcadia. The best-selling fiction of Gertude Atherton (1902) and others portrayed the Old Californians as an embattled elite, some of whom actually welcomed annexation by the United States; hence they became the direct ancestors of the Yankee upper classes in southern California (Starr 1990:255). Hugo Reid was considered to be an outstanding representative of this elite, and some civic-minded groups were intent upon preserving and restoring his adobe as evidence linking the emerging elite with perceived pre-Yankee roots. Between 1956 and 1958, William Wallace and his colleagues carried out extensive archaeological investigations inside and

Figure 6–5. Today's tourist can visit Father Junípero Serra's cell, the bedroom where he died at Mission San Carlos Borromeo on August 28, 1784. Hanging on a nail is Serra's iron-and-braided wire "discipline," his penitential scourge. Few have any inkling that this legendary locale is but a simulated reality, completely reconstructed from total ruins in 1937; see Figure 6–6. (Photograph courtesy of Bell Magazine Agency, Monterey, California)

Figure 6–6. This is what Father Serra's cell and the rest of the *convento* wing of Mission San Carlos Borromeo actually looked like in the 1920s, before extensive restorations; the cross marks the approximate location of Serra's cell. (Photograph courtesy of the California Section, California State Library, negative number 20,201)

outside the Reid adobe, which was probably built in the early 1840s (Wallace 1959). But problems soon arose.

The Reid adobe excavations were sponsored by the private Historical Committee of the County Arboretum, which had convinced the California State Division of Beaches and Parks to restore the adobe to its original appearance. But these same proponents were shocked when Wallace's excavations and research revealed that Reid lived not in baronial splendor, but rather in a rude rectangular shack with a packed dirt floor, La Brea tar roof, and windows probably covered with animal skins. When the restoration committee was presented with such startling findings, they recoiled, becoming hostile toward the archaeologists and denying permission for follow-up digging. Having ignored the compelling archaeological evidence to the contrary, the restoration of the Hugo Reid adobe sports a nifty tile floor and roof, elaborate anachronistic furnishings, and a Spanish-style patio. Even Governor Pio Pico's silver-encrusted saddle is displayed inside. Accommodating to public sentiment, Hugo Reid's simple adobe was upgraded to a rancho house considered suitable for a wealthy Don (see also Greenwood 1989).

Distortions also take place through omission. As so commonly happens with tourism-directed restorations around the globe, only the more spectacular, elite archaeological sectors are restored—the temples, the pyramids, the king's tomb. In California, "mission" was commonly equated with "church," and early restorers universally emphasized the latest colonial construction, to the exclusion of earlier forms and attendant structures (Barker and Costello 1991). Only rarely is the restoration extended to other important structures around the quadrangle —the *convento*, the *monjerio* ("women's quarters"), the workshops, and store-rooms. Today's visitor to most mission reconstructions cannot escape the feeling that these were feudal Mediterranean villages practicing European technologies.

Such restorations inflate the white, Catholic, European aspects of mission life. The surrounding, "lower-status" structures of the Indian ranchería are usually ignored. Although Franciscan graves are carefully marked and venerated, the mission reconstructions do not identify individual Indian graves. Most Indians are apparently interred in mass graves; some, such as those at San Juan Bautista, are not marked at all. This progressive Europeanization of California's missions denigrates, if not eliminates, Indians in the mission context. Unwittingly, these heavily restored meccas of tourism perpetuate the near invisibility of the Indian in California's past.

Archaeological sites and museum specimens are too often viewed as static me-mentos of a given time and culture, existing in their present-day setting unaf-fected by the values, needs, and desires of the numerous individuals who handle and use them. But, in fact, such remnants of the past exist within a dynamic environment in which cleaning, stabilization, repair, and restoration commonly take place. Great caution is required when reconstructing the physical evidence of the past. Although few will admit it publicly, even the experts are sometimes fooled by the restorations.[18]

Whatever Happened to Preservation?

The historic preservation movement in California has enjoyed a checkered ca-reer. The Landmarks Club started things off right, providing two decades of truly remarkable leadership—preserving and stabilizing, but not restoring. But by 1920, the Landmarks Club was no more, and most of the California missions fell into more unrestrained hands, which produced the unfortunate restorations discussed above.

A comparison between events in California and the American Southwest is instructive. Although both areas started down the same road to historic preser-vation, the paths diverged significantly along the way. As in California, the first Anglos occupying New Mexico typically derided the missions and other tradi-tional Hispanic churches as dank and moldy (Kessell 1980:15). But when *Ramona* arrived in the Southwest, it awakened many to the enchantment and marketabil-ity of their Hispanic antiquities. Not only did public protest save churches and chapels from demolition, but—unlike California—the area had an influential and vital scholarly community already in place.[19]

In 1907, the American Institute of Archaeology created the School of American Archaeology (in Santa Fe) to parallel those already in Rome, Athens, and Pales-tine, with Edgar L. Hewett serving as the first director. Ten years later, the school was reorganized to become the School of American Research (SAR). Although interest clearly centered on the prehistoric pueblo ruins, the SAR soon estab-lished a branch specifically to excavate and repair the seventeenth- and eighteenth-century missions. From the outset, the School of American Research, like California's Landmarks Club, explicitly emphasized preservation:

> We will preserve not only the stones of these venerable monuments, but the atmosphere of sanctity which should be their best protection. We will allow no vandal hands to destroy or restore them, but let their noble, broken walls testify to the spirit that built them. . . . We will not put back a single block of stone more than is necessary to arrest destruction, and we will let no work of our hands deface the work of their builders nor belie the spirit that wrought them; for that spirit lives in every chapel in our southwestern land and blesses simple native homes with a peace more precious than worldly wealth. When it is important for the information of the public, make a model of the building or a restoration on paper, clearly indicating where it is conjectural, and let it go at that [Hewett and Fisher 1943:205–206].

Despite a healthy start in California, the preservationists were now losing the battle. But through World War II, the historical preservation ethic in New Mexico was still holding firm against the would-be remodelers and embellishers.[20] Why the difference?

For the answer, once again, we return to the *Ramona* myth and its offspring. California's nineteenth-century demographic destiny was defined by the quest for gold and real estate. The flood of Anglos into California rapidly submerged all but selected, promotional aspects of Hispanic culture. Because the missions were integral to the search for a mythical identity, they were restored to appropriate heroic proportions.

But the Southwest, to late nineteenth-century America, was little more than a vast, otherwise-vacant desert between the great states of Texas and California. The major Anglo demographic influx to the American Southwest was postponed until the massive movement to the Sunbelt decades later. The badly outnumbered Anglos who did percolate into the turn-of-the-century Southwest found Hispanic and Native American populations going nowhere. There was no vacuum to fill. Although some of these same preservationists were later to live in highly romantic, even visionary dwellings of the "Santa Fe Revival," they still conserved the missions.[21] Anglo incentive to conjure up an instant Southwestern past was stifled by the reality at hand.

Confronting *Ramona*'s Archaeological Legacy

Only 500 miles separate the Californian and Southwestern missions, but they might just as well have been on different planets in the first half of the twentieth century. Mission archaeology in the Southwest was a going concern, with numerous professional excavations conducted in Arizona and New Mexico during the first quarter of the twentieth century (see the summary in Cordell 1989).[22] But during *Ramona*'s first half-century, impartial scholarly involvement in California lagged. With one rare exception, mission archaeology remained little more than a diversion for acquisitive friars and church bureaucrats, pot-hunters, and curious, if archaeologically innocent, historians.

Fortunately, that rare exception pointed toward a more spirited future for mission archaeology.

The La Purísima Alternative

The exception took place at Mission La Purísima Concepción, located east of Lompoc. Here, we find that a well-conceived, large-scale program of archaeological research was implemented to enhance and complement a colossal restoration effort. What makes La Purísima all the more remarkable is that this coordinated program of research and public outreach took place in the 1930s.

At first blush, La Purísima seems an unlikely candidate for such a successful program. After secularization, the mission buildings were quickly plundered of tiles and timber, leaving the unprotected walls to wash away. Before long, only the monastery was left standing, and, after considerable abuse as private residence and sheep ranch, it too collapsed. By 1934, only wall stubs and a few solitary pillars were left standing.

But on closer inspection, La Purísima was the ideal test case. Because the ruins at La Purísima were wholly unsuitable for church-related purposes, they became fair game for the preservation community. The first such attempt was sponsored by the Landmarks Club, which acquired La Purísima ruins from the Union Oil Company, on the condition that funds be raised and the ruins be preserved prior to 1917; neither the money nor the stabilization ever materialized (Butz 1985:70). In 1933, Santa Barbara County acquired part of the ruins, and after a much larger portion of the mission was acquired by the state, serious archaeology and restoration began as a joint venture involving the National Park Service, the Civilian Conservation Corps, and the state of California.

Under the direction of Arthur Woodward (archaeologist for the Los Angeles County Museum) and M. R. Harrington (archaeologist at the Southwest Museum), energetic excavations began in 1934. These important excavations unearthed the original water system and outlined the mission residences, tallow vats, workshops, outbuildings, cemetery, and the primary church. Significantly, Harrington and his crew also dug extensively beyond the central mission compound, highlighting the Native American presence by excavating large parts of the neophyte Chumash occupation areas and barracks. Robert Schuyler (1978:71) terms the La Purísima excavations "the earliest major project in historic-sites archeology on the West Coast." The archaeology was truly exceptional for its time, even when measured on a nationwide scale (Barker and Costello 1991).

Working with these professional archaeologists were some of the most knowledgeable authorities collaborating to restore Mission La Purísima, including the omnipresent Harry Downie and Edith Webb (a renowned historian specializing in mission lifeways). Eighteen major buildings and features were investigated and restored, among them the church, convento, workshops and living quarters, water system (including fountain and cistern), neophyte residence, blacksmith shop, warehouse, tallow and soap works, and cemetery. Original materials and techniques were employed wherever possible.

Sunset magazine claims that today's Mission La Purísima is the largest and most complete restoration in the American West (Krell 1981:206). Even though virtually no above-ground architecture remains from the original mission complex, the modern visitor is confronted not only with Hispanic mission lifeways, but also with the active involvement of Native Americans living at the mission, their hide processing, candle making, carpentry, cooking, irrigation, and other craft work.

The La Purísima alternative demonstrates the potential of coordinating archaeology with historic preservation and public education. Because the 1930s archaeologists and restorers worked hand in hand, unexcavated archaeological deposits were sufficiently protected so that subsequent excavations were possible in the same areas, as, for example, Deetz's pioneering work in the barracks, the blacksmith shop, and the tanning vats (Deetz 1962–1963). The same could hardly be said of the overly aggressive and ultimately destructive restorations at, say, San Carlos Borromeo de Carmelo (which were also conducted in the 1930s but without the benefit of archaeological input). However, aside from the prescient work of Harrington and his colleagues at La Purísima, no significant archaeological work took place in the California missions until the 1950s (Bennyhoff and Elsasser 1954). Why did Californian archaeology trail so far behind the Southwest?

One reason, of course, is that archaeologists had already descended in great numbers upon the Southwest's pre-Columbian sites. The consequential and picturesque pueblo ruins enchanted Anglo America, generating considerable institutional funding and numerous academic resources. The missions became part of an overall Southwestern excavation program designed, in part, to answer questions about prehistoric Indians.

But in California, the primary mission professionals were architects, not archaeologists. Until midcentury, A. L. Kroeber exerted tremendous influence over the practice of Californian archaeology because although Kroeber himself did very little archaeology, he had trained virtually all California archaeologists of the day. The resulting anthropological (rather than historical) orientation guided most Californians toward prehistoric sites. At midcentury, Robert Heizer and T. D. McCown note dismally, "California's record of historic archaeology cannot be called outstanding. [Merely] a bare beginning on an extensive program has been made." (1954:i). Not until the 1960s would the first archaeologist working in California explicitly identity with the field of historical archaeology —James Deetz (1962–1963), whose research at La Purísima set a new lofty standard for the historical archaeology and motivated a generation to continue in his footsteps (Chartkoff and Chartkoff 1984:304).

But to understand mission archaeology's slow start in California, we cannot forget *Ramona*. Although the missions helped give birth to a California regional identity, the *archaeology* of those mission sites never really mattered. To most, *Ramona* provided the tools necessary to deal with California's mission past, a perspective that became "fact" when the missions were reconstructed—generating a "reality" recapitulated again and again in Mission Revival architecture. Because *Ramona* already told us what went on at the missions, why, a curious public wondered, would anybody waste time doing archaeology? Why bother digging up fractured artifacts and melted adobe bricks when you could stroll right into the very room where Father Serra had breathed his last?

The Cost of Archaeological Inertia

The insignificance of pre–1950s mission archaeology in California would remain a minor, if somewhat dismal, footnote to the *Ramona* saga were not public indifference still an issue today. The problem for modern archaeologists is highlighted by a recent episode.

In 1985, the Roman Catholic Diocese of San Diego announced plans to construct an 8,000–square-foot parish hall on a portion of the original Mission San Diego de Alcalá quadrangle. The church wanted simply to bulldoze the area and pour a concrete slab. The city of San Diego, ignoring the historical significance of the site, agreed to issue a building permit based on an Environmental Impact Report (EIR) claiming "no adverse impact" of the proposed structure. This EIR, it turned out, was misleading (and ultimately incorrect). It was based on erroneous claims by certain misdirected archaeologists who felt that previous digging had exhausted the research potential and that no significant archaeological remains existed in the project area.

An immediate outcry issued from the San Diego County Archaeological Society, several professional archaeologists, parishioners, and local historians who argued that the proposed construction site must certainly contain important intact archaeological remains. As a result of aroused public opinion and threatened law suits and injunctions, the construction plan was modified in 1988; the church building was to rest on 20 concrete caissons, with archaeologists hired to excavate the holes.

Compelling Mission period archaeology was indeed discovered during the course of the excavations in the spring and summer of 1989, including numerous disturbed human burials. The archaeologists pleaded for more time and approached the church for permission to continue excavations. Since Mission San Diego is a national, state, and local landmark, the National Park Service concurred, asking the Roman Catholic Diocese to consider another site for the recreation hall.

Church officials refused, minimizing the archaeological findings. Msgr. I. Brent Egan claimed, "You can't appreciate anything on that site unless you're a scientist" (*San Diego Tribune*, July 10, 1989). He contended that the concrete piers and elevated structure would preserve the site beneath. Then Bill Finley, a public relations specialist retained by the diocese in part to orchestrate an antiarchaeology campaign, argued that the archaeologists were at fault. They had dawdled over the dig and run up the budget.

In the meantime, the Native American community had become understandably annoyed with the church's cavalier handling of what appeared to be a Mission-period Indian cemetery. At one point, Henry Rodriquez, a Luiseño, argued, "We want them to let the archaeologists continue and to preserve as much as they can" (*San Diego Tribune*, July 6, 1989). Other Indian representatives requested that all digging cease and everything be reburied.

Just as the increasingly ill-natured dispute was about to boil over at a town meeting, the Indian and church representatives cut a secret deal to abandon the construction plans, fill in excavations, and immediately rebury the bones. Following traditional Indian and Catholic services, an estimated 59 Mission period Indian burials were reinterred on August 4–5, 1989, without any analysis. Both Indian and church representatives came away happy. "We got pretty much what we wanted" said Fern Southcott, secretary for the Indian negotiating committee.

The excavations were simply filled in, with the burial artifacts and bones lost for analysis. It seems likely that the proposed construction zone contained the first mission church, built in 1774. Rarely do California archaeologists and physical anthropologists have the opportunity to work on well-excavated mission contexts, and the San Diego excavations could have produced extremely important results. While some form of reburial was clearly called for, the Catholic and Indian communities simply evaded the archaeologists as irrelevant bystanders.

The Mission San Diego fiasco of 1989 demonstrates the degree to which the *Ramona* myth survives. The diocese, the city of San Diego staff (including the Historic Sites Board), some members of the Native American community, and even a handful of archaeologists seemed perfectly content to live with the myth of the restored version of San Diego de Alcalá. After all, the restoration retains considerable commercial appeal—most recently as the backdrop for Nissan commercials and the logo for numerous local firms. The serene mission grounds, replete with gurgling fountains and fake adobe tiles, attract thousands of tourists each year. That the first, and probably second, mission structures, along with the associated Indian, Hispanic, and Anglo burials and thousands of artifacts, were threatened to make way for a Bingo parlor seemed not to matter.

The Future of the Past in Ramonaland

The past at times has been deliberately manipulated by nationalistically and religiously motivated ideologies that serve to convince the governed that those in power rule legitimately (see, e.g., the cases enumerated by Fowler 1987). The past has also been manipulated to advance national claims for some sort of physical or mental superiority; for instance, shouldering the white man's burden required that the British bring culture and civilization to the less fortunate parts of the world. The Nazis also marshaled considerable anatomical, linguistic, and archaeological data to support their claim of Aryan superiority, and hence their right to conquer and rule the globe. In these instances, the value of archaeology became inflated as the past was employed for political aims.

But in *Ramona*'s motherland, where the motivations were at times quite mercantile, maneuvering the past took a different course. Establishing a significant pre-Anglo heritage was good business and paid off handsomely in inflated land prices, increased tourism, packed railroads, and even cottage industries created to produce the trinkets and trappings of *Ramona*'s past.

That *Ramona* and her architectural legacy are mythical is not news. But the very magnitude and longevity of the myth sets California apart as a case study for all intrigued by the diverse uses of the past. Perhaps, as some feel, there may be little for archaeologists to do. California's counterfeit past has already been set in stone (or is it adobe?).[23]

Perhaps so. But with the coming of the Columbian Quincentenary, and all its attendant hoopla throughout the Spanish Borderlands, serious students of the past should perhaps consider assuming a more creative posture in confronting such fables. Nobody is suggesting that we tear out Serra's cell or rip out the bogus bougainvillea that adorn mission reconstructions. Still, the scholarly community needs to make a greater effort to expose some of the mission myths fostered by these Neo-Franciscan fantasies. There are some positive directions evident in today's mission archaeology.

Mission Reconstructions: Truth in Advertising

We have documented the damage done to California's missions by overzealous restorers and revisionists. Not only has such misguided overrestoration resulted in the unwarranted destruction of archaeological deposits, but the simulated realities of lush gardens and romanticized architecture have contributed numerous misinterpretations of history. The importance of high-quality historical and archaeological research has never been fully realized, and mission exhibitions still contribute to the near invisibility of Native Americans in California's past.

Fortunately, we can turn to a second California mission for guidance and inspiration. Most contemporary mission exhibits attempt to present themselves as bona fide heirlooms of the eighteenth and nineteenth centuries—and many succeed in giving that impression. Mission San Francisco Solano, located on the central plaza of downtown Sonoma, is a gratifying exception, a textbook example of how restorations *should* be presented to the public.[24]

Like so many missions, Solano passed through a series of hands after secularization, serving variously as a barn and a blacksmith shop. The Historic Landmarks League finally came to the rescue, purchasing the property in 1903. Badly damaged by the 1906 earthquake, the church was initially restored in 1911–1912, and title was handed over to the California State Parks Commission in 1927. More extensive restoration took place in 1943–1944. Significant state-sponsored archaeological excavations by James A. Bennyhoff, Albert B. Elsasser, and Adan E. Treganza in 1953 and 1954 (Bennyhoff and Elsasser 1954) were followed by more renovation. In the late 1960s, only a portion of the padre's quarters remained as original construction. *The Guide to Architecture in San Francisco and Northern California* says it all: today's Mission Solano is a "Mission Revival version of what a California Mission should be" (Gebhard et al. 1985:394).

But what sets this mission above its contemporaries is that Mission Solano explicitly owns up to what it is—a heavily reconstructed interpretation of the past. This disclaimer is not subtle; immediately after entering the *convento*, all visitors run squarely into an impossible-to-overlook sign, warning in boldface:

> Reconstruction of this mission and many others throughout the state was done
> around the first years of this century. Often accomplished without the benefit of
> historical or archeological research, these reconstructions were based on romanti-

cized paintings and accounts of the 19th century. Occasionally walls appeared or disappeared in these paintings and sketches. The reconstructions would reflect this misinformation.

Nearby are a dozen photographs and period sketches of various attempts at reconstructing Mission Solano, replete with a hard-hatted workman scratching his head and pondering what all the conflicting evidence means. Other prominent exhibit cases show how archaeology was conducted here, and how archaeologists interpreted what they found. Another caption, highly visible as one enters the chapel, explains the extent of restoration and discusses the evidence leading to the specific reconstructions.

The state of California has done a first-rate job presenting this reconstructed mission to the public. Only the most obtuse visitors could leave Sonoma Mission State Historical Park thinking they had observed the authentic, unrestored nineteenth-century Mission Solano—although I am certain that some still do.

California Mission Archaeology in the Twenty-First Century?

Before the 1950s, legitimate mission archaeology was largely irrelevant to California's high-profile veneration of the Hispanic past—in part because that reconstructed past was so readily available for all to see. And mission archaeology remained a low priority in Ramonaland for so long because archaeologists insisted on dealing with facts and had little to contribute toward romanticizing California's erstwhile past.

But over these past decades, a number of archaeologists have successfully brought California mission archaeology into the mainstream of American-based historical archaeology. Given the century of dilettante amateur excavations and overzealous restorations, it is a wonder that serious California mission archaeologists had anything left to excavate. But they did, and, in fact, there remains great potential for significant mission archaeology in future years.

Church-sponsored restorations typically concentrate on the latest mission buildings, often leaving earlier remains untouched. As a result, four unexcavated neophyte barracks and the foundations of the earliest church at Mission Buenaventura have been discovered on city-owned land. Unexcavated foundations and features associated with Mission San Gabriel Arcángel are also known to exist on private property adjacent to the restored Claretian-owned mission. A previously unknown foundation at Mission San Juan Capistrano was recently exposed in utility trenching under the adjacent street (Roberta Greenwood, personal communication). The State of California has purchased several parcels containing the archaeological remains of the original La Purísima Mission (Julia Costello, personal communication).

Many of California's missions exist today in urban settings, and historical archaeology has demonstrated time and time again that associational and architectural integrity may be present beneath streets, buildings, parking lots, and gardens. Although the church/mission quadrangle has often been heavily worked over, there is every reason to be optimistic that this new brand of off-site archaeology will divulge new insights into mission life, particularly hard-to-come-by data on economic, industrial, biocultural, and other ancillary activities. The preservation of this potential testifies to the importance of Culture Resource Management legislation requiring compliance with current environmental regulations.

Who Really Owns the Mission Past?

California's mission past is a promiscuous blend of truth and fiction, fact and fantasy. What began as Victorian romanticism ultimately escalated to lasting regional identity. Although in one sense this past belongs to everyone, several contemporary constituencies—the Roman Catholic Church, the Native American and Hispanic communities, archaeologists and historians, and an interested public—today compete for control over that past.

The Roman Catholic Church, which today owns all but 2 of the 21 California mission sites, will clearly play an important role in the future, but its direction remains undefined. Across the Spanish Borderlands, the church has actively encouraged archaeological investigations; the recent church-supported excavations at San Juan Capistrano and San Antonio de Padua are California cases that come immediately to mind (see also Harkins 1990).

But sometimes, as at Mission San Diego de Alcalá, the church has wielded a heavy hand—destroying, disturbing, remodeling, and otherwise quashing the archaeological record with impunity and disregard. While deploring such insensitivity, archaeologists must also recognize that the California missions were, and are, an integral part of a functioning religion. And everyone agrees that religious beliefs—be they Native American, Roman Catholic, or whatever—deserve respect.

The crux of the issue is not theology, but rather the precarious and ill-defined relationship between ownership and stewardship of the past. The Diocese of San Diego opted for ownership: "The basic issue is, is this an active church or a museum? Do the people of this parish own this property, or the archaeologists of San Diego?" (*San Diego Union*, July 7, 1989).

Good point. But nearly a century ago, Charles Lummis and his Landmarks Club made an articulate case for stewardship, at this very same Mission San Diego de Alcalá: "Those mighty piles belong not to the Catholic church but to you and to me, and to our children and the world. They are monuments and beacons of Heroism and Faith and Zeal and Art. Let us save them—not for the Church but for Humanity" (quoted in Fiske and Lummis 1975:88).

There will be no ironclad resolution of the ownership-stewardship dialogue. It is already a worldwide controversy. But it is worth noting that had Lummis and his Landmarks Club not come to the rescue of Mission San Diego, the present diocese would have precious little left to worry about. The future of the mission past depends upon how well these various parties balance their conflicting interests for the common good.

A similar equivocal relationship exists between archaeologists and the Native

American community, in California and elsewhere. For too long, archaeologists have shut Indians out of Native American archaeology; that ill-advised indifference has now returned to haunt us all. Not only are museum and university research collections endangered at present, but even well-meaning archaeologists are increasingly viewed with skepticism in Native American communities.

Monomaniac convictions (on both sides) to the contrary, plenty of common ground remains between archaeologists and Indians. For the past three decades, a host of archaeologists (beginning with James Deetz) have worked to explore and define the Indian presence at California's missions. As the transitions and perseverance of Indian culture are properly communicated to the Native American community—and to the public at large—archaeologists can help significantly to redress the extraordinary invisibility of Indians at today's California missions.

Some Native Americans readily recognize the importance of having such hard, empirical data to bolster their own views of California mission life. Was Serra a saint or a sinner? Were the missions uplifting institutions of higher learning or overcrowded concentration camps based on feudal domination and forced labor (Castillo 1989)? What is the real mission heritage: "God's great blueprint for man's abode on earth" (Weber 1988:103) or "a legacy of genocide" (Costo and Costo 1988)?

Convincing new insights into the realities of mission life and demography will only emerge from fresh, innovative, empirical explorations of the archaeological evidence. But this research will do nothing to bridge the gulf between Indians and archaeologists until Native Americans achieve meaningful involvement in things archaeological—not as "advisers" or "monitors," but as active, valued, hands-on collaborators and colleagues.

This is why, from the outset, the royalties from this three-volume *Columbian Consequences* series were specifically earmarked for scholarships to assist qualified Indians who wish to become professional archaeologists. Recognizing that significant tension has arisen between the archaeological and Native American communities over the past decade, and acknowledging the acute difficulties still facing Indians who seek higher education, the Native American Scholarship Fund (sponsored by the Society for American Archaeology) is designed to foster a new sense of shared purpose and positive interaction. This enterprise seeks to raise private donations and subsequent matching revenues to assist and encourage qualified American Indians in pursuing graduate education in the field of American archaeology.

All of us involved with this project hope that within a few years Native Americans will be directing programs such as the already successful Zuni Archaeological Project and the Navajo Nation Archaeology Department. We also look forward to the day when well-qualified Native American archaeologists will be conducting their own excavations at California mission sites. Not only will such informed leadership underscore the common ground between the archaeological and Native American communities, but the extended scope, innovative questions, and alternative explanations will undoubtedly broaden current perspectives on California's mission past. In this way, we hope that the *Columbian Consequences* seminars have materially contributed to the growing "cubist" perspectives on the Spanish Borderlands (Thomas 1989).

When Helen Hunt Jackson set out to write *Ramona* more than a century ago, she disguised the bitter reality for California's Indians in a sugar-coated Victorian romantic novel. Surely Jackson would have been shocked, had she lived, to see how deftly the Anglo public elevated the realities of mission life to lofty, even mythical proportions—yet forgot all about the plight of California's Indians. In effect, the Yankee public sucked off the romantic sugar coating, but never swallowed the prescription. Today's challenge is for all concerned—church advocates, Native Americans, Hispanics, archaeologists, historians, or an involved public—to seek the common purpose, to rework the *Ramona* myth, and ultimately to return California's mission heritage to a more realistic footing.

In short, all of us who care about California must define a more serviceable, more forthright past to propel us into the twenty-first century.

Acknowledgments

An earlier draft of this paper profited from numerous suggestions offered by Richard Ahlborn, Richard Carrico, Edward D. Castillo, Joyce Clevenger, Linda Cordell, Julia Costello, Dora Crouch, Margot Dembo, Don Fowler, David Gebhard, Roberta Greenwood, John Johnson, John L. Kessell, Valerie Sherer Mathes, Nicholas Megalousis, Lorann S. A. Pendleton, and David J. Weber. Although I did not always follow their advice, I am extremely grateful to these friends and colleagues for their concern and effort.

Notes

1. Several excellent reviews of California mission and rancho archaeology have appeared recently, particularly Barker and Costello (1991), Costello and Hornbeck (1989), and Greenwood (1989); see also Schuyler (1978).

2. A comprehensive discussion of relevant nineteenth-century ethics is far beyond the scope of this discussion, but these larger issues have been addressed by literary and intellectual historians. Kenneth Starr's *Americans and the California Dream, 1850–1915* (1973), *Inventing the Dream: California through the Progressive Era* (1985), and *Material Dreams: Southern California through the 1920s* (1990) are pivotal and highly entertaining sources. Langum (1978, 1983) addresses the strangely shifting perception of the *Californio* lifeway; see also Bolton (1921:290–293), Pitt (1966), Weber (1988:37; this volume), and Walker (1950).

3. This reaction to the California missions was closely tied to the eighteenth- and early nineteenth-century European tradition of the picturesque, the sense of a "pleasing gloom" (see esp. Weitze 1984:6–7, 140). Before long, the California missions became an integral part of the global cult of ruins.

4. Even Henry Wadsworth Longfellow was drawn to the missions: "A strange feeling of romance hovers about these old Spanish Missions of California, difficult to define and difficult to escape. They add much to the poetic atmosphere of the Pacific Coast" (cited in Weitze 1984:7).

5. Even the circumstances surrounding the writing and facts behind *Ramona* became the subject of considerable mythology. Several books were published almost immediately after *Ramona*, each attempting to set the record straight, conducting, in effect, an autopsy of the *Ramona* myth. Most notable were *The Genesis of the Story of Ramona* (Vroman and Barnes 1899), *Through Ramona's Country* (James 1913), and *The True Story of "Ramona": Its Facts and Fictions, Inspiration and Purpose* (Davis and Alderson 1914); see also references in Mathes (1990:192–193). For a less scholarly approach, see May (1989).

6. Jackson was aware of the problem. Although she died before *Ramona* achieved its ultimate impact, Jackson soon realized that many, perhaps most, of her readers missed her entire purpose: "I am sick of hearing that the flight of Alessandro & Ramona is an 'exquisite ideal,' & not even an allusion to the ejectment of the Temecula band from their homes" (cited in Mathes 1990:83). Jackson would, however, have been heartened to read Omer Stewart's (1978:705) more upbeat observation, that both *A Century of Dishonor* and *Ramona* "pricked the conscience of America and stimulated more federal help for California Indians."

7. Helen Hunt Jackson's stunning success was, of course, almost entirely posthumous. But in death, "H. H." became such a celebrity that her husband was forced to move her grave deep into the mountains outside Colorado Springs, to avoid the crass commercialism of those renting burros to tourists who longed to view the final resting place of *Ramona*'s famous creator (Davis and Alderson 1914:86).

8. Harte and Jackson were joined by a third novelist, Gertrude Atherton, in their growing sentimentality for Hispanic California. In *The Doomswoman* (1893) and *The Splendid Idle Forties* (1902), Atherton presented the rudimentary *Californio* culture as "the gayest, happiest, the most careless life in the world . . . But how long will it last? Curse the Americans! They are coming" (1902:4).

9. Surviving sketches and letters show the degree to which they relied on existing missions for inspiration. Particularly important was Mission Santa Bárbara, which had never fallen into a state of ruin. Curiously, because of the powerful presence of this surviving mission as a local symbol, the Mission Revival style never caught on in the Santa Barbara area (Starr 1990:275).

In 1890, a new San Francisco-based journal, *Architectural News*, ran an influential series of articles, dissecting the architectural significance of various California missions. The following year, *California Architect and Building News* added a month-by-month mission series, each emphasizing specific mission-related features such as wall surfaces, arcades, bell towers, and so forth (Weitze 1984:25–33).

10. Although the economic import of missions was often mentioned during this period, one must remember that many such pronouncements were in the true American spirit, which decreed that the best way to "sell" an idea or product was to wrap it in economic language. Although acutely aware of the economic potentials, Lummis and many other local color writers were truly enamored with the mission mystique; few were ever motivated by personal financial concerns.

11. Several literary historians have addressed the evolution of the Mediterranean analogy (esp. Langum 1983; Starr 1973:chap. 12; Walker 1950:chap. 5). The origins of the Mediterranean analogy can be traced to John C. Fremont, whose widely read *Report of the Exploring Expedition to Oregon* elaborated a California dripping with Mediterranean radiance. As it matured, the Mediterranean analogy mixed massive doses of fact and fancy. The shepherd became one key ingredient, not only Basques and Mexicans but also Indians like Alessandro, each watching over vast flocks scattered across the Central Valley and Southern California. The vine became another hallmark of the analogy, a common thread that, like the missions themselves, betokened romantic California's past.

12. Just in case the message might be lost, the publicity mill for the exposition drove this point forcefully home: "The fair was . . . a comparison of the old with the new . . . and, best of all, it will show how the old came to pass away and how the new came into existence" (quoted in Rydell 1984:209).

13. "Contrary to what the mission myth would have Americans believe, Lummis roared from the pages of 'The Lion's Den,' Southern California never supported such a pastel, pseudo-Castilian *mise en scène*. It had been a rugged frontier, true, but one touched by beauty. The Californian need not turn the mission into something resembling a La Scala production . . . in order to feel its ideality and charm" (Starr 1973:400).

Shortly before her death, Helen Hunt Jackson also campaigned for the restoration of California's missions. Speaking of Mission San Carlos Borromeo, she wrote: "It is a disgrace to both the Catholic Church and the State of California that this grand old ruin, with its sacred sepulchres, should be left to crumble away. If nothing is done to protect and save it, one short hundred years more will see it a shapeless wind-swept mound of sand. . . . The grave of Junípero Serra may be buried centuries deep and its very place forgotten; yet his name will not perish, nor his fame suffer. But for the men of the country whose civilization he founded [California], and of the Church whose faith he so glorified, to permit his burial place to sink into oblivion, is a shame indeed!" (Jackson 1883b:43, 47).

14. Lummis wrote: "In 1895, I founded the Landmarks Club, 'To Preserve for our Children, and the World, the Old Missions and other historic Landmarks of California'. It took a quarter of a century's campaign of education to interest the public at all in the unused Missions. But we lectured, published—and worked. We re-roofed an acre and a half of tiled buildings, and rebuilt half a mile of adobe walls, in all; we saved what is left at San Diego, at Pala, San Juan Capistrano and San Fernando. None of them would be more than mounds of adobe, today, except for this protective work. San Juan Capistrano and Pala are now restored to use as temples" (Lummis 1930:331–332).

15. As Heizer and McCown (1954:i) noted, "These early efforts at rebuilding or reconstruction, while undoubtedly well-intentioned, are in many cases most inaccurately done" (see also Heizer 1950:1). *The Architecture of Los Angeles: A Compleat Guide* is likewise critical of much mission restoration. Mission San Fernando Rey de España, for instance, is condemned for the "rather imaginative reconstruction . . . with few hints as to the details of the first building, [M. R.] Harrington set out [in 1935] to investigate the decoration of other missions and imitated what he found in order to give romantic appeal to the new church, an appeal which the good fathers have attempted to render in the 1974 building." The interior of the *convento*, "whose simplicity was earlier broken only by the Baroque headings of its windows, has now been enhanced by several gilt triumphal arches (source?) donated by some well-intentioned but misguided friend." Across the street from the *convento* "is a lovely park which, with its fountain, gardens, and statue of Junípero Serra, almost makes you forget the follies of contemporary restoration projects" (Gebhard and Winter 1985:326).

16. Although Santa Bárbara did boast the only nineteenth-century pleasure garden in the entire mission chain, it was not added until after secularization (Brown 1987:9–19).

17. Jonathan Reyman (1978) relays an amusing, if disconcerting tale. As part of a larger study of Anasazi subsistence and ceremonialism, Reyman attempted an archaeoastronomical analysis at Wupatki National Monument (Arizona). Using Hopi ethnographic data, he generated a series of astronomical predictions of solstice and equinox alignments through window openings at Wupatki. Selecting Room 44 because of its high elevation and unobstructed view of the eastern horizon, Reyman used a theodolite to shoot the necessary solar alignments through the east window. He was gratified that the measured azimuths "fit the predicted alignments within acceptable limits" (Reyman 1978:732).

But this empirical confirmation survived only overnight. When he examined a series of excavation records previously out on loan—including photographs dating as early as 1901—Reyman was appalled to find that Room 44 had been heavily reconstructed. The east window, through which he had just taken his azimuth readings, had not existed at all!

Reyman learned that after Room 44 had been excavated in 1933, this part of the pueblo was converted to a small museum and ranger station; the original walls were rebuilt and a small window was added to provide light for the room's interior. Three decades later, when Room 44 was re-restored back to its "original" condition, the wall reconstruction was so convincing that it became impossible to distinguish original twelfth-century construction from the 1933–1934 additions. Subsequent archaeological reports, prepared in the 1960s, also failed to detect any postexcavation modifications. As it turned out, none of Reyman's astronomical predictions for Room 44 could be confirmed for prehistoric Wupatki—"although they fit nicely with the Park Service and Museum of Northern Arizona stabilization and construction" (Reyman 1978:732). In this case, the investigator was fortunate to detect the foul-up before his results were published.

18. Another embarrassing case of unrecognized restoration—this time at the artifact level—eluded scholars for decades. The Thunder Pipe of the Blackfoot Indians was one of the best-known artifacts on display in the old Hall of the Plains Indians at the American Museum of Natural History in New York. The feather-bedecked stem and green stone bowl had been collected in the field in 1904 by Clark Wissler, acknowledged expert on the Blackfoot. Wissler later illustrated and described the artifact in a scholarly monograph, and the Thunder Pipe was also depicted in Robert Lowie's *Indians of the Plains*, for many years the classic source on Plains Indian culture.

This well-known artifact remained on display for more than 50 years. When the American Museum decided to renovate the old Plains Indian Hall, the Thunder Pipe case was opened, giving the new North American Indian curator, Stanley Freed, his first chance to examine this celebrated artifact. But upon picking up the pipe, Freed realized that something was amiss. Instead of the expected heavy green stone bowl, darkened from use, Freed found himself holding a lightweight plaster of paris copy. "Some 20 years later, I can still recall my shock at the realization that the bowl of this famed Thunder Pipe was not genuine" (Freed 1981: 229).

Searching the acquisition records, Freed found that Wissler had actually collected only the stem, and then apparently authorized a replica bowl to be added to the genuine stem for exhibition purposes. But then, forgetting this restoration, Wissler inadvertently published the imitation bowl with the stem in his definitive monograph on Blackfoot ceremonial bundles. "Even the seasoned scholar could easily be misled . . . by the Thunder Pipe . . . for it was sanctioned by an outstanding specialist on Blackfoot culture" (Freed 1981:231).

19. When, for instance, developers threatened to demolish the decrepit Mission San Miguel, newspapers and the citizenry of Santa Fe arose to halt destruction and raise funds to save this tourist mecca. San Miguel survived and today remains a local tourist attraction.

20. But exalted objectives are sometimes easier stated than done. Today's visitor to Pecos, for instance, will have difficulty distinguishing original adobe construction from the 1915 stabilization work on the church ruin, a job carried out under Hewett's general supervision (Kessell 1980:34). In 1922, architect John Gaw Meem (a prime mover in New Mexico's homegrown revival movement) joined Hewett and others in forming the Committee for the Preservation and Restoration of New Mexico Missions and Churches. The surviving architecture of the mission at Laguna was recorded and rerooted in 1922. Zia's received its new roof the next year. Work on Acoma followed in 1924, with Santa Ana, Las Trampas, and Chimayó soon after. Although economics were involved to some degree, and they did commit the occasional "restoration" (as at the sanctuario at Chimayó), the emphasis, still on stabilization and preservation, rather than outright restoration, was "to strengthen the fabric without altering the traditional appearance" (Kessell 1980:28).

21. The California-Southwest comparison does not end there. Even through the 1920s, Charles Lummis would not give up his preservationism. Having for decades promoted Hispanic imagery as a metaphor for Southern California, Los Angeles eventually outgrew both Spanish nostalgia and an aging Lummis, who became the symbol of a van-

ished era. "Every aspect of Lummis—his Spanish-cut green corduroy suit, his guitar and Spanish songs, his scholarly nostalgia for the Borderlands—seemed to go-ahead Los Angeles the imagery and preoccupations of a vanished era; and Lummis, progressively under-employed and perennially broke, had evidence enough of Los Angeles's opinion" (Starr 1990:276).

But Lummis correctly recognized that Santa Barbara might follow another path. In a widely distributed pamphlet, Lummis (1927) paired Santa Barbara with Santa Fe as the last two small cities in the United States that had not yet succumbed to "the Vandal Age" (Starr 1990:276). Citing his earlier work with the Landmarks Club to save the missions, Lummis argued that the *Ramona* myth had brought more prosperity to southern California than oil, oranges, or even the climate. By following the lead of Santa Fe, Santa Barbara could take the next step and capitalize on its legitimate Hispanic heritage by standing firm for the values of preservationism and controlled growth. The plan worked, and to this day, Santa Barbara is distinguished by its overtly preservationist mindset (Starr 1990:277).

22. We mentioned previously the excavations by Hewett and his colleagues at the School for American Research. Elsewhere in New Mexico, Nelson (1916) employed a direct historical approach to the Galisteo Basin, excavating seventeenth-century missions and associated Tanoan villages as a baseline for understanding precontact aboriginal sites. Other important Southwestern excavations include Pinkley's work at San Jose de Tumacacori from 1917 through 1921, and Kidder's (1924, 1958) decade-long extensive excavation at Pecos, beginning in 1915. In the mid–1930s, the Peabody Museum conducted exemplary, fully professional, multidisciplinary excavations at Awatovi, the Hopi town in northeastern Arizona; significantly, their excavation included work at the seventeenth-century Franciscan Awatovi churches (Montgomery et al. 1949).

23. As David Weber notes about a similar Texas mythology, "A number of the cherished stories about the Alamo have no basis in historical fact, but have moved out of the earthly realm of reality into the stratosphere of myth. . . . The sniping of scholars, no matter how true their aim, seems too feeble to bring these myths crashing down to reality" (1988:135–136).

24. Another possible avenue for mission interpretation is suggested by recent work at historic Annapolis. Spearheaded by Mark Leone and his colleagues, archaeologists working at Annapolis have pursued an innovative solution to a similar problem. Founded in about 1650, Annapolis became the capital of Maryland in 1695 and later experienced a prerevolutionary "golden age" of wealth and fame. Although the United States Naval Academy moved there in 1845, the nineteenth century signaled an era of "gentle eclipse" (Leone et al. 1987). For the past few decades, the area has experienced a commercial revival based on yachting, tourism, and new highways that define Annapolis as a suburb of Washington, D.C., less than 30 miles away.

With thousands of tourists buying guidebooks, listening to tour guides, and sauntering through the historic-house museums, historic preservation was important in the commercial renaissance of Annapolis. But this history-for-tourists evolved in the hands of diverse groups and institutions with overlapping and sometimes conflicting agendas. Annapolis history was actually several disconnected and disarticulated histories. Although the docks of Annapolis were featured in the television epic *Roots*—as the first American experience for many newly arriving slaves—black history became invisible in the talks of white tour guides, with slavery discounted as antecedent to relationships between contemporary groups. The histories of the city of Annapolis and the naval academy were likewise unconnected.

Ten thousand tourists visit Annapolis annually, and many want to view the ongoing archaeological excavations. But now, rather than hearing a pasteurized, white-bread version of Annapolis history, these visitors receive a carefully prepared excursion around town. Using examples drawn from the lives of George Washington and other historical figures, the guides underscore the ways in which history is sometimes manufactured for contemporary purposes, noting that current lifeways are not inevitable, that today's attitudes have origins and pretexts, that some taken-for-granted aspects of contemporary life evolved from the past. "The next time you see a presentation of history, visit a museum, take a tour, watch a television show about the past," the Annapolis guides caution, "you can ask yourself what that version of history is trying to get you to do" (Leone et al. 1987:290–291). These highly effective tours are designed to teach participants how to question and challenge their guides—and anybody else who would create and interpret the past (see also Leone 1983; Potter and Leone 1986). Something similar at California's historic missions and other Hispanic sites would provide an interested public with more effective tools for encountering its past.

References

Amero, Richard W.
  1990 The Making of the Panama-California Exposition 1909–1915. *Journal of San Diego History* 36(1):1–47.
Anonymous
  1892 California's Exhibition Building. *World's Fair Magazine*. February:62.
  1893 *Handbook of the World's Columbian Exposition*. Rand, McNally, Chicago.
Atherton, Gertrude
  1893 *The Doomswoman*. Tait, Sons, New York.
  1902 *The Splendid Idle Forties*. Macmillan, New York.
Barker, Leo R., and Julia Costello
  1991 *Archaeology of Alta California: A Sourcebook*. Garland, New York, in press.
Barton, Bruce Walter
  1980 *The Tree at the Center of the World: A Story of the California Missions*. Ross-Erikson, Santa Barbara, Calif.
Bennyhoff, James A., and Albert B. Elsasser
  1954 *Sonoma Mission: An Historical and Archaeological Study of Primary Constructions, 1823–1913*. University of California Archaeological Survey Reports, No. 27. Berkeley.
Bolton, Herbert E.
  1921 *The Spanish Borderlands: A Chronicle of Old Florida and the Southwest*. Yale University Press, New Haven, Conn.
Brown, Thomas
  1987 Mission Era Gardens and Landscapes. In *Early California Reflections*, edited by Nicholas M. Magalousis, pp. 9-1–9-28. Orange County Public Library, San Juan Capistrano, Calif.
Butz, Patricia A.
  1985 Landmark Club. In *Chas. F. Lummis: The Centennial Exhibition Commemorating his Tramp across the Country*, edited by Daniela P. Moneta, pp. 68–73. Southwest Museum, Los Angeles.
Castillo, Edward D.
  1989 The Native Response to the Colonization of Alta California. In *Columbian Consequences*, vol. 1: *Archaeological and Historical Perspectives on the Spanish Borderlands West*, edited by David Hurst Thomas, pp. 377–394. Smithsonian Institution Press, Washington, D.C.
Chartkoff, Joseph L., and Kerry Kona Chartkoff
  1984 *The Archaeology of California*. Stanford University Press, Stanford, Calif.
Cordell, Linda S.
  1989 Durango to Durango: An Overview of the Southwest Heartland. In *Columbian Consequences*, vol. 1: *Archaeological and Historical Perspectives on the Spanish Borderlands West*, edited by David Hurst Thomas, pp. 17–40. Smithsonian Institution Press, Washington, D.C.

Costello, Julia G., and David Hornbeck
1989 Alta California: An Overview. In *Columbian Consequences*, vol. 1: *Archaeological and Historical Perspectives on the Spanish Borderlands West*, edited by David Hurst Thomas, pp. 303–332. Smithsonian Institution Press, Washington, D.C.

Costo, Rupert, and Jeanette Costo (editors)
1988 *The Missions of California: A Legacy of Genocide*. Indian Historian Press, San Francisco, Calif.

Davis, Carlyle Channing, and William A. Alderson
1914 *The True Story of "Ramona": Its Facts and Fictions, Inspiration and Purpose*. Dodge, New York.

Deetz, James
1962–1963 Archaeological Investigations at La Purísima Mission. *Annual Reports of the University of California Archaeological Survey* 5:161–244. Los Angeles.

Eddy, Lucinda Liggett
1983 Lilian Jenette Rice: Search for a Regional Ideal. *Journal of San Diego History* XVI 4:262–285.

Farquhar, Francis P. (editor)
1930 *Up and Down California in 1860–1864: The Journal of William H. Brewer*. Yale University Press, New Haven, Conn.

Fiske, Turbesé Lummis, and Keith Lummis
1975 *Charles F. Lummis: The Man and His West*. University of Oklahoma Press, Norman.

Fowler, Don D.
1987 Uses of the Past: Archaeology in the Service of the State. *American Antiquity* 52(2):229–248.

Freed, Stanley A.
1981 Research Pitfalls as a Result of the Restoration of Museum Specimens. The Research Potential of Anthropological Museum Collections, edited by Anne-Marie Cantwell, James B. Griffin, and Nan A. Rothschild. *Annals of the New York Academy of Sciences* 376:229–245.

Gebhard, David
1980 Architectural Imagery, the Mission, and California. *Harvard Architecture Review* 1:137–145.

Gebhard, David, Eric Sandweiss, and Robert Winter
1985 *Architecture in San Francisco and Northern California*. Rev. ed. Peregrine Smith Books, Salt Lake City, Utah.

Gebhard, David, and Robert Winter
1985 *Architecture in Los Angeles: A Compleat Guide*. Peregrine Smith Books, Salt Lake City, Utah.

Gowans, Alan
1986 *The Comfortable House: North American Suburban Architecture 1880–1930*. MIT Press, Cambridge.

Greenwood, Roberta S.
1989 The California Ranchero: Fact and Fancy. In *Columbian Consequences*, vol. 1: *Archaeological and Historical Perspectives on the Spanish Borderlands West*, edited by David Hurst Thomas, pp. 451–465. Smithsonian Institution Press, Washington, D.C.

Harkins, Conrad, O.F.M.
1990 On Franciscans, Archaeology, and Old Missions. In *Columbian Consequences*, vol. 2: *Archaeological and Historical Perspectives on the Spanish Borderlands East*, edited by David Hurst Thomas, pp. 459–475. Smithsonian Institution Press, Washington, D.C.

Heizer, Robert F.
1950 Observations on Historic Sites and Archaeology in California. *University of California Archaeological Survey Reports* 9(6):1–5. Berkeley.

Heizer, Robert F., and T. D. McCown
1954 Preface to *Sonoma Mission: An Historical and Archaeological Study of Primary Con-*

structions, 1823–1913, by James A. Bennyhoff and Albert B. Elsasser. University of California Archaeological Survey Reports, No. 27, pp. i—ii.

Hewett, Edgar L., and Reginald G. Fisher
  1943 *Mission Monuments of New Mexico*. Handbooks of Archaeological History, edited by Edgar L. Hewett. University of New Mexico Press, Albuquerque.

Jackson, Helen Hunt
  1881 *A Century of Dishonor*. Harper and Brothers, New York.
  1883a Father Junipero and His Work. *Century* 10 (May).
  1883b *Glimpses of California and the Missions*. Roberts Brothers, Boston.
  1884 *Ramona*. Roberts Brothers, Boston.
  1912 [1884] *Ramona*. Grosset and Dunlap, New York.

James, George Wharton
  1906 *In and Out of the Old Missions of California*. Little, Brown, Boston.
  1913 *Through Ramona's Country*. Little, Brown, Boston.

Keeler, Charles Augustus
  1904 *The Simple Home*. P. Elder, San Francisco.

Kessell, John L.
  1980 *The Missions of New Mexico since 1776*. University of New Mexico Press, Albuquerque.

Kidder, Alfred V.
  1924 *An Introduction to the Study of Southwestern Archaeology*, with a Preliminary Account of the Excavations at Pecos. Papers of the Southwestern Expedition, No. 1. Phillips Academy. Yale University Press, New Haven, Conn.
  1958 *Pecos, New Mexico: Archaeological Notes*. Papers of the Robert S. Peabody Foundation for Archaeology, vol. 5. Phillips Academy, Andover, Mass.

Krell, Dorothy (editor)
  1981 *The California Missions: A Pictoral History*. Lane, Menlo Park, Calif.

Langum, David J.
  1978 Californios and the Image of Indolence. *Western Historical Quarterly* 9:181–196.
  1983 From Condemnation to Praise: Shifting Perspectives on Hispanic California. *California History* 61(4):282–291.

Leone, Mark P.
  1983 Method as Message. *Museum News* 62(1):35–41.

Leone, Mark P., Parker B. Potter, Jr., and Paul A. Shackel
  1987 Toward a Critical Archaeology. *Current Anthropology* 28(3):283–302.

Lummis, Charles Fletcher
  1895 In the Lion's Den. *Land of Sunshine* 4(1):43–46.
  1902 The Landmarks Club. *Out West* 16(2):184–185.
  1903a The Right Hand of the Continent. *Out West* 17(3):269–299.
  1903b The Sequoya League. *Out West* 18(3):355–365.
  1927 *Stand Fast, Santa Barbara!* Plans and Planting Committee of the Community Arts Association, Santa Barbara, Calif.
  1930 *The Spanish Pioneers and the California Missions*. New and Enlarged Edition. A. C. McClurg, Chicago.

McWilliams, Carey
  1973 *Southern California: An Island on the Land*. Peregrine Smith Books, Salt Lake City, Utah.

Manning, Agnes M.
  1884 San Carlos Borromeo de Monterey. *Overland Monthly*, July 1884.

Mathes, Valerie Sherer
  1983 Parallel Calls to Conscience: Reformers Helen Hunt Jackson and Harriet Beecher Stowe. *Californians* July/August:32–40.
  1990 *Helen Hunt Jackson and Her Indian Reform Legacy*. University of Texas Press, Austin.

May, Antoinette

1989 *The Annotated Ramona*. Worldwide Publishing/Tetra, San Carlos Borromeo, Calif.

Montgomery, Ross Gordon, Watson Smith, and John Otis Brew
1949 *Franciscan Awatovi: The Excavation and Conjectural Reconstruction of a 17th-Century Spanish Mission Establishment at a Hopi Indian Town in Northeastern Arizona*. Papers of the Peabody Museum of American Archaeology and Ethnology, Harvard University, vol. 36. Reports of the Awatovi Expedition. Peabody Museum, Harvard University, Report No. 3. Cambridge, Mass.

Morgado, Martin J.
1987 *Junípero Serra*. Mount Carmel, Pacific Grove, Calif.

Nelson, Nels C.
1916 Chronology of the Tano Ruins, New Mexico. *American Anthropologist* 18(2):159–180.

Neuerburg, Norman
1987 *The Decoration of the California Missions*. Bellerophon Books, Santa Barbara, Calif.

Nevins, Allen
1941 Helen Hunt Jackson, Sentimentalist vs. Realist. *American Scholar* 10:269–285.

Pitt, Leonard
1966 *The Decline of the Californios*. University of California Press, Berkeley.

Potter, Parker B., Jr., and Mark P. Leone
1986 History in Museums: A Critical Capacity in Museums versus Repeating Tradition. In *Education: The Spirit of the American Museum*, edited by Mary Ellen Munley and Carol Stapp. Journal of the Washington Academy of Sciences 75(3).

Reyman, Jonathan E.
1978 Room 44, Wupatki: Rejecting False Profits. *American Antiquity* 43(4):729–733.

Roosevelt, Theodore
1889 *Winning of the West*, vol. 1. G. P. Putnam's Sons, New York.

Rydell, Robert W.
1984 *All the World's a Fair: Visions of Empire at American International Expositions, 1876–1916*. University of Chicago Press, Chicago.

Schuyler, Robert L.
1976 Images of America: The Contribution of Historical Archaeology to National Identity. *Southwestern Lore* 42(4):27–39.
1978 Indian-Euro-American Interaction: Archeological Evidence from Non-Indian Sites. In *California*, edited by R. F. Heizer, pp. 69–79. Handbook of North American Indians, vol. 8, William C. Sturtevant, general editor. Smithsonian Institution, Washington, D.C.

Starr, Kevin
1973 *Americans and the California Dream, 1850–1915*. Oxford University Press, New York.
1985 *Inventing the Dream: California through the Progressive Era*. Oxford University Press, New York.
1990 *Material Dreams: Southern California through the 1920s*. Oxford University Press, New York.

Stewart, Omer C.
1978 Litigation and Its Effects. In *California*, edited by R. F. Heizer, pp. 705–712. Handbook of North American Indians, vol. 8, William C. Sturtevant, general editor. Smithsonian Institution, Washington, D.C.

Stevenson, Robert Louis
1895 *The Travels and Essays of Robert Louis Stevenson*. Charles Scribner's Sons, New York.

Temple, Sydney
1980 *The Carmel Mission: From Founding to Rebuilding*. Valley Publishers, Fresno, Calif.

Thomas, David Hurst
1989 Columbian Consequences: The Spanish Borderlands in Cubist Perspective. In *Columbian Consequences*, vol. 1: *Archaeological and Historical Perspectives on the Spanish Bor-*

derlands West, edited by David Hurst Thomas, pp. 1–14. Smithsonian Institution Press, Washington, D.C.

Vroman, A. C., and T. F. Barnes

1899 *The Genesis of the Story of Ramona*. Presses of Kingley-Barnes & Neuner, Los Angeles, Calif.

Wallace, William J.

1959 Historical Research Pertaining to the Original Reid Adobe House. *Lasca Leaves* 9(1):14–23.

Walker, Franklin

1939 *San Francisco's Literary Frontier*. A. A. Knopf, New York.

1950 *A Literary History of Southern California*. University of California Press, Berkeley.

Weber, David J.

1988 *Myth and the History of the Hispanic Southwest*. University of New Mexico Press, Albuquerque.

Weber, Francis J.

1988 *A Bicentennial Compendium of Maynard J. Geiger's The Life and Times of Fr. Junípero Serra*. 3rd ed. EZ Nature Books, San Luis Obispo, Calif.

Weitze, Karen J.

1984 *California's Mission Revival*. Hennessey & Ingalls, Los Angeles, Calif.

Williams, Stanley T.

1955 *The Spanish Background of American Literature*, vol. 2. Yale University Press, New Haven, Conn.

Part 2 ■

The Native Context of Colonialism in Southern Mesoamerica and Central America

Chapter 7 ■

Grant D. Jones and David M. Pendergast

The Native Context of Colonialism in Southern Mesoamerica and Central America: An Overview

Although divisible into two general physiographic zones (Figure 7–1)—the highlands and the tropical lowlands—southern Mesoamerica and Central America comprise so vast an array of microenvironments that it would take more than a Herculean effort to describe the terrain, vegetation, and climate of the region. Down the western side of the region runs one of the zones, the great spine of tropical highlands extending in a vast unbroken curving belt from the Isthmus of Tehuantepec to Nicaragua. The other portion of the highlands, narrow but no less dramatic in its dissection, begins in northern Costa Rica and terminates in southern Panama. The physical separation of the two highland belts is mirrored in vegetational assemblages, which are dominated by oak-conifer forests in the north and by a rain forest of South American affinity (rich in oak, laurel, and myrtle) in Costa Rica and Panama (West 1964:365).

The highlands—from the karstic limestone uplands of northern Chiapas (Chiapa in colonial times) through the granites in that state's southern portion to the volcanic zone from Guatemala south to Nicaragua—offered pre-Hispanic inhabitants a variety of plateaus, basins, and plains as the most attractive sites for occupation. Where there was reasonably level terrain there was generally also arable land, an adequate water supply, and a variety of other natural resources. Throughout the zone, but especially in the volcanic areas, the richness of the flatlands and the ruggedness of the remaining terrain played a vital role in population distribution.

The highlands are flanked both east and west for their entire length by the tropical lowlands. The Pacific slope is a plain largely composed of alluvium eroded from the volcanic uplands, and consequently of unsurpassed richness for agricultural purposes. Except in the extreme south, the forest of the plain is largely deciduous and interspersed with savanna. Ancient population was predictably high throughout this coastal region, but many parts of it are less well known archaeologically than the remaining lowlands.

On the east side of the highlands lie the vast Caribbean tropical lowlands that make up the Yucatán Peninsula, the Guatemalan Petén, and the east coast of the Central American states. This is an area of endlessly diverse topography, vegetation, rainfall, and natural resources. To the surprise of many first-time visitors, water is among the resources characterized by markedly differential distribution. This led inhabitants to focus their settlements on river valleys along parts of the Central American coast, although the modification of natural sinkholes and the construction of reservoirs in the rain forest of the southern Maya lowlands expanded the occupable area beyond the riverine environment into regions with little or no surface water. Water supply was even more critical in the northern Yucatán Peninsula, which is marked by low rainfall and lacks surface streams. On the coastal plain, scattered natural and modified caverns provided access to the relatively shallow water table, but to the west, in the limestone hills of the Puuc, no such solution was possible owing to the great depth of the water table. Nontheless, the undaunted Maya managed not only to settle the forbidding area but to develop in it a rich and distinctive tradition in architecture and other aspects of material culture.

To subsume the region of our concern within a few paragraphs is to risk perpetuating the uninformed view that everything from Chiapas south is verdant, hot, and wet. Close study shows that none of these adjectives applies throughout the region, and indeed none is entirely appropriate even for restricted parts of this vast and varied territory. The summary by West (1964) of the numerous papers produced under his editorship offers a more detailed account of the tropics than we can provide here.

Native American Context

The peoples of Southern Mesoamerica and Central America at the time of Spanish arrival were almost as diverse as the region's physiography. Therefore many studies of both the ethnographic present and the ethnohistorical and archaeological past have used the political boundaries of recent times as a convenient way of structuring their investigations. The seven modern political units of the region are by and large delimited by natural physiographic boundaries and reflect at least in part the much older cultural realities. It is, however, the narrative of the contact experience that often subsumes both modern and ancient entities and gives meaning to the treatment of so large an area as if it were a whole.

On their arrival in southeastern Mesoamerica (Figures 7–2, 7–3), the Spaniards encountered what they generally understood to be one people, the Maya. Although the European invaders soon learned that there was great variety even among small Maya polities, they never entirely lost their perception of the people of the Yucatán Peninsula, Guatemala, and western Honduras as a single entity. That perception did much to structure both the Spanish approach to problems in the Maya area and the written record of their successes and failures. The Spanish view remains meaningful in linguistic terms and also as an expression of the fact that there were elements of culture that once linked the inhabitants of this vast and varied region and that to some extent continue to do so today. That this was never the Maya perception of themselves is made clear by many lines of evidence, among which the archaeological is probably the most striking.

The city-state organization that characterized early Maya prehistory throughout the lowlands gave a degree of structure to what the Spanish first encountered in the northern Yucatán Peninsula, although upheavals in the centuries before Spanish arrival had altered and broken much of the power of the great centers of earlier times. In contrast, in most parts of the southern lowlands events had conspired to open an immense gulf between the archaeological Maya and their sixteenth-century descendants. Contributing greatly to the separation of past from present was the early tenth-century collapse of many city-states of the southern lowlands. Consequently, in the ensuing centuries populations were dispersed away from abandoned, decaying centers, and their pre-collapse social, political, and economic structure dissolved. Although islands of comparative calm remained in the sea of this upheaval, the net result of the collapse was the creation of an almost entirely village- and town-based rather than city-based way of life.

The southern lowlands probably seemed as much of a frontier to fifteenth-century northern lowland Maya as they did to the Spaniards who a century later followed Maya routes into the area in search of centers of religious and economic control. Whereas the north offered many such centers in the form of communities that had functioned for centuries as nodes in the network of Yucatecan life, only a few remained in the south. Hence the north always appeared the more settled and uniform area in Spanish eyes, while the south remained remote, heterogeneous, and immeasurably more difficult to exploit or control. This attitude persists to this day among the people of the north, strengthened by the shift from low to high forest as one moves south as well as by the political events of the centuries since the first European contact.

In the Guatemalan and Chiapas highlands, the Spaniards found peoples whose identity and territorial integrity had not suffered the onslaughts that had beset parts of the eastern lowlands. Although subject to periodic Spanish incursions from the earliest times onward, the highland peoples were successful in resisting assimilation, even into the present day. In many areas, resistance was given effective support by topography, but qualities of personality as rugged as the surroundings seem to have played a significant role as well. The results of that resistance can be judged in part by comparing the map of highland Guatemalan linguistic distribution about 1575 (Miles 1957:Figure 1) with a modern linguistic map of the area (Vogt 1969:Figure 1). In the Chiapas highlands, the Spanish were confronted by three groups: the Tzotzil, the Tzeltal, and the Tojolabal (Figure 7–3). Their immediate neighbors in the northwestern Guatemalan highlands were the Mam, the Jacaltec, and the Chuh, while the central highlands were held by the Quiché, the Cakchiquel, and the Tzutuhil, and the south by the Pokom, Chorti, Cholti, and the Xinca. It is in the south that the greatest change has occurred; elsewhere, modern and Contact period distributions are broadly the same. Miles's (1965) summary of the precontact ethnology of the highlands has been added to by subsequent research in some areas, most notably Chiapas, but still provides an excellent characterization of cultures and events in an area made complex by both its topography and its prehistory.

For most of the highland peoples, their homeland had long been both a fortress and a link with groups farther north. That link had over many centuries brought elements of central Mexican cultures into the region, but by late precontact times intrusions of this sort appear to have been fraught with danger to the intruders, at least in Chiapas (Adams 1961:348, 359). The Aztec view of the Chiapan highland people suggests the nature of the native context into which the Spaniards generally found themselves thrust, which was of the rather painful kind to be expected in the mountain fastness. Although no more united by centralized political power than were the lowland Maya, the highlanders were better equipped both with respect to their terrain and temperament than their eastern relatives to withstand the pressures set in motion by the arrival of the Europeans.

In facing the Spaniards, the peoples of highland Guatemala possessed yet another advantage in addition to the topography and their own indomitable qualities: For a considerable time prior to contact, territorial rivalries had given rise to defensive strategies that were manifested in community location as well as in architecture. This gave a number of the more important sites the sort of quality that would have caused a sinking feeling in a Spanish assailant's heart. Many of the crucial points were therefore bypassed by the Spaniards, and much of the native culture survived not only unscathed but also unassayed by the Europeans. The tactical situation led early to a concentration of Spanish power in a limited area; unfortunately, the difficulties of the highlands have also meant that much of the archaeological record of early highland Spanish-native contact, and even of immediate precontact native life, remains to be examined.

When we move from the Maya area into lower Central America (Figure 7–1), we enter a region that despite its cultural diversity can be characterized as having been occupied in the sixteenth century by two categories of native people, one of which was far larger than the other. The principal feature of the precontact population is that it comprised peoples for whom South American links have been postulated on linguistic grounds and on the basis of features of social structure and kinship, food habits, and aspects of material culture,

Figure 7–1. Sixteenth-century colonial provinces of southeastern Mesoamerica and Central America, with principal Central American language groups.

which included highly developed metallurgical skills. Nevertheless, early relations between the Maya area and other parts of Mesoamerica are recognizable in the ceramic record as far south as Nicaragua (Healy 1980:325–327). The most reasonable view of the bulk of indigenous lower Central American native cultural traditions is that they represent varied blendings of local developments with elements drawn from both south and north. Except where they had been supplanted or transformed by later immigrations, it was these heterogeneous cultures that remained for the Spaniards to encounter.

The second significant group in the area's precontact culture history consisted of Mexicans who had migrated south either as settlers or as conquerors. Such migrations may have forged Mesoamerican links with the southern part of lower Central America fairly early, beginning with the migration of Chorotegan peoples from Chiapas to Nicaragua (Healy 1980:337). It was, however, the arrival of the Nahua-speaking Pipil-Nicarao (Fowler 1989) that gave full effectiveness to the Mesoamericanization of lower Central America. Both the Pipil of the north, spread from Guatemala through Honduras and El Salvador, and the Nicaraguan Nicarao brought with them not only a language intelligible to those with conquest experience in central Mexico but also a suite of practices, beliefs, and elements of material culture that reflected their Mexican heritage. In some respects, this situation made it easier for the Spanish to move through Central America, but in others it probably was something of a hindrance, if only because it confused perception of the ethnic composition of an area that was already a very complex mosaic.

For a variety of reasons that have to do with both the political climate and the intellectual history of Central American archaeology, we are at present far better able to set the native context at the time of contact than to establish the effects of that contact as they may be reflected in the earth. It is nonetheless clear both from the archaeological record of earlier times and from the documentary evidence that the Spaniards' experience in lower Central America was as multifarious as the native cultures they confronted. The great initial surprise for the Spaniards as they entered the New World was the presence of civilization where they had expected something far less grand. The even greater continuing surprise as they passed from place to place was the endless richness and variety in the ways the New World's peoples had devised to meet life's challenges in so diverse a setting. The area with which we are concerned here embraces only a part of that diverse environment and culture; it nevertheless reveals, despite the comparative recentness of investigations in the sphere of Contact period archaeology, Columbian consequences that link its peoples to those whose stories lie elsewhere in this volume and its two companion works.

History of European–Native American Interaction

Spanish contact with southern Mesoamerica and Central America began with Christopher Columbus's seizure of a canoe-load of native people in the Gulf of Honduras during his fourth voyage in 1502. Yucatán was probably first encountered in 1511, when shipwrecked Spanish sailors were cast ashore on the eastern coast of the peninsula. In the following decades, exploration and conquest activities accelerated, although by piecemeal and diverse strategies. The actual conquest occupied a period of decades, in some areas nearly two centuries.

For most of its colonial history, Yucatán fell under the jurisdiction of the Audiencia of Mexico. The Audiencia of Guatemala, except for brief periods, governed the remaining areas of Central America from Chiapas to Costa Rica. The boundary between Guatemala and Yucatán remained ill-defined throughout most of the Colonial period, as did the jurisdictional and ecclesiastical control over the long unconquered region that is now the Guatemalan department of El Petén. Most of remote Belize was governed by Yucatán until the mid-1600s, when British smugglers and logwood cutters began to frequent its coastal waters (Figure 7–1).

The surviving landscape of native peoples today reflects a panorama of historical, cultural, and environmental variables. In some areas, native groups soon became nearly extinct, whereas in others they have survived in large numbers to the present day. In the Yucatán Peninsula, for example, Yucatec Mayan even today serves as the lingua franca of most rural areas, and Maya cultural traditions, although vastly changed as a result of nearly five centuries of acculturation and cultural syncretism, still identify the Mayas as a strong ethnic unit. Strong cultural survival likewise characterizes much of the highland, and some of the lowland, areas of Chiapas and Guatemala. Even in these areas, however, the process of ladinoization—the "hispanicizing" effects of cultural change— has brought about many changes, particularly in urban areas. Europeans did not settle everywhere but rather chose to live where they found the physical environment tolerable, communication routes adequate, and human and natural resources worth exploiting. Their choices inevitably left huge, less inviting areas of native territory in a state of semi-independence, particularly in the Guatemalan Petén and lowland eastern Nicaragua and Honduras. These contrasts between north and south in the peninsula and between east and west in lower Central America still affect the boundaries both of political jurisdictions and of cultural regions.

The Lowland Maya

The conquest of the northern Maya lowlands lasted for several decades (Figure 7–2). The Mayas of the northeastern Yucatán Peninsula attacked an exploratory mission led from Cuba by Francisco Hernandez de Córdoba in 1517. The next year, Juan de Grijalva claimed Cozumel Island for the Spanish Crown, but his party was later twice attacked at Campeche as it explored the western coast. Cortés, who encountered Cozumel Mayas in 1519, also led an expedition across the Petén on his way to Honduras in 1525–1526.

The first organized attempts to conquer Yucatán were initiated by Francisco de Montejo, who had participated with Cortés in the conquest of Mexico. His first expedition, in 1527–1528, focused on the eastern coast of the peninsula, where a temporary villa (administrative center) was established on the mainland near Cozumel. The interior Mayas, however, provided strong armed resistance, and these first conquest efforts were eventually abandoned. In 1529, Montejo renewed his efforts by establishing a new villa at Campeche, while his lieutenant Alfonso Dávila attempted without success to pacify the southeastern areas of the peninsula and to establish a second villa at Chetumal. Disappointed by the lack of gold, Montejo's men began to abandon him by 1534, and he evacuated his

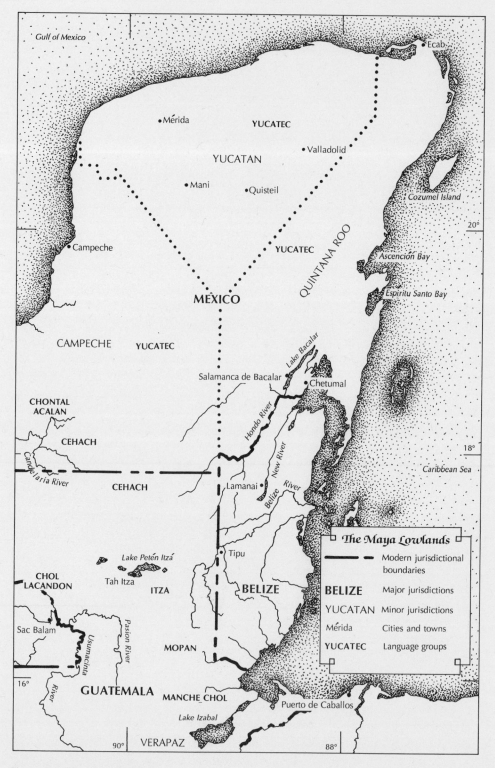

Figure 7–2. The Maya Lowlands.

forces from Yucatán for a second time. Finally, Montejo's son and nephew, beginning in 1540, succeeded in conquering much of northern Yucatán. The Maya groups of the northwestern part of the peninsula cooperated more fully with the Spanish during this phase of the conquest than did those of the northeastern regions, an event that reflected long-standing political conflicts among native populations. The Spanish founded Mérida at the Maya town of T'ho in 1542 and by 1544 had established the villas of Campeche, Valladolid, and Salamanca de Bacalar (Chamberlain 1948).

The conquest of the southeastern peninsula was publicized for the cruelty of its perpetrators, and in 1546 the area from Valladolid to Belize rose up in rebellion. Although the rebellion was quelled, many Mayas responded by fleeing southward to the unconquered interior in a pattern they were to follow for more than a century. Maya resistance to the first encomiendas (systems of tribute collection) and to the earliest Franciscan missionaries in Yucatán took the combined form of flight and the continued practice of their native religion. The discovery of "idolatry" among supposedly converted groups by zealous Franciscans led in 1562 to a controversial auto-da-fe, organized by the famous Franciscan friar Diego de Landa.

The independent interior regions attracted runaways from the northern encomiendas. At the heart of this zone were the Itzas of Lake Petén Itzá. As early as 1615 Spanish Franciscans in Yucatán attempted to convince the Itza"ruler" Can Ek that Maya prophecies called for the Itzas' peaceful surrender to Spanish rule and their conversion to Christianity. Franciscans visited Can Ek in 1618 and 1619 but were unsuccessful in pressing for Itza submission. Other Franciscans attempted to apply the same tactic beginning in 1695, claiming now that 1696 would be the year in which the prophecies would result in Itza surrender. This strategy also failed, and in 1697 Spanish troops defeated the recalcitrant Itzas, the last independent Colonial period Maya chiefdoms.

Estimates of the preconquest population of the Maya lowlands vary widely, but most scholars would agree that the entire lowlands contained well over one million people and possibly several millions. At the time of the first tributary count of 1549–1550 the conquered population of Yucatán represented only about 240,000 persons, and the losses—due to smallpox, influenza, measles, yellow fever, and other European diseases—were probably far greater in the southern lowlands (Farriss 1984). As the labor pool declined so did food production, and there ensued cycles of famine and flight to the forests.

In Yucatán, a resource-poor colony, the Mayas provided the principal source of Spanish income, in the form of encomienda tribute (primarily cotton cloth) and repartimiento payments. The latter usually consisted of finished crafts or forest products, demanded by local officials in return for very small remuneration. Commercial agriculture did not develop on a significant scale until the late eighteenth century (Patch 1985). Sugarcane production expanded widely in the early nineteenth century and contributed to the extensive loss of Indian lands. The devastating Caste War of Yucatán, the first major uprising since the brief Quisteil rebellion of 1761, broke out in 1847–1848, partly in response to these economic conditions (Reed 1964). This war resulted in the deaths of tens of thousands of people and in the collapse of Yucatán's economy. The surviving Maya rebels formed independent groups in the southeastern peninsula, and many sought refuge in Belize.

The Maya of Highland and Pacific Guatemala and Chiapas

The peoples of western Guatemala (Figure 7–3) were aware of Cortés's conquest of central Mexico as a result of preexisting diplomatic ties with the Aztecs. Thus they were not surprised when, early in 1524, Pedro de Alvarado, one of Cortés's principal officers, arrived in Soconusco with a large military party that included Mexican foot soldiers. Alvarado, whose reputation as a ruthless conqueror has been much debated (García Añoveros 1987), marched rapidly along the Pacific coast through Mam territory and headed directly for the Quiché capital of Utatlán. The Quichés were well prepared, offering strong resistance along Alvarado's route and attempting to trap the conquest troops in the walled town of Utatlán. Nonetheless, with assistance from the Cakchiquels, who regarded the Quichés as their enemies, Alvarado captured and burned Utatlán, rapidly secured the surrender of surrounding Quiché territories, and conquered the Tzutujil capital of Tzikinahay on Lake Atitlán (Bricker 1981:29–32).

In a matter of months, by means of conquest and peaceful surrender, most of the highlands of Guatemala and adjacent parts of neighboring El Salvador were under nominal Spanish control. Alvarado quickly established the first Guatemalan capital, Santiago de los Caballeros, at Iximche, the Cakquiquel capital. The eastern areas—especially Chorti territory—resisted full surrender, however, until 1530, and early postconquest resistance among the Cakquiquels, Quichés, and Pokomams suggest that the initial conquest was by no means completely successful (Bricker 1981:32–35). The northeastern predominantly Kekchi-speaking Verapaz region, so named because of mid-sixteenth century Dominican missionary efforts to "conquer" the area by means of peaceful conversion, also resisted Alvarado's attempts at military conquest. Only a few enclaves in coastal eastern Guatemala were effectively controlled by the Spanish, and most of the adjacent lowland territories of the Manche Chol, the Mopan, and the Chol-speaking Lacandon resisted conquest for nearly two centuries.

The conquest of Chiapas also began in 1524, with the occupation of Chiapanec territory in the vicinity of the Grijalva River by Spanish troops under Luis Marín (Figure 7–3). Just as Alvarado had had the support of the Cakquichels in his conquest of Guatemala, Marín was assisted by enemies of the expansive Chiapanec. Although Marín subdued the neighboring Chamulans and was offered no resistance by the Zinacantecos—both Tzotzil Maya-speaking polities—he abandoned the region without establishing a permanent Spanish presence. These areas of Chiapas were reconquered in 1527 by Diego de Mazariegos, who in 1528 established the Spanish town of Villa Real near the site of the old Chiapanec capital on the Grijalva River. The capital of Chiapas was later transferred to Ciudad Real (today San Cristóbal de las Casas) near Zinacantán (Bricker 1981:43–46).

Estimates of the demographic impact of Spanish conquest on these regions vary considerably, but there is wide agreement that depopulation during the first

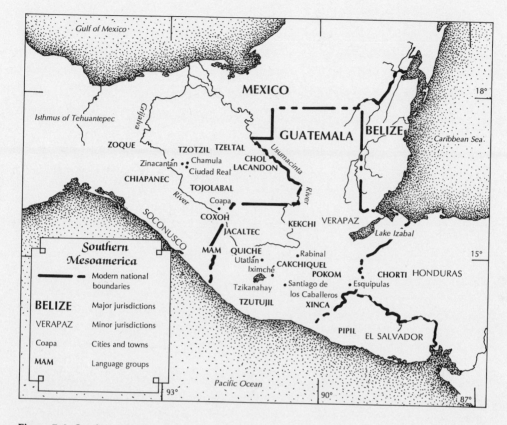

Figure 7–3. Southern Mesoamerica.

century of colonial rule was high. As in Yucatán, epidemics caused by European diseases actually preceded Spanish conquest and weakened the native ability to resist militarily. A variety of psychological, environmental, and organizational factors increased the impact of these diseases on the native population. Several recent studies indicate that these losses ranged from 70 to 90 percent of the contact population by the end of the sixteenth century, with slow recovery beginning in the seventeenth century (MacLeod 1984). Even in interior frontier lowland areas where native cultures survived much of the direct conquest and colonial disruption that affected the highlands, population losses were massive.

As in Yucatán, the principal institutions applied to the more densely populated areas of highland Guatemala and Chiapas were the encomienda, repartimiento, and other forms of forced or controlled labor. Populations were subjected regularly to intense forms of resettlement or congregación. In Soconusco cacao was left primarily in the hands of native cultivators, who paid taxes on their product. Spanish settlement in Guatemala concentrated around Santiago and the fertile plains to the south and east of the capital, well into El Salvador. In these regions Europeans controlled the production of such cash crops as indigo, cochineal, and sugar, and of cattle, sheep, and maize. They paid little commercial attention to the higher, colder mountainous regions to the north and west of Santiago.

Similar patterns also distinguished the mountainous areas around San Cristóbal de las Casas from the rich agricultural zones to the west and south of the Chiapan capital. There, as in Guatemala, the Indians from the *tierra fría* were utilized as a labor reservoir for the cultivation of crops grown in lower altitudes. The crops have changed over the centuries, but early colonial patterns of ethnic settlement distributions and labor utilization survived nearly everywhere well into the twentieth century. The highland Mayas, although beset by intense economic and spiritual colonialism, maintained a strong sense of cultural autonomy throughout the Colonial period (Lovell 1985).

This success was clearly due not to the Mayas' lack of experience with colonial interests but rather to the fact that they were able to adapt successfully to circumstances that permitted them to maintain their principal communities at some distance from dense European settlement and permanent commercial economic enterprises. Highland Maya rebellions in Chiapas and Guatemala during the eighteenth century were brief, as they were in Yucatán. On at least some occasions, however, these uprisings, as was apparently the case in the 1712 Tzeltal revolt in Chiapas, displayed a fervent desire for ethnic self-expression.

Lower Central America

Whereas the conquest of the territory that is modern-day Guatemala sent waves of Spanish influence from north to south, into adjacent areas of El Salvador and Honduras, that of southern Central America had its origins in the south (Figure 7–1). With the arrival of Pedrarias Dávila in Panama in 1514, a series of explorations was launched along the Pacific into Costa Rica and Nicaragua. Control over the region—both the Pacific and Atlantic sides—was bitterly and violently contested by would-be Spanish conquerors not only from Panama but also Mexico and the Caribbean. Pedrarias Dávila became governor of Nicaragua and Costa Rica in 1527 and soon attempted to lay claim to territories in Honduras and El Salvador, where he faced counterclaims already established by Pedro de Alvarado during the conquest of Guatemala. The initial conquest and colonization of the native populations, principally in the Pacific areas of Nicaragua and Honduras, was continued under Rodrigo de Contreras, who governed Nicaragua from 1535 to 1544.

The devastation wrought upon the native populations during these years was greater than elsewhere, particularly in the more densely populated, agriculturally rich Pacific regions. Encomiendas were established early and demanded payments in cloth, foodstuffs, and cacao. Gold was panned from streams and extracted from placer mines with Indian labor until this resource ran out. The principal source of Spanish income, however, was in slaves, who were exported primarily from Nicaragua to Peru via Panama and from Honduras to Cuba. MacLeod (1973:52) has suggested the conservative figure of 200,000 Indian slaves exported in this fashion from Nicaragua alone between about 1528 and the late 1540s. Diseases, famines, overwork, and mistreatment exacerbated the effects of the slave trade. By the time this industry had died out in 1550—in the wake of royally decreed reforms and fewer labor demands as colonial Peru came to rely on its own native labor resources—the native population of Pacific Nicaragua and Nicoya had been reduced by over 90 percent, from an estimated Contact period population of some 600,000 to about 45,000 (Newson 1987:337). Most of the remaining Pacific zone native population gradually merged into a ladinoized population, as it did in the intensive agricultural zones of El Salvador and Guatemala.

With certain exceptions, the less densely populated, less socially stratified eastern zone populations of Honduras and Nicaragua were so difficult to exploit that the region attracted little Spanish interest other than the eventual infusion of missionary activity and of selective use of the encomienda. These areas also suffered enormous population losses, although at a later date and to perhaps a somewhat lesser degree. Even today in Nicaragua, the Pacific zone remains the principal area of government control, while the Atlantic area has long been outside the principal sphere of "Spanish" influence. The Caribbean zones, barely colonized by the Spanish, served the British (as did the coast of Belize) beginning in the seventeenth century as staging grounds for bucaneering activities, slave raiding, and attacks on Spanish settlements (Floyd 1967). In these areas miscegenation and cultural contact among English, African, and Indian populations produced new cultural mixes, such as the Miskito, that can still be identified among the native populations.

With so few native peoples having survived between Costa Rica and El Salvador and Honduras, the study of the history of the native peoples of this region must depend largely on ethnohistorical and archaeological reconstruction. This situation contrasts markedly, of course, with the survival of large numbers of Native Americans in Guatemala, Chiapas, and Yucatán, where an understanding of historic native populations can be enriched by knowledge of the rich variety of living native cultures. Even these cultures, however, are today undergoing rapid change, both voluntary and involuntary. Tens of thousands of Guatemalan Mayas were massacred during the army's campaign to quell guerrilla opposition in the early 1980s. Such tragedy, coupled with army efforts to resettle and reorganize the rural Mayas, provides a harsh reminder that in some areas the mentalities of the conquest, set in motion nearly 500 years ago, have yet to be abandoned.

History of Scholarly Research

Only in recent years has our knowledge of Mesoamerica and Central America progressed to the point at which it is now possible to write a general synthesis of the colonial experience there. Only one comprehensive overview to date includes Central America as well as non-Mesoamerican Central America (Helms 1975), and only one collection provides full coverage for southern Mesoamerica alone (MacLeod and Wasserstrom 1983). The four-volume *Guide to Ethnohistorical Sources* of the Handbook of Middle American Indians (Cline 1972–1975) focused primarily on other regions, and much research has postdated this work. An extensive bibliography of colonial Central America was prepared by Markman (1977).

The Lowland Maya

John Lloyd Stephens's vivid nineteenth-century travelogues, illustrated by Frederick Catherwood, first exposed the modern North American and European community to spectacular ancient Maya monuments in Yucatán and northern Honduras (Stephens 1963, 1969). Stephens recognized that the living Mayas themselves were the descendants of the inhabitants of these ruined cities, and his speculations represent the beginnings of modern historical scholarship on the lowland Maya. Serious prehistoric research began around the turn of this century, and information on preconquest lowland Maya cultural history has since accumulated rapidly (Coe 1987; Hammond 1982; Henderson 1978; Morley and Sharer 1983). Research on the Postclassic period has lagged behind studies of the Classic period, but new syntheses are emerging (Chase and Rice 1985; Rivera and Ciudad 1986).

Under the leadership of Alfred A. Tozzer, Harvard's Peabody Museum broadened its early emphasis on archaeological research in the Maya lowlands to include both ethnographic and historical investigations (Means 1917; Tozzer 1907, 1941). The Carnegie Institution of Washington later established an ambitious program (1930–1958) whose investigators integrated archaeological, historical, and ethnographic approaches. Among the later Carnegie-sponsored archaeological projects was the excavation of Mayapan, an important Late Postclassic site in northern Yucatán for which substantial related historical data were analyzed (Pollock et al. 1962). Now classic ethnographic studies by Robert Redfield and Alfonso Villa Rojas in Yucatán (1934) and by Villa Rojas in Quintana Roo (1945), among others, also emerged from the Carnegie project (see also Villa Rojas 1969).

Above all, the Carnegie years resulted in seminal studies on lowland Maya colonial history, ethnohistory and literature, political history, and processes of Spanish colonization (Chamberlain 1948, 1951; Roys 1939, 1943, 1952, 1957, 1962, 1965, 1967; Scholes 1937; Scholes and Adams 1938; Scholes and Roys 1968). These Carnegie scholars applied sophisticated historical and ethnohistorical techniques and for the first time made extensive use of both Spanish and Maya-language documents.

A number of more recent studies, based on extensive documentary research, have examined the impact of Spanish colonialism upon the lowland Maya. The most important modern synthesis for colonial Yucatán is that of Nancy M. Farriss (1984; see also Farriss 1983, 1986, 1987). Peter Gerhard, a historical geographer, has provided a useful supplement to Roys's (1957) political geography of Yucatán, covering in addition Tabasco, Laguna de Términos, and Chiapas, and Soconusco (Gerhard 1979). García Bernal has focused on population history and the encomienda in Yucatán (1978), and Hunt and García Bernal have provided syntheses of Spanish Yucatecan society (García Bernal 1972; Hunt 1976). The importance of the Franciscan missionaries in the early conquest of Yucatán have been the focus of works by Clendinnen (1987) and González Cicero (1978). Documentary investigations of single Maya communities offer a promising new direction (P. C. Thompson 1978). For a useful general overview of Yucatecan history, see Mosley and Terry (1980).

Detailed historical demographic studies of the lowland Maya were initiated with Cook and Borah's longitudinal study of the population of Yucatán (1979). More recently, García Bernal (1978) has reinterpreted some of their conclusions, and Robinson has carried out a detailed case study of native migration demographics in eighteenth-century Yucatán (1981).

Anthropological linguists have produced new translations and interpretations of Yucatec Maya literature and other Maya writings (Edmonson 1982, 1986; Edmonson and Bricker 1985; Hanks 1986; Hanks and Rice 1989). Bricker has written an innovative comparative study (1981) of the colonial experience of the entire southern Maya region, including both the highlands and lowlands, that emphasizes the importance of native interpretations of history.

The southern frontiers of Yucatán, including the Petén and Belize, were long neglected by colonial historians and ethnohistorians. Hellmuth (1972) called attention to the importance of the available documentation for this region, and several detailed studies have appeared in recent years (Jones 1986, 1989; de Vos 1980) that build on the earlier work of Scholes and Roys (1968) and emphasize the role of the frontier in the wider colonial setting. New English translations of important Spanish materials have made this region more accessible to general readers (e.g., Avendaño y Loyola 1987; Villagutierre Soto-Mayor 1983).

The rapprochement of historical archaeology and ethnohistorical research is a recent phenomenon in the Maya lowlands, but several studies posdating Thompson's (1990) pioneering efforts have recently begun to fill this void. Andrews (1981) provides a useful overview for Yucatán (see also Benavides and Andrews 1979; Miller and Farriss 1979). The combination of archaeological and ethnohistorical approaches has been particularly fruitful at the colonial Maya towns of Lamanai and Tipu in Belize (Graham and Bennett 1989; Graham, Jones, and Kautz 1985; Graham, Pendergast, and Jones 1989; Jones et al., 1986; Pendergast 1977, 1981, 1986a, 1986b).

The Maya of Highland and Pacific Guatemala and Chiapas

Archaeological studies of the Precolumbian period in these areas, which are considerably less numerous than those of the lowlands, are synthesized in the general archaeological summaries cited above. Carmack's overview of ethnohistoric, ethnographic, and archaeological sources for the Quiché Mayas (1973) marked a turning point for the study of the prehistoric-colonial transition period in the western highlands of Guatemala. Carmack's subsequent long-term interdisciplinary project generated new approaches to the integration of archaeological and ethnohistorical data (Carmack 1981; Carmack and Weeks 1981; Wallace and Carmack 1977).

Murdo MacLeod (1973) has written the landmark study of colonial Central America, including present-day Guatemala and Chiapas. MacLeod's (1983) and

Carmack's (1986) more recent syntheses of Indian–Spanish relations in Guatemala are excellent overviews of the state of research in this area (as is also Sherman 1983). Other investigations covering the Colonial period in Guatemala, some strongly interdisciplinary in focus, include work on the early encomienda and colonial land tenure (Rodríguez Becerra 1977; Solano y Pérez-Lila), the Pokom Maya (Miles 1957), the Tzutujil Mayas (Orellana 1984), and the Quiché Maya of Rabinal (Bertrand 1983; Ichon 1979–1982), Verapaz (Saint-Lu 1968; Feldman 1985), and Sacapulas (Hill and Monaghan 1987).

Historical demographic studies, the focus of much recent research on colonial Guatemala, reflect a variety of perspectives on native depopulation and resultant changes in Spanish–Indian interaction. MacLeod's summaries of this and related work (1982, 1984) can be consulted in conjunction with several other recent studies (Carmack et al. 1982; Lovell 1985; Lutz 1982; Zamora 1983).

Guatemalan native literatures, especially in the Quiché and Cakchiquel languages, have long been of intense interest to scholars of this region. In addition to the English translations of Recinos's Spanish translations (Recinos et al. 1950, 1974), there are more recent English translations of the Popol Vuh directly from the Quiché-language original (Edmonson 1971; Tedlock 1981) and a collection of conference papers on this important example of native literature (Carmack and Morales Santos 1983).

Chamberlain's earlier study (1947) of the conquest period in Chiapas remains a valuable source, but modern ethnohistorical studies of the Chiapas highlands have been slow to emerge. Gosner (1983) has recently examined the Tzeltal revolt of 1712 (see also Klein 1966; Wasserstrom 1980) and the role of native elites (Gosner 1984). The prolific but largely ahistorical Harvard University Chiapas project of the 1960s and 1970s focused almost entirely on contemporary ethnographic research, but members of that project have recently offered historically based interpretations of the colonial experience of such municipios as Chamula and Zinacantán (Rus and Wasserstrom 1980; Wasserstrom 1981, 1983). The proceedings of a 1986 conference on the history and prehistory of Chiapas also offer a useful overview (Centro de Investigaciones Regionales de Mesoamérica 1989).

Among the most interesting examples of the combined use of archaeological and ethnohistorical research strategies is Lee's study of the Coxoh Maya town of Coapa in Chiapas (Lee 1979; Lee and Markman 1979). Cacao-producing Colonial period Soconusco on the Pacific coast of Chiapas has also been studied recently from both documentary and archaeological perspectives by Gasco (1989).

Lower Central America

The non-Mesoamerican areas of Central America have received much less scholarly attention in recent times than the Maya-speaking regions, although MacLeod's seminal history of colonial Central America (1973) did much to stimulate new research in this area, and Sherman's *Forced Native Labor in Sixteenth Century Central America* (1979) has shed light not only on slavery and labor conditions but also on broader aspects of the Indian experience in colonial society from Costa Rica to Guatemala. Archaeological work, particularly for the late

Precontact and early Colonial periods, has been less extensive in these areas than in the Mesoamerican regions. For various general studies, see Stone (1941, 1957) on Honduras; Healy (1980) on Nicaragua; and Stone (1972) and Lange and Stone (1984) on Central America as a whole.

Various modern scholars have examined the native populations of lower Central America during the Colonial period. Stone's synthesis of earlier ethnohistorical work (1966) is still useful, as is Chamberlain's study of the conquest of Honduras and adjacent regions (1953). Some of the more recent studies report on the sixteenth-century Lenca in Honduras (Chapman 1978), the Toles (Jicaques) in eighteenth-century Honduras (Davidson 1985), the native populations of Costa Rica (Ferrero 1985), Nahua-speakers from Guatemala to Nicaragua (Fowler 1985, 1989), the historical demography of El Salvador (Fowler 1988), and native populations of the Comayagua and Sulaco valleys in Honduras (Lara Pinto 1985).

The geographer Linda Newson has written detailed analyses of the Indian experience under Spanish colonialism in eastern and western Nicaragua and in adjacent Nicoya (1987) and in Honduras (1986), drawing together the scattered primary and secondary sources. Newson's work, while focusing on the factors that resulted in the early decline of native populations, provides an overview of native groups and colonial systems of native governance and economic control (see also Stanislawski 1983).

Much modern research on colonial Costa Rica is contained in the proceedings of a conference held in San José in 1978 (Costa Rica, Comisión Nacional Organizadora 1978).

Chronology: Key Dates in the History of Southern Mesoamerica and Central America

1502	Christopher Columbus's explorations of the Bay of Honduras
1511	First documented discovery of Yucatán
1514	Arrival of Pedrarias Dávila in Panama and beginning of Spanish exploration of the Pacific coast of Central America
1517	First Spanish conflicts with the Mayas of Yucatán under Francisco Hernández de Córdoba
1519	Arrival of Hernán Cortés at Cozumel, Yucatán
1521	Conquest of Tenochtitlán, the Aztec capital, by Cortés
1523	Conquest of the Pacific plain of Nicaragua by Francisco Hernández de Córdoba; establishment of León and Granada.
1524	Pedro de Alvarado's conquest of Quiché and other provinces in Guatemala; his establishment of Santiago de los Caballeros; initial conquest of Chiapas by Luis Marín
1525–1526	Cortés's journey across interior Maya lowlands, including visit to Tah Itza
1527–1528	Francisco de Montejo's first expedition to conquer Yucatán; reconquest of Chiapas by Diego de Mazariegos and establishment of Ciudad Real
1542–1544	Founding of the villas of Yucatán (Mérida, Campeche, Valladolid, and Salamanca de Bacalar)

1543	Establishment of the Audiencia of Guatemala
1545–1550	Phase-out of the lower Central American Indian slave trade
1546	Native rebellion in eastern and southeastern Yucatán
1562	Franciscan auto-da-fe in Yucatán
1563	Establishment of Cartago, Costa Rica
1618–1619	Visits by Franciscan friars to Can Ek, the Itza ruler
1638	Rebellion of the Belize Maya
1695	Spanish conquest of Sac Balan, Chol Lacandon center, from Guatemala
1697	Spanish conquest of Tah Itza, from Yucatán
1712	Tzeltal revolt in Chiapas
1761	Rebellion at Quisteil in Yucatán
1785	Beginning of phase-out of encomiendas in Yucatán
1821	Declaration of Mexican independence from Spain
1823	Declaration of independence of United Provinces of Central America from Mexico
1847–48	Outbreak of Caste War of Yucatán
1862	British Honduras (Belize) declared a British Crown Colony

References

Adams, Robert M.
  1961 Changing Patterns of Territorial Organization in the Central Highlands of Chiapas. *American Antiquity* 26:341–360.
Andrews, Anthony P.
  1981 Historical Archaeology in Yucatan: A Preliminary Framework. *Historical Archaeology* 15(1):1–18.
Avendaño y Loyola, Andrés de
  1987 *Relation of Two Trips to Petén Made for the Conversion of the Heathen Ytzaex and Cehaches.* Edited by Frank E. Comparato and translated by Charles P. Bowditch and Guillermo Rivera. Labyrinthos, Culver City, Calif.
Benavides, C. Antonio, and Antonio P. Andrews
  1979 *Ecab: Poblado y provincia del siglo XVI en Yucatán.* Instituto Nacional de Antropología e Historia, Mexico.
Bertrand, Michel
  1983 *Terre, indianité, et colonisations au Guatemala: histoire de communautés Maya-Quiché de la region de Rabinal de leurs origines au XXème siècle.* Centre National de Recherche Scientifique and Ecole de Hautes Etudes en Sciences Sociales, Paris.
Bricker, Victoria R.
  1981 *The Indian Christ, the Indian King: The Historical Substrate of Maya Myth and Ritual.* University of Texas Press, Austin.
Carmack, Robert M.
  1973 *Quichean Civilization: The Ethnohistoric, Ethnographic and Archaeological Sources.* University of California Press, Berkeley.
  1981 *The Quiché Mayas of Utatlan: The Evolution of a Highland Guatemala Kingdom.* University of Oklahoma Press, Norman.
  1986 Ethnohistory of the Guatemalan Colonial Indian. In *Supplement to the Handbook of Middle American Indians*, vol. 4, pp. 55–70. University of Texas Press, Austin.
Carmack, Robert M., John Early, and Christopher Lutz
  1982 *The Historical Demography of Highland Guatemala.* State University of New York, Institute for Mesoamerican Studies, Albany.

Carmack, Robert M., and Francisco Morales Santos
1983 *Nuevas perspectivas sobre el Popol Vuh*. Editorial Piedra Santa, Guatemala.
Carmack, Robert M., and John M. Weeks
1981 The Archaeology and Ethnohistory of Utatlan: A Conjunctive Approach. *American Antiquity* 46(2):212–341. Centro de Investigaciones Regionales de Mesoamérica and Plumsock Mesoamerican Studies
1989 Special issue on the prehistory and history of Chiapas. *Mesoamérica* 10 (18).
Chamberlain, Robert S.
1947 *The Governorship of the Adelantado Francisco de Montejo in Chiapas, 1539–1544*. Carnegie Institution of Washington, Publication 574, Contribution 46. Washington, D.C.
1948 *The Conquest and Colonization of Yucatan, 1517–1550*. Carnegie Institution of Washington, Publication 582. Washington, D.C.
1951 *The Pre-Conquest Tribute and Service System of the Maya as Preparation for the Spanish Repartimiento-Encomienda in Yucatan*. University of Miami, Hispanic-American Studies 10. University of Miami Press, Coral Gables, Fla.
1953 *The Conquest and Colonization of Honduras, 1520–1550*. Carnegie Institution of Washington, Publication 598. Washington, D.C.
Chapman, Anne
1978 Los Lencas de Honduras en el siglo XVI. *Estudios Antropológicos e Históricos* 2:8–11.
Chase, Diane Z., and Arlen F. Chase
1986 Archaeological Insights on the Contact Period Lowland Maya. In *Los Mayas de los tiempos tardíos*, edited by Miguel Rivera and Andrés Ciudad, pp. 13–30. Publicaciones de la Sociedad Española de Estudios Mayas, no. 1. Madrid.
Chase, Arlen F., and Prudence M. Rice (editors)
1985 *The Lowland Maya Postclassic*. University of Texas Press, Austin.
Clendinnen, Inga
1987 *Ambivalent Conquests: Maya and Spaniard in Yucatan, 1517–1570*. Cambridge University Press, Cambridge.
Cline, Howard F.
1972–1975 *Guide to Ethnohistorical Sources*. Handbook of Middle American Indians, vols. 12–15. University of Texas Press, Austin.
Coe, Michael D.
1987 *The Maya*. Thames and Hudson, New York.
Cook, Sherburne F., and Woodrow Borah
1979 The Population of Yucatan, 1517–1960. In *Essays in Population History: Mexico and the Caribbean*, by Sherburne F. Cook and Woodrow Borah, vol. 2, pp. 1–179. University of California Press, Berkeley.
Costa Rica. Comisión Nacional Organizadora
1978 *Centenario de Gonzalo Fernández de Oviedo, 5th, Nicoya, Costa Rica, 1978*. Memoria del Congreso sobre el Mundo Centroamericano de su Tiempo, 24–25–26 y 27 de agosto de 1978. Comisión Nacional Organizadora, San José.
Davidson, William V.
1985 Geografía de los indígenas toles (jicaques) de Honduras en el siglo XVIII. *Mesoamérica* 6(9):58–90.
Edmonson, Munro S.
1971 *The Book of Counsel: The Popul Vuh of the Quiche Maya of Guatemala*. Tulane University, Middle American Research Institute Publication 35. New Orleans.
1982 *The Ancient Future of the Itza: The Book of Chilam Balam of Tizimin*. University of Texas Press, Austin.
1986 *Heaven Born Merida and Its Destiny: The Book of Chilam Balam of Chumayel*. University of Texas Press, Austin.
Edmonson, Munro S., and Victoria R. Bricker
1985 Yucatecan Mayan Literature. *Supplement to the Handbook of Middle American Indians*, vol. 3, pp. 44–63. University of Texas Press, Austin.

Farriss, Nancy M.

1983 Indians in Colonial Yucatan: Three Perspectives. In *Indians and Spaniards in Southeastern Mesoamerica: Essays on the History of Ethnic Relations*, edited by Murdo J. MacLeod and Robert Wasserstrom, pp. 1–39. University of Nebraska Press, Lincoln.

1984 *Maya Society under Colonial Rule: The Colonial Enterprise of Survival*. Princeton University Press, Princeton.

1986 Indians in Colonial Northern Yucatan. In *Supplement to the Handbook of Middle American Indians*, vol. 4, pp. 88–102. University of Texas Press, Austin.

1987 Remembering the Future, Anticipating the Past: History, Time and Cosmology among the Maya of Yucatan. *Comparative Studies in Society and History*, 29(3):566–593.

Feldman, Lawrence H.

1985 *Tumpline Economy: Production and Distribution Systems in Sixteenth Century Eastern Guatemala*. Labyrinthos Press, Culver City, Calif.

Ferrero, Luis

1985 *Entre el pasado y el futuro: las culturas aborígenes de Costa Rica del sector de tradición sudamericana a principios del siglo XVI*. Editorial Costa Rica, San José.

Floyd, Troy S.

1967 *The Anglo-Spanish Struggle for Mosquitía*. University of New Mexico Press, Albuquerque.

Fowler, William R.

1985 Ethnohistorical Sources on the Pipil-Nicarao of Central America: A Critical Analysis. *Ethnohistory* 32:37–62.

1988 La población nativa de El Salvador al momento de la conquista española. *Mesoamérica* 9(15):79–116.

1989 *The Cultural Evolution of Ancient Nahua Civilizations: The Pipil-Nicarao of Central America*. University of Oklahoma Press, Norman.

García Añoveros, Jesús María

1987 Don Pedro de Alvarado: las fuentes históricas, documentación, crónicas y bibliografía existente. *Mesoamérica* 8(13):243–282.

García Bernal, Manuela Cristina

1972 *La sociedad de Yucatán, 1700–1750*. Escuela de Estudios Hispano Americanos, Seville.

1978 *Yucatán: Población y encomienda bajo los Austrias*. Escuela de Estudios Hispano-Americanos, Seville.

Gasco, Janine

1989 Economic History of Ocelocalco, a Colonial Soconusco Town. In *Ancient Trade and Tribute: Economies of the Soconusco Region of Mesoamerica*, edited by Barbara Voorhies, pp. 304–325. University of Utah Press, Salt Lake City.

Gerhard, Peter

1979 *The Southeast Frontier of New Spain*. Princeton University Press, Princeton, N.J.

González Cicero, Stella Maria

1978 *Perspectiva religiosa en Yucatán, 1517–1571: Yucatán, los franciscanos y el primer obispo fray Francisco de Toral*. Colegio de Mexico, Mexico.

Gosner, Kevin

1983 *Soldiers of the Virgin: An Ethnohistorical Analysis of the Tzeltal Revolt of 1712 in Highland Chiapas*. Ph.D. dissertation, University of Pennsylvania. Ann Arbor: University Microfilms.

1984 Las elites indígenas en los Altos de Chiapas, 1524–1714. *Historia Mexicana* 33(4):405–423.

Graham, Elizabeth, and Sharon Bennett

1989 The 1986–87 Excavations at Negroman-Tipu, Belize. *Mexicon* 11:114–117.

Graham, Elizabeth, Grant D. Jones, and Robert R. Kautz

1985 Archaeology and Ethnohistory on a Spanish Colonial Frontier: The Macal-Tipu

Project in Western Belize. In *The Lowland Maya Postclassic*, edited by Arlen F. Chase and Prudence M. Rice, pp. 206–214. University of Texas Press, Austin.

Graham, Elizabeth, David M. Pendergast, and Grant D. Jones
1989 On the Fringes of Conquest: Maya–Spanish Contact in Colonial Belize. *Science* 246(4935):1254–1259.

Hammond, Norman
1982 *Ancient Maya Civilization*. Cambridge University Press, New York and Cambridge.

Hanks, William F.
1986 Authenticity and Ambivalence in the Text: A Colonial Maya Case. *American Ethnologist*, 13(4): 721–744.

Hanks, William F., and Don S. Rice
1989 *Word and Image in Mayan Culture: Explorations in Language, History and Representation*. University of Utah Press, Salt Lake City.

Healy, Paul F.
1980 *Archaeology of the Rivas Region, Nicaragua*. Wilfrid Laurier University Press, Waterloo, Ontario, Canada.

Hellmuth, Nicholas M.
1972 Progreso y notas sobre la investigación etnohistórica de las tierras bajas mayas de los siglos XVI a XIX. *América Indígena* 32:172–244.

Helms, Mary W.
1975 *Middle America: A Culture History of Heartland and Frontiers*. Prentice-Hall, Englewood Cliffs, N.J.

Henderson, John S.
1978 *The World of the Ancient Maya*. Cornell University Press, Ithaca, N.Y.

Hill, Robert M., II and John Monaghan
1987 *Continuities in Highland Maya Social Organization: Ethnohistory in Sacapulas, Guatemala*. University of Pennsylvania Press, Philadelphia.

Hunt, Marta Espejo-Ponce
1976 Processes of the Development of Yucatan, 1600–1700. In *Provinces of Early Mexico*, edited by Ida Altman and James Lockhart, pp. 33–62. University of California Latin American Center, Los Angeles.

Ichon, Alain
1979–1982 *Rabinal et la vallée moyenne du Rio Chixoy: Baja Vera Paz, Guatemala*. Cahiers de la Recherche Coopérative sur Programme No. 500. Centre National de la Recherche Scientifique, Institut d'Ethnologie, Paris.

Jones, Grant D.
1986 The Southern Maya Lowlands during Spanish Colonial Times. In *Supplement to the Handbook of Middle American Indians*, vol. 4, pp. 71–87. University of Texas Press, Austin.
1989 *Maya Resistance to Spanish Rule: Time and History on a Colonial Frontier*. University of New Mexico Press, Albuquerque.

Jones, Grant D. (editor)
1977 *Anthropology and History in Yucatán*. University of Texas Press, Austin.

Jones, Grant D., Robert R. Kautz, and Elizabeth Graham
1986 Tipu: A Maya Town on the Spanish Colonial Frontier. *Archaeology* 39(1):40–47.

Klein, Herbert S.
1966 Peasant Communities in Revolt: The Tzeltal Republic of 1712. *Pacific Historical Review* 35(3):247–263.

Lange, Frederick W., and Doris Stone (editors)
1984 *The Archaeology of Lower Central America*. University of New Mexico Press, Albuquerque.

Lara Pinto, Gloria
1985 Apuntes sobre la afiliación cultural de los pobladores indígenas de los valles de Comayagua y Sulaco. *Mesoamérica* 6(9):45–57.

Lee, Thomas A., Jr.
  1979 Coapa, Chiapas: A Sixteenth-Century Coxoh Maya Village on the Camino Real. In *Maya Archaeology and Ethnohistory*, edited by Norman Hammond, pp. 208–222. University of Texas Press, Austin.
Lee, Thomas A., Jr., and Sidney D. Markman
  1979 Coxoh Maya Acculturation in Colonial Chiapas: A Necrotic Archaeological-Ethnohistorical Model. In *Actes du XLIIe Congrès des Américanistes*, vol. 8, pp. 57–66. Société des Américanistes, Paris.
Lovell, W. George
  1985 *Conquest and Survival in Colonial Guatemala: A Historical Geography of the Cuchumatán Highlands, 1500–1821*. McGill-Queen's University Press, Toronto.
  1988 Surviving Conquest: The Maya of Guatemala in Historical Perspective. *Latin American Research Review*, 23(2):25–57.
Lutz, Christopher H.
  1982 *Historia sociodemográfica de Santiago de Guatemala, 1541–1773*. Centro de Investigaciones Regionales de Mesoamérica, Guatemala.
MacLeod, Murdo J.
  1973 *Spanish Central America: A Socioeconomic History, 1520–1720*. University of California Press, Berkeley and Los Angeles.
  1982 An Outline of Colonial Central American Demographics: Sources, Yields, and Possibilities. In *The Historical Demography of Highland Guatemala*, edited by Robert M. Carmack, John Early, and Christopher Lutz, pp. 3–18. State University of New York, Albany.
  1983 Ethnic Relations and Indian Society in the Province of Guatemala ca. 1620–ca. 1800. In *Spaniards and Indians in Southeastern Mesoamerica: Essays on the History of Ethnic Relations*, edited by Murdo J. MacLeod and Robert Wasserstrom, pp. 189–214. University of Nebraska Press, Lincoln.
  1984 Modern Research on the Demography of Colonial Central America: A Bibliographical Essay. *Latin American Population History* 3:23–29.
MacLeod, Murdo J., and Robert Wasserstrom (editors)
  1983 *Spaniards and Indians in Southeastern Mesoamerica: Essays on the History of Ethnic Relations*. University of Nebraska Press, Lincoln.
Markman, Sidney David
  1977 *Colonial Central America: a Bibliography Including Materials on Art and Architecture, Cultural, Economic, and Social History, Ethnohistory, Geography, Government, Indigenous Writings, Maps and Plans, Urbanization, Bibliographic and Archival Documentary Sources.* Arizona State University Center for Latin American Studies, Tempe.
Means, Philip A.
  1917 *History of the Spanish Conquest of Yucatan and of the Itzas*. Peabody Museum of American Archaeology and Ethnology, Papers 7. Cambridge, Mass.
Miles, Suzanne W.
  1957 *The Sixteenth-Century Pokom-Maya: A Documentary Analysis of Social Structure and Archaeological Setting*. Transactions of the American Philosophical Society, vol. 47 (n.s.), part 4, pp. 733–781. Philadelphia.
  1965 Summary of Preconquest Ethnology of the Guatemala-Chiapas Highlands and Pacific Slopes. In *Handbook of Middle American Indians*, vol. 2, pp. 276–287. University of Texas Press, Austin.
Miller, Arthur G., and Nancy M. Farriss
  1979 Religious Syncretism in Colonial Yucatan: The Archaeological and Ethnohistorical Evidence from Tancah, Quintana Roo. In *Maya Archaeology and Ethnohistory*, edited by Norman Hammond and Gordon R. Willey, pp. 223–240. University of Texas Press, Austin.
Morley, Sylvanus, and Robert W. Sharer
  1983 *The Ancient Maya*. Stanford University Press, Stanford.

Moseley, E. H., and E. D. Terry
  1980 *Yucatan: A World Apart*. University of Alabama Press, Tuscaloosa.
Newson, Linda
  1986 *The Cost of Conquest: Indian Decline in Honduras under Spanish Rule*. Dellplain Latin American Studies, Westview Press, Boulder, Colo.
  1987 *Indian Survival in Colonial Nicaragua*. University of Oklahoma Press, Norman.
Orellana, Sandra Lee
  1984 *The Tzutujil Mayas: Continuity and Change, 1250–1630*. University of Oklahoma Press, Norman.
Patch, Robert W.
  1985 Agrarian Change in Eighteenth-Century Yucatán. *Hispanic American Historical Review* 65(1):21–49.
Pendergast, David M.
  1977 Royal Ontario Museum Excavation: Finds at Lamanai, Belize. *Archaeology* 30:129–131.
  1981 Lamanai, Belize: Summary of Excavation Results, 1974–1980. *Journal of Field Archaeology* 8:19–53.
  1986a Stability through Change: Lamanai, Belize, from the Ninth Century to the Seventeenth Century. In *Late Lowland Maya Civilization: Classic to Postclassic*, edited by Jeremy A. Sabloff and E. Wyllys Andrews V, pp. 223–249. University of New Mexico Press, Albuquerque.
  1986b Under Spanish Rule: The Final Chapter in Lamanai's Maya History. *Belcast Journal of Belizean Affairs* 3(1&2):1–7. Belize College of Arts, Science, and Technology, Belize City.
Pollock, H. E. D., Ralph L. Roys, Tatiana Prokouriakoff, and Ledyard A. Smith
  1962 *Mayapan, Yucatan, Mexico*. Carnegie Institution of Washington, Publication 619. Washington, D.C.
Radell, David
  1976 The Indian Slave Trade and Population of Nicaragua during the Sixteenth Century. In *The Native Population of the Americas in 1492*, edited by William M. Denevan, pp. 67–76. University of Wisconsin Press, Madison.
Recinos, Adrián, Delia Goetz, and Dionisio José Chonay
  1974 *The Annals of the Cakchiquels. Title of the Lords of Totonicapán*. University of Oklahoma Press, Norman.
Recinos, Adrián, Delia Goetz, and Sylvanus G. Morley
  1950 *Popol Vuh. The Sacred Book of the Ancient Quiche Maya*. University of Oklahoma Press, Norman.
Redfield, Robert, and Alfonso Villa Rojas
  1934 *Chan Kom: A Maya Village*. Carnegie Institution of Washington, Publication 448. Washington, D.C.
Reed, Nelson
  1964 *The Caste War of Yucatan*. Stanford University Press, Stanford.
Rivera, Miguel, and Andrés Ciudad
  1986 *Los mayas de los tiempos tardíos*. Publicaciones de la Sociedad Española de Estudios Mayas, no. 1. Madrid.
Robinson, David J.
  1981 Indian Migration in Eighteenth-Century Yucatan: The Open Nature of the Closed Corporate Community. In *Studies in Spanish American Population History*, edited by David J. Robinson, pp. 149–173. Westview Press, Boulder, Colo.
Rodríguez Becerra, Salvador
  1977 *Encomienda y conquista: Los inicios de la colonización en Guatemala*. Seminario de Antropología Americana, Universidad de Sevilla, Seville.
Roys, Ralph L.
  1939 *The Titles of Ebtun*. Carnegie Institution of Washington, Publication 505. Washington, D.C.

1943 *The Indian Background of Colonial Yucatan.* Carnegie Institution of Washington, Publication 548. Washington D.C.

1952 *Conquest Sites and the Subsequent Destruction of Maya Architecture in the Interior of Northern Yucatan.* Carnegie Institution of Washington, Contributions to American Anthropology and History, no. 11, pp. 129–182. Washington, D.C.

1957 *The Political Geography of the Yucatan Maya.* Carnegie Institution of Washington, Publication 613. Washington, D.C.

1962 Literary Sources for the History of Mayapan. In *Mayapan, Yucatan, Mexico,* by Harry E. D. Pollock et al., pp. 24–86. Carnegie Institution of Washington, Publication 619. Washington, D.C.

1965 Lowland Maya Native Society at Spanish Contact. In *Handbook of Middle American Indians,* vol. 3, pp. 659–678. University of Texas Press, Austin.

1967 *The Book of Chilam Balam of Chumayel.* Reprinted. University of Oklahoma Press, Norman. Originally published 1933, Carnegie Institution of Washington, Washington, D.C.

Rus, Jan, and Robert Wasserstrom

1980 Civil-Religious Hierarchies in Central Chiapas: A Critical Perspective. *American Ethnologist* 7(3):466–478.

Saint-Lu, André

1968 *La Vera Paz: Esprit evangelique et colonisation.* Centre de Recherche Hispanique, Paris.

Scholes, France V., and Eleanor B. Adams

1938 *Don Diego Quijada, Alcade Mayor de Yucatán, 1561–1565.* Editorial Porrúa, Mexico.

Scholes, France V., and Ralph L. Roys

1968 *The Maya Chontal Indians of Acalan-Tixchel: A Contribution to the History and Ethnography of the Yucatan Peninsula.* Reprinted. University of Oklahoma Press, Norman. Originally published 1948, Carnegie Institution of Washington, Washington, D.C.

Sherman, William L.

1979 *Forced Native Labor in Sixteenth Century Central America.* University of Nebraska Press, Lincoln.

1983 Some Aspects of Change in Guatemalan Society, 1470–1620. In *Spaniards and Indians in Southeastern Mesoamerica: Essays on the History of Ethnic Relations,* edited by Murdo J. MacLeod and Robert Wasserstrom, pp. 169–188. University of Nebraska Press, Lincoln.

Solano y Pérez-Lila, Francisco de

1977 *Tierra y sociedad en el reino de Guatemala.* Colección "Realidad Nuestra," no. 4. Editorial Universitaria, Guatemala, C.A.

Stanislawski, Dan

1983 *The Transformation of Nicaragua, 1519–1548.* University of California Press, Berkeley.

Stephens, John L.

1963 *Incidents of Travel in Yucatan.* Reprinted. Dover, New York. Originally published 1841, Harper & Brothers, New York.

1969 *Incidents of Travel in Central America, Chiapas and Yucatan.* Reprinted. Dover, New York. Originally published 1843, Harper & Brothers, New York.

Stone, Doris

1941 *Archaeology of the North Coast of Honduras.* Memoirs of the Peabody Museum of Archaeology and Ethnology 9, no. 1. Harvard University, Cambridge, Mass.

1957 *The Archaeology of Central and Southern Honduras.* Papers of the Peabody Museum of Archaeology and Ethnology 49, No. 3. Harvard University, Cambridge, Mass.

1966 Synthesis of Lower Central American Ethnohistory. In *Handbook of Middle American Indians,* vol. 4, pp. 209–233. University of Texas Press, Austin.

1972 *Pre-Columbian Man Finds Central America.* Peabody Museum Press, Cambridge, Mass.

Tedlock, Dennis
1981 *Popol Vuh: The Definitive Edition of the Mayan Book of the Dawn of Life and the Glories of Gods and Kings*. Simon and Schuster, New York.

Thompson, Donald E.
1954 *Maya Paganism and Christianity: A History of the Fusion of Two Religions*. Tulane University, Department of Middle American Research, Publications 19, pp. 1–36. New Orleans.

Thompson, J. Eric S.
1990 *Maya History and Religion*. Reprinted. University of Oklahoma Press, Norman. Originally published 1970.
1977 Proposal for Constituting a Maya Subgroup, Cultural and Linguistic, in the Petén and Adjacent Regions. In *Anthropology and History in Yucatán*, edited by Grant D. Jones, pp. 3–42. University of Texas Press, Austin.

Thompson, Philip C.
1978 *Tekanto in the Eighteenth Century*. Ph.D. dissertation, Tulane University. University Microfilms, Ann Arbor.

Tozzer, Alfred M.
1907 *A Comparative Study of the Mayas and the Lancandons*. Macmillan, New York.

Tozzer, Alfred M. (editor)
1941 *Landa's Relación de las cosas de Yucatán*, edited and translated by Alfred M. Tozzer. Papers of the Peabody Museum of American Archaeology and Ethnology 18. Harvard University, Cambridge, Mass.

Villa Rojas, Alfonso
1945 *The Maya of East Central Quintana Roo*. Carnegie Institution of Washington, Publication 559. Washington, D.C.
1969 The Maya of Yucatan. In *Handbook of Middle American Indians*, vol. 7, pp. 244–275. University of Texas Press, Austin.

Villagutierre Soto-Mayor, Juan de
1983 *History of the Conquest of the Province of the Itzá*, edited by Frank E. Comparato and translated by Robert D. Wood. Labyrinthos, Culver City, Calif.

Vogt, Evon Z.
1969 The Maya: An Introduction. In *Handbook of Middle American Indians*, vol. 7, pp. 21–29. University of Texas Press, Austin.

Vos, Jan de
1980 *La paz de Dios y del Rey: la conquista de la selva lacandona, 1525– 1821*. Fonapas, Chiapas, México.

Wallace, Dwight T., and Robert M. Carmack
1977 *Archaeology and Ethnohistory of the Central Quiche*. Institute for Mesoamerican Studies, Monographs 1. State University of New York, Albany.

Wasserstrom, Robert
1980 Ethnic Violence and Indigenous Protest: The Tzeltal (Maya) Rebellion of 1712. *Journal of Latin American Studies* 12(1):1–19.
1981 *Class and Society in Central Chiapas*. University of California Press, Berkeley.
1983 Spaniards and Indians in Colonial Chiapas, 1528–1790. In *Spaniards and Indians in Southeastern Mesoamerica: Essays on the History of Ethnic Relations*, edited by Murdo J. MacLeod and Robert Wasserstrom, pp. 92–126. University of Nebraska Press, Lincoln.

West, Robert C.
1964 The Natural Regions of Middle America. In *Handbook of Middle American Indians*, vol. 1, pp. 363–383. University of Texas Press, Austin.

Zamora, Elías
1983 Conquista y crisis demográfica: la población indígena del occidente de Guatemala en el siglo XVI. *Mesoamérica* 4(6):291–328.

Chapter 8 ■

William R. Fowler, Jr.

The Political Economy of Indian Survival in Sixteenth-Century Izalco, El Salvador

The Izalco region of western El Salvador was invaded by Spanish forces in 1524. By the early 1530s, Izalco was functioning as a key region in the Spanish colonial empire. Spanish domination of the Izalco Pipil resulted in demographic, economic, and cultural catastrophe. During the sixteenth century, Izalco went from one of the richest regions in Central America to one of the poorest. The cacao industry, which was the leading source of wealth for the crown and colonists, was a shambles by the end of the century. Reeling from epidemic disease and bearing the brunt of vicious exploitation by encomenderos, royal officials, clerics, and merchants, the local population struggled for survival against extremely long odds.

Yet, those Indians who survived the debacle somehow maintained a vigorous native cultural tradition. Traditional modes of production were preserved, while the Izalco Pipil simultaneously participated actively in the regional political economy. Although colonial tribute demands more or less leveled the high degree of social stratification that existed before the conquest, it seems that some degree of stratification was maintained. As with all other indigenous groups facing colonial exploitation, the strategies for survival that the Pipil worked out were vitally influenced by continuities in economic, social, and political structure from their pre-Columbian past. An important element in the political economy of their past was the production and exchange of cacao.

Because Izalco was one of the foremost regions in the world for the production of cacao (Bergmann 1969), the first monocultural source of wealth in colonial Central America, it became one of the richest and most renowned areas of the Spanish empire (Fowler 1987; MacLeod 1973:80–95). Its encomiendas (royal grants of Indians obligated to give service, tribute payment in kind, or both [Gibson 1964:58]) were among the most coveted, being assigned to influential friends and relatives of Alonso de Maldonado, the first president of the Audiencia (circuit court and its territory) of Guatemala. Its indigenous inhabitants—the producers of the wealth—were among the most heavily exploited of the empire.

No one would deny the brutal exploitation of Izalco's Indians during the sixteenth century. Yet the Indians themselves did not simply acquiesce and accept such treatment as some kind of divine plan. In their struggle for survival, they attempted to adapt to their new circumstances. In order to study the context for this adaptation, I provide some details on Izalco Pipil society at Spanish contact, the conquest, the colonial cacao industry, population collapse, forced labor and tribute, and the new lords of the land—encomenderos, royal officials, merchants, and secular clergy.

The Izalco Pipil at Spanish Contact

The native inhabitants of Izalco at the time of the conquest were Nahua-speaking Pipil whose ancestors had migrated from central and southern Mexico to Central America sometime during the Postclassic period (A.D. 900–1524). In the early sixteenth century, the Pipil were densely settled in the Escuintla region of southeastern Guatemala and in most of western and central El Salvador (Fowler 1983, 1988, 1989:51–65).

It seems likely that several separate movements or "waves" of Pipil migration to Central America occurred during the Postclassic (Fowler 1989:39–49). We do not have precise data on the time of the Pipil intrusion in the Izalco region. Archaeological sites with Early Postclassic (A.D. 900–1200) occupation in the Balsam Coast region, just to the south and east of Izalco, show close material culture ties with contemporary complexes in other regions of El Salvador that have been attributed to the Pipil (Fowler et al. 1989). But it is entirely possible that the Pipil did not take over the Izalco region until later in the Postclassic.

Once established in the western Pacific region of El Salvador (in the modern departments of Ahuachapan and Sonsonate), the Pipil of Izalco formed one of the most powerful pre-Hispanic regional states of southeastern Mesoamerica. At the time of the conquest, Izalco was the center of a small, independent polity, similar in structure to the Postclassic city-states of central Mexico before the foundation of the Aztec empire (Hodge 1984). The pre-Columbian Izalco state comprised about 15 principal settlements within its domain, with a territory of some 2,500 square kilometers and an estimated population of 54,000 in 1519

(Fowler 1990). The principal cacao-producing towns were Izalco, Caluco, Tacuscalco, and Naolingo (Figure 8–1).

Izalco was often referred to in sixteenth-century documents as "Tecpan Izalco." As Pedro Carrasco (1976:21–24) and others have shown, the Nahua term *tecpan* referred to the territory and dependents of a native lord; in other words, it was the seat of a noble lineage. Indeed, I believe that the very name "Pipil" (from Nahua *pipiltin*, plural of *pilli*, "noble") should be understood as a reference to noble lineages. As in central Mexico, the noble lineages among the Pipil had important political and economic functions that played an essential role in social stratification. The lineage was internally stratified among its titular head, nobles, and commoners subject to the noble house. Pipil commoners were members of *calpultin* (plural of *calpulli*), which were politico-territorial divisions that, also as in central Mexico, probably served as units of tribute collection and constituted the basic unit of production above the level of the household (Hicks 1982).

The Conquest

The conquest of the Pipil was directed by Pedro de Alvarado, who with 250 Spanish troops and some 5,000 to 6,000 native auxiliaries entered the province of Izalco in June 1524 and engaged Pipil troops in the battle of Acajutla, "donde

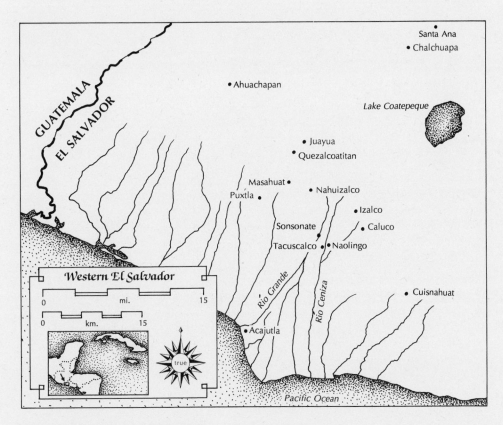

Figure 8–1. Map of western El Salvador.

bate la mar del sur" (Alvarado 1934:278). This was a characteristically brutal encounter. Alvarado reported that all the Pipil troops in this battle were killed (1934:279). Spanish losses were also heavy. Alvarado himself was among those permanently injured by Pipil arrows.

Five days after the battle of Acajutla, the Pipil fielded another army large enough to face the invaders again at Tacuscalco, only about 8 kilometers from Izalco. The outcome of this battle was another "great massacre and punishment" (Alvarado 1934:279), and thereafter the Pipil refused to meet the Spaniards on the open field, preferring to fight only in guerrilla skirmishes.

The battles of Acajutla and Tacuscalco appear to have been decisive for the Izalco Pipil. Unlike the neighboring Pipil of Cuscatlan, they did not join in the general uprising of 1526 (Barón Castro 1950:66), and there is no further evidence of even isolated resistance to the imposition of Spanish rule in the Izalco region.

The swiftness of the conquest of Izalco can be attributed to the extreme loss of lives in the two major battles as well as to the devastating impact of epidemic disease (see below). The smallpox epidemic that swept through Guatemala in 1520–1521 (Crosby 1972:47–51, 1986:200; Dobyns 1983:Table 1; Lovell 1988:7–10; MacLeod 1973:98) probably struck the Pipil as well. Although Newson (1987:119) maintains that there is no evidence of European disease spreading further south than Guatemala before 1527, it is extremely unlikely that El Salvador was spared this scourge (Crosby 1972:47–58; Dobyns 1983:11–14). Possibly involving pulmonary plague as well as smallpox (MacLeod 1973:19, 40–41), this was a "virgin soil epidemic" (Crosby 1976), meaning that affected populations had no previous contact with the pathogens and thus were immunologically defenseless. MacLeod (1973:41) has estimated that at least one-third of the population of highland Guatemala died in this epidemic. Assuming that the same proportion of the population perished in the Izalco region, which seems very likely, then epidemic disease, the "shock troops of the conquest" (Ashburn 1947:80), had probably weakened the Pipil of Izalco to the point that the high mortality of the battles of Acajutla and Tacuscalco was enough to break their resistance.

The Colonial Cacao Industry

Spanish conquistadors who settled in Central America first sought wealth through slaves, gold, and silver (MacLeod 1973:46–63). But most of them soon realized that the future lay in commercial agriculture. The sixteenth-century cacao boom in Central America—first in Soconusco, Chiapas (Mexico), later in Izalco—was largely a response to the collapse of slaving and mining as the basis of Spanish wealth immediately after the conquest. Cacao in Izalco had the advantage that it required no initial investment of capital: The plantations were already there, awaiting intensification of production. The appeal of cacao in Central America was also enhanced, from around 1530 until 1550, by an abundance of coerced cash-crop labor.

Spanish entrepreneurs in the region immediately recognized the potential value of cacao as a cash crop, and by 1535 small amounts of cacao were being exported from Izalco to Mexico (MacLeod 1973:80). By the 1540s and 1550s, the

Izalco cacao plantations had expanded to such an extent that the area was hailed as one of the richest in Central America (Marroquín 1542; Torre 1553; Robledo 1556; López de Yrarraga 1556). Early colonial travelers, historians, and royal officials extolled the region for exceptional cacao production (Benzoni [1565] 1857:158; López de Velasco [1572] 1894:296; García de Palacio [1576] 1983:74–75; Pineda [1594] 1925:352; Vázquez de Espinosa [1622–1630] 1969:pt. 1, bk. 5, ch. 12, p. 155).

In 1564, Francisco de Magaña, alcalde mayor (regional governor) of the newly settled Villa de la Santísima Trinidad de Sonsonate, a Spanish merchant settlement in the region, wrote that in a typical year 15 ships sailed from the nearby port of Acajutla to New Spain and that 25,000–30,000 *cargas* of cacao were shipped annually.[1] This trade was worth a sum of about 200,000 pesos annually (Magaña 1564). The oidor (associate justice) Diego García de Palacio (1983:75) reported in 1576 that more than 50,000 cargas of cacao were produced annually by only four of the towns of the Izalco region (Izalco, Caluco, Naolingo, and Tacuscalco).

The effect of an increased demand for cacao was intensified production. But before intensification was possible, changes in land tenure were necessary. According to both Spanish and Indian witnesses in a 1580–1581 land dispute between the towns of Naolingo and Tacuscalco, agricultural lands, especially cacao orchards and maize fields, had been held in common by these settlements in ancient (presumably late pre-Hispanic and early colonial) times. By the early 1580s, however, the lands in question were divided into numerous small plots owned by mestizos and mulattoes, as well as Indians (Indians of Tacuscalco 1580–1581). The orchards around Izalco and Caluco were divided into hundreds of small holdings, but these were owned almost exclusively by Indians (Pleitos contra Diego de Guzmán 1582–1585; Vissita y tasación de Caluco 1582).

MacLeod (1973:97, 126–127) has observed that sixteenth-century encomenderos of Central America were more interested in control of labor than in control or ownership of land. This was true in general, but some encomenderos of the Izalco region, especially those whose grants were relatively small, did acquire land, either through purchase or usurpation, and planted cacao and other crops. A common tactic was to purchase a small plot and then fence off more land than had actually been bought. Gomez Díaz de la Reguera, for example, the renegade encomendero of Naolingo, bought land from the Indians of Tacuscalco and then forcibly occupied an adjacent plot of land belonging to don Juan Chiname, the cacique of Tacuscalso (Indians of Tacuscalco 1580– 1581; Testamento de don Juan Chiname 1567:f. 1295v.).

Cacao cultivation was intensified in the 1560s. Many milpas of maize were converted to cacao, and the orchards were planted more densely than ever. Tacuscalco changed maize lands over to cacao in about 1566 (Indians of Tacuscalco 1580–1586). Gaspar de Cepeda, the encomendero of Nahuizalco, bought land near that town, which was already planted in cacao, and proceeded to plant more. Upon his death in 1567, assessors counted more than 20,000 cacao trees in three orchards (Cepeda 1567:f. 1023). The trees reportedly were planted only 7 to 8 feet apart, when they should have been spaced at least 12 feet apart.

Witnesses stated that because the trees were too densely packed and there was not enough irrigation water, they did not yield much cacao (Cepeda 1567:f. 1024v.). Indians also intensified production in an effort both to meet tribute demands and to produce a surplus for the market. Unlike some Spanish producers, however, they did not have the means to tend adequately the vast numbers of trees or to replace old ones. In Caluco, for example, it was reported that although an Indian may have had more than 10,000 trees planted, owing to a local labor shortage, he could not have tended more than 2,000 of them (Vissita y tasación de Caluco 1582:f. 9). The labor shortage was brought on by the sudden collapse of the local population in the sixteenth century.

Population Collapse

Epidemic disease had a devastating impact on population levels in the Izalco region. Three waves of virulent disease decimated the native population of Central America in the sixteenth century: the previously discussed preconquest smallpox pandemic of 1520–1521, *cocoliztli* or *gucumatz* (possibly pneumonic plague or typhus) in 1545–1548, and smallpox and typhus in 1576–1577 (Lovell 1985:148, 1988; MacLeod 1973:98). Each struck with tremendous mortality; the Izalco region was particularly hard hit, and the repercussions on the cacao industry were immediate. The precipitous decline of the Izalco Pipil population in the sixteenth century has been documented elsewhere (Fowler 1990), so here I present only a summary.

By 1548, the Izalco population had already declined so drastically that workers to tend the cacao orchards were in very short supply. The remedy for this situation was to import labor from other regions, especially the Verapaz region of Guatemala. From the 1540s until the 1570s, when this outside source of labor was exhausted, many laborers were brought in (MacLeod 1973:92). Encomenderos and royal officials conspired to enter these newcomers on the tribute rolls and thereby to inflate the number of tributaries. Despite the protests of a number of priests, the newcomers were often forced to marry in Izalco so that they would be counted as full tributaries (Villagómez 1580; García de Valverde 1584:f. 7).

What was the actual rate of population decline in the Izalco cacao towns? President Cerrato officially registered 400 tributaries in Caluco, 200 in Naolingo, and 100 in Tacuscalco in the 1549 tasación; the number of tributaries in Izalco was not recorded (Tasaciones de los naturales 1548–fl 1551:ff. 82, 82v., 86, 111v.). These figures appear to be substantial underestimates (Fowler 1989:143).

Many Indian, Ladino, and Spanish witnesses were called to testify on tribute and native population in the Izalco region in an exhaustive investigation of Diego de Guzmán, the encomendero of Izalco in the late sixteenth century (Pleitos contra Diego de Guzmán 1582–1585). Witnesses in the Guzmán investigation stated that in 1549 Izalco had 700 to 960 tributaries, Caluco 650 to 800, and Naolingo 350 to 400 (1582–1585:ff. 1429–1493). Tacuscalco is not mentioned in these proceedings.

The witnesses, all of whom knew the towns well, were asked to compare past and present population levels. A Spanish priest stated that only about one-twentieth of the Indians registered in 1549 survived in 1582. Another priest stated that Naolingo had 350 tributaries in 1568, and only 40 in 1582. The Indian cacique of Caluco recalled that his town had 700 to 800 tributaries in 1562, and only about 20 of these survived in 1582. An Indian witness from Izalco declared that his town had 800 tributaries in 1549, and no more than 60 survived in 1582. Another Indian witness from Izalco said that of approximately 800 tributaries in 1549, only 50 survived in 1582. Thus, consistent testimony sets the reduction of the native Pipil population of Izalco from 1549 to 1582 at around 90 to 98 percent. Most of the witnesses pointed out that the majority of the population of the principal cacao towns of Izalco were recent arrivals.

According to President Diego García de Valverde, who must have based his estimates on the testimony from the Diego de Guzmán investigation as well as the reports of his oidores and other reliable observers, the town of Izalco had 800 or 900 tributaries at the time of the Cerrato tasación, of which only 100 survived in 1584, but their number was augmented by 400 or 500 outsiders who had been brought in at the behest of the encomendero.[2] Of the 700 tributaries in Caluco at midcentury, Valverde reckoned that 60 survived, and they were complemented by 240 recent arrivals. The 600 original tributaries of Naolingo in 1549 had declined to 40 or 50 in 1584, but their number was increased by about 250 immigrant laborers (García de Valverde 1584:f. 7v.). The local work force therefore numbered just over 1,000 Indians, but this number was declining fast, and Valverde predicted that the province would be completely depopulated within 10 years (MacLeod 1973:92). He was exaggerating, but the decline did indeed continue. By 1636, Naolingo had only 70 to 80 tributaries, and Tacuscalco had only 9 or 10 (Autos e información 1636:f. 7v.).

Forced Labor and Tribute

Conquistadors and early settlers in the Spanish colonies were rewarded for their services to the Crown with encomiendas. Cacao production in Izalco was "preadapted" to the encomienda system. The plantations were already in place at the time of the conquest, and demand for the crop was on the rise. Since cacao had been an object of precolonial tribute, Indian producers were already accustomed to this sort of payment. What they were not accustomed to was the increase in tribute demands caused by pressures of the world market and the greed of the encomenderos.

A fairly precise idea of the increase in tribute demand may be gained from the case of Ateos, a Pipil town just to the east of the Izalco region. In 1532, half the inhabitants of Ateos paid their encomendero 20 xiquipiles of cacao tribute annually (Relación Marroquín 1968:222). By 1548, these villagers were ordered to pay the same encomendero 60 xiquipiles annually (Tasaciones de los naturales 1548–1551:f. 6v.). The latter assessment was made by Alonso López de Cerrato, the reformist president of the audiencia, known for his efforts to moderate excessive tributes (see Fowler 1989:26–27, 142–145; Lovell et al. 1984; MacLeod 1973:116–117; Sherman 1979:12, 153–188, 241), yet he increased tributes in this town by 300 percent over the 1532 levels.

In spite of the drastic native population decline, especially in 1545–1548 and in 1576–1577, Cerrato and other officials held tribute amounts constant in the Izalco region, and in some cases tributes were even increased. The earliest tasación (tribute assessment) of Izalco, made by Bishop Francisco Marroquín and President Alonso de Maldonado some time between 1536 and 1541 (Rodríguez Becerra 1977:117–118), required the town to pay 1,000 xiquipiles of cacao annually to its first encomendero (Pleitos contra Diego de Guzmán 1583:f. 1656). Caluco probably paid an equal amount to its first encomendero (1583:ff. 2180–2182v.).

According to the Cerrato tasaciones, 13 of the 15 Izalco towns paid tribute in cacao in 1549 (Fowler 1989:164). The most heavily assessed towns were Izalco, Caluco, Naolingo, and Tacuscalco. Both Izalco and Caluco were assessed 1,000 xiquipiles of cacao by Cerrato, while Naolingo was assessed 685 xiquipiles and Tacuscalco 400 xiquipiles (Tasaciones de los naturales 1548–1551:ff. 82, 82v., 86, 111v.). In 1570, Izalco was again assessed 1,000 xiquipiles of cacao tribute (Pleitos contra Diego de Guzmán 1583:f. 1673). In 1575, García de Palacio increased Izalco's tribute to 1,300 cargas (3,900 xiquipiles) (Autos del consejo 1587). In 1582, Caluco was assessed 1,104 xiquipiles of cacao tribute (Vissita y tasación de Caluco 1582:f. 4).

Tribute abuses reached their most extreme levels in the 1570s, but no attempt was made by the audiencia to rectify the situation until 1582. Although the population had declined drastically, encomenderos levied tribute on the number of tributaries specified in the 1548–1551 Cerrato tasación, causing many contemporary observers, including President Valverde, to observe that "the living were paying for the dead" (García de Valverde 1584:f. 4).

Tribute was also levied on property; the more cacao plantations an Indian owned, the more tribute he paid. Widows and orphans paid full tribute on inherited cacao lands. In many cases, Valverde noted, the Indians paid more in tribute than they could have gained from the sale of their lands (García de Valverde 1584:ff. 6–7). This was indeed an extraordinary case of exploitation in which ownership of the means of production brought poverty rather than wealth.

Encomenderos and Royal Officials

The most powerful encomenderos of early colonial Guatemala were favored by President Alonso de Maldonado with grants of cacao towns (MacLeod 1973:83–84, 117). Most were not conquistadors, but rather well-connected hidalgos on intimate terms with President Maldonado. The most notorious were Juan de Guzmán and his son Diego, encomenderos of Izalco and half of Naolingo. The elder Guzmán was a first cousin or nephew of Maldonado's (Residencia de Alonso de Maldonado 1548:ff. 41, 56; Residencia de Alonso López de Cerrato 1550: f. 746v.). He was originally granted the town of Machaloa, Honduras

(Residencia de Alonso de Maldonado 1548:f. 392), which brought healthy revenues to the encomendero from the illegal use of Indians as tamemes (porters). He became encomendero of Izalco through his marriage to Margarita Orrego, the widow of Antonio Diosdado, the first encomendero of Izalco, who had paid Maldonado 800 pesos for the encomienda (Alvarez de Ocampo 1572; Residencia de Alonso López de Cerrato 1550:f. 746).

Diego de Guzmán succeeded to his father's encomienda in 1569 (Residencia de Francisco Briceño 1568–1569:f. 317). For more than 10 years he collected more than 170 cargas of cacao annually over the amount to which he was entitled by the tasación (Pleitos contra Diego de Guzmán 1584:f. 1v.). In early 1580 the vicar of Izalco, Villalán de Villagómez, sent the audiencia a detailed account of Guzmán's activities (Villagómez 1580). Villagómez wrote that Guzmán had the Indians of the town so terrorized that they would not dare to speak against his abuses of them. On October 27, 1580, the audiencia began a criminal proceeding against Guzmán, charging him with excessive tribute collection, mistreatment of the Indians, and deception and bribery of government officials (Villagómez 1580). MacLeod (1973:94) notes that Guzmán, realizing that he would not escape conviction, fled the province, and his fiefdom was broken up.

Guzmán's escape from Guatemala did not remedy the situation, however, for his flight took him to the Spanish court in Madrid. Although the audiencia did indeed strip him of his encomienda (Pleitos contra Diego de Guzmán 1585:f. 416v.), Guzmán appealed to the Crown, and two years later the Council of the Indies restored his encomienda to him (Autos del consejo 1587). He returned to Guatemala, more ineffectual denunciations were filed, and the abuses continued (Audiencia of Guatemala 1601; Espinosa de la Plaza 1595; Ramírez 1603).

The Guzmáns' use of terrorism and bribery in their ruthless extortion of the Indians is well documented (MacLeod 1973:86–95; Fowler 1987:144–147). Their behavior appears to be typical of, if perhaps more extreme than, that of most encomenderos of cacao-producing towns of Guatemala in the sixteenth century.

Another brutal figure was Gomez Díaz de la Reguera, the encomendero of Naolingo, who, unlike most of his counterparts, was married to a Ladina, the daughter of a conquistador father and a Pipil mother (Costilla 1565:f. 13). Not fully accepted as a member of the nouveaux riches in the cacao clique (MacLeod 1973:84, 117), Díaz de la Reguera was an outlaw tyrant who maintained a private army of about 300 blacks, mulattoes, and mestizos that he used frequently to harass the local Indian population. In the previously mentioned land dispute with Tacuscalco, he ordered his irregulars to destroy the town's irrigation ditches (Indians of Tacuscalco 1580–1581; Residencia de Francisco Briceño 1568–1569:f. 250). He also kept a private jail in which he incarcerated those who ran afoul of him, and he was accused of torture and executions of Indians (Residencia de Francisco Briceño 1568–69:ff. 1250–1251, 1256v.).

The encomenderos were allied with royal officials at all levels of the bureaucratic hierarchy. The Guzmáns and their peers were closely connected with the audiencia until Cerrato replaced Maldonado as president in 1548. They also held office in and derived political support from the ayuntamiento of Santiago de los Caballeros (Guatemala City). Thus, after Cerrato was installed as president and under succeeding administrations, their power base was strong enough to allow them to defy the audiencia (MacLeod 1973:86, 94). The Guzmáns clashed with minor local officials because of an obvious conflict of interest. In Madrid in 1585, Diego de Guzmán petitioned the Council of the Indies for a royal decree prohibiting the local authorities of Sonsonate from using the Indians for personal service (Guzmán 1585).

Other encomenderos such as Gomez Díaz de la Reguera were more closely linked with alcaldes mayores (regional governors) and petty local officials, although Díaz de la Reguera was said to be an intimate friend of the oidor Antonio Mexía (Residencia de Antonio Mexía 1561:f. 634v.), who was also well known for his own excesses (see Sherman 1979:308–309, 314). Alcaldes mayores sometimes ignored the directions of the audiencia. Juan de Torres, for example, forced the Indians of Izalco to pay cacao tribute for a year in which the audiencia had declared them exempt owing to a poor harvest (Audiencia of Guatemala 1601:f. 14).

The judicial reviews of the alcaldes mayores consistently accuse them of illegally trading with the Indians, often through black and Ladino middlemen; selling them wine, clothing, and trinkets; interfering with the activities of merchants; using the Indians for personal and public service; beating Indian men and women; residing illegally in Indian towns; stealing and selling Indian children and young women and stealing cacao and other items from the Indians; and generally failing to uphold the law with regard to protection of the Indians (Residencia de Alonso Gasco de Herrera 1563; Residencia de Francisco de Magaña 1568; Residencia de Juan de Torres 1583).

Merchants

Spanish and casta merchants were attracted to the Izalco region by the lucrative cacao trade. The merchants first established themselves principally in the major cacao-producing towns of Izalco, Caluco, Naolingo, and Tacuscalco. As early as 1542, Bishop Marroquín informed the crown of the dangers of Spanish merchants trading in Indian towns (Marroquín to Crown 1542). The traders' presence was regarded as a threat by the encomenderos, who argued that the merchants and their black, mulatto, and mestizo servants took advantage of the Indians. The encomenderos successfully petitioned the crown to order the merchants out of the Indian towns.

As a result, the Villa de la Santísima Trinidad de Sonsonate was founded in 1552 (Lardé y Larín 1950; López de Velasco [1572] 1894:296; MacLeod 1973:82). Although the resettlement was an attempt to curb the merchants' activities, the town grew rapidly and became a strong center of merchant power (García de Valverde 1584:f. 2v.–3; Guzmán 1585; Nuñez de Landecho 1563; Torres 1578). In 1556, Sonsonate had 150 houses of merchants and traders (Audiencia of Guatemala 1556:f. 372). In 1564, its alcalde mayor estimated that there were about 300 men in the town, of whom roughly 80 were permanently settled, married men who lived by the cacao trade (Magaña 1564:f. 1v.). By 1572, the town had 400 Spanish vecinos (citizens, usually heads of families), merchants who traded in cacao and other items, not one of whom was an encomendero (López de Velasco [1572] 1894:296). In 1586, Sonsonate was described as a town of merchants and traders rather than soldiers and landowners (Ciudad Real [1586] 1873:1:403).

Reports abounded of abuse and mistreatment of the Indians by merchants, their servants, and slaves. They sold them wine, clothing, and trinkets at inflated prices. They sold them short measures of maize and other subsistence items. They extended credit and charged exorbitant interest rates. Worst of all, the castas were said to be guilty of teaching the Indians an idle and lascivious life-style (Nuñez de Landecho 1563; Espinosa de la Plaza 1585; Ungría Girón 1605).

The merchants, for their part, argued that their presence was beneficial, for it brought order (pulicía), Christianity, and good customs to the Indians who lived in the region (Zuleta 1556). They also pointed out that deleterious influences stemmed not from merchants and their servants but from the many vagrants and outsiders who came into the villa without any legitimate business (Residencia de Alonso Gasco de Herrera 1563:f. 35).

The Clergy

Like royal officials, merchants, and their servants, the secular clergy were also accused of trading illegally with the Indians (Reales Cédulas 1563:f. 102–103). But considering the moral and physical abuses of the Indians of Izalco, of which many members of the secular clergy were said to have been guilty, this was but a mild accusation. A notorious case was that of don Francisco Gómez, dean of the cathedral of Guatemala, who was tried before Bishop Marroquín (Proceso criminal contra Francisco Gómez 1556–1559). Before being appointed dean of the cathedral, Gómez had served as parish priest in Izalco in 1552–1553, where he was held by the Indians to be a "man of bad conscience." Native witnesses from Izalco and Caluco testified that Gómez customarily sold watered-down wine to the Indians, and that he sold them mantas and candles at inflated prices and illegally traded for cacao with them. The price of a jug of watered-down wine was as high as four xiquipiles of cacao (Proceso criminal contra Francisco Gómez 1556–1559:f. 85v.). Beyond his trading violations, Gómez was no ascetic. Not only did he have sexual relations with María, the daughter of the cacique of Izalco, as well as with several other women (Torre 1552), but he was also accused of molesting Pipil women in public. Witnesses said that he would often lie in wait by the river and expose himself to young women when they went to collect water (Proceso criminal contra Francisco Gómez 1556–1559:ff. 73v., 75v., 76v.).

The behavior of Gómez and other priests was well known as early as 1552, when Marroquín was prompted to appoint Fray Thomas de la Torre, provincial of the Dominican order in Guatemala, to conduct an investigation of all secular clergy in the Izalco region and all those along the road from Santiago to San Salvador (Proceso criminal contra Francisco Gómez 1552:f. 86v.). Torre's (1552) report is a litany of charges of physical abuse, extortion, and mistreatment of the Indians (see also Sherman 1979:293–294). He recommended to the Crown that the secular clergy be removed from the cacao-producing towns of Izalco and that a Dominican or Franciscan monastery be established there. The secular clergy, Torre claimed, ministered to these towns only to exploit the Indians; their real mission, he said, was to amass enough money to return to Spain (Torre 1553:40–40v.; Sherman 1979:242).

Strategies for Survival

I would like to offer two fairly self-evident but nevertheless important observations about the strategies for survival that the sixteenth-century Pipil of the Izalco region adopted to cope with the misery, oppression, degradation, and exploitation brought upon them by colonial domination. The observations are sufficiently general that they should apply to all similar situations. The first is that strategies for survival must be seen in terms of pre-Columbian continuities: It is impossible to comprehend the response to the colonial situation without reference to the historical antecedents.

The second obvious but significant point is that strategies for survival are mediated by social relations of production, and they should be studied within that context. The documents reveal complex productive relations among indigenous peasant producers, royal officials and encomenderos, merchants and middlemen, and the clergy. The tension and conflicts that prevailed between these different interest groups left many interstices in the social fabric that the Indians could turn to their advantage through both passive and active resistance. Not that their resistance was successful—it was doomed to failure—but we distort reality if we ignore the Indians' attempts to adjust to the new situation.

Consider, for example, the conflict between encomenderos and the clergy, both of whom were interested in taking maximum advantage of the Indians. Diego de Guzmán was instrumental in getting several parish priests removed from their posts, and he reportedly told the Indians that the priests had no authority over them (Villagómez 1580). If Guzmán successfully undermined sacerdotal authority, the Indians were probably encouraged or allowed to maintain aspects of their native religion such as the cacao-planting ritual described in 1576 by Diego García de Palacio (1983:74–75).

Cacao production was simultaneously the source of brutal exploitation and a way for the Indians to attempt to cope with the situation. At midcentury the cacao orchards around the Izalco villages were divided into hundreds of small holdings, owned almost exclusively by Indian families. While the holdings of the native nobility were much larger than those of commoners, virtually all Indian families owned at least a small plot. Rather than a postconquest novelty, this pattern had its roots in the precolonial mode of production. Cacao production appears to have been organized at the level of the household and the calpulli during both preconquest and early colonial times. While many documents record land transfers from Indians to Spaniards and Ladinos during the late sixteenth century, I am aware of none that records transfers between Indians. Private ownership and inheritance of cacao trees and orchards must have been in place at the time of the conquest, and preconquest antecedents determined the response to colonial exploitation. Thus, the Indians were owners of the most important resource in the region. Of course, Spanish tribute demands created the paradox that ownership of the means of production brought poverty rather than wealth (Fowler 1987:145–146). But the Indians did not simply submit passively to this fate. Those who were able, at least, attempted to adapt to the new tribute demands and the increased demand for cacao through intensified production. As mentioned previously, cacao cultivation in Izalco was intensified in the 1560s. Tacuscalco converted maize lands to cacao in about 1566 (Indians of Tacuscalco 1580–1581). This action was presumably the result of a conscious decision based on the relative value of maize versus cacao. Production figures indicate that from 1540 until about 1575 some households were capable of producing a surplus of cacao.

The native gobernador of Caluco in 1582, don Gregorio de Valencia, and his wife, doña Francisca, owned a total of 10 cacao orchards, seven of which she had inherited from her first husband. Other members of don Gregorio's extended family also owned orchards. Altogether, don Gregorio's household owned or controlled 29 orchards containing some 33,570 cacao trees; according to contemporary production estimates, these trees in their prime might have produced a total of about 50 xiquipiles of cacao annually (Vissita y tasación de Caluco 1582–1583:ff. 24v.–26v., f. 446v.). The total tribute levied against this household was 20 xiquipiles.

In theory, therefore, a surplus could have been produced for payment of labor and tribute and for trade in the marketplace. This was not the case, however, since the cacao industry of Izalco was in decline in the 1580s. The trees were old and exhausted. Native depopulation, soil exhaustion, and climatic change also contributed to the collapse of the industry. Production had dropped to about 25 percent of its previous levels (Vissita y tasación de Caluco 1582–1583:ff. 12, 440). The productive life span of a cacao tree was 30 to 40 years (Vissita y tasación de Caluco 1582–1583:f. 446v.), so from about 1540 until 1575 surplus production presumably would have been feasible for some households.[3] The surplus would have been the result of intensified production in response to both increased tribute demands and increased commercial demand for the crop.

Exchange relationships also played an important role in the struggle for survival. Again, this response was rooted in a behavior pattern that dates to preconquest times since it appears that the pre-Columbian Pipil had a vibrant system of market exchange (Fowler 1989:186–190). The Pipil under Spanish domination participated actively in the vigorous market economy that centered on Izalco and Sonsonate in the sixteenth century. While the intensive trade interaction described above was clearly a vector of exploitation of the underclass of cacao producers, it was also an accelerator of acculturation and "ladinoization" (Mörner 1964:139–142; Pineda [1594] 1925:333, 336). Simultaneously, it became a way for some Indians to escape from the onerous burden of tribute. Because of the severe loss of native population, poor soil conservation practices, irrigation problems, plant disease, inadequate care of plantations, and changes in climate, production declined and tribute demands became increasingly onerous from about 1550 to 1600. Many Indians simply "voted with their feet" and opted to reject the traditional way of life; they left the villages, donned European clothing, and eventually were dropped from the tribute rolls (Real Cédula ca. 1602). This flight from the villages to the obrajes and estancias would continue throughout the seventeenth and early eighteenth centuries (Alcaldes y tatoque de Tecpan Yzalco 1626; Registro Chancillería 1677; Testimonio de los naturales de Izalco 1721). Similar transformations occurred all over colonial Latin America as Indians discovered active means to avoid imperial domination (MacLeod 1984:230–232).

Acknowledgments

Primary archival research on the Pipil in the sixteenth century was sponsored by the U.S.-Spanish Joint Committee for Cultural and Educational Cooperation for work in the Archivo General de Indias in Sevilla in 1984–1985, and by the Wenner-Gren Foundation for Anthropological Research and the American Philosophical Society for work in the Archivo General de Centroamérica in Guatemala City in 1986 and 1987. Special thanks are in order to Murdo MacLeod for blazing the trail with his pioneering research on Izalco and its sixteenth-century cacao industry.

Notes

1. A *carga*, which weighed approximately 50 pounds, was composed of three *xiquipiles*, or 8,000 cacao "beans." A *xiquipil* in turn consisted of 20 *zontles*, or 400 "beans." The latter two terms, of Nahua origin, were used throughout the Colonial period in Guatemala and El Salvador (Fowler 1987:160–161).

2. According to a 1581 padrón conducted by Francisco del Valle Marroquín, the total population of Izalco in 1581 was 1,838, of which 617 were tributaries (Pleitos contra Diego de Guzmán 1581:ff. 707–1141).

3. By the end of the sixteenth century, the cacao industry of Izalco was dead. By 1605, many cacao orchards lay unattended, and many Indians of Naolingo and Tacuscalco had sold their holdings to Spaniards, blacks, and mestizos (MacLeod 1973:94–95).

Abbreviations

The following abbreviations are used in the references:

AGCA	Archivo General de Centroamérica, Guatemala City, Guatemala	
AGI	Archivo General de Indias, Seville, Spain	
	Sections:	
	AG	Audiencia de Guatemala
	EC	Escribanía de Camara
	JU	Justicia
	PR	Patronato Real

References

Alcaldes y tatoque de Tecpan Izalco
  1626 Alcaldes y tatoque del pueblo de Tecpan Izalco de la Real Corona [piden] que el dicho pueblo se contase, AGCA A3.16-534-5967.
Alvarado, Pedro de
  1934 Relación hecha por Pedro de Alvarado a Hernando Cortés; Otra relación hecha por Pedro de Alvarado a Hernando Cortés. In *Libro viejo de la fundación de Guatemala y papeles relativos a D. Pedro de Alvarado*, pp. 261–282. Sociedad de Geografía e Historia, Guatemala.
Alvarez de Ocampo, Leonor
  1572 Leonor Alvarez de Ocampo con Juan de Guzmán y Margarita Orrego, su mujer, vecinos de la ciudad de Salamanca, sobre que les den cuenta con pago de los vienes y herencia que quedaron de Alonso Diosdado, difunto en Yndias, AGI JU 1034.
Amaroli, Paul
  1986 En la búsqueda de Cuscatlán: Un proyecto etnohistórico y arqueológico. Unpublished manuscript on file, Department of Anthropology, Vanderbilt University, Nashville.
Ashburn, Percy M.
  1947 *The Ranks of Death*. Edited by Frank D. Ashburn. Coward McCann, New York.
Audiencia of Guatemala
  1601 Letter to Crown, AGI AG 11, 5-25-1601.
Autos del consejo
  1587 Autos del Consejo y la Audiencia de Guatemala sobre el pleito de Diego de Guzmán con sus Indios, AGI AG 57, 4-7-1587.
Autos e información
  1636 Autos e información hecha por el señor presidente de la Real Audiencia de Guatemala, AGI AG 125.
Barón Castro, Rodolfo
  1950 *Reseña histórica de la villa de San Salvador*. Ediciones Cultura Hispánica, Madrid.
Benzoni, Girolamo
  1857 *History of the New World*. Translated and edited by W. H. Smyth. Works issued by the Hakluyt Society, No. 21. London. Originally published 1565.
Bergmann, John F.
  1969 The Distribution of Cacao Cultivation in Pre-Columbian America. *Annals of the Association of American Geographers* 59:85–96.
Carrasco, Pedro
  1976 Los linajes nobles del México antiguo. In *Estratificación social en la Mesoamérica prehispánica*, by Pedro Carrasco, Johanna Broda, et al., pp. 9–76. Instituto Nacional de Antropología e Historia, Mexico.
Cepeda, Gaspar de
  1567 Cuenta y tasación de los pies de cacao que tenía Gaspar de Cepeda, AGCA A1.43–365–4171, 5-9-1567.
Ciudad Real, Antonio de
  1873 *Relación breve y verdadera de algunas cosas que sucedieron al Padre Fray Alonso Ponce en las provincias de la Nueva España . . . .* 2 vols. Imprenta de la Viuda de Calero, Madrid. Originally written 1586.
Costilla, Ysabel
  1565 Ysabel Costilla, vecina de la ciudad de San Salvador, con Gonzalo de Alvarado sobre el derecho a los pueblos de Yndios, Noacalco, Zitula, y Guacapa, AGI JU 285, No. 1, Ramo 1.
Crosby, Alfred W.

1972 *The Columbian Exchange: Biological and Cultural Consequences of 1492*. Greenwood Press, Westport, Conn.

1976 Virgin Soil Epidemics as a Factor in the Aboriginal Depopulation in America. *William and Mary Quarterly* 33:289–299.

1986 *Ecological Imperialism: The Biological Expansion of Europe, 900–1900*. Cambridge University Press, Cambridge.

Dobyns, Henry F.

1983 *Their Number Become Thinned: Native American Population Dynamics in Eastern North America*. University of Tennessee Press, Knoxville.

Espinosa de la Plaza, Thomas

1585 Letter to Crown, AGI AG 10, 3-30-1585.

1595 Letter to Crown, AGI AG 10, 6-15-1595.

Fowler, William R., Jr.

1983 La distribución prehistórica e histórica de los pipiles. *Mesoamérica* 6:348–372.

1987 Cacao, Indigo, and Coffee: Cash Crops in the History of El Salvador. *Research in Economic Anthropology* 8:139–167.

1988 La población nativa de El Salvador al momento de la conquista española. *Mesoamérica* 15:79–116.

1989 *The Cultural Evolution of Ancient Nahua Civilizations: The Pipil-Nicarao of Central America*. University of Oklahoma Press, Norman and London.

1990 The Living Shall Pay for the Dead: Trade, Exploitation, and Social Change in Early Colonial Izalco, El Salvador. In *Perspectives on Change: Ethnohistorical and Archaeological Approaches to Culture Contact*, edited by J. Daniel Rogers and Samuel M. Wilson. In press.

Fowler, William R., Paul E. Amaroli, and Barbara Arroyo López

1989 *Informe preliminar del Proyecto Izalco: Temporada de 1989*. Unpublished report submitted to the Administración del Patrimonio Cultural, San Salvador, El Salvador.

García de Palacio, Diego

1983 *Carta-relación de Diego García de Palacio a Felipe II sobre la provincia de Guatemala, 8 de marzo de 1576*. Versión paleográfica de María del Carmen León Cazares. Universidad Nacional Autónoma de México, Mexico.

García de Valverde, Diego

1584 Letter to Crown, AGI AG 10, 4-8-1584.

Gibson, Charles

1964 *The Aztecs under Spanish Rule*. Stanford University Press, Stanford, Calif.

Guzmán, Diego de

1585 Letter to Crown, AGI AG 56, 4-11-1585.

Hicks, Frederic

1982 Tetzcoco in the Early Sixteenth Century: The State, The City, and The *Calpolli*. *American Ethnologist* 9:230–249.

Hodge, Mary W.

1984 *Aztec City-States*. Memoirs of the Museum of Anthropology, University of Michigan, No. 18. Ann Arbor.

Indians of Tacuscalco

1580–81 Pleyto entre los yndios de Tacuscalco y los de Naolingo, AGCA A1.12-674-6178.

Lardé y Larín, Jorge

1950 Orígenes de la villa de la Santísima Trinidad de Sonsonate. *Anales del Museo Nacional "David J. Guzmán"* 1 (2):46–59. San Salvador.

López de Velasco, Juan

1894 *Geografía y descripción universal de las Indias*. Fortanet, Madrid. Originally written 1572.

López de Yrarraga, Nicolao

1556 Letter to Crown, AGI AG 52, 4-26-1556.

Lovell, W. George
1985 *Conquest and Survival in Colonial Guatemala: A Historical Geography of the Cuchumatan Highlands, 1500–1821.* McGill-Queen's Press, Kingston and Montreal.
1988 The "Secret Judgements of God": Disease and Depopulation in Early Colonial Guatemala. Paper presented at the International Congress of Americanists, Amsterdam.

Lovell, W. George, Christopher H. Lutz, and William R. Swezey
1984 The Indian Population of Southern Guatemala, 1549–1551: An Analysis of López de Cerrato's Tasaciones de tributos. *The Americas* 40:459–477.

MacLeod, Murdo J.
1973 *Spanish Central America: A Socioeconomic History, 1520–1720.* University of California Press, Berkeley and Los Angeles.
1984 Aspects of the Internal Economy of Colonial Spanish America: Labor; Taxation; Distribution and Exchange. In *The Cambridge History of Latin America*, vol. 2: *Colonial Latin America*, edited by Leslie Bethell, pp. 219–264. Cambridge University Press, Cambridge.

Magaña, Francisco de
1564 Letter to Crown, AGI AG 39, 2-18-1564.

Marroquín, Francisco
1542 Letter to Crown, AGI PR 184-1-35, 2-20-1542.

Mörner, Magnus
1964 La política de segregación y el mestizaje en la audiencia de Guatemala. *Revista de Indias* 24:137–151.

Newson, Linda
1987 *Indian Survival in Colonial Nicaragua.* University of Oklahoma Press, Norman.

Nuñez de Landecho, Juan
1563 Letter to Crown, AGI AG 9B, 3-2-1563.

Pineda, Juan de
1925 Descripción de la provincia de Guatemala. *Anales de la Sociedad de Geografía e Historia* 1:327–363. Guatemala. Originally written 1594.

Pleitos contra Diego de Guzmán
1582–1585 Pleitos seguidos por el señor Fiscal de la Audiencia de Guatemala, contra don Diego de Guzmán, AGI EC 331A and 331B.

Proceso criminal contra Francisco Gómez
1556–1559 Proceso criminal que se trató en la ciudad de Santiago de Goathemala ante el Obispo de la dicha Ciudad contra el dean de aquella santa yglesia, don Francisco Gómez sobre las causas de que le acusa. AGI JU 283-3-1, 10-6-1556-2-23-1559.

Ramírez, Juan
1603 Letter to Crown, AGI AG 156, 2-3-1603.

Real Cédula
ca. 1602 AGCA A3.16-534-5967.

Reales Cédulas
1563 AGI AG 394, libro 4, ff. 102–103, 3-15-1563.

Registro Chancillería
1677 AGCA A1.24-1565-10209.

Relación Marroquín
1968 El licienciado Francisco Marroquín, y una descripción de El Salvador, año de 1532. Archivo General de Indias, Sevilla. Audiencia de Guatemala, legajo 965. Paleografía de Francis Gall. *Anales de la Sociedad de Geografía e Historia* 41:199–232. Guatemala.

Residencia de Alonso de Maldonado
1548 Juicio de residencia de Alonso de Maldonado, AGI JU 299A.

Residencia de Alonso Gasco de Herrera
1563 Juicio de residencia de Alonso Gasco de Herrera, Alcalde Mayor de la Villa de la Trinidad, AGI JU 311, 10-4-1563.

Residencia de Alonso López de Cerrato
1550 Juicio de residencia de Alonso López de Cerrato, AGI JU 301.
Residencia de Antonio Mexía
1561 Juicio de residencia de Antonio Mexía, AGI JU 309.
Residencia de Francisco de Magaña
1568 Juicio de residencia de Francisco de Magaña, Alcalde Mayor de la Villa de la Trinidad, AGI JU 312.
Residencia de Francisco Briceño
1568–1569 Juicio de residencia de Francisco Briceño, AGI JU 317.
Residencia de Juan de Torres
1583 Juicio de residencia de Juan de Torres, Alcalde Mayor de la Villa de la Trinidad, AGI EC 344A.
Robledo, Diego de
1556 Letter to Crown, AGI AG 9A, 4-10-1556.
Rodríguez Becerra, Salvador
1977 *Encomienda y conquista: Los inicios de la colonización en Guatemala*. Universidad de Sevilla, Seville.
Sherman, William L.
1979 *Forced Native Labor in Sixteenth-Century Central America*. University of Nebraska Press, Lincoln and London.
Tasaciones de los naturales
1548–1551 Tasaciones de los naturales de las provincias de Goathemala, AGI AG 128.
Testamento de don Juan Chiname
1567 Residencia de Francisco Briceño, AGI JU 317, 2-16-1567.
Testimonio de los naturales de Izalco
1721 Testimonio de la pretensión de los naturales de el pueblo de Izalco, en razón de los gravamenes que padecen, AGI AG 226, 8-22-1721.
Torre, Thomas de la
1552 Ynforme de Fray Thomas de la Torre sobre los clerigos que residen en los yzalcos . . . , AGI AG 168, 11-12-1552.
1553 Letter to Crown, AGI AG 8, 5-22-1553.
Torres, Juan de
1578 Letter to Crown, AGI AG 55, 3-1-1578.
Ungría Girón, Manuel
1605 Letter to Crown, AGI AG 12, 3-20-1605.
Vázquez de Espinosa, Antonio
1969 *Compendio y descripción de las Indias Occidentales*. Edición y estudio preliminar por B. Velasco Bayón. Biblioteca de Autores Españoles, vol. 231. Ediciones Atlas, Madrid. Originally written 1622–1630.
Villagómez, Villalán de
1580 Memorial de las cosas que en el pueblo de Tecpan Izalco . . . pasan, AGI AG 170, 3-18-1580.
Vissita y tasación de Caluco
1582 Vissita y tasación de tributos de los Yndios del pueblo de Caluco, AGI JU 334.
Zuleta, Cristobal de
1556 Probanza de los méritos y servicios de Cristobal de Zuleta, AGI PR 60-5-5, 2-17-1556.

Chapter 9 ■

William Van Davidson

Geographical Perspectives on Spanish–Pech (Paya) Indian Relationships, Northeast Honduras, Sixteenth Century

For inhabitants of North America, the consequences of Columbus's encounters began along the coast of Central America, in August 1502. This was during Columbus's fourth voyage to America, 10 years since the first. The four Spanish ships had been at sea for three months—a nice, quick trip. The fleet had passed through the Lesser Antilles and had touched Hispaniola, Jamaica, and the south coast of Cuba before sailing past the Cayman Islands and eventually stopping in the Bay Islands, in sight of the mainland of Honduras. The islands and adjacent mainland were then occupied primarily by ancestors of the modern Pech Indians, or as they have been called by outsiders for over 300 years, the Paya.

The Pech did not live within the bounds of Mesoamerica, the realm of high culture dominated by the Aztecs and the Mayas, and perhaps for this reason northeast Honduras has remained historically vague. However, the story of Spanish—Indian relationships in one of the more peripheral areas is intriguing and invites investigation. What follows, therefore, in abbreviated form, is a chronicle of the century-long interplay between conquerors and the vanquished.

The particular perspective employed here is that of historical geography. To historical geographers, in their attempt to reconstruct the past, *places* and *physical environments* are of unusual importance. Exactly where did the past action take place is one of the first questions asked by historical geographers. Historical events may also be emphasized, but human activities must be located and placed within a specific geographical setting, thereby providing an enriching base for the action. A reconstruction of past landscapes and regional interactions based on archival research *and* fieldwork is the goal (Sauer 1941).

The approach of historical geography has special value in areas such as northeast Honduras where documentary evidence of the Spanish—Indian contact is so slight. Being alongside the zone of more active, successful Spanish colonization and possessing very few early Spanish towns, northeast Honduras left relatively little in the historical record to reconstruct past activities. In those marginal areas where the Spaniards did not immediately overwhelm the natives, the natural world becomes a more valuable avenue to understanding the period of culture contact and conflict. In such areas, one must wonder how the natives were able to resist European domination as long as they did. Perhaps at least part of the answer involves the nature of the physical environment—one aspect of the region that has changed little over the five centuries since the contact.

In this chapter, the primary themes are (1) the extent and geographical nature of the Pech culture region, (2) the erection of major Spanish centers therein, (3) the development of mining, (4) the Indian reaction to European presence, and (5) the eventual depopulation and territorial reduction of the Pech. All of these topics touch on the relationships between man and the natural environment, as well as the spatial and locational aspects of the early Spanish—Indian interaction.

The Fourth Voyage of Columbus in the Bay of Honduras

Most scholars who have written on the fourth, and final, voyage of Columbus to America have misinterpreted much information that is available from the primary accounts. The trip is, of course, a major event, but is yet to be understood satisfactorily. While it has not been given the attention that it deserves, the voyage (and its primary documents) remains the place to begin any serious discussion of native responses to Spanish incursions and of Spanish—Pech history specifically.

Confusion about the voyage stems primarily from the early determinations of Samuel Lothrop (1927), Frans Blom (1932), and Eric Thompson (1951) that the trading canoe found in the Bay Islands was operated by Mayas. Also some blame might be placed on those historians who followed Samuel Morison (1963) in his account of Columbus's route in the Bay of Honduras. A much better look at the trip and its implications can be found in Edwards's study of 1978.

This is not the place to discuss in detail the reformist notions of the trip; however, note that the Crown's historian, Peter Mártyr, who, it is believed, had access to Columbus's now lost account of the trip, clearly wrote in the first edition that the merchant in the trading canoe was the ruler of the island, returning home (Mártyr 1966:116). While most writers on the subject have concluded that the trading canoe was the first instance of Spanish contact with the high cultures of Mesoamerica, Mártyr's comment might indicate that the merchant was not necessarily a Mayan carrying Mesomerican trade goods to other Mayas. He could have been a local island merchant, a Pech, trading for his island and the adjacent mainland. Mártyr also wrote that Columbus sailed west from the Bay Islands, not south or east, as say the historians. From close inspection of all of the primary evidence, one could also conclude that Roatán Island, and not Guanaja, was the island visited by Columbus.

As will be seen below, documents of the voyage also provide insights into the nature of the sixteenth-century Pech of the mainland.

Extent and Nature of the Pech Region, Early Sixteenth Century

At the beginning of the sixteenth century, all lands in Honduras were obviously under the control of Indians. But it is also clear that there was great variation among the native populations there. One church chronicler of the late seventeenth century suggested that humans had lived in Honduras for 5,600 years and that over 30 different peoples could be then be identified (Vásquez 1944:4:77–79). That these groups often seem to be separated by features in the natural landscape indicates the close relationship between early man and his habitat. Therefore, a first step toward understanding the regionalizations among Honduran Indians, and specifically the Pech, might be to review the natural geography. Pech response to European contact was limited to their homeland alone.

Although the boundaries of the Pech culture region for the early sixteenth century cannot be determined with certainty, a general delimitation can be suggested from a perusal of the archeological, ethnohistorical, linguistic, toponymic, and geographical evidence.

Natural Environment

The physical geography of northeastern Honduras, at the greatest scale, is dominated by five mountain ranges that generally trend southwest-northeast and by the four hydrologic systems (Aguán, Sico, Paulaya, Plátano) enclosed by the mountains. In height, the mountains are not overpowering—they reach over 1,500 meters in only a few places and the maximum elevation is 2,333 meters— but they are quite difficult to traverse on foot because of their irregular topography. The few large intermountain flatlands—such as the Agalta Valley and the Olancho Valley—are 400–600 meters above sea level.

Climate is seasonal, with fairly sharp contrasts between the wet period (June —December) and the dry (January—May). Tropical temperatures are moderated as elevation increases. Natural vegetation is primarily a mix of hardwoods and pine in the sloping lands, with significant amounts of old savanna in the largest valleys (Johannessen 1959). Large waterways, particularly those that are navigable for the slight drafted *pipantes*, or dugout watercraft, are of importance to the

Indians. At the same time, obstacles to dugout travel, rapids and waterfalls that limit or make such travel difficult, are culturally prominent features. The head of dugout navigation on these eastern streams, or "canoe line," will later be examined as a possible cultural divide using the Wampú River as an example.

Limits of the Pech Culture Region

Archeological Record. At least 77 sites have been reported in the numerous archeological reports from northern and eastern Honduras, including the islands offshore (Craig 1965; Epstein 1957, 1978; Epstein and Véliz 1977; Feachem 1938, 1947–1948; Hasemann 1977; Healy 1974, 1978, 1987; Helbig 1956, 1964; Mejía C. 1954; Pownall 1779; Sapper 1899; Spinden 1925; Stone 1941, 1942; Strong 1934a, 1934b, 1935; Véliz 1972; Véliz et al. 1977). Many of the earlier surveyors, such as Spinden (1925), Strong (1934a, 1934b), and Stone (1941, 1942), after recognizing similar artifacts, particularly pottery and stylized metates, declared the zone to be "Paya" (see Figure 9–1). More recent archeologists (Epstein, Véliz, Healy), while continuing to recognize the similarity in remains, have cautiously avoided mentioning the possible ethnic relationship.

Given the site records, two distributional generalizations are apparent: (1) the Bay Island offertory sites are normally on the hilltops, and (2) the mainland sites are clustered along the major streams, particularly along the upper piedmont

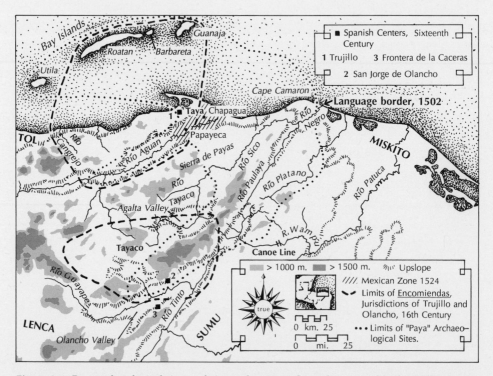

Figure 9–1. Paya archaeological sites and sixteenth-century Spanish centers, Northeast Honduras.

of the river valleys and away from stream banks (which might be subject to flooding or have been eroded away). Of course, the archeological survey can never be complete and does not encompass all Pech territory.

Ethnohistory, Language, and Toponyms. The ruler/merchant that Columbus first made contact with in the Bay Islands was taken as a translator along the coast as far as he could understand the language. He was released probably at the mouth of the Río Negro, some 100 kilometers east of Trujillo, where, as the eye-witnesses proclaimed, he was no longer useful. Obviously, he had come to the limit of his culture region. This is only one piece of evidence that incorporates the Bay Islands and the adjacent mainland into one linguistic and cultural region.

Other evidence is that in 1526, newly appointed Governor Diego Lopéz de Salcedo reported that a site in the Bay Islands and two mainland sites, one 4 or 5 leagues to the interior and the other 30 leagues inland, shared a common religious region. The three shrines, which sheltered green marblelike idols in the form of females, were cared for by a celibate Indian leader called "papa." A century later, islanders served as translators for Franciscan missionaries who worked on the mainland in Pech lands (Vásquez 1944:4:156).

Additional information on the distribution of Pech during the first century of contact with Europeans can be gleaned from local words of the period. If I am correct about the ethnicity of the aboriginal Bay Islanders, the first words recorded by the Europeans in the islands were Pech, although probably heard imperfectly by the untrained Spanish ear and transcribed incorrectly by the scribes of the day. Even with the great potential for misunderstanding, terms from the earliest documents can provide insights into the nature of the region. Table 9–1 lists the names of the people and places appearing in the four primary accounts of the Columbian voyage, the statements of eye-witnesses during the Columbian trials a decade later, reports of the Spanish entradas until 1527, and the missionary effort of 1622 that used island translators on the mainland.

Perhaps of most interest are the first place names attached to the mainland, *Taia* and *Maia* (Mártyr 1966:116). I believe these are simply Pech terms for "mine" and "theirs," referring to parts of the north coast of Honduras. *Taya*, *Tayaco*, and *Tayacon*, can still be located in a few places, all of which are associated with the past and modern Pech. The latter two toponyms are probably derived by fusing the Pech word (*Taia*) with the Nahuatl locative *co*. *Maia*, or "their land," probably referred to non-Pech territory in western Honduras, perhaps then occupied by the so-called Jicaque, or modern Tol-speakers. This group certainly occupied those lands during the seventeenth century (Davidson 1985). *Oaque cocao*, which refers to Barbareta Island and is taken from Bartholomew Columbus's map of about 1506, could possibly mean "five houses" in Pech. *Ebuya*, which was known to Yáñez Pinzón, one of the captains on the voyage as a mainland province associated with chief Camarona (CDIU 1892:7:269), was probably near modern Cape Camaron, at the mouth of Río Negro. Contact with natives there could have been made when Columbus stopped to let the Bay Island translator off ship. *Uya* is the Pech term for "large." *Eb* is a prefix for "snake." As a final example, the topo-

Table 9-1. Early Words from the Pech Region, 1502–1527, 1622

Dates of Event/Publication	Word	Refers to	Source
Places known from Columbian voyage			
1502–1506	oalaua	Utila Island	B. Columbus map
1502–1506	manaua	Roatán Island	B. Columbus map
1502–1506	oaque cocao	Barbareta Island	B. Columbus map
1502–1506	banassa	Guanaja Island	B. Columbus map
1502–1511	Guanassa	Guanaja Island	Mártyr 1966:116
1502–1511	Guanasa		Mártyr map
1502–1513	Guanaxa		Anonymous 1513:269
1502–1513	Guanasa		Anonymous 1513:255,274
1502–1515	Guanaca		CDIU 1892:7:96
1502–1515	Guacuaza		CDII 1893:39:415
1502–1515	Guanasa		CDIU 1895:9:165
1502–1515	Guana		CDIU 1892:7:348
1502–1515	Guanaja		Anonymous 1515:76
1502–1515	Guanasa		Anonymous 1515:80
1502–1511	Quiriquetánam Quiriquetana	Honduras mainland	Mártyr 1966:116
1502–1511	Taia	Mainland province	Mártyr 1966:116
1502–1506	Maiam		B. Columbus ca. 1506
1502–1511	Maia	Mainland province	Mártyr 1966:116
1502–1515	Maya	The mainland	CDIU 1892:7:348
1502–1515	Maya		CDIU 1892:7:92
1502–1515	Maya		CDIU 1894:8:76
1502–1515	Uiuya	The mainland	CDIU 1892:7:264
1502–1515	Ebuya	Mainland province, of the chief Camarona	CDIU 1892:7:269
Places known from early Spanish entradas			
1525–1526	Chapagua	Major town 7 leagues from Trujillo	Cortés 1971:265
1525–1526	Coabata town	Subject to Papayeca	Cortés 1971:266
1525–1526	Huitila	Utila Island	Cortés 1971:273
1525–1526	Huilacho	Olancho	Cortés 1971:271
1525–1526	Papayeca [Papaeca]	Province 7 leagues from Trujillo, with 18 subject towns	Cortés 1971:265 [271]
1525–1526	Telica	Town subject to Chapagua	Cortés 1971:266
1526–1526	Telicachequita	Town near savanna in Olancho	Ceparo 1526:61
1525–1563	Guaimura	Indian name for Trujillo or vicinity	Díaz 1982:674
ca. 1526	Gueymura	Port at Cabo de Honduras	Mendez ca. 1526
1525–1563	Olancho	Peaceful interior area	Díaz 1982:541
1525–1563	Olancho	Towns so-called, 55 leagues from Trujillo	Díaz 1982:559
1525-1563	Olancho	Town at peace	Díaz 1982:570

Table 9-1. (continued)

1527–1527	Nuylancho	A valley	Salcedo 1527a:250
1525–1563	Guayape	Later name for Olancho	Díaz 1982:570
1525–1563	Quemara	Coastal town 4 days' walk east of Tela	Díaz 1982:545
1526–1526	Agalta	Indian town	Ceparo 1526:60
1526–1526	Escamilpa	Indian town in province of Huylancho	Ceparo 1526:57
1526–1526	Escamilpachecita	Town near savanna in Olancho, slightly more than 1 league from Escamilpa Grande, which is up-valley	Ceparo 1526:61
1526–1526	Escamilpa Grande	Town a little more than 1 league from Escamilpa	Ceparo 1526:61
1527–1527	Chequilta	Town 17 leagues from Trujillo	Salcedo 1527a:247

Places known from 1622 mission trip

1622–1714	Azocecqua	*Aso-se-wa* (Pech)=*agua amarillo*(Spanish)	
	Barcaquer		
	Borbortabahca		
	Murahqui	Later name for Guampún	
	Río Guampún	Río Wampü	
	Río Xaruá		
		(Unidentified Pech word or mistranscription?)	
	Yaxamahá		
	Zuyy		Vázquez 1944:4:164

People known from Columbian voyage

1502–1515	Ynube	Island ruler	CDIU 1892:7:264
1502–1515	Yunbera		CDIU 1892:7:397
1502–1515	Junbe		CDIU 1894:8:37-38
1502–1515	Junhera		CDIU 1894:8:76
1502–1539	Yumbé	Island merchant-chief	F. Columbus 1959:231
1502–1515	Camarona	Chief of Ebuya Province	CDIU 1892:7:269

People known from early entradas

1525–1526	Cecoatl	Chief of Coabata, a town subjected to Papayeca	Cortés 1971:266
1525–1526	Chicohuytl	Chief of Chapagua Province	Cortés 1971:270
1525–1526	Mazatl	Chief of Papayeca Province	Cortés 1971:270
1525–1526	Mendoreto	Chief of Chapagua Province	Cortés 1971:270
1525–1526	Montamal	Chief of Telica, of the province of Chapagua	Cortés 1971:266
1525–1526	Pizacura	Chief of Papayeca Province	Cortés 1971:270
1525–1526	Poto	Chief of Chapagua Province	Cortés 1971:270
1525–1563	Papayeca	Chief of large town near Trujillo	Díaz 1981:541
1525–1563	Acaltecas	Unpacified Indians of interior	Díaz 1982:541

nym *Asocecgua*, reported in 1622 by Franciscan missionaries in "Paya" lands (Vásquez 1944:4:14), is still used by the modern Pech to mean a muddy stream (in Spanish, *agua amarillo*, or "yellow waters").

Apparently, Nahuatl toponyms, such as *Chapagua* and *Papayeca* (Cortés 1971:265), seem to have referred to the relatively large Mexican-led settlements in the lower Aguán valley. The names of their chiefs, also given to us in Mexican, support that notion.

A Modern Analogy. To test the possibility of a modern analogy relating toponyms to physical geography and cultural boundaries, in January, 1990, four geographers from Louisiana State University ventured down the Río Wampú in search of the boundary that separates the modern realms of the Pech and the Sumu.[1] After a day-and-a-half walk through mountains, we reached the upper Wampú, which is too shallow to float canoes, so balsa rafts were constructed. A day later, after passing through more than 50 minor rapids, we could not, with safety, pass the largest of the rapids (*Salto Grande*; in Sumu, *Kitan-non*). We reached the Sumu villages on the middle Río Patuca on the fifth day.

The Wampú trip confirmed our hypothesis that a "canoe line" might separate the upstream Pech from the downstream Sumu. It actually worked. As it turns out, upstream from the large waterfall the tributaries bear the Pech prefix *aso*, which means "water"; downstream the tributaries carry the Sumu suffix for "water," *was*.

A Final Demarcation. If the limits of the "Pech" archeological region, the distribution of the sixteenth-century Indian settlements in the hinterlands of Trujillo and Olancho, the sites of modern Pech place names, and the eastern limits of Bay Island speech on the shore at 1502 are drawn on the same map, the composite that emerges probably comes close to defining the cultural region of the Pech in the 1500s. This territory included the Bay Islands and the north coast of Honduras between the Río Cangrejo (near La Ceiba) and Río Negro. To the interior, Pech occupied the valleys of the Aguán, Sico, Paulaya, and Plátano, as well as the Agalta Valley and the Olancho Valley at least until the confluence of the Río Tinto. The headwaters of the Wampú were probably utilized as well.

Determining the limits of the region is perhaps easier than attempting to explain such a configuration. I am becoming convinced that certain aspects of physical geography play some role. The canoe line on the Wampú seems to correspond to a cultural border today and perhaps did so 400 years ago. The rapids on the upper Patuca might have played a similar role in separating the Pech and aggressive ancestors of the Sumu; the higher mountains of the coastal range west of Trujillo seem to separate the Tol and Pech; high mountains also separate the Lenca and Pech. The proto-Miskito and Pech, as mentioned first by the Columbian sailors, are still separated by upland and lowland habitats (see Figure 9–1).

This Pech area probably contained alien enclaves. Apparently, two Mexican-dominated settlements with their subjugated Pech towns occupied the lower Aguán Valley south and east of Trujillo.

The Early Spanish Centers at Trujillo and Olancho: Two Spatial-Environmental Settlement Models

After the Spaniards became established in México under Cortés and in Panamá under Pedrarias, the lands between became a battleground for Spaniards fighting among themselves for New World property. Pedro Alvarado eventually took Guatemala for Cortés and Hernando Córdova overwhelmed Costa Rica and organized Nicaragua for Pedrarias, but Honduras remained, and here the fraternal battles raged (see Chamberlain 1966 for the most exhaustive historical account). Eventually the Cortesians won Honduras, but in their rush to claim the land by right of settlement, the earliest attempts to build towns failed. Two early centers that had the most success and affected most directly the Pech population were Trujillo and San Jorge de Olancho.

Trujillo

The coastal site first explored by the Columbian sailors was settled under the orders of Cortés by his captain, Francisco de las Casas, in May 1525 (Saldaña 1525). The locale selected was an obvious choice—again emphasizing the importance of the physical world in historical activities. For the same reason that Columbus had first stepped ashore in the place, the Spanish colonizers were guided to the site—because it lies inside the largest protected bay on the Caribbean shore of Central America. For people using sailing vessels, such a site is of overwhelming importance. The enormous enclosure, some 13 kilometers wide across its mouth, was formed as a giant sand spit built westward. Sediments from the Río Aguán, whose mouth is just upwind, are pushed westward with the longshore drift by the constant Trade Winds. Inside the harbor, winds and waves are relatively calm, except in the rare cases of winter *nortes* that infrequently blow in from the northwest. Without this set of geographical features to attract the earliest explorers and colonists, Spanish contact with the Pech would have been much delayed. Without a doubt, the presence of a large, protected bay was the single most important physical factor that influenced Spanish settlements on the north coast of Honduras. Puerto Caballos and Tela, both to the west of Trujillo, are other examples.

Cortés himself visited the new villa in 1526 and assisted in cutting the forest from the site and in erecting the first houses. After dividing the pacified local Indians among the conquerors (Salcedo 1526:f.322,328), he returned to Mexico in the same year. The initial site of Trujillo was a swampy area beneath the foot of the mountain, but under Governor Salcedo the town was moved upslope, "where the setting sun could be seen" (Salcedo 1526:f.324).

Olancho

The large flat valley to the interior of Trujillo, over two difficult mountain ranges to the south, was known first as *Uilancho*, and then as *Huilancho*, before being finally corrupted into Olancho. The valley, one of the largest in all of Honduras, approximately 20 by 130 kilometers, quickly attracted the attention of rival Spaniards, who had a liking for the upland flatlands that reminded them of their Castille homeland. It was into this land that the Spaniards from Nicaragua traveled and thereby provoked a response by the allies of Cortés in Trujillo.

By late April 1526, Francisco Saavedra, left in Trujillo as Cortés's representative, had determined that a Spanish settlement should be established far to the interior near the heart of Indian populations—in the Olancho Valley. He therefore ordered Bartolomé de Celada to proceed inland in search of the best site for the proposed Spanish villa (Cepero 1526:57–59). The new settlement, named Villa de la Frontera de Cáceres, was erected "in a savanna near some Indian towns called Telica chequita and Escamilpa chequita" (Cepero 1526:61).

The town seems to have been located and constructed according to requirements of Spanish town planners of the time, because the site possessed the following characteristics: (1) it was in the territory of Indian settlements, where labor can be obtained without much effort and where Indians can serve the Spaniards without much work, (2) the place should be beautiful, airy, dry, and settlers must be able to see the setting sun, (3) waters nearby should be clear and flowing, (4) the site should be away from the marshes and mudholes, (5) there should be grass, pasture, and land for *ejido*, and all types of livestock, and (6) there should be forested land nearby for timber to use in framing building and to lay foundations for stone houses (see Cepero 1526:59; Salcedo 1527b:385–386).

At another scale of design, the internal layout of the villa followed another widely known model of new settlement by Spaniards in the New World. Celada and his men, with the help of the local Indians, laid out the first plots in the following order: (1) the church, (2) the plaza, (3) hospital, (4) the governor's house, (5) jail, (6) cabildo, and (7) other houses.

The Settlement Model

Within only two years of Spanish colonization, the two dominant models of colonial settlement had been placed on the landscape of eastern Honduras. One model focused on the coast and had a port as a node of transhipment. It was connected to the interior by a *camino real* (main highway), which had in turn a few tributary roads that reached into a hinterland. In those lands behind the port, products were gathered for use in the port or sent on to the mother country.

The second pattern of settlement was oriented to the interior and focused on a Spanish town built along the upper piedmont of an upland valley. Frontera de Cáceres was designed as this type, but San Jorge de Olancho was the permanent example for the Olancho Valley.

For at least half a century, the Spanish settlers in Honduras did not deviate from this pattern of settlement site selection. All of the Spanish centers (Lunardi 1946: 67–90) fit one of the two models: the ports were Puerto de Caballos (near modern Puerto Cortés), Triunfo de la Cruz (near modern Tela), and Trujillo; the interior piedmont sites were Villa de la Frontera de Cáceres, Choluteca, San

Pedro, Gracias a Dios, and Comayagua. Not until the attraction of mining in irregular upslope areas, such as at the silver mines near Tegucigalpa in the 1580s (West 1959), did the colonists abandon their propensity for coastal ports and upland interior piedmonts.

Early Mining

The acquisition of precious minerals, which attracted so much Spanish interest throughout the New World during the colonial period, twice dominated the economy of Honduras. Between 1530 and 1560, gold placering occurred along the streams entering the Caribbean Sea and in the adjacent valleys. The second period began in 1570 and centered on several gold and silver veins in the mountainous interior of western Honduras (West 1959:767). In eastern Honduras, the swiftly flowing streams on their way to the sea cut deeply into the old, highly mineralized crystalline rock and eroded flakes and nuggets of gold downstream into alluvial deposits probably known to the natives before the arrival of the Europeans.

Gold brought the Spaniards, less than two years after they established Trujillo, into the gravels of the Aguán Valley just over the mountains from the port (West 1959:768, citing AGI Guat 44/20 marzo 1530). By 1534, the placers were in full production (West 1959:768, citing AGI Guat 48/25 febrero 1534). Five years later, the richest of all Honduran placers was discovered near Guayape in the upper Olancho Valley (Chamberlain 1966:218, 233; Montejo 1539b). Pedraza (1544:402), shortly afterward, claimed Olancho to be the richest area in all of Central America, if one included its potential for agriculture and ranching.

The reputation of the Guayape finds immediately attracted other Spaniards. Initial exploitation by Alonso de Cáceres in 1540 was halted after less than two years because of jurisdictional disputes among the Spanish officials (Chamberlain 1966:217–219; see especially n. 7, p. 219), but he did found a new Spanish town—San Jorge de Olancho—across the Río Guayape from the abandoned Frontera de Cáceres. During the earliest mining of the Olancho Valley, Indians often resisted the new Spanish community through various means mentioned below, but gold was a powerful incentive and eventually Spanish success there led to further exploration into eastern lands and the establishment of Nueva Salamanca. While San Jorge can be located with some precision along the upper piedmont near the Río Olancho and the modern site of Boquerón, Nueva Salamanca, which existed from 1544 until at least 1550, was near the previously unknown Indian towns of Xoanya, Paragri, Xagua, and Tanguara (Chamberlain 1966:222–224), and until now remains unlocated. We know only that the *villa* was some "20 leagues" (80–100 kilometers?) beyond (east of?) San Jorge de Olancho (Chamberlain 1966:222–223).

By the mid-sixteenth century, gold production in Honduras had begun to decline. Deposits in some areas were depleted, but the main reason for decline was the disappearance of cheap labor. The decimation of Indian population had been such that the New Laws of 1542 forbidding aboriginal slavery did not have to be strongly enforced [West 1959:769].

Pech Reaction and Resistance

Native reactions to the conquest, with its numerous aspects—warfare and slaving, settlement construction, mining, agricultural development—were varied and in the Pech lands of sixteenth-century Honduras seem to have followed a rhythmic progression of resistance-retreat-resistance-retreat until the number of natives was so slight that they were overwhelmed and placed in several encomiendas, where they quietly declined.

When Cortés left Trujillo for the return to México, explicit instructions were left describing the proper good treatment of the local Indians (Cortés 1525). At the time, Indians were at peace with the Spaniards, but shortly after his departure for México, the officials who replaced him became known for their cruelty (Pedraza 1544:416–417). Governor Salcedo (1526:f. 322) complained that the Indians near Trujillo had to be ordered to work and after one year at his job, this governor conducted a successful slaving trip to León, Nicaragua (Salcedo 1529).

But the Indians on occasion had their reprisal. The earliest account of an Indian victory came under the leadership of the Lenca cacique Unito, the "Señor de Comayagua," whose own political headquarters was 170 kilometers to the west. Upon hearing of the fledgling Spanish presence in the Olancho Valley, Unito gathered local Indians and in the middle of the night attacked and destroyed Frontera de Cáceres, killing 15 "Christians" and 20 horses (Salcedo 1527a:250). No other attempts to build Spanish towns in Olancho took place until the discovery of the rich Guayape gold mines in 1539 led the bold conqueror Cáceres to erect San Jorge de Olancho in 1540 on the northern valley piedmont across the Guayape from the original villa.

While the building of Spanish towns in their midst provoked the Indians, nothing seemed to incite them more than the abuses accompanying mining. Throughout the 1540s, about every two years (1542, 1544, 1546) Olancho Indians fought the Christians (Chamberlain 1966:224–225). Some Indians refused to furnish supplies to the concentrated populations of the mines, some fled the valley, and others fought (Chamberlain 1966: 218). Late in 1542, negro slaves joined the rebellious Indians of the Olancho district and drove the Spaniards from their headquarters at San Jorge and from throughout the valley. The revolt was put down in early 1543 by Rodrigo de Anaya, who rebuilt San Jorge and restored some encomiendas in the valley, finally securing the valley for the Spaniards (Chamberlain 1966:221–222).

Perhaps one of the last notable instances of Indian reprisal was that reported by Alonso de Río (1546). In 1544, a widespread Indian revolt apparently took place and included the Guayape mines of Olancho, near Comayagua, at San Pedro, and in Nicaragua at Nueva Segovia. In these places, native warriors killed several Spaniards and their negro slaves who were working the mines; as a result, the mines became depopulated.

Some 80 years later, and 160 kilometers away, one report from Trujillo reminds us that Indian resistance probably continued throughout the sixteenth century (Tovilla 1635). Martín Tovilla, named alcalde mayor of Gulf Dulce and Verapaz by the king in 1629, left Spain with the famous Honduras flotilla in early 1630, and by way of Puerto Rico, Santo Domingo, and Jamaica, reached Trujillo in October 1630. He arrived in the small port of 150 *vecinos* with some apprehension because he had learned that the local "Jicaques," who are also called "Caribdis," had a reputation for eating human flesh. During his stay of 50 days, Tovilla learned that Trujillo's governor, Capitan Francisco de Via Montan y Santander, had prepared the town (of *manaca* palm-roofed dwellings) in defense with an enclosure and a fortified *morro* of 16 pieces of artillery. The defenses were primarily designed against the "Indios de Guerra," whose lands began in the mountains some 6 leagues south of the port and extended 300 leagues along the coast to Cartagena (Colombia). Between the Indian lands and Trujillo was a great plain where one Mateo Ochoa was the principal land and cattle owner. On occasion, the Indians raided the pastures and threatened the residents of the port nearby.

Seaward of the port, the Indians were no threat. In fact, the offshore Paya, from islands then named La Guanaja and La Guayaba (Roatán), served the Spanish settlement as provisioners and were paid four reales per person for each week's work. Produce from the Trujillo area most prominently included indigo, hides, zarzaparilla, pita grass, and cochineal.

The other mechanism that seemed to stir intense native anger was the intrusion of religious missions into their lands. Perhaps because of the associated martyrdom, the most famous colonial mission episodes of eastern Honduras are those of the Franciscans Esteban Verdelete (1604–1612) and Cristóbal Martínez de la Puerta (1616–1623). Both were killed on the eastern margins of Pech lands, in the untamed territory of "Taguzgalpa" (Vásquez 1944:4:99–122; 127–186) and probably by ancestors of the Sumu, not by the Pech.

Indian Depopulation and Territorial Reduction

Perhaps the most commonly expressed disappointment—an almost constant gripe—of the Spanish officials in the New World when writing home was the disastrous decline or lack of Indians in their neighborhoods. Native labor was vital to Spanish development in the colonies and without the local manpower European life was a hard one. Of course, the other side of the situation was the occasional attempt, notably by religious personnel, to protect native life and institutions.

Coasts and islands just offshore, easily accessible to foreigners who approached by watercraft, were the best places to raid for slaves. The Bay Islands had been looted for Indians to replenish the Cuban mines in 1516 and 1517, and even while Cortés proposed peace with the Indians on the adjacent mainland, other countrymen were slaving offshore (Davidson 1974:32–33). By 1526, one or two of the Bay Islands had been depopulated by slavers from Cuba (Salcedo 1526:f. 324).

When the Protector of the Indians,[2] Bishop Cristóbal de Pedraza, arrived on his second trip to Trujillo in 1544, he realized, perhaps in his own bias favoring the Indians, that the mainland as well had lost considerable native population. Only a few Indians, less than 400, remained in the vicinity of the port (Pedraza 1544:417). He blamed the reduction on the governors who followed Cortés and Saavedra. Pedraza claimed that Salcedo and Cereceda had captured the Indians and sold them as slaves in the Greater Antilles, where most natives had perished over a decade earlier (Sauer 1966:66; Denevan 1976:57). Near Trujillo the natives who had escaped the slaving raids ran into the *monte* behind Trujillo some 14 to 15 leagues away— in an area now known as the "Sierra de Payas." The bishop further remarked that since the days of Cortés, when population density near Trujillo was greater than that of México, now no towns of 1,000 and 1,500 houses were left.

The local story was perhaps best reported by a priest who wished the Crown to learn of the maltreatment of natives in Honduras (Irugillen 1547). He, echoing the words of his bishop three years before, wrote of the poor treatment of Indians near Trujillo at the hands of past governors Salcedo and Cereceda. The padre claimed that Indians were captured, placed on ships, and sold in all of the Greater Antillean Islands. Others were linked together by chains and transported overland to Nicaragua. This last episode is verified by the account of Governor Salcedo himself (Salcedo 1529). For the Indians who escaped slavery, they vanished into the rugged mountains across the Río Aguán behind Trujillo, where "many died of hunger and sickness." At the time of Irugillen's report, in all of the jurisdiction of Trujillo, including the Bay Islands, he believed only 150 to 180 Indians (probably meaning *tributarios*, or tribute-paying Indians) remained. These few had been divided (*repartidos*) among the Spanish citizens and conquerers of the port.

Although there are indirect indications of early encomiendas near Trujillo and Olancho (Salcedo 1526), the thorough Cerrato census of encomiendas (1549–1551) organized from Guatemala to cover the entire province of Guatemala, reports nothing for eastern Honduras. The implication, therefore, is that indeed few natives were organized and remained under the control of Spaniards.

So few Indians were left in the Trujillo vicinity to man the port (Robledo 1556) that with the decline in gold to the interior the prominence of Trujillo was reduced and Comayagua became the seat of the church in 1558 (Reina V. 1983:153).

Although the early documents portray a clear sense of the depopulation that took place in eastern Honduras, for no period is there better standardized documentation on the reduction of the Pech Indians than for the last quarter of the sixteenth century. Researchers must be aware, however, of the one great flaw to any analysis of population change for the period—most Pech territory was still outside the control of the conquerors.

Statistics were gathered only from the encomiendas within the hinterlands of Trujillo and San Jorge de Olancho. Still, some indication of population decline in the controlled areas is presented in the five sets of figures compiled between 1575 and 1592 (see Tables 9–2 and 9–3).

The most general document is that of Velasco (1575:469). Clearly, the reporter

Table 9-2. Indian Settlements/Population in the Trujillo Jurisdiction, Late Sixteenth Century, by Census Year

	1575	1582a	1582b	1590	1592
Number Indian towns	24	19	22	20	15
Number tributarios	600	440	413	496	301
Settlements					
Agalteca		50		60	
Agalteca		58			
Coyra		40		40	
Curubare, Curubarique			(counted with Tople and Minguepa)		14
Çapota					6
Elen, Elena (Isla)				15	18
Goacura, Guacura (counted with Moaca)		30		40	22
Guanaja, La (Isla)		40		60	56
Helen (Isla)		14			
Maloa		8		14	
Minguepa			(counted with Tople and Curubare)		
Moaca (counted with Guacura)			Moaca		
Monguiche		20	Monguiche	30	13
Monterjuca/Montiejuca/ Monte Xucar		35	Montejucar	30	44
Ninguepa		13			
Ochoa		10	Ochoa	20	14
Papaloteca		10		12	9
Papeyeca		10		8	
Roatan (Isla)		15		20	20
Tepusseca, Tepusteca		6		15	11
Tocoa		45		50	28
Tomala, Tomalamaugua, Tomalamazagual		10		20	16
Topel/Tople		4	22, counted with Minguepa and Curubare		
Utila					
Xagua		5	Xagua		5
Xuyxa/Xuyza/Juyja		30	Xuyxa	40	25

Source: 1575=Velasco (1575); 1582a=Contreras (1582); 1582b=Anonymous (1582); 1590=Valverde (1590); 1592=Anonymous (1592).

was acting from incomplete information as he wrote that the Trujillo area had 220 to 230 Indian towns with 8,000 to 9,000 tributarios. For the district around San Jorge de Olancho, the figures are as outlandish: 10,000 tributarios in an untold number of towns. Actually, Velasco might have been correct on the estimates of Indians living in the unexplored eastern parts of Honduras adjoining the districts of Trujillo and Olancho, but these areas were without even the most rudimentary exploratory surveys at the time, and any population estimates must therefore be mere guesses.

Two documents from 1582, one collected in April by secular officials in Valladolid (Comayagua) (Contreras 1582) and another in May by the church from Tru-

Table 9-3. Indian Settlements/Population in the Olancho Jurisdiction, Late Sixteenth Century, by Census Year

	1575	1582a	1582b	1590	1592
Number Indian Towns	s.n.	36	34-39	14	29
Number Tributarios	10,000	470	726	469	590
Settlements					
Agalteca			Present		69
Cacao Suchil/Cacaoçuchil		15	Present		11
Catacamas/Cataçamas		30			12
Chindona		80		60	45
Cilca Comayagua/Circacomayagua		30		20	21
Cilimongapa		8			
Coay					4
Comayaguela		8			
Comayaguilla		5			
Coroora		15			
Cotaciali/Cosacial/Cotaçialia		10	Present	20	14
Cuchiapa		8			
Çagua/Zaquay		20			19
Çanoara					6
Çapota/Capote				20	6
El Real, Santa María					
Goapinchiapa		4			
Gualaco		50			23
Gualpay		15	Present		6
Guanapo		25			
Gueycanola					37
Jano/Xano/Zano		30		30	41
Jutícalpa/Xuticalpa		20		20	8
La Guata		25		40	54
Laguína/Yalaguína		18		15	
Maguina		7+7			5
Malcao		6			
Maloa					4
Mantocanola		20		40	32
Matapique		30			
Metapa				30	24
Monte Xuca		40			
Punuara/Ponvara		12+12			10
Taloa			Talhua		16
Talsina		10			
Taporoora					9
Taycones, Los/Taycon		8+7+15		80 (in six barrios)	
Tepaneca					8
Texilque/Tijilque		25	Present	40	17
Tunpan/Taunpan		14	Taunpan		4
Xalapa		4			
Yaguale		3			
Yaroca					15
Yupiricano				40	
Yupite Yoron/Yupiteyocon		60			59
Yupitilenca/Yutipelenca/Lupite		10	Lupite	14	11
Zaquire		12			

jillo (Anonymous 1582), portray a much better and similar picture of the number of Indian towns and the tribute-paying adults in the hinterlands of Trujillo and Olancho. The governor's figures for the eastern Honduran zone totaled 1,139 tributarios in 56 villages; the church counted 1,060 "indios casados y tributarios" in 55 towns.

By the spring of 1584, Honduran officials had written to the king much concerned about the decrease in Indians throughout the country, especially around Trujillo and Olancho, where much sickness was reported because of the forced collection of zarzaparilla during the invierno (in Honduras, this is the rainy, cooler season, between June and December). To make their point to the Spanish officials, the oidores from Guatemala claimed that whole villages were full of widows (Anonymous 1584). Zarzaparilla was a leading item of tribute during this period.

There is some confusion between the summary of Valverde (1590) and the figures presented in the longer document, but in either instance the number of *indios casados* (tribute-paying natives) dropped to 965 for the hinterlands of Trujillo and Olancho, down by 9 to 15 percent from the previous census in 1582. According to Valverde's 1590 *relación*, of the 27,000 native miners along the Guayape River in 1542, when they were freed, none now remain. A further reduction to 899 *indios tributarios* is shown in the 1592 count of the "Naturales de los pueblos de esta Provincia de Honduras q consta en las 194 partidos de esta cargo" (Anonymous 1592).

Therefore, for the Spanish-controlled areas, among the encomienda populations for the decade after 1582, one could conclude that native population dropped about 20 percent.[3]

Conclusion

And finally, to answer the Pech the question posed by the editor of the *Columbian Consequences* volumes (Thomas 1989:11), "Why did some Native American groups survive while others disappeared?" Two factors, eminently geographical in nature, recommend themselves for the Pech region.

1. The Pech occupied, and still occupy, a location peripheral to Spanish permanent settlement. Aside from the Spanish centers at Trujillo and in the Olancho valley, which only during this decade have been joined by an all-weather road, no significant Spanish settlement was established in eastern Honduras. The Pech lived on the eastern edge of colonial success and even until today, Hispanic ways have not penetrated the Bay Islands or eastern Honduras.

2. The local physical geography, dominated by rugged topography and streams inaccessible by nonnative watercraft, provided innumerable sites of refuge for Indians retreating from the conquest. Although the valleys were virtually eradicated of natives by the close of the sixteenth century, the upland enclaves did allow isolated continuations of Pech life. Virtually all of the 1,200 remaining Pech live in the highest watersheds.[4]

Notes

1. Participants were Scott Brady, Peter Herlihy, and James Samson.

2. The position of Protector of the Indians was established in 1528 (Chamberlain 1966:224–225, see n. 1; Montejo 1539a).

3. For Honduras, the best account of population reduction is that of Newson (1986).

4. The bibliography of works on the modern Pech includes Anonymous (1977), Castillo V. (1967), Conzemius (1927–1928, 1928, 1930, 1932), Cruz S. (*s. f.*), Díaz E. (1922), Holt and Bright (1976), Honduras (1977), Lanza, et al. (1986), Lunardi (1943), and Massajoli (1970).

References

Anonymous
    1513 Probanza hecha a petición del fiscal relativamente a . . . cuarto viaje de D. Cristóbal Colón. *CDIU* 7(1892):241–283.
    1515 Provanza hecha a petición del almirante D. Diego Colón . . . *CDIU* 8(1894):61–87.
    1582 Ms., Archivo General de Indias (Sevilla), Guatemala 164, de Trujillo, 1 de mayo.
    1584 Ms., Archivo General de Indias (Sevilla), Guatemala 10, de Guatemala, 8 de abril.
    1592 Pueblos tributarios de Honduras . . . Ms., Archivo General de Indias (Sevilla), Contaduría 989.
    1977 Perspectivas de solución al problemas de los Payas. Ms., Instituto Hondureño de Antropología e Historia, Tegucigalpa, p. 9.
Blom, Frans
    1932 Commerce, Trade, and Monetary Units of the Maya. *Middle American Research Institute Series*, Publication No. 4:531–552. Tulane University, New Orleans.
Bonilla, Conrado
    1955 *Piraterías en Honduras*. Imprenta Renovación, San Pedro Sula.
Castillo Velásquez, Claudio.
    1967 *Cambios positivos logrados en la comunidad de Silim, a través de la educación*. Tesis de la Universidad Nacional Antónoma de Honduras, Tegucigalpa.
CDHN
    1954–1957 *Colección Somoza: documentos para la historia de Nicaragua*. 17 vols. Madrid.
CDII
    1864–1884 *Colección de documentos inéditos, relativos al descubrimiento, conquista y colonización de las posesiones españoles de América y Oceanía, sacados, en su mayor parte, del real archivo de Indias*. 42 vols. Imprenta Manuel G. Hernández, Madrid.
CDIU
    1885–1932 *Colección de documentos inéditos relativos al descubrimiento, conquista y organización de las antiguas posesiones españoles de ultramar*. 25 vols. Tipográfico "Sucesores de Rivadeneyra," Madrid.
Cepero, Francisco de
    1526 Testimonio de la fundación de la villa de la Frontera de Cáceres, en la provincia de Honduras . . . *CDII* 14(1870):57–64.
Cerrato, Alonso
    1549–1551 Las tasaciones de los naturales de las provincias de Guatemala. Ms., Archivo General de Indias (Sevilla), Guatemala 128. Copy also in Library of Congress, Washington, D.C.
Chamberlain, Robert S.
    1966 *The Conquest and Colonization of Honduras, 1502–1550*. Octagon Books, New York.

Originally published 1953, C.I.W. Publication 598, Carnegie Institution of Washington, Washington, D.C.

Columbus, Bartholomew
ca. 1506 Informatiō di Barto Colōbo della navieatiō di ponete et garbi di Beragna new mondo novo. Ms., Biblioteca Nazionale Centrale di Firenze, Banco Raro 234:fs. 31–34v. Also published in Harrisse 1866:471–474.

Columbus, Fernando
1959 *The Life of the Admiral Christopher Columbus by His Son Fernando*. Translated and annotated by Benjamin Keen. Rutgers University Press, New Brunswick, N.J.

Contreras Guevara, Alonso de
1582 Relación hecha a su Majestad por el gobernador de Honduras, de todos los pueblos de dicha gobernación. *Boletín del Archivo General del Gobierno* (Guatemala)11(1 y 2):5–19.

Conzemius, Eduard
1927–1928 Los indios Payas de Honduras: estudio geográfico, histórico, etnográfico, y linguístico. *Journal de la Societe des Américanistes de Paris* 19:245–302; 20:253–360.
1928 On the aborigines of the Bay Islands (Honduras). *Actas, XXII Congresso Internationale degli Americanisti, 1926, Roma* 2:57–68.
1930 Bibliografía referente a los indios payas de Honduras. *Revista del Archivo y Biblioteca Nacionales* (Tegucigalpa) 8(7 y 8):279–282; 8(9 y 10):349–353.
1932 *Ethnographical survey of the Miskito and Sumu Indians of Honduras and Nicaragua*. Smithsonian Institution, Bureau of American Ethnology Bulletin No. 106, Washington, D.C.

Cortés, Hernán
1525 Carta . . . a Hernando de Saavedra . . . *CDII* 26(1876):185–194.
1971 *Cartas de Relación*. Editorial Porrúa, México.

Craig, Alan K.
1965 Contributions to the Pre-history of the Bay Islands, Honduras. *Katunob* 5:70–79. For a Spanish translation see *Yaxkin* (Tegucigalpa) 2(1):19–27.

Cruz Sandoval, Fernando
s.f. La población indígena de Honduras. Ms., Instituto Hondureño de Antropología e Historia, Tegucigalpa.

Davidson, William V.
1974 *Historical Geography of the Bay Islands, Honduras: Anglo-Hispanic conflict in the Western Caribbean*. Southern University Press, Birmingham, Ala.
1985 Geografía de los indígenas toles (jicaques) de Honduras en el siglo XVIII. *Mesoamérica* (Antigua, Guatemala) 6(9):58–90.

Denevan, William M.
1976 *The Native Population of the Americas in 1492*. University of Wisconsin Press, Madison.

Díaz del Castillo, Bernal
1982 *Historia verdadera de la conquista de la Nueva España*. Instituto "Gonzalo Fernández de Oviedo," Madrid.

Díaz Estrada, David
1922 Apuntes generales del dialecto Paya, con datos geográficos e históricos. *Boletín de la Escuela Normal de Varones* (Tegucigalpa) 2(14):493–498; 2(15 y 16):566–568; 2(17):649–652.

Edwards, Clinton R.
1978 Pre-Columbian Maritime Trade in Mesoamerica. In *Mesoamerican Communication Routes and Cultural Contacts*, edited by T. A. Lee, Jr., and Carlos Navarrete, pp. 199–209. Papers of the New World Archaeological Foundation No. 40. Brigham Young University, Provo, Utah.

Epstein, Jeremiah F.

1957 *Late Ceramic Horizons in Northeastern Honduras.* Ph.D. dissertation, University of Pennsylvania. University Microfilms, Ann Arbor.

1978 Problemas en el estudio de la prehistoria de las Islas de la Bahía. *Yaxkin* (Tegucigalpa) 2(3):149–158.

Epstein, Jeremiah F., and Vito Véliz

1977 Reconocimiento arqueológico de la Isla de Roatán, Honduras. *Yaxkin* (Tegucigalpa)2(1):28–39.

Feachem, R. W.

1938 Antiquities from the Bay Islands, Honduras (a Notice of the Exhibition, Lord Moyne's Collection). *Man* 38:73–74.

1947–1948 *The Material Culture of the Bay Islands.* 2 vols. Unpublished Master's thesis, Department of History, Cambridge University, Cambridge.

Harrisse, Henry

1866 *Bibliotheca Americana Vetustissima: a Description of Works Relating to America Published between the Years 1492 and 1551.* George P. Philes, New York.

Hasemann, George E.

1977 Reconocimiento arqueológico de Utila. *Yaxkin* (Tegucigalpa) 2(1):41–76.

Healy, Paul F.

1974 The Cuyamel Caves: Preclassic Sites in Northeast Honduras. *American Antiquity* 39:435–447.

1978 La arqueología del noreste de Honduras. Informe preliminar de la investigación de 1975 y 1976. *Yaxkin* (Tegucigalpa) 2(3):159–173.

1987 The archaeology of Honduras. In *The Archaeology of Lower Central America*, edited by F. W. Lange and D. Z. Stone, pp. 113–161. University of New Mexico Press, Albuquerque.

Helbig, Karl

1956 *Antiguales (Altertümer) der Paya-Region und die Paya-Indianer von Nordost-Honduras.* Museum für Völkerkunde und Vorgeschichte, Hamburg.

1964 *Areas y paisajes del noreste de Honduras.* Traducción por Guillermo Cano. Banco Central de Honduras, Tegucigalpa.

Holt, Dennis, and William Bright

1976 La lengua paya y las fronteras lingüisticas de Mesoamérica. In *Las fronteras de Mesoamérica, XIV mesa redonda, Tegucigalpa, 1975* 1:149–156. México.

Honduras, República de. Secretaria de Cultura, Turismo e Información, Oficina de Planificación Sectorial. Departamento de Investigación Social

1977 *Estudio socio económico y cultural. El Carbón, Pueblo Nuevo Subirana, Olancho, y Silim, Colón.* Tegucigalpa.

Irugillen, Padre

1547 Carta al rey, de Trujillo, 1 de mayo. Ms., Archivo General de Indias (Sevilla), Guatemala 164.

Johannessen, Carl L.

1959 *The Geography of the Savannas of Interior Honduras.* Unpublished Ph.D. dissertation, Department of Geography, University of California, Berkeley.

Lanza, Rigoberto de Jesús, Marco Tulio Escobar, Mauren Denise Carías Moncada, and Rosa Carminda Castellanos

1986 *Los Pech (Payas), una cultura olvidada.* Editorial Guaymuras, Tegucigalpa.

Lothrop, Samuel K.

1927 The Word "Maya" and the Fourth Voyage of Columbus. *Indian Notes and Monographs* 4:350–362. Museum of the American Indian, The Heye Foundation, New York.

Lunardi, Federico

1943 *Los Payas, documentos curiosos y viajes.* Tipográficos Nacionales, Tegucigalpa.

1946 *La fundación de la ciudad de Gracias a Dios, y de las primeras villas y ciudades de Honduras.* Tipográficos Nacionales, Tegucigalpa.

Mártyr de Angelería, Petrus
   1966 *Opera. Legatio Babylonica, De Orbe Novo Decades Octo, Opus Epistolarum*. Facsimile of 1530 edition, Alcalá. Academische Druck-u. Verlagsanstalt, Graz, Austria.
Massajoli, Pierlone
   1970 Los Payas. *Revista de la Universidad* (Tegucigalpa) 3(2–3):62–79.
Mejía Chirinos, Beatríz
   1954 Zonas arqueológicas descubiertas en el pueblo de Dulce Nombre de Culmí, Departamento de Olancho. *Revista del Archivo y Biblioteca Nacional* (Tegucigalpa) 32(11 y 12):309, 312.
Mendez, Diego
   ca. 1526 Cedula real, descobar que en el puerto de Gueymura e Cabo de Honduras. Ms., Archivo General de Indias, Ind. Gen'l.1205(53), 31 de julio.
Montejo, Francisco de
   1539a Carta del adelantado . . . al emperador, sobre varios asuntos relativos á la gobernación de Honduras. *CDII* 2(1864):212–244.
   1539b Otra carta sobre el mismo asunto . . . *CDII* 2(1864):244–252.
Morison, Samuel E. (translator and editor)
   1963 *Journals and Other Documents on the Life and Voyages of Christopher Columbus*. Heritage Press, New York.
Newson, Linda
   1986 *The Cost of Conquest, Indian Decline in Honduras under Spanish Rule*. Dellplain Latin American Series No. 20. Westview Press, Boulder, Colo.
Pedraza, Cristóbal de
   1544 Relación de la provincia de Honduras y Higueras. *CDIU* 2(1898):385–434. Also in *Revista del Archivo y Biblioteca Nacional* (Tegucigalpa) 4(1908):280–306.
Pownall, Thomas
   1779 Observations Arising from an Enquiry into the Nature of the Vases Found on the Mosquito Shore in South America. *Archaeologia* (London) 5:318–324.
Reina Valenzuela, José
   1983 *Historia eclesiastica de Honduras, tomo 1, 1502–1600*. Tipográfia Nacional, Tegucigalpa.
Río, Alonso de
   1546 Alonso Río al Rey, 2 feb. . . Ms., AGI Guat 9, Sevilla.
Robledo, Diego de
   1556 Carta al Rey, 10 abril . . . Ms., AGI Guat 9, Sevilla.
Salcedo, Diego López de
   1526 Carta al Rey, de Truxillo, postrero de dic. . . . Ms., Colección Muñoz A–104, Simancas. Also published in *CDHN* 1(1954):176–177. Madrid.
   1527a Carta á su magestad, de Chequilta, 26 de Hebrero . . . Ms., Colección Muñoz A–105, Simancas. Also published in *CDII* 40: 244–251.
   1527b Instrucción y poder que dió . . . Salcedo á Gabriel de Rojas . . . *CDII* 14(1870):384–395.
   1529 [Carta al Rey] de Trujillo, puerto é cabo de Honduras . . . *CDII* 14(1870):70–77.
Saldaña, Juan de
   1525 Testimonio de la posesión y fundación . . . del puerto . . . de Trujillo, en el cabo de Honduras. *CDII* 14(1870):44–47.
Sapper, Karl
   1899 Die Payas von Honduras. Geschildert nach einem Besuche in Jahre 1898. *Globus* 75:80–83.
Sauer, Carl O.
   1941 Foreword to Historical Geography. *Annals, Association of American Geographers* 31:1–24.
   1966 *The Early Spanish Main*. University of California Press, Berkeley and Los Angeles.

Spinden, Herbert J.
1925 The Chorotegan culture area. *Actas, XXIe Congres International des Américanistes (1924)* 2:529–545. Goteberg.

Stone, Doris Z.
1941 Archaeology of the North Coast of Honduras. *Memoirs of the Peabody Museum of Archaeology and Ethnology*, Harvard University 9(1). Cambridge, Mass.
1942 A Delimitation of the Paya Area in Honduras and Certain Stylistic Resemblances Found in Costa Rica and Honduras. *Actas, de la primera sesión del Vigésimoséptimo Congreso Internacional de Americanistas (1939)* 1:226–230. México.

Strong, William D.
1934a Hunting Ancient Ruins in Northeastern Honduras. *Explorations and Field Work of the Smithsonian Institution in 1933*, pp. 44–48. Washington, D.C.
1934b An Archeological Cruise among the Bay Islands of Honduras. *Explorations and Field Work of the Smithsonian Institution in 1933*, pp. 49–53. Washington, D.C.
1935 Archaeological Investigations in the Bay Islands, Spanish Honduras. *Smithsonian Miscellanous Collections* 92(14). Washington, D.C.

Thomas, David Hurst
1989 Columbian Consequences: The Spanish Borderlands in Cubist Perspective. In *Columbian Consequences*, vol. 1, *Archaeological and Historical Perspectives on the Spanish Borderlands West*, edited by David Hurst Thomas, pp. 1–14 Smithsonian Institution Press, Washington, D.C.

Thompson, J. Eric S.
1951 Canoes and Navigation of the Maya and Their neighbors. *Journal, Royal Anthropological Institute* 79:69–78.

Tovilla, Martín Alfonso
1635 Relación histórica descriptiva de las provincias de la Verapaz y la del Manche del Reino de Guatemala. In *Relaciones Histórico-Descriptivas de la Verapaz, El Manche y Lacandon, en Guatemala*, edited by Frances V. Scholes y Eleanor B. Adams, pp. 39–59. Editorial Universitaria, Guatemala, 1960.

Valverde, Francisco de
1590 Relación geográfica de . . . Ms. 11-4-4, 855, Real Academia de Historia, Madrid. Also published in Conrado Bonilla 1955:240–245.

Vázquez, Francisco
1937–1944 *Crónica de la provincia de Santiago Nombre de Jesús de Guatemala*. 4 tomos. Biblioteca "Goathemala" de la Sociedad de Geografía e Historia, tomos 16–19. Guatemala.

Velasco, Juan López de
1575 Demarcación y división de las Indias. *CDII* 15(1871):409–572. Imprenta de José María Perez, Madrid.

Véliz, Vito
1972 *An Analysis of Ceramics from the Piedra Blanca Site, Northeastern Honduras*. Unpublished Master's thesis, Department of Anthropology, University of Kansas, Lawrence.

Véliz, Vito, P. F. Healy, and G. R. Willey
1977 Clasificación descriptiva preliminar de cerámica de Roatán. *Yaxkin* (Tegucigalpa) 2(1):7–18.

West, Robert C.
1959 The mining economy of Honduras during the colonial period. *Actas, XXXIII Congreso Internacional de Americanistas, 1958* 2:767–777. San José, Costa Rica.

Chapter 10 ■

Gloria Lara Pinto

Change for Survival: The Case of the Sixteenth-Century Indigenous Populations of Northeast and Mideast Honduras

Events at the beginning of the Spanish colonial period in Honduras can be divided into several phases on the basis of the policies and activities of the conquistadores (Lara Pinto 1980:8–11). The first two of these phases concern us here. The initial phase, from 1502 to 1524, comprises the discovery of the Caribbean coast and the offshore islands. No systematic attempt was made at that time to subjugate the indigenous populations or to impose an administrative network; even so, on at least one occasion, a slaving expedition from Cuba raided the Bay Islands (Las Casas 1958:391–394).

A second phase, from 1525 to 1536, signals the beginning of exploration as well as the uncoordinated conquest of the northwest, northeast, and southeast regions of Honduras. In the first half of 1526, the first repartimiento of Indian settlements took place in the northeast to establish an encomienda system.[1] The specifics of this event are not yet documented, but it was carried out under instructions from Hernán Cortés and represents the first direct Spanish interference in the native social and political organization in northeast Honduras (Salcedo 1526, in Rubio Sánchez 1975:40).

In concrete terms, an encomienda was represented by a settlement (or settlements) whose tribute the encomendero was entitled to collect for himself. He could also periodically claim personal services from the Indians of his encomienda to work in his household or on his landholdings. In those early days, claims on personal services seem to have been more common than tribute, probably because limits on labor were not regulated until the middle of the sixteenth century (Lara Pinto 1980:242–264). Indian tribute was delivered in species, for example, corn, manioc, and birds in the case of the northeast hinterland of Trujillo (Salcedo 1526, in Rubio Sánchez 1975:42). Eventually, metal bells and hachets (probably of tumbaga) made their way into the tribute inventories (Cereceda 1530, in CDHN 1954:426; Salcedo 1526, in Rubio Sánchez 1975: 53), but these were of almost no interest to the Spaniards given their low gold content.

During this period of incipient encomiendas, slaving by the local conquistadores, as well as those from elsewhere in the Caribbean (especially Cuba) (Salcedo 1526, in Rubio Sánchez 1975:47–48), continued in the Bay Islands and on the mainland in the region of Trujillo (Cereceda 1530 in CDHN 1954:406; García Lerma 1531, in Saco 1932:158; Salcedo 1527, in Saco 1932:155–156; Oviedo 1959:374). The local disruptions created by efforts to impose a more or less stable encomienda system was confused by these slaving activities and further aggravated by the internal conflicts existing among the conquistadores themselves.

In the second half of 1526, a newly appointed governor of Trujillo, López de Salcedo, began making changes in the encomienda privileges established by Cortés (Salcedo 1526, in Rubio Sánchez 1975:50). Shortly after Salcedo's death in 1529, encomiendas were again assigned (Cereceda 1530, in CDHN 1954:436). For the final time in this period, 1533 (Oviedo 1959:388), the authorities of Trujillo were advised to distribute the remaining Indian settlements among the 50 Spanish citizens who were to establish themselves permanently in the town.

The key word here is "remaining." The significance of this term derives from the number of Spaniards active in the Trujillo region during those early years. From 1525 to 1526, a small group of 50–60 were living there (Moreno 1525); in 1527 this number rose to around 140 (Castillo 1527, in Rubio Sánchez 1975:503–509); and from 1529 to 1533, at least 230 (Oviedo 1959:388) were actively involved in Trujillo in the slave trade and in the exploitation of gold mines in the Agalta Valley. I have been able to reconstruct the existence of at least 30 encomiendas in the region around Trujillo, including the islands, for the period between 1525–1533 (Lara Pinto 1980:106–110). Comparison of these data with the situations in other well-settled regions of Honduras—the northwest, northeast, and central regions—leads me to believe that Trujillo and its hinterland had at the time of contact a relatively high demographic potential (Lara Pinto 1980:149–182, 252–259). By 1533, however, increasing complaints indicate that the Trujillo region and the islands were becoming depopulated (Pedraza 1539, in Sherman 1979:44–47, 268, and 379). In other words, the demographic collapse was so critical that subsistence for the conquistadores was no longer guaranteed.

In sum, the years from 1525 to 1533 frame the beginning of the conquest in the Trujillo region and the subsequent abandonment of the area by the majority of the conquistadores. By that time, these adventurers had transferred their interests and efforts to the systematic conquest of the northwest, leaving behind a legacy of disorder. That is, the conquest in Trujillo was carried out under contradictory conditions of leadership (Cortés, Salcedo, Cereceda) and was characterized by internal struggles among the colonists themselves. The objective of this intervention was a rapid and complete exploitation of natural and human resources, the latter being ultimately abandoned and forced to restore some order to their own survival. This radical and fitful disruption produced deep and irreversible changes in the indigenous societies in this part of Honduras.

This impact translated into the disappearance of autonomous forms of organization and production more so than an adaptation of indigenous sociopolitical features to the new administrative model imposed by the Europeans. Many natives, in fact, had no opportunity to adapt as part of a group since survivors were commonly enslaved and relocated in foreign regions from which they probably never returned. This was not unusual for those times; a conquistador who participated in the conquest and colonization of other parts of the isthmus or in other regions of Honduras would take with him his slaves or naborías (see Konetzke 1965:165–166) on subsequent expeditions. Such was the case of the accountant for the province of Honduras, Andrés de Cereceda, a key figure in the colonial policies applied at Trujillo from 1530 to 1533. After his death in 1539, he claimed as personal property in his will the Indians of "su casa." Among these Indians were natives from Trujillo, the Bay Islands, the northwest, and mountainous southwest, and also from Guatemala, Yucatan, Nicaragua, and ultimately Panama (Cereceda 1539). This must have been common in those days; that is, there is no reason to believe that Cereceda was an exception.

These Indians, removed from their homelands, separated from their families, and dispossessed of a common language tie, must have constituted the first generation of "indios ladinos" (Hispanicized Indians) (Lara Pinto 1980:203–205), as some were already referred to in this document. In other words, the most viable form of adaptation for this indigenous conglomeration was integration into the emerging mestizo mass.

This panorama of accounts, events, and consequences during the first years of conquest should encourage a clearer understanding of the influences of native slave trade, the tribute system, forced labor in the mines, epidemics, and the weakened indigenous power structures upon the populations that managed to survive the impact of the third decade of the sixteenth century in northeast and mideast Honduras.

However, the discussion that follows focuses not only on the consequences of European contact in the sixteenth century, but also on the identity of the native populations in northeast and mideast Honduras at the time of the discovery and initial conquest. That is, an assessment of the consequences of contact depends to a large degree on our understanding of the native groups affected by such contact. Since there is some confusion and controversy over this question, I will devote significant space at the outset to identifying the indigenous groups in northeast and mideast Honduras.

The Problem of Identity

At the moment of Spanish contact, indigenous groups from northeast and mid-east Honduras were located along the Caribbean coast east and west of Trujillo and in the Aguán, Agalta, and Olancho valleys. A good part of this territory has been considered the mainland domain of the Pech (Paya) (Helbig 1956; Stone 1975). Davidson (1974:24, Map 8) offers a synthesis of boundaries proposed as Pech territory for the period immediately before and after the Spanish conquest. These delimitations all assert that Pech inhabited the continental area which extends in the north from the mouth of Aguán and Patuca rivers and reaches the confluence of the Guayape and Guayambre rivers to the south (Figure 10–1). Referring to this territory as the "continental" or "mainland" Pech area implies that the Bay Islands are also considered part of the "insular" Pech area during the same period (Davidson 1974:25, this volume; Stone 1975:42–47).

Analysis of the indigenous settlement pattern and reigning sociopolitical organization at the moment of contact has been the guiding theme for several of my investigations in recent years (Lara Pinto 1980, 1982, 1985, 1987, 1990). My reconstruction of these patterns in the regions mentioned above do not support the extension of a continental Pech area into the Agalta and Olancho valleys nor into the Aguán Valley, as has been deduced from comparative archaeological data at the beginning of the sixteenth century (Stone 1975:39–42). The ethnohistoric sources at my disposal suggest an ethnic and linguistic definition slightly different for this territory. In this context, the Nahua "colonies" recognized earlier by others (Fowler 1983:359–363; Reyes Mazzoni 1974:19–31; Richter 1971:77–79; Stone 1975:15) played a more important role and reached a greater expansion than previously believed (Lara Pinto 1980:72–76).

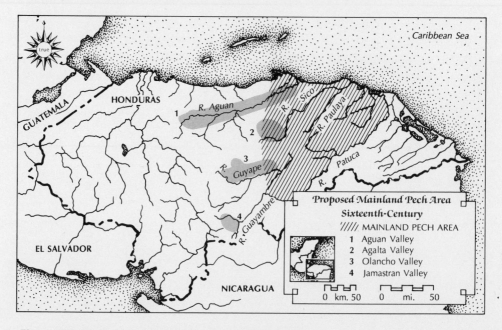

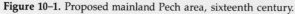

Figure 10–1. Proposed mainland Pech area, sixteenth century.

Basing my arguments primarily on the analysis of sixteenth- and seventeenth-century documents, I examine the sociopolitical organization, ethnic affiliation, interregional interactions, and territorial limits of the indigenous groups in the region described. Within this framework, I evaluate the obvious impacts of the Spanish conquest. We should be able to note the following at least superficially: the kinds of societies the Spanish confronted, the depth of the changes provoked by the imposition of the foreign political regime, the mechanisms of adaptation adopted by the indigenous groups, and cases of success and failure of these adaptations. Under these latter circumstances some groups lost their identity, and, if they managed to survive at all, were commonly absorbed into other indigenous groups or into the growing mestizo conglomerate.

It is important for the reader to understand at this point that I am aware of the contradictions emergent between my own work and that of Davidson (this volume). Davidson proposes a Pech region that included the Aguán, Agalta, and Olancho valleys in the sixteenth century; I propose for the same territory a region that shows the influences of Nahua culture and language. I do not necessarily exclude the Pech (or speakers of another language) from this setting in the sixteenth century, but I do argue for Nahua control of the bottomlands in these valleys. By extension, I am urging at the same time a reconsideration of the origins of the archaeological remains now credited to the Pech.

The names of the Indian settlements called "Pech" in Tables 9–2 and 9–3 (this volume) are taken from sixteenth-century sources that I have evaluated for this or other studies in the past; however, there is *no* allusion in these documents to the ethnic affiliations of these encomienda-villages.[2] I assume that this is the result of Davidson's own interpretation. That is, the region has been postulated as Pech, and the Indian settlements included in the encomiendas of that region are assumed to have been Pech as well.

Speaking as a nonlinguist, I would not deny the possibility of Pech terms in Tables 9–2 and 9–3, but I suspect that calling them Pech at this stage of the investigation would be misleading. In other words, my conclusions do not result from unawareness of the historical sources Davidson mentions, but from a different approach to the data at my disposal. I have chosen to present a case study using the ethnohistorical sources in a more selective manner to bring new light to an old issue.

Finally, the document I base the core of my interpretation on (vis-à-vis the survival of Nahua traits in the so-called Pech region) may not be known to Davidson. Had he been aware of its existence, some of our major discrepancies may never have emerged. In any case, the objective of my essay is not to provoke further controversy, but to encourage a critical reevaluation of the facts.

Discovery of the Islands and Mainland Honduras, 1502

The documentation of Columbus's fourth voyage is well known and will not be repeated here (see Chamberlain 1953:9–10; Davidson 1974:25–27; Lara Pinto 1980:31–45; Richter 1971:73–77). I *will* mention the consequences of that voyage that are pertinent to this discussion, namely, those that provide clues to ethnic identities. Without itemizing, I note as a first point of departure that a significant number of specific and complicated cultural traits were shared by the islanders from Guanaja and the indigenous mainlanders from the Punta Caxinas-Black (Sico) River coast.[3]

Columbus's meeting with a native trading vessel near Guanaja is equally well known. The impressment of an indigenous crewman as interpreter for the Spaniards is evidence that the native spoke at least one of the languages of the coast (Colón 1892:147–154). Davidson (1974:28; this volume) offers convincing evidence that Pech was spoken on Guanaja and the corresponding mainland; I would reiterate that Pech was but one of several languages spoken on the coast between Punta Caxinas and Black River.

However, the interpreter did not speak the language of any of the groups (called "savages" by the Spaniards) to the east of Black River. This corresponds well with the distinction also noted in characteristics of their material culture. These "savages" occupied the coast ("Costa de la Oreja") from Black River to the Cape of Honduras (Figure 10–2).

Settlement and Conquest of the Northeast Coast and Interior, 1525–1533

The original colonial settlement of Trujillo was founded in 1525 adjacent to an Indian settlement known locally as "Guaimura" (Díaz del Castillo 1964:402) and was probably moved at least once, but within the same bay area (Salcedo 1526, in Rubio Sánchez 1975:43). This bay area pertained to the territory or province known earlier also as "Guaymura" (Pedraza 1544, in CDID 1868:414). Nearby, old indigenous settlements had existed at the "Guaimoreta" Lagoon (Tamayo

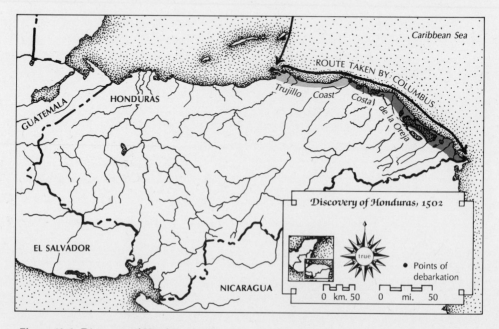

Figure 10–2. Discovery of Honduras, 1502.

1642) and the inland sierra was also known then as "Guaymoreta." This contiguous area seems to represent a circumscribed territory unified by one of the languages spoken on the coast, perhaps Pech.[4]

From the moment Trujillo was founded, interest shifted toward the native settlements 7 to 8 leagues inland. There, large agricultural populations with up to 500 houses (many of masonry) occupied rich flatlands where they harvested maize, cassava, and beans and raised ground fowl, deer, and dogs. Beyond, however, Spanish penetration was halted by distinct warrior groups who controlled the next 100 leagues (Moreno 1525).

Cortés arrived at Trujillo in 1526 and immediately sent emissaries to two of these same cooperating towns. The nearest was Chapagua, with 10 subject villages. Two leagues beyond was Papayeca with 18 subject villages (Cortés 1963:299–300). After a brief period of uneasy collaboration, these indigenous groups began open resistance against the Spanish. The resulting campaign carried the Spaniards 35 leagues inland to a town I have been able to locate in the Aguán Valley. This is the town of Agalteca (Acalteca), at that time in the vicinity of Sonoguera and later moved farther south (Lara Pinto 1980:72). The valley itself "de Papayela . . . tiene 30 leguas o mas de largo hacia Olancho, por lo que pasa por un rio caudaloso que se dice Huahuan" (López de Velasco 1971:157–158). In other words, Papayeca was a *pueblo de indios* in the Aguán Valley, apparently in the part closest to Trujillo. But not only the Aguán Valley was involved in this phase of Spanish conquest. Other settlements known to be subject villages of Chapagua and Papayeca were located in the Agalta Valley (Lara Pinto 1980:Map 5).

Of special note here is that two paramount leaders ("principales señores") were recognized in this so-called territory of the Papayeca. One of these ruled from the Agalta Valley (Lara Pinto 1980:72), indicating that some sort of political affiliation may have existed between the Aguán and Agalta Valleys, maybe in the form of an incorporated territory. For this reason I have included the Agalta Valley within the sphere of influence of what I will refer to from now on as the Province of Papayeca (Figure 10–3). Keeping in mind that one of Chapagua's subject villages lay in the southern part of the Agalta Valley, it seems likely that Chapagua was also drawn into the same political sphere.

Finally, we may speculate that the Bay Islands were somehow affiliated with this same province of Papayeca: At the request of Cortés, the *señores* of Chapagua and Papayeca provided the Spanish with labor in Trujillo; although the documentation is not clear on this point, Cortés was provisioned with fish from the Bay Islands, perhaps through this same link (Díaz del Castillo 1968:227–228).

In 1525, explorations of the Olancho Valley also began. A member of Cortés's expedition distinguished this "Province of Olancho" (later known as Guayape) in such a way that it is now possible to include part of its limits in Figure 10–3 (Díaz del Castillo 1968:250).[5]

It is important to mention that the lords of Chapagua submitted to the conquistadores. The Papayaca, on the other hand, opened war against the Spanish from their mountain retreats. As one result, the Papayeca lost their two lords— one was executed and the other carried in slavery to Mexico (Cortés 1963:306).

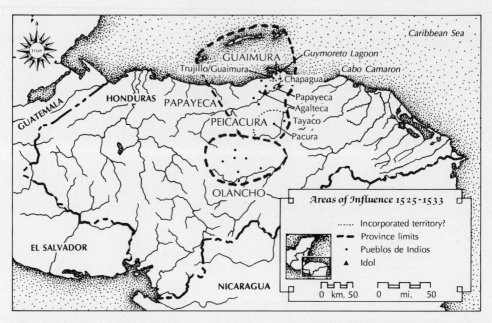

Figure 10–3. Area of influence of the provinces of Papayeca (I), Guaimura (II), Peicacura (III), and Olancho (IV), 1525–1533.

These events weakened the sociopolitical order in the Aguán Valley, leaving the Papayeca without their principal political leaders and, perhaps, their religious leaders as well, as I will explain below (see also Lara Pinto and Hasemann 1988).

By the middle of 1526, the conquistadores had explored the Aguán and Agalta valleys thoroughly enough to identify three places where idols were guarded. One of these, which we can associate with pilgrimages (see Davidson 1974:30), was located 3 to 4 leagues from Trujillo (near Chapagua?); another was located on an island that Davidson has identified as Guanaja; the third, some 12 to 15 leagues from Trujillo (Aguán Valley?). The guardians of these idols were known as *papas* and resided in special quarters. Even though they possessed religious attributes, a papa was also a *principal* and had in his care the sons of all the other *principales* of the land (Salcedo 1526, in Rubio Sánchez 1975:41).[6] These papas and their duties bring to mind the Aztec *papauaque*.[7]

In 1526, the idol closest to Trujillo was destroyed. In the Valley of Olancho, with settlement names suggestive of another area of Nahua influence, massive slave movements provoked open rebellion in that same year (Lara Pinto 1980:87). During the final months of 1526, slaving became the order of the day in the Bay Islands and the Aguán Valley as well (García de Lerma 1531, in Saco 1932:158). In these latter cases, the Spanish authorities justified slaving privileges, citing their understanding that the islands belonged to the jurisdiction of Trujillo at that time as well as in the preconquest past (Salcedo 1526, in Rubio Sánchez 1975:47–48).

By the beginning of 1527, the entire region was at war. Consequently, the Spanish authorities initiated a punitive expedition against the rebel settlements, mostly in the province of Olancho. Apparently the populations of the Aguán and Agalta valleys participated as well. Their villages were burned, and many, including caciques, were carried in chains to Nicaragua where they were executed (Lara Pinto 1980:87–96).[8] These data have helped establish the limits of the province of Olancho to the west, north, and east (Figure 10–4).

Between 1527 and 1528, events shifted to the recently discovered gold deposits at Tayaco, some 18 leagues from Trujillo (Cereceda 1530, in CDHN 1954:410–411, 426). The lord of Peicacura (his name survived in the village name Pacura), as the Agalta Valley was then called, was considered the most powerful of the region (Cereceda 1530, in CDHN 1954:436). These mines were probably within his domain (Cereceda 1530, in Oviedo 1959:371). This suggests that at least some of the many Aguán Valley settlements were abandoned, had decreased in population, or lost the political cohesion necessary to mount an uprising like the one that broke loose in the Agalta Valley shortly thereafter. Nahua influence in the Agalta Valley also seems to have declined around this time. I will return to this point below.

The indigenous populations fled to the mountains as a result of the Agalta uprising, ending for the time being the extraction of gold deposits. But this also came at great sacrifice to the natives: They abandoned their harvests and left behind their stored foods, forcing them to descend in dark of night to recover supplies. Between 1530 and 1533, a measles epidemic swept through all of eastern Honduras, further debilitating the indigenous populations (see Herrera 1601–1615:28).

Summarizing briefly, the indigenous populations in the Aguán, Agalta, and Olancho valleys were decimated, and, at least in the Aguán, the sociopolitical

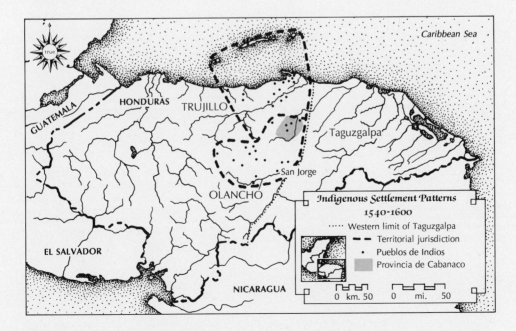

Figure 10–4. Indigenous settlement patterns, jurisdictions of Trujillo (I) and Olancho (II), 1540–1600.

structure had been radically weakened. This process was completed in just eight years (1525–1533). Contributing factors included the treatment of slaves, abuses in the mines, epidemics, starvation, and frequent relocation of the enco-menderos and personal native servants, not to mention the constant state of war which kept the natives holed up in their mountain retreats (see Newson 1986: 95–116).

Survival of the Nahua Cultural Tradition in the Agalta Valley, 1540–1600

From 1533 to 1540, expeditionary activity focused on the west and central sections of the country. Not until the consolidation of control in this territory did the Spanish shift their interest back to the Olancho Valley, where they founded San Jorge in 1540 (Lara Pinto 1980:197). From here the Agalta Valley was reoccupied. At this time, the Agalta reappears in the documentation, but not as Pecaicura. It was then known as the "Provincia" or "Comarca de Çabanaco," an area inhabited by the Taicones (Corella 1561), a name probably derived from Tayaco (mines) of 1527–1528 (Figure 10–4). From that time on, some of these Taicones reinitiated the native resistance.

The events described next are based on declarations made by conquistadores who knew the Agalta Valley and had observed characteristics of the native culture still surviving between 1541 and 1545. First, the papa (papuauque) functioned as they had in the province of Papayeca in 1525. According to informants, the papas directed secret ceremonies and sacrifices and continued to command the obedience and respect of the native communities. Accordingly, they were provided with elaborate dwellings in the mountains similar to those described by archaeologists in the Bay Islands (cf. Davidson 1974:20) and by early ethnohistoric evidence (see Sherman 1979:46–47). In one case, a Spanish observer found a papa in a large house at the hub of paved walkways. The papa was accompanied by 25 juvenile males 10–12 years old and 2 apprentice/assistants who would replace him at his death.

This same witness recognized the remains of another Spaniard who had apparently been sacrificed and buried with other humans, many macaws, and various offeratory items. This papa, of course, was torn protesting from his temple and escorted to town. He hid his eyes with his knee-length hair so that he would not look upon any woman; having done so, he would have been disqualified from his office.

One form of ritual observed by the Spanish included bloodletting. Papas, as well as the general native population, drew blood from their own ears, noses, and tongues with stingray spines. This was also practiced with *macanas* in front of stone idols. They also let blood from their backs with spiny branches of ceiba trees.[9] But what bothered the Spanish most was the rumored sacrifice of those youngsters in the papa's service, including, among other rituals, their live burial upon his death.

One additional point of interest in this context is the language of communication between the Spanish interpreters and the Taicones: In the mid-sixteenth century, the language usually learned by the conquistadores for their use in this territory was Nahuatl (see Richter 1971:113–114).

These data indicate a vigorous cultural tradition still active among the Taicones, that is, the Nahua tradition, which had already been lost in the Aguán Valley and the remainder of that sphere of influence. In 1561, the Crown proposed to eradicate the religious practices described above and to eliminate permanently the residues of social and political power held by the papas. To do this, it introduced Catholic clergy into Taicon settlements. According to Bishop Corella (1561), however, the Taicones were lazy and poor and would not plant maize or raise chickens, despite the excellent conditions. Less than 40 years before, the Taicones were not only harvesting seed crops, but also storing food supplies. By 1561, however, they had apparently adapted to another, less stable and less sedentary subsistence strategy, which they probably developed during their periodic retreats to the mountains. This radical change of lifeways from permanent and densely settled agricultural communities with fairly rigid sociopolitical structure to small, temporary, and dispersed settlements based on foraging must have brought as a consequence the weakening of existing social norms. Shortly thereafter, the Taicones disappeared as their numbers dwindled (at the end of the sixteenth century the six towns of *taicones* included 80 "indios casados" [Memorial, n.d.]), Catholicism overcame native religion, and neighboring indigenous groups offered better alternatives for survival.

The Native Populations of Taguzgalpa, Seventeenth Century

A contemporaneous definition of the rest of eastern Honduras, that is, the area populated by the "savages," allows me to assume that the province of Taguzgalpa began in the mountains to the east of Trujillo (Espino 1674, in CLDHA 1908:369) or east of the mouth of the Aguán River.[10] (Although the account of Espino dates to 1674, it refers to missionary work begun in 1622). The southern limit of this territory was the Guayape and Guayambre rivers (Espino 1674, in CLDHA 1908:368). In the central section the boundary can be drawn in the neighborhood of the Agalta Valley (Vásquez 1716, in CLDHA 1908:LI-LII). The Agalta and Olancho valleys were therefore not considered lands of the Paya nor other Taguzgalpa groups at that time. In 1664, as evidence of this, Spanish colonists who lived in the Agalta Valley unsuccessfully tried to settle the Pech there (Vásquez 1716, in CLDHA 1908:LII).

We have another boundary definition, although a little confusing, which nevertheless supports the boundary described above (Vásquez 1716, in Stone 1975:8). In this latter case, the northern boundary of Taguzgalpa is located in the area around the Guaymoreto Lagoon; to the west, the Agalta, Olancho, and Jamastrán valleys; to the south, the Guayambre and Guayape rivers. This same source adds that the northern limits of Taguzgalpa begin at the Black River and reach the confluence of the Guayambre and Guayape rivers (Figure 10–4).[11]

Other post-seventeenth-century sources place the Pech on the Black River (Rubio Sánchez 1975:Mapa del siglo XVIII between pp. 350 and 351). An early nineteenth-century report from missionaries declares that the Pech "habitaban unas 30 leguas de las montañas de Agalta" (Goicoechea 1838, in Stone 1975:19). Note that the document states "mountains" and not Agalta Valley. This is not surprising since we already know that the Agalta was inhabited by a different indigenous group from the moment of contact until the end of the sixteenth century before being overtaken by Spanish colonials. As we saw above, the colonials wanted to settle Pech in the valley from the middle of the seventeenth century on. So, the natives who settled in the missions at the beginning of the nineteenth century relieved somewhat the labor shortage for 20 cattle ranches there. However, the colonials complained that this would not do (Goicoechea 1807–1808, in Lunardi 1943:15) since the Pech were accustomed to abandoning the missions from time to time without warning.

The Archaeology of Northeast and Mideast Honduras

The archaeology of the Agalta Valley, site of the Pech missions from the end of the seventeenth century on, has been identified as Pech. Since the archaeology of the Aguán Valley, the Bay Islands, and parts of the Olancho Valley are similar, these regions have been declared Pech as well. The analysis of ethnohistoric documentation does not support this interpretation for the moment of contact. Instead, these data suggest that the Nahuas held those territories, either under total political control or at least under strong cultural influence. This does not deny the possible coexistence of other native groups in a substratum or as populations marginal to the territory of Nahua influence. Groups with other cultural affiliations are known for the Valley of Olancho (Richter 1971:107, 121–126), but this does not change the general panorama for the Aguán and Agalta valleys proposed above. On the other hand, recent archaeological discoveries in the Miskitia (ancient Taguzgalpa) suggest that we will have to redefine the cultural character of the area for the preconquest period (see Lara Pinto and Hasemann 1988).

The combined analysis of ethnohistoric and archaeologial data is very suggestive. Fowler (1983:361) submits that the archaeological site of Río Claro in the Aguán Valley (Healy 1978:163) could be the Papayeca mentioned by Cortés. According to Fowler, the architectural remains show Mexican features, even though the typical talud-tablero construction style is absent. On the other hand, the appearance of these Mexican architectural features and other specific innovations in the material culture of the so-called Cocal period (A.D. 1000–1530) (Healy 1978:172) coincide with the time frame (A.D. 800–1300) of the proposed Nahua migration from central Mexico and the lowlands of the Gulf of Mexico to Guatemala, El Salvador, and Honduras (Fowler 1983:348). For example, Cocal period sites tend to be larger and more densely populated than those corresponding to the preceding period (Healy 1976:6); there is a marked dependence on maize cultivation, in contrast to the earlier subsistence economy based primarily on molluscs and game (Healy 1978:167); and the year A.D. 1000 marks the appearance of elaborate metate sculpture in the area (Healy 1978:164). This all conforms to Fowler's assertion that Mexican migrants introduced changes in the architecture, settlement pattern, economy, and technology (1983:351).

Curiously, the community plan of Río Claro/Papayeca(?) (Healy 1978:170), with its three paved walkways, one of which enters the site from the south-southwest and ends just before one of the largest and highest structures, lends credence to the witnessed account presented above (Corella 1561). Once more, as suggested in the documents indicated earlier, a relationship emerges between the Agalta and Aguán valleys.

Conclusions

At the beginning of the seventeenth century, the Aguán and Agalta valleys were inhabited by Nahua groups that exercised a strong regional influence and left their own particular mark on the culture of this part of Honduras. This influence seems to have extended to the Bay Islands and, to a lesser extent, to the coast east of Trujillo and toward the Black River. The use of a Nahua variant in the valleys mentioned above and in the rest of their area of influence does not pre- clude the simultaneous existence of other languages (most notably Pech), espe- cially along the coast between Trujillo and the Black River. The Olancho Valley also seems to have been settled by groups with ties to central Honduras.

In a short period (1525–1533), the Nahua influence was neutralized in the Aguán Valley. A Nahua remnant survived in the Agalta Valley until the end of the sixteenth century by altering its survival strategies. Although the Spanish did redirect their attention away from the Nahua, however, the Nahua were ac- celerating their own political and economic deterioration and, ultimately, the disappearance of their own original culture. Apparently they were able to incor- porate themselves into the numerous warlike societies of Taguzgalpa. For their part, the groups indigenous to that part of Taguzgalpa began to cross into areas left vacant by the Nahua. The Taguzgalpa groups showed in the long run a greater capacity for adaptation within the colonial regime, perhaps because they were not constrained by such rigid sociopolitical structures.

Notes

1. *Encomienda* means "patronage"; that is, a Spanish encomendero comitted himself to protect the king's property (e.g., tribute and labor of the Indian vassals) and to Chris- tianize these same Indians. In compensation for his efforts in the conquest and these other services, the encomendero was allowed to profit in a very specific way from his encomienda.

2. The sixteenth-century sources Davidson refers to are López de Velasco 1575 (also published in 1971); Contreras Guevara 1582, (also published in 1946); Valverde 1590 (also found in Memorial, n.d.). As further clarification, I also should point out that all the sixteenth-century Indian place names mentioned in Davidson's Tables 9–2 and 9–3 have been known to me since 1980 and were included in my dissertation of that year (pub- lished in Germany).

3. Diego de Porras, one of the witnesses of this event, calls the boundary between these two distinct cultural traditions "Río de la Poseción." From geographic descriptions made by Porras and others (Colón 1892), it seems clear that Porras identified the Río Sico,

Tinto o Negro (Black River) and *not* the Río Patuca. In addition the distance between Punta Caxinas and Río de la Poseción, according to Porras, is 15 leagues, which coincides with the approximate distance between Punta Caxinas and Río Tinto. His observation that the coastal lowlands began there (which corresponds to the actual situation) constitutes another factor favoring the identity of today's Río Tinto as the Río de la Poseción in 1502.

4. The towns of the Guaymoreto Lagoon, which appear for the last time in my inventory toward the end of the sixteenth century, were located three leagues from Trujillo and were populated by fishermen. By 1642, they were explicitly recorded as nonexistent.

5. The Nahua presence in the Olancho Valley can also be speculated from this inventory: Hueitapalán, Huictlalo, Huilacho, Olancho (Lara Pinto 1980:76); according to Cortés (1963:303) Olancho was known in another language(?) as "Xucutaco."

6. For a discussion of this see Lara Pinto and Hasemann (1988).

7. *Papauaque - guedejudos;*
   papatli   - long, tangled/matted hair of the custodians
                  of the idols (Molina-1977:79);
   papauaque - indigenous priests who met with nobles
                  when the latter selected a chief or king;
   papatli   - long and disordered hair of the Indian
                  priests (Siméon 1986:375).

8. López de Salcedo, governor of Honduras at that time and in charge of this expedition, was denounced for capturing 22 chiefs and 300 natives in Olancho and escorting them in chains to León, Nicaragua, where he executed 200 (Castillo 1527 in Rubio Sánchez 1975:503–509). He brought with him to Trujillo on his return from León 102 naborías who came from the towns between Trujillo and Olancho (Testimonio 1529).

9. It is difficult to ignore here the comparison with the self-imposed penances of the youngsters of the *calmecac* (illustration from the Mendocino Codex in Macaza 1981:92).

10. It has been said that this area was Pech in the seventeenth century (Stone 1975:9) since the missionaries appeared to have taken native interpreters from the Bay Islands. However, Espino (1674, in CLDHA 1908:368) asserts that one of the clerics knew the language. This individual lived on that coast for several years after having been shipwrecked there as a young man. That is, the presence of Indians would not have been strictly necessary to establish communication.

11. The information from Vásquez seems to have caused some confusion since Stone says that "the Río Tinto is the Patuca" and traces the western limits of Taguzgalpa along this river. I believe that the data at my disposal suggest a more congruent boundary departing from the Río Tinto to the confluence of the Guayape and Guayambre rivers.

References

CDHN
   1954 *Colección Somoza: documentos para la historia de Nicaragua,*vol. 2. Madrid.
CDID
   1864–1884 *Colección de documentos inéditos relativos al descubrimiento, conquista y organización de las antiguas poseciones españolas de América y Oceanía, sacados de los archivos del reino y muy especialmente del de Indias.* 42 vols. Madrid.
Cereceda, Andrés de
   1539 Bienes de Andrés de Cereceda. San Pedro de Puerto Caballos. Archivo General de Indias, Contaduría 987. Seville.
CLDHA
   1908 Relaciones Históricas y Geográficas de América Central. In *Colección de libros y documentos referentes a la historia de América*, vol. 8. Madrid.

Colón, Fernando
1892 *Historia del Almirante Don Cristóbal Colón*, vol. 2. Madrid.

Contreras Guevara, Alonso
1946 Relacion hecha a su Magestad por el gobernador de Honduras de todos los pueblos de dicha gobernación, año 1582. Valladolid del Valle de Comayagua. *Boletín del Archivo General del Gobierno*. Year IX, nos. 1 and 2. Guatemala.

Corella, Gerónimo de
1561 Letter from the Bishop of Honduras, Gerónimo de Corella, to the Crown, 1561. San Jorge de Olancho. Al.29/Leg4672/Exp40137. Archivo General de Centroamérica. Guatemala.

Cortés, Hernán
1963 Quinta Carta, Relación de Hernan Cortes al Emperador Carlos V. Tenuxtitan, 3 de septiembre de 1526. *Cartas y Documentos*. Mexico.

Chamberlain, Robert S.
1953 *The Conquest and Colonization of Honduras, 1502–1550*. Carnegie Institution Publication No. 598. Washington, D.C.

Davidson, William V.
1974 *Historical Geography of the Bay Islands, Honduras: Anglo-Hispanic Conflict in the Western Caribbean*. Southern University Press, Birmingham, Ala.

Díaz del Castillo, Bernal
1968 *Historia Verdadera de la Conquista de la Nueva España*. Editorial Porrúa, Mexico.

Fowler, William R. Jr.
1983 La Distribución Prehistórica e Histórica de los Pipiles. *Mesoamérica* 6:348–372.

Healy, Paul F.
1976 Informe Preliminar sobre la Arqueología del Período Cocal. Noreste de Honduras. *Yaxkín* 2:4–9.
1978 La Arqueología del Noreste de Honduras: Informe Preliminar de la Investigación de 1975 y 1976. *Yaxkín* 2:159–173.

Helbig, Karl
1956 *Antiguales (Altertümer) der Paya-Region und die Paya-Indianer von Nordost Honduras. Beiträge zur mittelamerikanischen Völkerkunde*. Selbstverlag des Hamburgischen Museums fur Völkerkunde und Vorgeschichte, Hamburg.

Herrera y Tordesillas, Antonio de
1601–1615 *Historia General de los hechos de los castellanos en las Islas i Tierra Firme del Mar Oceano*. Decade V, Book I, Chapter 10. Madrid.

Konetzke, Richard
1965 *Süd-und Mittelamerika I. Die Indianerculturen Altamerikas und die Spanisch-portuguisische Kolonialherrschaft*. Frankfurt am Main.

Lara Pinto, Gloria
1980 *Beiträge zur indianischen Ethnographie von Honduras in der 1. Hälfte de 16. Jahrhunderts, unter besonderer Berücksichtigung der Historischen Demographie*. Repro Lüdke, Hamburg.
1982 La Región de El Cajón en la Etnohistoria de Honduras. *Yaxkín* 5:37–50.
1985 Apuntes sobre la Afiliación Cultural de los Pobladores Indigenas de los Valles de Comayagua y Sulaco, Siglo XVI. *Mesoamérica* 9:45–52.
1987 Indigenous Communication Networks in 16th Century Honduras: The Ethnohistorical Evidence. Paper presented at the annual meeting of the Society for American Archaeology, Santa Fe.
1990 Sociopolitical Organization in Central Honduras at the Time of the Conquest: A Model for the Formation of Complex Society. In *The Formation of Complex Society in Southeastern Mesoamerica*, edited by William Fowler. Telford Press, in press.

Lara Pinto, Gloria, and George Hasemann
1988 Sixteenth Century Indigenous Society in Northeast Honduras: Are Ethnohistory

and Archaeology Contradictory? Paper presented at the annual meeting of the Association of American Anthropologists. Phoenix.

Las Casas, Bartolomé de
1957–1961 *Obras Escogidas*. 5 vols. Biblioteca de Autores Españoles, Madrid.

López de Velasco, Juan
1971 *Geografía y Descripción Universal de las Indias*. Biblioteca de Autores Españoles, Madrid.

Lunardi, Federico
1943 Los Payas: Documentos Curiosos y Viajes. *Boletín de la Biblioteca y Archivo Nacionales*, no. 6. Tipografía Nacional de Honduras, Tegucigalpa.

Macaza Ordono, César
1981 *Diccionario de la Lengua Nahuatl*. Editorial Inovación, Mexico.

Memorial
n.d. Memorial de todos los pueblos que ay en la juridizion de st miguel y villa de la choluteca que es comarca de fonseca y de la probincia de honduras. Archivo General de Indias, Audiencia de Mexico 257. Seville.

Molina, Fray Alonso de
1977 *Vocabulario en Lengua Castellana y Mexicana y Mexicana y Castellana*. Editorial Porrúa, Mexico.

Moreno, Pedro
1525 Relación e información del viaje que hizo a las Higueras el bachiller Pedro Moreno. In CDID (1870), Tomo XIV:237–264. Madrid.

Newson, Linda
1986 *The Cost of Conquest: Indian Decline in Honduras under Spanish Rule*. Dellplain Latin American Studies No. 20. Westview Press, Boulder, Colo.

Oviedo, Gonzalo Fernández de
1959 *Historia General y Natural de las Indias*. Biblioteca de Autores Españoles, Madrid.

Pedraza, Cristóbal de
1544 Relación de la Provincia de Honduras y Higueras. In CDID (1868). Tomo XI:379–434. Madrid.

Reyes Mazzoni, Roberto
1974 El Nombre de Olancho y los Grupos Nahuat en Honduras, *Notas Antropológicas* 5:31–39. Instituto de Investigaciones Antropológicas. Universidad Nacional Autónoma de México.

Richter, Ernesto
1971 *Untersuchungen zum "Lenca"-Problem*. Fotoschnelldruck R. Kohler, Tubingen.

Rubio Sánchez, Manuel
1975 *Historia del Puerto de Trujillo*. Banco Central de Honduras, Tegucigalpa.

Saco, Jose Antonio
1932 *Historia de la Esclavitud de los Indios en el Nuevo Mundo, seguida de la Historia de los Repartimientos y Encomiendas*. Havana.

Sherman, William L.
1979 *Forced Native Labor in Sixteenth-Century Central America*. University of Nebraska Press, Lincoln.

Siméon, Rémi
1986 *Diccionario de la Lengua Nahuatl o Mexicana*. Siglo Veintiuno, Mexico.

Stone, Doris
1975 *Arqueología de la Costa Norte de Honduras*. Reprinted by original publisher. Originally published 1943, Memoirs of the Peabody Museum of Archaeology and Ethnology, Cambridge, Mass.

Tamayo, Melchor Alonso
1642 Informe sobre el sitio de Puerto de Caballos y el traslado de los indios de las islas a tierra firme, Trujillo. Archivo General de Indias, Audiencia de Guatemala 39. Seville.

Testimonio de los Esclavos y Naborías que trajeron de
1529   León a la Villa de Trujillo en Honduras, de orden de Pedrarias Dávila, los español-
oles que fueron a ella con el Governador Diego López de Salcedo. In CDID (1870)
Tomo XIV:70–76. Madrid.

Chapter 11 ■

John M. Weeks and Nancy J. Black

Mercedarian Missionaries and the Transformation of Lenca Indian Society in Western Honduras, 1550–1700

The encounter between Europeans and the indigenous populations of northern Central America during the sixteenth century was one of the more brutal episodes in the history of Hispano–Indian relations. Although population loss from military campaigns and various Indian revolts was immediate and significant, the primary causes of the population decline were more protracted, and included the use of Indians as local slave labor and their exportation to the Caribbean Islands and South America (Cerrato 1875; Montejo 1875:250, 292).

Infectious diseases, particularly smallpox, measles, and possibly typhus and influenza, eliminated large parts of the Indian population, and the impact of this decimation was felt for several generations. Programs of forced relocation, reduced reproductive capacity, and the collapse of local native food production and distribution systems by conquest and colonization resulted in malnutrition and starvation. The situation was exacerbated by the Spaniards' appropriation of Indian food and other supplies and the Indians' scorched-earth defensive tactics. Europeans and African slaves contributed to the decline by removing women as concubines or mistresses from the indigenous gene pool (Chapman 1978; Newson 1986).

Spanish colonial expansion into western Honduras during the sixteenth century resulted in widespread social, economic, political, and ecological disruption. After 1550, the major cultural changes that occurred in the region were related to the expansion of agriculture and mining and the gradual integration of native populations into the economic and social life of the province. Such a process could not occur without the disintegration of indigenous communities. At the same time that the social fabric of Indian communities was disintegrating, the Catholic Church was converting the Indians to Christianity (Newson 1986:203).

The effect of the mission system on the indigenous cultures of western Honduras remains poorly understood despite the recent publication of several excellent ethnohistorical studies (Chamberlain 1953; Chapman 1978; Lara Pinto 1980; Newson 1986). It should be possible, through focused archaeological, historical, and ethnographic research, to identify, define, and monitor some of the processes of interaction between the Lenca Indians of northern Central America and European missionaries. The purpose of this chapter is to summarize the progress of recent historical and archaeological research on the mission system in the colonial province of Tencoa of western Honduras.

The Mission as a Colonial Institution in Northern Central America

The protohistoric Lenca Indians were distributed in hereditary chiefdoms throughout central and western Honduras and adjacent El Salvador east of the Lempa River (Figure 11–1). These chiefdoms comprised complex regional polities that included focal settlements supported by several subordinate communities (Chapman 1978; Herrera y Tordesillas 1727; Richter 1971; Weeks et al. 1987). The Spaniards faced a relatively sparsely populated, hostile, and economically unprofitable area, with little possibility of dominating a strong territorial leader to secure control over subordinate groups, as had been done in central Mexico and western Guatemala. Sustained institutionally based interaction between the Lenca and Europeans could not begin until political stability in the area was established.

Physical conquest was the first step in attaining the ultimate goal of spiritual conversion. The Crown ordered civil and religious authorities to formulate plans for the conversion of the Indians in 1536, when the region of western Honduras was approaching pacification, and in 1538 an order followed instructing civil authorities to intervene with religious orders to establish convents in indigenous centers known as *pueblos de indios*. In 1540, the bishop of Guatemala was instructed to bring the Indian nobility (*caciques*) together in order to instruct them in the Christian faith (AGCA A1.24–2197–15752, f.54). However, conversion could not be effectively carried out until the regular orders arrived (Fuentes y Guzmán 1932–1933:3:194; Remesal 1932:1:403; Ximénez 1929–1931:1:440).

Initially, the secular clergy was charged with instructing the Indians gathered into encomiendas in western Honduras. The task proved difficult because the indigenous settlements were dispersed and only a few parish priests were available. In addition, the small size and relative poverty of Indian villages kept away

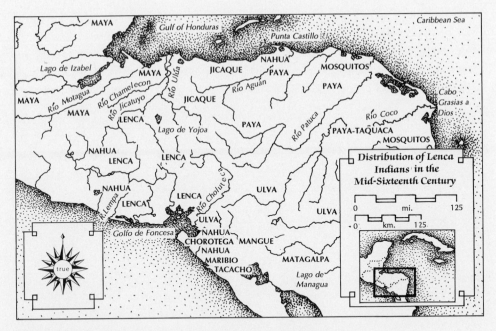

Figure 11–1. Distribution of Lenca Indians in the mid-sixteenth century.

the high-quality clerics, who generally preferred ministering to Spaniards in urban centers. As a result, regular clergy were permitted to minister to Indians in tributary villages, although the Crown had originally intended to let missionaries undertake the preliminary conversion of Indians remaining outside of Spanish control.

The mission was a frontier institution par excellence. As Bolton (1917:43) has pointed out: "Whoever undertakes to interpret the forces by which Spain extended her rule, her language, her law, and her traditions, over the frontiers of her vast American possessions, must give close attention to the missions, for in that work they constituted a primary agency." The mission system was designed as a temporary institution to convert an indigenous population to a manageable community within a 10–year period (Ricard 1966). The duties of the clergy were to provide regular instruction in the Catholic faith, hear confessions, arrange for the celebration of special masses and festivals, and perform the ceremonies of baptism, marriage, and burial. The priests were also required to suppress idolatry, witchcraft, concubinage, drunkenness, truancy, and other evils by punishing offenders with flogging and imprisonment (AGCA A1.24–2195–15749, f.251v). The missionary was usually assisted in his duties by Indians, initially catechists, who acted as appointed assistants and administrators of church affairs.

Pueblos de indios were divided into parishes for purposes of ecclesiastical administration (AGCA A1.23–1513, f.534). Each had a *cabecera de doctrina*, or a focal town where the local clergy lived and from which they made their rounds. In contrast to the cabeceras de doctrina, which were essentially towns created for colonizing Spaniards who voluntarily chose to reside in them, pueblos de indios were founded to impose European colonial institutions on the indigenous populations who were forced to settle there. These were essentially closed communities as Spaniards and blacks were prohibited from residing in them (AGCA A1.23–1513, f.579; AGCA A1.23–4575, f.433v–434). The large scale on which hundreds of pueblos de indios were founded throughout northern Central America is directly linked to intensive Christianization campaigns and the consequent Europeanization of indigenous populations.

The missionaries not only built a church organization, they structured communities along European lines. The principal native officials in these Indian villages were appointed to their offices by missionaries or other Spanish officials and exercised restricted judicial and administrative authority. Church officials were strongly supported by the Crown in their conversion attempts, and missionaries became essentially political, economic, and social agents who helped extend, control, and Europeanize the colonial periphery (Gibson 1966:68–70).

Lenca Archaeological and Historical Project

Since 1985 the authors, together with Julie C. Benyo (Boston University), have conducted archaeological, historical, and ethnographic research relating to the mission system in the colonial province of Tencoa in western Honduras.

History

The province of Tencoa is an appropriate place to study the late Prehistoric and early Colonial periods for a variety of reasons. Available historical documentation, although certainly not extensive, indicates that the region supported a relatively large protohistoric population (Alvarado 1871; Montejo 1875). Recent archaeological investigations in the vicinity of the ruins at Gualjoquito by the Santa Barbara Archaeological Project (Ashmore 1987; Schortman and Urban 1987) indicate a temporal depth to at least the Late Preclassic period (400 B.C.–A.D. 200). Perhaps most important, Tencoa lies on an important pre-Hispanic and colonial commercial route between eastern Guatemala and the interior of Honduras, and so the natives were undoubtedly exposed to and forced to adapt to a variety of changing external stimuli.

The Tencoa region is characterized by rough topography and numerous small and isolated intermontane depressions. An eighteenth-century narrative by the bishop of Honduras (Cadiñanos 1893:111) states: "The roads of this curacy are terribly rugged and surrounded by rough mountains. The many swift rivers are without bridges and impede the travel of the priest and parishioners. For this reason many souls die without confessing at the hour of their death." The eighteenth-century manuscript map of the curacy of Tencoa shown in Figure 11–2 indicates the relative positions within the district of pueblo de indios settlements, as well as the locations of savannas, rivers, and other physiographic features. Until the late eighteenth century, the settlements of Posta and Quesailica were situated on the important commercial network from Guatemala to Puerto Caballos on the north coast of Honduras.

Sustained European presence in the region began about 1536 when Pedro de Alvarado, the conqueror of Guatemala, arrived at the settlement of Tencoa with a force of Spaniards and Guatemalan Indians to suppress an insurrection near Buena Esperanza in the Naco Valley to the north. Alvarado sent several expeditions from a staging area at Tencoa to reduce the indigenous Lenca population of western Honduras and to establish the settlement of Gracias a Dios (AGI Guatemala 44).

In 1549 Alonso López de Cerrato, president of the Audiencia of Guatemala, instructed Fray Marcos Pérez Dardon, provincial vicar of the Order of the Blessed Virgin Mary for the Ransom of Captives (Mercedarians) at Santiago de Guatemala, to found three convents in central and western Honduras (Borges Morán 1960; Castro Seoane 1945; Reina Valenzuela 1983). Within two years, Mercedarians were evangelizing in the vicinity of Gracias a Dios, and by 1554 convents had been established at Valladolid de Comayagua (1552), Gracias a Dios (1554), and Tencoa (1554).

The earliest missionary activity in the Tencoa region probably began in 1553 when a Lenca Indian named Luis Pérez received 25 pesos to instruct local Indi-

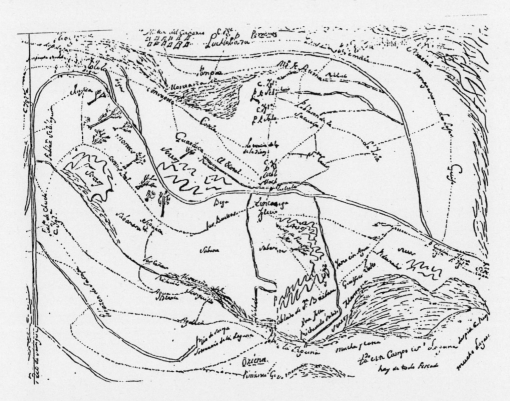

Figure 11–2. Eighteenth-century map of the Partido of Tencoa. The *cabecera de doctrina* of Tencoa is situated in the center of the map, slightly below (east) of the Río Ulúa; the *pueblos de indios* of Macholoa, Jalapa, Celilac, Yamala, and Posta are above (west); Gualala and Llama to the right (north); and Chuchepeque and Ojuera to the left (south).

ans in the Christian doctrine. The following year, the Mercedarian Nicolás del Valle began evangelizing work at Tencoa. Valle was associated with the convent until 1565 and apparently had great success in mastering the Lenca language and in eliminating the indigenous images found "in great quantity among the Indians" (Pérez Rodríguez 1966:99–102). In 1556, chalices, a complete *ornamento* or outfit of sacred vestments, and a bell were purchased for the convent with money from the Royal Treasury. Gerónimo de Corella, bishop of Honduras, visited Tencoa in 1559. He reported to the Crown the lack of clergy, general poverty, and difficult travel in the region. The documentation for the early operation of the convent is extremely limited, although the missionaries there appear to have been reasonably successful in their efforts. By 1568, missionary work was being carried out at Celilac, Ilama, Jalapa, and Quesailica, and *reducciones*, or settlements of previously unconverted Lenca Indians, were founded at La Magdalena (possibly Macholoa), San Nicolás Colinas, and San Pedro Zacapa before 1579.

Tencoa must have had a large enough population to warrant being selected as the site of a cabecera de doctrina. The majority of Mercedarian centers began as doctrinas that were transformed into convents as the number of resident missionaries increased (AMERGUA leg. 1). Convent status brought these centers privileges within the Mercedarian Order as well as increased support from the Spanish Crown.

By 1582, the Mercedarians were administering five subordinate administrative districts (*partidos*) in Honduras, including Tencoa. Together they comprised some 50 villages with an estimated tributary population of 1,800 (Contreras Guevara 1946), or about 35 percent of the entire tributary population of western Honduras at that time. By 1632, the partido of Tencoa consisted of 1,100 converts from 12 settlements and was administered by three Mercedarians. The language spoken at this time was identified as being similar to that in the Lenca regions of Cururú and Gracias a Dios (Samayoa Guevara 1957).

After secularization, Tencoa remained an important though peripheral regional center until 1787, when, as a result of litigation, it was forced to relocate to Santa Bárbara de Cataquiles, a few kilometers to the north (AGCA A1.10–39–328). Negotiations were difficult and the relocation was bitterly opposed by the Indian populations of Jalapa, Macholoa, Ojuera, Quesailica, and Yamala. A few years later, the region was decimated by a series of catastrophes including outbreaks of cholera and malaria, as well as flooding along the Río Ulúa and Río Jicatuyo (Vallecillo A. 1944). Thereafter, most of the settlements were abandoned and eventually relocated.

The conversion to Christianity of the Lenca Indians proceeded slowly as the Mercedarian missionaries stuggled to overcome their problems, which were much like those that mission programs were experiencing elsewhere in the Audiencia of Guatemala. Little is known about explicit responses of the Lenca Indians to missionization. Triennial reports kept up by the main Mercedarian convent in Guatemala for over a century reveal only general information about the difficulties experienced by the regular orders (Black 1989). Two recurring problems for the missionaires were the antagonism of resident Spaniards and the lack of religious paraphernalia (AGCA A1.18–211–5028, f.56v; AGCA

A1.23–1512, f.305). They kept all that was necessary to celebrate the Mass on portable altars, including a chalice, cross, candlestick, and a transportable *retablo* (ornamental screen or painting) in a small chest (Remesal 1932:1:431–432).

The reaction of many of the missionaries in their initial encounters with the Indians must have been one of astonishment in the light of European neo-medieval attitudes regarding society and culture. In partial justification of missionary activities in Guatemala, the sixteenth-century Dominican Remesal (1932:1:430–431) wrote that evangelization not only saved Indian souls, but also "civilized" them, pointing out that Indians would defecate and urinate in public and when they came to hear a sermon would leave the church "fouler than an animal corral." Such behavior surely can be interpreted as an indigenous response to the imposition of European colonialism.

Remesal argues further that the Indians were treated inhumanely before the arrival of the regular orders, because neither the Spaniards nor the secular clergy showed sensitivity to them or paid much attention to their physical or spiritual needs. He blames the Europeans for the loss of many positively perceived aspects of indigenous culture and native beliefs. As an example, Remesal states that when asked why they stole, killed, profaned, lied, or raped, the Indians would respond that they merely wished to become more Christian.

Evaluating the success of the conversion efforts is problematic, because conversion did not come easily. Baptism, for example, was not universal as many Indians resisted the imposition of Christianity and refused to be convinced of the merit of Christian concepts. At the same time, those who did not resist often misunderstood the spiritual significance of baptism and saw it as a rite that conferred tributary status rather membership in the Christian community (Ximénez 1929–1931).

The partial acceptance of Christian concepts also complicated matters. For example, some Maya Indians considered the Virgin Mary to be the Christian deity because the first churches were dedicated to her (Remesal 1932:1:392), while Indians at Mexicanos in El Salvador in the late eighteenth century brought flowers and incense not to venerate the image of Santiago but rather the horse on which he rode (Cortés y Larraz 1958:1:102). The Mercedarian bishop Andrés de las Navas y Quevedo issued an order in 1684 prohibiting the display of San Miguel, San Gerónimo, San Juan Evangelista, and other saints that have animals at their feet since the Indians tended to venerate the animals rather than the saints.

The Indians would have found some aspects of Christianity novel and exotic, to be sure, but they would have had difficulty comprehending the abstract theological concepts, which were probably only partly explained in any case. The Indians were frequently converted en masse and often with economic, moral, and even physical coercion (Ricard 1966). The concept of "god" was particularly difficult to explain, and the Dominicans and Franciscans debated the relative merits of trying to do so in the vernacular languages (Fuentes y Guzmán 1932–1933:2:365–366; Remesal 1932:2:254–255).

They were unable to adequately explain theological concepts in part because they lacked proficiency in these languages (AGCA A1.23–1513, f.607; AGCA A1.23–1514, f.45). The clergy tried unsuccessfully to instruct the Indians in

"Mexicana," a lingua franca. The Mercedarians used indigenous languages and initiated the practice of removing a small number of children to convents, where they were raised in the Catholic faith, and later returning them to help assist friars preach in native languages (AGI Guatemala 168; Pérez Rodríquez 1966: 100).

The dispersed character of the pueblos de indios and the small number of clergy produced intermittent and probably superficial instruction in the Catholic faith. Although there were several Mercedarians working within the jurisdiction of Tencoa, each of them had to minister to several villages as well as to individual families living on scattered plots (Pérez Rodríguez 1966:101). To make matters worse, many villages could not provide sufficient food and services to support visiting priests for any length of time.

In some *visitas*, or settlements that were visited at intervals by clergy residing at a cabecera de doctrina, the regular instruction of Indians was undertaken by *cantores*, or Indians who provided music, maintained the ornamentos, and cleaned the church. Their effectiveness is questionable since in 1584 ecclesiastical authorities in Honduras persuaded the Crown to order the congregation of Indian villages. Despite the order, there is no evidence that massive congregation took place, and the difficulties of ministering to a dispersed population continued throughout the Colonial period (Newson 1986:236).

Although the obvious external symbols of religious adherence, such as indigenous temples and images, were largely destroyed and replaced by churches and convents containing Christian statuary, Indian communities often managed to conceal their images and continued clandestine worship. Both secular and ecclesiastical officials continued to be instructed to suppress idolatry throughout most of the Colonial period (Fuentes y Guzmán 1932–1933:7:376; García de Palacio 1927–1928:76; Vázquez 1937–1944:3:265; Ximénez 1929–1931:2:381–382). Goicoechea (1936–1937:203–204) complained that the Jicaque Indians of Nombre de Jesús Pacura in the Olancho region of Honduras would repeatedly return to Franciscan convents to be baptized in order to get clothing and food, yet persisted in their native worship. In 1685, the Dominican Agustin Cano used a similar strategy among the Chol Maya of northern Guatemala, but the Indians returned to apostasy (Ximénez 1929–1931:2:433–434). Vázquez (1937–1944:4:387) notes that idols were concealed behind the church altar at Moyuta in the parish of Conguaco in El Salvador, and Ximénez records similar practices for Chiapas and Guatemala (1929–1931:2:191–192, 203).

Parish priests assumed a prominent position in the spiritual life of Indian communities, but never entirely replaced indigenous religious practitioners (Herrera y Tordesillas 1726). Although Christian symbols of religious adherence dominated indigenous ones, Indian beliefs remained in essence aboriginal, with aspects of Christianity grafted on to them (Newson 1986:238). Colonial perceptions regarding the effectiveness of the Mercedarian mission system among the Lenca Indians in western Honduras were perhaps best summed up by the late eighteenth-century bishop of Honduras, Fernando de Cadiñanos (1893:105):

> For some faithful to find themselves so far removed from one another in the most hidden of mountains and away from the settlements, a lifestyle originally totally

abandoned to hatred and stained with abominable vices. Public cohabitation is in excessive numbers. Sins of incest are of the most prohibited degrees [and] the crass ignorance that they endure in the principles of the Catholic religion, and obligation of their state is well noted.

Archaeology

The terminal Postclassic period (ca. A.D. 1200–1535) has been difficult to define archaeologically in western Honduras (Healy 1984), and the apparent lack of massive architecture, the reduced platform size, and conservative ceramic inventories have led Urban (1986:286) to characterize the period as being "invisible." No discussion of cultural adaptation can afford to ignore the period, however, since it represents the important transition from independent to subordinate social development.

The archaeological component of our study has emphasized the relationship between the colonial Mercedarian mission system and the Lenca Indian population, as well as the need to evaluate and improve methods of examining the archaeological remains of Historic period societies. Our first goals were to characterize the location, size, and configuration of protohistoric and early colonial Lenca settlement patterns and to identify and extend the existing regional ceramic chronology into the Postclassic and Historic periods (Weeks et al. 1987).

The fieldwork has been guided by a broad assumption that Colonial period centers with significant Indian populations, that is, pueblos de indios settlements, replaced pre-Hispanic centers (Markman 1984). It is reasonable to suggest that pre-Hispanic ceremonial or administrative centers, even those lacking monumental architecture, were focal points for these populations. The Mercedarian mission system was dedicated not only to converting the Lenca Indians to Christianity, but also to tranforming them from subsistence agriculturalists into European peasants by forcing them to live in closer proximity to other peasants, near the church, and near civil authorities, where they could be taxed, counted, and used as a source of labor.

The archaeological study area extends from Posta and Quesailica in the west to Tencoa in the east, and from Ilama in the north to Malera in the south (Figure 11–3). The survey emphasized valleys associated with historically described mission stations at Celilac, Chuchepeque, Gualala, Jalapa, Macholoa, Malera, Ojuera, Yamala, and the reducción at San Pedro Zacapa. Each survey area was systematically examined and all visible architectural surface remains were mapped using transit and stadia. Prehistoric sites in the vicinity of Ilama and in the valley of Tencoa were recorded by the Santa Barbara Archaeological Project, and sites in the vicinity of Posta and Quesailica were included in the settlement surveys by La Entrada Archaeological Project (Nakamura 1987) and the La Canteada Archaeological Project (Pahl 1988).

The most tangible result of the archaeological component of the project has been the unexpected number of prehistoric and historic sites identified and, in particular, the large number of late prehistoric remains in the vicinity of mission settlements. Over 75 pre-Hispanic and historic sites were identified during the survey, and a series of 125 test units and clearing operations revealed human

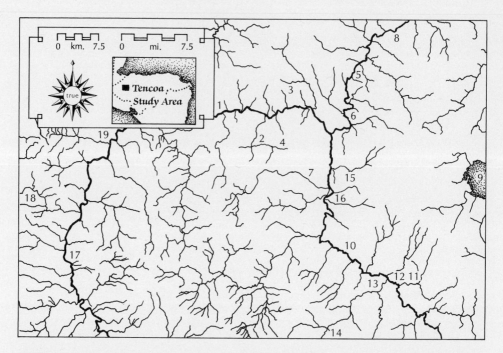

Figure 11–3. Map of the Tencoa study area: *1*, Yamala; *2*, Celilac; *3*, Colinas; *4*, Jalapa; *5*, Ilama; *6*, Gualala; *7*, Macholoa; *8*, Río Ulúa; *9*, Lago de Yoyoa; *10*, Río Ulúa; *11*, Zacapa; *12*, Chuchepeque; *13*, Ojuera; *14*, Malera; *15*, Santa Bárbara; *16*, Valle de Tencoa; *17*, Río Jicatuyo; *18*, Quesailica; *19*, Posta.

occupation in mission locations dating from the Late Preclassic (ca. 400 B.C.–A.D. 200) through the Historic period.

The Late Postclassic period (ca. A.D. 1200–1535) is characterized by a continuation of Early Postclassic settlements, with substantial revivals at Viejo Jalapa (Site 345) and Yamala (Site 503) along the Río Jicatuyo, and at Gualala (Site 347) north of the confluence of the Río Ulúa and the Río Jicatuyo. Several pottery types typical of the earlier period continue and some local monochromes are added to the ceramic assemblage. Architectural modification is evident in the increased use of adobe as a primary construction material and by the movement away from alluvial flats to more elevated terrace locations.

The size and configuration of many late pre-Hispanic sites conform to the expectation of a substantial chiefly settlement and several of these sites can be correlated positively with settlements described in historical documents. The valley at Yamala is located about 25 kilometers west of the Río Ulúa in a long narrow floodplain near the confluence of the Quebrada Grande and the Río Jicatuyo. The valley is surrounded by exceedingly rugged terrain, which makes the location well adapted to the defensive needs of the Lenca Indians. Between 1537 and 1539, the success of the colonial system was threatened by a regional insurrection under the leadership of the cacique Lempira. The Lenca concentrated at summits that were strengthened with fortifications and stocked with arms and prepared for a siege (AGI Guatemala 9; Chamberlain 1953; Herrera y Tordesillas

1726; Montejo 1875). The destruction in 1539 of one of these refuges in the study area has been described by Francisco de Montejo (1864:216):

> They were building many houses on a great, very strong rock which they have [at Yamala], and providing them, with provisions. The Spanish chieftain sent a Negro spy, who knew the language of the Indians, to enter the stronghold and bring back a report. The frightened Negro found there four houses built very large, and four more larger ones full of corn, and set fire to the houses and to the corn.

Site 503 is located about 750 meters west of the ruins of the colonial church on an alluvial terrace above the floodplain at Yamala. The site consists of a small multiple-plaza platform group and generally corresponds to the refuge described by Montejo. Ceramics excavated from the site indicate a predominant Late Postclassic period occupation.

Another locus, Site 628, high in the mountains about 7 kilometers southeast of San Antonio de Malera, consists of three major mound groups. This site probably corresponds to the refuge of Urvera, the target of a week-long siege and the outstanding victory of the Alonso de Caceres Comayagua campaign of 1537 (Chamberlain 1953:94; Funes 1952). None of the platforms at the site has been tested, although the architectural configuration suggests a probable late prehistoric occupation.

The transition from the Protohistoric to Colonial periods is marked in the archaeological record by several pottery types and the introduction of colonial glazed ceramic inventory as well as by the extinction of many aspects of the pre-Hispanic settlement system. The location of most mission stations was made possible by remarkable continuity and similarities in toponyms from the sixteenth century to the present. The survey revealed that mission stations are positioned between three and six linear kilometers apart and are located near significant prehistoric archaeological remains and adjacent to major rivers. These floodplain surfaces were probably characterized by open savanna in the sixteenth century, although centuries of intensive agriculture have converted this vegetation type to thorny brush and low forest.

The remains of at least three sixteenth-century churches associated with the mission system have been identified near substantial Lenca remains from the Late Postclassic period at Jalapa, Chuchepeque, and Tencoa. Site 345 at Jalapa comprises two groups of significant prehistoric ruins. Group A includes over 20 visible constructions arranged in multiple plaza groups, and is one of the largest sites in the region. Ceramics recovered from excavations into Structures 1 and 14 indicate extensive Early Classic through Postclassic assemblages. Group B appears to be a single-component Late Postclassic assemblage to the north of Group A. A small excavation into a rectangular platform within Group A revealed a deposit of deteriorated adobe construction with Late Postclassic and colonial glazed ceramics. The surface configuration of the platform and associated ceramic artifacts suggests the possible remains of the early pueblo de indios church at Jalapa.

Site 315 is one of two colonial church constructions identified in the Tencoa Valley and possibly represents the site of the original cabecera de doctrina at Tencoa. The building includes sections of a tamped earth or adobe wall on a foundation of massive riverine cobbles. Trenching into the interior revealed the extensive use of fired clay flooring tiles in the presbytery as well as partly disarticulated skeleton accompanied by black jet rosary beads. Excavation also revealed large accumulations of pottery, broken glass, iron nails, and roofing tiles. Unfortunately there was not enough recovered material to correlate it with historically described church inventories for Tencoa (AMERGUA 27b).

Other abandoned pueblos de indios churches, typically constructed between 1575 and 1725, were located at Celilac, Gualala, Ilama, and Yamala. Most of these buildings are large rectangular halls with a pitched wood-frame roof, and rarely any constructional device to separate functional areas, such as choir, nave, or presbytery. In more formally conceived plans the interior space is divided by piers abutting on the side walls near the rear or presbytery. The frontal facade was an enormous masonry screen or backdrop fronting the courtyard or *atrio*, which usually served as a town plaza or square. The walls of the nave are usually not bonded to the facade, especially if they are made of adobe (Markman 1984:206). A report on the condition of churches in Tencoa for 1791 indicates 40 percent of pueblos de indios churches were still roofed with thatch at the time and 30 percent constructed with wattle and daub (AMERGUA 27a).

Obviously, much archaeological research still needs to be completed and synthesized before a conservative model of settlement change can be formulated. In particular, further excavation is necessary to provide temporal information for prehistoric and historic sites identified south of Tencoa at Chuchepeque, Malera, Ojuera, and San Francisco Zacapa. In addition, the sampling of churches needs to be expanded in order to refine local historical sequences.

Conclusions

The mission system established by the Mercedarian friars provided an alternative structure for Hispano–Indian interaction and a mechanism for organizing indigenous labor and production in areas remote from effective Spanish administrative control. Any appraisal of the effectiveness of the mission system must consider a balance of environmental conditions, personnel, financial resources, the nature of local indigenous society, the rules and regulations of the religious order, the regional secular hierarchy, and the Crown.

Such an appraisal must also consider the cultural and religious enlightenment Europeans brought to the New World along with the Black Legend view of arrogant opportunists. In this, as in other historical dilemmas dealing with New World exploitation, the meticulous record-keeping tradition of early missionaries must be balanced with the ideological declarations of the European church and state. Pronouncements such as papal bulls, laws made by the Council of the Indies, and other similar contemplating bodies and warnings of elites from the peninsula should not be equated with actual behavior toward indigenous peoples working in the fields and mines in the Western Hemisphere, far from Europe's surveillance and control.

The study of Late Prehistoric and Early Historic period indigenous settlements has been a recent development in northern Central American archaeology, both because of the traditional research interests in prehistoric chronology, origins, and population movements, and simply because of the difficulty in recognizing Contact period sites.

Knowledge and understanding of culture change through time and space in the Lenca region of western Honduras has been increased through archaeological and historical research. The archaeological component has thus far emphasized the identification, location, and definition of ancient remains located near colonial mission stations in the Tencoa region. Such a nonrandom survey strategy was determined by a specific interest in the colonial transformation of late prehistoric settlement patterns. It was assumed, and demonstrated through archaeological fieldwork, that the location of colonial missions was not fortuitous but rather a reflection of the desire to maximize large, late pre-Hispanic populations.

When the analysis of our archaeological and historical data is complete, we expect to be able to better identify, define, and monitor changes in the location, size, and configuration of pre-Hispanic Lenca Indian settlements through time in the Tencoa region. These data, in conjunction with primary historical information, will be used to describe and ultimately to explain patterns of Lenca cultural continuity and change and adaptive responses to Spanish colonialism. At a more general level, the effects of European domination on local indigenous cultures and the complex process of Hispano-Indian accommodation may be examined from a social historical perspective.

Acknowledgments

Research summarized in this chapter was conducted with the approval of the Instituto Hondureño de Antropología e Historia (IHAH), Lic. Ricardo Agurcia F. and Lic. Victor C. Cruz Reyes, directors during the field research period. We gratefully appreciate support provided by the following archives: Archivo General de Centro América and the Archivo de los Padres Mercedarios de Guatemala in Guatemala City, Archivo Eclesiástico de Comayagua, and the Archivo Nacional de Honduras in Tegucigalpa. Initial funding was provided by the National Geographic Society to the Santa Barbara Archaeological Project, co-directed by Wendy Ashmore, Edward Schortman, and Patricia Urban. Subsequent funding has been made available by the National Endowment for the Humanities and the National Geographic Society, as well as the University of Minnesota Graduate School Grant-in-Aid and College of Liberal Arts McMillan-Faculty Travel Grant, and a Benevolent Association Fellowship from the State University of New York at Albany.

References

Archivo General de Centro América (AGCA)

AGCA A1.10–39–328. Instancia de las habitantes del pueblo de Tencoa, acerca de que no se proceda a la traslación de la cabecera al pueblo de Santa Bárbara Cataquiles, 1797.

AGCA A1.18–211–5025, f.56v. Real cédula: Recuerdase el cumplimiento de las disposiciones sobre que a los indígenas de la provincia de Guatemala que viven dispusos por los montes sean reducidos a poblado urbana, el 28 de enero de 1541.

AGCA A1.18–211–5028, f.56v. Real cédula: Para que la Audiencia evite que los encomenderos obstan la libre enseñanza del evangelio entre los indios, el 10 de septiembre de 1550.

AGCA A1.23–1512, f.305. Su Magestad: Ordena que a los frailes doctrineros de Nuestra Señora de las Mercedes Redención de Cautivos y que tienen a su cargo varios pueblos de Guatemala solamente se les de los necesarios para su alimentación y vestuario, el 21 de junio de 1562.

AGCA A1.23–1513, f.534. Real cédula: Que el presidente y oidores previo informe, resolvan lo mas conveniente en cuanto a la reducción y concentración de varios pueblos de indios para su mejor evangelización como lo habia propuesto el obispo de Honduras, Fr. Alonso de la Cerda, el15 de diciembre de 1580.

AGCA A1.23–1513, f.579. Queda prohibido que los negros tengan sus residencias en los pueblos de indios o en las inmediaciones de ellos, el 23 de septiembre de 1580.

AGCA A1.23–1513, f.607. Real cédula: Que en todas las partes donde hay audiencias y cancillorias reales, se instituya catedra de lengua indígena para que los sacerdotes destinados al servicio de doctrina puedan hacerse entender de los indígenas, el 27 de mayo de 1582.

AGCA A1.23–1514, f.45. Real cédula: Para que por parte del presidente y de los oidores de la Audiencia, se comunique a los provinciales de las ordenes de religiosos, que tienen a su cargo el servicio de doctrinas que para admitir algún religiosos como tal doctrinero debe conocer la lengua predominante de su doctrina, el 14 de noviembre de 1603.

AGCA A1.23–45745, f.433v. Sobre carta a la cédula de 25 de noviembre de 1578, prohibiendo que en los pueblos de indígenas viven negros, mulatos y mestizos, el 3 de febrero de 1587.

AGCA A1.23–45745, f.434. Llamase la atención al presidente y audiencia, por haber otorgado licencia a española para residir en pueblos de indios, el 18 de febrero de 1587.

AGCA A1.24–2195–15749, f.215v. Real cédula: Prohibe se a los regulares doctrineros a castigar a los indígenas por medio de azotes, rapado, cárcel, y cepo, el 4 de septiembre de 1560.

AGCA A1.24–2197–15752, f.54. Su Magestad: Recomienda al gobernador y al obispo de Guatemala, que periodicamente reunen a los indios libres y esclavos para enseñarles la doctrina, buenas costumbres industriales, el 9 de noviembre de 1540.

Archivo General de Indias (AGI)

AGI Guatemala leg. 9. Relación de sucesos ocurridos en Honduras y del estado en que se hallaba esta provincia, enviada a Su Majestad, por el obispo Lic. Cristóbal de Pedraza, el 18 de mayo de 1539.

AGI Guatemala leg. 44. Cartas y expedientes de varios cabildos seculares del distrito de la audiencia, 1530–1695.

AGI Guatemala leg. 168. Cartas y expedientes de personas eclesiásticas del distrito de dicha audiencia, 1532–1570.

Archivo Mercedario de Guatemala (AMERGUA)

AMERGUA leg. 1 Secreta del monasterio de Nuestra Señora de la Merced de Guatemala, 12 de marzo de 1581.

AMERGUA leg. 27a. Estado que manifesta el número de almas que se han confirmado en su ultima visita episcopal, las capellanias, y cofradías que obtiene, curato de Tencoa, 11 de junio de 1791.

AMERGUA leg. 27b. Reconocimiento de los bienes por fin y muerte del R. P. Cura Fr. Joaquín Borqueno, 28 de diciembre de 1795.

Alvarado, Pedro de
1871 Repartimiento de la ciudad de Gracias a Dios y su fundación por Pedro de Alvarado [1536]. *Colección de documentos ineditos relativos al descubrimiento, conquista y organización de las antiguas posesiones españoles de America y Oceania*, vol. 15, pp. 5–20. Imprenta Española, Madrid.

Ashmore, Wendy
1987 Cobble Crossroads: Gualjoquito Architecture and External Elite Ties. In *Interaction on the Southeast Mesoamerican Frontier: Prehistoric and Historic Honduras and El Salvador*, edited by Eugenia J. Robinson, pp. 28–48. British Archaeological Reports, International Series, 327. Oxford, England.

Black, Nancy J.
1989 *Transformation of a Frontier Mission Province: The Order of Our Lady of Mercy in Western Honduras, 1525–1773*. Unpublished Ph.D. dissertation, State University of New York at Albany.

Bolton, Herbert E.
1917 The Mission as a Frontier Institution in the Spanish American Colonies. *American Historical Review* 23:42–61.

Borges Morán, P.
1960 *Métodos misionales en la cristianización de América, siglo XVI*. Consejo Superior de Investigaciones Científicas, Madrid.

Cadiñanos, F. de
1893 Censo levantado por fray Fernando de Cadiñanos, obispo de esta diócesis, en 1791. In *Primer Anuario Estadístico Correspondiente al Año de 1889, Républica de Honduras*, edited by Antonio R. Vallejo, pp. 105–118. Tegucigalpa: Tipografía Nacional.

Castro Seoane, José.
1945 La expansión de La Merced en la América colonial. *Anales de la Sociedad de Geografía e Historia de Guatemala* 20:39–47.

Cerrato, Alonso López de
1875 Carta a Su Magestad del dicho licenciado Cerrato, 1549. *Colección de documentos ineditos relativos al descubrimiento, conquista y organización de las antiguas posesiones españoles de America y Oceania*, vol. 24, pp. 463–473. Imprenta Española, Madrid.

Chamberlain, Robert S.
1953 *The Conquest and Colonization of Honduras, 1501–1550*. Carnegie Institution of Washington, Publication 598. Washington, D.C.

Chapman, Anne M.
1978 *Los Lencas de Honduras en el siglo XVI*. Instituto Hondureño de Antropología e Historia, Tegucigalpa.

Contreras Guevara, A.
1946 Relación hecha a su magestad por el gobernador de Honduras, de todos los pueblos de dicha provincia [1582]. *Boletín del Archivo General del Gobierno de Guatemala* 11:5–19.

Cortés y Larraz, Pedro de
1958 *Descripción geográfico-moral de la diócesis de Goathemala* [1770]. Biblioteca Goathemala de la Sociedad de Geografía e Historia de Guatemala, vol. 20. Tipografía Nacional, Guatemala.

Fuentes y Guzmán, Francisco Antonio de
1932–1933 *Recordación Florida: Discurso historial y demonstración natural, militar y política*

del Reyno de Guatemala [c.1675]. Biblioteca Goathemala de la Sociedad de Geografía e Historia de Guatemala, vols. 6–8. Tipografía Nacional, Guatemala.

Funes, Alonso de
1952 Probanza de los méritos y servicios de Alonso de Funes, vecino de Comayagua [1548]. *Boletín del Archivo General del Gobierno de Guatemala* 7:183–193.

García de Palacio, Diego
1927–1928 Relación hecha por el licenciado Palacio al Rey D. Felipe II, en la que describe la provincia de Guatemala, las costumbres de los indios y otras cosas notables [c.1575]. *Anales de la Sociedad de Geografía e Historia de Guatemala* 4:71–92.

Gibson, Charles
1966 *The Aztecs under Spanish Rule: A History of the Indians of the Valley of Mexico, 1519–1820*. Stanford University Press, Stanford, Calif.

Goicoechea, José Antonio
1936–1937 Relación del R. P. Dr. Fr. José Antonio Goicochea, sobre los indios gentiles de Pacura, en el obispado de Comayagua [c.1800]. *Anales de la Sociedad de Geografía e Historia de Guatemala* 13:303–315.

Healy, Paul F.
1984 The Archaeology of Honduras. In *The Archaeology of Lower Central America*, edited by Frederick W. Lange and D. Z. Stone, pp. 113–161. University of New Mexico Press, Albuquerque.

Herrera y Tordesillas, Antonio de
1726 *The General History of the Vast Continent and Islands of America, Commonly Called the West Indies* [1601]. J. Batley, London.

Lara Pinto, Gloria E.
1980 *Beitrage zur indianischen Ethnographie von Honduras in der 1. Halfte des 16. Jahrhunderts unter besonderer Berucksichtigung der historischen Demographie*. Unpublished Ph.D. dissertation, University of Hamburg.

Markman, Sidney D.
1984 *Architecture and Urbanization in Colonial Chiapas, Mexico*. American Philosophical Society, Memoir vol. 153. Philadelphia.

Montejo, Francisco de
1864 Carta del adelantado don Francisco de Montejo a la gobernación de Honduras [1539]. *Colección de documentos ineditos relativos al descubrimiento, conquista y organización de las antiguas posesiones españoles de America y Oceania*, vol. 2, pp. 212–252. Imprenta Española, Madrid.
1875 Carta a su magestad del adelantado don Francisco de Montejo sobre el estado y accidentes de la provincia de Guatemala [1539]. *Colección de documentos ineditos relativos al descubrimiento, conquista y organización de las antiguas posesiones españoles de America y Oceania*, vol. 24, pp. 250–297. Imprenta Española, Madrid.

Nakamura, Seiichi
1987 Archaeological Investigations in the La Entrada Region, Honduras: Preliminary Results and Interregional Interaction. In *Interaction on the Southeast Mesoamerican Frontier: Prehistoric and Historic Honduras and El Salvador*, edited by Eugenia J. Robinson, pp. 129–141. British Archaeological Reports, International Series, 327. Oxford, England.

Newson, Linda A.
1986 *The Cost of Conquest: Indian Decline in Honduras under Spanish Rule*. Westview Press, Boulder, Colo.

Pahl, Gary W.
1988 The Survey and Excavation of La Canteada, Copán, Honduras: Preliminary Report, 1975 Season. In *The Periphery of the Southeastern Classic Maya Realm*, edited by Gary W. Pahl, pp. 227–261. Latin American Center, University of California at Los Angeles.

Pérez Rodríguez, Pedro Nolasco

1923 *Religiosos de La Merced que pasaron a la América española.* Tipografía Zarzuela, Seville.

1966 *Historia de las misiones mercedarias en América.* Revista Estudios, Madrid.

Reina Valenzuela, J.

1983 *Historia eclesiástica de Honduras, 1502–1600.* Tipografía Nacional, Tegucigalpa.

Remesal, Antonio de

1932 *Historia general de las Indias Occidentales y particular de la gobernación de Chiapa y Guatemala* [c.1619]. Biblioteca Goathemala de la Sociedad de Geografía e Historia de Guatemala, vol. 4–5. Tipografía Nacional, Guatemala.

Ricard, Robert

1966 *The Spiritual Conquest of Mexico: An Essay on the Apostolate and Evangelizing Methods of the Mendicant Orders in New Spain, 1523–1572.* University of California Press, Berkeley.

Richter, Ernesto

1971 *Untersuchungen zum "Lenca"-Problem.* Unpublished Ph.D. dissertation, University of Tübingen.

Samayoa Guevara, Humberto H.

1957 Historia del establecimiento de la Orden Mercedaria en el reino de Guatemala, desde el año de 1537 hasta 1632. *Antropología e Historia de Guatemala* 9:30–43.

Schortman, Edward M., and Patricia A. Urban

1987 Survey within the Gualjoquito Hinterland: An Introduction to the Investigations of the Santa Barbara Archaeological Project. In *Interaction on the Southeast Mesoamerican Frontier: Prehistoric and Historic Honduras and El Salvador,* edited by Eugenia J. Robinson, pp. 5–27. British Archaeological Reports, International Series, 327. Oxford, England.

Urban, Patricia A.

1986 Precolumbian Settlement in the Naco Valley, Northwestern Honduras. In *The Southeast Maya Periphery,* edited by Patricia A. Urban and Edward M. Schortman, pp. 275–295. University of Texas Press, Austin.

Vallecillo A. C.

1944 Santiago de Posta, como se extinguio? Naranjito, como se fundo? *Revista del Archivo y Biblioteca Nacionales de Honduras* 22:385–387.

Vázquez, Francisco

1937–1944 *Crónica de la Provincia del Santísimo Nombre de Jesús de Guatemala de la Orden de N. Seráfico Padre San Francisco en el reino de la Nueva España* [c.1675]. Biblioteca Goathemala de la Sociedad de Geografía e Historia de Guatemala, vol. 14–17. Tipografía Nacional, Guatemala.

Weeks, John M., Nancy Black, and J. Stuart Speaker

1987 From Prehistory to History in Western Honduras: The Care Lenca in the Colonial Province of Tencoa. In *Interaction on the Southeast Mesoamerican Frontier: Prehistoric and Historic Honduras and El Salvador,* edited by Eugenia J. Robinson, pp. 65–94. British Archaeological Reports, International Series, 327. Oxford, England.

Ximénez, Francisco

1929–1931 *Historia de la provincia de San Vicente de Chiapa y Guatemala de la Orden de Predicadores* [c.1700]. Biblioteca Goathemala de la Sociedad de Geografía e Historia de Guatemala, vols. 1–3. Tipografía Nacional, Guatemala.

Chapter 12 ■

Wendy Kramer, W. George Lovell, and
Christopher H. Lutz

Fire in the Mountains: Juan de Espinar and the Indians of Huehuetenango, 1525–1560

We focus here on the controversial career of Juan de Espinar, a humble Spanish tailor who, in 1525, received the encomienda of Huehuetenango, the largest award of Indian goods and services in the Cuchumatán Highlands of Guatemala (Figure 12–1). In an attempt to increase his quota of native tribute and labor, Espinar manipulated Indians into burning their homes and taking up residence within the boundaries of his encomienda. Early archival documentation, containing testimonies of both Indian and Spanish witnesses, offers a unique view of native life under European domination and reveals the cunning, malevolent behavior of an ambitious man committed to making himself master of the region.

The Issues

How, as an early privilege of conquest, the encomienda functioned in Guatemala has never been adequately determined (Kramer 1990; Rodríguez Becerra 1977). Hitherto, only sparse documentation on the subject has come to light.[1] Prior to the stabilizing presence of royal government, which in Guatemala did not materialize until 1544, conquerors themselves set the requirements for what goods

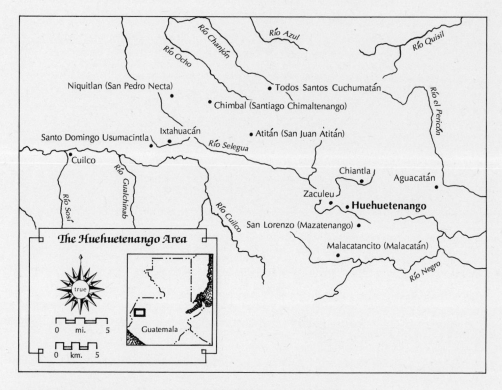

Figure 12–1. Settlements of the Cuchumatán Highlands of Guatemala.

and services were expected from the Indians they held in encomienda. It should not surprise us that Spaniards deliberately overlooked recording this kind of information, for the amount of tribute and the variety of services provided by Indians often exceeded the legal limits established by the Crown. We know, from passing references, of the existence of several documents that may contain such information, but these sources have not yet been found. It is for this reason that uncovering data relating to the early operation of encomienda in and around Huehuetenango, the largest town in the Cuchumatán highlands, is so exceptional. Our principal source is the correspondence of a complex pleito, or lawsuit, that took place from 1529 to 1537 between an obscure Spanish conquistador, Juan de Espinar, and the man who spearheaded the conquest of Guatemala, Pedro de Alvarado (AGI Justicia 1031). Litigation between conquerors was most frequent in the period immediately following subjugation. Bickering was exacerbated in the Guatemalan case by the constant reassignment of encomiendas on the part of those individuals charged between 1524 and 1548 with the day-to-day business of running the country (see Table 12–1). It was the reassigment of Huehuetenango, from Juan de Espinar to Francisco de Zurrilla, by Pedro de Alvarado in 1530, that triggered the lawsuit we examine here. Our examination, however, requires beforehand a brief outline of Preconquest and Conquest period history in order to contextualize certain events and circumstances discussed later on.

Table 12–1. Distribution of Encomiendas in Spanish Guatemala, 1524–1548

Governors, Lieutenant Governors, and Interim Governors	Tenure	Number of Towns Granted	Number of Encomenderos
Pedro de Alvarado	1524–1526	30	22
Jorge de Alvarado	1527–1529	94	72
Francisco Orduña	1529–1530	11	10
Pedro de Alvarado	1530–1533	90	50
Jorge de Alvarado	1534–1535	8	6
Pedro de Alvarado	1535–1536	19	10
Alonso de Maldonado	1536–1539	12	8
Pedro de Alvarado	1539–1540	7	3
Francisco de la Cueva	1540–1541	14	5
Beatriz de la Cueva	1541	—	—
Bishop Marroquín and Francisco de la Cueva	1541–1542	20	16
Alonso de Maldonado	1542–1548	—	—

Source: Kramer (1990).

Preconquest Huehuetenango

Archaeological and ethnohistorical evidence indicates that, by the middle of the fifteenth century, Huehuetenango had fallen under the political and tributary jurisdiction of the Quiché of Gumarcaah, later known as Utatlán (Carmack 1973). The precise extent of Quiché control, however, is still unclear. While strong all across the south, Quiché influence appears to have been less pronounced in the north and west, where small Mam chiefdoms may have held out against the expansionist aims of Gumarcaah. The secession of the Cakchiquel from the Quiché, which occurred around 1475, led to civil war between the two groups, a development that weakened considerably the rule of Gumarcaah over subjugated peoples. At least three Cuchumatán groups then seem to have thrown off the yoke of Gumarcaah, for the Indian chronicle known as the *Título de Santa Clara* exhorts the Quiché to be on guard against the Agaab people of Sacapulas, the Balamiha people of Aguacatán, and the Mam people of Zaculeu (Recinos 1957:197). Certainly by the time the Spaniards arrived in Guatemala, in 1524, the Mam of Zaculeu were treated by the Quiché more as allies than as vassals, for it was reported by none other than Pedro de Alvarado that the Mam ruler, Caibil Balam, was received with great ceremony and respect at Gumarcaah (Woodbury 1953:10).

The primacy of Zaculeu in the preconquest scheme of things is unequivocal, even if the nature of its political hold over surrounding communities is as difficult to establish as the spatial range of its domination. We know that warriors from Cuilco and Ixtahuacán fought alongside the Mam of Zaculeu against the Spaniards in 1525, so its sphere of influence extended at least 50 kilometers to the west. Northward, also, it commanded allegiance and affiliation, perhaps as far as the valley of Todos Santos, for it was from these parts that a relief force descended to assist Caibil Balam during the Spanish siege of Zaculeu (Woodbury 1953:16–19).

Spanish Conquest of the Mam

Spanish penetration of Huehuetenango began in 1525, when Gonzalo de Alvarado led an expedition against the Mam. Alvarado had been informed, so Fuentes y Guzmán (1932–1933:3:110) tells us, that Mam country was "great and rich" and that "abundant treasures" would be among the spoils of victory. He set off early in July 1525 with a party of 40 cavalry, 80 infantry, and 2,000 Mexican and Quichean warriors. Assisted by another contingent of several hundred Indians who served as pack bearers, the party proceeded first to Totonicapán, which functioned as military and supply headquarters for the duration of the campaign. After a brief encampment at Totonicapán, the party then journeyed north, entering Mam country proper. In the days that followed, Alvarado's men defeated two sizable Mam armies, one from Mazatenango (San Lorenzo) and the other from Malacatán (Malacatancito), before marching on toward Huehuetenango, which they found abandoned. Having heard of the Spaniards' approach, Caibil Balam had ordered the evacuation of Huehuetenango and had retreated with his forces to the nearby stronghold of Zaculeu, where Mam forces waited in hostile confrontation.

The task confronting the Spaniards was indeed formidable, for Zaculeu exhibited a distinct air of impregnability. Although located on an open plain, the site was surrounded on all sides but one by ravines, and further protected by a man-made system of walls and ditches. A reconstruction of the fortress as Fuentes y Guzmán imagined it to be (Figure 12–2) appears in the *Recordación Florida*. While the chronicler's drawing is certainly fanciful, it nonetheless imparts a sense of Zaculeu as a safe and secure stronghold. Inside its defenses Caibil Balam had gathered 6,000 warriors, which meant that the Spaniards and their Indian allies were outnumbered some two to one.

By early September, however, Alvarado had steered his men successfully through two separate armed engagements. During the second clash, 8,000 warriors are reported to have come down from the mountains to the north in an attempt to break the siege laid to Zaculeu following the first exchange of fire. On both occasions, victory on the part of the invaders can in large part be attributed to the murderous impact of Spanish cavalry on Indian foot soldiers. Following their double defeat on the field of battle, the Mam never again ventured outside their stronghold, where they were effectively besieged until Caibil Balam finally surrendered a month or so later. Satisfied that the subjugation of the Mam had been accomplished, Gonzalo de Alvarado left for Spanish headquarters, at that time located in Iximché, with news of his triumph.

The fall of Zaculeu, in October 1525, meant that Spanish rule was considered to prevail throughout Huehuetenango. In his account of the conquest, Fuentes y Guzmán talks in exalted tones about the valor of Gonzalo de Alvarado, whose

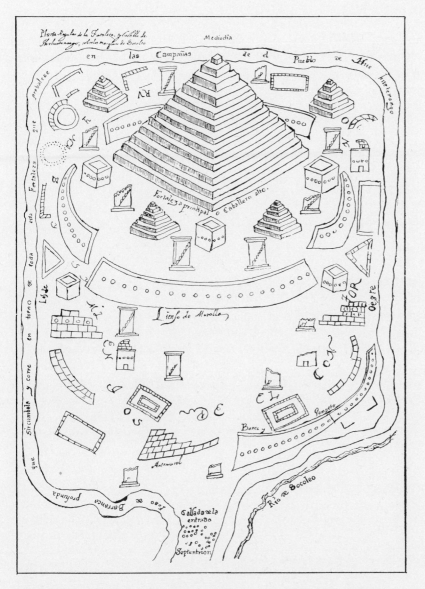

Figure 12–2. The fortress of Zaculeu, as depicted by Fuentes y Guzmán (1933).

own account of the conquest (alas, no longer extant) the chronicler relied upon heavily. Using Fuentes y Guzmán as a historical source is always problematical (Sáenz de Santa María 1969), but the chronicler does make it clear in this case that he was working directly from Gonzalo de Alvarado's firsthand descriptions. Alvarado's account may likewise have been imperfect, weighted perhaps in his own personal favor, but the fact remains that Fuentes y Guzmán's filtered version is the only surviving source we have for the conquest of the Mam. Fuentes y Guzmán also singles out the key role played in the campaign by Antonio de Salazar and Gonzalo de Solís. Salazar was credited with maintaining the siege of Zaculeu when Alvarado led other Spaniards into battle against the relief force that attacked from the north. After Alvarado's departure for Iximché, Solís was left in command of Spanish and allied troops stationed in Huehuetenango and was charged with conducting a reconnaissance of all Mam communities either subject to, or aligned with, Zaculeu. None of these three conquerors, however, received the encomienda of Huehuetenango for the part they played in bringing the natives to heel. That prize, the right to exact unspecified goods and services from Indian communities in the newly conquered land, fell to Juan de Espinar, a Spaniard whose name passes without mention in the story so far.

Juan de Espinar, Encomendero of Huehuetenango

The documents are silent about both Juan de Espinar's place of origin and his family background. This is hardly surprising, given that Espinar himself would have had no wish to dwell on his humble lineage, and in view of the fact that it is difficult generally to identify the place of origin and family background of many of Guatemala's early conquerors. Perhaps a good number of them, like Espinar, were of low social standing and so had little reason to dwell on where they were born or who their families were—standard refrains that surface in the depositions prepared by conquerors and their offspring when they sought recompense from the Crown for services rendered. Men who did include information of this kind in legal solicitations were ones who usually had something to boast about (Kramer 1990:390). Unfortunately, nothing exists for Guatemala that is remotely comparable to the census of the first encomenderos of Panama used by Mario Góngora (1962:68–90), or the roll of Cajamarca analyzed by James Lockhart (1972:90–102), or the survey carried out in 1514 in Hispaniola, which Frank Moya Pons (1987:99–118) gleaned so effectively. In her study of the hidalgos, or noblemen, of Guatemala, Pilar Sanchíz Ochoa (1976) notes that the intense interest among Spanish residents to become hidalgos spread even to nonconquerors, tradesmen, and laborers. Sanchíz, however, was able to add but little to our knowledge of either the regional or social origins of Spanish residents, observing only that, in spite of vociferous claims to "hidalguía," there were probably very few "hidalgos peninsulares" in the area.

Espinar was awarded Huehuetenango by Pedro de Alvarado in 1525. He held the encomienda until 1530, when Don Pedro had it temporarily removed. Although no mention is made of him, we assume that Espinar must have served under Gonzalo de Alvarado, for he gained control of Huehuetenango around the time the Mam surrendered at Zaculeu.[2] Huehuetenango was then a prize catch, but there were other encomiendas of comparable size or even larger, encomiendas held by such men as Pedro and Jorge de Alvarado, Pedro Puertocarrero, Pedro de Cueto, Sancho de Barahona, Diego de Rojas, and Bartolomé Becerra (Kramer 1990:357–358). In spite of the fact that, after Huehuetenango was returned to him in 1531, Espinar no longer had the usufruct of some neighboring towns, his encomienda continued to be substantial (AGI Justicia 295).

Unlike most of his peers, Espinar was quite content with his lot. He announced with obvious pride that, since the time of the conquest, he had never traveled outside of Mexico or Guatemala, a thinly veiled slight about the high mobility of the first conquerors, many of whom left the area disappointed with their gains, seeking greater enrichment elsewhere (AGCA, A1.29 legajo 4678, expediente 40244).

Two important chroniclers make mention of Espinar, but they are unable to furnish specific information either about his services in the conquest or his place of birth. The main reason why Espinar attracted their attention is because of the money he made in America. Bernal Díaz del Castillo (1962:284) claimed that he remembered when, at the time of the conquest of Mexico, Juan de Espinar disembarked in Villa Rica from Spain and the Canary Islands, noting that Espinar went on to become a "very rich" resident of Santiago de Guatemala. Fuentes y Guzmán (1932–1933:3:99–101) also noted that Espinar became a wealthy man, but depicted Espinar's circumstances prior to his alleged discovery of silver mines at Chiantla as one of consummate poverty. Espinar is described, before fortune smiled on him, as a "miserable subject, with a wife and many children but with no means to feed so many mouths." The chronicler, once again, may have confused fact with fancy, for our archival sources say nothing about Espinar having been impoverished, nor ever having married and fathered children, even out of wedlock. We do have evidence that Espinar benefited considerably from gold placer mining in the Río Malacatán to the south of Huehuetenango, an enterprise he became involved in soon after the conquest. Espinar may indeed have played a role in the discovery, later on, of silver mines within the boundaries of his encomienda, but by then he was already a man of some means. A fellow conqueror, one Francisco López, made the unsolicited remark as early as 1539 that Espinar (AGCA A.1.29, legajo 4678, expediente 40244) "has very fine *haciendas* and good profits from them." Years later, President Alonso López de Cerrato (AGI Justicia 301) also observed that Espinar had "good Indians," probably meaning an ample or sufficient number at his command. Espinar himself reveals little, concerned in one deposition (AGCA, A1.29, legajo 4678, expediente 40244) with telling the Crown that he was a conqueror of Mexico and a first conqueror of Guatemala. It meant a lot to him to establish that he had a rather good horse (AGI Justicia 1031), a point others also did not fail to make.[3]

Besides his soldierly deeds and his owning a horse, nothing about Espinar's stature prepares us for the award of such a prime encomienda as Huehuetenango. We must bear in mind that Espinar was neither a member of the Alvarado clan nor one of its favored cronies. Don Pedro, the original grantor, was himself hard-pressed to explain why Huehuetenango landed in the hands of such an unworthy recipient. In 1530, the only explanation he could offer (AGI Justicia 1031) ran as follows:

> As a result of continuous warfare in the region, the distribution of encomiendas had been irregular. Consequently, there were men like Espinar to whom the captains, to placate the appetites [of their soldiers], had given disproportionately large encomiendas, while others who deserved good encomiendas ended up with very little.

It is to Alvarado's investigations into Espinar's background that we owe some specific evidence as to whom the encomendero of Huehuetenango might have been.

There was certainly no love lost between Pedro de Alvarado and Juan de Espinar. The enmity between them dated from the time of Francisco de Orduña's governmental inquiry of 1529–1530, when Espinar presented damaging testimony against Alvarado. Upon Don Pedro's return to Guatemala in 1530, he set his sight on Huehuetenango as an appropriate reward either for himself or for one of his new followers. Alvarado, accustomed to getting his way, was unprepared for Espinar's bold refusal to relinquish his encomienda. Even though Don Pedro had originally granted Huehuetenango to Espinar, changed conditions in the former's own fortunes and the influx of worthy new colonists made it necessary to usurp or divide large encomiendas held either by members of the first conquering expedition or distributed by Jorge de Alvarado in 1528. Besides, reports that Espinar mistreated Indians and had burned several of their towns in order to get them to reside within the boundaries of his encomienda, provided Alvarado with ample justification for the removal of Huehuetenango.

Don Pedro had this to say (AGI Justicia 1031) about the man he regarded as an artisan upstart:

> Espinar is a lowly person and of little disposition, someone who has lived by his trade as a tailor. His Majesty orders that tradesmen of the mechanical arts should not be given Indians but, rather, that they use their trades so that they ennoble newly settled lands and kingdoms and that the Indians should be given to the nobility and to those of a disposition other than that of tradesmen similar to the aforementioned Espinar.

For most men, Alvarado's wrath would have been good cause to back down, but Espinar stood firm. While careful always to downplay his knowledge of a manual skill, Espinar was not ashamed of the fact, prevailing prejudices aside, that he had once worked as a tailor (AGI Justicia 295). Don Pedro and his supporters also tried to denigrate Espinar by accusing him of gambling huge sums of money. Gambling, however, was so widespread among early Spanish settlers that this accusation likely did little to erode Espinar's reputation. Ironically, the former tailor lost especially large sums to Alvarado himself. Gambling debts evidently forced Espinar to make onerous demands on his Indians for gold and jewels (AGI Justicia 1031). His imperious character and his staunch belief that encomienda rewards should rest on military service and seniority in the region alone help explain how Espinar was able to frustrate Alvarado's attempts to appropriate or reassign Huehuetenango for any great length of time. Thus, regardless of his past and his growing infamy as a Spaniard who abused Indians, Espinar argued tenaciously that Huehuetenango was his from the time of the first assignment and should continue to be so.

Encomienda: The Spanish Reward

Juan de Espinar held the encomienda of Huehuetenango from 1525 until his death in the early 1560s, with one 10- to 12–month haitus. For more than 35 years, many of them turbulent and fraught with uncertainty, a combination of tenacity, cleverness, and political savvy, together with a toughness that drifted, at times, into cruelty, made Espinar the master of Huehuetenango. He also had keen business instincts, controlling the sale of Indian tribute and developing an elaborate infrastructure of mining and agricultural activities in and around Huehuetenango. Land titles that cover Espinar's tenure as encomendero have yet to be located. It seems safe to assume, however, that by virtue of the power he wielded, Espinar could use the land much as he pleased, even though encomienda theoretically had nothing to do with seigneurial rights.[4] Espinar, for example, owned a pig farm next to the town of Huehuetenango, and laid claim to enough land to raise large quantities of corn and beans, which he stored for consumption throughout the year.

About 10 kilometers to the south of Huehuetenango, along the course of the Río Malacatán, Espinar was fortunate enough to be one of the first Spaniards to exploit local deposits of gold. Good fortune for Espinar proved to be an onerous burden for the Indians he controlled. There is no evidence to show that Espinar owned the gold deposits. Rather, he staked claim to a part of them, as did other Spaniards in the same area. Since Espinar held the largest encomienda close to the placer mines, he wisely took advantage of his position to sell food supplies to other Spaniards who had gangs of Indian slaves (cuadrillas) working the gold deposits. While his encomienda gave him a foothold in the region and supplied him with foodstuffs, cloth goods, and labor services, it was panning for gold that made Espinar a wealthy man (AGI Justicia 1031).

Espinar claimed in his litigation with Alvarado that he earned approximately 9,000 pesos a year from his mining operations and another 3,000 pesos from his agricultural enterprises. From these earnings it would be logical to deduce that the rewards from the encomienda itself were insignificant because Espinar was an entrepreneur, not a feudal lord. That conclusion, however, would be misleading. In the case of Espinar, and many other encomenderos as well, the two roles were intertwined. Without his encomienda, and all that a rapacious encomendero could extract, Espinar's mining and agricultural enterprises may never have been more than modest or insignificant operations.

It is difficult to chart the course of Espinar's fortunes throughout his lifetime. We are on reasonably firm ground, however, in assuming that the most profitable years occurred prior to midcentury. Indian numbers were at their highest levels in the first decades after conquest. Population decline (Table 12–2) set in quickly and precipitously, the result of warfare, disease, and culture shock (Lovell and Swezey, 1982; Lovell et al. 1984). Espinar lived long enough to see the native population of Huehuetenango plummet to a small percentage of what it had been when he first arrived in 1525. One factor that affected the population size of his encomienda was that during the first five years of his tenure (until 1530) he claimed not only the cabecera (head town) of Huehuetenango but a handful of other settlements he lost the right to later on, when they were granted to other Spaniards.

Added to the woes of an encomieda shrinking both in population numbers and territorial extent, with the enforcement of the New Laws (1542) under President Cerrato (1549–1555) came restrictions on the amounts of tribute collected, the numbers of Indians given in personal service, and the outright abolition of most Indian slavery (Sherman 1979:129–152). Also, gold deposits in the Río Malacatán probably did not continue to provide as rich a payoff in the 1540s and 1550s as in earlier decades. In short, native numbers and riverine gold declined at the same time (MacLeod 1973:60–61,110–111). These developments must have made Espinar's later years somewhat less prosperous than his first quarter-century as encomendero of Huehuetenango. Even though his fortune declined, it was his varied and creative use of Indian labor and resources that helped him sustain a position of high economic status until the time of his death. Measured only in terms of population size, Espinar's encomienda in the mid-sixteenth century was the eleventh largest in a list of over 90 holdings, not including those of the Crown (AGI Guatemala 128).

Juan de Espinar did not run this complex operation, especially the panning of gold, all by himself. He had Indian servants (naborías) work exclusively in the mines, a Spaniard who served as a mining expert, a foreman (mayordomo or calpixque), and several pig herders (pastores) in Huehuetenango. To the south, whether Santiago's capital site was Almolonga (1527–1541) or Panchoy (1541–1773), Espinar built a house that must have been maintained by servants. By 1530, possibly even earlier, he was a council member (regidor) on the body (cabildo) that governed the most important city in Central America. As well as

Table 12–2. The Population of Huehuetenango and Subject Towns, 1530–31 and 1549

Head/Subject Town	1530–1531	1549
Huehuetenango (includes Chiantla)	3,000–3,500[a] tributaries	500[b]
Santiago Chimaltenango (Chimbal, Chinbal)	500 casas[c]	35[d]
San Juan Atitán (Atitán)		
San Pedro Necta (Niquitlán, Niquetla)	200 casas[e]	20

a. Estimate based on calculations by Kramer 1990.
b. All 1549 figures are from AGI Guatemala 128.
c. 200 houses in the town center, or cabecera, and 300 in outlying settlements, or estancias. AGI, Justicia 1031.
d. Santiago Chimaltenango and San Juan Atitán, together, had 35 tributaries in 1549.
e. AGI Justicia 1031.

an urban household in the capital, Espinar also owned agricultural lands nearby. On this estate, Espinar likely settled Indian slaves, who would be joined by groups of encomienda Indians to produce wheat and other foodstuffs, for both domestic consumption and sale at market (AGI Justicia 1031; *Libro viejo* 1934:34; Lutz 1982).

Encomienda: the Indian Burden

Litigation between Pedro de Alvarado and Juan de Espinar provides the earliest details on the tribute and labor obligations of a Guatemalan encomienda. We compare in Table 12–3 native obligations for 1530–1531, when Zurrilla held Huehuetenango, and 18 years later, in 1549, when Espinar had long since regained control. Circumstances clearly altered over time. First, the encomienda of Huehuetenango in the early 1530s consisted of the population of the cabecera itself plus the inhabitants of at least four smaller, outlying towns. In 1549, the encomienda contained only the head town and one subject town, Chiantla. Second, the total number of Indian tributaries dropped from an estimated 3,000–3,500 to only 500 during these two decades (Table 12–2). Third, the more stringent enforcement of Crown laws, especially the reforms regarding Indian tribute and labor and the abolition of Indian slavery, must have greatly reduced the burden on the remaining population. Since an information void exists between the early 1530s and the late 1540s, we are forced to reconstruct how Huehuetenango's Indians fared during the interim. Espinar's loss of some subject towns, and their tributaries, in the 1530s, together with depopulation and encomendero freedom to exploit as the master saw fit, meant increasingly hard times for the Indians. While his encomienda holdings were rapidly spiraling downward, Espinar was undoubtedly desirous of maintaining his mining operation, his income, and his status in Santiago society. In short, if the year under Zurrilla presented in Table 12–3 looks bad for the Indians, most likely there were even more difficult years later on.

On the other hand, the year that Zurrilla held Huehuetenango might well have been an unusually demanding one for the Indians. Zurrilla took advantage of this opportunity to direct considerable native resources toward supporting the mining operations run by himself and Pedro de Alvarado. During his tenure, Zurrilla had the gang of 120 Indian slaves taken from the encomienda. He also owned outright, from his days in Mexico, a second cuadrilla of 100 Mixtec slaves. To the feeding and clothing of these slaves we must add an unknown quantity of goods and services given to Pedro de Alvarado for the Indian slaves belonging to him, for they worked the same gold deposits as the slaves of Zurrilla. Forty laborers known as indios de servicio, along with honey, fowl, and some clothing, went to Zurrilla's house in Santiago and the estate he owned nearby. Most other goods and services—cotton cloth, reed mats, foodstuffs, and the labor of men and women—were deployed in the support of the Indian slaves and the Spanish miner. We lack information on precise tribute schedules, but if payment followed the pattern used in subsequent periods, then half was furnished on the tercio de San Juan (June 24) and half at Christmas on the tercio de navidad. Juan, an Indian leader of Huehuetenango, stated that each time tribute was paid to Zurrilla he counted the items and turned them over to the foreman (a Spaniard) who distributed the items between the mines and Santiago (AGI Justicia 1031). Most of the crops harvested to feed the local population and meet their obligation to feed the indios de servicio and Indian slave miners would probably have been furnished in the December payment. In his litigation with Alvarado, Espinar claimed that he had 3,000 fanegas (4,500 bushels) of corn and 300 fanegas of beans and chile stored at Huehuetenango, which he lost when Zurrilla held

Table 12–3. Tribute Paid in Huehuetenango in 1530–1531 and 1549

	1530–1531	*1549*
Clothing:	800 mantas[a] 400 masteles[b] 400 xicoles[c] 400 guipiles[d] 400 naguas[e] 400 cutaras[f]	300 mantas
Foodstuffs:	Unspecified amounts of maize, beans, chile, and salt[g]	1 sementera of 15 fanegas (maíz)[h]
	108–126 large jugs	1 sementera of 5 of honey[i]fanegas (frijoles)[j]
		100 cargas/loads of agí[k] 100 panes/loaves of salt
Fowl:	2,268 gallinas[l]	12 dozen gallinas de Castilla[m]
Other Items:	400 petates[n]	1 sementera of 4 fanegas of cotton[o]
Labor Obligations:	40 indios de servicio: Indian men to the city every 20 days all year[p]	6 indios de servicio
	120–200 indios de servicio: Indian men to the gold mines every 20 days all year[q]	
	30 indias de servicio: Indian women to the gold mines in order to make tortillas and prepare food for the Indian laborers and the Indian slaves.[r]	

the encomienda. Espinar's 600 pigs, likewise, were lost, although Zurrilla denied any responsibility.

It seems, on the testimony of several witnesses, that Zurrilla and his partner Alvarado were more rapacious in their exploitation of Huehuetenango than was Juan de Espinar. While, with hindsight, we know that Zurrilla only held the

Table 12–3. (continued)

Slaves	80 male and 40 female slaves, siezed from other towns, delivered to Zurrilla in Santiago. Used in the mines.[s]

a. A standard length of cotton cloth. Half of this amount paid during each of two tributary payments. The same was true in the cases of the masteles, xicoles, guipiles, naguas, cutaras, and petates.

b. From the Nahuatl, *maxtlatl*, a type of loincloth.

c. A doublet or jacket.

d. Huipil, or type of woven blouse worn by women.

e. Womens' skirts.

f. A type of sandal, with deerhide soles, probably worn by men.

g. See below in the labor part of this table and text.

h. The harvest from a planting (sementera) of approximately 22.5 bushels of maize. A large planting.

i. Honey (miel) delivered to the encomendero in the city by the 40 personal service Indians sent to the city on 20 day shifts. They carried six or seven large jugs (jarros) each trip.

j. Most likely a type of black bean.

k. Chile.

l. At this early date, probably turkey hens or native fowl. Each group of 40 Indians sent to work for the encomendero in the city of Santiago (see below) carried 126 every 20 days of the year for an annual total of approximately 2,268.

m. European chickens introduced by the Spaniards from the Iberian peninsula were more commonplace than 20 years earlier.

n. Woven reed mats used for sleeping.

o. A planting of four fanegas, equal to approximately six bushels, of which the encomendero would receive the entire crop.

p. These Indians carried the gallinas (turkey hens) and honey listed above on a regular basis to the encomendero's house in Santiago. The total of 720 Indians gave approximately 14,400 days of labor in house construction, domestic service, and agricultural work in the encomendero's estate in the valley of the city. Each time a group of 40 traveled to the city they provided and carried their own supply of corn.

q. These laborers hauled firewood and dug out dirt to aid the mining of the gold. Every time they went to the mines they brought five gallinas for the miner, and all the chile, beans, salt, and corn necessary to feed themselves and the 200 slaves Zurrilla had mining for gold. These 2,160 to 3,600 Indians provided approximately 43,200 to 72,000 days of work in a year.

r. Over an entire year, approximately 540 women served in this capacity producing about 10,800 days of labor for the encomendero.

s. Newly enslaved Indians from towns included in the encomienda of Huehuetenango. About 70 Indians were branded. All were taken to work the gold mining operations but most returned to their towns, according to Zurrilla, when he lost the encomienda.

Source: AGI Justicia 1031; AGI 128; Kramer (1990); Fowler (1989:159,185); Díaz del Castillo (1962:5); Simeón (1981:765).

town for 10 months to a year, it makes no sense to think that he wished to consume its worth as quickly as possible, for he could not have known he would hold it so briefly. On the other hand, unlike Espinar, Zurrilla did not intend to stay in a backwater like Guatemala all of his life. So neither Zurrilla nor his mentor Alvarado, the latter ever anxious to amass large sums of cash for his foreign ventures, acted as if preserving the encomienda and its population were important.

Espinar claimed, and witnesses supported him, that the population of Huehuetenango declined by half during the brief time Zurrilla was encomendero. Apart from attrition due to disease, numbers fell because Indians fled to the mountains to escape the clutches of Zurrilla's hired administrators. In an unidentified subject town, Indians were said to be (AGI Justicia 1031) "very hostile and did not want to serve, running off always into the wilds. Sometimes Indians from the cabecera [together] with the Spaniard working as foreman went to look for them. They would bring them back forcibly as prisoners, and make them work. [Zurrilla] had them put in chains in order that they might work at the mines as did [the Indians] in the other towns." Indian resistance, perhaps more passive than in the subect town just mentioned, also occurred in the cabecera. When two high-ranking leaders of Huehuetenango did not cooperate with Zurrilla in mobilizing Indian labor, he ordered that they be sent before Pedro de Alvarado in Santiago. It was said by one witness (AGI Justicia 1031) that Zurrilla "had had a lord and a lord who was a translator punished."

Another witness, Luis de Bibar, testified that he had heard it said that Indians from Huehuetenango had been mistreated, perhaps even killed, when they refused to serve Zurrilla and Alvarado. Bibar stated that when Espinar arrived back in Guatemala in 1531, with the order from the Audiencia of Mexico returning Huehuetenango to him, that Indian leaders (principales) were in prison for having fled. Among those jailed was Coatle, the lord of Chiantla. Bibar also stated, however, that Coatle fled later on from Espinar, himself not above reproach for harsh treatment of Indians. In his defense, Espinar's attorney stated (AGI Justicia 1031) that when "his client had mistreated his Indians it was a long time ago, when the Indians were uncivilized and half at war and [because] they did not want to feed nor maintain some slaves that their encomendero had in the mines, on account of which some of them [slaves] died of hunger." Ignacio de Bobadilla, on the other hand, noted that on two occasions he had written letters on Espinar's behalf, instructing his foreman to give the Indians more supplies of corn, if they were in need, even though they had received their regular supplies (AGI Justicia 1031). This suggests that, while no saint, Espinar was understandably concerned for the welfare of his Indians, for their work in the mines kept him rich. Ironically, these two factors, Indian survival and maintaining the flow of gold, appear to have played a key role in the burning of several of Huehuetenango's subject towns in early 1530, perhaps the most startling revelation offered by the documents at hand.

The Burning of the Towns

Analysis of testimony concerning the burning, in January 1530, of four or five subject towns, the motivations for these actions, and the subsequent migration of Indians down from the mountains to the fertile plain close to Zaculeu leads us to conclude that it was Juan de Espinar who ordered this course of action, probably in collusion with the native lords of Huehuetenango and, perhaps also, with the Indian leaders of the outlying towns themselves. In order to understand this unusual course of action we must briefly invoke Preconquest antecedents.

From testimony we learn that many of the Mam settlements west and north of Huehuetenango, as well as the cabecera itself, began to pay tribute to Utatlán after Quiché expansion into the region in the early fifteenth century. Not only did Mam communities begin to pay tribute, but the conquering Quiché are said to have displaced local populations from traditional lands in the lower and more fertile plain around Zaculeu, forcing them to move to colder, less salubrious upland locations. Even with the decline of Quiché influence in the late fifteenth century, and with the increasing independence of Huehuetenango from Utatlán, the smaller Mam settlements (each with its own patio and temples, as the witnesses testify) continued to pay tribute to the Quiché lords. This would suggest that places such as Chimbal, Atitán, Niquitlán, Chiantla, and others were under the indirect rule of Utatlán, and that the authority of Huehuetenango and Zaculeu was somehow bypassed. Contradicting this assumption, however, is the evidence that, after the Spanish conquest, the lords of Huehuetenango ordered these same places to pay tribute to the new master of Huehuetenango, Juan de Espinar, an order the rulers of the subject towns obeyed. Their apparent willingness to pay tribute to Espinar upon orders from Huehuetenango suggests that the latter held considerable sway over outlying communities. Justified or not, the lords of Huehuetenango referred to the nonelite inhabitants of the subject settlements as "their commoners." The close ties between these places and Huehuetenango is indicated by their involvement, outlined earlier, in Mam efforts to defeat the Spaniards at Zaculeu.

Taking these relations into account, it becomes more understandable why, in early 1530, under orders from Espinar and the lords of Huehuetenango, families in several mountain towns (see Table 12–4) would burn their houses (apparently having first removed their personal possessions and food supplies), abandon both home and community, and move a relatively short distance to the plain surrounding Zaculeu. Other motives, however, are less apparent, and involve a necessary departure, on our part, from historical fact to historical imagination.

Espinar tried to cover up his involvement in the plot by telling the then governor, Francisco de Orduña, that the Indians had burned their towns because they were in rebellion against the Spaniards. At the same time, Espinar, through his intermediaries, ordered Indian leaders to proceed with this destruction, and indeed flee to the mountains, in order that armed Spaniards whom he claimed would be passing through the region on missions of conquest and pacification might not see them. Afterward, those who fled were to come and live near

Table 12–4. Settlements Burned, Wholly or in Part, in Huehuetenango (1530)

Identified Places	Unidentified Places
Huehuetenango	Amala
Cozumaçutla, Xozumaçutla (Sto. Domingo Usumacinta)	Mocoga
Chiantla	Esquinel
Atitán[a]	
Chinbal, Chimbal (Santiago Chimaltenenago)	
Niquitlán, Niquetla, Necotla (San Pedro Necta)	

a. Acatepeque "en lengua de México y [en lengua de] la tierra Muachi y agora se llama Atitán." *Source:* AGI Justicia 1031.

Zaculeu, also referred to as Zacualpa Huehuetenango. Cotoha, an Indian leader of Huehuetenango, testified that Espinar's native messenger told the lords (AGI Justicia 1031) that his master had said that "everyone should go down to the plain and gather themselves so that the Christians could not distribute them [in the encomienda]." The same witness said that Espinar had ordered that the towns be burned quickly, before informants of Orduña could see them, for if they did not proceed in haste then the Spaniards would kill them.

Espinar's initial reason behind razing thousands of houses was his anger over what he saw as intrusions into his encomienda jurisdiction by two other Spaniards, García de Salinas and Juan Niño. Preliminary evidence suggests that these men laid claim, based on official grants, to Chimbal, Atitán (claimed by Salinas) and Nequetla (claimed by Niño).[5] In order to eliminate the case made by them—that he was usurping *their* towns—Espinar planned with his allies, the lords of the cabecera of Huehuetenango, the burning of subject towns and the resettlement of inhabitants in other locations. Because, under Spanish law, a grant of encomienda was for the use of the production and labor of a specified population, and not the lands or territory on which people lived, by this daring move Espinar wiped out the real resource base of his enemies while, simultaneously, consolidating his own holdings. As well as asserting and strengthening his own authority, Espinar's action also served to bolster the authority of the lords of Huehuetenango.

Investigations ordered by Orduña soon revealed that the Indians of the subject towns were not in rebellion but, rather, were simply following, as they had on previous occasions, the instructions of both Espinar and the lords of Huehuetenango. Espinar's motives were thus ones of unabashed greed, the desire for optimal enrichment. They also reflect a spitefulness and sense of territoriality against what he saw as the intrusion of García de Salinas and Juan Niño. To these must be added his wish to protect the rather elaborate infrastructure he had developed in the environs of Huehuetenango within a scant five years of the Spanish conquest.

Indian motives are more complex and less obvious to discern. Throughout the lawsuit, there is evidence of a congruence of interests between Espinar and the Indian leaders of both the cabecera and the outlying towns. Even though the solution chosen—to burn entire towns—was a radical one, inhabitants of these places had legitimate complaints about where they lived. Indian witnesses complained that town sites in the sierra were unhealthy, excessively cold, and that soils there were inferior to those of the plain around Huehuetenango and Zaculeu. By contrast, the same witnesses noted that they, their families, and their children especially would live in a warmer, more hospitable environment.[6]

Equally important, the return to the plain, after the displacement caused by Quiché conquest, relocated these populations near the best land for growing corn, where they and their ancestors had raised far better crops than was possible at more lofty altitudes. Olín, the chief of Huehuetenango, testified that the lords and Indians of the other towns were living close to Zaculeu, where they guarded their corn fields.

Without exception, all witnesses speak favorably of moving from higher elevations to the lower altitude of the Zaculeu plain. Even the leaders of Huehuetenango mentioned this as a factor, which suggests that the town of Huehuetenango of the late 1520s must have been at a higher elevation and in a different location than the modern city of the same name.

Another reason that Indian witnesses gave for having burned their towns was that the Cuchumatán region was no longer at war, meaning that disruptions caused both by Quiché invasion and Spanish conquest were over. Testifying in 1530, Olín stated that the main justification for burning part of the old cabecera of Huehuetenango and moving closer to Zacualpa Huehuetenango (Zaculeu) was that there was no more war and so, by implication, the inhabitants could move to less defensible, open locations on the plain.

If, as the Indians declared, there was lower morbidity, warmer temperatures, and better harvests on the plain, all this was beneficial both for the former inhabitants of the subject towns and their leaders. On the negative side, the subject towns, and especially their leaders, must have lost some of their autonomy, for they were apparently now under the direct authority of the lords of Huehuetenango and, through them, Espinar. If there were benefits for the people of the subject towns, burning and resettlement appears to have been a boon for the encomendero and his native accomplices. In short order, the cabecera's leaders and their Spanish master concentrated most of the scattered population of some half dozen towns. Since, as they claimed, these people had their best, traditional milpas near Zaculeu, not only would a larger labor supply be mobilized for the use of the native elite and Espinar but, at the same time, there could be greater agricultural productivity for everyone. The concentration of the region's labor pool could have relieved some pressure on Huehuetenango's own local population while at the same time increasing the productivity of Espinar's varied enterprises in agriculture and mining.

While the burning of the towns and the gathering of their inhabitants near

Zaculeu had benefits for all parties involved, the main beneficiary was Juan de Espinar, not the Indians. Unfortunately for him, his trickery and scheming came to the attention of Francisco de Orduña, whose investigative findings were passed on to Pedro de Alvarado. Don Pedro, in turn, used the disclosures against Espinar. This resulted, about eight months after the incidents occurred, in Espinar losing his encomienda, and in the collapse of related agricultural and mining enterprises. It also resulted in Espinar being thrown in jail and then forced into exile, albeit temporarily, in Mexico. After Francisco de Zurrilla's one-year tenure as encomendero, Espinar regained control of Huehuetenango and of his agricultural and mining operations. The economic power and political authority he and his Indian allies asserted during that brief period in 1530, however, was gone forever. Because of excessive exploitation by Zurrilla, Huehuetenango's congregated population fell by about half during Espinar's year-long absence. Furthermore, when Espinar regained control of Huehuetenango, the encomienda known by that name no longer included Chimbal, Atitán, or Niquetla, which were apparently ceded to Francisco de Zurrilla (AGI Justicia 295). The parts of Huehuetenango that remained under Espinar's entitlement incorporated only the cabecera itself and nearby Chiantla. As a consequence, Espinar's economic power and the political authority of local native elites suffered a sharp decline.

By 1537, when Espinar's litigation with Alvarado over losses suffered under Zurrilla's tenure in 1530–1531 came before the courts, the Indian rulers of Huehuetenango were at least nominal Christians with new baptismal names. Their conversion to Christianity may indicate a continued willingness to cooperate with Espinar in order to maintain their status even as the human resource base around them was shrinking. Huehuetenango was still an important encomienda at mid-century, but decidedly a lesser place than it had been in preconquest times and, briefly again, in the months immediatly following the fire in the mountains of 1530.

Notes

1. William L. Sherman (1969) has written about the estate of Pedro de Alvarado but his study does not deal in any detail with early encomienda.

2. Formal title to the encomienda of Huehuetenango is dated October 3, 1525. Even though it seems that Zaculeu did not actually capitulate until toward the middle of the month, the Spaniards must by early October have felt confident of victory.

3. The witness Hernando de San C[h]ristóbal states that Espinar "has served in the conquest . . . on foot and on horseback." This suggests a rise from more lowly to higher status. Ygnacio de Bobadilla notes that Espinar "is among the first conquerors of this province of Guatemala and that in this war he has seen him serve with his arms and horses and sometimes saw that he had a servant." Pedro de Paredes, a witness for Pedro de Alvarado, knew of Espinar serving "in the war of the conquest of this province and in that of Tututepeque." See AGI Justicia 1031.

4. See Lovell (1985:118–139) on Spanish and Indian landholding patterns in the region. On the often close link between encomienda and the birth of the hacienda, of which this appears to be a good example, see Lockhart (1969) and MacLeod (1973:129–130).

5. Espinar (AGI Justicia 1031) refers to García de Salinas and Juan Niño as "enemies

who have endeavored to dispute with me [my rights] over some of the aforementioned towns." Our evidence that these three towns were in contention is more circumstantial than direct. Chimbal, or Chimaltenango, and Atitán were considered one encomienda when President Cerrato assessed them for tribute in 1549 (AGI Guatemala 128). Juan Niño volunteered (AGI Justicia 1031) detailed testimony on Niquetla, suggesting more than just passing interest in the settlement. He notes that, during a visit there, he found the cabecera of Niquetla to be a burned-out shell, a place empty of people. Niño therefore journeyed one league (4 kilometers) to sleep "at some outlying parts, for they were populated." The people there, however, fled when they saw the Spaniard. Among the inhabitants, Niño says he did not see any men. It is also important to remember that Espinar held Huehuetenango and Chiantla until his death in the early 1560s.

6. Because of the conspiracy between Espinar and Indian leaders to tell Spanish authorities the same story, reinforced by the encomendero's apparent threats to harm or kill anyone who told of his involvement, it is difficult to discern Indian concerns from those suggested by Espinar himself. Added to this confusion of motives is the problem of accurate translation from Mam to Spanish at this early date.

References

The following abbreviations are used in these references: Archivo General de Centroamérica (AGCA), and Archivo General de India (AGI).

AGCA A.1.29, legajo 4678, expediente 40244
  1539 Probanza de Juan de Espinar.
AGI Guatemala 128
  1549–1551 Las tasaciones de los pueblos del termino y jurisdicción de Santiago de Guatemala.
AGI Justicia 295
  1535 Residencia de Pedro de Alvarado.
AGI Justicia 301
  1555 Residencia de Alonso López de Cerrato.
AGI Justica 1031
  1529–1537 Juan de Espinar con Pedro de Alvarado.
Carmack, Robert M.
  1973 *Quichean Civilization: The Ethnohistoric, Ethnographic, and Archaeological Sources*. University of California Press, Berkeley and Los Angeles.
Díaz del Castillo, Bernal
  1962 *Historia verdadera de la conquista de la Nueva España*. Editorial Porrua, México, D.F.
Fowler, William R., Jr.
  1989 *The Evolution of Ancient Nahua Civilizations: The Pipil-Nicarao of Central America*. University of Oklahoma Press, Norman.
Fuentes y Guzmán, Francisco Antonio de
  1932–1933 *Recordación florida*. Biblioteca "Goathemala," vols. 6–8. Sociedad de Geografía e Historia de Guatemala, Guatemala.
Góngora, Mario
  1962 *Los grupos de conquistadores en Tierra Firme (1509–1530)*. Universidad de Chile, Centro de Historia Colonial, Santiago de Chile.
Kramer, Wendy
  1990 *The Politics of Encomienda Distribution in Early Spanish Guatemala, 1524–1544*. Unpublished Ph.D. dissertation, University of Warwick, England.
Libro viejo de la fundación de Guatemala y papeles relativos a D. Pedro de Alvarado.

1934 Prólogo del Lic. Jorge García Granados. Biblioteca "Goathemala" vol. 12, Sociedad de Geografía e Historia de Guatemala, Guatemala.

Lockhart, James

1969 Encomienda and Hacienda: The Evolution of the Great Estate in the Spanish Indies. *Hispanic American Historical Review* 49:411–429.

1972 *The Men of Cajamarca: A Social and Biographical Study of the First Conquerors of Peru.* University of Texas Press, Austin.

Lovell, W. George

1985 *Conquest and Survival in Colonial Guatemala: A Historical Geography of the Cuchumatán Highlands, 1500–1821.* McGill-Queen's University Press, Kingston and Montreal.

Lovell, W. George, Christopher H. Lutz, and William R. Swezey

1984 The Indian Population of Southern Guatemala, 1549–1551: An Analysis of López de Cerrato's Tasaciones de Tributos. *The Americas* 40:459–477.

Lovell, W. George, and William R. Swezey

1982 The Population of Southern Guatemala at Spanish Contact. *Canadian Journal of Anthropology* 3(1):71–84.

Lutz, Christopher H.

1982 *Historia sociodemográfica de Santiago de Guatemala: 1541–1773.*

Serie Monográfica 2. Centro de Investigaciones Regionales de Mesoamérica, Antigua, Guatemala.

MacLeod, Murdo M.

1973 *Spanish Central America: A Socioeconomic History, 1520–1720.* University of California Press, Berkeley and Los Angeles.

Moya Pons, Frank

1987 *Después de Colón: Trabajo, sociedad y política en la economía del oro.* Alianza Editorial, Madrid.

Recinos, Adrian (editor and translator)

1957 *Crónicas indígenas de Guatemala.* Editorial Universitaria, Guatemala.

Rodríguez Becerra, Salvador

1977 *La encomienda en Guatemala: Análisis de una sociedad en formación (1524–1554).* Universidad de Sevilla, Sevilla.

Sáenz de Santa María, Carmelo

1969 Estudio preliminar, in *Obras históricas de D. Francisco Antonio de Fuentes y Guzmán.* Biblioteca de Autores Españoles, vol. 230:v– lxxxii. Editorial Atlas, Madrid.

1969–1972 *Obras históricas de D. Francisco Antonio de Fuentes y Guzmán.* Edited by Carmelo Sáenz de Santa María. Biblioteca de Autores Españoles, vols. 230, 251 and 259. Editorial Atlas, Madrid.

Sanchíz Ochoa, Pilar

1976 *Los hidalgos de Guatemala: Realidad y apariencia en un sistema de valores.* Universidad de Sevilla, Sevilla.

Sherman, William L.

1979 *Forced Native Labor in Sixteenth-Century Central America.* University of Nebraska Press, Lincoln and London.

1969 A Conqueror's Wealth: Notes on the Estate of don Pedro de Alvarado. *The Americas* 26:199–213.

Simeón, Rémi

1981 *Diccionario de la lengua Náhuatl o Mexicana.* Siglo Veintiuno, México, D.F.

Woodbury, Nathalie F. S.

1953 The History of Zaculeu. In *The Ruins of Zaculeu, Guatemala*, 2 vols., edited by Richard B. Woodbury and Aubrey S. Trik, 1:9–20. United Fruit Company (William Byrd Press), Richmond, Va.

Chapter 13 ■

Robert M. Hill II

The Social Uses of Writing among the Colonial Cakchiquel Maya: Nativism, Resistance, and Innovation

In the most general sense, the social use of writing is everywhere the same: to preserve ideas and information. Yet, societies may differ considerably in the kinds of information deemed worthy of preservation, the types of documents produced, and the social context of that production. An analysis of these three aspects of a society's documents can reveal a great deal about its general social conditions and people's concerns. Such an analysis may be particularly useful when applied to a subordinate people in a colonial society whose views do not generally enter either the public consciousness of the dominant society or the wider historical consciousness of contemporary world society. The spectrum of information contained in such documents is the subject of this chapter. We shall be looking at the types of documents produced by and for a Mesoamerican people, the Cakchiquel Maya of highland Guatemala during the Spanish Colonial period, as well as the contexts in which they were created. This exercise should provide some new insight into the range of Cakchiquel responses to colonial rule, including nativism, innovation, and cultural resistance.

The Cakchiquel are well known to the thousands of visitors to Guatemala who have made the pilgrimage from the national capital to Lake Atitlán or

Chichicastenango, since their route takes them across the heart of Cakchiquel country. Indeed, the Cakchiquel are "the Maya" as far as many tourists are concerned. In early colonial history, they are famous (or infamous, depending on one's point of view) for having first invited the Spaniards to the region to assist them in their wars with the Quiché and Tzutujil. After a series of stunning victories in the spring of 1524, however, the Spaniards under Pedro de Alvarado decided that they had no further need for their Cakchiquel allies and attempted to impose on them the same harsh tribute and labor obligations they had placed on their former enemies. The Cakchiquel rebelled against this betrayal beginning in August of 1524 and continued to do so sporadically all through the 1530s.

A proper royal administration did not begin until the arrival of Alonso López de Cerrato in 1548. Intent on implementing the New Laws of 1542, Cerrato abolished many of the most egregious excesses of the conquistadores. By the 1550s, the colonial system had assumed the basic form that would remain in place for the next several centuries. It was clearly an inequitable system. Although slavery had been abolished, the Cakchiquel were still subject to Spanish demands on their labor and its products and, although Spaniards could not summarily expropriate Indian lands, the Cakchiquel still had to prove prior ownership or use in order to protect against usurpation. Despite the obvious inequities, the colonial regime was a stable system and one to which the Cakchiquel quickly adapted, although not always in ways that their Spanish overlords would have liked. Nowhere is this more apparent than in the uses to which the Cakchiquel put the new, European writing technology.

Like other indigenous Mesoamerican peoples, the Cakchiquel were heirs to an ancient writing tradition, complete with fairly conventional types of documents, long antedating the Spaniards' arrival in the New World. But, because the Spaniards identified indigenous writing and its documents with traditional Mesoamerican religions, the former was banned and most of the latter were destroyed. Indigenous writing in preconquest Mesoamerica was probably only the province of the higher aristocracy, priesthood, and perhaps a few scribes, who had always made up a small segment of the population. This was also the segment to suffer the greatest losses during the initial conquest of the region.

Among the highlands of Guatemala, as elsewhere in Mesoamerica, the new alphabetic writing system was introduced in the sixteenth century by the Spanish friars. Those working among the Cakchiquel quickly adopted the symbols developed by Francisco de la Parra, himself a Franciscan, to denote the different stops in highland Maya languages (stops are sounds unfamiliar to Spanish ears). Initially, the Spanish idea seems to have been to educate the native Mesoamerican aristocracy, although this class rapidly became superfluous in the emerging colonial society in which the Spaniards had established themselves as the highest social stratum. Even so, the they realized that literacy was still necessary for at least a few Indians, especially town scribes who would assist with the administration of the newly formed Indian communities. These individuals would be needed to read the instructions sent by Spanish officials, to make entries in the account books of the *caja de comunidad*, and (ideally, much more rarely) to initiate administrative correspondence.

But, having let the genie out of the bottle, the Spaniards were unable to control the range of uses to which the Cakchiquel and other Mesoamerican peoples put writing. Some of the resulting highland Maya documents have long been known to Mesoamericanist ethnohistorians, who have mined them primarily for the information they contain concerning preconquest culture and history. Another approach has been to focus on some of the longer documents (such as the Popol Vuh of the Quiché) as literature. These are certainly valid and valuable undertakings. Yet these same documents have another, equally compelling potential; to enlighten us about social conditions of the Colonial period as the Cakchiquel perceived them.

Conquest Document Types and Nativism

According to Bartolomé Las Casas, the preconquest Mexicans (and, by extension, other Mesoamerican peoples) had five "books" or, more properly, five *kinds* of "books." These he defined as (1) histories and narratives of the years and ages; (2) books giving notice of the solemn and festal days of each year; (3) books about dreams and augeries; (4) books that told about the "baptism" and naming of children; and (5) books describing rites and ceremonies, specifically those relating to marriage, perhaps also (according to Las Casas) those describing the sacrifices made to their gods (Las Casas 1958:2:341). Of course, Central Mexican peoples created other, shorter kinds of documents, as opposed to "books," such as tribute records (i.e., the Codex Mendoza) and land records/maps (the *lienzos*). While Las Casas described Central Mexico specifically, a similar, if not identical, range of "books" and other documents was clearly produced by the late preconquest Cakchiquel, since at least three of these types survived the conquest and continued to be produced well into the Colonial period.

The Xahil

Of these document types, the "histories" are the most numerous and best known. Las Casas's description of their contents as they were written by the preconquest Mexicans makes them sound like medieval European chronicles, compilations of very diverse kinds of information and events. According to Las Casas, such books contained notices of general events, fiestas, and the passage of the years; accounts of their wars, victories, and heroic deeds; the origin, succession, and genealogies of their principal lords; the history of their reigns; the weather, both good and bad; misfortunes, pestilences, other adversities, and under whose reign they occurred; and the provinces that had been conquered by the group in question up until the arrival of the Spaniards (Las Casas:2:341). This inventory appears to describe perfectly the content of the most famous colonial Cakchiquel document, the so-called Memorial Tecpán-Atitlán, or "Annals of the Cakchiquels," written by and for members of the Xahil family.

This document has been known to several generations of scholars, who have tended to focus on those parts of the chronicle that recount preconquest events, interpreting them as a "national history" of the Cakchiquel. They have downplayed or even ignored the explicitly postconquest portion (Brinton 1885; Recinos 1950). Yet, it is in the postconquest portion that the true nature of the document is revealed (Recinos 1950; Teletor 1946). The "Annals" is, in reality, a history of the Xahil family, in the same way that the Popol Vuh is, ultimately, a history of the Cavek family of the Quiché. In both cases, family history and "national history" are merged to some extent (especially in the remote past) and extend back to semimythical events to give both families (and the respective polities that they helped to lead) the legitimacy of ancient lineage, all the way back to the legendary times of the fantastic Toltecs. The Xahil document follows the history episodically through the major events of the Cakchiquel association with the Quiché of the Utatlán polity and their eventual separation from the Quiché after the revolt against the ruler Quikab around 1470. Episodic history ends here and absolute history (i.e., with dates) begins with the Cakchiquel abandonment of their old center, Chiavar (near present-day Chichicastenango).

From here on, the structure of the document is identical to that of the traditional Mesoamerican histories as outlined by Las Casas. Recounted are the genealogies, accessions, and deaths of the rulers and their wars and political intrigues, culminating in the Tukucheé revolt of 1493 which, henceforth, served as a chronological reference point for the rest of the chronicle.

As best as can be reconstructed, the compiler of most of the document was one Francisco Hernández Arana (Xahil), a direct lineal descendant of Oxlahuh Tzii (d. 1508), the most successful Ahpoxahil (head of the Xahil) and co-leader (along with the Ahpozotzil) of the Iximché polity. Francisco was born early in the sixteenth century (he recounts having seen Moctezuma's messengers at Iximché in 1510), yet he apparently did not begin to compose his chronicle until about 1573 (Recinos 1950:124). Much of the preconquest part of the document was probably based directly on oral tradition and indigenous manuscripts such as those described by Las Casas. For the period of the 1520s on, Francisco was at least partly relying on his own memory and even noted the date of his marriage (in 1522). His chronicle continues as a personal account of the conquest, but with dates tied to the Cakchiquel calendar. This suggests that either he or someone else had been keeping a running record during this tumultuous period so that in 1573 he could place events in an accurate relative and absolute chronological framework. However, the important point here is that Francisco's chronicle does not end with the conquest but continues, following the same preconquest format, up to the time of his death around 1582. By the 1560s, one can already detect a pronounced change in the entries, which become ever more localistic, personal, and mundane.

From 1583 to 1605, entries were made by another descendant of Oxlahuh Tzii, Pacal Francisco Diaz (Xahil), a collateral relative of Francisco Hernández, though two generations younger. The tendency toward a more personal account becomes even more pronounced in Pacal Francisco's entries. The succession of *cabildo* officers replaces that of hereditary rulers. Assaults, petty disputes, bouts of drunkenness, and marital infidelity replace the wars and palace intrigues of earlier times. The births and all-too-frequent deaths of children replace the passing of lords. With Pacal Francisco's passing (evidently with no surviving male children to inherit the chronicler's task), the effort ends. The other surviving Xahil were apparently no longer interested in keeping up the record.

This raises the question of why Francisco Hernández should have begun the work in the first place and why Pacal Francisco should have continued it for another generation. To me, the intent of both authors was clearly nativistic. Theirs was a conscious attempt to preserve and perpetuate the memory of a glorious past by attaching an ongoing account of postconquest events to the end of a traditional, preconquest Mesoamerican family history, using the same basic format, chronological reference points, and system of computing time and including much of the same kind of information, despite the fact that the Xahil no longer enjoyed anything like their former preeminent social position. Indeed, it was precisely because of this declining status that the chronicle was undertaken. We are looking at one aspect of an aristocratic family's almost desperate efforts to maintain a social status that the conquest and colonial society had rendered obsolete.

If (as seems likely from Las Casas's brief description and the other surviving chronicles) having a family history/genealogy was one of the characteristics of aristocratic status, what could be a more logical strategy for preserving that status than continuing the chronicle? At the same time, for those of Francisco Hernández's generation who had been born and had grown up before the Spaniards arrived, some of the anxieties and psychological dislocation of the conquest could be ameliorated through the simple act of maintaining the chronicle's continuity and, in so doing, retaining a direct, physical link with the past. The passing of Francisco Hernández marked the end of the preconquest generation, and Pacal Francisco could only record the mundane events of community life in an attempt to maintain a status with which he and his generation were personally unfamiliar. With his death, and in the absence of any obvious heir, the task of family historian would have passed over two more generations to individuals who had even less understanding of the past and who, by this time, were probably well on their way to the peasant status occupied by almost all of their fellow Cakchiquel.

The Xpantzay

Only slightly less well-known to scholars is the corpus of documents created by or attributed to the Xpantzay family, which ruled a *chinamit* (a territorially based social unit of the late preconquest highland Maya; see Hill and Monaghan 1987:24–42) of that name within the Iximché polity. These were originally published by Berlin (1950) as the "Historia de los Xpantzay," but it is clear that the six documents he includes were created at different times and for a variety of reasons and thus do not constitute a single text. Recinos (1957) published the three longer documents, giving them separate titles, while Carmack (1973:50–53) renamed five of the six texts published by Berlin. For ease of reference and so as not to characterize the nature and content of these documents inappropriately, I shall refer to them according to the letter order employed by Berlin.

Berlin's "A" is not specifically an Xpantzay document but a combined history of the main sociopolitical groups that composed the Iximché polity. It is similar in structure to the early part of the "Annals," suggesting a traditional format, but the traditional origin in Tula has been replaced by a biblically inspired account in which these Cakchiquel now claim to have crossed the ocean like the Spaniards before disembarking in the New World. Although the document was dated 1524, Recinos has noted inconsistencies that indicate it was probably written after 1544 (Recinos 1957:125). The document also claims that the Iximché people were favored by Alvarado for having gone to greet him when he first entered the region. However, the main body of the document consists of a description of the Iximché groups' collective boundaries, and this suggests that its true function was to act as evidence of their prior possession of the land in order to safeguard against Spanish encroachment. Indeed, this document and the others in the corpus were presented (and thus preserved) in at least one litigation with a Spaniard over land ownership in 1659 (and it should be noted that the documents were instrumental in bringing the Indians their ultimate victory). Despite the fact that this document was created to meet some postconquest need, the boundary description itself is completely traditional, narrating the circuit of the groups' territory, proceeding from boundary marker to boundary marker. The information it provides about territories controlled prior to the arrival of the Spaniards closely resembles one category of knowledge Las Casas attributed to native Mesoamerican histories in general.

Berlin's "F" is another document that is probably of genuine traditional origin but that also has only a tangential connection to the Xpantzay. Written down in 1554, document "F" is a history of the wars conducted by the Zotzil and Tukucheé divisions of the Cakchiquel when they were still allies of the Quiché. Since the Tukucheé rebelled against and were expelled from the Iximché polity in 1493, the document clearly represents a traditional class of information that also conforms to one of Las Casas's categories of Mesoamerican historical record keeping. Since the Xpantzay are only mentioned at the end of the document, they may well have "borrowed" some of the history of their Zotzil confederates, tacking a brief notice of themselves onto the end of the narrative, in just the same way that the Xahil tacked their family history onto the end of the traditional Cakchiquel "national" history.

It is Berlin's "D," also written in 1554, that constitutes a true family history similar to the specifically Xahil portion of the "Annals." Set down by one Alonso Pérez (Xpantzay), it contains a similar range of information, including genealogy, the succession of rulers, their marriages, migrations, and wars. A generation later in 1581, his son, successor as cacique, and then-alcalde Felipe Vázquez, wrote a description (Berlin's "B") of the boundaries of his Xpantzay chinamit, following the usual practice of proceeding from marker to marker. This description was validated by the other current alcalde and the town's Indian governor, whose signatures occur at the end along with don Felipe's.

The final document in the corpus, Berlin's "E," was also written by Felipe Vázquez, as an old man in 1602. This fascinating document is specifically concerned with genealogy and attempts to bridge the immediate Pre- and

Postconquest periods. Don Felipe's main concern was to demonstrate that his own immediate family, including his father's other children and their children, were the legitimate, direct descendants of Hunlahuh Can, the last of the preconquest Xpantzay leaders, and that certain pretenders of the Orozco family were in reality the children of concubines or slaves with no authentic claim to noble status. As with the postconquest portion of the Xahil history, we see here don Felipe still very much concerned with maintaining ties to preconquest times and ancestors as a way of validating and perpetuating his family's aristocratic status. Apparently, he took time late in life to write this document in order to define the true line of descent so that his own descendants would have a document to present in case their status should ever be challenged by any of Orozco's descendants. However, just as entries in the Xahil history end in 1604 with the death of the last of the second generation born after the conquest, so too do Xpantzay documents. The challenge by the Orozcos seems never to have come.

Clearly, the documents were carefully preserved as "títulos"—a generic term for documents that could prove land ownership or occupancy—but no additions were made. They were presented as evidence in the 1659 litigation (Berlin's "C" is one of the complaints against an encroaching Spaniard), but almost as antiques, revered relics of another age, which, by that time, in a real sense they were. Just as questions of noble status had apparently become moot among the Xahil by the early seventeenth century, they were apparently becoming similarly irrelevant to the Xpantzay.

The Chajomá

A final group of historical writings in the indigenous tradition pertain to the eastern Cakchiquel. These people were called the Akajal by their more westerly cousins of the Iximché polity, but they called themselves the Chajomá. The documents containing their histories were penned in the middle of the sixteenth century. The best known of these is the "Título de los del pueblo de San Martín Xilotepéque," published by Crespo (1956). The 1555 document contains a synopsis of the western Chajomá group's history since leaving the Joyabaj area (probably in the late 1400s), which focuses on their migrations, the sites they occupied at various times, and, of course, the succession of their rulers. Also included was a description of the territory they occupied at the time of the conquest, defined in the traditional manner as a circuit of the boundary markers (which, in fact, describe the boundaries of the present-day municipio of San Martín Jilotepéque). As with most other examples of this type, it was preserved because it had been presented as a título in a later land litigation, in this instance a dispute with some Indians from neighboring Xenacoj in 1689 (Hill 1990).

Three much briefer documents were prepared in 1550 by the eastern Chajomá of San Juan and San Pedro Sacatepéquez, with the participation and agreement of their western Chajomá neighbors, with whom they shared a common boundary (Hill 1988; Borg 1986). These were likewise presented in a later 1707–1708 litigation as títulos, in this case involving the Pirir family, whose members resided in the town of San Juan (see below). The documents include a brief historical synopsis that mentions places occupied prior to the conquest, the succession of rulers, and a description of the circuit of boundary markers. Accompanying these is a map noting 34 such markers, which encompass an area corresponding to the northern third of the Department of Guatemala. The map is a rarity for this part of Mesoamerica in the sixteenth-century period, but it clearly was executed in the indigenous tradition. Like other such maps, the crucial information was the boundary markers. These were represented by rectangles arranged along the edges of the paper. Next to each rectangle was written the name of the particular boundary marker. The map itself forms a rectangle, the corners of which seem to correspond to the main corners of the territory that they describe. Unlike other Mesoamerican maps, this one contains no internal topographic detail, but rather what appears to be a list of the names of the area's noble families, including the Pirires, who did not challenge the map's authenticity in the 1707 litigation.

Calendar Books and Divinatory Manuals

The final group of surviving preconquest documents of the colonial Cakchiquel seems to encompass at least two of the kinds of "books" described by Las Casas: those giving notice of solemn and festal days, and those concerned with the naming of children. Perhaps we should also include books concerning dreams and auguries, since the Cakchiquel calendar books were evidently used for all three purposes. However, since there are no extant examples of these books, we cannot tell if they constituted a single document type or if there was truly a variety of such books used for different purposes. In their descriptions, the Spanish chroniclers often indicate all three functions but make no such distinctions among the books used. That may be due simply to their lack of familiarity with Cakchiquel calendrics, or it may be that some contraction of calendrical information into a single, multipurpose book occurred some time after the conquest. In any case, we are clearly dealing with a preconquest document tradition, examples of which continued to be produced and used well into the Colonial period.

Although there are no surviving examples of this document tradition, they are described, or at least defined, in the works of colonial Spanish friars. Tomás Coto's late seventeenth-century Spanish-Cakchiquel dictionary, the "Thesaurus Verborum," contains brief though important entries under both "calendar" and "divination." Under *calendario*, we find "vuh ahilabal q'ih," which he renders as "book for counting birth dates." He added that in San Antonio (Aguascalientes) there was a wise man who, everyone knew, kept a book for calculating the days (Coto: 68). Under his entry for *advinar*, he stated that, among other forms of divination, those who thus count the days and so perform divinations are much esteemed among the Indians (Coto: 10). Coto clearly was describing the book used to keep track of the *cholol q'ih*, the Cakchiquel variant of the 260–day Mesoamerican divinatory calendar, so important in determining individuals' fates on the basis of the day of their birth.

Common among the highland Maya in the past, and enduring in many parts of the area today, was a form of divination that involved the casting and counting of seeds and crystals. These were counted as days of the 260–day calendar, yielding information on a variety of topics. (See Colby and Colby [1981] and Tedlock [1982] for extended discussions of this form of calendrically based divination among contemporary highland Maya peoples.) At least some diviners using this technique, the *ah tzité* (he of the tzité, or divining seeds) had some kind of book or manual to which they could refer when interpreting the meaning of their lots. This was called a *tzité q'am vuh*, according to the anonymous seventeenth-century Cakchiquel-Spanish dictionary, the "Vocabulario de la lengua Cakchiquel."

A much more detailed description of a seventeenth-century Cakchiquel solar calendar book (*q'amutz*) is contained in a fragment of the now-lost, anonymous "Crónica Franciscana" (see Carmack 1973:193–194). The author must have had an Indian calendar book of some sort to refer to, since he presented a detailed enumeration of the month and day names, the numeration system, and a systematic comparison of the Mexican and Cakchiquel calendars. He also noted the main events of each month (such as planting, harvesting, and the beginning of the rainy season) and the auspicious days of each month. Finally, the chronicler explained in some detail the ways in which the Cakchiquel calendar differed from the European calendar, especially with regard to the beginning of the year. In order to clarify his exposition, the author noted the different days on which the Maya new year fell in the European calendar in the years immediately preceding 1585 (in which the account was written). It seems likely that he could only have done this if he had some calendar book before him (and quite possibly some informant as well). He went on to state:

> There were among the Indians some who were masters of this diabolical art [of divination], called among the Mexicans Tonalpouhquiy, among the Guatimaltecas [Cakchiquel] Ahquitz, the book or hide in which they kept the characters or signs of these counts the Mexicans called Tonalamatl and these [Cakchiquels] K'amutz, and both of them mean "book of fortune" or "roll of the days" [Anon. 1956:19].

Although the author of this chronicle wrote in the past tense, it is clear from Coto (and also Fuentes y Guzmán for the Quiché of the Totonicapán area) that both calendrical divination and the calendar books continued at least through the seventeenth century.

But much more is involved here than the mere survival of a form of divination. By preserving their way of tracking time, the Cakchiquel preserved much more than a divinatory technique, more even than a link to their past and ancestors. They preserved the very structure and dynamics of their universe. Perhaps the one Spanish writer who came closest to appreciating the significance of this was Fuentes y Guzmán who wrote:

> They believed with certainty in the immortality of the soul and afterwards, in a universal resurrection, they would return to have all their possessions such that they would not have to repair the defects and bad condition of their houses, saying that *thus they were left by their ancestors, and that they will return to possess the same*

lands that they possess at the time of their death. And for this reason they keep hidden the silver mines and rich gold deposits. There is among them no promise or threat sufficient to reduce them to show them [to Spaniards]. And, seeing themselves pressed, they respond that they know where they [the mines] are but, *since the treasures are not theirs but rather of their ancestors who left them, they must exculpate themselves before the ancestors when they return to this world* [Fuentes y Guzmán 1972:3:273].

. . . and this they did [bury grave goods in preconquest times with their dead] because they believed in the immortality of the soul. In this belief they demonstrated their errors down to the present day [ca. 1690] as they say that there [after death] they needed to work to eat, needed servants to attend them, and that *they will return from there and once again possess their lands and treasures left buried and mines they left covered up*; growing from this error, not being able to discover anything that they know [about mines, treasures, etc.] because they say *what account would they give their ancestors when they return from that other world*; thinking and believing that they had gone to remote lands in which they had to labor as they did when they were here and that *they would return in the same appearance and beauty as when they had died* [Fuentes y Guzmán 1969:1: 389–390, emphasis added].

The question of how much of this reflects indigenous belief and how much (if any) represents accretions from Christianity need not detain us here. The important point is that the Cakchiquel concept of cyclical time meant that, someday, the ancestors would return and life would be as it was before the coming of the Spaniards. A necessary precondition of this, of course, and one that Fuentes in his exasperation over failing to get information from the Indians did not notice, would be that the Spaniards themselves would have to disappear. Viewed in this light, the Cakchiquel future takes on a millenarian quality, but one that is nativistic in nature since it explicitly involves a return of the good old days. Such beliefs obviously had profound implications for the Cakchiquel in terms of dealing emotionally, psychologically, and spiritually with their situation as a politically subordinated and economically exploited population. The conquest and their resulting subjugation could be understood as only a phase in time, not as a permanent condition. Like all phases, it would eventually pass and all Cakchiquel would be reunited in a world free of Spaniards and their domination. Preserving their order of time through their calendar thus ultimately preserved both a vision of an orderly, comprehensible universe and hope for the future.

Colonial Document Types and Adaptation

The Cakchiquel did not use writing just to perpetuate their past. They also put writing to a variety of pragmatic uses in response to the exigencies and possibilities of life in the Colonial period. While writing was used in both public and private spheres, in both areas most concerns revolved around land: acquiring it, keeping it, and passing it on. A full discussion of land tenure principles is beyond the scope of this discussion, but land was clearly the crucial commodity in this agricultural society and, whatever its status in preconquest times, it had become a true commodity by the end of the sixteenth century at the latest. At the same time, the Cakchiquel population had declined to its lowest level of the Colonial period, so land was relatively abundant. Even the great tracts patented by the Spaniards at this time did not impair the Indians' subsistence. Under these conditions, venturesome individuals, in particular, could acquire land through unofficial purchases and build up considerable estates (Hill 1989). Yet two problems had to be addressed: how to secure these holdings against subsequent claims by the Spanish or other Indians, and how to pass on such holdings securely to heirs in the face of possible contradictory claims. The Cakchiquel innovated three document types to deal with these problems: *cédulas*, *convenios*, and *testamentos*.

Cédulas were simple bills of sale, executed between an Indian buyer and seller of land. Of course, in the absence of a royal title, no one could legally transfer property, but this practice was commonplace throughout the Colonial period in much of Guatemala (see, e.g., Hill and Monaghan 1987:126–132; Hill 1990). Clearly, the Cakchiquel needed to adjust holdings from time to time as families increased or declined in size or as economic necessity forced people to raise cash quickly, and small sales were a way to do this. In order to protect the buyer from any future claims by descendants or relatives of the seller, and to have a título to present as proof of prior possession should a Spaniard claim the land, these cédulas were drawn up, typically by the town scribe. A Spanish translation of a later seventeenth-century cédula is presented below (see Appendix A).

Yet, evidently, more was involved in such transfers of property than just the document. A brief passage dating to the late sixteenth century in the "Annals of the Cakchiquels" indicates that all of a community's leaders attended a fairly formal ceremony that constituted the "official" transfer and witnessed the cédula, after which they were the guests of the buyer at a banquet (Recinos 1950:179–180). The Pirir cédula presented below probably lacks the signatures of town officials since it was a transaction among relatives, all of them with the Pirir surname. It was thus probably drawn up to protect the new owner from Spanish claims rather than those of other Indians.

Convenios, or covenants, are recorded agreements concerning the ownership, division, and/or use of land, typically between corporate entities such as families, chinamitales/parcialidades, and towns. These documents seem to have been executed in order to avoid or settle disputes over land, especially when it seemed to the parties involved that the Spanish courts might intervene to their mutual detriment. An early seventeenth-century convenio from San Juan Sacatepéquez is presented in Appendix B. In it the town officials and all the *principales* and *calpules* (leading citizens and parcialidad heads) define the uses to which a tract of land would henceforth be put.

Finally, in terms of securely passing land on to descendants, the Cakchiquel innovated testamentos, or wills, apparently reaching a peak of development in the seventeenth century, when social stratification among the Cakchiquel was still present to some extent and before population growth in the eighteenth century led to the fragmentation of the larger native estates (Hill 1989). Yet, as the document presented below demonstrates, wills were not produced just for the wealthy in colonial Cakchiquel society, but could be commissioned by anyone with landholdings to protect and, presumably, the fee for the scribe (see Appendix C).

Ttulos: Writing as Cultural Resistance

While the Cakchiquel waited for the flow of time to free them from foreign domination and some of them attempted to perpetuate the past and their fast-disappearing status, on a practical level they faced ongoing challenges from Spaniards eager to change their culture and take their lands. Direct, overt resistance to the Spaniards was out of the question, but the entire range of passive, covert resistance activities was open to and used by the Cakchiquel. Among these was writing.

The very act of writing in the Cakchiquel language was a form of cultural resistance, a conscious refusal by these Indians to adopt the conqueror's language, while simultaneously co-opting his writing technology for their own purposes. The uses of writing to perpetuate the calendrical system, the associated worldview, and ties to the past were also clearly efforts to resist Spanish acculturative pressures. In addition, writing allowed the Cakchiquel to create a countercorpus of documents in their own language that would thus be unintelligible to all but a few Spaniards (mostly clergy) who knew Cakchiquel, in response to Spanish documents, the content of which was, in turn, unintelligible to all but a few Cakchiquel (mostly town scribes, whose knowledge of Spanish was often limited at best). The unique Cakchiquel identity and a sense of apartness from the foreigners were thus reinforced any time one wrote, referred to, read from, listened to, or presented as evidence a document in that language.

Yet it was, perhaps, in the defense of their lands that the Cakchiquel won some of their most significant battles with the intruders, for without the land base to support their agricultural economy, there would be no chance of perpetuating their culture. Almost as soon as they had pacified the region, the Spaniards began to acquire landholdings, but their appetites grew during the seventeenth-century period of depression when more and more otherwise urban-oriented residents of the colonial capital at Santiago (present-day Antigua) were forced to the countryside and agriculture as a means of economic survival (see MacLeod 1973:217–221). As the Maya closest to the capital, the Cakchiquel saw that their lands were in the greatest danger. To preserve their lands, to have them ready for their ancestors' return, and of course to continue to subsist, they had to find some way effectively to resist Spanish encroachment. Armed resistance was out of the question, but the Cakchiquel found another way: by using their documents in conjunction with Spanish law and lawyers, before Spanish courts.

Spanish colonial land law as embodied in the Laws of the Indies was based on centuries of development during the reconquest (see Vassberg 1984:5–56). All lands taken by force of arms technically became *tierras realengas*, or royal lands. But, morally, the Crown was concerned that its new, New World subjects would retain possession of whatever lands they had held before the conquest and the royal administration was charged with ensuring that Indian claims were given priority in any disputes with colonists. The question was, how could prior Indian possession be proven? In the immediate Postconquest period, the testimony of aged witnesses concerning the occupation of preconquest land was often sufficient since similar evidence had long been accepted in Spain (Vassberg 1984:20). However, as time passed, such witnesses eventually disappeared. In their place, the Cakchiquel offered all of the document types described above (with the exception of their calendar books) as "títulos." Of course, the only true title from the Spanish viewpoint was a royal one, granted via *composición*, in which the recipient effectively purchased land from the Crown. Yet the Crown was generous with its vast New World holdings and permitted its Indian and non-Indian subjects alike to use unoccupied land. As evidence of prior occupancy or use, Spanish practice admitted almost any written document, and the Cakchiquel soon discovered the potency of their títulos before Spanish courts, containing as they did fairly detailed boundary descriptions that antedated any possible colonist's claim.

However, given the cronyism, the favoritism shown fellow Spaniards, and the outright bribery of underpaid or venal colonial officials by colonists, these títulos, by themselves, might have counted for little. Yet, along with their documents, the Cakchiquel also quickly learned how to retain Spanish legal counsel, who, in turn, knew how to utilize their clients' títulos as evidence to force official recognition of their claims. With this combination of documentary evidence and professional representation, the Cakchiquel consistently were able to frustrate colonists' attempts to usurp their lands throughout the seventeenth and eighteenth centuries. While the foreigners could not be eradicated and land already in their hands could not be recovered, the Cakchiquel were at least able to fight a spirited and largely successful holding action, until the "liberal" reforms of the land laws in the later nineteenth century drastically changed the rules of the game and made títulos irrelevant.

Conclusion

While the effects of the Spanish conquest and colonial administration of native Mesoamerican peoples were overwhelmingly detrimental, these peoples themselves were by no means completely disorganized and demoralized by their experience. Nor did they play a passive role in the colonial regime, complying with every demand made on them. By focusing on the social uses of writing by one colonial Mesoamerican people, the Cakchiquel Maya of highland Guatemala, we have been able to glimpse some of their responses to their situation. The adoption of European writing technology was itself an innovative act, but the Cakchiquel soon discovered how to make it serve their own purposes. To a certain extent, writing was used nativistically to perpetuate preconquest document types, which, in turn, contained both the traditional Cakchiquel worldview and the social statuses threatened by Spanish policies and programs of directed culture change. The Cakchiquel also innovated new uses for writing in order to both solve problems and take advantage of opportunities created by the colonial situation, particularly with regard to land. Finally, the Cakchiquel used these documents as ammunition in their generally successful guerrilla war against Spanish encroachment on their lands, waged in the invader's own courts. Above all, extant examples of colonial Cakchiquel writing stand out as monuments to the perserverance, innovativeness, and adaptability of the human spirit.

Appendix A: The Pirir Cédula

[From the official Spanish translation of the original Cakchiquel document, now lost, in document A3.15 Legajo 2787 Expediente 40301, Archivo General de Centro America]

> I, Pedro Pirir, son of Domingo Pérez Pirir, state that it is true that I make and entrust this instrument to Melchor Pirir and state that I receive the sum of thirty *tostones* in the form of *Reales*, for which I sold him and made him keeper of a piece of land, a ranch site.
>
> And I state that my father, Domingo Pérez Pirir, left it to me in his testament and as owner I sell it without any dispute and I indicate for him the bounds and markers of said land.
>
> The first goes from two *madre de cacao* trees and goes by the hill and the road and goes straight to some old fields of our grandfather, Miguel Pirir, and goes down a gully to join with the big ravine and later it runs to a farm called Cuajilote, which is on the bank of the Piscaya [River].
>
> And it goes down the Piscaya River and runs into the stream called Cuspu by the big gorge.
>
> It goes up the gorge to a big pine which is on the hill and from there it goes down to a big oak and from there it goes to a marsh and from there it goes down the stream bed to a copal tree and from there it comes to the big gorge beside a big boulder which borders with my brother, Diego.
>
> And it comes up the gorge to the two *madre de cacao* trees, the first marker where we began.
>
> And this is true that there is no dispute and this land has in its favor a Royal Decree, which our grandfather [sic] obtained when he settled said land in order that, if one day a dispute should arise, one can depend on said Decree.
>
> Now my instrument which I execute and entrust is ready and it goes signed before witnesses on the 27th of December of the year 1674. This is the truth.
>
> Witness

Marcos Pérez Cian	Francisco Pérez Pirir	Melchor Pirir
Gaspar Pérez Pirir	scribe	he who bought it
Juan de la Cruz Pirir		for thirty *tostones*
Cristóbal Pirir		
Pedro Pirir who sold it		

Appendix B: Convenio of the Principales and Calpules of San Juan Sacatepéquez

[From the original Cakchiquel text and the official Spanish translation, in document A3.15 Legajo 2787 Expediente 40301, Archivo General de Centro America]

> Jesus, Mary, and Joseph
>
> On the first day of December of the year 1607, we the *principales* and *calpules* who call ourselves Chajomá, Cakchiquel, and Akajal, [are] all together in this *cabildo* of our town of San Juan Sacatepéquez.

And we state that these lands called Zaq'tzuy are of our ancestors, the said land is for the commonage of our town, in order that its produce assist the *principales* and provide for the necessities of the Holy Church, such as candles and the rest that is offered in the church of our father San Juan in all the major festivals, feast days, and patronal fiesta of our town.

And thus we state that from said lands will come everything necessary for the Holy Church. Now and in times to come may our children always protect this community land. All of us in agreement and concurrence together in this *cabildo* write this, our charter.

And at the same time we state and in concurrence decide that this other piece of land we destine to the *cofradía* of Our Lady of the Rosary, in order that she intercede for us before her precious son.

And this other piece of land which is named Hurbachoy, and Piedras de Cal, and Navoron is also destined to and appointed to the Virgin, Our Lady of the Rosary.

And thus all the *principales* in agreement we make this our charter in our *cabildo* of San Juan.

And we name and indicate the boundary markers and landmarks of said lands.

First, one leaves the first marker of the Tapanal River and goes down to join the Piscaya River.

And from there it goes into the Big River at the place called Chichip.

And later it goes to the place named Oronic Chun.

And it continues along the Big River to the place named Chaq'uihsanayi.

And it goes up to the place called Xiquin Chiq'ina which is on the road.

And by said road it comes to the place called Chuitzaq'.

And from there it goes to the place we call Holon Quej.

And it goes to San Raimundo.

And these lands which we call Chinimaquin and Zaq'tzuy which the Father Fray Benito, and the Father Fray Sebastián de Aguilar, and the Father Vito de Carvajal, vicar for twelve years, and also Cristóbal Rodríguez, these Fathers know the shape of our lands.

And these lands called Navoron, Hurbalchoy, and Pachun are also known by Father Fray Pedro de Vargas.

And the Piscaya and Big River lands are all for Our Lady of the Rosary by the common will of all of us, we Big Men of the *cabildo* of the town of San Juan Chajomá.

And this our charter is signed on the first day of the month of December of the year 1607.

Alcalde, Domingo Pérez Set	Alcalde, Domingo Alvarez Ahzic Ajau
Joseph López, Regidor	Francisco López Coh, Regidor
Juan Tubiih, Nima Uinaq'	Domingo de Castro
Martin Pérez, Nima Uinaq'	Miguel Pérez Xpeq'
Pedro Culpatan Tzunun	Miguel Cheztzunun
Juan Culpatan Tzeq'en	Miguel Pérez Pirir
Estéban Rámos Tacatic	Diego López Chocojay
Estéban Rámos Coc	Benito Alvarez Tzeq'uen
Andrés López Tzeq'en	Benito Cuxe
Pedro López Coh	Diego Cama Mutzuc
Gaspar López Tavas	Francisco Camey
Bernabé Yap	Nicolás López Zaclahay
Nicolás Queh	Sebastián Pérez Patan
Ambrosio Pirir	Marcos Coy
Benito de la Cruz	Juan Pinera Patcan
Mateo Ahzic Ajau	Andrés Ahtzalam Boch

Matheo Ahzicaha   Estéban Rámos Culahay

These are the names of the 32 *principales* who were witness to this.

Appendix C: Testament of Miguel Sanom

[From the original Cakchiquel text and two official Spanish translations, documents contained in A1.45.1 Legajo 5322 Expediente 44813, Archivo General de Centro America]

In the name of God the Father, God the Son, and God the Holy Spirit, so be it. Amen. Jesus.

This is my word, my testament, I the infirm Miguel Sanom.

I find myself now very ill with my infirmity and, thus, I want to make this statement before God and before the lords and officials.

I am a poor man who has no riches except his children and let no one contradict what I have to say in this my statement.

And let not the heart of my father, Melchor Pérez, say anything, because he threw me out of his house in the presence of those Cakchiquel called Juan Pérez, Baltasar Tumauac, Francisco Ch'och', and Melchor Pandevel; as witnesses that my father threw me out of his house.

And I state that, when I left, my father told me in the presence of said witnesses that thus I have gone.

And he has nothing to say concerning my children or about Diego Xgue, my maternal uncle, to whom I went with my children, which are three boys and two girls, five in all, so that he should raise them. Let no one take them from this said Diego.

If he raises them, they should stay with him.

Thus is my testament that I now make.

A grinding stone and muller for my son, Melchor.

A hoe for my son, Pedro.

A cape for my son, Diego.

A stool for each of them, Diego and Pedro.

My farmland in Pachojob, a tree is its marker,it runs to another tree, and to another marker called Cuachuachjac, which borders the land of Diego Ajcuc, and another marker all along the road to Godines.

It must be divided into three parts for my [three] sons and the said Diego must make the division of the said land for my sons.

Five *tomines* I owe to Francisco Atzih Guinac, and two *tomines* to his younger brother.

And I ask the Padre for a mass to aid my soul before God.

I state no more in this my testament, I the infirm Miguel Sanom, before God and the lords and officials, on the 13th day of October, the year 1627.

Diego Sánchez, alcalde   Estéban García, alcalde
Gaspar López, regidor   Juan Hernández, regidor
Melchor Méndez, scribe   Juan Tzu, regidor

References

American Philosophical Society Library. Vocabulario de la lengua Cakchiquel [ca. 1675]. Manuscript.

Anonymous
1956 Calendario Cakchiquel de los indios de Guatemala (1685). *Antropología e Historia de Guatemala* 9(2). Guatemala.

Berlin, Heinrich

1950 La Historia de los Xpantzay. *Antropología e Historia de Guatemala* 2(2). Guatemala.

Borg, Barbara E.

1986 Ethnohistory of the Sacatepéquez Cakchiquel Maya, ca. 1450–1690 A.D. Unpublished Ph.D. dissertation, Department of Anthropology, University of Missouri, Columbia.

Brinton, Daniel G.

1885 *The Annals of the Cakchiquels*. Brinton's Library of Aboriginal American Literature, Philadelphia.

Carmack, Robert M.

1973 *Quichean Civilization*. University of California Press, Berkeley.

Colby, Benjamin N., and Lore M. Colby

1981 *The Daykeeper: The Life and Discourse of an Ixil Diviner*. Harvard University Press, Cambridge, Mass.

Coto, Tomás

n.d. Thesaurus Verborum: Vocabulario de la lengua Cakchiquel u Guatemalteca (ca. 1690). Manuscript at the American Philosophical Society Library, Philadelphia.

Crespo, Mario

1956 Títulos Indígenas de Tierras. *Antropología e Historia de Guatemala* 8(2). Guatemala.

Fuentes y Guzmán, Francisco Antonio de

1969–1972 *Recordación Florida* (ca.1690), 3 vols., Biblioteca de Autores Españoles, nos. 230, 251, 259. Ediciones Atlas, Madrid.

Hill, Robert M. II

1990 *Colonial Cakchiquels: Highland Maya Adaptations to Spanish Rule, 1600–1700*. New York: Holt, Rinehart Winston, in press.

1988 Defining the Eastern Chajomá Territory. Paper presented at the 1988 meetings of the American Anthropological Association.

1989 The Pirir Papers and Other Colonial Period Cakchiquel-Maya Testamentos. Vanderbilt University Publications in Anthropology, no. 37. Nashville, Tenn.

Hill, Robert M. II, and John Monaghan

1987 *Continuities in Highland Maya Social Organization: Ethnohistory in Sacapulas, Guatemala*. University of Pennsylvania Press, Philadelphia.

Las Casas, Bartolomé de

1958 *Apologética Historia de las Indias*, 2 vols. Biblioteca de Autores Españoles, nos. 105, 106. Ediciones Atlas, Madrid.

Macleod, Murdo J.

1973 *Spanish Central America: A Socioeconomic History*. University of California Press, Berkeley.

Recinos, Adrián

1950 *Memorial de Sololá: Anales de los Cakchiqueles. Título de los Señores de Totonicapán*. Fondo de Cultura Económica, Mexico.

1957 *Crónicas Indígenas de Guatemala*. Editorial Universitaria, Guatemala.

Tedlock, Barbara

1982 *Time and the Highland Maya*. University of New Mexico Press, Albuquerque.

Teletor, Celso N.

1946 *Memorial de Tecpán Atitlín* (Ultima Parte). Guatemala.

Vassberg, David E.

1984 *Land and Society in Golden Age Castile*. Cambridge University Press, Cambridge.

Chapter 14 ■

Janine Gasco

Indian Survival and Ladinoization in Colonial Soconusco

Introduction

Visitors to the Soconusco region of Chiapas, Mexico (Figure 14–1) are often struck by the stark contrast between the people in this area and the populations in the nearby highlands. Whereas the Chiapas highlands are home to several Maya groups, coastal Chiapas has no easily recognizable Indian population at all. This difference is reflected in the amount of anthropological research that has been conducted in these two regions. Whereas the Chiapas highlands have been the focus of numerous anthropological studies, Soconusco is (to my knowledge) the subject of only a single published article that can be considered ethnographic (Medina Hernández 1973).

The Soconusco has received only slightly more attention from historians and historical anthropologists. My own work in the region has been concerned with changes in the Indian population of colonial Soconusco from both an archaeological and ethnohistorical perspective (Gasco 1987a, 1987b, 1989a, 1989b). Several other recent studies have focused primarily on social and economic history (Báez Landa 1985; Ortiz Hernández 1985; Toraya Toraya 1985; García de León

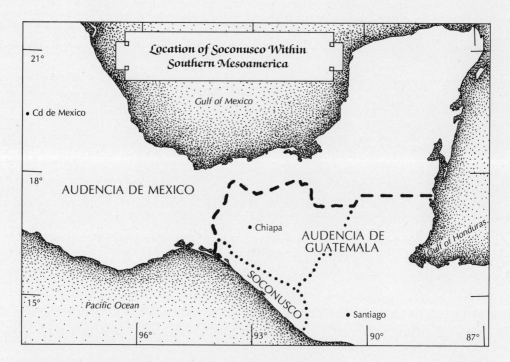

Figure 14–1. Location of Soconusco within southern Mesoamerica.

1984). And a recent study by Campbell (1988) examines the linguistic history of the region. The region also is discussed in other, more general histories of Mexico and Central America (MacLeod 1973; Sherman 1979; Gerhard 1979; Wortman 1982).

Presumably, a primary reason for this relative lack of interest in both historic and modern Soconusco is that the modern population there is not Indian. In southern Mesoamerica (Chiapas and portions of Central America), people are classified as being either Indian or Ladino (non-Indian), and for the most part, anthropologists and others have gravitated to the Indian communities. Areas like Soconusco, where the modern populations are classified as Ladino, have been largely ignored.

My general objectives in this chapter are to broaden our understanding of some of the factors that led to the transformation of Indian populations into Ladino populations and to explore how these changes took place. The process of Ladinoization was complex—it was not always simply the case that a greatly diminished Indian population was replaced by a non-Indian population. Instead, in some areas Ladino populations emerged, in part, because Indians adopted traits that would later result in their being called Ladino in response to certain situations and pressures.

On a more specific level, I examine the process of Ladinoization in colonial Soconusco, particularly the extent to which the population of Soconusco had become Ladino by the close of the Colonial period and the underlying causes for the changes in the makeup of the population. I begin with an overview of how the term "Ladino" is used today and discuss how it was used in the Colonial period. I then look at the demographic, archaeological, and other historical evidence for Ladinoization in colonial Soconusco.

Ladinos in Modern Central America

In the most widely used definition today, Ladino means a person who is culturally non-Indian. Ladinos are "the carriers and practitioners of modern Latin American culture" (Gillin 1952:198). They are the "cultural descendants of the Spanish colonists" (Warren 1989:ix). Typically, Ladinos and Indians are portrayed as being polar opposites. "The Ladino orients toward the city, to the center, to power, and despises manual labor. The Indian orients to the field, the *campo*, the periphery. He . . . sees manual labor not only as his lot but as his preference" (Hawkins 1984:10). In many cases, differences in the material culture of Indians and Ladinos are also stressed (Marino Flores 1967).

Despite the claim that Indians and Ladinos have very different material cultures, worldviews, and value systems, there is also an implicit and sometimes explicit recognition that some proportion of the modern Ladino population was formerly Indian. Hawkins, in his study of Indian and Ladino communities in the western highlands of Guatemala, states that "those who no longer wish to be Indian move, usually toward a larger urban center or to the symbolically Ladino lowlands" (1984:10). To be Ladino, then, one does not necessarily have to be a genetic descendant of Spaniards. Instead, the emphasis is on cultural traits. In this sense, the Ladino/Indian dichotomy is not the same as the mestizo/Indian dichotomy. Mestizaje implies miscegenation while Ladinoization does not. More often, Ladinoization is equated with acculturation.

The identification of people as either Ladino or Indian is a uniquely Central American phenomenon (see discussion in de la Fuente 1952:94–96). The term "Ladino" is simply not used today in other parts of Spanish America (see Mörner 1967). In Mexico, for example, a distinction is often made between mestizos and Indians, and the folk/urban dichotomy (or continuum) (Redfield 1941), in a sense, mirrors the Indian (folk)/Ladino (urban) dichotomy.

There are a number of problems with this bipartite approach to the study of modern populations of southern Mesoamerica. First, it is an ahistorical approach that ignores the region's complex cultural and demographic history. While recognizing that Indians today can and do move into the Ladino population, it fails to address the underlying causes for such a seemingly important change that, by definition, must result in a complete reversal in one's values.

This approach also ignores the tremendous diversity that exists within both Indian and Ladino populations. It is impossible, for example, to distinguish between Ladino finca owners of European descent and Ladino peasants whose roots are more closely linked to colonial and perhaps even prehispanic Indian societies.

Even scholars who have attempted to identify the important differences between Indians and Ladinos recognize that people do not always fall easily into one category or the other. Rural Ladinos can be "similar in custom and way of life to Indians and acculturated Indians" (de la Fuente 1952:79). Moreover, "there may be even in a small family both Ladino and Indian members" (de la Fuente 1952:85).

A final problem that I see is that the term "Ladino" too often carries a negative connotation. Ladinos are seen as the exploiters of Indians. Moreover, Ladinos have betrayed their traditional culture. It is true, of course, that Indians have been and continue to be exploited by some Ladinos. Yet it is just as true that many Ladinos are themselves exploited by other Ladinos. Smith (1977:38) notes that in Chiapas there is a "large population of rural Ladino subsistence farmers and wage laborers whose economic position is no different from that of most Indians." It is also true that Indians who have become Ladinos have usually given up native language and dress, two of the criteria most widely used to categorize people as Indians. But again, in terms of many other cultural traits that are used to identify Indians such as occupation, subsistence practices, participation in the *compadrazgo* system, and religious practices (see de la Fuente 1952; Marino Flores 1967; Gillin 1952; McBryde 1947:9–13; Van den Berghe and Colby 1961), the life-style of many Ladinos is very similar to that of Indians.

While these modern views of Ladinos and Indians have some serious shortcomings, I am not suggesting that the term "Ladino" is without meaning or importance. Instead, I would argue that we need to pay closer attention to its historical uses and to the historical development of populations that are now called Ladino. Given the large population of Ladinos today, surprisingly little has been written about this subject (but see Luján Muñoz 1976; Lutz and Lovell 1990; Lutz 1984, 1990a, 1990b; MacLeod 1979).

Ladinos in Colonial Spanish America

The term "Ladino" was used in colonial Central America, as it is today, to classify people. In the early eighteenth century, the *Diccionario de Autoridades* ([1732] 1969:347) defined "Ladino" as someone who was skilled with language. The word was said to have originated during the Roman occupation of Spain when Romans were called "Latinos" by native Spaniards, and the term came to mean someone who was wise. In the Spanish colonies, the term apparently was used originally to refer to Indians who spoke Spanish (Farriss 1984:438; Lutz 1984:433–434) and to blacks who spoke Spanish (Mörner 1967:16). In a more general way, it presumably was used to refer to Hispanicized Indians, that is, Indians who had adopted certain elements of Spanish culture including language, dress, and names (Luján Muñoz 1976:52; Sherman 1979:332) or who were Christian (Adams 1964:156). In time, the term also came to include mulattoes, mestizos, and *castas* (people of mixed racial origins). By the late eighteenth century, the term "Ladino" was used to classify the population that was neither Spanish nor culturally Indian (Luján Muñoz 1976:53; Lutz 1984:433–434). McBryde (1947:13) cites a late eighteenth-century document from Chiapa that stated that certain people were called Ladinos "because they speak Spanish, they are mulattoes, zambos, and other castes which are not Indian." Lutz (1990b) notes that by the late eighteenth century the boundaries between ethnic groups had all but disappeared. Even mestizos and mulattoes could not be easily distinguished, and both groups were sometimes included in the Ladino category.

From this brief overview it becomes clear that a Ladino population could emerge in two ways. First, Indians could be called Ladino if they learned Spanish and perhaps adopted other Spanish traits. In other words, Indians who became acculturated to some degree were, at least in some cases, called Ladinos. This did not necessarily mean that they ceased to be classified as Indians for tribute purposes, however. Second, as the Colonial period progressed, other non-Spanish ethnic groups came to be called Ladino.

Within the Audiencia of Guatemala (Central America and Chiapas) the Indian, Ladino, and Spanish populations were not evenly distributed across the landscape. MacLeod (1973:308) and others (Lutz 1990a, 1990b; Lutz and Lovell 1990) have noted that within Guatemala there was a fundamental difference between the Indian "west" (and north) and the Ladino "east" (and south). Others have focused on the major concentrations of Ladinos in cities and large towns that were centers of Spanish population (Luján Muñoz 1976:54). Generally, demographic and economic factors have been suggested to explain the differences between Indian and Ladino regions. The areas where native depopulation was extremely high and where the resource base attracted the greatest Spanish interests (e.g., the east and south of Guatemala) were the areas that by the end of the Colonial period had the largest Ladino populations (Lutz and Lovell 1990).

In one of the few studies that focuses exclusively on the Indian population that became Ladino, MacLeod (1979) also notes that demographic and economic factors, particularly the nature of Indian work, affected levels of Indian acculturation or Ladinoization in colonial Mesoamerica. By comparing and contrasting the nature of production of three monocultural crops—cochineal, indigo, and sugar—MacLeod identifies an "acculturative continuum," in which the Indians involved in cochineal production are the least acculturated and those involved in sugar production exhibit the greatest levels of acculturation (1979:82–92). The critical variable that distinguished these three crops was the nature of Spanish involvement in the cultivation and production processes. In the case of cochineal, a native dye extracted from insects that live on the nopal cactus plants, dye production required special knowledge and skills that the Spaniards did not have. Cochineal production remained in Indian hands, even though non-Indians tended to control the trade. As a result, rural Oaxaca, the center of cochineal production, remained more "Indian" than did many other regions (MacLeod 1979:88).

Indigo was also a native dye crop, but in contrast to cochineal, Europeans were familiar with its production, which required little skilled labor. As a result, the Spaniards were quick to gain control of the colonial indigo industry (MacLeod 1979:88–90). In El Salvador, a center of indigo production, Indians became "undifferentiated peasants," and by the end of the Colonial period the natives in indigo areas "were mostly ladinos" (MacLeod 1979:90).

Sugar, a crop introduced by Europeans, required large outlays of capital and a large pool of semiskilled labor. It was a completely Spanish-dominated enterprise, and even more than indigo, the sugar industry tended to dominate and influence people's lives and lead to greater Indian acculturation (MacLeod 1979:90–91).

In summary, Colonial period definitions of "Ladino" varied through time (and perhaps across space). Initially, the term referred to Indians (and sometimes blacks) who had adopted, or at least knew, the Spanish language, but it later came to include other non-Spanish groups. During the Colonial period, the term was always used in a narrower sense than is the case today. Spaniards and criollos clearly were *not* Ladinos. Finally, the areas that by the end of the Colonial period had large Ladino populations (whether acculturated Indians or other groups) tended to have several things in common. These areas had experienced heavy native depopulation, and they were also areas where there was a sustained Spanish presence because of a resource base that attracted Spanish-run enterprises.

Keeping in mind the colonial meanings of the term "Ladino" and the factors that are generally thought to give rise to a Ladino population, I turn now to the evidence for Ladinoization in colonial Soconusco.

Ladinoization in Colonial Soconusco

The process of Ladinoization in colonial Soconusco can be examined from several perspectives: how the term "Ladino" was used in the region; the economic and demographic history of the Soconusco, particularly the interaction between Soconusco Indians and immigrants; and the relationship between material culture and Ladinoization in colonial Soconusco.

Use of the Term Ladino in Colonial Soconusco

The term "Ladino" was used in two contexts in colonial Soconusco. First, it was used in legal documents to describe Indian witnesses and interpreters. By at least the mid-seventeenth century, the terms "Indios ladinos" or "Indios Ladinos en lengua" appear in documents.[1] In these cases, it is clear that the Indios Ladinos were simply tribute-paying "Indios de pueblo" who spoke Spanish.

Later, the term "Ladino" came to be used to classify people in census documents. The term first appears in 1735 when a portion of the population of the town of Pijijiapan was classified as Ladino. By 1765, a few tribute-paying Indians were married to people classified as Ladinos. The implication in the 1765 census documents is that Ladinos were no longer Indian tributaries. By the close of the Colonial period, there was a clear distinction in census documents between Spaniards, Ladinos, and Indian tributaries. It would appear then, that at least in the Soconusco, by the 1730s the term Ladino had come to mean something significantly different, although the precise identity of the people now being called Ladino is unclear. But whether they were former Indians or members of some other ethnic group, they were no longer obliged to pay tribute. There were certainly advantages to becoming a Ladino in eighteenth-century Soconusco.

Economic and Demographic Background—Northwest versus Southeast Soconusco

The economic and demographic factors that might have influenced the magnitude of Ladinoization or acculturation in colonial Soconusco cannot be fully uncovered until one recognizes that the colonial Province of Soconusco consisted of two fairly distinct subregions. The northwestern half of the province, from Tonalá to Mapastepec, was very different from the southeastern half in both demographic and economic terms. Since most of my research has been concerned with the southeastern portion of the province (Figure 14–2), I concentrate on that region here. Note, however, the basic differences between the northwest and the southeast illustrate how economic activities and demographic trends influenced levels of Indian acculturation.

The northwest half of the colonial province of Soconusco was apparently sparsely populated at the time of the conquest, and in the Colonial period it came to be called "Despoblado." In this area, cattle ranching and indigo production, both dominated by Spaniards, were the primary economic activities. We would expect this combination of demographic and economic factors to result in high levels of Indian acculturation and a large non-Indian population.

The southeastern portion of the province had a higher population density at the time of the Spanish conquest and many more settlements. In the southeast, cacao was the most important product in the Colonial period, and cacao cultivation was dominated largely by the Indian population. The bulk of the annual

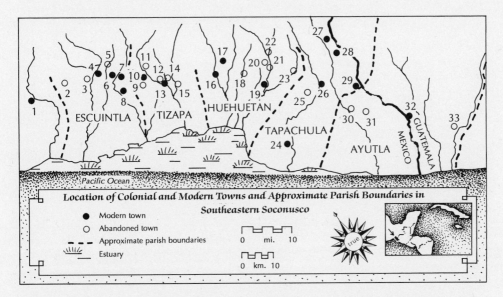

Figure 14–2. Location of colonial and modern towns and approximate parish boundaries in the southeastern Soconusco: *1*, Mapastepec; *2*, Cececapa; *3*, Cacaluta; *4*, Soconusco; *5*, Ocelocalco; *6*, Acacoyagua; *7*, Escuintla; *8*, Acapetahua; *9*, Zapaluta; *10*, Tizapa; *11*, Gueypetagua; *12*, Guilosingo; *13*, Pueblo Nuevo; *14*, Amastlán; *15*, Mazapetagua; *16*, Huixtla; *17*, Tuzantán; *18*, Islamapa; *19*, Huehuetán; *20*, Tepeguis; *21*, Tlacoaloya; *22*, Cuilco; *23*, Nexapa, *24*, Mazatán; *25*, Copulco; *26*, Tapachula; *27*, Cacahuatán; *28*, Tuxtla Chico; *29*, Metapa; *30*, Coyoacán; *31*, Chiltepeque; *32*, Ayutla; *33*, Tilapa.

cacao crop was available for trade with non-Indian merchants, while a smaller portion of the crop (probably less than 20 percent) was paid to the Spanish Crown in tribute (Gasco 1987a, 1987b, 1989a).

This set of economic factors falls somewhere in the midground of the extremes that existed in the Spanish colonies. The cacao-producing region of Soconusco was not dominated by Spanish-run enterprises, yet there was a fairly sustained Spanish presence in the form of merchant activity. In terms of the MacLeod's cochineal-indigo-sugar continuum, the nature of cacao cultivation probably falls somewhere between cochineal and indigo. If this is true, we might expect a modest degree of Indian acculturation in southeastern Soconusco but certainly less than in the northwestern part of the province.

The demographic profiles of these two regions are distinctly different and generally conform to the expectations outlined above.

In the Province of Soconusco as a whole, the decline in the native population was extremely high. Within the first 50 years after the arrival of the Spanish, the Indian population declined by 90 to 95 percent (Gasco 1987a:78ff.). In Soconusco, however, the high rate of native depopulation was not accompanied by a heavy influx of Spaniards or other non-Indians.

The earliest population data for the entire province that enumerate the various segments of the population are from 1611, at which time there were 1,786 married Indian couples (*casados*) and another 168 Indian widows or widowers in 39 towns.[2] At that time there were also 36 Spanish couples in 5 towns, 6 of whom owned cacao plantations, and 150 blacks and mulattoes in the indigo workshops in the northwest part of the province (in Tonalá and vicinity). The extreme differences between the northwestern and southeastern parts of the province are illustrated in this population count. In 1611, 94 percent of the Indian population and 89 percent of the Spanish population resided in the southeast, while the entire mulatto and black population was found in the northwest.

By 1683, the Indian population in the entire province had dropped to 800 tribute-paying Indians.[3] The mulatto, mestizo, and free black population had climbed to 259, but they apparently again were concentrated in the northwestern part of the province (in Tonalá, Pijijiapan, and Mapastepec) and in the far southeast (Ayutla). In addition, at this time there were 100 Spaniards who were either cattle ranchers, owners of cacao plantations, or merchants.

In 1733, the Indian population in the 25 towns in the southeast had dropped to 461 families, while there were 18 mulatto families, 29 families classified as mulatto or mestizo, and 125 families in a more general category of Spaniards, mestizos, and mulattoes.[4] Thus, 73 percent of the families in the southeast were Indian. The northwest, still had a much smaller population with a total of 122 families. However, only 40 (33 percent) of these families were classified as Indian, and even these were described as "very Spanish" ("muy castellano"). The remainder of the population was classified as Spanish, mestizo, mulatto, black, and Ladino.

Toward the end of the eighteenth century, in 1778, the total population in the 19 towns in southeastern Soconusco was 6,875.[5] Of these, 5,024 (73 percent) were classified as Indian and *navorías* (usually Indian wage-earners—see discussion below), 871 (13 percent) were black and mulatto, 649 (9 percent) were *castizos* (Spanish-mestizo mix), and 330 (5 percent) were Spanish. In contrast, in the northwest, the total population was 2,740. Only 968 (35 percent) were Indians and *navorías*, while the majority, 1,662 (61 percent) were black and mulatto, 51 (2 percent) were *castizo,* and 59 (2 percent) were Spanish.

By the end of the Colonial period, several Soconusco communities in the southeast had relatively large non-Indian populations that included Ladinos, Spaniards, mestizos, mulattoes, and blacks. Tapachula, which had become the provincial capital in 1792, had the largest non-Indian population. Nevertheless, the majority of the population was still classified as Indian, and in fact, over half of the Soconusco communities in the southeast were 100 percent Indian. The proportion of Indians in the 14 towns in the southeast may have dropped to around 61 percent by this time, with the Ladino population climbing to 33 percent. Mulattoes made up 5 percent of the population and Spaniards only 1 percent. Unfortunately, the two population counts for this period, one from 1818,[6] and a second from 1821,[7] give somewhat conflicting figures.

I do not have data for the northwest part of the province for the nineteenth century, but there is no reason to believe that the trend toward a smaller Indian population and a larger non-Indian population established by the seventeenth century was reversed after 1778.

In summary, the demographic data from Soconusco show that in the northwest portion of the province, what was a small Indian population to begin with continued to decline, and by at least the early eighteenth century it was outnumbered by other groups. In southeastern Soconusco, Indians constituted the majority of the population throughout the Colonial period, although the proportion of the population classified as Indian declined as the Colonial period progressed. Although this area did not retain the high proportions of Indians that highland regions did (see Lovell 1985; Lutz 1990a, 1990b), neither did it become predominantly non-Indian.

In the remainder of this report, I focus only on the southeastern, cacao-producing region of Soconusco and the process of Ladinoization there. The two aspects of cacao cultivation and trade that presumably would have had the greatest influence on Indian acculturation were (1) the cacao trade attracted Spanish, mestizo, and other non-Indian merchants to the region and thus resulted in intermittent but sustained contact between Indian cacao farmers and non-Indian merchants; and (2) because cacao is a labor-intensive crop (at least at certain times of the year), it attracted migrant laborers, both Indian and non-Indian.

The importance of migrant labor is a common theme in colonial documents as both Indians and Spaniards were concerned about labor shortages. In 1582, for example, a number of Indians and Spaniards cite the shortage of "Indios tlaquehuales" as a cause for the decline in the cacao industry.[8] *Tlaqueualli* is defined as "aquilados" or "mercenarios" by Molino (1970:134), and here the term presumably refers to Indians who worked for wages. Again, in 1685, Francisco de Quintana Dueñas, an ex-governor of Soconusco, defended his practice of lending money to the Indians of Soconusco so they could pay the"taqueguales" (also called "Indios forasteros") for their work in the cacao orchards.[9] According to Quintana Dueñas, these "taqueguales" would only work for money, not cacao, so the Indians were accustomed to borrowing money from him so they could pay their workers during the harvest.

From the sixteenth century on, people variously called *naborías* (or *naboríos*), *laboríos*, and less frequently *forasteros*, could be found in the Soconusco. Basically, all these terms refer either to Indians who had left their communities, so were no longer "Indios de pueblo," or to free blacks and mulattoes. Legally, members of these groups were supposed to pay a special tribute, but this practice met with limited success (see Lutz 1984:449–451).

Although *naborías* and *laboríos* were often associated with Spaniards, either working as servants in Spanish households or working for wages in Spanish-run enterprises, in Soconusco they are often found in Indian villages. In 1665, the Indian *alcaldes* (mayors) of several Soconusco communities actually paid the "paga de naborío" for the *naboríos* who presumably were working in the cacao orchards of community residents.[10]

In addition to the *naborías* and *laboríos* who worked in Soconusco, Indians who were still being counted as tributaries in communities outside the province came to the Soconusco to work, and in some cases they remained and eventually became tributaries in Soconusco towns.

In sum, there was a considerable movement of people, Indian and non-Indian, into and out of the colonial province of Soconusco. Whereas in other areas (including the northwestern part of the province) Indian acculturation or Ladinoization can be attributed to Indians losing their lands and becoming involved in Spanish-dominated enterprises as wage laborers, in southeastern Soconusco commercial activities and interaction among a number of different ethnic groups may have been more influential factors. The effects of these kinds of contacts are explored below.

Interaction between Soconusco Indians and Immigrants

The nature and effects of interaction between the Indians of Soconusco and the immigrant population, both Indian and non-Indian, can be deduced from patterns of intermarriage between the two groups and from the nature of the presence of foreign Indians in the Soconusco.

Intermarriage between Soconusco Indians and Non-Indians or Foreign Indians

I have suggested that the extensive movement of *laboríos*, *naborías*, mulattoes, blacks, and foreign Indians into and out the province of Soconusco contributed to the process of acculturation and eventually to the growth of the non-Indian population in the province. Presumably, extensive intermarriage between Soconusco Indians and either non-Indians or even Indians from other regions would also have accelerated this process.

Before the eighteenth century, we find virtually no evidence to indicate the extent of intermarriage between the Indians of Soconusco and people from outside the province, Indian or non-Indian. There undoubtedly were unions (legal or otherwise) between Spanish men and Indian women, and other immigrants may have married local Indians, but at the present time I cannot even speculate about their frequency. Then, in the eighteenth century, details about patterns of marriage begin to emerge from a series of *padrones* (census documents) of the tributary population of several Soconusco towns. The *padrones* were taken to record the tributary population, that is, the Indian population that was affiliated with a certain town for tribute purposes (the "Indios de pueblo"). The large majority of marriages recorded in these documents were between Indians from the same town. These marriages were simply recorded as "casados enteros." In other words, the marriage of two Indians from the same town simply meant that for tribute purposes, they paid as a whole tributary. Indians who were widows, widowers, or single paid tribute as half a tributary. Finally, Indians who were married to anyone other than an "Indio de pueblo" were assessed as half a tributary. In these cases spouses could fall into one of a number of categories, including *Indio laborío, laborío, naboríos, Indio forastero, forastero,* mulatto, mestizo, or "Indio de otro pueblo."

The *padrones* can be divided into three groups. The first group consists of censuses taken from 1718 to 1735 in 13 towns.[11] The second covers the period 1750 to 1755 and gives details on 7 towns.[12] And the third covers 1765 and 8 towns.[13]

The earliest group of *padrones* provides information on 790 Indians over the age of 14; the 1750–1755 group covers 1,014 adult Indians; and the 1765 *padrones* cover about 1,299 Indians over the age of 14. Because these censuses consistently state the tribute status of spouses, it is possible to examine patterns of marriage between Soconusco Indians and non-Indians (in which I am including all of the above-named groups except for "Indios de otro pueblo") and between Soconusco Indians and "Indios de otro pueblo."

Throughout the eighteenth century, women showed a greater tendency to choose spouses from outside their communities, whether Indian or non-Indian, than did men (Figure 14–3). Legally, children inherited the status of their mothers, yet it seems likely that children from the union of an Indian mother and a non-Indian father would have been more likely to move into non-Indian status at some later date. It is surprising to see that, in fact, the frequency with which Indian women in Soconusco towns married non-Indians actually declined after the 1718–1735 period, and only rose slightly from 1750–1755 to 1765. For women, there was virtually no change in the frequencies of marriage to "foreign Indians" for the years covered by these *padrones*. The frequency with which men married non-Indians also declined after the period of 1718–1735. Fewer Indian men married foreign Indian women in the 1750–1755 period than either earlier or later.

This situation contrasts sharply with patterns of intermarriage documented by Lutz (1984:404) for the parishes around Santiago de Guatemala. For this same period, anywhere from 50 to 75 percent of the Indians were marrying non-Indians. In terms of marriage between Soconusco Indians and either non-

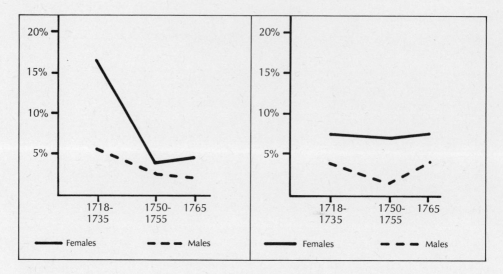

Figure 14–3. Percentages of *indios de pueblo* marrying non-Indians (left) and marrying *indios de otro pueblo* (right).

Indians or foreign Indians, then, rates in Soconusco were well below the rates documented for a more urban Indian population.

Foreign Indians in Eighteenth-Century Soconusco

Another aspect of immigration into the province of Soconusco can also be examined through the eighteenth-century census documents. In this case, I simply examine who the foreign Indians were and how they were integrated into the Soconusco communities.

Although temporary migrant laborers probably were never recorded, the eighteenth-century *padrones* do record the foreign Indians who married local Indians (discussed above), and in the 1750–1755 *padrones*, and particularly in those for 1765, it becomes clear that many foreign Indians had permanently settled in Soconusco and had been added to the tribute rolls in the Soconusco communities.

The extent to which foreign Indians were integrated into the Soconusco towns is illustrated in the 1765 *padrón* from Cacahuatán (see note 13), where we are told that a male immigrant from Colotenango served as *alcalde*.

Foreign Indians from 43 towns outside the province of Soconusco are recorded in the eighteenth-century *padrones*. These immigrants may have spoken as many as 13 languages, including Mam, Quiché, Teco, Cakchiquel, Sipacapec, Chicomuseltec, Zoque, Tzotzil, Tzeltal, Coxoh, Motozintlec, Zapotec, Chiapanec, and possibly others (I have not been able to determine the linguistic affiliation of several towns). A particularly interesting aspect of this immigration is the distribution of the immigrants within the province of Soconusco. There is no evidence to suggest that people who spoke the same languages settled together in the same towns. In 1750–1765, immigrants from Chicomuseltec towns, for example, could be found in eight Soconusco communities. Immigrants from Mam towns lived in five communities, and immigrants from Quiché towns resided in four communities. Similarly, in any one town a wide range of linguistic groups could be found. In Escuintla, at that time the provincial capital, as many as nine different languages were represented in addition to Nahuatl, which was allegedly the mother tongue of the community. It is possible, of course, that the immigrants were already Spanish speakers before they migrated to the Soconusco. In the *padrones* they all appear with Spanish surnames (as do the Indians from Soconusco).

It seems likely that this kind of immigration as much as any other single factor may have led to the adoption of Spanish as a lingua franca, and quite likely to a number of other cultural changes that contributed to the growth of the Ladino population.

Material Culture and Ladinoization

As I noted earlier, Indians and Ladinos are sometimes distinguished on the basis of material culture. Documentary evidence about the material culture of Indians and Ladinos in colonial Soconusco is relatively poor, but archaeological data from the predominantly Indian town of Ocelocalco provide information about the consumption patterns of colonial Indians in this region.

Ocelocalco existed from at least 1572 until 1767, when it was abandoned by its last three residents. Excavations were carried out in eight residential structures, the church, and a structure whose function remains unknown. Although a small number of Spaniards lived in Ocelocalco during part of the seventeenth century, it seems likely that the excavated structures were the homes of Indians (Gasco 1987a).

The most striking aspect of the archaeological record is the relatively large amount of Spanish-introduced goods (e.g., glazed wheel-thrown pottery, metal goods, and glass) recovered. Compared with other colonial Indian communities that have been excavated in Central Mexico (Charlton 1979), in the Grijalva Valley of Chiapas (Lee and Markman 1979), and in Belize (Jones et al. 1986), the Indians of colonial Ocelocalco clearly had much greater access to, and desire for, Spanish-introduced goods than did Indians in these other regions. At first glance, this might suggest that the Indians of colonial Soconusco were much more acculturated than were Indians in other areas. Nevertheless, the large majority of artifacts from Ocelocalco were in the native tradition (e.g., unglazed, hand-molded pottery, ground stone).

Elsewhere (Gasco 1989c), I have examined in more detail the extent to which the artifacts from Ocelocalco suggest culture change or acculturation among the Indian residents of the community. Briefly, I have argued that in spite of the large quantities of Spanish-introduced goods, there was considerable continuity in material culture from Postclassic to Colonial periods. This conclusion is based on a functional analysis of the Spanish-introduced goods. Most of these goods (e.g., majolica plates and bowls, metal knives) simply replaced something that was already in use. The only class of artifacts found at Ocelocalco that represented a completely new function was horse-related paraphernalia (horseshoes, horseshoe nails).

The material culture of the Indians of Ocelocalco suggests that within the continuum of acculturation, the Indians of southeastern Soconusco again fall somewhere in the middle range. Unfortunately, because we know so little about the material culture of Ladinos or acculturated Indians in the Colonial period, it is difficult to say just how different the material culture of Indians in Soconusco was from that in more heavily Ladino areas.

Conclusions

Indians throughout Spanish America used a variety of strategies in the Colonial and Postcolonial periods to ensure their survival as individuals, as communities, and as members of larger linguistic and ethnic groups. The strategies varied, depending on a range of economic, political, and demographic factors. In southeastern Soconusco, the main economic considerations that influenced Indian strategies involved the cacao trade. The earliest record of Ladinos in colonial Soconusco refers to Indians who spoke Spanish. Given the importance of trade between Indian cacao farmers and non-Indian merchants, it is easy to imagine that Indians who had a good command of Spanish would have been more successful than Indians who knew no Spanish. The cacao trade also gave Soconusco Indians the means to acquire the glazed pots and metal goods found in the archaeological record. The main demographic factor was the heavy native depopulation and the resulting low population density. In response to both the demands of the cacao trade and the labor shortages, immigration was encouraged. Even though the majority of immigrants may have been Indians themselves, a likely result of this immigration was the reduced "Indianness" of all parties concerned.

At the end of the Colonial period, the majority of the population in southeastern Soconusco was still nominally Indian, although the Ladino and other non-Indian segments of the population had grown. It was only with the dramatic changes of the nineteenth century that the transformation of Soconusco's Indian population to a Ladino population was complete. If the cacao economy fell somewhere in the middle of the range of the economic situations discussed above, the coffee economy of the late nineteenth century exhibited all the characteristics of the most extreme form of Spanish-dominated enterprises (Spenser 1984). The final chapter of the history of Ladinoization in Soconusco cannot be written until the demography of the nineteenth and twentieth centuries is better understood.

Acknowledgments

Research in the Archivo General de Indias was supported by a Graduate Humanities Grant, University of California, Santa Barbara. Work in the Archivo General de Centroamérica and the Archivo Histórico Diocesano de San Cristóbal de las Casas was supported by a grant from the National Endowment for the Humanities and the Wenner-Gren Foundation. Permission to conduct archaeological excavations at Ocelocalco was granted by the Instituto Nacional de Antropología e Historia in Mexico, and funding was provided by the National Science Foundation, Grant BNS82–14029. Finally, I would like to thank Greg Luna, Lorena Martinez, and John Patton who, with support from the Faculty Mentorship Program at the University of California, Santa Barbara, compiled the data base for the eighteenth-century *padrones* used in this study.

Notes

The following abbreviations were used in this chapter:

AGI	Archivo General de Indias, Sevilla.
AG	Audiencia de Guatemala.
AM	Audiencia de México.
EC	Escribanía de Cámara.
Cont	Contaduría.
AGCA	Archivo General de Centroamérica, Guatemala.
AHDSCLC	Archivo Histórico Diocesano de San Cristóbal de las Casas, Chiapas.

1. In 1653 "Indios ladinos en lengua" from Ocelocalco and Escuintla, AGCA A1.43 127 970. In 1692 "Indio ladino" from Escuintla, AGI EC 350A, Residencia of Juan Ramirez y Valdez. In 1718 "Indio Ladino, interprete" of Soconusco, AGCA A3.16 358 4613. In 1720 several Indians from Escuintla described as "todos ladinos," AGI EC 356A, Residencia of Capt. don Joseph Damián Fernández de Córdoba. In 1726 "Indio Ladino y principal de Escuintla," AGI EC 356C, Residencia of Francisco Pimentiel y Sotomayor. In 1731 "Indio Ladino de Acapetahua," AGCA A1.45 316 2276.

2. AGI, AM 3102, Report by Fructos Gómez Casillas, 20 November, 1611.

3. AGI Cont 815, "Razón de las ciudades, villas y lugares. . . .de este Audiencia," 1683.

4. AGI AG 375, Report by Gabriel de Laguna, 22 December 1733.

5. AHDSCLC, "Estado de los Vasallos que tiene su Magestad en este Obispado de Cd. Real de Chiapa," 1778.

6. AHDSCLC, "Descripción de la Subdelegación de Tapachula," 1818.

7. AGCA A1.44 46 549, *Padrón* of Tapachula, 1821.

8. AGI EC 331A, "Provisión a Francisco de Santiago. . .para la Provincia de Soconusco," folios 1537–1545v.

9. AGI EC 348C, "Residencia de Francisco de Quintana Dueñas," 1685.

10. AGCA A3.16 290 3910, Paga de *naborío*, 1665.

11. All *padrones* are from the AGCA. 1718–Soconusco, A3.16 358 4613; 1729–Acacoyagua, A3.16 359 4629; 1729–Acapetahua, A3.16 367 4758; 1729–fl Escuintla, A3.16 359 4631; 1729–Guilosingo, A3.16 359 4628; 1729–Huehuetán, A3.16 359 4632; 1729–Huixtla, A3.16 358 4625; 1729–Tuzantán, A3.16 358 4626; 1729–Ilamapa, A3.16 359 4627; 1735–Cacahuatán, A3.16 359 4648; 1735–Mazatán, A3.16 359 4045; 1735–Tecolocoya, A3.16 359 4647; 1735–Nahuatán, A3.16 359 4643.

12. AGCA, 1750–Acacoyagua, A3.16 361 4668; 1750–Cacahuatán, A3.16 361 4669; 1750–Tuxtla, A3.16 361 4671; 1750–Mazatán, A3.16 361 4672; 1755–Huixtla, A3.16 361 4679; 1755–Tapachula, A3.16 361 4680.

13. AGCA, Acacoyagua, A3.16 300 4056; Cacahuatán, A3.16 300 4051; Escuintla, A3.16 1254 21758; Guilosingo, A3.16 290 3908; Tapachula, A3.16 300 4053; Nahuatán, A3.16 300 4055; Tepeguís, A3.16 300 4052; Tuxtla, A3.16 300 4054.

References

Adams, Richard N.
  1964 La Mestización Cultural en Centroamérica. *Revista de Indias* Año XXIV Nums. 95–96:153–176.
Báez Landa, Mariano
  1985 Soconusco: Region, Plantaciones y Soberanía. In *La Formación Histórica de la Frontera Sur.* Centro de Investigaciones y Estudios Superiores en Antropología Social, Cuadernos de la Casa Chata 124, Mexico, D.F.
Campbell, Lyle
  1988 *The Linguistics of Southeast Chiapas, Mexico.* Papers of the New World Archaeological Foundation, No. 50. Brigham Young University, Provo, Utah.
Charlton, Thomas H.
  1979 The Aztec-Early Colonial Transition in the Teotihuacan Valley. In *Actes du XLII Contres International des Americanistes*, vol. 9, pp. 199–208. Paris.
de la Fuente, Julio
  1952 Ethnic and Communal Relations. In *Heritage of Conquest*, edited by Sol Tax, pp. 76–96. Free Press, Glencoe, Ill.
Diccionario de Autoridades
  1969[1732] Edicion Facsimil. Real Academia Española, Madrid.
Farriss, Nancy
  1984 *Maya Society under Colonial Rule: The Collective Enterprise of Survival.* Princeton University Press, Princeton, N.J.
García de León, Antonio
  1984 *Resistencia y Utopia.* Ediciones Era, México, D.F.
Gasco, Janine
  1987a *Cacao and the Economic Integration of Native Society in Colonial Soconusco, New Spain.* Ph.D. dissertation, University of California, Santa Barbara. University Microfilms, Ann Arbor.
  1987b Economic Organization in Colonial Soconusco, New Spain: Local and External Influences. In *Research in Economic Anthropology*, vol. 8, edited by Barry Isaac, pp. 105–137. JAI Press, Greenwich, Conn.
  1989a The Colonial Economy in the Province of Soconusco. In *Ancient Trade and Tribute: Economies of the Soconusco Region of Mesoamerica*, edited by Barbara Voorhies, pp. 287–303. University of Utah Press, Salt Lake City.
  1989b Economic History of Ocelocalco, a Colonial Soconusco Town. In *Ancient Trade and Tribute: Economies of the Soconusco Region of Mesoamerica*, edited by Barbara Voorhies, pp. 304–325. University of Utah Press, Salt Lake City.
  1989c Material Culture and Colonial Indian Society in Southern Mesoamerica: The View from Coastal Chiapas, Mexico. Paper presented at the meetings of the Society for Historical Archaeology, Baltimore, Md.
Gerhard, Peter
  1979 *The Southeast Frontier of New Spain.* Princeton University Press, Princeton, N.J.
Gillin, John
  1952 Ethos and Cultural Aspects of Personality. In *Heritage of Conquest*, edited by Sol Tax, pp. 193–222. Free Press, Glencoe, Ill.
Hawkins, John
  1984 *Inverse Images: The Meaning of Culture, Ethnicity, and Family in Postcolonial Guatemala.* University of New Mexico Press, Albuquerque.
Jones, Grant D., Robert Kautz, and Elizabeth A. Graham
  1986 Tipu: A Maya Town on the Spanish Colonial Frontier. *Archaeology* 39(1):40–47.
Lee, Thomas A., and Sydney Markman
  1979 Coxoh Maya Acculturation in Colonial Chiapas: A Necrotic Archaeological

Ethnohistorical Model. In *Actes du XLII Congres International des Americanistes*, vol. 8, pp. 57–66. Paris.

Lovell, W. George
  1985 *Conquest and Survival in Colonial Guatemala: A Historical Geography of the Cuchumatán Highlands, 1500–1821*. McGill-Queen's University Press, Kingston.

Luján Muñoz, Jorge
  1976 Fundación de Villas de Ladinos en Guatemala en el Ultimo Tercio del Siglo XVIII. *Revista de Indias* Año 36 Nums. 145–146:51–81.

Lutz, Christopher
  1984 *Historia Sociodemográfica de Santiago de Guatemala 1541–1773*. 2d ed. Centro de Investigaciones Regionales de Mesoamérica, Antigua, Guatemala.
  1990a Evolución Demográfica de la Población No Indígena, 1524–1700. In *Historia General de Guatemala*, vol. 2, edited by Jorge Luján Muñoz. Fundación para la Cultura y el Desarrollo, Guatemala, in press.
  1990b La Población No Española y No Indígena, Sus Divisiones y Evolución Demográfica, 1700–1821. In *Historia General de Guatemala*, vol. 2, edited by Jorge Luján Muñoz. Fundación para la Cultura y el Desarrollo, in press.

Lutz, Christopher, and George Lovell
  1990 Core and Periphery in Colonial Guatemala. In *Guatemalan Indians and the State: 1540–1988*, edited by Carol A. Smith (with the assistance of Marilyn M. Moors). University of Texas Press, Austin, in press.

MacLeod, Murdo J.
  1973 *Spanish Central America: A Socioeconomic History 1520–1720*. University of California Press, Berkeley.
  1979 Forms and Types of Work and the Acculturation of the Colonial Indian of Mesoamerica: Some Preliminary Observations. In *El Trabajo y los Trabajadores en la Historia de México*, edited by Elsa Cecilia Frost, Michael C. Meyer, Josefina Zoraida Vázquez, and Lilia Díaz, pp. 75–92. El Colegio de México, México, D.F. and University of Arizona Press, Tucson.

Marino Flores, Anselmo
  1967 Indian Population and Its Identification. In *Social Anthropology*, edited by Manning Nash, pp. 12–15. Handbook of Middle American Indians, vol. 6. Robert Wauchope, general editor. University of Texas Press, Austin.

McBryde, Felix Webster
  1947 *Cultural and Historical Geography of Southwest Guatemala*. Smithsonian Institution, Institute of Social Anthropology Publication No. 4. Washington, D.C.

Medina Hernández, Andrés
  1973 Notas Etnográficas sobre los Mames de Chiapas. *Anales de Antropología* 10:141–220.

Molino, Fray Alonso de
  1970 *Vocabulario en Lengua Castellana y Mexicana y Mexicana y Castellana*. Editorial Porrua, México, D.F.

Mörner, Magnus
  1967 *Race Mixture in the History of Latin America*. Little, Brown, Boston.

Ortiz Hernández, María de los Angeles
  1985 Formación Histórico-Político de la Region del Soconusco, Chiapas. La Oligarquía de Tapachula, 1842–1890. In *Concentración de Poder y Tenencia de la Tierra. El Caso de Soconusco*. Centro de Investigaciones y Estudios Superiores en Antropología Social, Cuadernos de la Casa Chata 125, México, D.F.

Redfield, Robert
  1941 *Folk Culture of Yucatan*. University of Chicago Press, Chicago.

Sherman, William
  1979 *Forced Native Labor in Sixteenth Century Central America*. University of Nebraska Press, Lincoln.

Smith, Waldemar

1977 *The Fiesta System and Economic Change*. Columbia University Press, New York.
Spenser, Daniela
1984 Soconusco: The Formation of a Coffee Economy in Chiapas. In *Other Mexicos: Essays on Regional Mexican History, 1876–1911*, edited by T. Benjamin and W. McNellie, pp. 123–143. University of New Mexico Press, Albuquerque.
Toraya y Toraya, Bertha Rosa
1985 Origin y Evolución de la Tenencia de la Tierra en el Soconusco, Chiapas. El Caso de Santo Domingo. In *Concentración de Poder y Tenencia de la Tierra. El Caso de Soconusco*. Centro de Investigaciones y Estudios Superiores en Antropología Social, Cuadernos de la Casa Chata 125, México, D.F.
Van den Berghe, Pierre L., and Benjamin N. Colby
1961 Ladino-Indian Relations in the Highlands of Chiapas, Mexico. *Social Forces* 40:63–71.
Warren, Kay
1989 *The Symbolism of Subordination: Indian Identity in a Guatemalan Town*. University of Texas Press, Austin.
Wortman, Miles
1982 *Government and Society in Central America 1680–1840*. Columbia University Press, New York.

Chapter 15 ■

Elizabeth Graham

Archaeological Insights into Colonial Period Maya Life at Tipu, Belize

The subject of this chapter is the dynamics of cooperation and conflict along the colonial frontier in Mayan Mesoamerica (for background details, see Graham et al. 1989; Jones 1989). During the Colonial period, communities in Belize and in parts of Campeche and Quintana Roo served as refuges for Mayas fleeing centers of tight Spanish control. As a result, they became the loci of resistance movements. But even in times of cooperation, their remoteness permitted the Maya greater control than in fully administered areas throughout the course of relations with the Spanish. My intention here is to complement Jones's (1989) pioneering ethnohistorical research on the details and complex character of Maya resistance to Spanish rule along the Yucatan frontier with data from the archaeological investigation of the frontier community of Tipu in Belize (see Pendergast, this volume, Figure 16–1).

Negroman, the modern Belizean name for the place where the community of Tipu once flourished, has a history of occupation that stretches back into the Preclassic period (about 300 B.C.). At the opposite end of the continuum the re-verberations of Spanish occupation and economic exploitation were probably felt in 1544, although the name "Tipu" is not actually noted in the documents as part of an encomienda until 1568 (Jones 1984). The Colonial period ruins at Negroman, barely perceptible as undulations in the cleared pastures of a cattle ranch, lie near an elbow of the Macal River, on the left bank. The Macal, one of Belize's most beautiful rivers, drains the dramatic granites of the Maya Mountains and the forested limestones of the Vaca Plateau. With such diverse parent material, the resulting alluvium is inherently fertile and apparently served the Maya well in both prehistoric and historic times.

During the Spanish Colonial period, Tipu was one of a number of communities in the Dzuluinicob Province (of which it was apparently the political center) that grew cacao for both tribute and trade in orchards along the rich soils of the riverbank (Jones 1989:10, 103, 120; Muhs et al. 1985). Tipuans maintained close relationships with the independent Itzá Maya kingdom in the central Peten. Unlike the Itzá, however, Tipuans became Christians and a *visita* mission was established at the site. The mission consisted of a small thatch-roof church bordering a courtyard and a semidetached, church-related structure, possibly a residence, which were built near the edge of the second terrace overlooking the river. These buildings and others arranged around a rectangular plaza area, as well as various cobblestone pavements, concealed a considerable spread of debris from Postclassic occupation, as well as Late Postclassic buildings, the foundations of which were incorporated into Colonial period construction. This combination of Pre- and Postcolumbian foundations was to affect community character and stability over the years between 1544 and 1707 as Tipu passed back and forth between Maya and Spanish control (Graham et al. 1989; Jones 1989:5).

Conditions of Discovery and Initial Excavation

My interest in the historic phase of Maya occupation in Belize began at Lamanai (Graham 1987; Pendergast 1981, 1986a, 1986b, 1986c) in northern Belize, a site that has been occupied for over 3,500 years. Between 1980 and 1984 I excavated and recorded the remains of a number of Postclassic (A.D. 900–1500) and Colonial period buildings at this site. The excavations were directed by David Pendergast, who, by 1977, had already been fitting the results of Colonial period archaeological work into the documentary framework that Grant Jones had begun to erect. My deeper involvement in the Colonial period thus developed as an offshoot of what Jones and Pendergast had started, and it was Jones and Pendergast who, on a visit to Negroman in 1978, spotted the barely perceptible but distinctive relief in one of the cattle pastures that turned out to represent the remains of historic Tipu.

The excavations conducted at Negroman-Tipu from 1980 to 1982, under the direction of Robert Kautz, have been outlined in previous publications (Graham et al. 1985; Jones et al. 1986). During this period the entire site was mapped, an area of about 0.5 square kilometers. Negroman contains mostly prehistoric structures, but quadrats were sampled in an attempt to locate Colonial period buildings. Selected Classic and Postclassic period structures were also investigated. The church (Str. H12–13) was the first historic structure to be identified.

Its parallel sides and polygonal ends, the presence of steps to an altar at the east end, and the orientation, character, and placement of associated burials clearly represented Postcolumbian, non-Maya practices. In addition, test pits in the quadrat in which the church was located turned up sherds from European-made olive jars and Majolica ware.

The Colonial Period Focus

In 1984, the structures near the church that appeared to be oriented around a rectangular plaza were partly excavated, as were buildings that lay between the plaza area and the ruins of a Postclassic ceremonial center to the east (Figure 15–1). Except for what we had learned at Lamanai in the excavation of two churches (Str. N11–18) and other buildings (see Pendergast, this volume), nothing was known about southern lowlands Colonial period architecture, or about the shapes and styles of Colonial period pottery of native manufacture. We hoped to uncover this sort of information for central Belize and the area of the Belize River drainage by focusing on the plans of buildings and the nature of construction. Intensive excavation and processing were devoted to stratified midden deposits with well-preserved remains with a view to (1) establishing a Late Postclassic-Colonial period ceramic and lithic chronology; (2) charting the course of changes in resource exploitation from Postclassic to historic times; and (3) determining the range of Colonial period technology and the impact, if any, of Spanish technological imports.

Architecture

Our initial excavation procedure was based on what we knew about the shapes and sizes of Precolumbian Maya structures; as it turned out, the approach was unsuitable for Colonial period architecture. In fact, it was not until 1987, when we excavated the latest phase of a building just north of the church, that the nature of Colonial period construction became intelligible. Precolumbian Maya buildings, whether masonry or thatch, are normally built on faced platforms of earth or stone. The platforms can be low and, as was often true in Late Postclassic times, bordered by a single row of stones. Alternatively, they can be elaborate terraced masonry structures. In both cases, there is a regularity of form that is distinctively Maya, but the regularity disappears in colonial times. Some colonial construction incorporates earlier postclassic buildings, and in these cases height is provided by the remains of the earlier building. In other cases, no formal, or at least no rectangular-shaped, platform seems to have been built. River stones and a mixture of shaped and unshaped limestone were laid down to form a rough sort of cobblestone pavement. The church and related buildings were built around a cobblestone courtyard, and a cobblestone pavement formed at least part of the plaza surface. Cobblestone pavements were also formed into amorphous, platformlike, raised areas that may have supported perishable buildings. It is unclear, however, whether such a pavement was meant in all cases

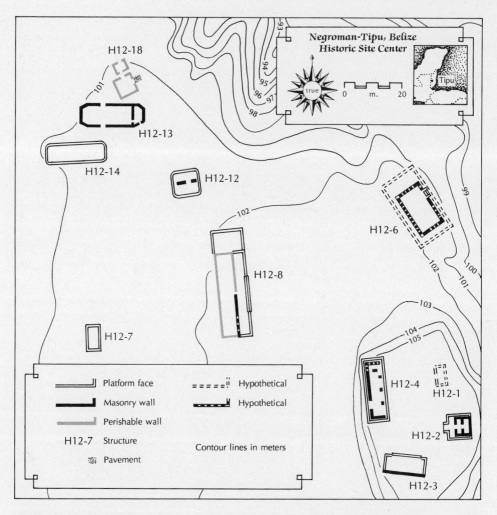

Figure 15–1. Map of Colonial period (H12–6, 7, 8, 12, 13, 14, 18) and Postclassic (H12–1, 2, 3, 4) buildings. Structures H12–6, 8, 18 have Postclassic components. An unexcavated structure lies under a cattle corral southwest of H12–8, and more probably south of H12–14, and west of the excavated area. (Drawing by David Jones)

to support enclosed structures. The plans of buildings at both Tipu and Lamanai suggest that the pavement areas may have supported parts of buildings that were roofed but lacked walls. Roofed buildings with walls either of masonry or thatch seem to have had earth floors, and the pavement areas perhaps served as roofed-over forecourts or as exterior walkways between houses, courtyards, or other usable but not necessarily enclosed spaces.

The model for such construction is partly Maya. It is not uncommon for Postclassic buildings to consist of two long, parallel rooms. The outer room is roofed, but in place of walls there are masonry or timber supporting columns, whereas the inner room is enclosed by a masonry wall. Unfortunately, the colonial pattern is not as easily "readable" as the Maya pattern. For example, there seem to be all kinds of building extensions, represented by stone-lined terraces and irregular pavements, that are difficult to translate into a three-dimensional model. The concept of interior and exterior roofed space is, however, a common tropical pattern, and what we may be witnessing is an amalgam of Maya and Spanish traditions. As we increase our inventory of excavated buildings, colonial planning and construction will no doubt become clearer.

The colonial pattern of building represents far more of a break with Maya tradition than anticipated. Changes in building styles form the Preclassic through Classic and Postclassic periods would lead one to expect greater continuity and a greater prevalence of the Maya pattern. Despite the possible continuity from the Postclassic to Colonial periods in the definition of interior and exterior space, a major break with the Precolumbian architectural tradition is indicated by the absence of formal platforms, the introduction of cobblestone pavements for an apparent variety of structural uses, changes in the overall plans of buildings, and changes in the nature of construction techniques. It is difficult to attribute this break to pressure from the Spanish, since the documentary evidence suggests that the Spanish exercised only intermittent control at Tipu.

There are a number of possible explanations. The documentary evidence may be patchier than we thought; records of frequent visits and strict supervision by religious and secular authorities may have been lost. Or, as I have suggested elsewhere (Graham et al. 1989), the community of Tipu may, by 1544, have already been decimated by European diseases. Moreover, the communication links between generations so essential in passing on information and technological expertise may have already been broken, leaving the remaining community members with far less expertise on which to draw. It is also possible that the Tipuan builders acknowledged limited Spanish authority over construction and were not permitted to direct work according to traditional methods.

The Artifact Inventory: Continuity

In contrast to the apparent break in architectural traditions, there is continuity in the artifact inventory from the Postclassic to Colonial period. My comments here are guarded, however, because so little is known about the immediate preconquest artifact inventory of the Maya in Belize. The work done at Lamanai and Tipu indicates that regional differences in ceramic and lithic types were significant and that the pace and direction of change differed in the two areas. This makes it almost impossible to generalize about conquest effects, at least at present.

What we can say is that the conquest seems not to have affected local pottery production at all. There are changes in some pottery forms, but these are well within the range expected had the conquest never taken place. That is, there are minor and gradual changes in such features as rim profiles and lip forms that are consistent with the nature of change in earlier times. European Majolica and olive jars were clearly present, but the overall quantity is relatively small. The context of the European pottery—buildings near the church and around the plaza—suggests that the olive jars and Majolica plates were used either by visiting Spaniards or by Christianized Mayas of status.

The number of Postclassic-style figurines in midden deposits, which for the most part are not primary but reused in construction, suggests that the Tipuans continued to follow a number of Precolumbian practices frowned on by Spanish clerics. In one case, an effigy actually formed part of a cache deposited in a Colonial period building. To this extent, then, we have corroborating archaeological evidence of the "idolatry" reported in the documents. (Other evidence, however, does not entirely bear out the clerics' claims of apostasy, as discussed below.)

Changes in lithic technology and production also seem to have been minimal. Metals make their appearance in the form of copper and brass needles and rings associated with individuals in burials, but iron seems to have made little impact. Friars are known to have brought knives to Tipu (see below), but the iron in the archaeological inventory appears as coffin nails, or as locks from chests. One lock, probably from a Spanish-made vargueño chest, is associated with a structure built in colonial times. The other, recovered from the cemetery, is from a smaller Spanish chest that contained a secondary burial.

Owing to the scarcity of European metals, chert continued to be the main material used in tool production. Two forms predominated: small side-notched points, most probably arrowheads (Figure 15–2a and b); and small, bipointed bifaces. The other chert artifacts consist of informal tools—flakes with various kinds of edge wear. As with the pottery, so little is known about the lithic inventory from the Late or Terminal Postclassic period in the area that it is difficult to comment on change or continuity from preconquest times. The inventory is certainly unlike that of the Middle Postclassic period—spanning the twelfth and thirteenth centuries—when points or knives, though side-notched, were larger and were probably designed for use with atlatls and spears. Small bipointed bifaces were also absent in Middle Postclassic times, although large, carefully chipped ceremonial bifaces were not uncommon. The near-blank part of the record is the Late Postclassic period, and until the technology of this time becomes better known, we will not be able to comment on pre- to postconquest change.

The Artifact Inventory: Change

Although chert, locally mined, remained available in historic times, there is evidence that raw obsidian was unobtainable. Hydration dating of obsidian from stratified deposits that were also dated ceramically suggests that in postconquest times, trade in the material was disrupted and that the Maya of Tipu were forced to recycle implements that they found lying about or buried in archaeological deposits.

The possibility that obsidian trade was disrupted is currently being examined in more detail, but two other changes in the native artifact inventory also deserve close attention. The first of these is the appearance at Tipu in historic times of a type of pottery made in a style characteristic of the Historic period at Lamanai. Called the Yglesias phase at Lamanai, the pottery of this period replaces the local Tulum-style ceramics (Graham 1987). It is characterized by thin walls, relatively crude shapes, and a washlike slip. In contrast to the Lamanai

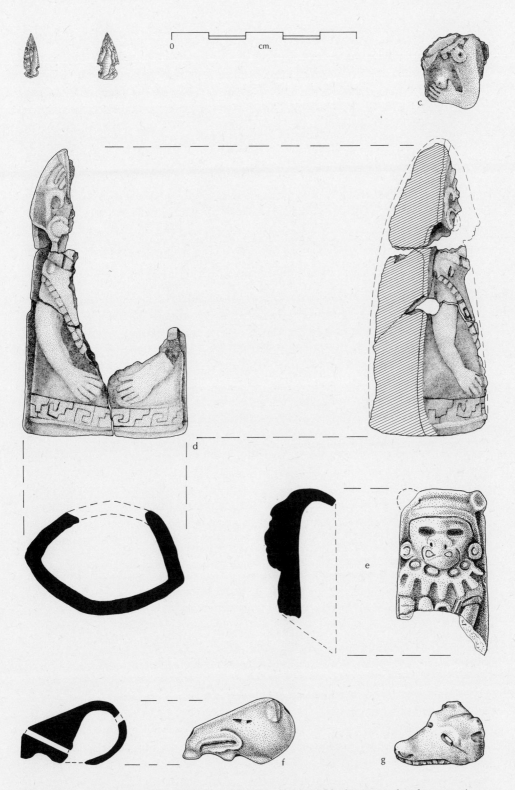

Figure 15–2. Artifacts from Tipu, Belize: *a* and *b* are small side-notched points; *c, d,* and *e* are portions of female figurines; *f* is a tapir; and *g* is a dog. (Drawings by Emil and Mariana Hustiu)

pottery, Yglesias-like pottery at Tipu adds to, rather than replaces, the local ceramic tradition.

Second, the data assembled from Lamanai thus far suggest that the Yglesias style of pottery making is associated with the first appearance of bow and arrow technology in the area. The genesis of Yglesias pottery occurred just prior to the conquest. We have not excavated extensively or intensively enough at Tipu to be certain of the time Yglesias-style pottery and arrowpoints were introduced, but the only primary or well-dated contexts in which the two are found are of the Postconquest period. Both the pottery and the weapons technology may reflect the influx of Yucatec Maya—individuals or families—into the southern lowlands in the last half of the sixteenth century, as recorded extensively in the documents (Jones 1989:17). I am well aware how dangerous it can be to posit a people-pot association. The proposition can, however, be examined and corroborated, or refuted, by future work.

I suggested this link between changes in different facets of the artifact inventory and population movements not only to convey something about how archaeological interpretation is proceeding, but also to show how archaeology and enthnohistory can complement one another in unexpected ways. Jones (1989:332) recently supplied additional information on Martín Chan, who headed a delegation to Merida in 1695. The delegation was purportedly sent by Can Ek, the ruler of the Itzás at Tayasal, as an act of submission to Spanish authorities (Jones 1989:262). Martín Chan related that his father was married to Can Ek's sister, a woman named Can Te, who had originally come from Chichén Itzá. Jones suggests that Martín Chan must have meant that his mother's *ancestors* came from Chichén Itzá, because the Chichén occupation is thought by archaeologists to have ended in the latter part of the twelfth century. The small side-notched points from Tipu and Lamanai that are indicative of bow and arrow technology also turn up at Chichén (Dan Potter, personal communication). If our dating of these points at Lamanai is correct, then their presence at Chichén documents a sixteenth-century occupation, in which case Martín Chan meant just what he said: His mother's birthplace was Chichén Itzá.

The gradual appearance of small side-notched point technology in the northern and southern lowlands may well mark the movements of groups of people who used the bow and arrow, rather than the spread of a technologically useful idea. In the northern lowlands, these movements seem to have predated the Colonial period, but the picture changes, at least in the Tipu region, where the new technology may be a Colonial period phenomenon. Unfortunately, the documents are not likely to yield detailed information on bow and arrow technology, and hence on the nature of Maya population shifts, because the Spanish were not inclined to comment on material culture, native or otherwise. Herein lies one of the largest disjunctions between archaeology and ethnohistory, particularly for remote frontier areas with weaker documentation than the metropolitan centers (Jones 1989:vii). The archaeologist works predominantly with material remains, the ethnohistorian with documents in which material goods, particularly native ones, receive little attention.

Archaeology and Ethnohistory

There are a number of ways in which the facets of archaeological and ethnohistorical evidence can be joined to reflect Tipu's colonial past. However, the data from ethnohistory and archaeology often lie in planes that do not intersect. As Jones (1989:4) has commented, "So different are the archaeological and historical records that each to some extent requires its own reflections." Although this disjunction would seem, at first, to dash all hope of integrating the information from these records, it happens that the disparity, as well as the complementarity, of archaeological and ethnohistorical data can shed light on Maya–Spanish relations. Disparity is productive in another critical sense; it forces us to examine our assumptions concerning the relationship of our data to any one vision of reality. In the paragraphs that follow I discuss some of our initial assumptions concerning the perspectives of the chroniclers, the meaning of the archaeological record, and the nature of data integration and disparity. My emphasis on complementarity and positive disjunction accords well with Thomas's caveat against pursuing any one "true" past (1989:9). My intention is not to imply that all pasts are equally valid (see Shanks and Tilley 1987:27), but that there are ways in which we can learn from the past without nailing every scrap of evidence onto the same structural framework.

Conjunction/Disjunction

Despite the lack of documentary evidence on material culture, we are learning about the nature of the contacts maintained by Tipuans in colonial times. The approximately 600 burials from the church cemetery at Tipu (Graham and Bennett 1989), as well as reused midden deposits in buildings, yielded European glass beads, Spanish pottery, and metal artifacts. Needles are the most common grave accompaniment; about 50 have been recovered so far. Ongoing analysis by Michael Wayman (Graham and Wayman 1989) has revealed that a number of the needles are brass, and hence are European imports. Needles probably reached Tipu as part of the inventory of gifts that priests carried to the Maya during their proselytizing efforts. In Guatemala, Dominican friars and other missionaries distributed gifts of machetes, knives, needles, scissors, hatchets, hats, rings, blankets, and other useful articles (Van Oss 1986:16), and the Franciscan Fathers Bartolomé de Fuensalida and Juan de Orbita carried crosses, knives, needles, rosaries, and glass beads, presumably to give as gifts, when they left Merida in 1618 bound for Tipu and Tayasal (Jones 1989:136).

A number of other items from Tipu are not mentioned in the documents: silver earrings; copper, silver, and brass rings; beads of jet and amber; gunmetal; iron nails; Precolumbian-style bells; chests, presumably used to transport goods from Yucatan; and other miscellaneous objects. Chemical analysis suggests the amber is Baltic (Joseph Lambert, personal communication). The jet appears to have a European source as well, although at present no profiles of New World jet are available for comparison.

The bells are interesting because they vary in composition. Twelve of 16 have been analyzed so far: 10 are copper, some with phosphorus and some with lead, and the other 2 are bronze (Graham and Wayman 1989). Since the forms are native ones, it is possible that the Maya were in some cases recasting European bronze. Analysis of the technology of some of the Lamanai metal artifacts reveals evidence of reworking of Precolumbian metal (D. Hosler, personal communication to D. Pendergast, 1990). Both Lamanai and Tipu have turned up "pigs," that is, small lumps of copper that are a by-product of smelting, and the Lamanai data suggest that a Maya copperworking tradition predated the conquest. It is also possible that the Maya at Tipu and Lamanai were receiving copper through native trade networks even after the conquest. Lead isotope analysis is expected to shed some light on the possible Mesoamerican sources of the native copper, and hence on the direction of Colonial period native trade. Jones (1981) long ago suggested that native trade was relatively brisk in frontier regions after the conquest. The presence of marine fish in Colonial period midden deposits at Tipu suggests that ties with coastal communities were maintained, but whether these coastal communities were still serving as way stations for trade (for example, in copper bells) remains uncertain.

One of the phenomena at Tipu that has touched me deeply is the fact that many of the children buried in the cemetery were more elaborately adorned than the adults. Most of the silver earrings and glass bead necklaces and bracelets were worn by children, and it saddened us all to record the details of burials of ones so young and so lovingly adorned in death. Why European baubles were more commonly worn by children rather than by adults has yet to be explained. What Maya girls and boys wore does not seem to have been of interest to the chroniclers. It is possible that the rosaries carried by Fuensalida and Orbita were intended for the adults, whereas the bead jewelry was meant for the children. Although it is not entirely clear, Van Oss's reading of a document concerning missionization in Guatemala implies that rosaries were among the status items reserved for caciques (1986:16, n. 31). We know that children were certainly the focus of early catechizing efforts (Scholes 1938:Ser. 5, Doc. 18, p. 28; Peñalosa 1969:69, 70), and although the archaeology and ethnohistory in this circumstance are far from conclusive, the data suggest that the beads and earrings were gifts specifically for the children at Tipu from priests responsible for teaching the catechism.

"Idolatry"

"Idols" are common at Tipu and indeed form a large part of the Postclassic and Colonial period inventory, although they are only occasionally from primary deposits such as a cache and have been recovered largely from middens reused in construction. They comprise a fascinating array of animals, people (particularly women), and figures that combine human and animal characteristics. What meaning they had for the Maya is, however, unclear, for on this point the documents are silent. Idols are mentioned frequently by chroniclers, but always with horror and repugnance. "Idolatry" was not uncommon at Tipu (Jones 1989:148,

190), and Jones quotes a vivid passage, maddening for what it lacks in description of the idols, from López de Cogolludo, in which Fray Juan de Orbita discovers a cache of idols at Tipu in 1619:

> He found a great quantity of idols, and next to the house of the cacique, who had been D. Luis Mazun (who, as was said, died in jail in Merida), he discovered an alcove [*retrete*] with some idols and vestments from their priests inside that had been owned by that cacique and that now belonged to his wife Doña Isabel Pech. The religious called her, and when they asked her who the idols and vestments belonged to, she answered that her husband had left them there and that they were from the Itzás. Although they whipped her a few times to make her tell the truth, she was not able to say any more. Father Orbita addressed the Indians with such a spirit that they themselves showed him a great multitude of idols, so many that Father Fuensalida says they could not be counted, because they made a different idol to worship each thing that they felt like. The Father destroyed all that they found and threw them into the deepest part of the river [Jones 1989:148–149].

Excavation, and not the written record, has provided archaeologists with information on the forms of the "idols," but the other types of data we would like to have—concerning the customs, rituals, or worship the figurines were associated with, the rooms they were placed in—would never have been sought, let alone recorded, by the chroniclers. Even modern historians (e.g., Clendinnen 1987:73, 80; Warren 1985:96–97) continue to refer to figurines and statues of native manufacture as "idols." Archaeologists usually refer to them as "gods."

The Impact of Christianity and the Nature of Syncretism

The term "idol" is loaded with cultural bias, and its use by Catholic missionaries is particularly ironic. Their statues were saints, but the Maya statues were idols. Without exception, the chronicles mention "idols" only to note the recalcitrance of the Maya and the presence of the devil. The critical point here is that the Spaniards had great difficulty conceptualizing native religion as anything other than the work of the devil.

This bias in the chroniclers' accounts has had far-reaching and long-lasting effects, as can be seen in our lack of understanding of native religion. The bias also underscores the disparity in the nature of the archaeological and ethnohistorical data. The archaeological record at Tipu provides a rich inventory of figurines with regularities of dress and visage that unquestionably had symbolic meaning. Clearly, Tipuans cannot be characterized, as Father Fuensalida put it, as having a "different idol to worship each thing that they felt like."

One style of female figurines shows the individual clasping her left breast with her left hand (Figure 15–2c); two such figurines occur at Tipu. Another depicts a woman dressed in a huipil with a decorated border (Figure 15–2d). She wears a necklace on which is suspended a circular object, perhaps an obsidian mirror. In the one instance in which the face is preserved, it combines human and ape-like features (Figure 15–2e). Overall, there are strong parallels with the saints of Christendom, each of whom is depicted in a particular style and color of clothing and is usually associated with an object, or even an animal, that has symbolic significance.

A number of depictions of animals occur at Tipu: turkeys, a tapir, dogs, and a variety of birds (Figure 15–2f and g). In most cases, the figures are whistles; in others, the image is fragmentary, and it is difficult to visualize the complete object. In the documents, Spanish priests lump all Maya statues together as "idols" and accuse the Maya of worshipping them as "gods" no matter what the statue's appearance (archaeologists are very good at this as well). There is by no means conclusive or even suggestive evidence that all the animal figurines were gods. The problem in interpretation can be illustrated by an example from Catholic worship. Most churches have special alcoves in which crèches are set up each Christmas. Statues of the principal figures (Jesus, Mary, Joseph, the Wise Men) are usually arranged around and in a stable, along with figurines depicting the animals normally found in such a circumstance, a donkey and a cow. A bird with outstretched wings is almost always centered on the peak of the stable roof. Catholics know the symbolism behind each image, and I think it is generally agreed that the donkey, for example, is not a god. Neither are the Wise Men, for that matter. Yet the donkey, the Wise Men, and indeed all of the figurines are important religious symbols with a complex history. Anyone without knowledge of the tenets of Catholicism might easily interpret the lot as gods.

The technique of using the Catholic framework of images to understand Maya religion is a tantalizing one (Graham 1989). I draw attention to it in this context because it is an alternative approach to an old problem, and as such probably answers Thomas's (1989:8) call for fresh perspectives and new viewpoints. It also bears on his discussion of the futility of a search for a true past (1989:9). This approach can sensitize us to details of form or context that we might not have noticed before and make us aware that the term "idol" has little meaning except to signify the superstitions of "the other."

Up to this point, I have focused on native religion in order to provide an example of the disjunction between archaeology and ethnohistory and to demonstrate that the existence of such a disjunction actually has the positive effect of sharpening our critical faculties and causing us to rework our assumptions and our approaches to interpretation. A further reason for such a focus is that the data from Tipu call into question our assumptions about the character of native religion after the conquest, and about the nature of what is most often called religious syncretism.

Our original assumption about the attitudes of Tipuans toward the Spanish was based on the ethnohistorical record, which reports that initial conversion and incorporation into the encomienda system were followed by dissatisfaction and ultimate rebellion in 1638, after which all vestiges of Spanish politics, economics, and culture were rejected. This state of affairs continued until 1695, when Tipu was again incorporated into the colonial system (Graham et al. 1989:1257). Information from the excavations indicated that the course of Contact period life at Tipu was not quite so straightforward. There is evidence, in the form of burials cut through construction deposits that overlie church collapse, that the Maya continued to bury people in the church cemetery according to

Christian practice even after the rebellion of 1638. At first this evidence seemed confusing, but then I realized that my thinking had been heavily influenced by the tone of the documents, which implied that the only good Christian was a Hispanicized one. In addition, I assumed that the rejection of Spanish political and economic authority in 1638 meant the rejection of Spanish religion as well.

The documents attest that the Maya of Tipu, unlike the Peten Itzás, were Christianized, and the relatively large number of burials in the cemetery is a good indication that the Maya were not nominal but practicing Christians. This is especially significant since the Tipuans were subject to infrequent visits from churchmen and were far from the centers of Christian power and authority. That they had internalized at least some aspects of the Christian belief system seems the best explanation. The period from Spanish contact in 1544 to rebellion in 1638 covers 94 years, which is long enough for two or three generations of Maya to have adopted a worldview that was significantly affected by Christian teaching. If my interpretation of the association between the glass bead necklaces and the children in the cemetery is correct—that the beads were given to catechized children at Tipu—it provides us with a tangible image of Tipuans growing up in a world in which an unadulterated preconquest belief system existed only as memory. The religion of Tipuans after 1544 was suffused with images of saints and angels and a heaven and hell that meshed well with the spirit world of Precolumbian times. This blending was probably facilitated by the powerful image technology of Christendom: colorful perspective paintings of martyred saints that were carried into the bush by friars, or polished medals and medallions depicting ascensions into heaven and the descensions of holy spirits.

All of this should have some bearing on our concept of religious syncretism and on what we like to interpret as the persistence of Precolumbian practices. Many scholars have maintained that Christian teachings were simply a veneer on a Precolumbian base. This, in fact, is what the priests ultimately came to believe. In their view, they had successfully preached the faith to the Maya, and they rejoiced at the ready acceptance of the word of the Christian God, but they despaired when the Maya carried out rituals that were not part of Spanish practice. The Maya then became liars and deceivers in the minds of the priests and Spanish authorities. They were seen as having simply adopted enough Christianity to deceive their overlords without believing what they were taught. How, one might ask, did Maya children who had grown up under Christian teaching, however sporadic, and had been exposed to the superior image technology of the Spanish Christians develop faith only as a veneer? The concepts of a "base" of Precolumbian thought and a "veneer" of Christianity may be appropriate in describing the conversion of adults during the first years of contact, but they are totally inadequate to depict the Maya worldview once the Spanish had clearly come to stay.

The problem in interpreting Maya/Christian syncretism lies not in Maya insincerity, but in Spanish bias. There is no reason to believe that the Maya were insincere about adopting Christian beliefs, but every reason to believe that they may have interpreted Christian practice in their own terms. The Spanish could not understand what seemed to them to be an incongruity, but then they could not see themselves as the bearers of a spirit world that was as complex and colorful as that of the Maya. It is doubtful whether the average Maya or the average Spaniard contemplated Christian doctrine in Augustinian or Aquinian terms. The commonality between the Christian and Maya worldviews lay in the fact that *both* were an everyday adaptation to a world of spirits and demons. The Maya saw this; the Spaniards did not. Therefore when the Maya practiced ritual in a way that seemed to them to be a logical extension of what they already believed, the Spaniards quite predictably attributed the phenomenon to deception and cunning. Had the priests only looked back to the early Christianization of Europe, they would have seen that their cherished images of heaven and hell, their devils and their archangels, were merely transformations of the pagan imagery of the time—products of the sincerity of early Christians whose rituals were logical extensions of their beliefs.

Closing Perspective

The above examples have served, I hope, to demonstrate that the interplay between archaeology and ethnohistory is complex. Ethnohistory can, in fact, stand entirely on its own and present a lively narrative, a colorful story, dynamic characters, and vivid historical reconstruction. The chink in the otherwise smooth ethnohistorical armor is that the documents are written almost entirely from the Spaniards' point of view. Where this problem can be accommodated, we are still faced with the fact that the Spanish were least interested in recording those things that loom largest in the archaeological record: the components of Maya material culture. Nevertheless, it is possible to derive glimpses of the interaction between Mayas and Spaniards, although these insights are often disparate. Thomas (1989:9) suggests that we might learn how to depict the past from seemingly disparate elements by heeding the cubist dictum in art. To the cubists, "humans learn not from the single, all-encompassing glance, but rather from an infinite number of momentary glimpses, unified into a whole by the spectator's mind. Cubist paintings depict objects as one knows them to be . . . from several angles at once" (1989:9).

My discussion of the differing interpretations of Maya-Spanish belief systems can be seen as an example of the productiveness of the cubist perspective. No one side is right and none is wrong. All angles are critical in deriving meaning and significance from the experiences. Furthermore, individuals should not necessarily be subsumed within the group response. Of the many scenes brought to life by ethnohistoric research in Belize and Yucatan (Jones 1989), the most deeply moving are often those in which individuals struggle to come to terms with the Spanish presence and set courses of action that are not necessarily those of their neighbors. A struggle of particular interest to me was that between Can Ek, the Itzá ruler, and his wife, who was said to have persuaded her husband to throw the proselytizing Franciscan friars Fuensalida and Orbita off the island of Tayasal in 1619 (López de Cogolludo as cited in Jones 1989:152). She and several Itzá priests were opposed to capitulating to Spanish rule.

I have no wish at this juncture to replace the cubist perspective with a feminist one, but I cannot let pass the opportunity to note the almost total absence of the voices of women in the colonial documents with which I am familiar. Women will continue to be ignored unless we adopt an approach that defines women in "group strategy" terms. Although I am loath to say this, a little dose of culturology (White 1987) might be helpful here—women as communicators of cultural information to children, as filters of Spanish ideas and processors of new information, as dietary planners and maintainers of health and hygiene, and as wives, advisers, and companions of the first Spaniards—the primary weavers of the first tapestry to include threads of Old and New World cultures.

It might be asked how women can be brought into the picture if they do not appear in the documents. To provide but one example, there is a contrast in the general health of the Colonial period population between Tipu and Lamanai. According to skeletal indicators of health (Cohen et al. 1989; White 1988), the Lamanai population had a high frequency of porotic hyperostosis, and by inference anemia, whereas the Tipu population apparently had a low incidence of this and related bone disorders (Graham et al. 1989:1258). In addition, reconstruction of dietary strategies (Emery 1990) demonstrates that continuity in resource exploitation from the Late Postclassic to Colonial period was characteristic of Tipu, whereas Lamanai experienced significant changes in the same period as fish and birds came to make up a much larger part of the diet after the conquest at the expense of mammals. Such evidence could be interpreted in a number of ways, but women must have played no small part in maintaining a high standard of general health and hygiene at Tipu, despite the stress of conquest and conversion, whereas Lamanai's inhabitants were apparently not so successful. Differences in population composition or ethnic affiliation may have played a role in the contrasting health histories of the two communities, but even here the dietary strategies were in all likelihood culturally mediated, and women would have had a major role in maintaining health standards through food growing, preparation, and processing.

Information from the documents is vital to interpreting the archaeological evidence on women's roles in Maya life during the Spanish period. Lamanai was closer to the Spanish center of control at Bacalar. It served as a reduction center for runaways from the Bacalar region and as such was a colonial community in flux. Tipu was more remote, and it remained, perhaps because of its early conversion and general attitude of initial accommodation to Spanish rule, a stable center (Graham et al. 1989:1258). In such an environment, family life was probably not as severely damaged as it was at Lamanai. The extended family networks so necessary to childrearing and to maintaining one's diet and health would not have been as severely disrupted; husbands would not have had to flee from Spanish tribute collectors, women would not have had to raise children on their own, mothers would not have lacked sufficient breast milk for their babies. Some essential information would still have passed from mother to daughter, from grandmother to grandchild, from parents to children. Obviously, we do not know for certain whether what I have suggested is a "true" picture. In my view, it is a reasonable extension of the conditions indicated by the archaeological evidence, and it reflects a reality with which we are familiar. Whatever the truth turns out to be, the part women play in the answer may not be as important in the long run as whether women are part of the question.

Back to the Future

Thomas, in the stimulating introduction to which I repeatedly refer, encourages scholars to depart from the notion of pursuing "truth" in history. This does not mean that we should reject goals that call for a synthesis of disparate data or that call on us to reconstruct cultural history or to generalize about human behavior. What it means is that, although the conclusions we reach may be important, revealing, and even beneficial to society, they will not be the way things really were. They may reflect truth (Graham 1990), and they may reflect us, but they will not be true. In other words, multivariate approaches offer the only hope of extracting from the record of the past, in all its forms, the many, and often disparate, versions of reality it contains.

References

Clendinnen, Inga
   1987 *Ambivalent Conquests, Maya and Spaniard in Yucatan, 1517–1570*. Cambridge University Press, Cambridge.
Cohen, Mark N., Sharon Bennett, and Carl Armstrong
   1989 *Health and Genetic Relationships in a Colonial Mayan Population*. Final Report to the National Science Foundation on Grant 85–06785. SUNY, Plattsburgh, N.Y.
Emery, Kitty
   1990 *Colonial Period Dietary Strategies in the Southern Maya Lowlands: Spanish Conquest or Maya Conservatism?* Unpublished Master's thesis, Department of Anthropology, University of Toronto.
Graham, Elizabeth
   1987 Terminal Classic to Historic-Period Vessel Forms from Belize. In *Maya Ceramics: Papers from the 1985 Maya Ceramic Conference*, edited by Prudence M. Rice and Robert J. Sharer, pp. 73–98. BAR International Series 345(i).
   1989 The Ecclesiastical Context of Early Maya–Spanish Relations in Belize. Paper presented at the American Society for Ethnohistory Meetings, Chicago, November 2–5.
   1990 Science and Athena's Shield: Reflections of Reality. *Rotunda* 23(1):50–54.
Graham, Elizabeth, and Sharon Bennett
   1989 The 1986–1987 Excavations at Negroman-Tipu, Belize. *Mexicon* 11(6):114–117.
Graham, Elizabeth, Grant D. Jones, and Robert R. Kautz
   1985 Archaeology and Ethnohistory on a Spanish Colonial Frontier: An Interim Report on the Macal-Tipu Project in Western Belize. In *The Lowland Maya Postclassic*, edited by Arlen F. Chase and Prudence M. Rice, pp. 206–214. University of Texas Press, Austin.
Graham, Elizabeth, David M. Pendergast, and Grant D. Jones
   1989 On the Fringes of Conquest: Maya—Spanish Contact in Colonial Belize. *Science* 246:1254–1259.
Graham, Elizabeth, and Michael Wayman
   1989 Maya Material Culture at Conquest: Copper and Other Artifacts from Colonial Tipu, Belize. Paper presented at the 88th Annual Meeting of the American Anthropological Association, Washington, D.C.
Jones, Grant D.

1981 Agriculture and Trade in the Colonial Period Southern Maya Lowlands. In *Maya Subsistence, Studies in Memory of Dennis E. Puleston,* edited by Kent V. Flannery, pp. 275–293. Academic Press, New York.

1984 Maya—Spanish Relations in Sixteenth Century Belize. *Belcast Journal of Belizean Affairs* 1(1):28–40.

1989 *Maya Resistance to Spanish Rule: Time and History on a Colonial Frontier.* University of New Mexico Press, Albuquerque.

Jones, Grant D., Robert R. Kautz, and Elizabeth Graham

1986 Tipu: A Maya Town on the Spanish Colonial Frontier. *Archaeology* 39:40–47.

Muhs, Daniel R., Robert R. Kautz, and J. Jefferson MacKinnon

1985 Soils and the Location of Cacao Orchards at a Maya Site in Western Belize. *Journal of Archaeological Science* 12:121–137.

Peñalosa, Joaquin A.

1969 *La Práctica Religiosa en México: Siglo XVI.* Editorial Juan, Mexico City (Colección Mexico Heróico No. 95).

Pendergast, David M.

1981 Lamanai, Belize: Summary of Excavation Results, 1974–1980. *Journal of Field Archaeology* 8:19–53. University of New Mexico Press, Albuquerque.

1986a Lamanai, Belize: An Updated View. In *The Lowland Maya Postclassic,* edited by Arlen F. Chase and Prudence M. Rice, pp. 91–103. University of Texas Press, Austin.

1986b Under Spanish Rule: The Final Chapter in Lamanai's Maya History. *Belcast Journal of Belizean Affairs* 3(1, 2):1–7.

1986c Stability through Change: Lamanai, Belize, from the Ninth to the Seventeenth Century. In *Late Lowland Maya Civilization,* edited by Jeremy A. Sabloff and E. Wyllys Andrews V, pp. 223–249. University of New Mexico Press, Albuquerque.

Scholes, France V., Carlos R. Menéndez, J. Ignacio Rubio Mañe, and Eleanor B. Adams (editors)

1936–1938 *Documentos para la Historia de Yucatán.* 3 vols. Compañía Tipográfica Yucateca, Merida.

Shanks, Michael, and Christopher Tilley

1987 *Social Theory and Archaeology.* University of New Mexico Press, Albuquerque.

Thomas, David Hurst

1989 Columbian Consequences: The Spanish Borderlands in Cubist Perspective. In *Columbian Consequences,* vol. 1, *Archaeological and Historical Perspectives on the Spanish Borderlands West,* edited by David Hurst Thomas, pp. 1–14. Smithsonian Institution Press, Washington, D.C.

Van Oss, Adriaan C.

1986 *Catholic Colonialism, A Parish History of Guatemala, 1524–1821.* Cambridge University Press, Cambridge.

Warren, J. Benedict

1985 *The Conquest of Michoacan, The Spanish Domination of the Tarascan Kingdom in Western Mexico, 1521–1530.* University of Oklahoma Press, Norman.

White, Christine

1988 The Ancient Maya from Lamanai, Belize: Diet and Health over 2,000 Years. *Canadian Review of Physical Anthropology* 6(2):1–21.

White, Leslie A.

1987 *Ethnological Essays.* Edited by Beth Dillingham and Robert L. Carneiro. University of New Mexico Press, Albuquerque.

Chapter 16

David M. Pendergast

The Southern Maya Lowlands Contact Experience: The View from Lamanai, Belize

Introduction

The extraction of historical perspective from the earth once trodden by the ancient Maya has in many respects proved as difficult a task as the reconstruction of Maya life in the Precontact period. Nevertheless, excavations carried out in the southern lowlands in recent years have provided at least a moderate degree of insight into the impact of the Spanish arrival on Maya material and social culture. The archaeological evidence available at present is frequently unclear and often conflicting from site to site, as of course it is for the pre-Spanish period as well. Unhappily, this situation is compounded by the effects of frontier conditions in the Dzuluinicob Province (Jones 1989), which exacerbated the thinness of the documentary record that characterizes much of the Maya area. As a result, congruence between archaeological and ethnohistorical data, the great hope that fuels the excavator's approach to remains from the sixteenth and seventeenth centuries, is the exception rather than the rule. The nature of many of the problems that confront both archaeologist and ethnohistorian in attempting to develop an understanding of the Spanish period in the southern lowlands is set forth in Graham et al. (1989).

Although archaeological investigation of Spanish period sites in the southern lowlands is still in its comparative infancy, the work at Tipu (Graham, this volume) and Lamanai (Pendergast 1984a, 1986b) has begun to provide us with a sense of what shape the record is likely to take when it is augmented by the identification and investigation of additional historic towns. The messages conveyed by the data acquired thus far suggest, however, that far too many facets of the record will remain amorphous no matter how many Contact period communities we succeed in examining. As a result, Columbian consequences for the southern lowlands will almost certainly continue to find their fullest expression in the documents. Nonetheless, the many questions and the small number of answers that emerge from the Lamanai data give us a picture of the early Contact period more fully illuminated than it would be if the light were cast by the written record alone.

Lamanai at the Time of Spanish Arrival

Founded by or before 1500 B.C., the northern Belize site of Lamanai (Figure 16–1) survived the decline that afflicted most southern lowlands sites in the ninth century and came through the collapse with most of its political and religious structure intact and its population probably diminished little, if at all (Pendergast 1986a). Throughout the Postclassic, the community continued to flourish despite the decay and abandonment of most neighboring sites and the similar fate that befell Lamanai's ancient central precinct. By the early sixteenth century, settlement was concentrated in the southern third of the site with what was apparently a small satellite community near the northern limit of the ancient site.

Although our investigation of the terminal Postclassic and early Historic community at Lamanai was as thorough as anything short of complete dissection of the southern third of the site would permit, it remains impossible to provide a secure population estimate for the sixteenth century. It is beyond question that the peak figures of the seventh through the fourteenth century were not sustained through the Terminal Postclassic period, but the extent of population dispersion from the ancient center is impossible to determine. The principal difficulty in this respect, the impermanent nature of much of the late architecture, obtains in the Historic period as well. The slim documentary evidence suggests a community of about 72 souls in 1637 (Jones 1989:117, 310), but the date is too late to relate to the archaeological picture or to indicate the size of the precontact Lamanai polity.

Despite the community's dwindling size, its fortunes appear not to have waned appreciably in the last years before Spanish arrival. Importation from both Maya and non-Maya suppliers continued to be of importance to the end of the Prehistoric period, and local technological change was equally significant in maintaining and possibly even expanding Lamanai's terminal Postclassic economy. Chief among the late innovations were the emergence of a new ce-

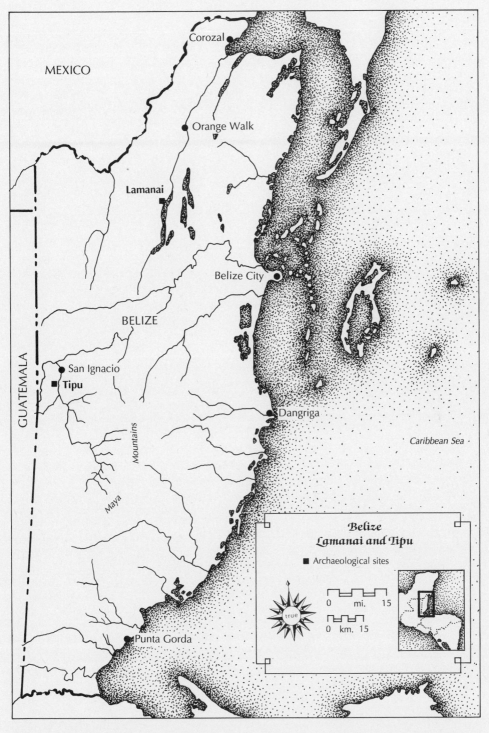

Figure 16–1. Map of Belize showing locations of Lamanai and Tipu, as well as modern communities.

ramic tradition, the Yglesias phase (Graham 1987:91–95), and the development of metalworking technology focused on the casting of large celts using material produced by melting down earlier artifacts. Data available at present do not document distribution of either metal objects or Yglesias pottery from Lamanai to centers farther north or to communities within Belize, but the potential for economically productive exchange clearly lay in both of these classes of material.

Although one of the better measures of Lamanai's Terminal Postclassic importance may be the Spaniards' view of the community in succeeding years (Pendergast 1986b:4–5, 1988), the latest noble burial at the site provides unequivocal evidence that wealth and power remained aggregated in the shrunken sixteenth-century surroundings. Although the tomb lacked the sheet gold objects of a twelfth-century interment of similar scale (Pendergast 1981:44), it contained metals, ceramics, and other goods in sufficient quantity to bespeak noble status in unmistakable form (Pendergast 1984b). With a date very probably later than A.D. 1525, the burial is quite likely to be that of the last pre-Hispanic ruler of Lamanai. Like the polity he ruled, he may have been trading a bit on the dimming glories of times long past, but his and the community's strength and status clearly rested on a foundation of continuing vitality and productivity.

The Effects of Spanish Arrival

The establishment in 1544 of an encomienda that may have encompassed Lamanai (Jones 1989:41–43, 301, 306) was probably followed quite quickly by Spanish contact with the community's inhabitants. Although the first European entrants to what is now Belize encountered numerous hardships, the dynamics of explorer–native contact appear not to have developed as they did in the American southeast and elsewhere. Partly as a consequence of this and perhaps partly as a reflection of the economic realities of the Yucatan Peninsula, neither the encomenderos and their minions nor the clerics, most probably seculars, appear to have found it necessary or desirable to dispense European goods in quantity. The need to establish relations with the Maya, to provide recompense to guides and porters, and to purchase other services seems to have been met in some manner that did not leave recognizable material traces.

One would hardly expect to encounter St. Augustine's profusion of European material (Deagan 1983:Tables 5.1–5.3) in the Maya towns and villages of a remote encomienda, but a kind of parity with peninsular Florida (Mitchem 1990), if anything a less economically attractive area than the Maya lowlands, might be expected. In fact, however, even the items that are plentiful in the American southeast generally range from rare to unknown in the extant archaeological record for the southern Maya lowlands. A principal difficulty in assessing the reasons for the comparative dearth of European goods is the fact that we have no information regarding the specific motivations behind the gifts of such material to Maya individuals. Furthermore, we have no means whatsoever of identifying the givers. The records for other times and places suggest that it would be almost equally easy to attribute the presence of most European goods either to political and economic maneuvering or to attempts at Christian persuasion. There are, however, some classes of artifacts for which both motive and—within limits—use can at least be postulated. Together with architectural, burial, and community planning data, such artifacts create a sense, albeit restricted and structured, of the consequences of Spanish presence for Maya economic, political, and spiritual life.

The Establishment of the Church

Erection of the first permanent religious edifice at Lamanai (Figure 16–2) followed the practice widely in use elsewhere in the Americas of superposing the Christian building on a native ceremonial structure. Superposition had the eminently practical aim of perpetuating precontact patterns of activity while supplanting one form of religious practice with another. At Lamanai, this entailed demolition of most of a small, fresco-decorated temple of probable fifteenth-century date and the raising of an earth platform around and over the remains as support for a structure that was partly of masonry and partly of perishable construction. In plan and probably in general appearance the structure closely paralleled the Tipu church, which appears to have been built some 20 to 25 years later (Graham et al. 1989:1256).

The ability of the Spanish to establish Christianity in substantial physical form quite early at Lamanai suggests that the new religion quickly made major inroads on precontact patterns of life at the site. It is probable, however, that the inroads were in truth limited by the fact that a single cleric, operating in the *visita* (circuit-riding) system made necessary by understaffing and the great distances between Christianized communities, brought Catholicism to Lamanai and initiated the construction of the church. As was probably to be expected in a frontier area, the building was a blend of Christian structural requirements and local construction techniques rather than the syncretic combination of Spanish and native techniques commonly found in the northern part of the peninsula (Benavides and Andrews 1979) and elsewhere in New Spain (Saunders 1990).

Far less grand than the temple it supplanted, the church surely had few exterior features other than its dimensions to distinguish it from precontact residences. Similarities with other early Historic period churches suggest that the form was a relatively standard peninsular accommodation between Christian precept and lowlands necessity. Variations in both exterior and interior features such as those that distinguish the Lamanai church from its Tipu counterpart were probably the products of differing abilities of friars as interpreters of the standard plan. In addition, the builders at Lamanai were confronted by bedrock outcrops that dictated unusual architectural solutions, just as they had done in precontact times. The constraints on the friar's time imposed by the visita system may have meant that the construction itself was overseen by a native manager, whose skills and experience added another element to the syncretic mix. Later events in the church zone obscured the history of the area north of the first church. It appears probable, however, that a precontact structure north of the church was converted to use as either a *convento* (religious residence) or a

Figure 16–2. The platform of the earlier church at Lamanai, in the foreground, with the chancel of the later church in the background.

bodega (warehouse). The first type of structure would have been a standard element in the ideal Spanish plan, but might have seen little use in a visita system. The second would also have been an expectable presence in a church complex and would presumably have been needed no matter how episodic a cleric's presence might have been. The presence of a moderate quantity of olive jar sherds at the rear of the structure suggests the warehouse identification, but scarcely makes such an identification irrefutable.

It would be reasonable to take the small size of the church, with a nave approximately 6 meters wide by 9 meters long, as evidence of a small number of parishioners. It is not certain, however, whether the building was designed to house all worshippers during Mass or intended as shelter only for a specific portion of the faithful. In the absence of documentary evidence for the period, we cannot be sure that the church is an architectural reflection of community size rather than a product of other concerns or even of limitations imposed by time, funds, and the cleric's skills.

As was true everywhere in the Maya area, syncretism was as much the mode in religious belief and practice as in church construction at Lamanai. At the start, it was given its finest physical expression in a small event that occurred during demolition in preparation for the construction of the church platform. Though nominally a Christian, one of the workers must have felt it necessary to copper his bets by appeasing the old gods for the destruction of their temple. Seizing a moment when no unwavering Christian could stay his hand, he opened a small hole at the ruined temple front and deposited a small bat effigy vessel (Figure 16–3b). This done, he presumably found it possible to immerse himself in Christianity while knowing that the safety net of ancient belief was stretched securely beneath him. In this drawing of the best from both worlds, most or all of Lamanai's inhabitants appear to have followed suit from the beginning to the end of Spanish hegemony and beyond.

Spanish Impact on Community Planning

The limitations imposed by isolation appear to have combined with Lamanai's distinctive precontact plan, the product of a lakeside setting, to prevent redevelopment of the community center along Spanish lines. In contrast with Tipu, where a fairly standard Spanish plaza was created out of the heart of the

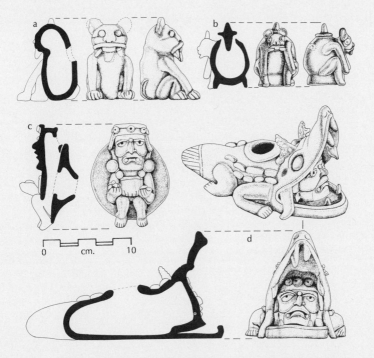

Figure 16–3. Maya ceramic figurines of the sixteenth and seventeenth centuries: *a* and *c* are precontact, *b* was interred during construction of the first church, and *d* is of a class that both antedates and postdates the Spanish presence. (Drawings by Louise Belanger)

precontact settlement (Graham et al. 1989:1256), Lamanai was given only the church and one or more related buildings as a sixteenth-century community focus superposed on the past. Topography in the church zone and the proximity of bedrock to ground surface would in any event have made creating a Spanish-style town center a near-impossible task. The labor force necessary for such an undertaking may have existed in the community and its neighboring settlements, but the Spaniards seem to have seen the effort as disproportionate to the return.

Lamanai had functioned in strip form in precontact times, and clearly continued to do so through the period of Spanish control. Whatever the nature of Spanish expression and exercise of secular authority, it must not have required the architectural definition of the town plaza. Hence, although its consequences for daily life may have been appreciable, Spanish hegemony would go undetected in settlement pattern were it not for the church itself. It is possible to conclude from this that the authority of the church was paramount at Lamanai, and that Spanish political and economic control was weakly defined at best. There is danger in such a reconstruction from planning evidence, however, because the community's early Historic period plan is the exception rather than the rule. It is more likely that the interplay of sacred and profane that characterized Spanish presence elsewhere in the lowlands was equally in evidence at Lamanai, but was given no physical expression for purely practical reasons. The lesson this provides in reading events from architectural data hardly needs underscoring.

The Consequences for Native Health and Diet

Although the visita system should have joined with native population movement to provide a means of spreading introduced diseases, the susceptibility of the Lamanai population to this range of the Spaniards' gifts is impossible to gauge at present. This is because the history of church development and use at Lamanai, coupled with the luck of archaeological sampling, leaves us without a solid basis at the moment for establishing a reliable mortality curve for the Spanish period. The church described above served as a burial site for at least part of the period, and it is from this context that all of the analyzed skeletal material comes. There was, however, a second cemetery, possibly of greater size than the one examined. Discovered at the very end of the excavation program, it remains to be explored. As a result, we cannot now compare the effects of European pathogens at Lamanai with those reflected in the extensive data from La Florida (Larsen et al. 1990), and comparisons with nearby Tipu are equally fraught with problems.

In the area of general population health, the Lamanai data are considerably more useful. Differences in the health profiles of Lamanai and Tipu suggest that a variety of factors structured the health consequences of the Spanish presence. Foremost among the bases for difference is probably the fact that Lamanai served as a center for reducciones throughout most of its colonial history, whereas Tipu remained a settled community into which reduced native population appears to have been introduced only on a small scale. Recurrent reducciones tended to destabilize a community's agricultural endeavor and also to impose heavy burdens on the subsistence activities of the permanent population. As a result, Lamanai may have found itself at a distinct disadvantage compared with Tipu, and indeed compared with its subsistence situation in precontact times.

Unfortunately, conditions for the preservation of food remains are even poorer in the near-surficial Spanish period deposits than they are generally in the Maya Lowlands. As a result, we cannot assess directly either the dietary impact of Spanish arrival on the native population or the degree of accommodation to native diet by the rarely present Europeans. The documentary evidence on this matter is, unhappily, almost as slim as the archaeological data base. It is beyond question, however, that the southern lowlands offered little opportunity to pursue traditional European subsistence strategies. I suspect that very little if any of the crop and import inventory documented for La Florida (Ruhl 1990) was enjoyed or even dreamed of at Lamanai or anywhere else in the southern lowlands.

Although the inhabitants of Lamanai should have suffered no Spanish disruption of the lake fishing and turtle collecting they had practiced since time immemorial, reducciones may have lessened the per capita protein intake, just as they stressed the agricultural subsistence base. Presumably the same would have held true for hunting, with the added difficulty of greater noise and activity in the bush to militate against the hunters' success. Very heavy dependence on large turtles (*Dermatemys*) is in evidence in middens of the Spanish period, but the pitfalls in any attempt to assess available protein per individual or residential unit are as numerous here as in any midden. The dietary disadvantage that Lamanai appears to have experienced is mirrored in a high frequency of porotic hyperostosis, an indicator of anemia, in the skeletal sample (White 1988), which contrasts sharply with the picture at Tipu (Cohen et al. 1989). Dental analyses currently under way appear to alter the picture somewhat, by suggesting less difference between Lamanai and Tipu as well as less of a decline in health at Lamanai during the Spanish period. In sum, although the Spanish introduction of disease and impact on general health are not open to question (Graham et al. 1989:1256), we are left at present with a range of possibilities from "catastrophic" to "relatively limited" in defining the magnitude of their consequences at Lamanai.

Later Church Construction and Its Significance

The first church probably served the needs of Lamanai and its Spanish controllers until almost the end of the sixteenth century. Early in the succeeding century, Spanish plans for the community must have undergone radical transformation, probably in the direction of increased service as a reduction center. One would not expect such a change to be reflected in domestic architecture, for individuals and families brought to Lamanai in reducción campaigns were surely given housing of which no traces are likely to remain. The change is, however, manifested by a new church of far greater size (Graham et al. 1989:1256, Figure

2), placed just north of its unpretentious predecessor (Figure 16–2). It is not possible to determine whether the church was built in contemplation of a greatly increased body of parishioners or was a solution to problems already in existence, but the change in Lamanai's fortunes is nonetheless unmistakable.

The second church boasted a masonry chancel to which a pole and thatch nave was attached. In overall plan and in some details, the structure resembled the church at Ecab, built 25 to 50 years earlier, as well as others in the northern part of the peninsula (Benavides and Andrews 1979:16, Figures 18, 19). The resemblances suggest that, like its predecessor, the second church was one of many variations on a standard peninsular blend of Christian and local requirements. Unlike the first church, however, the later building exhibits wholly European characteristics in the surviving masonry portion. Fully cemented wall core, facings of undressed spalls and cobbles capped with the heavy plaster characteristic of Spanish period construction, and massive quoins at the chancel entrance all bespeak the tradition of the European rather than the Maya. Although it is conceivable that, as before, the work was supervised by a native, it is far more likely that Maya hands were given direction by a Spaniard. This in itself suggests a view of Lamanai's future in which Spanish influence might come to be more strongly felt than it had been over the first half-century of contact.

Whatever the hopes for Lamanai may have been, they began to ravel early in the seventeenth century and by 1638 had come entirely to pieces as the community joined a widespread revolt. In 1641, Franciscan Fathers Fuensalida and Orbita found the church and other buildings burned and abandoned (López de Cogolludo 1971:bk. 11, chap. 13; Jones 1989:214–224). The uprising signaled the end of Spanish influence at Lamanai, as it did throughout most of Belize until 1695 (Jones 1989:189–211).

The Aftermath of Apostasy

The disappearance of the Spaniards and of native sacristans who had frequently been the only representatives of Spain on the southern lowlands visita circuit (Cárdenas Valencia 1639) might be expected to have meant the death of Maya Christianity as well. Left behind as the Spaniards and their lieutenants withdrew were only local Mayas trained to carry on Catholic rituals and catechization (Peñalosa 1969:70), scarcely a real force for the preservation of Christian practice and belief in the face of apostasy. The archaeological evidence suggests, nonetheless, that elements of Christianity survived the uprising. The blend of Christian and ancient belief remained as it had always been, with the difference that syncretism was now overt and Maya practice, if not belief, was at the fore.

We were at first inclined to see evidence of post-rebellion Maya activity in the nave of the second church as a manifestation of apostasy. Erection of a stela, complete with the required substela cache, near the chancel entrance seemed to be evidence of the resurgence of precontact belief and a forceful statement of the rejection of Spanish Christian values. A small plastered altar near the stela and several offerings interred near the chancel front could also be taken to represent the reestablishment of ancient ways. This is especially true of the offerings because among other material they included pottery figurines (Figure 16–3) that represent a revival, or more probably a reemergence, of precontact material culture. Reconsideration of the evidence in the light of data from Tipu (Graham et al. 1989:1257) suggests, however, that the choice of location for the stela, altar, and offerings rested not on an attempt to repudiate Christianity, but rather on a continuing reverence for the church as sanctified ground. Although the chancel ultimately came to serve as a residence for a native family, it is clear that the lessons taught by Spanish clerics and their native assistants did not fall on deaf ears and continued to bear fruit long after the Europeans had departed.

The Spanish Impact on Native Material Culture

As I noted above, the quantity of European goods at Lamanai is small. It is, in addition, highly structured both in content and in context. In all of these respects, the picture at Lamanai parallels that at Tipu, although the inventories from the two sites exhibit a number of significant differences. Apart from the uncertainty regarding the motivation behind the importation of most goods, the slimness of the Lamanai sample of European material raises questions as to the overall material importance of Spanish hegemony in the southern lowlands. As we shall see, however, certain items in the inventory may give us insights into the nonmaterial Spanish impact, even if their distributions within the site do not.

Olive Jars and Other Ceramics. With the exception of fragments found in contexts disturbed by nineteenth-century British activity, the entire sample of olive jar sherds comes from the church zone and from lakeside refuse dumps immediately to its south. A considerable portion of the olive jar sherd sample lay scattered with other refuse over the surface of the community's second cemetery, situated between the rear of the second church and the lake. None of this distribution can be fixed in time within the century of Spanish influence, and the fact that most of the material consists of sherds without joins indicates that the material is redeposited. Redeposition or extensive disturbance is also indicated by the condition of material associated with the putative warehouse. In only one case, from the cemetery-area refuse, can a large part of a jar body be reconstructed. The distribution and condition of the material is probably best interpreted as evidence of the long-term reuse of a small number of jars. As a result, specific context is not necessarily a basis for interpreting building or area use, although it is surely significant that the olive jar sherds are concentrated in the church zone.

In comparison with many other parts of New Spain, Lamanai seems almost to have done without the products that are thought to have been contained in olive jars. The entire sample, which consists of 487 sherds, could represent no more than 40 to 60 jars, a seemingly minuscule number when spread over the full period of Lamanai's Contact period history. One possible interpretation of the small quantity is that it represents solely the importation of oil and wine for sacramental use, with an average of less than one jar of each every 2 years for the 80 years between 1544 and 1624. The amount of guesswork in such a calculation is readily apparent and makes clear the opportunities for any number of entirely different interpretations. In any event, the distribution of the sample argues for church-related use, and probably limits the range of possibilities as regards contents. The sample size shows that the jars and their contents were never among the major imports to the community. The fragmentary condition of the material suggests that extensive reuse, apparently never for domestic purposes to which the jars would have been well suited, followed the arrival of the jars at Lamanai.

If the olive jar sample is minuscule, the amount of other European ceramics recovered is almost microscopic. Columbia Plain small plates and shallow bowls are represented by just 47 sherds that are almost entirely from the cemetery refuse scatter, with a few from residential areas north of the church zone. A single green-glazed bowl base comes from near what appears to have been the principal Contact period residence (Pendergast 1985), Structure N11–18 (Figure 16–4), and floor surfaces of the building yielded two small sherds of Sevilla Blue on blue Majolica plus one of Sevilla Blue on white. The only other European ceramics consist of 11 sherds of what appears to be black-decorated Columbia Plain and four Sevilla Blue on blue fragments that came from a structure some distance north of the second church that may have been an important Contact period residence, but was too extensively disturbed during nineteenth-century British occupation to permit certainty regarding its history. Most structures that appear fairly likely to have been built or used between 1544 and 1638 yielded no Spanish earthenware whatsoever.

As is true of other classes of European material, sampling error may have skewed the frequency of Spanish tablewares at Lamanai slightly, but there can be no question that such imports were never of economic significance to the community. Even more strongly than in the case of the olive jars, the significance and use of the European pottery remain in question because the amount is so small. One logical conclusion is that Spanish wares were used only by Spaniards, who probably carried their mess kits from town to town and left behind only pieces broken by their user or a careless (and probably hapless) servant. It is equally possible that Spanish tableware was presented to community leaders as a mark of distinction, a kind of tabletop badge of office. If the first explanation is adduced, one has to envision Maya retention of fragments because of their association; if the second is chosen, one is forced to conclude that the Spaniards were extremely stingy.

Middens associated with N11–18 and with other structures quite likely to have been occupied during the Contact period make it clear that pre-Hispanic Yglesias ceramics continued in use throughout the time of Spanish presence. It would therefore have been very likely that any Spaniards resident at Lamanai for protracted periods would have found it both necessary and desirable to adopt locally made pottery for household use, as was the practice in St. Augustine (Deagan 1990:309). It follows that the tiny quantity of Spanish ceramics cannot be used as evidence that all Spanish presence at Lamanai was transient any more than it can document the period in which importation took place.

Figure 16–4. Structure N11–18, the principal Contact period residence.

Beads. Almost 90 percent of the sample of European glass beads comes from the midden associated with Structure N11–18 and from floor ballast surfaces within the structure. The fact that approximately 82 percent of the 46 specimens are Nueva Cadiz Plain and twisted suggests importation quite early in Lamanai's Contact period history. Both the date and the distribution of the beads open the door to several assessments of the significance of the material, no one of which can be given primacy over the rest. In this case, as opposed to other classes of European material, sampling error is moderately likely to have structured interpretation, and although the source of the error can be identified, no resolution of the problem is currently possible.

Dating appears to offer clearer evidence than does distribution, but even here there are two alternatives. If the dates commonly ascribed to the Nueva Cadiz type apply throughout the Yucatan Peninsula, it would be possible to conclude that all of the beads reached Lamanai as a single lot within the first decade of Spanish presence. Unfortunately, we have no way of knowing whether a stock of the beads was maintained in Merida or in Salamanca de Bacalar, the villa that was the control center for the encomienda of which Lamanai was a part (Graham et al. 1989:1255, Figure 1). Such a stock might have been paid out over a considerable period in return for favors, to validate the status of local authorities, or for countless other reasons. The beads would, of course, have had the same range of uses, although greater impact, had they been brought to Lamanai in a single lot.

The questions that surround the history of bead importation and use are diffi-cult to resolve, either by dating or by distribution. Although the beads come from a limited context, there is nothing in their association to indicate that they were originally one lot rather than individual specimens brought to Lamanai throughout at least the first half of the Contact period. Furthermore, their scat-tered distribution over floor ballast and particularly their presence in middens seems to belie the importance they presumably would have had on arrival at the site. It may be that a particularly striking kind of conspicuous consumption was the agency behind midden deposition, but this is hardly the stuff of which a real explanation of the beads' significance can be constructed. Therefore, although N11–18 was clearly the principal residence of the Contact period, it does not necessarily follow that the beads served to signify the rank or status of the structure's occupants. As we shall soon see, however, the conglom-eration of European goods on and around N11–18 surely does tell us some-thing about the importance of the building's residents in sixteenth-century Lamanai.

The matter of sampling error is worth noting because of the sharp distinction between Lamanai and Tipu as regards bead quantity and distribution. Beads are unknown in midden and other residential contexts at Tipu and are most common as necklaces that adorn burials of children (Graham and Bennett 1989:116). The use of beads as burial accompaniments is not in evidence at Lamanai, but because burials in the earlier church are uniformly adults it is clear that beads may be seriously underrepresented in the current sample. The appar-ent presence of a children's cemetery within a larger burying ground in the Apalachee (Jones and Shapiro 1990:502) suggests the possibility of a similar fea-ture in the yet-unexcavated second cemetery at Lamanai, and it is our hope that exploration of the possibility will ultimately resolve the question of whether the difference between Lamanai and Tipu is apparent or real.

Metal Implements and Other Objects. Apart from nails, which are widely dis-tributed in the Spanish period community but pose special problems because of the nineteenth-century British use of the area, all identifiable sixteenth- or seventeenth-century European metalwares come from either the church zone or Structure N11–18. The first context produced only two lockplates, and the sec-ond yielded implements in a quantity far from sufficient to have had any eco-nomic impact at Lamanai, as well as a small number of nonutilitarian objects. In this category, as in all others, one must conclude that importation had nothing to do with an attempt to impose European technology on the Maya, but rather was intended either to serve the Spaniards themselves or to repay native effort and provide material recognition of rank or status.

The implements, all recovered from floor ballast surfaces and exterior (proba-bly paved) areas of N11–18, comprise one or possibly two knives, what may be a wedge, several pieces of strapwork (including one pierced by several nails), and a single axehead. Taken together, they constitute less than one would expect in a household minimally equipped with European goods in many other areas of New Spain. Perhaps more than any other category of Spanish imports, the tools seem to give voice to the Europeans' guiding principle, which was that they gave in proportion to what they got—and in this region, one would judge, they got very little.

It is the lockplates and two objects from a floor ballast surface in N11–18 that broaden our picture of Spanish presence in some measure. Although the lockplate from the core of the platform that supported the first church has not yet been satisfactorily identified, it probably represents either a chest or some other European container. The other plate, from a stone alignment behind the second church, is of a more elaborate sort that would have adorned a chest of high quality. Though small for the purpose, the lock might have been part of a *vargueño*, the distinctive multicompartmented chest-on-stand. In either case, the complete container might have been something transported from community to community, but it is far more likely that the objects were meant to remain at Lamanai, perhaps to hold the items necessary for the Mass and other sacraments. Although their number is small, the lockplates suggest a fairly substantial evocation of Spanish hegemony, and perhaps of Catholicism, through furnishings.

The final items, though tiny, convey a message at least as important as that of the coffers. The two objects are single gilt leaves of two book hinges. They resemble in general the hinges on volumes illustrated by Penney (1967:Plates I, V, VIII) that range in date from 1401 to 1600. The illustrations suggest that surface mounting of hinges persisted until about 1600, after which concealment of hinges within the binding was characteristic. The elaborate decoration of the Lamanai specimens suggests surface mounting, and hence may indicate that one or more books reached Lamanai and remained there prior to 1600. Of course, two hinge leaves do not necessarily make a book, but they are reasonable presumptive evidence for retention of a handsomely bound tome at Lamanai, something rather unexpected in view of the paucity of other European goods and the obviously high value of such a volume. It is intriguing to think that the book might have been kept secure by a native sacristan or held by the community's leader as proof of his links with the European world, but one wonders whether the work's contents can have had any great importance other than as a near-mystical expression of distant authority.

Conclusions

Sixteenth-century Maya response to Spanish entry into the southern lowlands probably found expression in ways as varied as the histories of precontact communities. The strategies and techniques that permitted the endurance of some functioning centers up to the arrival of the Spanish made the Maya vulnerable and at the same time resistant to the physical and spiritual incursions that followed. One the one hand, the Maya saw the Spaniards as cruel, obdurate oppressors, and they responded with a variety of resistance techniques that ultimately culminated in successful rebellion. On the other hand, they saw in the Spanish religion a different but partly parallel view of the world and the cosmos that they could adopt and adapt to conform to their own value system. It is, or has been, the archaeologist's expectation that the drama of conflict and accommodation set forth in the ethnohistorical record would find reflection in evidence from the earth. The truth is, of course, that the reflection is there, but often so unclear that we cannot discern it.

The evidence now in hand suggests that Lamanai may in many respects be as flawed a mirror of Contact period events as any other single Spanish-controlled community would be. Although Lamanai and Tipu are but a tiny sample of the whole, the numerous contrasts between the two prime us to expect that the lessons learned in one excavation will not necessarily emerge from another. Yet Lamanai does tell us some fundamental things about the impact of the Spanish arrival on the Maya. It also informs us that a place of considerable importance in an area neither easily dominated nor readily productive may yield precious little evidence of its importance. Were it not for the second church, we would in fact probably feel safe in concluding that Lamanai lay at the far end of nowhere in Spanish thinking from beginning to end.

Although the European material record at Lamanai is, to put it kindly, quite thin, it is that very thinness which, as we have seen, permits some hesitant judgments regarding Spanish, if not native, uses for imported goods. The evidence makes it appear that the Spaniards never made a serious attempt to bring the wonders of European material culture to the southern lowlands. As people living beyond the pale, the Maya of Belize and their neighbors may have seemed worth changing only in the spiritual realm; the material investment for this purpose was not great, but even here the Spaniards stinted wherever possible. Otherwise they distributed their very limited largesse only where and when it was likely to bring good return on the money. The result was that they gave very little to the Maya overall, and nothing that supplanted traditional native technology. Where glass beads are found, there also are clay beads in equal or greater numbers. The bits of European crockery lie amidst masses of Maya ceramics, and the seemingly useful olive jars never made it to Maya households well supplied with locally made counterparts. The single axe is figuratively flanked by its stone cousins, and one can imagine a Spaniard learning to shave with an obsidian blade rather than suffering the dullness of his culture's solution to that ever-present problem. In these as in other respects that surely included eating habits as well as preferences, the Spaniard became part Maya just as the Maya became part Spaniard.

Every aspect of Maya–Spanish relations that is reflected in the archaeological record bespeaks mutual adaptation between two competing value systems, probably with more change on the Spaniards' part than they realized or would have been willing to admit. The greatest irony is that when the Spaniards found the people of Lamanai risen in rebellion and the community abandoned in 1641, they concluded that they had lost. The truth is that they had lost on the secular field but not on the spiritual. The events that followed the burning of the church show that although the Spaniards had clearly failed to Hispanicize the Maya they had succeeded, probably more fully than they realized, in Christianizing them.

Acknowledgments

The Lamanai excavations were funded by the Social Sciences and Humanities Research Council of Canada and the Royal Ontario Museum, with capital grants from the Richard Ivey Foundation (London, Ontario).

References

Benavides, Antonio, and Anthony P. Andrews
  1979 *Ecab: Poblado y Provincia del Siglo XVI en Yucatán*. Cuadernos de los Centros Regionales: Sureste. Instituto Nacional de Antropología e Historia, Mexico City.
Cárdenas Valencia, Francisco de
  1639 *Relación Historial Eclesiástica de la Provincia de Yucatán de Nueva España, escrito en el año de 1639.*
Cohen, Mark N., Sharon Bennett, and Carl Armstrong
  1989 *Final Report to the National Science Foundation on Grant 85–06785 Health and Genetic Relationships in a Colonial Mayan Population*. SUNY, Plattsburgh, N.Y.
Deagan, Kathleen A.
  1983 *Spanish St. Augustine: The Archaeology of a Colonial Creole Community*. Academic Press, New York.
  1990 Accommodation and Resistance: The Process and Impact of Spanish Colonization in the Southeast. In *Columbian Consequences*, vol. 2, *Archaeological and Historical Perspectives on the Spanish Borderlands East*, edited by David Hurst Thomas, pp. 297–314. Smithsonian Institution Press, Washington, D.C.
Graham, Elizabeth
  1987 Terminal Classic to Early Historic Period Vessel Forms from Belize. In *Maya Ceramics*, edited by Prudence M. Rice and Robert J. Sharer, pp. 73–98. BAR International Series, 345(i). BAR, Oxford, England.
Graham, Elizabeth, and Sharon Bennett
  1989 The 1986–1987 Excavations at Negroman-Tipu, Belize. *Mexicon* 11:114–117.
Graham, Elizabeth, David M. Pendergast, and Grant D. Jones
  1989 On the Fringes of Conquest: Maya—Spanish Contact in Colonial Belize. *Science* 246:1254–1259.
Jones, B. Calvin, and Gary Shapiro
  1990 Nine Mission Sites in Apalachee. In *Columbian Consequences*, vol. 2, *Archaeological and Historical Perspectives on the Spanish Borderlands East*, edited by David Hurst Thomas, pp. 491–509. Smithsonian Institution Press, Washington, D.C.
Jones, Grant D.
  1989 *Maya Resistance to Spanish Rule: Time and History on a Colonial Frontier*. University of New Mexico Press, Albuquerque.
Larsen, Clark Spencer, Margaret J. Schoeninger, Dale L. Hutchinson, Katherine F. Russell, and Christopher B. Ruff
  1990 Beyond Demographic Collapse: Biological Adaptation and Change in Native Populations of La Florida. In *Columbian Consequences*, vol. 2, *Archaeological and Historical Perspectives on the Spanish Borderlands East*, edited by David Hurst Thomas, pp. 409–428. Smithsonian Institution Press, Washington, D.C.
López de Cogolludo, Diego
  1971 *Los Tres Siglos de la Dominación Española en Yucatán, o sea Historia de esta Provincia*. Facsimile of 2nd ed. Campeche-Merida 1842–1845; Akademische Druck und Verlagsanstalt, Graz.
Mitchem, Jeffrey M.

1990 Initial Spanish—Indian Contact in West Peninsular Florida: The Archaeological Evidence. In *Columbian Consequences*, vol. 2, *Archaeological and Historical Perspectives on the Spanish Borderlands East*, edited by David Hurst Thomas, pp. 49–59. Smithsonian Institution Press, Washington, D.C.

Peñalosa, Joaquin A.
1969 *La Práctica Religiosa en México: Siglo XVI*. Editorial Juan, Mexico City.

Pendergast, David M.
1981 Lamanai, Belize: Summary of Excavation Results, 1974–1980. *Journal of Field Archaeology* 8:29–53.

1984a Excavations at Lamanai, Belize, 1983. *Mexicon* 6:5–10.

1984b The Hunchback Tomb: A Major Archaeological Discovery in Central America. *Rotunda* 16(4):5–11.

1985 Lamanai 1984: Digging in the Dooryards. *Royal Ontario Museum Archaeological Newsletter*, ser. 2, no. 6.

1986a Stability through Change: Lamanai, Belize, from the Ninth to the Seventeenth Century. In *Late Lowland Maya Civilization: Classic to Postclassic*, edited by Jeremy A. Sabloff and E. Wyllys Andrews V, pp. 223–249. University of New Mexico Press, Albuquerque.

1986b Under Spanish Rule: The Final Chapter in Lamanai's Maya History. *Belcast Journal of Belizean Affairs* 3(1&2):1–7. Belize College of Arts, Science, and Technology, Belize City.

1988 What's in a Name? Lamanai and Early Maps of Mayaland. *Rotunda* 20(4):38–42.

Penney, Clara Louisa
1967 *An Album of Selected Bookbindings*. Hispanic Society of America, New York.

Ruhl, Donna
1990 Spanish Mission Palaeoethnobotany and Culture Change: A Survey of the Archaeobotanical Data and Some Speculations on Aboriginal and Spanish Agrarian Interactions in La Florida. In *Columbian Consequences*, vol. 2, *Archaeological and Historical Perspectives on the Spanish Borderlands East*, edited by David Hurst Thomas, pp. 555–580. Smithsonian Institution Press, Washington, D.C.

Saunders, Rebecca
1990 Ideal and Innovation: Spanish Mission Architecture in the Southeast. In *Columbian Consequences*, vol. 2, *Archaeological and Historical Perspectives on the Spanish Borderlands East*, edited by David Hurst Thomas, pp. 527–542. Smithsonian Institution Press, Washington, D.C.

White, Christine
1988 The Ancient Maya from Lamanai, Belize: Diet and Health over 2,000 Years. *Canadian Review of Physical Anthropology* 6(2):1–21.

Chapter 17 ■

Anthony P. Andrews

The Rural Chapels and Churches of Early Colonial Yucatán and Belize: An Archaeological Perspective

The chapels and churches of early colonial Yucatán and Belize (Figure 17–1) represent some of the most important historical remains on this peninsula. Designed and administered by Spanish friars, and built and used by the Maya, they lie at the core of the initial process of acculturation that resulted in the Spanish domination of the culture and daily life of the newly conquered natives. These structures, often built with stone from Maya pyramids, became the new focus of the cultural and social life of native communities. They were the seat of indoctrination, in which the Maya were taught to shed their old ways and adopt the new, to give up their gods for the Catholic Cross, to learn a new language and the ways of a foreign culture. The chapels and churches were also the social hub of the communities, the locale for baptisms, weddings, fiestas, civic gatherings, and funerals. And, to complete the life cycle, the members of the community were often buried underneath these structures.

To the historian and archaeologist, these structures represent an important setting for the study of early colonial life, and of the process of acculturation.

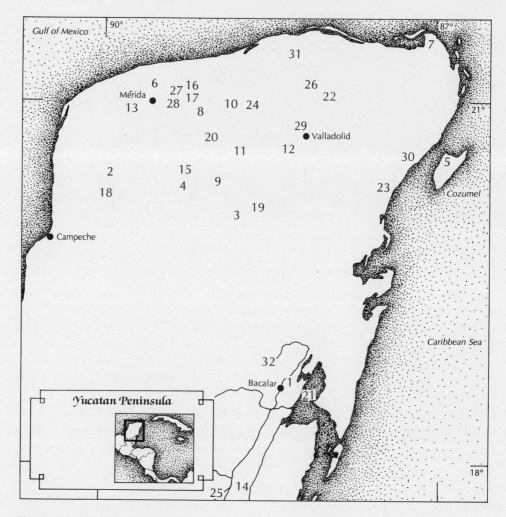

Figure 17–1. Map of the Yucatán Peninsula, showing the location of sites discussed in the text; numbers are keyed to Table 17–1.

As many of the surviving chapels and churches lie in rural areas, often on the frontiers of the Spanish domain, they also provide a context for examining the tensions that accompanied the acculturation process, the dynamics of cultural interaction on the frontiers, and the nature of the tenuous European control over the native Maya.

The study of these structures is still in its early stages, and the results to date are mainly of a descriptive nature. In this chapter, I discuss the results of past research, the typology of the known structures, and potential avenues for further study.

Early Missionary Activity in Yucatán

The Catholic missionization of Yucatán began with the arrival of eight Franciscan friars in 1544, during the final stages of the Spanish conquest. The Franciscans were the main evangelical arm of the church in the early Colonial period. They established the first convents in Campeche and Mérida in 1545 and began their missionary activities in the rural areas with the founding of a third convent in Maní in 1547. In the next three decades, convents were established at Valladolid, Izamal, Calkiní, Tizimín, Tekax Dzidzantún, Motul, Conkal, Homún, Hunucmá, Hocabá, Oxkutzcab, Sotuta, Tekantó, Chancenote, and Ichmul. The friars resided at these convents. Most of the convents included a private chapel (for the friars), a large thatched church for public religious rites and instruction of the doctrine, and in some cases, an infirmary.

From their convents, the Franciscans carried their religious activities to native communities throughout the rural areas, where they built dozens of chapels and churches. By 1580, they had established a presence across the peninsula, with outposts in what is now southern Campeche, Quintana Roo, and Belize, as far south as Tipú (for the history of early missionary activity see Carrillo y Ancona 1895; Clendinnen 1987; Farriss 1984; González Cicero 1978; López de Cogolludo 1957).

The process of conversion went hand in hand with the settlement programs of congregation and reduction. In the former, members of native communities were relocated in new towns laid out in Spanish grid fashion, around a main square with a church and civic buildings. The purpose of the reduction programs was to force refugees and natives from remote rural communities to resettle in new towns under Spanish control.

The process of missionization was most successful in the north and west of the peninsula, where the Spanish established a secure presence throughout the Colonial period. The regions to the far east and south were more difficult to secure. Even though missions had been established from northern Quintana Roo to Bacalar and Tipú in central Belize, they lacked a strong enough military and administrative presence to keep the frontier zone stable. At the same time, they suffered a shortage of friars. As a result, the area was increasingly neglected and became a haven for refugees from the north and west, while pirates roamed freely along its coasts. Military reduction campaigns along the Caribbean coast, in which thousands of natives were captured and forced to resettle, failed to stem the flow of refugees, or to discourage piracy. In the early seventeenth century, Maya resistance to Spanish rule became acute in the far southern regions of Quintana Roo and Belize, and by 1650 most of the eastern and southern mission outposts had been abandoned (Farriss 1978, 1984; Jones 1984, 1989). Some of the best-preserved examples of early rural religious architecture are found at these remote abandoned mission communities.

Past Research

Although the literature on the colonial architecture of Mesoamerica is quite extensive, the data on early Spanish religious construction in Yucatán are limited (most of the reports are listed in Table 17–1.)

One of the earliest and most successful efforts to record the religious architecture of Yucatán was carried out by a group of scholars in the 1930s; their report, the *Catálogo de Construcciones Religiosas del Estado de Yucatán* (Fernández 1945) contains architectural plans of hundreds of churches throughout the state. This useful catalog is primarily an inventory of churches that were in use at the time but includes a few early structures, all of which had been heavily modified. A few years later, Ralph Roys, in the course of his historic research for the Carnegie Institution of Washington, located and reported several abandoned sixteenth-century churches in the Yucatecan countryside; his reports include detailed historical data on the communities in which the churches were located, but the descriptions of the structures are brief and do not include architectural plans (Roys 1952).

Subsequent research on early colonial religious architecture was heavily influenced by John McAndrew's *The Open-Air Churches of Sixteenth-Century Mexico* (1965). Although the primary focus of this study was structures throughout Mexico, its detailed description of architectural features provided researchers in Yucatán with a large body of comparative data. To date, the only extensive study of colonial Yucatecan religious architecture is Miguel Bretos's *Arquitectura y Arte Sacro en Yucatán* (1987a; see also Bretos 1983, 1987b). Other useful sources include *Capillas abiertas aisladas de México,* by Juan Artigas (1983), which includes studies of several early churches in Yucatán, and *Maya Missions,* an illustrated guidebook to Yucatecan churches written by Richard and Rosalind Perry (1988).

Of particular interest to researchers have been the small rural chapels and churches of the sixteenth century, which have been reported at a variety of locations throughout the peninsula. Several of these have been the subject of detailed study.

Most of the early colonial religious structures reported in the Maya area were discovered in the course of archaeological surveys concerned primarily with the location of prehispanic sites. In Yucatán, the first such structure to be reported was the chapel of San Miguel de Cozumel, which John L. Stephens encountered in 1842. Unfortunately, Stephens only mentioned the structure in passing, and provided few details of its construction (1843:255–256); subsequent visitors added little information (William of Sweden 1922:96–97; Escalona Ramos 1946:560–610), and the structure was destroyed in the late 1940s or early 1950s.

The next structure to be reported was a ramada church at Lamanai in northern Belize, located by F. de P. Castells in 1902 (see Pendergast, this volume). At the time, the site was known as "Indian Church," and local mahogany cutters believed that the structure was an early Roman Catholic church; Castells, however, mistakenly argued that it was a Postclassic Maya temple (1904).

In the course of an archaeological reconnaissance in 1912, Raymond E. Merwin located an abandoned church near Chetumal in southern Quintana Roo. This structure, which lies in the midst of a large prehispanic and early colonial settlement on the western shore of Chetumal Bay, was reported as being near the ranch of San Manuel; Merwin's report provides a brief description and

Table 17-1. Selected Chapels and Churches of Early Colonial Yucatán

Locality	Type of Structure	Major Sources
1. Bacalar, Q.R.	Enclosed ramada church	Escalona Ramos (1943)
2. Calkimí, Camp.	Open ramada church	McAndrew (1965); Artigas Hernández (1983); Bretos (1987a,1987b)
3. Calotmul, Yuc.	Enclosed ramada church	Roys (1952)
4. Cauich, Yuc.	Undetermined	Roys (1952)
5. Cozumel, Q.R.	Ramada chapel	Stephens (1843); Williams of Sweden (1922); Escalona Ramos (1946)
6. Dzibilchaltún, Yuc.	Open ramada church	Folan (1970); Artigas Hernández (1983)
7. Ecab, Q.R.	Enclosed ramada church	Benavides Castillo and Andrews (1979); Andrews et al. (n.d.)
8. Hoctún, Yuc.	Open ramada church	Author's field notes (1988)
9. Hunacti, Yuc.	Enclosed ramada church	Roys (1952)
10. Izamal, Yuc.	UD ramada church	Fernández (1945); McAndrew (1965); Bretos (1987a)
11. Kanchunup, Yuc.	UD ramada church	Roys (1952)
12. Kava, Yuc.	UD ramada church	McAndrew (1965)
13. Kizil, Yuc.	Open ramada church	Roys (1952)
14. Lamanai, Belize ("Indian church")	Ramada chapel	Castells (1904); Pendergast (1975, 1981, 1984, 1986a, 1986b)
15. Maní Yuc.	Open ramada church	Fernández (1945); McAndrew (1965); Artigas Hernández (1983); Bretos (1987a, 1987b)
16. Motul, Yuc.	Open ramada church	Fernández (1945); McAndrew (1965); Bretos (1987a)
17. Muxupip, Yuc.	UD ramada church	Fernández (1945); McAndrew (1965)
18. Pocboc, Camp.	UD ramada church	Messmacher (1966); Artigas Hernández (1983)
19. Sacalaca, Yuc.	UD ramada church	Bretos (1987a)
20. Sanahcat, Yuc.	UD ramada church	Fernández (1945); Bretos (1987a, 1987b)
21. Tamalcab, Q.R. (also reported as San Manuel, La Iglesia, and Oxtancah)	Open ramada church	Merwin (1913); Gann (1926,1928); Escalona Ramos (1943, 1946); Bautista Pérez (1980); Artigas Hernández (1983); Jones (1984, 1989); Andrews and Jones (1987)
22. Tahcabó, Yuc.	UD ramada church	Fernández (1945)
23. Tancah, Q.R.	Ramada chapel	Miller and Fariss (1979); Miller (1982)
24. Tecoh, Yuc.	Open ramada church	Roys (1952)
25. Tipú, Belize	Ramada chapel	Jones and Kautz (1985); Jones et al. (1986); Graham and Bennett (1989)
26. Tizimín, Yuc.	Open ramada church	Fernández (1945); McAndrew (1965)
27. Tixcuncheil, Yuc.	UD ramada church	Fernández (1945)
28. Tixpehual, Yuc.	UD ramada church	Fernández (1945)
29. Valladolid Yuc. (San Bernardino de Sisal)	Open ramada church	Fernández (1945); McAndrew (1965); Bretos (1987a, 1987b)
30. Xcaret, Q.R.	Ramada chapel	Andrews and Andrews (1975)
31. Xlacah, Yuc.	Enclosed ramada church	Gallareta Negrón et al. (1990)
32. Xocá Q.R.	UD ramada church	Grant Jones (1988 field notes)

two sketches of the structure (Merwin 1913:2–4, Figure 1). A few years later, the church was visited by Thomas Gann; he provided a brief description and photographs of the structure, which he dated to the seventeenth century (1926:55–56, 1928:30–38). In 1937, the church was rediscovered by Alberto Escalona Ramos, who was unaware of the earlier visits of Merwin and Gann. He renamed the site "La Iglesia" and published a report and sketch of the building (Escalona Ramos 1943, 1946; see also Roys 1952:164). Escalona believed that this was the church built by Alonso Dávila at the prehispanic site of Chetumal in his campaign of conquest in 1531; Dávila's short-lived community was named "Villa Real de Chetumal." In a recent history of the region, Bautista Pérez (1980:65–67, 76) includes a more detailed map of the church and also asserts that it is the Dávila church of Villa Real. The location of the prehispanic site of Chetumal is a matter of some debate, and it is unlikely that the church of San Manuel/La Iglesia (also known as Oxtancah) was the structure built by Dávila, as he dismantled his church before leaving the area. Research by Grant Jones indicates that the church was the focus of the late sixteenth-/early seventeenth-century community of Tamalcab, which may have been located near the ancient site of Chetumal (Andrews and Jones 1987; Jones 1984:29, 1986:80, 1989:280–282).

The structure is a typical open *ramada* (thatched) church of the early colonial period (Figure 17–2). It consists of an arched chancel, or presbytery, flanked by two rooms, one a baptistry, the other a sacristy. This structure was built of heavy Spanish stone and mortar known as *mampostería*, and the rooms were covered with either a barrel vault roof, or a flat beam- and-mortar roof known as an *azotea*. The nave, a long open-thatched ramada, extended out from the chancel.

In 1955, E. Wyllys Andrews IV located a small early chapel at Xcaret, on the Quintana Roo coast opposite Cozumel (Figures 17–3, 17–4). It consisted of a simple rectangular structure with an apsidal end housing the altar; its mampostería walls supported a thatched roof. From historic documents, we know that this chapel was part of the sixteenth-century community of Polé, which was the main port of embarkation for Cozumel during prehispanic and colonial times (Andrews and Andrews 1975; Con and Jordan n.d.).

During the 1960s, two sixteenth-century structures were the subject of detailed reports. These include the ramada churches of Dzibilchaltún, in northwest Yucatán, and Pocboc, on the Camino Real in Campeche. The church at Dzibilchaltún (Figures 17–5, 17–6) was consolidated and restored by William Folan in 1962; the large open ramada nave was attached to a "T"-shaped masonry structure. The room on the south side of the chancel is missing; it was either never completed, or was of perishable materials. Near the church are the partly standing remains of a *casa cural*, or curate's residence (Folan 1970). The Pocboc structure, reported by Miguel Messmacher (1966), had a typical "T"-shaped layout, but the perishable ramada had been replaced by a masonry nave in the eighteenth century. This "T"-shaped layout of three masonry rooms with a perishable nave was a common design in sixteenth-century Yucatán (Figure 17–6; Benavides Castillo and Andrews 1979; Bretos 1987a, 1987b).

Two more early structures were reported in the decade that followed. An early chapel at Tancah, on the central coast of Quintana Roo, is the simplest structure

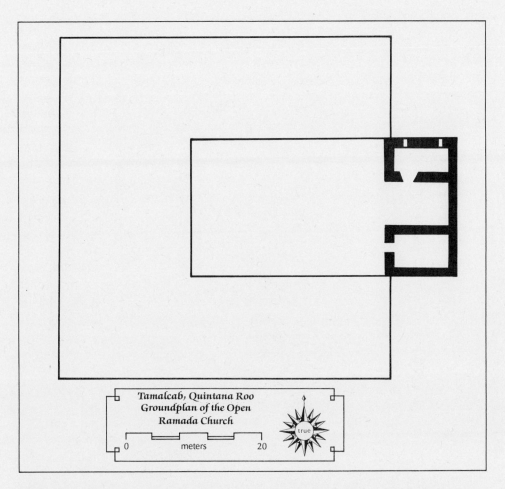

Figure 17–2. Tamalcab, Quintana Roo. Groundplan of the open ramada church, redrawn from Bautista Pérez (1980:76).

yet reported: a thatched chancel enclosed by three mampostería walls in a "half-hexagon" layout, from which extended an open ramada nave (Figure 17–3). This chapel was part of the early colonial community of Tzama, which later came to be known as Tulúm and Tancah (Miller and Farriss 1979; Miller 1982). One of the most impressive early churches on the peninsula is that of Ecab, a remote early colonial community near Cabo Catoche in far northeast Quintana Roo (Figures 17–6, 17–7). This building, which is well preserved, is a large "T"-shaped ramada church, with high barrel vaults over all three rooms. The nave, which had solid masonry walls, was covered by a large ramada. Nearby is a large curate's residence with five rooms; two of the rooms had large barrel vault roofs, one had a thatched roof, and two had flat azotea roofs. One of the vaulted rooms was a chapel for visiting friars (Figure 17–8; Benavides and Andrews 1979; Andrews et al. n.d.).

Recent studies have yielded information on several new structures, three of which have been excavated. At Lamanai, in northern Belize, the remains of an

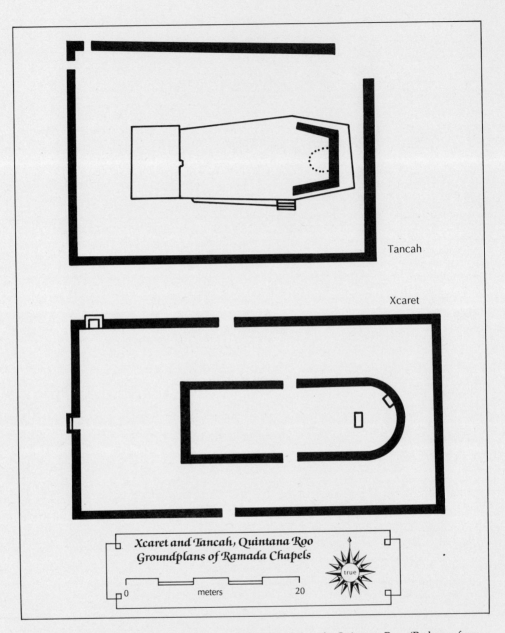

Figure 17–3. Groundplans of ramada chapels at Xcaret and Tancah, Quintana Roo. (Redrawn from Andrews IV and Andrews 1975:40; and Miller 1982:35).

early chapel and a later ramada church have been excavated by David Pendergast (this volume) and his colleagues. The ramada church is the structure originally located by Castells in 1902 (see above). The chapel, similar to those of Xcaret and Tancah, has a half-hexagon-shaped apse; the church displays the "T"-shape design of the churches of northern Yucatán (Pendergast 1975, 1981, 1986b) Further south, in west central Belize, Grant Jones and several colleagues have located the ramada chapel of Tipú, a Spanish frontier outpost of the early Colonial

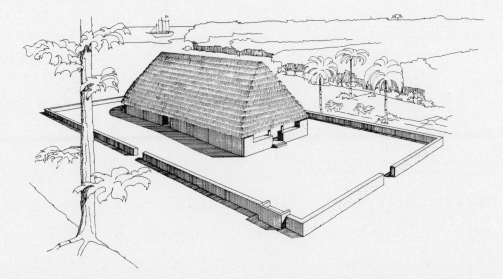

Figure 17–4. Xcaret, Quintana Roo. Restored perspective drawing of ramada chapel, by Gordon and Ann Ketterer. (From Andrews IV and Andrews 1975:39).

period. Excavations have revealed the design of this structure, which closely resembles those of Lamanai and Xcaret; the main difference is that both ends of the building show the half-hexagon layout characteristic of Tancah and Lamanai (Graham and Bennett 1989; Graham et al. 1985, 1989; Jones and Kautz 1985; Jones et al. 1986; Graham, this volume).

In 1988, two additional structures were briefly studied in northern Yucatán. One is located north of Panabá, in the northeastern part of the state. A typical "T"-shaped building, it had an enclosed nave and a couple of additional rooms on the north wing of the chancel. It is remarkably similar to the church at Ecab. The community in which this church lies has yet to be identified, although it may be the short-lived sixteenth-century village of Temul (Gallareta Negrón et al. 1990). The second structure, briefly mentioned in the 1945 *Catálogo*, is the early chapel at Hoctún, halfway between Mérida and Chichén Itzá. This building has a "T"-shaped layout and an open ramada in the front (author's 1988 field notes).

A third structure located in 1988 by Grant Jones and Richard Leventhal lies at Xocá, in south-central Quintana Roo. This is a small ramada church, but it is unclear whether the nave was enclosed or not (Jones, personal communication 1990). Xocá was a prominent town in the sixteenth century, and may have been the same town as Chablé, one of the communities visited by Alonso Dávila in his 1531 entrada (Jones 1989:278–279).

In 1989 and 1990, three projects to study early colonial sites were under way. These were all under the supervision of the Instituto Nacional de Antropología e Historia of Mexico. Fernando Cortés, Director of the Centro Regional de Quintana Roo, continued his project to restore the church at Tamalcab, north of Chetumal. María José Con and Craig Hanson conducted excavations at the church

Figure 17–5. Dzibilchaltún, Yucatán. Restored perspective drawing and reconstruction of west elevation of open ramada church, by Gordon and Ann Ketterer. (From Folan 1970:182)

at Xcaret, and have located several burials (Hanson 1990). Luis Millet is conducting a survey of the site of Tecoh, near Izamal, where Roys originally reported an early church. This site has several early colonial structures, and their eventual excavation should provide important data on this little-known community.

Typology of Structures

During the early Colonial period, hundreds of ramada chapels and churches were built across the Yucatecan landscape. Most of these were subsequently re-

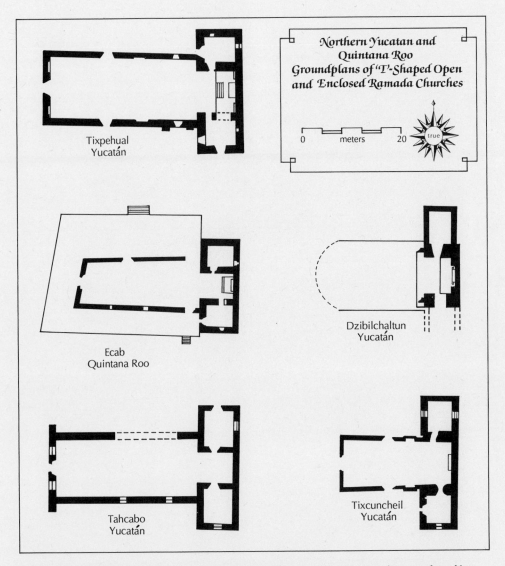

Figure 17–6. Groundplans of "T"-shaped open and enclosed ramada churches from northern Yucatán and Quintana Roo. (Redrawn from Fernández 1945; Folan 1970; and Benavides et al. 1979)

placed by more substantial masonry structures, and only a handful of the original ramada structures have survived. They are often referred to as "open chapels," following McAndrew's 1965 pioneering analysis of these buildings in various parts of Mexico. The unifying criterion for this designation has been the presence of a thatched roof over the nave. As Bretos has argued, however, this term is not appropriate for many of the early structures in Yucatán, as the naves of many of the chapels and churches were enclosed by either masonry or perishable walls (1987a, 1987b). Moreover, there is considerable architectural variation in these structures, both in terms of layout and size. Some of them (such as the ramada churches at Maní, Calkiní, and Ecab) had massive masonry

Figure 17–7. Ecab, Quintana Roo. Restored perspective drawing of enclosed ramada church, by Gordon and Ann Ketterer. (From Benavides Castillo and Andrews 1979:37)

cores, and the naves could accommodate several hundred people; it is difficult to think of them as "chapels."

Even the Spanish were inconsistent in labeling these structures. The massive ramada structures that abutted the sixteenth-century convents of Maní and Calkiní were known as *capillas de indios*, while many rural structures (such as those of Ecab, Polé [Xcaret], and Lamanai) were often referred to as "*yglesias*." In a preliminary attempt at classifying these early structures, Bretos has defined two formal categories: "*capillas de indios*," and "*capillas de visita*." The first are ramada structures that formed part of the earliest convents; these are quite large, and in some cases (e.g., at Maní) have a two- storied masonry vaulted choir balcony above the presbytery. The nave could have easily accommodated several hundred people. The second category, the capillas de visita, included all other free-standing rural ramada structures (Bretos 1987a, 1987b; see also Artigas Hernández 1983, for a similar dichotomy). This classification is useful for distinguishing between convent and rural structures, but it does not encompass the full range of architectural variation. Although a formal architectural typology of these structures may have to await detailed architectural studies, aided in many cases by excavation, it is nonetheless possible at present to define four main types of buildings: ramada chapels, open ramada churches, enclosed ramada churches, and undetermined ramada churches.

Ramada Chapels (Figures 17–3, 17–4). These include the small, simple rectan-

Figure 17–8. Ecab, Quintana Roo. Restored perspective drawing of the *casa cural*, by Gordon and Ann Ketterer. (From Benavides Castillo and Andrews 1979:38)

gular structures in which the chancel and nave form a continuous space under a thatched roof. Examples of these are the chapels at Xcaret (Polé), San Miguel de Cozumel, Tancah (Zama), Lamanai, and Tipú. In most cases, these were enclosed by mampostería or dry-laid stone walls on all sides. The apse of these chapels was enclosed by either a half-hexagon (e.g., Tancah, Tipú, and Lamanai), or a semicircular wall (Xcaret). Doors were set into the side and/or west walls. In some cases, for example, at Xcaret and Tipú, the side and west walls did not reach all the way up to the thatch, leaving an open space between the top of the wall and the ramada. At Tancah, only the chancel is walled; the remaining sides may have had a wall made of perishable materials, or may have been open.

This type of structure may have been a predecessor of the more elaborate ramada structures described below. This was clearly the case at Lamanai, where the ramada chapel was replaced by a larger structure with a solid masonry chancel and side rooms. In many cases, however, these structures may have been built to satisfy the needs of a small congregation, and their simple design may reflect the marginal nature of the community they were part of. They are all located in frontier zones—the Quintana Roo coast and Belize—and most of the communities were abandoned by the late seventeenth century.

Open Ramada Churches (Figures 17–4, 17–5, 17–9). This category includes most of the structures described in the literature as "open-air chapels." For the most part, these had a masonry chancel flanked by a baptistry and sacristy, with an open ramada nave facing the chancel. This was the typical "T"-shaped design discussed above, and the main distinguishing feature is the absence of a masonry wall enclosing the nave. Examples include the structures at Dzibilchaltún, Hoctún, Tamalcab, and the later church at Lamanai. This categorization does not preclude the possibility of a perishable wall around the nave. Such walls may been made of wattle and daub, thereby rendering a totally enclosed nave, or of a lattice of poles and sticks, which would have allowed breeze and sunlight into the structure (see Bretos 1987a:Figures 19–21, 23). However, the existence of these perishable walls may never be ascertained, even with the aid of archaeological excavation.

Enclosed Ramada Churches (Figures 17–6, 17–7). These structures are essentially the same as the above type, but differ in that the nave is enclosed by a masonry wall. The wall generally reaches up to the ramada roof, or rises part way; in the latter case, the wall may have been superseded by perishable materials that filled in the open area. The nave walls in these structures have one or more doorways and occasionally one or more windows. These structures also tend to be somewhat larger that the open type and may include additional architectural features, such as bell screens, ornamented doorway and window frames, and roof merlons. Examples of these structures include the churches at Xlacah, Calotmul, Hunactí, Ecab, and Bacalar.

Many of these structures may have originally been open churches; the walling in of the nave would have transformed them into enclosed structures.

Undetermined Ramada Churches (Figure 17–6). Many of the colonial masonry churches found in villages and towns across Yucatán were once ramada structures. The original chancel and flanking rooms are still preserved, but the ramada has been replaced by a later colonial masonry nave with a barrel vault, flat, or tiled roof. The problem is that there is no way of determining whether the original structure was open or enclosed; it may originally have been open, and later enclosed. Such a transformation has been documented by Messmacher at the church of Pocboc in Campeche, which was originally a sixteenth-century ramada church; the ramada was subsequently replaced by a masonry roof in the seventeenth or eighteenth century (Messmacher 1966). Other examples include the churches of Kanchunup, Sanahcat, Tahcabó, Tixcuncheil, and Tixpehual, all in Yucatán.

The large variation in size among the above types of structures can be explained by several factors. The large ramada churches of northern Yucatán were designed for the growing communities in which the Spanish were relocating the natives in a process known as *reducciones* (reductions); most of these towns retained stable populations during the Colonial period, a fact reflected in the conversion or replacement of many of the ramada churches with full-fledged masonry structures. In smaller communities, such as Dzibilchaltún, Xlacah, and Tecoh, where the population was in decline, the original ramada structures were eventually abandoned without ever having been modified. As noted earlier, the small chapels of Quintana Roo and Belize were designed for small communities acting as frontier missions of the Spanish domain; their populations were also dwindling, and most were abandoned in the seventeenth century. Still, the construction of large structures at remote sites such as Ecab, Tamalcab, and Lamanai

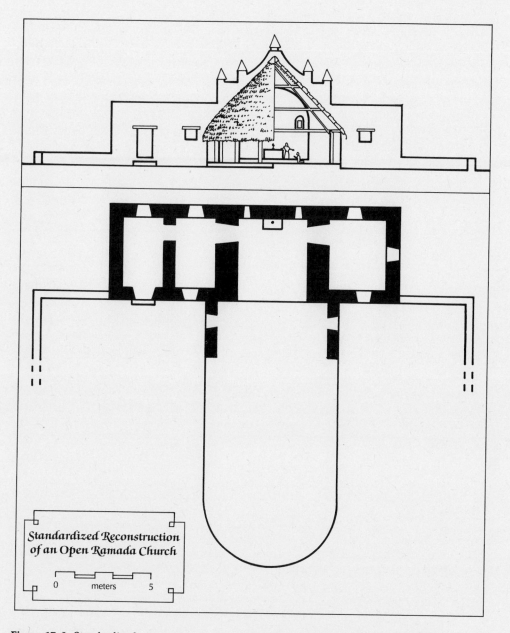

Figure 17–9. Standardized reconstruction of an open ramada church. (From Roys 1953:149)

(the second church) seems puzzling. As Jones (personal communication 1990) has suggested, these may have been designed with the expectation of congregating large populations around them, which never took place.

Chronology

The above typology would appear to be an evolutionary one, and in some respects it is. At Lamanai, for example, a ramada church replaced a ramada chapel, and many of the open ramada churches throughout the peninsula were converted into enclosed structures. At the same time, most of the structures discussed here were contemporary, so the different types do not represent an absolute chronological sequence.

Several Colonial period authors have noted that most of the religious structures of sixteenth century Yucatán were ramada buildings. Antonio de Ciudad Real, who accompanied Father Alonso Ponce on an inspection tour of Yucatán in 1588, reported that of the 22 towns they visited, 21 had ramada churches, whereas only 6 full masonry structures had been built—in Mérida, Campeche, Izamal, Valladolid, Dzidzantún, and Maní (Artigas Hernández 1983; Noyes 1932). Despite orders issued in 1583 that all churches were to be built of stone, most ramadas were not replaced with masonry naves until well into the seventeenth century (McAndrew 1965:519; Artigas Hernández 1983). We know from historic sources that most of the structures discussed in this chapter date to the sixteenth century. However, given the paucity of historic data, it is difficult to determine more precise dates of construction. Some of the structures were built shortly after the conquest; the ramada church of Maní, for example, was built in 1549 (Bretos 1987b:4). Most of the rural chapels and churches were built after the establishment of encomiendas in 1546. As most of the structures discussed here are listed in a 1582 catalog of churches of Yucatán (Scholes et al. 1936:Vol. 2), we know that they were built before that date. Thus, we can safely say that most of the structures were erected in the 36–year period between 1546 and 1582. The structures in northern Quintana Roo can be dated to between 1546 and 1571, a 25–year period.

During the late seventeenth and eighteenth centuries, most of the ramadas were replaced by masonry naves. Few ramada structures survived into the nineteenth century, and a only a few rare examples have been reported in the twentieth century (see Artigas Hernández 1983; Bretos 1987a; Fernández 1945).

Assessment of Past Research and Future Potential

The historical archaeology of Yucatán is still in an exploratory and descriptive stage (see Andrews 1981, 1985; Benavides and Andrews 1985). Most of the work conducted to date on the early religious architecture of Yucatán consists of surveys and architectural recording, occasionally accompanied by historical documentation of the communities in which the churches have been found. Detailed analysis of this architecture has been limited to the studies of McAndrew (1965), Artigas Hernández (1983), and Bretos (1983, 1987a, 1987b), which offer an informative overview of the history and evolution of Yucatecan religious architecture. Nonetheless, we are dealing with a body of data that is fragmented and primarily descriptive; much still remains to be done. Many historically known structures have yet to be located, and future surveys will undoubtedly yield many new buildings. However, more intensive research needs to be conducted at individual sites. For example, many architectural details can only be ascertained through excavations, which can also yield chronological data that are not available from the historical record. Furthermore, as the few excavations have shown, there is a wealth of data to be had from artifacts and burials.

So far, excavations have been carried out at only three sites—Tancah, Tipú, and Lamanai—and while the results are not yet fully reported at the latter two sites, it is clear that such efforts are very productive. The excavations led to detailed plans of the structures, exposing many important architectural features. In the case of Tipú, it was only through excavation that the church was identified, thereby confirming the location of the site.

The artifacts recovered from the excavations are also valuable sources of information on past activities. At all three sites, the excavations yielded evidence of native Maya rituals carried out within the structures, raising important questions about Maya-Christian religious synchretism, and resistance to the Catholic faith. Moreover, large cemeteries or *camposantos*, which are almost always associated with these buildings, have been uncovered at all three sites and have yielded the largest early colonial burial samples in the Maya area. The analyses of these remains are yielding data on mortuary practices, physical characteristics, Maya—Spanish racial mixing, population structure, diet, and disease, which will tell us much about daily life in these communities.

Future work at early colonial sites in Yucatán might be approached in several ways. In the area of survey, the location of early religious structures will play a critical role in identifying certain sites. For example, two early colonial communities on the Quintana Roo coast—Conil on the north coast, and Nuestra Señora de la Limpia Concepción on Espiritu Santo Bay—have yet to be located. From historic sources, we know they had religious structures, probably ramada chapels; confirmation of the identity of these sites will hinge to a large extent on the location of the chapels. In northern Belize and southern Quintana Roo, a number of historically documented communities have yet to be located (Jones 1989:277–291); some of these had chapels, the location of which would enable researchers to identify the communities. Some of these chapels may not be easily identifiable, and, as was the case at Tipú, excavations may be necessary.

As the results from Tancah, Tipú, and Lamanai demonstrate, excavations can yield important data on religious and mortuary practices, as well as information about the physical characteristics of the population of the community. Future research projects should note the likely presence of large quantities of burials under and around these structures and should plan accordingly; excavation teams should include a physical anthropologist with experience in osteological excavation and recovery.

As many of the structures discussed here are located in communities that were abandoned early in the Colonial period, future excavations will likely focus on other structures and features at these sites. Some work along these lines has already been carried out at Tipú and Lamanai, with informative results (Graham and Bennett 1989; Pendergast 1984, 1986a, 1986b). We know very little about the daily life of early colonial Maya communities, and many of the sites discussed above offer excellent laboratories for this type of research, given their undisturbed condition. Research on settlement patterns and households will likely be among the top priorities as we develop a more holistic community-wide research strategy at these sites. Only through a broader approach will we begin to uncover the more subtle patterns of community life, and their significance in the larger processes of acculturation.

Acknowledgments

Grant Jones generously allowed me to include unpublished data from his work, and he, David Pendergast, David H. Thomas, and Mary Andrews offered valuable suggestions in the preparation of this manuscript, for which I am most grateful.

References

Andrews, Anthony P.
  1981 Historical Archaeology in Yucatán: A Preliminary Framework. *Historical Archaeology*, 15(1):1–18.
  1985 La arqueología histórica en el Area Maya. *Revista Mexicana de Estudios Antropológicos*, 31:9–14.
Andrews, Anthony P., and G. D. Jones
  1987 Sitios coloniales en la costa de Quintana Roo. *XX Mesa Redonda de la Sociedad Mexicana de Antropología* (Mexico 1987), in press.
Andrews, Anthony P., A. Benavides Castillo, and G. D. Jones
  n.d. Ecab: A Remote Encomienda of Early Colonial Yucatán. Ms.
Andrews, E. Wyllys IV, and A. P. Andrews
  1975 *A Preliminary Study of the Ruins of Xcaret, Quintana Roo, Mexico*. Middle American Research Institute, Publication No. 40. Tulane University, New Orleans.
Artigas Hernández, Juan B.
  1983 *Capillas Abiertas aisladas de México*. Universidad Nacional Autónoma de México, Mexico.
Bautista Pérez, Francisco
  1980 *Chetumal*. Tomo I. Chetumal.
Benavides Castillo, Antonio, and A. P. Andrews
  1979 *Ecab: Poblado y Provincia del Siglo XVI en Yucatán*. Cuadernos de los Centros Regionales. I.N.A.H., Mexico.
Benavides Castillo, Antonio, and A. P. Andrews (editors)
  1985 Arqueología Histórica en el Area Maya. *Revista Mexicana de Estudios Antropológicos*, 31. Sociedad Mexicana de Antropología, Mexico.
Bretos, Miquel A.
  1983 Yucatán: Franciscan Architecture and the Spiritual Conquest. In *Franciscan Presence in the Americas*, edited by F. Morales, pp. 393–420. Academy of American Franciscan History, Potomac, Md.
  1987a *Arquitectura y Arte Sacro en Yucatán*. Editorial Dante, Merida.
  1987b Capillas de Indios Yucatecas del Siglo XVI: Notas sobre un complejo formal. *Cuadernos de Arquitectura de Yucatán*, 1:1–12. Facultad de Arquitectura, Universidad Autónoma de Yucatán, Mérida.
Carrillo y Ancona, Crescencio
  1895 *El Obispado de Yucatán. Historia de su fundación y de sus obispos*. 2 vols. Mérida.
Castells, F. de P.
  1904 The Ruins of Indian Churches in British Honduras. *American Antiquarian and Oriental Journal* 26(2):32–39.
Clendinnen, Inga

1987 *Ambivalent Conquests: Maya and Spaniard in Yucatán, 1517–1570.* Cambridge University Press, Cambridge.

Con, María José, and E. Jordan D.
n.d. Polé: notas sobre un puerto maya. Ms.

Escalona Ramos, Alberto
1943 Algunas construcciones de tipo colonial en Quintana Roo. *Anales del Instituto de Investigaciones Estéticas* 3(10):17–40. Universidad Autónoma de México, Mexico.
1946 Algunas ruinas prehispánicas en Quintana Roo. *Boletín de la Sociedad Mexicana de Geografía y Estadística* 61(3):513–628.

Farriss, Nancy M.
1978 Nucleation vs. Dispersal: The Dynamics of Population Movement in Colonial Yucatán. *Hispanic American Historical Review* 58(2):187–216.
1984 *Maya Society under Colonial Rule.* Princeton University Press, Princeton, N.J.

Fernández, Justino (editor)
1945 *Catálogo de Construcciones Religiosas del Estado de Yucatán.* Texts by J. I. Rubio Mañé, L. Vega Bolaños, J. García Preciat, and A. Barrera Vásquez. 2 vols. Talleres Gráficos de la Nación, Mexico.

Folan, William J.
1970 *The Open Chapel of Dzibilchaltún, Yucatán.* Middle American Research Institute, Publication No. 26. Tulane University, New Orleans.

Gallareta Negrón, Tomás, A. P. Andrews, and P. J. Schmidt
1990 A 16th Century Church at Xlacah, Panaba, Yucatán. *Mexicon* 12:33–36.

Gann, Thomas
1926 *Ancient Cities and Modern Tribes.* Duckworth, London.
1928 *Maya Cities.* Duckworth, London.

González Cicero, Stella María
1978 *Perspectiva Religiosa en Yucatán, 1517–1571.* El Colegio de México, Mexico.

Graham, Elizabeth, and S. Bennett
1989 The 1986–1987 Excavations at Negroman-Tipu, Belize. *Mexicon* 11(6):114–117.

Graham, Elizabeth, G. D. Jones, and R. R. Kautz
1985 Archaeology and Ethnohistory on a Spanish Colonial Frontier: An Interim Report on the Macal-Tipu Project in Western Belize. In *The Lowland Maya Postclassic*, edited by A. F. Chase and P. M. Rice, pp. 206–214. University of Texas Press, Austin.

Graham, Elizabeth, D. M. Pendergast, and G. D. Jones
1989 On the Fringes of Conquest: Maya–Spanish Contact in Colonial Belize. *Science* 246(4935):1254–1259.

Hanson, Craig A.
1990 The Spanish Chapel at Xcaret, Quintana Roo, Mexico. Ms., Middle American Research Institute, Tulane University, New Orleans.

Jones, Grant D.
1984 Maya–Spanish Relations in Sixteenth Century Belize. *Belcast Journal of Belizean Affairs* 1(1):28–40.
1986 The Southern Maya Lowlands during Spanish Colonial Times. *Handbook of Middle American Indians*, Supplement, vol. 4:71–87. University of Texas Press, Austin.
1989 *Maya Resistance to Spanish Rule. Time and History on a Colonial Frontier.* University of New Mexico Press, Albuquerque.

Jones, Grant D., and R. R. Kautz
1985 Arqueología e Historia de una Frontera Española Colonial: El Proyecto Macal-Tipú en el Oeste de Belize. *Revista Mexicana de Estudios Antropológicos* 31:145–154.

Jones, Grant D., R. R. Kautz, and E. A. Graham
1986 Tipu: A Maya Town on the Spanish Colonial Frontier. *Archaeology* 39(1): 40–47.

López de Cogolludo, Diego
1957 *Historia de Yucatán.* Prólogo, Notas y Acotaciones de J.I Rubio Mañé. 2 vols. 5th ed. Mexico. Originally published 1688.

McAndrew, John
1965 *The Open-Air Churches of Sixteenth-Century Mexico*. Harvard University Press, Cambridge.

Merwin, Raymond E.
1913 *The Ruins of the Southern Part of the Peninsula of Yucatán, with Special Reference to Their Place in Maya Culture*. Unpublished Ph.D. Thesis, Harvard University, Cambridge.

Messmacher, Miguel
1966 Capilla abierta en el Camino Real de Campeche. *Boletín I.N.A.H.* 24:13–21. I.N.A.H., Mexico.

Miller, Arthur G.
1982 *On the Edge of the Sea: Mural Painting at Tancah-Tulum*. Dumbarton Oaks, Washington, D.C.

Miller, Arthur G., and N. M. Farriss
1979 Religious Synchretism in Colonial Yucatán: The Archaeological and Ethnohistorical Evidence from Tancah, Quintana Roo. In *Maya Archaeology and Ethnohistory*, edited by N. Hammond and G. R. Willey, pp. 223–240. University of Texas Press, Austin.

Noyes, Ernest
1932 *Fray Alonso de Ponce in Yucatán, 1588*. (Report written by Antonio de Ciudad Real, translated and annotated by E. Noyes). Middle American Research Institute, Publication No. 4. Tulane University, New Orleans.

Pendergast, David M.
1975 The Church in the Jungle: the ROM's First Season at Lamanai. *Rotunda* 8:32–40.
1981 Lamanai, Belize: Summary of Excavation Results, 1974–1980. *Journal of Field Archaeology* 8(1):29–53.
1984 Excavations at Lamanai, Belize, 1983. *Mexicon* 6(1):5–10.
1986a Historic Lamanay: Royal Ontario 1985 Excavations at Lamanai, Belize. *Mexicon* 8(1):9–13.
1986b Under Spanish Rule: The Final Chapter in Lamanai's Maya History. *Belcast Journal of Belizean Affairs* 3(1–2):1–7. Belize.

Perry, Richard, and R. Perry
1988 *Maya Missions. Exploring the Colonial Churches of Yucatán*. Espadaña Press, Santa Barbara, Calif.

Roys, Ralph L.
1952 *Conquest Sites and the Subsequent Destruction of Maya Architecture in the Interior of Yucatán*. Carnegie Institution of Washington, Publication No. 596. Washington, D.C.

Scholes, France V., C. R. Menéndez, J. I. Rubio Mañé, and E. B. Adams (editors)
1936–1938 *Documentos para la Historia de Yucatán*. 3 vols. Cia. Tipográfica Yucateca, Mérida.

Stephens, John L.
1843 *Incidents of Travel in Yucatán*. 2 vols. Harper & Brothers, New York.

William, Prince of Sweden
1922 *Between Two Continents*. E. Nash and Grayson, London.

Chapter 18 ■

Murdo J. MacLeod

Indian Riots and Rebellions in Colonial Central America, 1530–1720: Causes and Categories

Human geography played a significant part in the different indigenous responses to Spanish rule in Spanish America. The Audiencia de Guatemala, with its seat in Santiago de los Caballeros, stretched from Tehuantepec's border with Chiapas to the western borders of Panama, but its core was very much a mountain and Pacific unit. Yucatan belonged to another jurisdiction, and the Caribbean zones, stretching down from the Petén and Belize along the Caribbean coasts of Honduras, Nicaraguan Mosquitía, and Costa Rica, were interrupted by only a few tiny Spanish corridors to the Caribbean. In colonial Central America, all of these settled areas faced open frontiers and "unreduced" peoples all the way from Belize to Talamanca.

Colonial Resistance

The study of the colonial Indian, now ethnohistorical in large part, has changed in emphasis in recent years. From a perspecitve that stressed Spanish oppression and its effects—the Indians as they were acted upon—the new scholarship has swung to a dialectic in which the two groups act upon another, against one another, with one another, and even at times, autonomously (Stern 1988; Jones 1989).[1] Indeed, reading the new research, one is sometimes led to wonder who won, such is the emphasis on Indian success at resisting and surviving colonial rule.[2]

Part of this new emphasis on Indian reaction and action has been the result of increased research on Indian revolts. One might even say there has been an overemphasis on revolts, not only in Spanish American studies but in all studies of colonial situations (e.g., Katz 1988; Stern 1987). Such uprisings are dramatic, romantic, heroic, and usually well-documented struggles for greater justice. What few scholars care to reflect upon is that rebellions are only one form of resistance to exploitation. If resistance in its many forms is thought of as a continuum, the rebellions are only one end of that continuum, and not often a very impressive end as far as the results are concerned. Revolts by peasants and by conquered peoples mean poor and unorganized leadership. Lacking cohesive direction, rebels frequently drift away and revolts fail, bringing retribution for the survivors and a renewal of colonial oppression. Far more important, if one wants to understand Indian life and survival, are the quieter, daily forms of resistance, little known to the scholar but of great importance to the Indian. It is these "weapons of the weak," tiny in themselves but cumulatively of great importance, that helped conquered oppressed peoples to survive, certainly far more than dramatic rebellions did (Farriss 1984; Isaacman 1988; Scott 1985). Rebellions are brought on by desperation where daily resort to the weapons of the weak has failed or by calculations, usually miscalculations, of the subordinate peoples that the oppressors and their government have become weak, distracted, or riven by internal conflict. (The last case is unusual because such conflict is seldom perceived, or even misperceived, by conquered peoples.)

Two examples of daily quiet resistance will suffice here. After all, this essay is about the rebellions that I have just depreciated. Time and again, colonial administrators noted that nuclear villages had dispersed and ended up in *rancherías* or scattered settlement patterns. Many modern researchers have assumed that this demographic act of scattering is related to surviving precolumbian settlement patterns or to land hunger in the face of growing cattle and *hacienda* intrusions. Yet the demographic facts strongly support the idea that dispersal was a form of resistance. The period after the demographic disaster caused by the European invasions up to about 1700 was one of low rural population, and in many parts of Central America, such as Chiapas, the Cuchumatanes, Verapaz, much of Honduras, and central Costa Rica, there were few cattle or Spanish would-be *hacendados* to intrude. So the villagers who moved to distant *milpas* were seldom reacting to land hunger and demographic pressure, or to intrusions by Spanish-owned farms. And, as many cases seem to show, these migrants were not making economically or communally rational choices, at least not on the surface of things. They placed themselves away from easy routes of communication and central village markets, making it harder to sell their tiny surpluses and buy what they needed. They also placed themselves in a cultural dilemma. They relied on the village for identity, solidarity, ceremony, and to some extent for protection against intrusive forces, yet they fled it. Why did they make these economically, demographically, agriculturally, logistically, and culturally unproductive migrations? They were avoiding the colonial head counter, the tribute collector, and the confiscatory priest, merchant, or colonial official. Some of them in Chiapas lived two days' walk from their primary village, marketplace, and fiesta of allegiance, although vacant land was available near it.[3]

Another example is the colonial Indian *cofradía*. Implemented by the Spaniards on a Spanish model, supervised by the local parish priest, often used by the *párroco* and by other local Spaniards as a way of extracting some cash and produce, becoming an institution that cost Indians large sums of money for masses, fiestas, feasts, and processions, it was nevertheless, at least at some times and places, welcomed by Indians. Spanish officialdom and high clerics often complained of excesses of enthusiasm in the Indian cofradías, of proliferation in their numbers, and of the amount of money expended in ceremonies (Pardo 1978:chap. 6). Here, too, was an institution that some Indians were able to turn to their advantage. At least these extravagances were spent within the villages. But at a higher level Indians perceived an unwritten contractual exchange. Priests and officials were able to obtain cash and produce from the cofradías, which in exchange were able to obtain some cultural and religious autonomy, or at least a modicum of control of their ritual lives (MacLeod 1983; Meyers and Hopkins 1988).

Colonial Violence

Why then study revolts? There are two main groups of reasons. The historian's view of colonial Indian society comes to him or her through a heavy filter. The main source is documents written in Spanish by Spaniards, documents, moreover, that have Spanish priorities, perceptions and misperceptions, and that cannot reply to cross-questioning. Indian voices are often muffled as they come to us, and both Indians and Spaniards prevaricate on sensitive matters, as people do today. As a result, the ethnologist must look for corroborated accumulations on what then seemed minor matters, using the general proposition that people, even reluctant witnesses speaking to their oppressors, are less likely to lie about matters that are of little importance to them.

Revolts are of all-consuming interest to participants and to those who try to suppress them. They are followed by self-justificatory, detailed investigations and often by criminal trials against selected participants. These trials set out in general to defend colonial rule, to cast the blame on the rebels, to obtain Indian agreement that Spanish government and religion were right and that the rebels were wrong. Because of the intensity of the scrutiny of individuals' lives and the concentration on one subject—the revolt and the events and motivations of which it was composed—both Indians and Spaniards produce detailed comments on their daily actions and lives, often about things mutually understood but not normally mentioned in official documents. To divert Spanish attention from dubious activities, Indians talk frankly and fully about nondangerous matters: "I was there doing this and that and my wife and children were somewhere else doing something else." In short, details of material life emerge in the contemporary accounts of revolts. Also, to a much smaller but even more revealing extent, revolts produce the rare defiant witness whose frank testimony is reluctantly recorded and sometimes distorted by the *escribano*. One tack often taken by defiant and frank witnesses is to justify the revolt and their own activities in it by describing local legal infractions by Spaniards in the appeal to higher temporal or spiritual authorities.

Another reason for taking a fresh look at revolts is that in general, but especially in colonial Central America, these few and generally unsuccessful types of resistance have been treated too simply. Every such event—whether a fistfight between two *caciques*, a rock-throwing and window-smashing spree by anonymous and resentful night prowlers, murders and mayhem in a village, or a large uprising of 20 or more villages lasting almost a year—has been classified as a revolt (Martínez Peláez 1974). Such inclusiveness obscures our view of Indian society. It masks the nuances of Indian social structure, discontent, and changes over time, the very details which the ethnographer seeks. So violent incidents and revolts themselves need to be categorized if they are to be accurately depicted and useful to us.

One must begin with various dubious categories. Many so-called revolts were rationalizations for Spanish activities, especially in frontier zones where local Spaniards needed excuses for having attacked unconquered or refugee groups across the frontier. At times, the Spanish were responding to the Indian attacks or making certain there would be no threat of Indian attacks; at others, the Spanish or the clergy were attempting to extend Spanish conquests, or were simply recruiting forced labor. Many of these frontier "revolts" were little more than *entrada y saca* in which expeditions entered unconquered areas, captured native peoples, and took them out to resettle them in new or old villages within the areas already controlled by Spaniards. The entradas were a clear response to labor shortages. Often these frontier crossings were inspired by a mixture of all the above motives, but whatever their cause, they were not undertaken to quell revolts.[4]

Other variations on these themes occurred within Spanish-dominated territory. Sometimes Spanish or *casta* bravos or private enforcers made drunken village raids and sometimes private armies or "the boys" from nearby haciendas attacked unsuspecting villages, simply to keep them in line or to remind them of the violence behind every colonial regime. Some of these raids were little more than high-spirited badgering by bored yahoos looking for some drunken fun on a Saturday night. These *razzias* were sometimes passed off as revolts if the Indians complained to the authorities and there was need for a "cover-up."[5] Such activities were usually messages to Indian society about the true underlying basis of colonial power and only now and then did they signify the great colonial fear, revolt from those below. In such cases the Spanish incursions were, in their message and real meaning, a preemptive strike, a battering of Indian villages before they could do what rumors and the panic-stricken Spaniards suggested they were going to do (Rus 1983).[6]

Another dubious category of "revolts" sprung from cases in which Indian villagers took one side in a dispute between Spaniards. The bitter, bloody, and divisive rivalry and hatred between the president of the Audiencia Gabriel Sánchez de Berrospe, whose faction was known as the *Berrospistas*, and the *visitador* or *pesquisidor* sent by the Crown, Francisco Gómez de la Madris, whose partisans were known as the *Tequelíes*, led to a civil war (1700–1701) on the Pacific coast of Guatemala. Major battles were fought in Soconusco, for a time the visitador's stronghold. He received support from the Indians of Soconusco and the Pacific side of Chiapas, where a substantial affray occurred in the village of Chicomucelo.

Free blacks and mulattoes, who by this time were the largest population group on the Pacific coast of Guatemala, took the side of the visitador because the audiencia and especially President Sánchez de Berrospe had threatened the lands, fisheries, and salt pans they owned in Guazacapán. Indian participation is harder to fathom because usually their attitude was "a plague on both your houses," a more or less adroit reluctance to take sides and a hope that such disputes would not bring them further depredations from marauding partisans of one Spanish side or the other. It is also possible that they were duped by false promises from Gómez de la Madris, or that they optimistically forecast that his side would win. What is more likely is that Gómez de la Madris, backed by clerical authorities in Soconusco and Chiapas, including Bishop Francisco Núñez de la Vega, convinced Indian leaders, the institutional brokers between authority and their own people, of the legitimacy, of the royal and divine favor, behind Gómez de la Madris's opposition to what they claimed was a criminal, deposed, usurper of a president (León Cázares 1988).

It was a bitter lesson for the Indians of Soconusco. Sánchez de Berrospe was able to use his location in Santiago, the largest population center in all of Central America, to his advantage when it came to collecting troops and armaments. Moreover, he drew attention to the participation of free blacks from the coast and of Indians from Totonicapán, Soconusco, and Chiapas on the Gómez de la Madris side, thus stirring up the colonial fear of urban whites. By manipulating this fear, President Sánchez was able to turn people against Gómez de la Madris and to raise large militia units to send against the disaffected peoples. Thus Gómez de la Madris, the blacks, and the Indians all lost, while the president successfully argued that his previous actions and his raising of armies were responses to Indian and black rebellion against the colonial order.[7]

Similar Indian participation in the armed quarrels of the dominant classes can be found in the local revolts leading to Central American independence, but these upheavals occurred after the 1780s or 1790s and fall outside the scope of this essay. They are, at any rate, of a distinct politcal type.[8]

We now turn from the very dubious revolts, either fictional or Spanish-inspired and led, to more legitimate but still questionable categories. Indians fought among themselves, of course. Some villages were racked by internal conflict, and several were notorious for such violence. When village violence caused damage or bodily harm or affected the property and goods of local hacendados or merchants passing through, it invited Spanish officials to intervene. At times such intervention was opportunistic and self-serving, with *alcaldes mayores* or *corregidores* levying fines or collecting what fees they could while "investigating" the riot. When internal village quarrels were about elections to the *cabildo*, the contending parties took a somewhat greater risk. Spanish investigators in these cases were apt to appoint the candidate most liked by officialdom, presumably the most manipulable, without much regard to the disputed election results. Often officials were more solomonic, perhaps because of a lack of interest, and would decline to apportion blame or punishment, simply insisting that both sides refrain from public demonstrations of any kind in the future. Sometimes *calpul* or *barrio* factions, or rival caciques or cofradías, became so enraged with one another that they took the risky step of actually inviting the intervention of Spanish officialdom in the optimistic belief that their side would be vindicated. Then, as now, it was often a mistake for two quarreling sardines to invite the shark to settle their differences (Hill 1989).[9]

Quarrels between two or more villages were usually over land—over boundaries and boundary markers or the antiquity and validity of land titles. (This emphasis on ancient titles seems to have created quite an industry in counterfeit documents.) Disputes between villages tended to be more serious than those within the village and often involved valuable property rather than personal honor, precedence, or village offices, and so they attracted more official attention. Whenever Indians invited such attention, they were required to show not only quiet title, but probably, at least in the seventeenth century, also a certificate that they had paid the latest *composición*. Some Spanish judges insisted that villagers prove they were using the land and refused to accept foraging or use of the *monte* as an adequate response. At times, both villages might lose the case and find the disputed land taken over by a Spaniard or turned into *tierras realengas* or *baldías*.[10]

Such changes in land title tended to occur early in the Colonial period, when shrinking villages required less land to maintain themselves. In general, land disputes between villages have much to tell us about Indian demographic recovery, Malthusian pressures, and land hunger. Such disputes began to turn violent in the late seventeenth century and grew even worse in the eighteenth century. The strife increased not only because of a higher survival rate for late colonial documents, but also because villages were growing and pressing against one another. Few disputes occurred in areas of little or no demographic recovery, but many erupted in congested valleys or in well-established Indian villages where land that could be used for expansion was owned by non-Indian haciendas.

Many of these disturbances stemmed from other types of conflicts. Two Indian villages struggling over land, for example, might both be trying to attract official attention to a marauding or encroaching local hacendado. A village chronically involved in litigation against others was sometimes the scene of a power struggle between rival caciques, each attempting to dominate the cabildo by winning more land for the village.

Yet another category of disturbance was aggression against Spaniards, which on the surface seems closer to a riot or revolt in the usual sense. But even here the historian must be careful. Many of these activities should not be interpreted as attacks on the colonial regime, or even as attacks on its officials. Some simply consisted of exasperated villagers turning on rustlers or on thieving farmhands from a nearby hacienda, or even on the hacienda owner himself. The hostility ranged from pushing and shoving or releasing a shower of stones to giving the offender a thorough beating with broken bones. When the offenders, scared and often vengeful, escaped home or to the nearest Spanish settlement, they would cry sedition and call out the *vecinos* or the militia and complain to local officials. Some of these officials panicked and shouted revolt.[11]

Even attacks on government officials or their servants cannot always be construed as riots or revolts. Exploitation, oppression, and fee gouging were expected in the Indian countryside. Indians knew that tribute would be overcollected (and so they underreported), that officials had to be bribed to allay their wrath or the full force of the law, and that royal officials would oppress them by running private businesses on the side. But there was a shifting and difficult-to-perceive limit, a "moral economy" to such exploitation, which, if breached, left the overexploitive or naive official at some peril. Often Indian violence was little more than a first warning to such an individual, as a not-so-gentle reminder that the villagers were becoming upset by his heavy-handed or greedy exploitation. In such cases his servants or lieutenants, sent to collect tribute and illegal fees such as the *salutación* in Verapaz, would be chased out of town, hurried along by a hail of stones, by a roughing up, or by the theft of their horses or even their clothes.[12]

Priests sometimes overreacted to such milder forms of violence. Again, overcollection of fees for such matters as masses, baptisms, marriages, confirmations, or funerals was often the cause of violence against them. But priests fled town for other more culturally interesting reasons. Some found themselves in trouble because of what villagers felt to be overenthusiastic or fervent proselytizing against local "witchcraft and superstition," or against "excesses" by a local cofradía during its fiesta. A *cura* who confiscated or smashed a local icon might find himself besieged in the parish house or the village church by an angry rock-throwing crowd that would disperse in the evening, its warning having been suitably delivered and in some cases duly noted. Sometimes such events took a more serious turn, as they did in 1722 for the parish priest of Ocozocuautla in Chiapas, a *mestizo* named Fray Sebastián de Grijalva. He was a native of Copainla, also in Chiapas, and had been cura in Ocozocuautla since 1697 and seemingly had caused no trouble during his long tenure.

One day he noticed that a large *ceiba* growing close to his house was beginning to cast a little too much shade on it and was also damaging one of the walls. He ordered the village caciques and *principales* to have the ceiba trimmed. Very quickly several hundred villagers gathered under its shade. (Or so the report says—although a few such trees have been known to grow large enough to shelter that many.) For these villagers, the ceiba was the symbol of continuing life and their lineage descended from its roots. The cura, alarmed, canceled the tree trimming, and the crowd dispersed.

Grijalva then began a preaching campaign against what he saw as idolatrous worship of the tree, calling it an agent of the devil and demanding that it be cut down. Soon he was besieged in his house by a shouting, whistling, stone-throwing crowd, which returned at various hours to frighten him for the next 12 days. Finally, the priest spoke to the village *alcaldes*, who persuaded the crowd to disperse.

A few days later, four villagers spat in his face repeatedly in public, and the cura decided to flee and to inform the authorities. The *alcalde mayor* of the province arrived in the village with a small force, the tree was cut down and the villagers were warned against future misbehavior. One mulatto ringleader was exiled from the village, and a few Indians may have been flogged. Later Fray Sebastián returned to the village and the record shows that he lived on there, in seeming tranquility, for many years ("Motín" 1953).

In all these incidents the path of communication went from the Indians to the officials or priests. These Spaniards were being told that they had overstepped the bounds. Some then pulled back; others, such as Grijalva, invoked a higher authority and had their way. In no way did the Indians mean to challenge the regime, or even the ultimate authority of the official to whom they objected. They were, to use Hobsbawm's phrase, simply "bargaining by riot." Records of this can tell us about local understandings, mentalities, and power relationships and give us a window to local customs, rites, and beliefs.

We now shift to a much more dangerous category, still not seditious or revolutionary, but much closer to it, and much more bloody. There are a few cases in which villagers were unable to persuade the offending royal official to moderate his extortions. Usually this was because the official in question had easy access to force and so did not need to listen to complaints. Or if he had a high rank, say, that of an alcalde mayor of a whole district, this might have inhibited Indian violence. In such cases some villages sank into apathy, used new varieties of passive resistance, or fled. A few, perhaps those more conscious of their corporate solidarity, appealed to a higher authority. If the village did not fully understand the lines and divisions of authority, it might mistakenly appeal to the bishop, but most village leaders had an astute and flexible understanding of Spanish law and government, at least insofar as their own interests were concerned. So some, in such circumstances, appealed for relief to the audiencia, which, through its president and *oidores*, represented the king in the whole of Central America. The principle behind their appeals was an old one, well recognized by all, and not basically seditious. It was "down with bad government and long live the king."

If the audiencia ruled against the village, that was the end of the matter. The villagers either had to submit to extortions or find new informal ways of circumventing them. If the audiencia found for the Indians, there was a feeling of great triumph. The danger point came if the abusive official ignored the audiencia's *auto* and *real provisión* ordering him to cease his depredations and continued to act as before. This was the case in the large Zoque village of Tuxtla in 1693. The authorities and commoners of the village were roused to a frenzy of exasperation and frustration, and when the alcalde mayor of Chiapas, a notoriously corrupt and greedy official named Manuel de Maisterra y Atocha, next appeared in the village with his followers to collect tribute and other fees, he was first admonished by a local principal to mend his ways as the audiencia had decreed. Having ignored this warning, he was stoned to death by an enraged mob, together with one of his lieutenants and a local Indian who had been his agent. The Tuxtlecos then chased the remaining Spaniards and the village priest into the parish church and robbed two merchants passing through. The next day, after the Spaniards escaped up the road to Chiapa de los Indios, the people realized what they had done and begged for mercy. They received none. Spanish forces arrested hundreds of villagers. More than 20 were executed and dozens were banished to Guatemala. Clerics and government investigators talked of a rebellion, and the village was watched closely for years. The extortions of the alcaldes mayores continued.[13]

The Tuxtlecos had miscalculated and lost all the small advantages they might have gained from the use of the "weapons of the weak," such as evasion, bargaining, bargaining by riot, or appeal to the audiencia. By going one step too far, by murdering a royal official and taking total control of a village, however briefly, they aroused the full colonial fear of the Spaniards, even though they did not wish to challenge the legitimacy or existence of the colonial regime. Most Indians at most times knew that to do so would be a fatal and counterproductive step. They took great pains, even when driven by hardship and desperation, to use tactics that would not foster such fear. Once full Spanish repression came, it was swift, cruel, exaggerated and even hysterical, and the Indians on whom it was imposed seldom gained anything by their actions (Taylor 1976).[14]

Revolts against the Colonial Order

Evidence of Indian caution and their measured use of limited violence can be found when we analyze the few genuine rebellions themselves. Even some of the mass attempts by several *pueblos* to overthrow the colonial regime and to expel all Spaniards, such as the one by the Cakchiquel nation in the years immediately following the Spanish conquest, are not true revolts against the colonial order, which in many of these cases had not been established when these "conquest" or "first-generation" revolts broke out. The religious or "spiritual conquest" had hardly started. In some places the great missionary orders had not yet arrived. These revolts were, in fact, part of the late conquest (Ximénez 1971–1977:1:163–168). The revolts leading up to Central American independence, as I have already argued, are also a case apart. They were usually limited to a few villages, and *ladinos* or city people were involved in them to a greater or lesser extent.

The only real rebellion by the native population against Spanish rule during the entire established Colonial period was the so-called Tzeltal Revolt of 1712–1713 in highland Chiapas, and it happened only because of a large set of background circumstances and a unique conjunction of events. Economic exploitation increased after about 1690 as the alcaldes mayores had by then achieved a near total monopoly on tribute collection and trading, and trade had revived with Guatemala, Tabasco, and Mexico. During the first decade of the eighteenth century, an especially vigilant and orthodox bishop, Francisco Núñez de la Vega, who had campaigned against nagualism and other "superstitions" in the Indian communities, died and was replaced by a less puritanical but much more rapacious bishop, Juan Bautista Alvarez de Toledo from Guatemala, whose frequent and thorough pastoral *visitas* were little more than looting expeditions in the Indian countryside. According to one source, it was the announcement and start of yet another of the bishop's money-collecting expeditions through the Tzeltal countryside that precipitated the revolt (León Cázares and Ruz 1988; Ximénez 1971–1977:1:267–271).

The severity of exploitation after 1690 and especially around 1710 caused devastation among the remnant population of highland Chiapas, probably close to its smallest total since the conquest. Some of the lesser Indian elites, reasonably faithful brokers for Spanish priests, friars, and officials up until then, fell out of their class because of indigence, became disaffected, and increased their rivalries with other calpuls and with the more established elites that dominated some of the villages (Gosner 1984a).

Although the strain on these village communities was as severe as it had been since the conquest, economic hardship was nothing new and had not previously caused revolts. Nor was internal village strife unknown. Village elites had often divided bitterly under pressure or because of old calpul and lineage rivalries, and these situations had irritated or even amused local Spaniards but certainly had not frightened them.

Now, however, the desperate Indian leaders sensed weakness on the Spanish side. The War of Spanish Succession had been raging for over a decade, with battles taking place on Spanish soil. Taking advantage of Spanish weakness, the British from Jamaica had increased their piracy and logging in Campeche, Laguna de Términos, and Tabasco, sometimes raiding upriver Mayan villages. Above all, the ever-alert Indians noticed schism and disarray nearer home. The civil war that began between the visitador and the president in Santiago in 1700 soon included the black and mulatto populations of the Pacific coast of Guatemala, and in 1701 Chiapan Indians were persuaded to join the visitador as the true representative of the king in his war against the president of the audiencia. The visitador and the Indians lost, and the man they had been persuaded was a usurper won. For them, this severely damaged the political legitimacy of the regime (León Cázares 1988).[15]

Even closer to home, the new powers of the alcaldes mayores provoked bitter hostility from the bishops and the vecinos of Ciudad Real. Excommunications, denunciations, and even skirmishing in the streets became common. None of this was edifying to the subject population, which became more convinced that the regime was falling apart and that their window of opportunity was at hand. This still would not have been enough. Out of the village of Cancuc came a unique rebel leadership, the family and advisers of the prophetess and visionary María Candelaria, whose apparitions and messages from the Virgin Mary touched off and fueled the revolt. To this Cancuc leadership came another individual of high intelligence, Sebastián Gómez de la Gloria, who found ways in which the Indians could appropriate Catholicism, put their own stamp on it, and turn it against the Spanish regime (Gosner 1984b).

Just as in Tuxtla, the Indians had miscalculated, which they did so seldom. Many provinces failed to rise in support, the viceroy in Mexico sent financial aid to Ciudad Real, and invading armies from Tabasco and Guatemala came to help out the *ladinos* of Chiapas. The revolt was crushed after bitter fighting and was followed by devastation and many executions. All the leading Spanish figures received awards, while the Indian leadership in the province was destroyed. Chiapas remained a devastated land far beyond 1720. Oppression continued as before and grew worse later in the century.

Overt rebellions against the regime or even all-out attacks on important officials were not the main means of Indian resistance in colonial Central America, and they failed miserably when they were tried. So, too, did the sole Indian attempt to join one Spanish faction against another. Survival and day-to-day existence were better managed by subtle resistance, by turning Spanish institutions to advantage, by using Spanish law when it was advantageous to do so, and by avoiding it when it was not. Judicious and modified violence could be used as a bargaining chip. All of the tactics, avoidances, and confrontations were propelled by the age-old Indian realization that the wheels of time turn slowly but that if one survives they will ineluctably turn against the oppressors.

Notes

1. See the critique of Wallerstein's "world systems" approach in Stern (1988). The recent book by Grant D. Jones (1989) has a similar perspective for a peripheral area between Yucatan and Central America. This dialectic is explained for Africa in Isaacman (1989).

2. I sometimes found myself facing this question when reading Nancy M. Farriss's brilliant book, *Maya Society under Colonial Rule: The Collective Enterprise of Survival* (1985).

3. These patterns become apparent, much to the annoyance of Spaniards, in postrevolt surveys of Chiapas. See Archivo General de Indias, Audiencia de Guatemala (AGI/AG) 294. Honduran officials faced the same problems. See Archivo Nacional de Honduras (ANH), paquete 2, legajo 77 (1673); ANH, paquete 5, legajo 41 (1695); ANH, paquete 6, legajo 2 (1700), and many other documents. The Archivo General de Centroamérica (AGCA) contains many similar colonial documents.

4. There are many examples. For the Honduran Caribbean lowlands, see ANH, paquete 5, legajo 66 (1698), a resettlement of Payas near the mines of Corpus, and especially ANH paquete 6, legajo 2 (1700) that discusses "wild Indians" and their resistance to Franciscan resettlement plans. For Costa Rica, see Archivo Nacional de Costa Rica (ANCR), Cartago 029 (1639); ANCR Guatemala 137 (1707); and, a much larger case, ANCR, Complementario Colonial 5204 (1620). (The report given in this last document is attacked as false and as no more than a pretext for enslaving "wild" Indians, in ANCR Guatemala 058 (1626). For the Verapaz entradas to the Petén and Lacandón, see Stone (1932).

5. For example, AGCA, A1.15, 32515, 4102 (1617); AGCA, A1.15, 2953, 151 (1696).

6. The only example of this kind of raid that has been described fully is from the nineteenth century. It resembles several colonial cases. See Rus (1983).

7. AGI/AG 287–289 contains much of the story. The chronicler Francisco Ximénez, a supporter of the president, gave a full partisan account (Ximénez 1971–1977:1:98–178). (This volume also contains an account of an entrada y saca against the Chol, 216–219.)

8. The quarrel over the wars of independence and over the roles played by classes and ethnic groups has a large bibliography. See the contribution by Martínez Zelda (1979).

9. The variations in types of Indian village disagreements and in Spanish official responses are discussed in Hill (1989). Other cases of the kind described can be found

in AGCA, A1.24, 10204, 1560, f. 2 (1649); AGCA, A1.24, 10208, 1564, f. 35 (1672); AGCA, A1.24, 10211, 1567, f. 208 (1683); AGCA, A1.21.11, 47829, 5533 (1713); AGCA, A1.15, 32636, 4119 (1675).

10. See, for example, AGCA, A1.24, 10220, 1576, f. 334 (1707); AGCA, Tierras, 52132, 5951 (1692); AGCA, A1.24, 10218, 1574, f. 7 (1705); AGCA, A1.21–10, 47529, 5505, (1716): AGCA, Tierras, 51988, 5941 (1600). There are many more.

11. AGCA, A1.39, 11756, 1762, f. 42v. (1688); AGCA, A1.24, 10204, 1560 (1649); AGCA, A1.19–7, 47170, 5481 (1715); AGCA, A1.24, 10213, 1569, f. 191 (1694); AGCA, A1.24, 10215, 1571, f. 494 (1700).

12. AGCA, A1.24, 10226, 1582, f. 156 (1717); AGCA, A1.19–7, 47170, 5481 (1715); AGCA, A1.21, 15586, 2165 (1710); AGCA, A1.39, 11756, 1762, f. 42v. (1688).

13. Some of the AGCA documentation about the Tuxtla murder and riot has been collected ("Motín" 1953). There are also several documents on these events in AGI/AG 37. See also MacLeod (1991).

14. There are different interpretations of these matters. For other views see Taylor (1976).

15. León Cázares (1988) contains a lengthy appendix of letters from Indian village leaders touching on these matters.

References

Farriss, Nancy M.
    1985 *Maya Society under Colonial Rule: The Collective Enterprise of Survival*. Princeton University Press, Princeton, N. J.
Gosner, Kevin
    1984a Las élites indígenas en los Altos de Chiapas (1524–1714). *Historia Mexicana* 33:405–423.
    1984b *Soldiers of the Virgin: An ethnohistorical Analysis of the Tzeltal Revolt of 1712 in Highland Chiapas*. Unpublished Ph.D. dissertation, University of Pennsylvania.
Hill, Robert M. II
    1989 Social Organization by Decree in Colonial Highland Guatemala. *Ethnohistory* 36:170–198.
Isaacman, Allen F.
    1989 *Peasants and Rural Social Protest in Africa*. Institute of International Studies, University of Minnesota, Minneapolis.
Jones, Grant D.
    1989 *Maya Resistance to Spanish Rule: Time and History on a Colonial Frontier*. University of New Mexico Press, Albuquerque.
Katz, Friedrich (editor)
    1988 *Riot, Rebellion and Revolution: Rural Social Conflict in Mexico*. Princeton University Press, Princeton, N. J.
León Cázares, María del Carmen
    1988 *Un levantamiento en nombre del rey nuestro señor*. Universidad Nacional Autónoma de México, Mexico.
León Cázares, María del Carmen, and Mario Humberto Ruz (editors)
    1988 *Constituciones diocesanas del Obispado de Chiapas*. Universidad Nacional Antónoma de México, Mexico.
MacLeod, Murdo J.
    1983 Papel social y económico de las cofradías indígenas de la colonia en Chiapas. *Mesoamérica* 4:64–86.
    1991 Motines y cambios en las formas políticas y económicas de control; el ejemplo de Tuxtla (Chiapas) en 1693. *Mesoamérica*, in press.

Martínez Peláez, Severo
1974 Los motines de indios en el período colonial guatemalteco. *Ensayos de historia centroamericana*. CEDAL, San José, Costa Rica.

Martínez Zelada, Eliseo
1979 *Antes que criollos el pueblo forjó la independencia*. Impr. Galindo, Guatemala.

Meyers, A., and D. E. Hopkins (editors)
1988 *Manipulating the Saints: Religious Brotherhoods and Social Integration in Postconquest Latin America*. Wayasbah, Hamburg.

Motín indígena de Ocozocoautla, 1722
1953 Boletín del Archivo General del Estado (Chiapas) 2:25–51.

Pardo, José Joaquin
1978 *Miscelanea histórica. Guatemala, siglos 16 a 19: vida, costumbres, sociedad*. Editorial Universitaria, Guatemala.

Rus, Jan
1983 Whose Caste War? Indians, Ladinos and the "Caste War" of 1869, In *Spaniards and Indians in Southeastern Mesoamerica: Essays on the History of Ethnic Relations*, edited by Murdo J. MacLeod and Robert Wasserstrom, pp. 127–168. University of Nebraska, Lincoln.

Scott, James C.
1985 *Weapons of the Weak: Everyday Forms of Peasant Resistance*. Yale University Press, New Haven, Conn.

Stern, Steve J.
1988 Feudalism, Capitalism, and the World System in the Perspective of Latin America and the Caribbean. *American Historical Review* 93:829–897.

Stern, Steve J. (editor)
1987 *Resistance, Rebellion, and Consciousness in the Andean Peasant World, 18th to 20th Centuries*. University of Wisconsin, Madison.

Stone, Doris Z.
1932 Some Spanish Entradas. *Middle American Research Series*, pp. 200–296. Tulane University, New Orleans.

Taylor, William B.
1976 La Indiada: Peasant Uprisings in Central Mexico and Oaxaca, 1700–1718. Unpublished paper.

Ximénez, Francisco
1971–1977 *Historia de la provincia de San Vicente de Chiapa y Guatemala, orden de predicadores*. 4 vols. Sociedad de Geografía e Historia, Guatemala.

Chapter 19 ■

Robert M. Carmack

The Spanish Conquest of Central America: Comparative Cases from Guatemala and Costa Rica

This essay is part of a long-term study in which I am attempting to compare the social history of the Indians of Central American countries. To date, I have carried out both field and archival research on the Indian communities of Momostenango, Guatemala, and Buenos Aires, Costa Rica. Through such case studies I hope to gain a clearer understanding of how these nation-states have developed through time and why they are experiencing political conflict today. The Indians have had a profound impact on the political and cultural processes that have operated in the region, despite the fact that the Indians per se have been relatively neglected in historical research. The comparative nature of my study derives from the widely accepted claim that comparison is social science's experimental method, the means by which we can generalize about our subjects in order to then find explanations for generalizations about them.

The Spanish conquest of Central America is a propitious historical process to investigate. It provided the context for the meeting of radically different social systems, that of the Spaniards and those of the many indigenous societies. The conquest differed greatly from one area to another in Central America, and the results were highly variable. These differences in turn were undoubtedly signifi-

cant for subsequent political developments in the region, possibly with repercussions down to the present day and on into the future. Some scholars might
dismiss such a notion as anthropological romanticism, but recent thinking in
the social sciences would seem to support the idea, at least in principle. Unfortunately, in this brief essay I am not able to marshall the kind of evidence that
would be necessary to convince the skeptic of the very long historical shadow
cast by the conquest in Central America. Nevertheless, I hope that I can at least
make the idea plausible.

Momostenango and Buenos Aires provide interesting cases for comparison
within the Central American region, as do the two countries in which they
are found: Guatemala and Costa Rica, respectively. They are both municipios
with relatively large Indian populations—Quiché-Mayas in the case of
Momostenango, Chibchan speakers in the case of Buenos Aires. Both figured
in the conquest, both were established early in their respective provinces of the
Guatemalan colony, and both were somewhat peripheral to the main centers of
provincial development. Yet, as I attempt to clarify below, the conquest encounter was quite distinct for the two communities, and their subsequent social histories have taken vastly different courses. Their respective provinces (and later
the countries of Costa Rica and Guatemala) have also had different historical trajectories, which is precisely the reason I believe it is instructive to compare the
two cases.

Theoretical Comment

The Spanish conquest of Central America was an extremely complicated process, and we will need some framework to guide us. Although any number of
theoretical and methodological positions might be profitably adopted, I find the
Weberian model to be particularly useful for the study of the Central American
conquest. It is explicitly historical and comparative, and it takes account of economic, political, and cultural factors. Its analytical units include status and cultural groups, as well as class and political divisions. As I conceptualize the conquest process, these are the factors and units with which we must necessarily
deal.

In a recent summary of Weberian political theory, Randall Collins (1986) says
that conquest and colonization are to be conceptualized first and foremost as
expressions of "imperialism." For Weber, imperialist tendencies universally
characterize state-level politics, and economic goals are not the sole or even necessarily the most important cause of conquest. In contrast to many historians,
Weber argued that in early modern times manufacturing and trading interests
could be quite nonimperialist, whereas state-directed economic interests were
often highly imperialistic: "Where business interests . . . rely on the state to provide exploitable land, monopolized trade, or opportunities for tax farming, then
capitalism favors imperialism" (Collins 1986:150).

For Weber, competition for status in the global arena of states, especially
through emulation of the most powerful state, is always an important cause of
imperialism and can drive polities to conquer even when the economic benefits

may be negligible. Conquest is driven by the internal political groups (classes, status groups, and parties) who gain legitimacy thereby (but also illegitimacy if the conquests are unsuccessful) and the right of rule. Weber believed that out of such military successes and status elevations arise the sentiments and ideas that constitute "nationalism"; hence, the close relationship between imperialism and the modern nation-states.

Anthony Smith (1983) has applied Weberian theory to the conquest and colonization of Africa to good effect, and his framework would appear to be applicable to the Central American case as well. Studies of colonization, he claims, have generally followed one of two models: the "mode-of-production" model, exemplified by Immanuel Wallerstein; or the "communications" model, exemplified by Daniel Lerner or Karl Deutsch. Smith finds value in both models, but argues that the first places too much stress on economic factors, while the second overemphasizes cultural considerations. We need models that give more attention to the political system, especially the nature of the state and its relations with other states, as well as to specific historical developments. In particular, Smith (1983:18ff.) argues for the need to focus our studies on the "colonial state," for, despite the claims of Lenin and others, imperialism has been as much a political as economic issue (especially with respect to the issue of interstate struggle). The colonial state was a conscious, "rationalistic" European product, quite constant in form and function, and therefore potentially more significant for understanding the colonial societies than the oft-mentioned capitalist mode of production (which varied greatly from place to place and time to time). This is an important issue because the colonial state has become a model widely followed in defining later state and nationalist developments: "It was this encounter between an alien 'rationalized' bureaucratic system and the congeries of traditional cultures and societies it sought to incorporate and mould, that determined the subsequent evolution of most . . . [Third World] societies" (Smith 1983:28).

The main characteristics of the colonial state, according to Smith, were as follows: (1) its primary concern was territorial protection and thus it considered boundaries to be almost "sacred" while ignoring ethnic and cultural divisions; (2) its authority was mainly executive and bureaucratic, imposed from outside, and hence radically different from the native polities, "which it remolds to its own ends"; (3) it created parallel societies, within which racial and cultural lines of inequality would separate European rulers from native peoples; (4) it adopted an educational ideology that assigned a "civilizing mission" to the colonial rulers.

Smith warns that focusing on the colonial state gives considerable weight to the European factor and therefore must be offset by paying closer attention to the "differing relationships with the pre-existing cultures, religions, and societies it encountered" (Smith 1983:35). The important relationships during the conquest phase of colonization, he points out, are those involved in "primary resistance," at the period of contact, and the subsequent "millenial" movements by native groups. Although these movements have been historically important, at least in the African region, they were largely reactions against the colonial state rather than nationalist processes based on the colonial model.

With this sketch of a Weberian framework in mind, we turn now to the conquest of Guatemala, and then of Costa Rica.

Conquest of Guatemala

Murdo MacLeod (1973) has admirably summarized the main events and the factors behind these events for the conquest of Central America as a whole. The conquest of this region is said to have been especially difficult and violent, taking place "in bits and pieces, revolts and reconquests" (MacLeod 1973:404). The more important factors that came to play in this conquest, says MacLeod, were ecological, especially the demographic variations associated with highland-lowland contrasts, the sociopolitical condition of the native societies, and the character and activities of the Spanish conquistadores themselves. The main ecological divide in Central America is between the highlands and Pacific piedmont to the west and the Atlantic tropical lowlands to the east. This ecological division accounts for the most important preconquest cultural cleavage, that between the Mesoamerican-influenced native societies on the Pacific side, and the South American–influenced societies on the Atlantic side. Paradoxically, the conquistadores themselves divided along a somewhat similar line, the Cortés faction operating out of Mexico along the Pacific corridor, the Pedrarias faction of Panama along the Atlantic coastal strip. This Spanish factionalism, which involved other divisions as well, greatly complicated and prolonged the Central American conquest.

MacLeod documents the drastic decline in the native population with the conquest and demonstrates its profound impact on the economy of the emerging colonial society. He employs a mode-of-production model to explain developments in the region, arguing that from early on the Spaniards were preoccupied with finding a suitable export commodity for the world market. The conquistadores are said to have been entrepreneurially rather than feudally oriented, men who would turn to landed estates only if commerce were closed to them. As the conquest battles ended, the Spaniards engaged in a frenetic search for gold, converting the Indians into virtual slaves at the mining sites. When the gold ran out, the Spaniards turned to cacao trade (though a few became cattle ranchers), the Indians again providing the essential labor force—for the most part as transported workers from the highlands to the Pacific Piedmont area. The encomenderos played a role in this, but the main players were the Spanish merchants who earned profits by exporting the cacao beans.

MacLeod's interpretation of the Central American conquest is of undeniable scholarly importance, and it has been widely followed—in some cases almost word for word (Zamora 1979). Nevertheless, in the light of the theoretical framework described above, we need to keep in mind that it places much more emphasis on economic than on political or cultural factors, and that the native societies after the initial Contact period receive attention almost exclusively in the context of the Spanish economic system. Fortunately, more recent studies of the individual colonial provinces of Central America complement the strong economic orientation of MacLeod's conquest account (see, for example, the studies by Newson [1986, 1987], on Honduras and Nicaragua, as well as the studies to be discussed below on Guatemala and Costa Rica). I hope that the present essay will also serve as a small contribution in this sense.

Conquest of the Quichés

Let us begin with a summary of my own previous published account of the conquest of the Quiché-Mayas of central Guatemala (Carmack 1981; for the location of places mentioned below, see Figure 19–1). In that study I attempted to provide an inside view of how the Quichés prepared to meet the Spanish invaders and later fought decisive battles against them outside Quezaltenango (Carmack 1981:143ff.). Next I described the entry of the Spaniards into the Quiché capital of Utatlán, and the execution by burning of the two highest officials of the Quiché state (whom I identified as the *Ajpop* and *Ajpop C'amjá* officials). Finally, I tried to explain how the Spaniards defeated the rebellious Quiché forces in the fighting in and around Utatlán, a defeat partly made possible by the material aid (some 4,000 warriors) provided by the rival Cakchiquel state.

I also described developments in the central Quiché area during the first decades of Spanish rule, especially as these affected the political structure of the native society (Carmack 1981:305ff.). I argued, for example, that the Spaniards clamped on an extremely repressive system of political controls. This resulted in the fragmentation of the centralized Quiché state into several quasi-independent towns, the assignment of the Quiché Indians who had not been carried off as slaves into encomiendas held by Alvarado's lieutenants, and the stripping of former ruling class members of their past privileges.

I further documented the Quichés' fierce and violent resistance to such political controls, led by the recalcitrant survivors of the ruling class. They rebelled against each and every Spanish imposition, launching guerrilla warfare from rural zones surrounding Utatlán (especially from Santa María Chiquimula). While precise numbers are lacking, it is known that several ruling class leaders were killed in battle or captured and executed as a result of these military actions. The Quiché Indians also rose up in millenial-type movements under the leadership of prophets who found similarities between the natives' oppressed condition and the Christian stories being taught to them by the friars.

By midcentury, the situation had changed for the conquered Quichés (Carmack 1981:31lff.). The Crown had gained greater control over the conquistadores, the Dominican friars had become protectors and benefactors of the Indians, and a new generation of "caciques" had come under Spanish influence. Descendants of the Quiché ruling class were able to recoup some important privileges from the past: namely, tributary rights, a degree of authority over other towns and regions, and, for a while, an office at the Spanish capital where the Quiché "king" held court.

On the cultural side, by midcentury the Quichés had worked out an accommodation between their autochthonous religion and Christianity, thanks largely to Dominican tolerance and the intellectual leadership provided by members of the Quiché royal lineages. The accommodation reached was expressed in classic

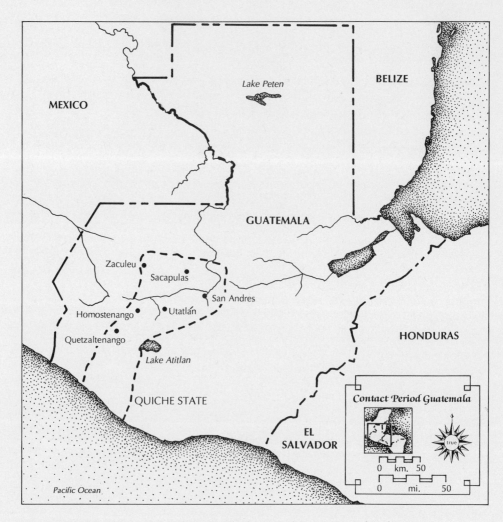

Figure 19–1. Map of Contact period Guatemala showing places mentioned in the text.

form by fairly sophisticated syncretistic entries in the colonial version of the Popol Vuh. In this native text we find an origin myth that links the Quiché homeland with ancient Palestine, a creation story in which the gods form humans out of maize and earth, and a monotheistic concept that somehow merges the many Quiché gods into a divine unity (*cabawil*).

I am aware, of course, that my account of the conquest refers only to the Quiché sector of colonial Guatemala. Nevertheless, in the context of the theoretical framework outlined above, I believe its thrust to be a useful complement to other, more economic-oriented studies of the Guatemalan conquest. It focuses on the emerging colonial state and the role played in that state by the Indians. In particular, it is an attempt to describe the changing relations of power as a result of the Quichés' incorporation into the Spanish authority system. It reveals the emergence of major resistance movements among the natives, even after the end of the conquest battles, and explains some of the ways these movements

were defused after the mid-sixteenth century. And it takes cultural developments seriously, seeing them in nativistic as well as ideological terms. Most important, the study helps us go beyond the Spanish vision of the conquest in
search of a better understanding of what agendas the Indians were pursuing
during this difficult and restive period.

Let us turn now to another work on the conquest of the Quichés that contrasts
in many ways with my own study: the late Jean Piel's (1989) important history
of the Quiché-speaking community of San Andrés Sajcabajá. Piel applies a
"mode of production" approach, although he also attempts to reconstruct the
regional history of the the Quichés' political system (or as he calls it, the "Utatlán
Kingdom").

Piel distinguishes three phases of conquest: a first one (1524–1550) of brutal
sacking and outright slavery, gradually ameliorated by Crown regulation; a second phase (1550–1580) of increased Crown control, largely exercised by Dominican friars operating from the town of Sacapulas; and a third phase (1580–1600)
of commercial influence, as both church and private groups utilized political
and private forms of native labor to work their cattle ranches.

During the first conquest phase, according to Piel, the political structure of
the Quiché Kingdom was irreparably disorganized, and did not become an important mediating structure thereafter. Santa Cruz Utatlán, the old Quiché capital, was seen by the Spaniards as a threat to the emerging colonial state and
therefore was excluded from activities that might have allowed it to continue
as a political force. Thus, while the caciques from elsewhere were called on by
the Spaniards to help in the conquest of rebellious Indian groups, the caciques
of Santa Cruz were reduced in number and allowed to exercise authority based
only on social (vs. economic) prerogatives. In essence, the caciques were reduced to the role of mediating between their respective "parcialidades" (rural
divisions) and the Spanish rulers. This transformation of the native political
structure explains, Piel says, the "ethnic personality" of the Santa Cruz area,
but also the absence of serious resistance there during the sixteenth century following the conquest wars.

By the second phase, the center of power had shifted from Santa Cruz to
Sacapulas, where the Dominican friars had established their base for the conquest of the *tierras de guerra*. The Dominican order exercised both political and
economic dominion over the eastern part of the old Quiché Kingdom. Few Spaniards resided in the area, and encomenderos were specifically kept out. Even
at Santa Cruz the Indians paid tributes to the Crown rather than to encomenderos. The Dominican control resulted in both a religious and native
(ethnic) "tinge" relative to other areas. But Piel insists that many of these cultural features—for example, dispersed settlements, cofradía cults, the use of
native language—were not carryovers from prehispanic institutions, but
rather Spanish-induced constructions (even if syncretistic).

Piel claims that during the third phase the area had already developed an economic structure that has been perpetuated in important ways down to the present day. Central Quiché became a marginal zone of reserve natives, whose surplus goods, natural resources, and labor were transferred to commercial centers

far removed from Quiché itself. As in recent times, many Quiché Indians were migrating to the Pacific Coast to work on plantations, and significant numbers of them never found their way back to the highland home.

Piel's study warrants serious consideration, although here I can only comment on it from the perspective of the framework outlined above. From that perspective, we should note Piel's tendency to see the Indians primarily as "objects" rather than "subjects" (Farriss 1983). Too little attention is given to the native political institutions, especially as these might be represented in the native sources. Piel gives so much credence to the Spanish administrative sources that he does not always determine the extent to which the policies they describe were actually carried out. It could be argued, too, that Piel gives so much weight to political and economic forces operating outside the Quiché area that possibly he exaggerated the area's involvement in these more global processes. A view from within central Quiché would reveal, I believe, important local political and economic processes (e.g., market activities), which are dealt with by Piel only superficially. Finally, although it is understandable that Piel would deal with the eastern part of the Quiché kingdom (given the French Mission's research focus on Sajcabajá), it should nevertheless be pointed out that developments in the western part of the kingdom might well have been quite different (as I will attempt to demonstrate below through the Momostenango case).

Before turning to Momostenango, I would like to mention a few other important works dealing with the conquest of Guatemala that fit fairly well into the framework outlined above. In this category I would include Francis Polo Sifontes's (1974) account of the involvement of the Cakchiquels in the conquest, Carol Smith's (1984) essay on Guatemalan history as seen in global context, Elías Zamora's (1983, 1986) essays on Conquest-period native demographics and resistance movements in the Western Highlands, George Lovell's (1989) moving essay on the cycles of conquest in Guatemalan history, and Wendy Kramer's (1988) thesis on the early allocations of encomiendas in Guatemala. Many additional studies might be mentioned (see the references in Carmack 1986), but space will not permit even a brief summary of the works just cited despite their relevance to the issues raised at the beginning of this essay.

The Momostenango Case

We now turn to the conquest of Momostenango, as both a contrasting case to the central and eastern Quiché areas (see above) and as a study carried out within the theoretical framework outlined at the beginning of this essay. I do not claim that Momostenango is an exemplary case, but only that it is relevant to the issues under discussion. The description of the conquest to follow is taken from a more detailed study of the political history of Momostenango now nearing completion (Carmack n.d.; see also Carmack 1983, 1988; Cook 1981; Tedlock 1982).

Our documentary sources indicate that the Quiché Kingdom's province known as Momostenango (*Chuwá Tz'ak* in the Quiché language) was not directly conquered by the Spaniards. Rather, it fell to Pedro de Alvarado and his forces as a result of the defeat of the main Quiché army on the plains outside

Quezaltenango. Momostenango's leading provincial chief, Izquín (he came from the second-ranked ruling lineage of Utatlán), apparently led the provincial warriors in battle against the Spaniards. Shortly after the death of the Quiché leader Tecum on the battlefield, Izquín accepted a peace offer from Alvarado, and appears to have remained loyal to the Spaniards from that time forward.

Izquín offered gold, food, and jewels to the Spaniards while they remained in the vicinity of Quezaltenango, and he was soon rewarded with Spanish cacique privileges: the continued right to exercise authority within the native communities, to ride horses and carry a sword, and to use the title of *don*. Momostenango's people apparently followed Izquín's lead, and en masse peacefully submitted to Spanish rule. We have no solid evidence of subsequent resistance or large-scale revolt on the part of Momostecan Indians during the early years of conquest. In fact, the creole chronicler, Fuentes y Guzmán (1932–1933:8:109) suggests that the Momostecans aided the Spaniards in both the conquest of the Mam Indians of Zaculeu (1525) and the quashing of a Quiché rebellion centered in the Quezaltenango valley (1526). I think it likely that the Momostecans' close collaboration with the Spaniards during those early years— given their later propensity for resistance to outside rule—had to do with a deepseated dissatisfaction with their subordinate position within the Quiché Kingdom. Indeed, the indigenous peoples of the area had to be reconquered at least once by Quiché military forces shortly before the Spanish conquest.

Momostenango suffered drastic population losses as a result of the conquest and its aftermath. I estimate the losses at about 70 percent of the aboriginal population between 1524 and 1580 (from about 10,000 to 2,400 persons), and the decline continued after that, although more slowly. Some of the losses must have resulted from the killing of Momostecan warriors by the Spaniards in the conquest battles outside Quezaltenango (up to 2,000 warriors from Momostenango might have participated). Other losses occurred when the Spaniards took slaves from Momostenango, although we do not know how many people were carried off in this fashion. Most of the decline, however, came from massive deaths caused by Spanish-introduced diseases, although again the specific details are lacking.

Spanish-imposed economic changes in Momostenango were modest during the sixteenth century. Apparently the gold mined in the mountains of Momostenango during prehispanic times was limited, and its exploitation under Spanish rule was probably of brief duration. Momostecans paid tributes to the Spaniards, as they had done to their Quiché overlords, mostly in the form of foods—maize, beans, turkeys, venison, honey. One important change introduced into the tributary system by the Spaniards, however, was the obligation to make a certain part of the payments in cacao beans and later in Spanish money. Unfortunately we lack specific information on how the Momostecans obtained these currencies in order to meet this new obligation.

The imposition of the Spanish political system in Momostenango was surprisingly gradual. The caciques played an active role in setting up the local government and staffing it thereafter. As early as 1530, the province was granted in encomienda to Alvarado's captain, Juan Pérez Dardón, but Pérez Dardón's influence appears to have consisted almost exclusively of collecting tributes and appropriating a limited amount of labor from the Momostecans. The Spanish project of congregating the dispersed settlements of the area into a town was carried out primarily by the former provincial chief, Francisco Izquín (the same chief who fought alongside Tecum in the conquest battles). One consequence of leaving the task to such local officials was that Momostenango's colonial boundaries corresponded closely to the prehispanic provincial boundaries.

The congregation activities of Cacique Izquín left the Momostenango community overwhelmingly rural. The vast majority of its inhabitants continued to be organized by and identified with rural patrilineages and hamlets, referred to in the documents as "parcialidades." Cabildo and church organizations were not formally established until late in the century, when the town center was moved from its original prehispanic location to its present site. This move took place under the direction of the Franciscan friars, and it allowed the Spaniards to modify some of the traditional structures that the natives had reproduced during the initial contact period. For example, Momostenango's 22 parcialidades were aggregated into four ward divisions, and then cabildo, cofradía, and tributary organizations were integrated into this new arrangement. Nevertheless, members of the native ruling class continued to serve as leaders of these divisions and the political-religious organizations associated with them. In providing this leadership, the caciques were assisted by principal families whose forefathers had originally been sent from the central Quiché area (in prehispanic times) to provide military security.

Contact between Momostecans and Spaniards was quite limited throughout the sixteenth century. Pérez Dardón, the first encomendero, had a small ranch nearby, and Momostecan Indians supplied him with workers. Regional Spanish authorities seated in the Zapotitlán-Suchitepéquez and later Totonicapán headquarters remained geographically and politically distant from Momostenango, especially before the organization of the cabildo. Even the Franciscan friars only paid brief visits to the community until late in the century, although they succeeded in making a good impression on the Momostecans. After founding a convent at the town center in 1587, the friars became the main Spanish influence in the community. Only in the seventeeth century did other Spaniards begin to penetrate the Momostenango community in small numbers, as they established cattle ranches in the Sija Valley north of the town center.

What can we learn from the Momostenango case that might be relevant to our previous discussion? To begin with, we should note the contrast between the limited "primary resistance" offered by the Momostecans and the strong oppostion of the central Quichés. Nor did the Momostecans engage in millenial movements during the years following the conquest battles, in contrast to the central Quichés and, for that matter, the Quichés of Quezaltenango (Zamora 1986). As we have already suggested, Momostenango's reaction to the Spanish conquest must have been conditioned in part by its prior subordinate position within the prehispanic Quiché Kingdom. The capitulation to the Spaniards by the Momostecan chief and the willingness of the masses to follow him sheeplike into subordinate relations with the Spaniards suggest that both native rulers and commoners expected to benefit from their acquiescense to Spanish rule. In a perverse sense, then, the Quiché Kingdom paved the way for the Spanish conquest of places like Momostenango. It created hostile peoples who rather easily sided with the Spaniards at the time of the conquest encounter, and it politically conditioned large numbers of rural peoples to submit to authority, whether native or Spanish. An important related question about the Momostenango case that we cannot discuss here is why in later centuries the community became so rebellious to outside rule.

The Momostenango case also tells us that despite Spanish rule the Momostecan Indians and their leaders exercised considerable agency in reproducing much of their indigenous political system. In contrast to what Piel argues for the central Quichés, these reconstituted native political forms operated on several levels and not just the parcialidad level (on this point see also Smith 1984). It is noteworthy that the Spanish-defined community of Momostenango had important roots in the prehispanic provincial structure and that the provincial chief himself played an active role in "creating" the new township. Mediated by the friars, the Spaniards later began to chip away at the native community structure, but the Momostenango case makes it clear that the Indians were tireless social engineers who moulded each and every new Spanish institution to their own specifications. That they were so successful in this nativistic enterprise probably goes a long way toward explaining the nonrebellious nature of the Momostecans during the sixteenth century.

What can we say about the role of capitalism at this early period? Relatively weak capitalist forces were at work in the community. This is not surprising, of course, and even those historians who adopt a rigid mode-of-production model recognize that areas like Momostenango, which were not rich in exportable resources, were affected only indirectly by capitalist forces. Nevertheless, the extent to which labor and goods were politically rather than commercially controlled in Momostenango is impressive. Furthermore, there is no good evidence that Momostecans at this time were a significant reserve of resources for commercial ventures on the coast or elsewhere. A possible exception to this would be the Momostecans' involvement in the production and exchange of cacao, but as Zamora (1983) has pointed out for the Western Highlands as a whole, early colonial Indians could draw upon preexisting native institutions (such as politically controlled coastal estancias) to fulfill their tributary obligation of cacao beans. Perhaps the central Quiché area described by Piel was more subject to capitalist forces than Momostenango at this early time, but the apparent difference could also be an artifact of employing an overly deterministic mode-of-production model.

We turn now to the conquest of Costa Rica, and to an examination of the early history of the Buenos Aires community.

Conquest of Costa Rica

In this section, I rely heavily on the numerous and high-quality studies of the conquest of Costa Rica in the literature (see especially Fonseca 1983; González

1981; Meléndez 1972; Quirós 1987; Rivas 1979; Zamora 1980). A recent essay by the late Paulino González (1988) is a useful place to begin, since he provides a convenient overview of the Costa Rican conquest and his approach is consistent with the framework outlined above. González argues that the key to any conquest is military and economic superiority, but political and ideological interests are also always at work. In the case of the Spanish conquest of Costa Rica, he says, Spain's economic interests derived from its fragile situation within the mercantile system of European markets and from its search for a Central American "straits" that would allow it to control trade with the Spice Islands. Ideologically, the conquest may be seen as Spain's version of the civilizing "crusades" (see Figure 19–2 for the location of places mentioned below).

Conquest of Diverse Indian Groups

At the time of the Costa Rican conquest, González notes, the native societies consisted of two broad types, Mesoamerican and South American. Both were at a great military disadvantage relative to the Spaniards, but nevertheless fiercely resisted the conquest and even in defeat stubbornly held out against submission to the colonial state. As elsewhere in Central America, political subordination came in the form of Spanish gobernadores and corregidores, Spanish town officials and cacique-led Indian officials operating within newly congregated native

Figure 19–2. Map of Contact period Costa Rica showing places mentioned in the text.

communities. The economic conquest of the Indians consisted of first seizing them as slaves, taking their goods as booty, and then forcing them to pay encomienda tributes to the conquistadores. Next the friars came to take "charge of making concrete the ideological subordination," by converting the Indians to Catholicism and organizing them into cofradía cults.

The Mesoamerican societies concentrated in the Nicoya Peninsula were the first to be contacted and conquered in Costa Rica, beginning in the 1520s. Working under the direction of Pedrarias in Panama, Francisco Hernández de Córdoba converted the Nicoya area into an exportation center for moving slaves and goods from Nicaragua to Panama. The Indians, mostly Chorotegas, were forced to serve as tamemes and provide food for resident Spaniards in the area. The aboriginal ruling councils (*monexico*) were abolished and replaced by Spanish-appointed individual caciques. The Indians were assigned to encomiendas, which later fell into the hands of Pedrarias and his comrades in Nicaragua. Encomienda Indians in Nicoya were forced to perform hard labor, including that of transporting commercial cargo, while many fell into outright slavery.

By the 1550s, the Mesoamerican Indians of Nicoya were fully subject to Crown authority, and a corregidor was assigned to the area. The Mercedarian friars baptized and congregated the Chorotegas into towns, although some Indians fled to the mountains at this time. Between 1529 and 1558, the number of available native working men in Nicoya dropped from 2,000 to 500 as a result of disease and slave-taking. Meanwhile, the culturally South American Indians (the Huetares) on the mainland side of the Nicoya gulf had up to this point successfully resisted Spanish rule.

The conquest of the Indians of the Central Plateau area was begun in 1561 by Juan Vázquez de Coronado, the alcalde mayor of Nicaragua. Vázquez attempted to "pacify" the Indians through persuasion, and some groups at first agreed to provide the Spaniards with tributes and services. It soon became evident, however, that the Indians would not conform to Spanish rule. A Huetar cacique, Garabito, united the dispersed native settlements of the western part of the plateau and led them in an uncontrollable revolt. The Spanish forces moved their base of operations from the western to the eastern part of the plateau, where they founded the town of Cartago. Like their western neighbors, the Indians of this zone also refused to accede to Spanish rule. They repeatedly rose up in rebellion, and the Spaniards finally had to resort to "terror tactics" ("quartering some Indians") in an attempt to bring a degree of order to the area.

For over a decade the Spaniards were confronted with native rebellion, culminating in 1568 with an insurrection led by Cacique Turrichiquí (in coalition with such powerful native polities as Guarco, Turrialba, Ujarrás, Corrosí, and Atirró). The Spaniards put down the insurrection, and with the onset of hunger and disease in the central area, native resistance waned. For the first time, González (1988:103) says, "the foreign yoke began to affect to some extent the structures of power of the Indian communities of this region." Gobernador Perafán de Rivera's 1569 encomienda grants finally allowed the conquering Spaniards to enjoy some tangible benefits from the conquest of the Central Plateau area.

The Spaniards' success in the Nicoya and Central Plateau areas was not matched on the Atlantic Coast, however, where they were unable to establish even a foothold, despite many attempts during the conquest years. The Indians from that area received the Spaniards peacefully at first, but thereafter fiercely resisted all attempts to subjugate them to the colonial state. They engaged in guerrilla warfare against the Spaniards, and even employed "scorched earth" tactics to prevent the conquerors from gaining access to their food supplies. On several occasions, the Spaniards founded towns along the Atlantic Coast (e.g., Santiago de Talamanca), but none of these lasted very long. The culturally South American Indians of the Atlantic Coast, then, were never really conquered by the Spaniards, although they were plundered and persecuted throughout the Colonial period.

González's important essay makes clear that the conquest of Costa Rica differed from area to area (the conquest of the Pacific South is discussed below in connection with the Buenos Aires case). He attributes these differences to ecological factors, as well as the native polities. He also emphasizes the severe economic exploitation of the Indians during the conquest and the Indians' violent political reaction in most areas (cf. Zamora 1980). Furthermore, González recognizes the importance of the emerging colonial state in facilitating the exploitation of the Indians (Fonseca 1983; Quirós 1987). Almost totally lacking from González's account, however, is any serious consideration of the internal organization of the native societies or of their cultural systems. For information on that topic, we must turn to the important work of Eugenia Ibarra Rojas (1984, 1989).

Ibarra (1984) documents the existence at contact of a series of aboriginal chiefdoms in the Central Plateau and Atlantic Coast areas of Costa Rica. The main structural components of the chiefdoms were ranked matrilineal clans. The clans were exogamous and through marriage and other forms of "reciprocal" exchange they provided integration within the chiefdoms and linkages with other polities. The chiefs received tributes from inferior clans and exercised authority over subject community leaders (*Ibuxes*) and other local authorities (known as *Taques* and *Oris*). These various authorities were bound together by kinship ties. Even the Atlantic coastal polities under the leadership of "Mexican" chiefs were similarly organized. Guarco, the largest of all the chiefdoms, was located near the place that was to become Cartago. It may have incorporated as many as 12,000 inhabitants within its political jurisdiction.

Ibarra (1989) demonstrates that these native polities contributed greatly to the events of the conquest in Costa Rica. For example, much of the native resistance to the Spaniards came specifically from the Guarco chiefdom. The first conquistadores found the Guarco leaders to be hostile, and in 1569 they led a revolt against Cartago. As late as 1590, the Spaniards tried to intervene in the Guarco chiefly succession in order to bring an end to rebellious activity, but without success. Later, when the rebellions shifted to the Atlantic Coast, Guarco military leaders began to appear among the ranks of the coastal rebels. Ibarra believes that prehispanic kin relations between the chiefdoms—possibly mediated by shared clan affiliation—explain the spread of rebellion from the Central Valley to the Atlantic Coast. Apparently, members of the Guarco chiefly line provided leadership for the rebellious coastal polities, and even the famous eighteenth-century Talamanca rebellion may have been directed by chiefs from the same Guarco clan line.

Ibarra (1989:28) concludes that "The Indian resistance was constant in the Central Valley and Talamanca from 1561 until 1710" and that "cultural continuity within . . . (the) chiefly societies . . . was not broken . . . as a result of the European presence." Her willingness to take seriously the "differing relationships with the pre-existing cultures" and the conquering powers is something that has often been lacking in studies on the conquest of Costa Rica (but see Rivas 1979; Quirós 1987; Zamora 1980). Her political and cultural focus also fits within the framework I promote in the present essay.

The Buenos Aires Case

The conquest of what later became the township of Buenos Aires was initiated in the 1560s by Spanish expeditions to the South Coast. In González's (1988) summary of the conquest of the Pacific South, he points out that the conquistadores first made contact with the coastal settlement of Quepo, which then became the launching point for incursions into the interior. Vázquez de Coronado originally "pacified" the native groups of the interior area in 1563, largely without violence according to González. Nevertheless, near what is today Buenos Aires, Vázquez encountered stiff resistance from Coctú and other militant chiefdoms. The Spanish forces quickly overpowered these native polities, however, and took the first steps toward establishing colonial rule in the area. A Spanish town was soon established near present-day Buenos Aires, although apparently it lasted for only a few weeks. Among the chiefdoms subdued by Vázquez were those of the Boruca and other Indian groups residing in territory that would later become part of the Buenos Aires township.

Quepo became the headquarters for the Spaniards in the Pacific South, but heavy exploitation of the natives and a friar's mistreatment of a cacique from there led to revolts by the local population. Many of the Indians dispersed to the nearby mountains, and Spanish control deteriorated so greatly by the seventeenth century that Quepo lost its position as the corregimiento headquarters of the area. Meanwhile, beginning around 1600, a mule route leading from Nicaragua to Panama was opened up in Boruca territory. This enabled the Spaniards to bring the Boruca Indians under more intensive control. In 1604, the Franciscan missionaries tried unsuccessfully to congregate the Boruca Indians into a Spanish-type town, but in 1629 a friar was sent to reside among them and the Indian towns of San Diego de Acuña and San Juan de Calahorra were finally established. With the decline of Quepo as a Spanish base, Boruca became the colonial center of the Pacific South. Soon the Spaniards were settling rebellious Indians from Quepo, Coctú, and the Atlantic Coast within or adjacent to the Boruca towns.

González concludes that the conquest process in the Pacific South resulted in no significant Spanish settlement or expropriation of lucrative tributes. Instead, the area came to function as an important commercial passageway between

Central America and Panama and as a place of refuge for semisubjugated Indian groups.

Luz Alba Chacón (1986) presents compelling evidence that the large savannas heavily populated with Indians when the first conquistadores entered the interior part of the Pacific South area were in fact located in the Valle del General. One of the most powerful chiefdoms of the valley was Cía, which Chacón believes occupied the site of the present-day town center of Buenos Aires. The Cía chiefdom may have had more territory and members than Coctú, the latter apparently being located to the south near the modern township of Coto Brus. Like Coctú, Cía had a large, fortified center (surrounded by a double stockade), with over 1,600 persons residing inside its fences. The basic social units of the Cía chiefdom appear to have been matrilineal clans, presided over by a chief, who in 1569 was named Quizicará. As with the Boruca and Coctú chiefdoms, the Cía polity resisted postcontact Spanish control, and many of its Indians fled to the mountains. In 1571, the Spaniards again tried to establish a Spanish town (Nombre de Jesús) nearby, but, like its predecessor, the town lasted only a short time. As late as 1680, when a Spanish official was sent to determine the condition of the Indians in the Valle del General, he found only "some 500 families, very belicose and dispersed" (Chacón 1986:36).

María Eugenia Bozzoli's (1979) reconstruction of the basic cultural patterns of Contact period natives of the Buenos Aires zone provides a useful backdrop to the events of the Spanish conquest and colonization there. She points out that the natives of the zone cultivated maize, cacao, beans, squash, yucca, and tropical fruits. They also grew cotton and extracted a drug by chewing the native Piper plant. Native craftsmen fabricated an attractive polychrome pottery (painted with animal designs), wove colorful cotton cloth, mined and worked gold, carved elaborate stone figures, and extracted a purple dye from the Murex shell. Most of these manufactured goods were traded along elaborate networks that extended well beyond the Pacific South area.

Bozzoli (1979:11–13) reports a drastic decline in the native population of the Buenos Aires zone as a result of the conquest. From an estimated population of about 3,000 persons at contact, the Indians of the zone were reduced by disease and migrations to about 1,400 persons in only six years. These losses were followed by the imposition of a heavy tributary regime on the Boruca Indians, who were forced to provide the missionaries with maize and canoes and to carry such goods to the Pacific Coast for shipment to Nicoya. In addition, they had to serve (free of charge) the mule trains passing through the zone. On top of all that, they were required to sponsor cofradía cult masses paid for with purple thread and cotton cloths.

Let us now attempt to view the Buenos Aires case in relation to the conquest of Costa Rica as a whole and the framework outlined at the beginning of this essay. The first thing to note in this regard is that the conquest of the Buenos Aires zone shares many features with developments in the Central Plateau and Atlantic Coast areas but contrasts significantly with the conquest of the Nicoya area. This strongly suggests that the cultural contrast between the Mesoamerican (Chorotegas of Nicoya) and South American (Chibchans of the Central, Atlantic Coast and Pacific South) native societies was an important factor in shaping the overall conquest of Costa Rica.

The Chorotegas of Nicoya were more vulnerable to the Spaniards than the Huetares or Borucas by virtue of their more complex sociopolitical organization (Rivas 1979). As we saw, the Mesoamerican Indians of Costa Rica eventually yielded to the colonial state, with its onerous tributary obligations, while the South American Indians either belatedly became unreliable colonial subjects (the Central Plateau) or never really fell under Spanish control (the Atlantic Coast and Pacific South). To some extent, this outcome is related to the ecology of the region. That is, Nicoya is less tropical and more strategically located for commerce than either the Central Plateau or Pacific South areas, and so the Spaniards made a greater effort to subjugate the Nicoya Indians. Furthermore, since the Pacific South is more tropical than the Central Plateau, ecology might explain some of the more subtle differences between the conquests of these two areas.

The chiefdoms inhabiting Buenos Aires and the Central Plateau at contact appear to have been quite similar, and their chiefly organizations helped determine the kind of strong resistance they offered to the Spaniards. The natives of the two areas were culturally similar as well, and the "level" of integration of their cultural systems differed radically from the Spanish cultural level. This made it difficult for these Indians to understand or accept the Christian religion, and as a result syncretic religious synthesis does not appear to have gone very far. As a result, the Costa Rican chiefdoms offered considerable (but only moderately effective) "primary" resistance but virtually no "millenial" opposition to the Spanish conquest and early colonization processes. Relations between the native and Christian religious systems gradually changed as the Colonial period wore on, but even in recent times the native religions in Buenos Aires are relatively poor in syncretic terms (Bozzoli 1986; Constenla 1979).

Finally, we should note with González (1988) that the Spaniards were unable to establish successful commercial agricultural ventures based on Indian labor in the Pacific South. On at least two occasions, Spanish towns were laid out in the Valle del General, and stretches of land were allocated to Spaniards with a view to developing food-producing estates. But the Indians could not be brought under encomienda control, and without their labor the Spanish settlers soon departed for the Central Plateau (Quirós 1987:139ff.; Zamora 1980:79–80). Nor was the supply of Indian labor or tributes abundant in the central area, and so the Spaniards there inceasingly turned to trade and cattle ranching (Fonseca and Quirós 1987). Eventually, the commercial forces unleashed in the central area reached the Buenos Aires zone in the form of mule trains passing through Boruca. But this activity does not appear to have radically transformed the native societies or their relations with colonial society.

Capitalist impulses at this early period were weak in Costa Rica as a whole and almost negligible in Buenos Aires. This clearly was an important factor in determining the nature of relations between the colonial state and the Indians, but in turn the particularities of that relationship had already in large measure determined the limited nature of the capitalist impulses reaching Costa Rica.

Conclusions

Commercial interests were a major factor driving the Spanish conquest of Central America, as has been argued by MacLeod and others. The exploitation of cacao in Pacific coastal Guatemala and slaves in the Nicoya Peninsula of Costa Rica for purposes of export trade would seem to support the "mode-of-production" thesis about conquest. Nevertheless, the specific cases of Momostenango and Buenos Aires reveal that political interests could also direct conquest and colonization processes in many areas. Even where the natives did not prove to be particularly useful for commercial ventures, the Spaniards' attempt to establish a colonial state based on territoriality, monopoly political control, and aristocratic privilege led to the relentless subjugation of the Indians through conquest. This is not really surprising, given Spain's state-directed monopoly capitalism and deeply entrenched tributary policy at that time.

The Momostenango and Buenos Aires cases reveal even more clearly how important the nature of the indigenous political systems was to the outcome of the conquest. As Mesoamericans, the Momostecans, and to a less extent the Nicoya Indians, were politically preconditioned to accommodate to the colonial state, while the Indians who were culturally South American Indians—those of Buenos Aires and to a less degree those of the Central Plateau—were not. Momostecans quickly became reliable, even faithful servants of the Crown, whereas the Boruca and other Buenos Aires Indian groups never really accepted Spanish rule at any time during the Colonial period. These differences have had important political repercussions through time for these two townships (Momostenango and Buenos Aires), and probably for their respective nation-states as well.

Finally, the issue of culture and its relationship to the conquest is illuminated by the case studies. Guillermo Céspedes (1985) has argued that the limited "world horizons" of the native Americans prevented them from understanding the threat the European world posed for them. This is undoubtedly true, but the native Americans' world horizons varied, depending on whether they were organized into states and on the kind of interstate system to which they were tied. The Momostecans, led by chiefs originally from the capital of the Quiché state, certainly understood conquest, tribute taking, and the relationship between such political processes and local authority. Culturally, they were in a position to comprehend their plight and to "creatively adapt" (Farriss 1984) their political and religious institutions to the new Spanish-dominated world. The Buenos Aires Indians, in contrast, had lived outside a state system, and indications are that they never understood the nature of the colonial state or ever made a concerted attempt to culturally adapt to it. Instead, most of them fled from Spanish society, and even today they appear to be extremely maladapted to the complex world of state-level society in which they find themselves (Carmack 1989). Differences between the natives' world horizons within Guatemala and Costa Rica must also have differentially affected the development of nationalism in the two countries, but that is a topic for another essay.

The problems that the Buenos Aires Indians face in accommodating to the modern world raise an issue that should always be uppermost in our minds as scholars: Our objects of study are really subjects, and ancient occurrences such as the Spanish conquest continue to have relevance for all of us. Unless we take this into account in our studies, so-called objective analysis will easily become a weapon that can be used by latter-day conquerors engaged in "cycles of conquest" (Lovell 1988) against the Central American Indians. Let us remember with Weber that conquest is always an expression of imperialism and that its causes are political and cultural as well as economic.

References

Bozzoli, María Eugenia
  1979 *Encuesta socioeconómica en la zona del P.H. Boruca.* ICI, San José, Costa Rica.
  1986 *El Nacimiento y la Muerte entre los Bribris.* 2nd ed. Editorial Universidad de Costa Rica, San José.
Carmack, Robert M.
  1981 *The Quiché Mayas of Utatlán.* University of Oklahoma, Norman.
  1983 Spanish—Indian Relations in Highland Guatemala, 1800–1944. In *Spaniards and Indians in Southeastern Mesoamerica: Essays on the History of Ethnic Relations*, edited by Murdo MacLeod and Robert Wasserstrom, pp. 215–252. University of Nebraska, Lincoln.
  1986 Ethnohistory of the Guatemalan Colonial Indian. In *Supplement to the Handbook of Middle American Indians*, vol. 4, *Ethnohistory*, edited by Ronald Spores, pp. 55–87. University of Texas, Austin.
  1988 State and Community in Nineteenth-Century Guatemala: The Momostenango Case. In *Guatemala Indians and the State: 1540–1988*, edited by Carol A. Smith, pp. 116–140. University of Texas, Austin, in press.
  1989 Indians in Buenos Aires, Costa Rica. *Cultural Survival Quarterly* 13:30–33.
  n.d. A Political Ethnohistory of Momostenango. Ms. in possession of author.
Céspedes, Guillermo
  1985 La conquista. In *Historia de América Latina*, vol. 1, by Pedro Carrasco and Guillermo Céspedes, pp. 267–371. Alianza Editorial, Madrid.
Chacón Umaña, Luz Alba
  1986 Buenos Aires, Cantón de Puntarenas. Apuntes para su historia. *Revista del Archivo Nacional* 44:5–166.
Collins, Randall
  1986 *Weberian Sociological Theory.* Cambridge University Press, New York.
Constenla, Adolfo
  1979 *Leyendas y Tradiciones Borucas.* Editorial Universidad de Costa Rica, San José.
Cook, Garrett
  1981 *Supernaturalism, Cosmos, and Cosmogony in Quichéan Expressive Culture.* Unpublished doctoral dissertation, State University of New York, Albany.
Farriss, Nancy M.
  1983 Indians in Colonial Yucatan: Three Perspectives. In *Spaniards and Indians in Southeastern Mesoamerica: Essays on the History of Ethnic Relations*, edited by Murdo MacLeod and Robert Wasserstrom, pp. 1–39. University of Nebraska, Lincoln.
  1984 *Maya Society under Colonial Rule: The Collective Enterprise of Survival.* Princeton University, Princeton, N.J.
Fonseca, Elizabeth
  1983 *Costa Rica Colonial. La Tierra y el Hombre.* EDUCA, San José, Costa Rica.
Fonseca, Elizabeth, and Claudia Quirós
  1988 Economía colonial y formación de las estructuras agrarias. In *Desarrollo*

Institucional de Costa Rica: De las Sociedades Indígenas a la crisis del 30, introduction, selection, and notes by Jaime Murillo, pp. 121–162. Guayacán, San José, Costa Rica.

Fuentes y Guzmán, F.A. de
1932–1933 *Recordación Florida*. 4 vols. Biblioteca Goathemala, vols. 6–8, Guatemala.

González, Paulino
1981 *Les resistences indiennes au royaume de Guatemala (1523–1720)*. Thèse pour le doctorat de 3ème cycle, Toulose, France.
1988 La Conquista. In *Desarrollo Institucional de Costa Rica: De las Sociedades Indígenas a la crisis del 30*, introduction, selection, and notes by Jaime Murillo, pp. 79–120. Guayacán, San José, Costa Rica.

Ibarra R., Eugenia
1984 *Los cacicazgos indígenas de la Vertiente Atlántica y Valle Central de Costa Rica*. Tésis de Grado, University of Costa Rica, San José.
1989 La organización clánica en el Valle Central y Talamanca en el momento de la conquista (s. XVI y XVII). In *Costa Rica Colonial*, edited by Luis F. Sibaja et al., pp. 13–37. Guayacán, San José, Costa Rica.

Kramer, Wendy
1988 *The Politics of Encomienda Distribution in Early Spanish Guatemala, 1524–1544*. Unpublished Master's thesis, Department of History, University of Warwick, England.

Lovell, E. George
1988 Surviving Conquest: The Guatemalan Indian in Historical Perspective. *Latin American Research Review* 23:25–57.

MacLeod, Murdo
1973 *Spanish Central America: A Socioeconomic History, 1520–1720*. University of California, Berkeley.

Meléndez, Carlos
1972 *Conquistadores y Pobladores, Orígenes Históricas-Soles de los Costarricenses*. EUNED, San José, Costa Rica.

Newson, Linda
1986 *The Cost of Conquest. Indian Decline in Honduras Under Spanish Rule*. Westview, Boulder, Colo.
1987 *Indian Survival in Colonial Nicaragua*. University of Oklahoma, Norman.

Piel, Jean
1989 *Sajcabajá: Muerte y resurrección de un pueblo de Guatemala (1500–1970)*. Centre d'Etudes Mexicaines et Centramericaines, Mexico.

Polo Sifontes, Francis
1974 *Los Cakchiqueles en la Conquista de Guatemala*. University of San Carlos, Guatemala.

Quirós V., Claudia
1987 *La Encomienda en Costa Rica y su Papel Dentro de la Estructural Socioeconómica Colonial: 1569–1699*. Unpublished Master's thesis, University of Costa Rica, San José.

Rivas, Francisco
1979 *La conquista de Costa Rica: Primera Fase (1502–1560)*. Tésis de grado, University of Costa Rica, San José.

Smith, Anthony D.
1983 *State and Nation in the Third World*. St. Martin's, New York.

Smith, Carol A.
1984 Local history in global context: social and economic transitions in Western Guatemala. *Comparative Studies in Society and History* 26:193–228.

Tedlock, Barbara
1982 *Time and the Highland Maya*. University of New Mexico, Albuquerque.

Zamora, Elías
1979 La conquista de America Central. *Historia* 16:69–79.
1980 *Etnografía Histórica de Costa Rica (1561—1615)*. Publicaciones de la Universidad de Sevilla, Sevilla.

1983 Conquista y crisis demográfica: la población indígena del occidente de Guatemala en el siglo XVI. *Mesoamerica* 6:291–328.

1986 Resistencia maya a la colonización: levantamientos indígenas en Guatemala durante el siglo XVI. In *Los Mayas de los Tiempos Tardíos*, edited by Miguel Rivera and Andrés Ciudad, pp. 197–214. Sociedad Española de Estudios Mayas, Madrid.

Chapter 20 ■

Mary W. Helms

Survivors of Conquest: A Survey of Indigenous Cultures of Lower Central America during the Sixteenth and Seventeenth Centuries

To many of the indigenous peoples of the territory now known as Lower Central America (the region between Mesoamerica and Colombia, including the eastern half of Honduras and Nicaragua and all of Costa Rica and Panama), the opening decades—indeed the first half—of the sixteenth century must have appeared as a terrifying apocalypse. Suddenly, with little or no warning, extreme perils, against which there were no known defenses, destroyed high chiefs and large numbers of ordinary population alike and threatened to eradicate—in some instances did eradicate—life-styles that had flourished for a thousand years or more. The agents of these disasters appeared as strangers from a distant and unknown realm, possibly, some thought, from the sky (e.g., Anderson 1938:219). Although at times the newcomers seemed to come in peace, proclaiming to curious and perplexed but initially hospitable chiefs the wisdom and power of new gods, the newcomers also frequently behaved otherwise, as beings apparently bereft of normal human courtesies and decencies who endlessly demanded gold beyond the expected limits of the usual gifts and presentations, inflicted torture and death and enslavement without regard for rank or condition, and, albeit unwittingly, introduced new and fatal diseases.

The newcomers initially appeared in eastern Panama and moved across the narrow isthmus. Then, from their encampment in western Panama, on the shores of the South Sea, they proceeded north, by sea and land trails, along the Pacific Coast to Nicoya and the western lake district of Nicaragua. From there, small bands of conquistadores moved further north into central Honduras, where they encountered comparable exploratory parties moving south from Guatemala. A generation or so later (in the 1560s and 1570s), similar exploratory bands moved south into the central highlands of Costa Rica to initiate small settlements in the upland basins known as the *Meseta Central*. Generalizing broadly, the basic intent of these initial intrusions into parts of western Central America (where virtually all Spanish colonial settlements were established) was to acquire portable wealth with which a soldier could return enriched to Spain. Long-term occupation generally was not an initial intent, but followed as a by-product of the fact that the extractable wealth of Central America was limited in comparison with the vast amounts of gold and silver and jewels flowing from the heartland of Mexico and Peru. Consequently, by mid-sixteenth century many hopeful conquistadors had left Central America to seek their fortunes in these new theaters of colonial activity. Those who stayed behind (if they lived in Nicaragua, Honduras, or Costa Rica) gradually, of necessity, adopted agrarian life-styles focusing on subsistence and a series of boom-and-bust cash crop endeavors. Those remaining in Panama administered the traffic of the *trajín*, the transisthmian river and trailway cargo route that linked Peru and the Andean colonies with the Caribbean and formed the major focus of Spanish interests in Panama in the years following the initial conquest.

Native communities and polities in the direct path of early Spanish conquest were severely disrupted, and the fate of the population was soon determined. In Panama, the disruptive passage of expeditions (*entradas*), the initial search for gold, the subsequent labor requirements for gold mining and washing, and conditions of general servitude, especially in the vicinity of Panama City and its supply area, led to the rapid extermination of natives who fell into Spanish hands, a repeat of the demographic and cultural destruction that had decimated Hispaniola. To meet the continuing labor demands of Hispanic Panama, particularly those relating to the trajín, large numbers of Indians were enslaved in western Nicaragua and shipped, with tremendous loss of life, to the Isthmus (and also to Peru). (When this labor supply also became depleted, tens of thousands of African slaves were imported to Panama to meet the Spaniards' labor demands). Those natives of western Nicaragua who were not enslaved were subject to disrupted life-styles and a series of serious epidemics. In central Honduras, forced labor in mines took a toll of native lives, while in Costa Rica over 90 percent of the population of the central mountain valleys died in massive epidemics within a few years of Spanish settlement.

Although significant regions of western Central America were seriously disrupted by the Spanish presence and a large percentage of the native population of these regions lost, the central mountains and the eastern lowlands remained by and large unconquered. The isolation of these hinterlands, the militancy of the indigenous populations living there, and the economic de-

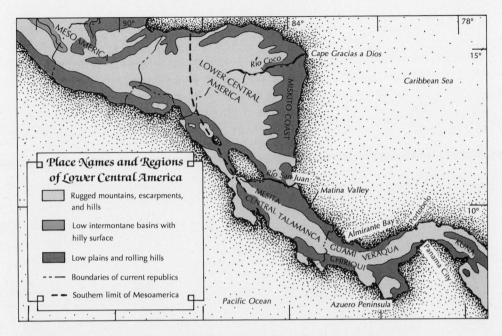

Figure 20–1. Significant place names and regions of Lower Central America.

pression and official disinterest that limited Hispanic expansion in the centuries following the initial establishment of colonial settlements allowed these regions to serve as a refuge for native populations and a place where indigenous culture patterns could continue with considerable protection from direct Spanish impact. These survivors and the nature of their adaptations are the focus of this essay. We must keep in mind, however, that the same isolation that protected these peoples and cultures during the sixteenth and seventeenth centuries has also greatly limited the amount of ethnohistorical data available for the reconstruction of the nature of their lives during this time.

Panama: The Kuna and the Guaymí

The presence of the Spaniards in Panama was limited to (1) the general environs of Panama City and the lowlands and smaller towns to the west, where cattle were raised and food was grown to supply the city; (2) the trajín that crossed between Panama City and the Caribbean terminus of Nombre de Dios, later replaced by Portobelo; and (3) gold mines and washings such as those on portions of the Tuira river (eastern Panama) and in the mountains of Veragua (northwest Caribbean versant) (Anderson 1938:272–286; Sauer 1969:280, 282). Except for various unsuccessful mission attempts to "reduce" the native population into nucleated settlements (Stier 1979:66–73; Young 1970), large stretches of territory both east and west of the major Spanish settlements and the transisthmian trail remained unsettled by Europeans after the initial entradas, and provided sanctuary both for communities of runaway African slaves and for native populations seeking safety by withdrawing from contact with outsiders. Presumably these populations were the survivors of the dozens of small chiefdoms that had existed in the isthmus prior to contact, although refugees from northern Colombia may well have settled in eastern parts of the isthmus, too (see note 2).

In eastern Panama (known as the Darién region), epidemics and the presence of the Spaniards on the Pacific shores led native societies to withdraw from the Pacific slopes into headwater regions of the central mountains and then, gradually, along the riverways of the Caribbean versant, a region that had been depopulated during the initial Spanish entry (Stier 1979:48–58, 353; Wafer 1934:78). The native population of this mountainous eastern region now became known as the Kuna,[1] and the essential question regarding their initial adaptation to the postconquest era asks to what extent did the political organization indigenous to Precolumbian Panama remain or in what manner was it changed.[2] Unfortunately, the data from the late sixteenth and especially the seventeenth centuries are limited. In the following discussion, I rely heavily on remarks by Lionel Wafer (1934) regarding the Bayano headwater region. Wafer's observations, however, may not be entirely appropriate for regions farther east, closer to Colombia.

General trends suggested by Wafer indicate considerable continuities with preconquest life-styles during the sixteenth and seventeenth centuries, at least for the population clustered in the Bayano headwater area. (In general, major acculturative changes did not occur for the Kuna until the eighteenth and nineteenth centuries). The greatest adjustments may have occurred at the highest level of chiefship with respect to those persons known as *quevís* in the literature of the conquest. Many of the traditional activities of these high chiefs seems to have revolved around "foreign affairs" involving interpolity alliances or warfare with other quevís or would-be quevís and trade, pilgrimages, and/or diplomatic contacts with leaders of polities even farther afield, particularly in northern and north-central Colombia. Much of this long-distance activity probably ended with the Spanish conquest (during which many quevís also died) and with it, presumably, a major context for chiefly activity, identification, and legitimation. Consequently, the title that is associated with native leadership in the centuries following the conquest (generally referring to heads of multigenerational extended family households or villages) is *saka* (or *sakla*), a title probably derived from the term for the second tier of elite status positions (*saco*) in precontact chiefdoms (Elliott Joyce 1934:173–174; Helms 1979:12–13; Howe 1986:12).

On the other hand, the Kuna continued to oppose the Spaniards militarily when necessary (hence the lack of missionary success), and prestigeful chiefly war leaders with supralocal or regional influence are still in evidence in the seventeenth century. One such leader was Lacenta, a chief visited by Lionel Wafer in 1681 (Wafer 1934:17–18) who resided at the headwaters of the Río Bayano, which was where the compound of the also highly influential Precolumbian chief, Comogre, had been located a century and a half earlier (Helms 1979:40, 189 n. 7, 190 n. 20). Some gold and silver ornaments indicative of rank and status, such as large ear and nose plates worn by men and nose rings worn by women, although now fewer and simpler in form, also were still used in Lacenta's time, as was body and face painting (Wafer 1934:85–86; nose rings and other gold jewelry continue to be worn and displayed by twentieth-century Kuna women). Yet many of the benefits and much of the esotericism of chiefly rank and office enjoyed by Precolumbian lords—and evidenced before the conquest in the services of war captive slaves, in the long-distance activities and skilled artisanry that produced the hugh quantities of exquisitely crafted regalia of chiefship, and in the preservation of mummified remains of ancestral chiefs in the inner rooms of chiefly compounds—apparently were gone (see Helms 1979:9).

The basic unit of Kuna society in the centuries immediately after the conquest may have been the extended family occupying a single dwelling with interior divisions, such as was described by the buccaneers in the vicinity of the lower Chucunaque river (Wafer 1934:xviii). Alternatively, Wafer notes that a separate house was built for a newly married couple, although where this house was located vis-à-vis other relatives is not indicated (1934:98). At the present time, Kuna marital residence is matrilocal and features strong ties between the father-in-law and son-in-law, as well as strong ties among the core group of consanguineous females. There has also been some tendency for neolocal residence by young men who become impatient with the dictates of their fathers-in-law (Helms 1976:137, 139, 151–152). Precontact evidence suggests that alliances, including those formed by marriages, were important among men, particularly as they allied a queví with supporters. It is possible that a mode of family organization in which ambitious family or community leaders supported one or more wives and their children (who may have had separate or combined households) and thereby commanded the services of numerous sons, and especially of sons-in-law, has existed unchanged in fundamental respects from preconquest patterns, when, although commoners were probably monogamous, nobles and chiefs practiced polygyny. Although monogamy has now become the norm, in the late seventeenth century a regional chief such as Lacenta continued to have numerous (seven for Lacenta) wives and presumably benefited from the alliances facilitated by his own marriages and those of his children (Helms 1976:159–60, n. 5, 1979:9–10; Wafer 1934:96).

Also in keeping with preconquest sociopolitical organization and settlement patterns is Wafer's description of larger community houses serving the somewhat dispersed homesteads constituting a "community" or "neighborhood" as council chambers (1934:xviii, 90), as did the compounds (*bohíos*) of high chiefs before the conquest. It is also likely that families living along the same river considered themselves a "people" and were identified by the name of the river (Wafer 1934:89; Wassén 1949:24; Stier 1979:126, 354–355).[3] This point is particularly interesting in light of the possibility that Precolumbian lords, particularly sacos, may have held authority over the peoples and territory identified with a given river system (Helms 1979:57). It would also appear that the Precolumbian subsistence base provided by hunting and fishing (men) and agriculture (men clear and burn; women plant, tend, and harvest) still persisted (Helms 1976: 141–142, 145, 153–154; Wafer 1934:92–93, 100–101).[4] Aboriginal tools[5] continued to be used to conduct these activities, although some metal implements (e.g., machetes) had been adopted. (Widespread use of metal implements did not occur until the eighteenth century, and firearms, though available in limited quantity in the eighteenth century, did not become widespread until the nineteenth [Stout 1947:61, 69]).

By the late seventeenth century, however, men's activities were diversified by a new type of long-distance activity involving sometimes extended periods of travel away from home as sailors on European ships, particularly those of English and French buccaneers raiding the shipping of the Caribbean Sea and the terminal ports of the Panamanian trail.[6] This penchant for travel, suggestive of Precolumbian interest in long-distance contacts, may have been a factor supporting (or encouraging further development toward) matrilocal residence. It has continued unabated during later centuries, ultimately acquainting hundreds of Kuna men over the years with the customs of foreign cities and the ways of non-Hispanic Europeans and North Americans (Stout 1947:57). In Panama itself, a limited amount of occasional trading was conducted indirectly with Spaniards as well as with buccaneers during the seventeenth century (Wafer 1934:83), but trade with full-time professional foreign traders would not develop until the nineteenth century. Nonetheless, by the late seventeenth century trade beads had been added to the more traditional materials (shells, animal teeth) used for necklaces and chains, and manufactured cloth joined cloth made of native cotton. Clothing, however, was minimal, except during ceremonial occasions, when long cotton mantles were worn. Shirts and trousers were adopted during the nineteenth century, as were the distinctive women's chemises, modified to become the colorful appliquéd blouses known as *molas*, for which Kuna women are famous today.

In the mountains and foothills of western Panama, the indigenous population known today as the Guaymí presented a somewhat parallel case of postconquest adaptation. Once again, however, data directly relevant to sixteenth- and seventeenth-century conditions are extremely limited, while data concerning the societies of this region on the eve of the conquest are close to nonexistent. Generally speaking, however, it appears that the Guaymí of the central mountains may be descendants of interior polities, probably small chiefdoms, that were centered in the foothills and higher Pacific and Caribbean slopes of the western cordillera, adjacent to other centralized polities centered on the Pacific coastal plains and on the lower Caribbean valleys (cf. Helms 1979:56, 60–63, 190 n. 17). Whereas the coastal chiefdoms faced the effects of more direct Spanish contact, the interior polities, protected by the isolation of their rugged mountains, maintained considerable demographic and, apparently, cultural continuity.

The fate of the lowland polities is not known in detail. Some of the chiefdoms of the Caribbean territory, a gold-bearing region known to the Spaniards as Veragua, undoubtedly were affected by Spanish efforts during the sixteenth century to mine gold on the Caribbean slopes (Anderson 1934:272–273). Other populations of the north coast were seized as slaves or driven into the mountains in the early eighteenth century by raids conducted by Miskito Indians from eastern Nicaragua (Lothrop 1950:15; see below). The population of the chiefdoms of the Pacific lowlands (Chiriquí) either fled into the hinterland or were "reduced" by missionaries during the sixteenth and early seventeenth centuries, meaning that they were resettled in towns and were subject to the encomienda. Although large-scale uprisings occurred and many "settled" Indians fled to the safety of the mountains, others stayed and gradually were Hispanicized into a ladino peasantry (Linares 1968:78; Young 1970:16, 1971:50–53, 55). From these mission towns friars moved toward the populations living in the highlands, and it is from their reports (especially that of Fray Adrian de Ufeldre, who lived with the Guaymí between 1622 and 1637)[7] that we have some account of Guaymí customs of the time (see also Fray Antonio de la Rocha's account of neighboring highland peoples summarized in Linares 1968:79–80).

Even more than was the case with the Kuna of eastern Panama, the Guaymí have shown considerable cultural continuity from the early conquest era until the present. Presumably these stable conditions, already noted in the sixteenth and early seventeenth centuries, reflect considerable continuity with precontact culture, too. Basic subsistence practices apparently remained essentially unchanged. The Guaymí, like other neighboring mountain populations,[8] were primarily farmers growing mainly root and tree crops (pejivalle palm). They also hunted and fished. Their settlement pattern also appears to have been particularly consistent, for all ethnohistoric sources refer to scattered residences, "widely dispersed small hamlets" reflecting kin groupings with no nucleated towns, at least not in the mountains (Linares 1968:79; Young 1970:17–18). The absence of obvious elite centers in the mountains has led some researchers to question whether the Guaymí (and native peoples in western Panama in general) were politically centralized as chiefdoms prior to Hispanic contact, although the weight of the little evidence that exists suggests they were. For example, the account of Columbus's fourth voyage notes the use of the term *queví* ("Quibian") to designate the "cacique" (political leader) of one of several chiefdoms along the Caribbean Coast of western Panama (Helms 1979:60–63; Sauer 1969:131–132). On the Pacific Coast (west of Azuero Peninsula), the names of chiefs and relative locations of (presumably) chiefly centers are known (Helms 1979:60; Linares 1968:76). Finally, and with reference to populations of the mountains, Fray Adrian in the seventeenth century noted small chiefdoms in a portion of Guaymí territory (Miranda Valley—Cricamola River) and indicates the use of the term *çabra* to designate the second in command to the cacique and war leader. Fray Antonio de la Rocha reported a comparable practice among other mountain groups (Linares 1968:79). Among Precolumbian Panamanian chiefdoms in general, *çabra* was the term used to identify the lowest level of elite (below *saco*), an achieved position with local administrative responsibilities accorded to select commoners in recognition of exceptional valour in warfare (Helms 1979:13; Young 1970:24). Fray Adrian also mentions war captive-slaves among the mountain Guaymí (who were also noted for their extreme belligerance toward the Spaniards) and thus suggests a social division among elites, commoners, and slaves (Young 1970:25), while Fray Antonio notes one or two "caciques" per territory. Young points out, however, that this centralized political organization had disintegrated by the late eighteenth century.

Marital residence and household organization seems to have consistently leaned toward patrilocality (virilocality), although a period of bride-service by son-in-law for father-in-law was expected before the wife joined her husband's place of residence (Young 1970:18–19). Polygyny also persisted. In such cases, according to Fray Adrian, the first and primary wife lived with her husband while additional wives (four to six), who may have been betrothed at a very early age, remained with their parents. The husband visited them (accompanied by his senior wife) and spent part of the year working, as in the sense of bride-service, in the parental households of these other wives. Eventually, when they came of age, the additional wives, with the permission of their parents and brothers, joined the husband at his own residence (Young 1970:18–21).[9] In Fray Adrian's time, such polygyny could be afforded and therefore was practiced by the rich and powerful, that is, by the elite.

Costa Rica: The Talamancan Tribes

In Costa Rica, as in Panama, permanent Spanish settlements were few. Most were clustered in the centrally located temperate upland basins known as the *Meseta Central*. Prior to the arrival of Europeans, this region, which included ready access to the headwaters of rivers leading to both the Caribbean and the Pacific, had been well populated by a number of chiefdoms. These polities apparently were further allied into two large regional groupings known to us as the Eastern and Western Güetar (Huetares), whose chiefly leaders were recognized by elites of other centralized polities of the Pacific and Caribbean versants, respectively (Fernández Guardia 1913:12–13; Ferrero 1981:101; Ibarra 1984).[10]

Unfortunately, the influx of Spanish settlers in the Meseta Central led to the servitude and then the demise of the resident native population, primarily because of the inadvertent introduction of foreign disease. The epidemic of 1576–1581 was particularly devastating, leading to the loss of as much as 90 percent of the indigenous population of the central valleys and destroying most of the native labor available there for Spanish use (MacLeod 1973:205–206,332). Consequently, the Spanish settlements of Costa Rica were maintained largely by the settlers themselves, and the Hispanic colonial population contained very little Indian admixture.

Other regions of Costa Rica, however, remained essentially free of permanent Spanish settlement after the initial entradas had passed. Particularly noteworthy here are the Caribbean sector and the mountainous region south of the central valleys known as Talamanca, a rugged and isolated territory constituting a continuation, both geographically and as a zone of refuge, of the mountain fastness of western Panama. Here a number of native societies, following traditional culture patterns, continued to survive in spite of periodic Spanish attempts at conquest. Some indigenous populations, most notably the Bribri, Cabécar, Térraba, and Boruca, still remain in the tributary headwaters of the Sixaola and the Térraba (or Diquís) rivers, following traditional cultural practices well into the twentieth century (Fernández Guardia 1918:7–8; Hill 1973; Stone 1949, 1962). This cultural survival continued in spite of periodic Spanish attempts to establish settlements and "reduce" and christianize the Talamancan peoples during the seventeenth century. In addition, during the late seventeenth to early eighteenth-century inhabitants of both the Caribbean coast and the Talamancan hills were afflicted with raids by pirates and by Miskito Indian marauders from eastern Nicaragua seeking captives to sell as slaves to English planters on Jamaica (Fernández Guardia 1913:372–373, 1918:20; Helms 1983; MacLeod 1973:336, 387) and with Spanish planters' use of Indians from the northern fringe of Talamanca as forced labor on cacao plantations established in the Matina Valley of eastern Costa Rica (MacLeod 1973:330, 333). These raids and labor drafts encouraged many surviving natives to withdraw even farther into the greater safety of the mountainous Talamancan interior, joining the population already sheltered there.

The isolation of these mountains and the paucity of ethnohistorical data make reconstruction of the nature of indigenous culture among the Talamancan people of the sixteenth and seventeenth centuries and assessment of the impact of Spanish contact, whether direct or indirect, a rather tenuous and frustratingly generalized enterprise (but see Ibarra 1984). It would appear, however, that on the local level much day-to-day subsistence and domestic activity continued relatively unchanged, particularly that focusing on style of home architecture, household organization and operation, and personal appearance including style of dress and ornamentation (use of ear, nose and lip plugs and of gold ornaments). A certain amount of political centralization seems to have continued, too, although it seems safe to assume that the destruction of the apparently very influential *Meseta Central* chiefdoms must have led to some reduction in the regional activities (and perhaps overall status) of the highest level chiefs, called *caciques majores* ("grand chiefs") by the Spaniards (as distinguished from several grades of *caciques principales* or "principal chiefs"; see Ibarra 1984:191–193; Ferrero 1981:100). On the other hand, Talamanca itself contained political-ideological centers with regional significance, such as San José Cabecar (Ferrero 1981:102; Stone 1962:42), and some degree of distinction between elites and commoners continued to prevail during colonial times (see Ferrero 1981:101). The high-status Precolumbian activity of crafting gold ornaments is still reported in seventeenth-century accounts, too (Bray 1981:156; Zevallos 1886:158). This artisanry undoubtedly continued an ancient tradition, for the Talamancan-Almirante Bay area apparently was well known as a gold-working region for a considerable period of time prior to the conquest.

Polygyny, too, continued as a practice apparently open to all but exercised particularly by "principal men" of higher social standing (Zevallos 1886:157). These leaders also continued to command the corporate labor of the population for enterprises such as war or building construction (Fernández Guardia 1918:12). Indeed, the Talamancan tribes (like Costa Rican tribes in general) were famous for bellicosity both among themselves and against the Spaniards (Fernández Guardia 1913:6, 1918:18–19; Ibarra 1984:133), and the continuation of warfare (using traditional weapons such as lance-darts, bows and arrows) may have contributed to the continued recognition of high-status positions. According to missionary accounts (Urcullu in Fernández Guardia 1918:18–19; Zevallos

1886:156; see also Fernández Guardia 1913:6), raids provided additional women and children for labor and captives for religious sacrifices, part of the continuing practice of traditional rites involving renowned priests who "talked with the devil" and served as diviners of the future and of events in distant places.

Everyday life continued to rest on swidden agriculture in which men cleared and women and older men planted and harvested. Root and tree crops were emphasized and some maize was grown as a secondary crop. Bananas and plantains were introduced after contact. Hunting and fishing were productive, too (Ferrero 1981:96; Stone 1962:12–13; Zevallos 1886:157–158). The settlement pattern was generally dispersed. Small settlements of two or three large pole-and-thatch houses, each sheltering an extended family (each wife had a separate hearth) stood several kilometers apart. Such settlements were located along waterways, at river headwaters, or at junctions of tributaries with mainstreams. There are occasional references to larger, more compact, palisaded settlements at strategic, topographically defensive localities reminiscent of the type of location chosen for Lacento's compound as described by Wafer in Panama (Ferrero 1981:98–99; Stone 1962:16–18; cf. Ibarra 1984:112–124, 133–134).

Residence seems to have been patrilocal, although matrilineal ties directed the inheritance of status positions and matrilineal kinsmen were not suitable marriage partners. Traditional death ceremonies and secondary burial in clan or lineage communal tombs also continued, as did the burial of a slave with deceased elites (Fernández Guardia 1918:22–27; Ferrero 1981:102; Stone 1962: 29–34; Zevallos 1886:159). Seventeenth-century observers also described exchange networks involving a range of utilitarian and ceremonial goods that undoubtedly were traditionally part of such systems. These included tame tapirs and tame peccaries used in ceremonies and feasts, aromatic tree resin for embalming, strings of small tubular shell beads, war captive-slaves, cotton textiles, gold ornaments, cacao, and salt. By the end of the seventeenth century, European goods were being included in this traffic (Fernández Guardia 1918:16; Ibarra 1984:154–167; Stone 1949:24, 1962:40–41; Zevallos 1886:157–158).

Although Spanish attempts to conquer and control the Talamancan population by military means were by and large unsuccessful, during the seventeenth century a series of missions were established in the coastal lowlands and in Talamancan territory in an attempt to pacify and reduce the population. In addition, mission villages as well as the short-lived Spanish "city" of Santiago de Talamanca (situated on the Tarire river, a region of considerable potential for agriculture and cattle raising and as a Caribbean port for trade with Panama) succeeded in attracting and settling (or apportioning among the Spanish population as servants) "Christianized" Indians numbering in the hundreds, perhaps thousands (Fernández Guardia 1913:319–323, 334–335, chap. 8).

Ultimately, however, the missions achieved very little, partly because of native uprisings in protest against punishments inflicted by the Spanish military and sacrileges against traditional sacred shrines, partly because of persistent attacks by non-Christianized "wild" Talamancans against the Christian converts, partly because of attacks by Miskito slavers against mission villages, and partly because of the often limited and sporadic support offered the missions by the colonial government in distant Guatemala City (Fernández Guardia 1913: 330–331, 339–341, 372–373, 378–379). Eventually, in 1709, a general native uprising destroyed most of the missions and the Spanish population they housed, and the mission effort was abandoned in practice (Fernández Guardia 1913: 380–382; Floyd 1967:41, 44, 46–52). In reprisal for the most destructive raids, the colonial government captured a number of Talamancans and transferred them to other areas of the country. Some soon died, while the descendants of the rest became part of the mestizo population (Fernández Guardia 1913:344–345, 383; Floyd 1967:52–53; Stone 1962:8).

Lasting mission impact on traditional life-styles in Talamanca seems to have been almost negligible, although such material items as European clothing and agricultural implements were made available by the priests and welcome periods of peace were achieved at times by mission influence (Fernández Guardia 1913:351–352, 370–372). Even Christianized natives, although they adopted Spanish practices when in the presence of the priest (e.g., dressing in cotton garments), reverted to traditional habits and practices when at work or at home (e.g., wearing coverings of barkcloth and skins) (Stone 1962:19; see also Stone 1949 regarding the Boruca, the most acculturated of the Talamancan tribes). More significant in terms of long-term survival prospects was the gradual decline in population by the mid-eighteenth century as a result of the persistent raids and warfare, forced relocations, loss of population to Miskito slavers (who probably successfully abducted several thousand Talamancans), and inroads of disease during prior decades (Fernández Guardia 1913:389).

Nicaragua: The Miskito "Indians" and Frontier Tribes

At the time of European discovery, the territory now encompassed by the Republic of Nicaragua (and also Honduras) formed the cultural divide between societies associated with Mesoamerica and those characterized by culture patterns associated with Lower Central America and northern South America. Peoples encountered by the first Spanish entradas moving north from Panama into the lake country of western or Pacific Nicaragua revealed Mesoamerican cultural influences. The societies of the Caribbean versant of the country, to the east of the central mountains, were non-Mesoamerican; these peoples constituted part of the cultural sphere of Lower Central America, as did the indigenous population of eastern Honduras. (The limits of the zone of Mesoamerican influence is generally demarcated on maps by a line running from the Gulf of Nicoya north through the mountains of north-central Nicaragua and Honduras to the Gulf of Honduras).

The dense native population of the chiefdoms or small states indigenous to Pacific Nicaragua was seriously depleted during the first decades of the Spanish presence (1530s and 1540s), partly by the general upset to normal family life-styles and partly by epidemics, but primarily by extensive deportation of hundreds of thousands of able-bodied individuals as slaves to Panama or Peru and the consequent hardships visited upon the young and aged left to fend for themselves. The overall population decline in Pacific Nicaragua may have exceeded

90 percent by 1550 and may have continued through the remainder of the six-teenth and seventeenth centuries as the surviving native population struggled to cope with labor and tribute demands that eventually forced them to abandon their villages and to seek employment as wage laborers. Ultimately, these fami-lies and individuals were absorbed into the developing mestizo population that became predominant in western Nicaragua during the colonial era (MacLeod 1973:51–55; Newson 1987:101–107, 118–122, 336–342).

The fate of the more scattered indigenous population in the central mountains and Caribbean lowlands of eastern Nicaragua varied. During the sixteenth and seventeenth centuries, inhabitants of the more mountainous regions were af-fected primarily by disease, by removal through encomienda, and by efforts to establish missions (see below), all of which also led eventually to the loss of vir-tually the entire native population and indigenous culture (Newson 1987:336, 338). The eastern or Caribbean lowlands escaped significant Spanish inroads, however, and were not directly contacted by a European colonial presence until the middle of the seventeenth century.

Prior to contact, the natives of this isolated eastern or Caribbean region lived as egalitarian tribesmen organized into small kinship units differentiated by di-alects. This population apparently was settled in small communities scattered along the gallery-forested rivers and the shores of coastal lagoons.[11] Women tended agricultural plots of maize, manioc, and other root crops while men hunted and fished. After contact, this traditional population was forced to adjust in varying ways, but two broad patterns can be readily discerned. During the eighteenth and nineteenth centuries, in particular, some groups sought to in-crease their isolation by withdrawing farther into the interior. Their numbers gradually declined so that by the end of the twentieth century they were close to total extinction. Others, however, made a more positive adaptation during this time such that their contemporary descendants, the Miskito (Miskitu) Indi-ans, have increased their ethnic autonomy, territorial extent, and population size and (along with the San Blas Kuna of Panama and the so-called Black Carib or Garifuna of northern Honduras) have become one of the major "indigenous" ethnic groups of Lower Central America today. Although much of this adjust-ment occurred during the later colonial decades and following the independence of the Hispanic colonies from Spain, and thus falls outside the time frame of this essay, important beginnings were made during the late seventeenth and early eighteenth centuries and are outlined briefly here.

During the latter decades of the seventeenth century, African and mulatto slaves and freedmen began to settle on the coast of eastern Nicaragua, seeking sanctuary in a region that had become a secluded backwater and, therefore, a zone of refuge in the Caribbean theater. Many of these new arrivals (including survivors of a wrecked slaving vessel and freedmen from the short-lived English plantation and trading colony on the island of Providencia) settled in the vicinity of Cape Gracias a Dios, at the mouth of the Río Coco (also known as the Wangks or Segovia River, the current boundary between Nicaragua and Honduras). There they intermingled with the local natives and established a population of mixed African-Indian descent and fierce reputation, known in the colonial literature as the Miskito (Mosquito)-Zambos.

During the late seventeenth and early eighteenth centuries, the Miskito-Zambo also became willing allies of French and English privateers and buccaneers who utilized the security of the isolated "Miskito Coast" as a rest and rendezvous area between raids on Caribbean shipping and on Hispanic settlements of the Spanish Main (Helms 1978:128–131). During this same period, the Miskito, armed with guns and ammunition received (along with other items of European manufacture) from the buccaneers, began to expand north and south from Cape Gracias along the east coast of Nicaragua and of Honduras, absorbing some local natives and driving others (known collectively today as the Sumu) to seek sanctuary by moving farther into the interior to the protection of the mountains (Helms 1971:14–19). The Miskito also found allies in English planters and traders who settled at river mouths along the coast (including buccaneers who had survived their hazardous pirating and settled down to a safer if more mundane existence) and were associated with their counterparts established in Jamaica by 1655.[12] These settlers, who used the Miskito as trading "middlemen" vis-à-vis interior groups, provided another source of European products that further supported the emergence of the Miskito-Zambo as a new "colonial tribe" and as the predominant local or "native" population of eastern Nicaragua and Honduras (Helms 1978:131–136).

Their English contacts also enabled the Miskito to range even farther afield during the first half of the eighteenth century and to conduct damaging raids against other native populations in the mountains of central Honduras and Nicaragua (i.e., on the Spanish mission frontier there), in coastal Costa Rica (the Matina Valley), Talamanca and the Almirante Bay area, and in the Petén and Yucatán, seeking slaves for further profitable exchange with the English in Jamaica. These raids did not subside until about 1740, when labor requirements in Jamaica could be adequately met by African slaves (Helms 1983).

The changes in indigenous patterns and practices that accompanied the emergence of the Miskito as a distinctive ethnic group and as the politically dominant native population of the east coast of much of Lower Central America during the late seventeenth and early eighteenth centuries were considerable. Traditional precontact preference for settlements along riverways was replaced by a preference for coastal locations near river mouths, where natives could readily make contact with buccaneer stations and then with English traders and planters (Helms 1978). Cooperation with buccaneers included stints of travel at sea for many Miskito men, whose skill as fishermen and turtlers placed them in great demand as ships' provisioners. Raids to distant frontier settlements also kept them away from home for long periods. These prolonged absences probably encouraged the rapid development of matrilocal residence as the preferred marital norm and the strong cohesiveness of mother-child and especially mother-daughter ties and, by extension, of the unit of maternal relatives in general. This pattern of marital residence possibly developed from a precontact pattern of patrilocality prefaced with periods of bride-service similar to that described above for other Lower Central American groups. As opportunity for travel developed, men simply extended the period of bride-service, leaving their wives and children with the wives' own families on a more permanent basis, and taking up residence with their in-laws on their periodic returns.

Economically productive travel by men (and later wage-labor opportunities) augmented their continued interest in hunting and fishing, while women continued their traditional roles as horticulturalists, a division of labor that has proven to be particularly flexible and adaptive to the conditions of contact faced by the Miskito over the years (Helms 1971:23–26, 1976). Access to European products and especially guns and ammunition not only facilitated territorial expansion and frontier raids but also provided the means (via prestigious English "middlemen" contacts and raid-and-trade activities) for the emergence and recognition of regional men of influence or "big men," who augmented the traditional village council of elders as persons with political authority. Population growth and perhaps agricultural productivity was further encouraged by keeping some of the women and children captured in slave raids and incorporating them into Miskito communities (another probable continuity with precontact raid-trade behavior; Helms 1983). Distinctive ethnic identity was also bolstered by conscious attempts (particularly by men of influence) to identify with and imitate English customs, language, and behavior, and by recognition of the British Crown as the rightful source of ultimate political legitimacy (Helms 1983).

Finally, a few words should be said about the Catholic missions established in the thinly populated mountains of central Nicaragua on the frontier of Spanish territory and at the edge of the non-Hispanic east soon to be controlled by the Miskito and the English. The establishment of these settlements, like those in Talamanca, was basically yet another example of Spain's traditional approach to the frontier regions of its colonial claim and to the zones of still "wild" or unconquered natives that lay beyond the settled colonial world. In Hispanic Nicaragua, missionary efforts on the frontier began in 1606, when small stations were established in the mountains of north-central Nicaragua (Matagalpa–Chontales), and lasted until the end of the century, followed by a few further attempts in the first half of the eighteenth century (see Floyd 1967:chap. 7). These efforts met with little success for a variety of reasons, which are by now familiar: the lack of support from the Crown; the diversity of the indigenous languages involved; epidemics and native fear of the new diseases; native resentment of forceful removal to mission settlements when persuasion failed; and the unwillingness or inability of traditionally seminomadic forest dwellers to accept sedentary village life (Newson 1987:16–17, 167–169). In addition, by the end of the seventeenth century the populations clustered in mission villages offered prime targets for Miskito raiders traveling into the mountain frontier via the numerous rivers that linked the cordilleras with the east coast (see Floyd 1967:43–44, 95, 99). It is not surprising, then, to find that the native populations brought to such settlements made every effort to slip away into the relative safety of the mountains, where they might hope to escape disease, mission life, and the Miskito or, in some cases, might join in common cause with the Miskito in retaliatory attacks on Spanish settlements (Floyd 1967:90–91).

While living in the mission, however, natives were confronted with radical cultural changes. Here, as elsewhere in New Spain, mission villages were established as miniature versions of Spanish settlements, with buildings organized around a central plaza. Subsistence was to be obtained by tending plots of land and raising domestic animals—chickens, cattle, horses—with European tools and techniques. Hunting and fishing and traditional agricultural practices as well as a more mobile life-style could not continue, and contacts with persons outside the missions were discouraged. Traditional native community life obviously could no longer continue, either. In addition, the missionaries frequently setiled natives from mutually hostile groups in the same mission, further enhancing tensions. The mission population also tended to be composed primarily of children, women, and the elderly, as able-bodied men were best able to escape. Added to this, of course, were missionary efforts to inculcate the formalities and beliefs of a new religion.

The difficulty of coping with such changes and overall lack of acculturative success at all levels and domains of cultural adjustment was reflected in both the natives' persistent efforts to flee and by the equally persistent supervision required of missionaries if their charges were to be kept in residence (Newson 1987:199–200).

Conclusions

The indigenous populations of Lower Central America in the centuries immediately following the arrival of the Spaniards generally seem to have faced three alternative fates. First, populations directly contacted by Spanish conquistadores and Hispanic settlers, who were clustered primarily in parts of western Central America, were frequently all but destroyed, with survivors either fleeing or melting into the foundations of a new mestizo population component. Thus a castelike colonial society containing ethnic sectors composed of powerful Spanish landowners and subservient, culturally Indian, laborers did not develop in Hispanic Lower Central America.

Second, indigenous populations who were initially resident in the central mountains or Caribbean lowlands or groups able to flee to these regions were able to resist outright foreign conquest to a considerable extent, although to varying degrees they remained vulnerable to Spanish entradas, missionary activities, or destructive raids by an emerging "colonial tribe" from the Miskito Coast. Nonetheless, during the sixteenth and seventeenth centuries the survivors in the mountains, most notably in Panama and Costa Rica, seem to have retained their domestic economy virtually unchanged, showed strong continuities in marital residence patterns and marital practice, and maintained significant elements of their precontact centralized political organization. However, the highest level of chiefdom organization, specifically the status of high chief and the long-distance activities associated with this office, apparently were most vulnerable to Spanish impact and were quickly lost. Efforts to establish mission villages temporarily affected the daily life-styles of natives attracted or taken to these settlements, but the impact of new practices and perspectives introduced by the friars seems to have been largely ephemeral in the long run. Consequently, significant alterations in culture patterns do not appear until the eighteenth, nineteenth, and twentieth centuries, particularly for surviving indigenous populations of Panama and Costa Rica.

The third pattern of postcontact experience can be seen in that portion of the indigenous population of eastern Nicaragua that intermingled with newcomers to the coast and then was able not only to accommodate the presence of a colonial power but to turn that presence to positive political and economic advantage for themselves. This pattern of adjustment not only allowed population survival but led to the development of a new cultural (ethnic) entity specifically adapted to the colonial milieu that gave it birth.

Notes

1. This move toward the Caribbean culminated in the late nineteenth- and twentieth-century exodus to the islands of the San Blas archipelago.

2. There has been considerable debate as to how much continuity actually existed between postcontact populations and the Precolumbian chiefdoms of the isthmus and how much of the postcontact population of the Darién in particular derived instead from northern Colombia via the Gulf of Urabá (see Stier 1979:40–48, 110, 114–115). I am assuming a significant degree of continuity with precontact isthmian chiefdoms, at least for the regions for which I have the most data for the period under discussion (e.g., the Bayano headwaters, one of the more heavily populated areas). It is entirely possible, however, that the Darién was a refuge for both Panamanian and Colombian groups. The population clustered around the Gulf of Urabá, especially during the seventeenth century, may well have included native peoples moving away from Spanish areas of northern Colombia.

3. Villages were relocated to accommodate agricultural practices or when the Spaniards became "too much acquainted with the place of their abode" (Wafer 1934:89).

4. The present-day involvement of Kuna men with agriculture did not develop until the late nineteenth century.

5. These included stone knives and hatchets, bows and arrows, clubs, lances, and darts. Points were made of wood, bone, or fish spine (Stout 1947:61).

6. With help from independent Indian (Kuna) and black populations of the forest, buccaneers also raided traffic of the transisthmian trail itself, as well as Spanish towns (see Anderson 1938:chaps. 20–23; Stout 1947:5).

7. Sometimes known as Fray Adrian de Santo Tomás. Brief excerpts from Fray Adrian's report can be found in Lothrop (1950:Appendix II).

8. Particularly Doraces and Zuries in the area of Caldera, Boquete, and the skirts of the Volcán Baru (Linares 1968:79).

9. It is possible that this practice was followed elsewhere in the isthmus and may, in fact, provide the basis for later adjustments to matrilocal (uxorilocal) residence preference among groups such as the Kuna.

10. In Costa Rica, as in Panama, chiefly domains probably focused on the numerous fertile valleys drained by rivers flowing from the central ranges to Caribbean or Pacific waters. Rivers may have served as political-ideological focal points for domain identification and also served as boundary lines between chiefly domains. Domains in some cases are specified as centering on coastal regions or lowland plains. In other cases they are situated in mountain interiors, on mountain slopes or inland savannas, or on headwater areas of rivers. In overall structure and organization, these chiefdoms resembled those of Panama, and vice versa. See Ibarra (1984) and Helms (1979).

11. Perhaps some sense of the riverine life-styles of this precontact era may still be found in the description by C. Napier Bell (1989) of life in an upriver Sumu (Twaka) community during the nineteenth century.

12. The English were interested in maintaining contact with Spanish activities in Central America via the "backdoor" of eastern Nicaragua and Honduras for various reasons of their own, including vigorous and profitable smuggling operations conducted through this same region (MacLeod 1973:chap. 20).

References

Anderson, C. L. G.
 1938 *Old Panama and Castilla del Oro.* North River Press, New York.
Bell, C. Napier
 1989 *Tangweera. Life and Adventures among Gentle Savages.* University of Texas Press, Austin. Originally published in 1899.
Bray, Warwick
 1981 Gold Work. In *Between Continents/Between Seas: Precolumbian Art of Costa Rica,* text by Suzanne Abel-Vidor et al., pp. 153–166. Harry N. Abrams, New York.
Elliott Joyce, L. E.
 1934 The Cuna Folk of Darien. In *A New Voyage and Description of the Isthmus of America,* edited by Lionel Wafer, pp. 166–184. The Hakluyt Society, Oxford.
Fernández Guardia, Ricardo
 1913 *History of the Discovery and Conquest of Costa Rica.* Translated by Harry Weston Van-Dyke. Thomas Y. Crowell, New York.
 1918 *Reseña Histórica de Talamanca.* Imprenta, Libreria y Encuadernación Alsina, San José.
Ferrero A., Luis
 1981 Ethnohistory and Ethnography in the Central Highlands-Atlantic Watershed and Diquís. In *Between Continents/Between Seas: Precolumbian Art of Costa Rica,* text by Suzanne Abel-Vidor et al., pp. 93–103. Harry N. Abrams, New York.
Floyd, Troy S.
 1967 *The Anglo-Spanish Struggle for Mosquitia.* University of New Mexico Press, Albuquerque.
Helms, Mary W.
 1971 *Asang: Adaptations to Culture Contact in a Miskito Community.* University of Florida Press, Gainesville.
 1976 Domestic Organization in Eastern Central America: The San Blas Cuna, Miskito, and Black Carib Compared. *Western Canadian Journal of Anthropology* 6:133–163.
 1978 Coastal Adaptations as Contact Phenomena among the Miskito and Cuna Indians of Lower Central America. In *Prehistoric Coastal Adaptations,* edited by Ann Pescatello, pp. 121–149. Academic Press, New York.
 1979 *Ancient Panama: Chiefs in Search of Power.* University of Texas Press, Austin.
 1983 Miskito Slaving and Culture Contact: Ethnicity and Opportunity in an Expanding Population. *Journal of Anthropological Research* 39:179–197.
Hill, Carole E.
 1973 Convirtiendóse en campesinos: los boruca de Costa Rica. *América Indígena* 33:447–456.
Howe, James
 1986 *The Kuna Gathering.* University of Texas Press, Austin.
Ibarra Rojas, Eugenia
 1984 Los Cacicazgos indígenas de la Vertiente Atlántica y Valle Central de Costa Rica: un intento de reconstrucción etnohistórica. Tesis para Obtar por el Grado de

Licenciado en Antropología con énfasis en Antropología Social, Universidad de Costa Rica, Facultad de Ciencias Sociales.

Linares de Sapir, Olga
1968 *Cultural Chronology of the Gulf of Chiriquí, Panama*. Smithsonian Contributions to Anthropology, Vol. 8. Washington, D. C.

Lothrop, Samuel K.
1950 *Archaeology of Southern Veraguas, Panama*. Memoirs, Peabody Museum of Archaeology and Ethnology, vol. 9, no. 3. Peabody Museum of Harvard University, Cambridge, Mass.

MacLeod, Murdo
1973 *Spanish Central America*. University of California Press, Berkeley.

Newson, Linda A.
1987 *Indian Survival in Colonial Nicaragua*. University of Oklahoma Press, Norman.

Sauer, Carl Ortwin
1969 *The Early Spanish Main*. University of California Press, Berkeley.

Stier, Frances R.
1979 *The Effect of Demographic Change on Agriculture in San Blas, Panama*. Ph.D. dissertation, University of Arizona. University Microfilms, Ann Arbor.

Stone, Doris
1949 *The Boruca of Costa Rica*. Papers of the Peabody Museum of American Archaeology and Ethnology, vol. 26, no. 2. Peabody Museum of Harvard University, Cambridge, Mass.
1962 *The Talamancan Tribes of Costa Rica*. Papers of the Peabody Museum of Archaeology and Ethnology, vol. 43, no. 2. Peabody Museum of Harvard University, Cambridge, Mass.

Stout, David B.
1947 *San Blas Cuna Acculturation: An Introduction*. Viking Fund Publications in Anthropology No. 9. New York.

Wafer, Lionel
1934 *A New Voyage and Description of the Isthmus of America*. Edited by L. E. Elliott Joyce. The Hakluyt Society, Oxford.

Wassén, S. Henry
1949 Contributions to Cuna Ethnography. *Etnologiska Studier* (Göteborg) 16:7–139.

Young, Philip D.
1970 Notes on the Ethnohistorical Evidence for Structural Continuity in Guaymí Society. *Ethnohistory* 17:11–29.
1971 *Ngawbe: Tradition and Change Among the Western Guaymí of Panama*. University of Illinois Press, Urbana.

Zevallos, Fr. Augustín de
1886 Memorial for our Lord the King concerning the Province of Costa Rica. In *Colección de Documentos para la Historia de Costa Rica* published by Lic. D. León Fernández, pp. 156–161. *Documentos Especiales sobre los límites entre Costa Rica y Colombia*, vol. 5. Imprenta Pablo Dupont, Paris. Originally published in 1610.

Part 3 ■

Portents for the Future of Borderlands Scholarship

Chapter 21 ■

Ann F. Ramenofsky

Beyond Disciplinary Bias: Future Directions in Contact Period Studies

The observance of the Columbian Quincentenary provides an opportunity to examine all aspects of the Contact period. Archaeologists, ethnohistorians, and ethnologists have capitalized on this opportunity, disseminating their knowledge of the period through a variety of formats. The volumes in this series amply demonstrate the breadth of that knowledge. In addition, scholars are concerned with the creation and advancement of knowledge, and the Quincentenary provides an opportunity to reflect about the nature of our knowledge of the Contact period. Assumptions, methods, and theories employed to construct past and present knowledge can be evaluated, and suggestions for the continued development of this field of study can be offered.

The chapters in this section summarize what is known in a particular region or on a particular topic, but they go further. They evaluate not only what is known, but *how we know*. Explicit in these evaluations is the recognition that we have been naive about the complexity of the Native American postcontact record, that assumptions governing descriptions or explanations have been reductionist and simplistic, that our knowledge of the period is in its infancy.

The contributions derive from different disciplines, and they vary in the amount of detail incorporated. Despite these differences, the essays share a number of commonalities. First, scholars have limited their contributions to only a few issues: disease introduction and native population decline, the historiography of texts, and the historical and archaeological analysis of trade. Second, certain themes appear repeatedly. This independent examination and confirmation is important because it implies that, despite disciplinary boundaries, scholars are reaching the same conclusions about the nature and limitations of knowledge. Recognizing these limitations is the beginning of the development of new knowledge.

The topic of disease contact and native population decline has become one of the most contentious in American anthropology (Borah 1976; Denevan 1976; Ramenofsky 1982, 1985, 1987; Roberts 1989; Ubelaker 1976). On the surface, the debate revolves around Native American population size just before European contact. If this were the only problem under investigation, its resolution would come more quickly. Researchers are invested in dichotomous assumptions regarding (1) the timing of disease contact relative to the earliest documents and (2) the magnitude of discontinuity between prehistory and history. Intellectual differences on these issues affect the methods of estimating native populations. Not surprisingly, scholarly opinion on the size of Native American populations is divided.

Individuals who produce low estimates (Helm 1980; Kroeber 1939; Steward 1949) either fail to consider disease as a factor in Contact period change or assume that it postdated documents. Scholars such as Cook and his associates (e.g., Cook 1937, 1973; Cook and Borah 1960; Cook and Simpson 1948) and more recently Dobyns (e.g., 1963, 1966, 1983) have arrived at high estimates of native populations. They argue that most documents postdate epidemics. Native populations were drastically reduced, and cultural systems were fundamentally altered or terminated long before documentation. Because the Cook-Dobyns position raises deep and fundamental questions about the integrity and structure of traditional, Boasian anthropology, cultural anthropologists and ethnohistorians continue to debate the meaning of numbers in historical documents and to revise precontact estimates of population (for a review, see Roberts 1989). A high estimate, for instance, is countered by a low one.

Within the last decade, archaeologists have entered this arena of research (Campbell 1989; Milner 1980; Ramenofsky 1987; Perttula 1989; Smith 1987; Snow and Starna 1989; Upham 1982). Because the nature of population data in the archaeological record (Perttula, this volume) is fundamentally different from that present in historical documents (Stannard, this volume), archaeological studies of population change do not duplicate historical demographic studies. Whereas historical demographers produce absolute counts of people, archaeologists build ordinal trends (Campbell 1990; Ramenofsky 1987). In addition, because archaeological evidence of population incorporates time, it is possible to evaluate empirically the timing of decline from disease relative to the beginning of documentation. While complementing historical investigations of population change, archaeologial investigations are emerging as a separate realm of inquiry.

Three of the following essays (Robert Dunnell, Timothy Perttula, and David

Stannard) deal explicitly with the issue of disease contact and native depopulation. One chapter is archaeological and focuses on the Trans-Mississippian South (Perttula). Stannard's chapter on historical demography uses documents to reestimate native Hawaiian populations in the light of disease. Finally, Dunnell's contribution is synthetic and explores the methodological consequences of the Cook-Dobyns assumptions for archaeology. Dunnell terms the population debate an "academic quibble" that draws attention away from the heart of the matter, the fundamental discontinuity between prehistory and history.

Although the issue of disease and depopulation is Dobyns's point of departure, in this chapter he is not concerned with the debate per se. Like Dunnell, Dobyns is interested in the implications of his assumptions. If his assumptions about the timing of disease contact are correct, then discontinuties of the first order separate prehistory from history. In such a setting, the use of ethnographic analogues to build descriptions of the past and the assumption of isomorphism between present and past must be seriously questioned. Dobyns questions this method of explanation and provides answers relevant for archaeologists.

As suggested by the debate surrounding population, documents are clearly an important source of information for all scholars working in the Contact period. The importance and critical evaluation of the meaning embedded in documents are separate issues. Thus, even though archaeologists use documents, this use does not imply intellectual sophistication in identifying and unraveling the biases that are an implicit part of the narratives. Indeed, part of the unique training in historical archaeology involves the "decoding" of documents. Three chapters in this section (Patricia Galloway, David Stannard, and William Swagerty) deal primarily with texts.

Galloway argues that the interpretations of texts made by archaeologists are superficial. Quite simply, the assumption that the meaning of a sixteenth-century narrative is knowable on the surface is wrong. Archaeologists must "excavate" a text to determine meaning. This excavation is comparable to stratigraphic excavation. Rather than evaluating the archaeological use of documents, Stannard focuses on biases inherent in documentary histories of native Hawaiian population size. This evaluation is crucial, given his own bias that all previous estimates of native Hawaiians are too low by at least an order of magnitude. Swagerty reviews archaeological and ethnohistorical models of Native American trade during the Postcontact period in western North America. Although largely descriptive, this essay exposes several important problems, including the tenuous relationship between ethnohistorians and archaeologists and the development of new models despite limited archaeological and documentary knowledge of trade. Ewer's Middle Missouri trade centers, for instance, were actually primitive central places. R. Wood defines and expands this hierarchical model in his Middle Missouri system. A world systems model, in which Mesoamerica is the core and the Southwest is the periphery, is the most recent attempt to elucidate the hierarchical structure of trade relationships. Clearly, both archaeological analysis of trade materials and historical excavation of texts are crucial for evaluating the reliability of these models.

As mentioned above, a second contribution of this suite of essays is the repetition of themes that transcend disciplinary boundaries. These themes range from simple references, for example Kidder's excavation at Pecos or the introduction of the horse, to evaluations of method, for example, the use of ethnographic analogy. The intersections between the discussions play themselves out as point and counterpoint and suggest an unexpected unity of thought and, therefore, direction.

My essay is the only one that deals explicitly with the need for theory in Contact period studies, but this need emerges as an implication in the work of others. According to Galloway, for example, theory of text construction is as important as theory in archaeology. Had archaeologists approached the mound builder problem with the same simplistic assumptions they employ in reading texts, the debate would still be raging.

Scholarly inquiry is not divorced from society. Questions asked and answers given are influenced by the cultural complexion of the times. Given the connection between scholarship and society, the historical context of knowledge provides a depth of understanding otherwise unobtainable. The historical context of knowledge is a theme that runs through the chapters by Galloway and Dunnell. Galloway points out that because standards of scholarship in sixteenth-century Spain were vastly different from those present in twentieth-century America, contemporary standards cannot be employed to discover sixteenth-century meaning. Dunnell views the "racist" argument about mound builders as a post hoc justification proffered by twentieth-century archaeologists. Eighteenth-century naturalists who wondered about mound origins operated within a different cultural matrix.

The use of methods that assume continuity from prehistory through history are considered in a number of chapters. Whereas Dobyns exposes the problems of ethnographic analogy from a perspective of cultural anthropology, Dunnell and I consider the consequences of analogical reasoning from an archaeological perspective. According to Swagerty, the direct historical approach that linked history to prehistory was a methodological breakthrough because archaeologists began exploring and utilizing information in documents. Dunnell's view of the direct historical approach is less complementary; he is concerned with the implied continuity that results from the use of this method.

In conclusion, the topics in these essays range from the historiography of sixteenth-century texts and the mound builder debate to the investigation of the disease hypothesis and the relevance of historical science to Contact period research. Although the Quincentenary has been a vehicle for the dissemination of knowledge, this set of essays emphasizes that our knowledge of the period is far from complete. I am hopeful that the reflections and analyses of the authors will stimulate new questions and investigations that, in turn, can be evaluated in A.D. 2090.

References

Borah, W. W.
  1976 The Historical Demography of Aboriginal and Colonial America. In *The Native*

Population of the Americas in 1492, edited by W. M. Denevan, pp. 13–34. University of Wisconsin Press, Madison.

Campbell, S. K.
1989 *Post-Columbian Culture History in the Northern Columbian Plateau: A.D. 1500–1700.* Unpublished Ph.D. dissertation, University of Washington, Seattle.
1990 How Wide the Ripples: The Case for Early Sixteenth-Century Epidemics in Non-agricultural North America. Paper presented at the 55th Annual Meeting of the Society for American Archaeology, Las Vegas.

Cook, S. F.
1937 *The Extent and Significance of Disease among Indians of Baja California, 1697–1773.* Ibero-Americana No. 12. Berkeley.
1973 The Significance of Disease in the Extinction of New England Indians. *Human Biology* 45: 485–508.

Cook, S. F., and W. W. Borah
1960 *The Indian Population of Central Mexico: 1531–1610.* Ibero-Americana No. 44. Berkeley.

Cook, S. F., and L. B. Simpson
1948 *The Population of Central Mexico in the Sixteenth Century.* Ibero-Americana No. 31. Berkeley.

Denevan, W. M. (editor)
1976 *The Native Population of the Americas in 1492.* University of Wisconsin Press, Madison.

Dobyns, H. F.
1963 An Outline of Andean Epidemic History to 1720. *Bulletin of the History of Medicine* 37: 493–515.
1966 An Appraisal of Techniques for Estimating Aboriginal American Population with a new Hemispheric Estimate. *Current Anthropology* 7:395–416.
1983 *Their Number Become Thinned.* University of Tennessee Press, Knoxville.

Helm, J.
1980 Female Infanticide, European Diseases and Population Levels among McKenzie Dene. *American Ethnologist* 7:259–285.

Kroeber, A. L.
1939 *Cultural and Natural Areas of Native North America.* University of California Publications in American Archaeology and Ethnology No. 38. Berkeley.

Milner, G.
1980 Epidemic Disease in the Post-Contact Southeast: A Reappraisal. *Midcontinental Journal of Archaeology* 4:39–56.

Perttula, T. K.
1989 *Contact and Interaction between Caddoan and European Peoples: The Historic Archaeological and Ethnohistorical Records.* Unpublished Ph.D. dissertation, University of Washington, Seattle.

Ramenofsky, A. F.
1982 *The Archaeology of Population Collapse: Native American Response to the Introduction of Infectious Disease.* Unpublished Ph.D. Dissertation, University of Washington, Seattle.
1985 Book Review. *Their Number Become Thinned*, by H. F. Dobyns. *American Antiquity* 50:198–199.
1987 *Vectors of Death: The Archaeology of European Contact.* University of New Mexico Press, Albuquerque.

Roberts, L.
1989 Disease and Death in the New World. *Science* 246:1245–1247.

Smith, M. T.
1987 *Archaeology of Aboriginal Culture Change in the Interior Southeast.* Riply P. Bullen Monographs in Anthropology and History No. 6. Florida State Museum, Gainesville.

Snow, D., and W. A. Starna
   1989 Sixteenth-Century Depopulation: A View from the Mohawk Valley. *American Anthropologist* 91:142–149.
Steward, J. H.
   1949 The Native Population of South America. In *Handbook of South American Indians*, vol 5., edited by J. H. Steward. Bureau of American Ethnology Bulletin 143:655–668. Washington D. C.
Ubelaker, D.
   1976 The Sources and Methodology of Mooney's Estimates of North American Indian Populations. In *The Native Population of the Americas in 1492*, edited by W. M. Denevan, pp. 243–288. University of Wisconsin Press, Madison.
Upham, S.
   1982 *Politics and Power: An Economic and Political History of the Western Pueblo.* Academic Press, New York.

Chapter 22 ∎

Ann F. Ramenofsky

Historical Science and Contact Period Studies

In the past 100 years, empirical knowledge of the Columbian period in the Americas has increased greatly. We know, for instance, the locations of some of the "lost Spanish missions" in the Southeast (Thomas 1988, 1990). We have inventories of Spanish artifacts useful in dating archaeological deposits and for building descriptions of cultural contexts (Deagan 1987). Towns visited by Coronado have been tested archaeologically (Kidder 1951; Nelson 1916). And we have a preliminary understanding of diseases introduced to native populations by European explorers and settlers (Cook 1973; Ramenofsky 1990b; Stearn and Stearn 1945).

Despite these advances in knowledge, we have barely begun to outline the nature, magnitude, or direction of change that occurred throughout the Contact period. To account for change requires theory, or a system of knowledge, that addresses "why" kinds of questions. Were such a theory in place, we could advance models and testable propositions that aim at explaining the nature of change incorporated in archaeological and historical records. Because models are always simpler than the events they seek to explain, the complexity of empirical events would force us to evaluate and refine our ideas. In the end, the interaction between models and phenomena would lead to a greater understanding of the changes that occurred.

My approach to the study of the Contact period is clearly within the realm of science. Yet "science in archaeology" is not as fashionable in 1990 as it was in 1970. Postprocessual critiques of the "objectivity" and deductive methodology of Hempelian positivism (Hodder 1985; Leone 1986; Tilley 1984; Trigger 1990) have raised questions about the feasibility of science as an archaeological goal. Were Hempelian positivism the only form of science, criticisms would carry greater weight. A commitment to science, however, does not entail a commitment to positivism.

I suggest that historical science (Dunnell 1982; Gifford 1981; Gould 1986; Teltser 1989), with its commitment to Darwinian evolution, is an appropriate framework for explaining Contact period change. The goal of historical science is to explain the differential persistence of variation, and the Contact record is one of the most readily available and dramatic examples of this phenomenon (Ramenofsky 1990a). Historical science is a "second style of science" (Gould 1986:60) that accommodates history and science, deduction and induction. Because both ideographic and nomothetic approaches exist within historical science, the use of this framework for explaining Contact period change would render meaningless Trigger's long-held dichotomy of archaeology as history or science (Trigger 1978, 1990) or the debates over induction versus deduction (Shanks and Tilley 1988).

In an earlier study (Ramenofsky 1990a), I suggested that the products of an approach of historical science will be different from those currently recognized. Dunnell (1982) has differentiated spacelike from timelike sciences and has suggested that most archaeological explanations develop within a spacelike framework. In this framework, the world is composed of essential types that have boundaries and can be discovered. Accordingly, documenting similarities and differences between discoverable types constitutes the necessary and sufficient conditions for demonstrating regularities, developing explanations, and establishing laws or statements that are true for all time and all space. Historical science, by contrast, is timelike in that phenomena are in a constant state of becoming. Types cannot be discovered because they have no reality. Consequently, variation, not types, is the focus of investigation. Rather than searching for laws, historical scientists seek to identify mechanisms of change that, in turn, account for the persistence of some variation and the loss of other.

The goal of this discussion is to (1) review the development of Contact period studies in both ethnology and archaeology and (2) evaluate that development from the perspective of historical science. In this review, I deliberately use the term "Contact period," as opposed to "Columbian period." The Columbian period refers to the age of exploration in the Americas, that is, the sixteenth and seventeenth centuries. My analysis, however, employs a cross section of all literature of native North Americans from the last 500 years. Consequently, Contact period is a more appropriate description of the temporal focus of my discussion.

The framework of historical science is important in this evaluation. The use of historical science points out that currently a spacelike perspective accounts for events that are clearly timelike. Because change has no meaning within a spacelike framework, a logical contradiction exists between the contact record and the framework of explanation. Moreover, because essentialism inheres in a spacelike science, the record of change through the Contact period reduces to a series of discoverable stages or types. Although difficult to obtain, the implementation of a timelike framework for explaining change would generate new types of questions, create a logically coherent system, and advance our knowledge of the Contact period.

Ethnology

Between 1890 and 1910, Boasian ethnology became the dominant paradigm in American academic institutions (De Laguna 1976; Hallowell 1976; Harris 1968). Ethnographic and linguistic descriptions proliferated, museum collections swelled, and the unilineal paradigm came under stringent attack.

Within the developing intellectual structure, investigation of the Contact period was of no interest. The focus was on reconstructing the past, not investigating the present. Consequently, changes in native culture since Europeans were viewed as obscuring rather than elucidating the past, and these changes were overlooked or ignored. Viewed in this light, it is not surprising that the first study of Contact period change in North America had no intellectual impact.

Mooney published the *Ghost Dance Religion* in 1896. Grinnell reviewed the monograph in 1897. The review demonstrates that the developing science of ethnology did not know how to accommodate discussions of change or termination. Although Grinnell praised Mooney for his ethnographic scholarship and diligent fieldwork, he confined his discussion of the reasons for the Ghost Dance to two sentences.

Even after the development of acculturation studies, Mooney's work on the Ghost Dance remained something of an anomaly. When Herskovits defined and reviewed acculturation studies, he cited Mooney's work as "the basis for all later contributions." He did not, however, review Mooney's description because it had "no particular significance for the study of acculturation either in theoretical statement or in methodology" ([1938] 1958:76).

Because Boasians assumed that significant change postdated European contact, it followed that before contact native cultures were largely static, relating to "one culture period comparable to the neolithic of Europe" (Wissler 1914b:501). The failure of American archaeologists to document an American Paleolithic (Meltzer 1983) contributed additional evidence that native societies were static.

Despite the static assumption regarding native societies, reconstructing that past remained a formidable task. The magnitude of European-induced changes since 1492 meant that precontact societies were either extinct or transformed and were represented in the present by memories and traits. In 1888, for instance, Boas lamented that the disintegration of native Canadian customs compelled the student "to collect reports from old people who have witnessed the customs of their fathers, who heard the old myths told over and over again"

(1888:234). Boasians mined these sources of information to reconstruct past societies.

The assumed static nature of native societies coupled with a focus on the past had an important consequence. Although Boasians, or the American Historical School, dealt with the past, it was atemporal. Without time, change could not be considered. From the perspective of historical science, the developing science of ethnology was spacelike. Static cultural types could be discovered from traits and memories.

Time and the consideration of some types of Contact period change came into Boasian ethnology through culture-area (Wissler 1914b, [1917] 1950) and age-area studies (Boas 1907; Lowie 1916; Sapir 1916). Geography became the organizational principle with which material traits could be counted and described. Time was inferred from space and form through the mechanism of diffusion. Diffusion accounted for the dispersion of traits with a near linear correlation posited between geographic breadth and age.

While asserting that the spatial distribution of the bow and arrow reflected great temporal depth, the success of the equation of space + form = time depended on demonstrating diffusion. Without temporal depth, this demonstration was most successfully accomplished by studying diffusions of European introductions. In the context of history, time could be controlled. Wissler's description of the horse in Plains culture (1914a) epitomizes this demonstration.

Wissler (1914a) judiciously employed history to estimate the arrival times of the horse among ethnic units of the Plains. His stated goal, however, was to determine whether the horse significantly altered Plains culture. His answer was equivocal and within the domain of historical reconstruction. Although the horse complex created "the typical Plains culture of the nineteenth century" (1914a:17), the diffusion was successful because the horse and related traits were similar to precontact traits. The adoption required minimal adjustment.

When diffusion became the mechanism for reconstructing culture history, historical period diffusions became important test cases for validating precontact invention and spread. The change in approach, in part, accounts for the acceptance of Wissler's work and denial of Mooney's. Of equal, though unstated, importance is that in the Wissler case, the horse was interpreted as having a positive effect. In the Mooney case, Europeans had a disastrous effect. It mattered little that the same groups who formed the "typical Plains culture" participated in the Ghost Dance.

The ethnological development of a timelike science began with acculturation, or culture contact, studies that appeared after 1930 (e.g., Herskovits 1937, 1958; Mead 1932; Redfield 1930; Redfield et al. 1935). The explicit purpose of these studies was to employ historical documents to build descriptions of culture change during the Postcontact period. Because the first generation of Boasians had not considered culture change, there was no precedent indicating how to proceed. In the absence of a method or theory for analyzing or describing change, these studies attempted to identify and describe specific details of change in particular settings.

While attempting to overcome the atemporal bias of Boasian ethnography, researchers were limited by the intellectual tradition in which they were trained. Accordingly, space or diffusion were viewed as mechanisms of change; why spatial differences or diffusion were causal was of less concern. In Redfield's Tepoztlan study (1930), geographic divisions between urban and rural settings accounted for the flow of change into rural Mexican culture. Although Herskovits (1937) argued that diffusion and acculturation were not synonymous, diffusion remained the mechanism of change. Diffusion, however, is an inference of process derived from comparisons of traits. Because diffusion is not a mechanism of change, it does not explain the differential transmission or adoption of traits.

The lack of a theoretical framework for explaining postcontact change became a more serious problem after World War II when Native Americans began to press land claims. Substantial amounts of money were involved in these cases, and it was crucial to have primary data for delineating native histories. In such a setting, acculturation, now termed ethnohistory, needed a product that could stand up in a court of law.

According to Steward (1955), there was no such product. All primary data were problematic in one way or another. Memory culture was of limited duration; historical documents were incomplete and subject to recorder bias. Acculturation studies were headed down the wrong path. When Steward and Omar Stewart reviewed the postcontact history of Northern Paiute, they reached opposite conclusions regarding the nature of precontact organization. Whereas Omar Stewart argued that bands and chiefs were present before European contact, J. Steward supported a postcontact, European-induced origin.

Even though there was no product, ethnohistoric studies continued to proliferate. Spicer's *Perspectives in American Indian Culture Change* (1961) typified studies of the 1960s. This edited volume contained six case studies. Spicer considered abstract issues of culture contact in the last chapter. He first integrated specific descriptions by redefining Linton's contact types of directed and nondirected change (Linton 1940). He then defined processes of change that correlated roughly with each type. Although the definitions provided a framework for discovering some regularities among native societies with different contact histories, Spicer could not account for variation in rates of change or for differential persistence of similar or different traits. In his own words:

> The same group sometimes changed rapidly its ceremonial interests and practices and under other conditions clung desperately to them; under some circumstances material culture items were replaced or changed rapidly while little else changed, but in other situations social structure and religion changed rapidly while material culture underwent small change. In some circumstances there was rapid change in all aspects of culture at the same time; under other circumstances there were marked differentials. . . . In short, the comparative analysis . . . led to an abandonment of a search for generalizations framed in terms of universal differential susceptibility to change of aspects of culture [Spicer 1961:542].

Although not deliberate, Spicer's quotation epitomizes the potential of historical science as a framework for explaining change. Differential persistence of traits varies according to selective pressures operating on those traits. Because all histories are unique, selective pressures among the Kwakiutl will be different from those on the Yaqui. These differences will lead to variable trajectories and rates of change, as well as a differential survival of traits. Despite this variability, selection operates on variation, leading to differential persistence.

Since 1970, Contact period studies have entered another period of growth stimulated, in large part, by the reexamination of the Columbian period. Dobyns's work in disease and historical demography (e.g., 1963, 1966, 1983), Crosby's research on the Columbian Exchange (1972) and ecological history (1986), and Trigger's work in Huron-Iroquoian history (e.g., 1962, 1976, 1985) play significant roles in these developments.

Trigger's work is useful to consider within the framework of historical science. Although committed to a historical and dynamic perspective of Iroquoian, and particularly Huron, history (1976, 1981, 1985), his explanations do not tell why differential trajectories of change met with differential success. Nor can "cultural differences" (Trigger 1976:843) explain why the Five Nations of the Iroquois persisted after the Huron collapsed. Terms such as cultural differences derive from a spacelike conception of the world that contradicts Trigger's commitment to a historical perspective. To explain why the Five Nations, but not the Huron, persisted one would have to (1) define classes of variation appropriate for measuring change or persistence, (2) document those classes present in archaeological and historical records; (3) create hypotheses and tests regarding the operation of selection in each of these settings through time. The framework of historical science leads to questions that require different types of answers.

In summary, my evaluation of ethnology has suggested several trends. The Boasian focus on the past did not include a temporal dimension. Without time, historical reconstructions were mounted from a spacelike framework in which cultural "types" could be discovered from memories and traits. The movement from synchronic and spacelike to timelike and dynamic began with age-area studies that in turn developed into acculturation and ethnohistory. Despite the current ethnological emphasis, in which "History matters" (Gould 1986:60), any explanation of change is still viewed as a comparison of similarities and differences, not as a measure of differential success of variable traits. To carry this dynamism further, we need a theory that explains the differential persistence of variation.

Archaeology

Archaeological interest in the Contact period developed with the mound builder debate in the late eighteenth century (Ramenofsky 1990a; Silverberg 1968; Willey and Sabloff 1980). The controversy was publicly resolved by Cyrus Thomas (1894) in the same decade that Mooney's description of the Ghost Dance was published.

In the century before Thomas's publication appeared, controversy arose over the cultural origin of the mounds. At the time of European settlement, areas rich in mounds were thinly populated. The disparity between mound and population density led some researchers (Atwater 1820; Gallatin 1836; Harris 1835; Squier and Davis 1948) to conclude that Native Americans could not have built mounds.

To demonstrate that Native Americans had been mound builders, Thomas (1894) had to reduce the disparity between population and mound density. First, he divided mounds spatially and demonstrated regional variability. He then argued that labor pools were smaller than imagined because building episodes were at regional scales. Second, he employed Columbian period descriptions of native mound use to argue that particular historic tribes were responsible for regional building efforts.

The conjunction of history and archaeology has had lasting consequences. First, Thomas's work marked the beginning of the direct historical approach in archaeology (Trigger 1985; Meltzer 1983; Ramenofsky 1990a). Second, the use of documents to explain the past implied that major disruptions postdated documentation. Consequently, the interval between disruptions and ethnographic descriptions decreased, and the decrease could serve Boasian-style historical reconstructions. Because native societies were pristine for longer periods, memories could be profitably employed to resurrect the past. Although developing from different origins, late nineteenth-century archaeology concurred with Boasian ethnology: Because native populations were static prior to European contact, there was no past. A spacelike framework was employed to account for the origin of the mounds.

The weight of the Boasian paradigm affected much of archaeology between 1910 and 1930. Because Boas was an ethnologist, not an archaeologist, a stepchild relationship developed between ethnology and archaeology in which ideas diffused from parent to offspring (Trigger 1990). Thus, Holmes (1914) created archaeological areas comparable to Wissler's culture areas. Dixon (1913:565) commented that archaeological investigations were "largely barren if pursued in isolation and independent of ethnology." Because historical reconstruction was the stated anthropological goal, archaeologists pursued that goal through excavation; they hoped to discover the historical roots of ethnographically defined groups.

Archaeologists began to dismantle the spacelike view of native populations through stratigraphic excavation. Nelson (1916) and Kidder (1926; Kidder and Kidder 1917) established the method in the Southwest. San Cristobal and Pecos were the foci of these excavations, and both were occupied historically. Nonetheless, the Historical period was of little interest other than providing a known temporal baseline. In proceeding from the known to the unknown, Nelson and Kidder discovered through the imposition of arbitrary levels that the past did not mirror the present. Pottery styles changed through time, and these changes could be employed to build chronologies.

From this point until well into the 1950s, chronology-building became the accepted goal of archaeology. By the 1930s, this goal had led to the establishment of the paradigm of culture history (Dunnell 1986; Willey and Sabloff 1980). This development was triggered in part by the Depression and New Deal archaeology. With a wealth of data generated by the Works Progress Administration and the rudiments of chronology from the Southwest, regional culture histories grew quickly.

Culture history made lasting contributions to prehistoric archaeology. Just as acculturation studies had done for ethnology, the paradigm of culture history built the temporal dimension of archaeology that, in turn, provided the rudiments of a timelike science. Armed with stylistic classes and stratigraphy, culture historians demonstrated the fallacy of the Boasian, age-area studies. Position in a stratigraphic profile was now a more important indicator of age than was geographic distribution. Because styles changed through time, culture historians inferred that cultures changed. Although mechanisms of change were post hoc and simplistic, the major conclusion could not be ignored: Change, not stasis, dominated the archaeological record.

The contributions of culture history to archaeology of the Contact period were more ambiguous. Major Contact period sites such as Bayou Goula (Quimby 1957) and Hiwassee Island (Lewis and Kneburg 1979) were excavated during the 1930s in order to round out developmental histories. Culture historians formalized the direct historical approach (Steward 1942; Strong 1940; Wedel 1938), but the method had both positive and negative effects.

The assumption of isomorphism between history and archaeological places allowed archaeologists to employ documents to discover archaeological sites (Ford 1961). The assumption of continuity between history and prehistory helped link the two records. This linkage could spatially anchor developing chronologies (e.g., Ford 1936). As a legacy of Thomas's mound research, documents were equated with the beginning of contact with two results. The duration of European contact at regional scales remained attenuated; the attenuation obscured evidence of earlier post-European disruptions. This legacy would not change until the 1980s (Ramenofsky 1987). Because of the continuity assumption, documents were used to reconstruct the nature of earlier cultures (Ramenofsky 1987, 1990a).

Archaeological investigation of the Contact period became more prevalent in the 1950s. Once again, the Plains area was an important focus because of the large number of historical documents about the Plains, the burgeoning interest in ethnohistory, and governmental funding of the River Basin Surveys. This fortunate circumstance led to the excavation of both historically known locations such as Sakakawea (Ahler 1978) and previously unknown protohistoric sites such as Buffalo Pasture (Lehmer and Jones 1968) and Phillips Ranch (Lehmer 1954). Not surprisingly, the first publication of the *Plains Anthropologist* appeared in this decade.

These investigations, largely within a culture historical framework, contributed a great deal to our knowledge of postcontact change. Lehmer (1971, 1977; Lehmer et al. 1978) defined the terminal culture history unit of the Middle Missouri as "disorganized" (1780–1850). Mandan, Hidatsa, and Arikara societies disintegrated as smallpox decimated their numbers. Unfortunately, because archaeology was already changing its focus to culture reconstruction, the construction of temporal units and the empirical recognition of change became less fashionable. Accordingly, Middle Missouri culture history received less attention than it deserved.

Dunnell (1986) has argued that the Ford-Spaulding debate marked the beginning of culture reconstruction in American archaeology. In pursuing culture history goals, Ford (1936, 1954a, 1954b, 1954c) constructed etic types that could serve temporal problems. Spaulding (1953, 1954a, 1954b), by contrast, wanted to discover "emic" types that could make archaeology more ethnological. When judged by the direction of classification studies in later decades (Hill and Evans 1972; Whallon and Brown 1982), Ford lost the debate. It is important to recognize, however, that Ford's perspective wasn't wrong. In fact, his documentation of stylistic variability and his general approach to classification has much utility within a historical science framework. Rather, the goal of the discipline had changed from chronology building to culture reconstruction.

The new archaeology (Binford 1962; 1965; Binford and Binford 1968) became the bridge between culture reconstruction in classification and culture reconstruction as a stated archaeological goal. With the exception of Deetz's study of the Arikara (Deetz 1965), the implementation of the goal reduced the duration of the Contact period to a temporal interval of zero.

Culture reconstructions are based on arguments by analogy in which the number of traits shared between a known and an unknown suggests the presence of still other similarities (Binford 1967). All analogical arguments are based on the principle of uniformity, but there is a fundamental difference between methodological and substantive uniformity (Gould 1986; Gould and Watson 1982; Teltser 1989), or between what Hookyas (1970) defines as actualism and uniformitarianism (Binford 1981; Ramenofsky 1987).

The arguments employed to reconstruct cultures derive from substantive uniformity. Consequently, ethnographies, drawn from the ethnographic present, serve as analogues. If the number of traits shared between the analogue and the archaeological manifestation are deemed sufficient, it follows that the past is not different from the present. In effect, by ignoring the change during the Postcontact period, substantive uniformity converted the archaeological record into a spacelike science.

Analogues are also employed in historical science, but they are methodological in nature. Thus, natural laws are constant temporally and spatially, and processes observed in the present operated in the past. Processes responsible for the eruption of Mount St. Helens, for instance, may also have caused eruptions of Rainier, Hood, or Adams. However, the similarity among processes does not imply that the configuration of the world is constant. In other words, St. Helens, Hood, and Rainier are unique historical events and, therefore, differ morphologically.

Although the new archaeology made lasting contributions to the study of prehistory by introducing the philosophy of science, multistage sampling strategies, and deductive methods of explanation, the approach curtailed the development of Contact period research. Because postcontact societies became the analogues for describing the nature and structure of prehistoric societies, the postcontact record was treated in essentialist terms. Quite simply, culture reconstruction with its reliance on ethnographic analogy made it impossible to investigate Contact period change.

Other developments in archaeology, especially historical archaeology and ethnohistory, counteracted the exclusion of archaeological studies of European contact that developed because of culture reconstruction. During the most recent period, postcontact studies have proliferated. Deagan's research has greatly influenced these recent developments.

Deagan's temporal focus is the last 500 years; consequently, she is comfortable moving between eighteenth-century St. Augustine and sixteenth-century Haiti. Within the period, she is interested in reconstructing lifeways and describing change that occurred in contact settings. The work from St. Augustine (1978a, 1983) elucidated Spanish, Indian, and mestizo adjustments in a missionary setting; the eastern Timucua work (1978b) described change in native culture. In addition, because Deagan is both an archaeologist and a historian (1982), she uses both sets of data in building descriptions.

Although these contributions are important, Deagan's work is not directed toward answering "why" questions. Like Trigger, she structures her descriptions of change and persistence within a spacelike science. Consequently, similarities and differences derived from real, discoverable entities are the necessary and sufficient conditions that suggest reasons for change. In the eastern Timucuan case, for instance, Deagan suggested directed contact through missions accounted for the change in social organization, religion, and politics; nondirected contact affected material culture and demography. In St. Augustine, the cultural value of "Spanishness" was responsible for the structure of the settlement.

Missionization or Spanish values are important reasons for change. Reasons, however, are not causes. Selective pressures cause change or stability, and these pressures operate on the variables that Deagan has identified.

Over the last 100 years, archaeological treatment of the Contact period has changed as the intellectual climate of the discipline has changed. There is no question that culture history was successful in overturning the older static, spacelike conception of native societies. By focusing on chronology, culture historians provided the temporal baseline crucial for the development of a timelike science. This success was limited largely to prehistoric periods. In Contact period research, the direct historical approach implied continuity between history and prehistory. Three consequences followed. The Contact period could be treated from a static, or spacelike perspective. That perspective, in part, facilitated the success of analogical arguments in culture reconstruction of the New Archaeology. As suggested, substantive analogy established a spacelike framework for Contact period studies.

Only recently have archaeologists truly begun to document the archaeological record of change that began in the sixteenth century. Now, we must begin to explain the nature and direction of these changes. The presence of theory that addresses "why" kinds of questions could integrate much of descriptive wealth that has been generated.

Conclusions

Contact period research holds a unique position in anthropology. Because this research is interdisciplinary, the presence of theory could eliminate the factionalism between science and antiscience that pervades the entire discipline. The result could be a powerful story. European discovery of the Americas established a new set of conditions in which both Europeans and native populations changed. Although there were "failed experiments" on both sides, there was also persistence. This persistence is the reflection of a flexibility that we have hardly begun to describe or explain. Because historical science makes "history doable" (Gould 1986:61) as science, implementing this framework would not sacrifice the rich and unique histories of postcontact America to the generalizing goal of the spacelike sciences. Consequently, I suggest that historical science can not only tell the stories of change that have occurred in the past 500 years, but can also explain the persistence.

Acknowledgments

I would like to thank James Houk who, as a graduate student, stimulated me to delve into the acculturation literature. Charlotte Beck, Bob Leonard, and Patrice Teltser provided thoughtful and important comments on earlier drafts of this essay. As usual, Tom Wood showed me that I am still learning how to write. Dave Thomas deserves special thanks for his organizational vision, editorial assistance, and intellectual support. His commitment to diverse perspectives is a rare and valued trait.

References

Ahler, S. A.
1978 *A Research Plan for Investigation of the Archaeological Resources of the Knife River Indian Villages, National Historic Site.* U. S. National Park Service, Midwest Archaeological Center, Lincoln, Nebr.
Atwater, C.
1820 *Description of the Antiquities Discovered in the State of Ohio and Other Western States.* Transactions and Collections of the American Antiquarian Society, Archaeological Americana No. 1. Worcester, Mass.
Binford, L. R.
1962 Archaeology as Anthropology. *American Antiquity* 28:217–225.
1965 Archaeological Systematics and the Study of Culture Process. *American Antiquity* 31:203–210.
1967 Smudge Pits and Hide Smoking: The Use of Analogy in Archaeological Reasoning. *American Antiquity* 32:1–12.
1981 *Bones: Ancient Man and Modern Myths.* Academic Press, New York.
Binford, S. R., and L. R. Binford
1968 *New Perspectives in Archaeology.* Aldine, Chicago.
Boas, F.
1888 The Northwestern Tribes of Canada IV. Report of the Committee. *British Association for the Advancement of Science* 1:233–242.

1907 *The Eskimo of Baffin Land and Hudson Bay.* American Museum of Natural History Bulletin 15. New York.

Cook, S. F.

1973 The Significance of Disease in the Extinction of the New England Indians. *Human Biology* 45:485–508.

Crosby, A. W.

1972 *The Columbian Exchange: Biocultural Consequences of 1492.* Greenwood Press, Westport.

1986 *Ecological Imperialism: The Biological Expansion of Europe, 900–1900.* Cambridge University Press, Cambridge.

Deagan, K. A.

1978a The Material Assemblage of Sixteenth-Century Spanish Florida. *Historical Archaeology* 12:25–50.

1978b Cultures in Transition: Fusion and Assimilation among the Eastern Timucua. In *Tacachale: Essays on the Indians of Florida and Southeastern Georgia during the Historic Period*, edited by J. T. Milanich and S. Proctor, pp. 89–119. University of Florida Presses, Gainesville.

1982 Avenues of Inquiry in Historical Archaeology. In *Advances in Archaeological Method and Theory*, vol. 5, edited by M. B. Schiffer, pp. 151–177. Academic Press, New York.

1983 *Spanish St. Augustine: The Archaeology of a Colonial Creole Community.* Academic Press, New York.

1987 *Artifacts of the Spanish Colonies of Florida and the Caribbean, 1500–1800*, vol. 1. Smithsonian Institution Press, Washington D.C.

Deetz, J.

1965 *The Dynamics of Stylistic Change in Arikara Ceramics.* Illinois Studies in Anthropology No. 4. Urbana.

De Laguna, F.

1976 The Development of Anthropology. In *Selected Papers from the American Anthropologist*, edited by F. De Laguna, pp. 91–104. American Anthropological Association, Washington D.C.

Dixon, R.

1913 Some Aspects of North American Archaeology. *American Anthropologist* n.s., 15:549–566.

Dobyns, H. F.

1963 An Outline of Andean Epidemic History to 1720. *Bulletin of the History of Medicine* 37:493–515.

1966 An Appraisal of Techniques for Estimating Aboriginal American Population with a new Hemispheric Estimate. *Current Anthropology* 7:395–416.

1983 *Their Number Become Thinned.* University of Tennessee Press, Knoxville.

Dunnell, R. C.

1982 Science, Social Science, and Common Sense: The Agonizing Dilemma of Modern Archaeology. *Journal of Anthropological Research* 38:1–25.

1986 Methodological Issues in Americanist Artifact Classification. In *Advances in Archaeological Method and Theory*, vol. 9, edited by M. B. Schiffer, pp. 194–207. Academic Press, New York.

Ford, J. A.

1936 *Analysis of Village Site Collections from Louisiana and Mississippi.* Department of Conservation, Louisiana State Geological Survey, Anthropological Study No. 2. Baton Rouge.

1954a Comment on A. C. Spaulding, "Statistical Techniques for the Discovery of Artifact Types." *American Antiquity* 19:390–391.

1954b Spaulding's Review of Ford. *American Anthropologist* 56:109–111.

1954c The Type Concept Revisited. *American Anthropologist* 56:42–54.

1961 *Menard Site: The Quapaw Village of Osotouy on the Arkansas River*. American Museum of Natural History, Anthropological Papers 48(2). New York.

Gallatin, A.
1836 *A Synopsis of the Indian Tribes of North America*. Transactions and Collections of the American Antiquarian Society 2:9–422.

Gifford, D. P.
1981 Taphonomy and Paleoecology: A Critical Review of Archaeology's Sister Disciplines. In *Advances in Archaeological Method and Theory*, vol.4, edited by M. B. Schiffer, pp. 365–439. Academic Press, New York.

Gould, R. A., and P. J. Watson
1982 A Dialogue on the Meaning and Use of Analogy in Ethnoarchaeological Reasoning. *Journal of Anthropological Archaeology* 1:355–381.

Gould, S. J.
1986 Evolution and the Triumph of Homology, or Why History Matters. *American Scientist* 74:60–69.

Grinnell, G. B.
1897 The Ghost Dance Religion, by James Mooney. *American Anthropologist* 10:230–232.

Hallowell, I.
1976 The Beginnings of Anthropology in America. In *Selected Papers from the American Anthropologist*, edited by F. De Laguna, pp. 1–90. American Anthropological Association, Washington D.C.

Harris, M.
1968 *The Rise of Anthropological Theory*. Crowell, New York.

Harris, T.
1835 Researches into the Origin of the Indigines of North and South America. Ms. on file, American Antiquarian Society, Worcester, Mass.

Herskovits, M. J.
1937 *Life in a Haitian Valley*. J. Knopf, New York.
1958 *Acculturation: The Study of Culture Contact*. Smith, Gloucester. Originally published 1938.

Hill, J. N., and R. K. Evans
1972 A Model for Classification and Typology. In *Models in Archaeology*, edited by D. Clarke, pp. 231–273. Methuen, London.

Hodder, I.
1985 Postprocessual Archaeology. In *Advances in Archaeological Method and Theory*, vol. 8, edited by M. B. Schiffer, pp. 1–26. Academic Press, New York.

Holmes, W. H.
1914 Area of American Culture Characterization Tentatively Outlined as an Aid in the Study of Antiquities. *American Anthropologist* 16:413–446.

Hookyas, R.
1970 Catastrophism in Geology, Its Scientific Character in Relation to Actualism and Uniformitarianism. *Mededlingen der Kominkleke Nederlandse Academie Van Weterschappen AFD. Letterkunde Nieune Reeks-Deel* 33–7:271–316.

Kidder, A. V.
1926 The Excavations of Pecos in 1925. Archaeological Institute of America. Papers of the School of American Research n.s. No. 14. Santa Fe.
1951 The Story of Pecos. *El Palacio* 58(3):3–10.

Kidder, M. A., and A. V. Kidder
1917 Notes on the Pottery of Pecos. *American Anthropologist* 19:325–360.

Lehmer, D. J.
1954 *Archaeological Investigation in the Oahe Dam Area, South Dakota, 1950–1951*. Bureau of American Ethnology Bulletin No. 158. Washington D.C.
1971 *Introduction to Middle Missouri Archaeology*. National Park Service, Anthropological Papers No. 1. Washington D.C.

1977 Epidemics among the Indians of the Upper Missouri. *Reprints in Anthropology* 8:105–111. Lincoln, Nebr.

Lehmer, D. J., and D. T. Jones
1968 *Arikara Archaeology: The Bad River Phase.* River Basin Surveys Publications in Salvage Archaeology No. 7. Lincoln, Nebr.

Lehmer, D. J., W. R. Wood, and C. L. Dill
1978 *The Knife River Phase.* Department of Anthropology and Sociology, Dana College. Submitted to Interagency Archaeological Service Center, Denver. Contract No. C3537 (68). Blair.

Leone, M. P.
1986 Symbolic, Structural and Critical Archaeology. In *American Archaeology Past and Future: A Celebration of the Society of American Archaeology, 1935–1985*, edited by D. J. Meltzer, D. D. Fowler, and J. A. Sabloff, pp. 413–438. Smithsonian Institution Press, Washington D.C.

Lewis, T. M. N., and M. Kneberg
1979 *Hiwassee Island: An Archaeological Account of Four Tennessee Indian Peoples.* University of Tennessee Press, Knoxville. Originally published 1946.

Linton, R. (editor)
1940 *The Acculturation of Seven American Indian Tribes.* D. Appleton, New York.

Lowie, R. H.
1916 *Plains Indian Age-Societies: Historical and Comparative Summary.* American Museum of Natural History, Anthropological Papers 11(13). New York.

Mead, M.
1932 *The Changing Culture of an Indian Tribe.* Columbia University Contributions to Anthropology No. 15. New York.

Meltzer, D. J.
1983 The Antiquity of Man and the Development of American Archaeology. In *Advances in Archaeological Method and Theory*, vol. 6, edited by M. B. Schiffer, pp. 1–51. Academic Press, New York.

Mooney, J.
1896 *The Ghost Dance Religion and the Sioux Outbreak of 1890.* Fourteenth Annual Report of the Bureau of Ethnology, Part 2. Washington D.C.

Nelson, N. C.
1916 Chronology of the Tano Ruins. *American Anthropologist* 18:159–188.

Quimby, G. I.
1957 *The Bayou Goula Site, Iberville Parish, Louisiana.* Fieldiana: Anthropology 47(2). Chicago.

Ramenofsky, A. F.
1987 *Vectors of Death: The Archaeology of European Contact.* University of New Mexico Press, Albuquerque.
1990a Loss of Innocence: Assessing Archaeological Explanations of Aboriginal Change in the Sixteenth-Century Southeast. In *Columbian Consequences*, vol. 2, *Archaeological and Historical Perspectives on the Spanish Borderlands East*, edited by D. H. Thomas, pp. 27–43. Smithsonian Institution Press, Washington D.C.
1990b Viral, Bacterial, and Protozoal Disease Introductions to the Americas: A.D. 1492–1700. In *The History and Geography of Human Disease*, edited by K. Kiple. Cambridge University Press, Cambridge, in press.

Redfield, R.
1930 *Tepoztlan, A Mexican Village.* University of Chicago Publications in Anthropology.

Redfield, R., R. Linton, and M. J. Herskovits
1935 A Memorandum for the Study of Acculturation. *American Anthropologist* 38: 149–192.

Sapir, E.

1916 *Time Perspective in Aboriginal American Culture, A Study in Method.* Geological Survey of Canada Memoir 90. Ottawa.

Shanks, M. and C. Tilley
1988 *Social Theory and Archaeology.* University of New Mexico Press, Albuquerque.

Silverberg, R.
1968 *Mound Builders of Ancient America: The Archaeology of a Myth.* New York Graphic Society, Greenwich.

Spaulding, A. C.
1953 Statistical Techniques for the Discovery of Artifact Types. *American Antiquity* 18:305–314.
1954a Reply. *American Anthropologist* 56:112–114.
1954b Reply to Ford. *American Antiquity* 19:391–393.

Spicer, E. H. (editor)
1961 Perspectives in American Indian Culture Change. University of Chicago Press, Chicago.

Squier, E. G., and E. H. Davis
1848 *Ancient Monuments of the Mississippi Valley.* Smithsonian Contributions to Knowledge No. 1. Washington D.C.

Stearn, E. W., and A. E. Stearn
1945 *The Effects of Smallpox on the Destiny of the Amerinidan.* Bruce Humphries, Boston.

Steward, J. H.
1942 The Direct Historical Approach in Archaeology. *American Antiquity* 7:337–343.
1955 Theory and Application in Social Science. *Ethnohistory* 2:292–302.

Strong, W. D.
1940 From History to Prehistory in the Northern Great Plains. In *Essays in Historical Anthropology of North America, in Honor of John R. Swanton.* Smithsonian Miscellaneous Collections 100:353–394. Washington D.C.

Teltser, P.
1989 Archaeology and the Historical Sciences. Paper presented at the 54th Annual Meeting of the Society for American Archaeology. Atlanta.

Thomas, C.
1894 *Report on the Mound Exploration of the Bureau of Ethnology.* Smithsonian Institution Bureau of Ethnology Annual Report 12:17–742.

Thomas, D. H.
1988 *St. Catherines: An Island in Time.* Georgia History and Culture Series. Georgia Endowment for the Humanities. Atlanta.
1990 The Spanish Missions of La Florida: An Overview. *Columbian Consequences,* vol. 2, *Archaeological and Historical Perspectives on the Spanish Borderlands West,* edited by D. H. Thomas, pp. 357–397. Smithsonian Institution Press, Washington D.C.

Tilley, C.
1984 Ideology and the Legitimation of Power in the Middle Neolithic of Southern Sweden. In *Ideology, Power and Prehistory,* edited by D. Miller and C. Tilley, pp. 111–146. Cambridge University Press, Cambridge.

Trigger, B. G.
1962 Trade and Tribal Warfare on the St. Lawrence in the Sixteenth Century. *Ethnohistory* 9:240–256.
1976 *The Children of Aataentsic: A History of the Huron People to 1660.* 2 vols. McGill-Queen's, Montreal.
1978 *Trend and Tradition: Essays in Archaeological Interpretation.* Columbia University Press, New York.
1981 Archaeology and the Ethnographic Present. *Anthropologica* 23:3–17.
1985 *Natives and Newcomers: Canada's "Heroic Age" Reconsidered.* McGill-Queen's University Press, Kingston.
1990 *A History of Archaeological Thought.* Cambridge University Press, Cambridge.

Wedel, W. R.

1938 *The Direct-Historical Approach in Pawnee Archaeology*. Smithsonian Miscellaneous Collections 91:1–21. Washington D.C.

Whallon, R., and J. A. Brown (editors)

1982 *Essays in Archaeological Typology*. Center for American Archaeology, Evanston, Ill.

Willey, G. R., and J. A. Sabloff

1980 *A History of American Archaeology*, 2d ed. W. H. Freeman, San Francisco.

Wissler, C.

1914a Influence of the Horse in the Development of Plains Culture. *American Anthropologist* 16:1–25.

1914b Material Cultures of the North American Indians. *American Anthropologist* 16:447–505.

1950 *The American Indian*, 3d ed. Peter Smith, New York. Originally published 1917.

Chapter 23

Patricia Galloway

The Archaeology of Ethnohistorical Narrative

Effective use of ethnohistorical narratives from the early Contact period by archaeologists and anthropologists has been hindered by a frequent failure to apply adequate rigor to the evaluation of written sources. With few exceptions, these sources portray Indian peoples and their motivations as various sets of Europeans' preconceptions demanded that they be; and these verbal images are embedded in a Western European discourse that is still so congenial with our own modes of apprehending reality that we often fail to recognize the problematic aspects of the texts themselves. In the hope of conveying the historiographical complexity of histories of the Contact period, I attempt to explain these very real concerns using the metaphor of archaeological site formation and excavation.

Rhetorical Dimension of Historical Evidence

It is a truism that documentary evidence is seldom exactly what it seems. For the past 20 years, historiographers have been debating whether we can expect to learn anything from it at all. In evaluating a historical text, we must consider not only the obvious factor of intentional misrepresentation, but whether, first, it is possible in principle to represent any event at all in a way that is closely congruent with the facts; second, what form that representation should take; and third, whether a reader from a subsequent reality might be capable of truthfully reconstructing the event on the basis of that representation (always assuming that we know what "truthfully" means). American historians, initially bemused by European philosophers' debates about the precarious status of historical narrative, have reacted to this fundamental paradigm shift in predictable ways, and a lengthy theoretical dialogue dominated by younger scholars—not unlike the theoretical ferment of postprocessual archaeology—has become a notable feature of recent historical writing. Older historians generally try to ignore this debate long enough to produce a last major work and retire, but most of them also seem to have decided to stipulate that although documents are probably capable of granting us some kind of access to the past, there is still much to be learned about what kind of access this may be (see Kellner 1987; White 1987:26–57).

It is disconcerting, then, as the approach of the Columbian Quincentenary enlivens interest in the early Contact period, to find archaeologists and anthropologists taking the evidence from ethnohistorical documentary materials so confidently at face value. Just when we would expect fresh revaluations of all questions connected with the explorations of the sixteenth century, we see instead a rash of research based on manifestly problematic but still virtually unexamined texts, such as the so-called log of Columbus's voyage (Henige and Zamora 1989) or the narratives of the Hernando de Soto expedition (Galloway 1990). Yet instead of demanding critical elucidation of such problematic texts by historians, archaeologists and anthropologists have been content to approach these sources alone, armed only with the "normal science" of a historical method generations old.

This issue is particularly serious because of the nature of the most crucial sources for early contact. Nearly all of these sources, as even cursory examination makes abundantly clear, are secondary narrative histories, narratives consciously composed by nonparticipants with the aim of presenting a coherent account of events that happened in the past. It is precisely this narrative form that has come in for such harsh historiographical judgment over the last generation (White 1987:26–57). The extraction of individual facts from such narratives requires, first and foremost, the recognition that the form itself carries ideological implications no different from those of the narrative form in fiction. Such awareness must then support a critical attitude toward narrative history that permits it to be converted back into the collection of facts with which the historian supposedly started.

The failure of archaeologists and anthropologists to achieve this critical stance with respect to the narrative histories of early contact is especially strange at a time when there is lively debate among social scientists themselves on the contingency of anthropological field observations and the inadequacy of narrative as a vehicle for reporting them. Even if we grant that good ethnographic observations are possible in principle, conquerors and colonialists were certainly not trained participant observers by any stretch of the imagination. Which is not to claim that no Colonial period observer observed truly or learned a great deal in his contact with native peoples; for the moment, we may also stipulate that there might be such an ideal observer. But to use ethnohistorical narrative, we must recognize that we are dealing with what is now not an observation but a *reported* observation; not an experience, but a *text* describing it. If the information itself is potentially valuable, we must still solve the problems raised by the form in which it reaches us.

A simple example can suggest the significance of these problems. Even in our own day of much less rigidly prescribed communication formats, there are still formal and informal rules that constrain both the presentation of information and the kind of information that can be included, regardless of its "reality": one need only consider the wedding invitation, with its conventional expression of gratification on the part of the bride's parents; or the job application with its résumé carefully tailored to the requirements of the job. Furthermore, where specific rule does not govern these features, other factors may come into play, such as public taste in the case of genres that aim at communicating with the public or disciplinary convention in scholarly writing (Foucault 1972; Kuhn 1970). This rhetorical dimension to all communication resides in the material form it takes and determines some of its content and all of its presentational features. Hence there is virtually no such thing as a useful "face value" for a historical text.

Cultural Hegemony of the Narrative Text

Unfortunately, the song of narrative history makes that history appear more attractive than it is unless we can stop our ears against it. Archaeologists and anthropologists wishing to extract evidence about native cultures from the narratives of the early Contact period in the Southeast have assumed from the beginning of serious investigations into these problems that what parts of documentary evidence to take seriously and what parts to discard were easily determined by common sense, without the application of any detailed analysis (e.g., Phillips et al. 1951:349; Swanton 1939:4–11). This conviction continues unexamined in more recent work (Brain 1985:105–106; Brain et al. 1974:239–243; Hudson 1987:1), where researchers have proceeded to create their own composite narratives of the de Soto expedition by choosing segments from the several accounts of it according to ill-defined and ill-documented criteria.

The reason for this naive approach to historical texts is not far to seek. Anthropologists and archaeologists have simply made use of assumptions about the structure of narrative that they acquired during the exposure normal schooling gave them to the "text-based" disciplines of literature and history. The teaching methods used in both disciplines at the undergraduate level were and unfortunately still are designed to hustle students as quickly as possible through surveys meant to prepare them for literate behavior in their society, requiring that they extract and manipulate meaning from texts without having been taught how—or even that—meaning was constructed by the texts in the first place. Hence the ironic spectacle of well-trained social scientists, professionally attuned to the analysis of complex patterns of behavior in preliterate societies, placing blind trust in a set of narratives whose underlying assumptions reenforce the social formation that produced them (cf. White 1987:13–14). This can happen because the victims of this kind of teaching command no way of talking about texts belonging to their own culture except as somehow primarily meaningful, as the exact representation of something someone actually said or thought, so that any reservations about a text's truth value are expressed in terms of a characterization of the author's veracity. This phenomenon is very similar to the approach to archaeological analysis that takes every feature of every site as a primary deposition reflecting precisely the behavior of its inhabitants, another assumption that has been discarded as broadly inaccurate.

General Theory of the Narrative Text

There are, however, very much more precise and accurate ways of talking about texts, based not only upon the past 30 years' theoretical development through phenomenological, structuralist, deconstructionist, and reception theories of the analysis of discourse, but also drawing upon a heritage that goes back in the western tradition to the detailed analysis of biblical texts in the Middle Ages (Baldwin 1928; Culler 1975; Holub 1984; Norris 1982). A first fundamental distinction is made between what is being said and how it is articulated.

In formalist discussions of narrative in general, a distinction is made between the *story* as the underlying "matter" that is to be communicated (the "content," so to speak) and the *plot* as the "manner" in which the story is communicated (the "form" of the text and its interpretive component). Historical "truth" is then apparently easily discovered: We need simply extract the underlying story from the clutches of the plot in a historical narrative and thereby discover what "really happened." Alas, however, the solution is never that simple. Just to begin with, the story is most of the time so thoroughly interwoven with the plot—that is, the plot determines so much about how much and what parts of the story reach the reader—that it is impossible to disentangle them without damage to both. Since we have access to the story only through the plot, we have to understand the cultural contingencies of the plot very well indeed if we intend to have a hope of recovering any part of the story.

An additional complexity arises because the underlying matter, the story, will have been conceived, either by the observer who reported the events or by the historian who assembled them into a narrative, or both, as a story that "made sense" in terms of his own culture, that expressed one of its master metaphors (White 1987), and the power of that story will have lent form and color to detail that was originally unspecified. Thus all the narrators of the de Soto expedition, from the participant Biedma to the three historians who later assembled secondary narratives, viewed the expedition as an admirable expression of Iberian determination in the face of hardship, whatever else they may have thought of it, and as a result they all conventionalized to some degree the purposes and indeed the characters of the participants in order to portray at least some of them as heroes.

This is not to say simply that a narrative history is the product of its culture, but also to make the point that the narrative history is also an agent of the reproduction of the culture that produced it, and part of its function is to idealize that culture, to make its imperatives "come true" by lending them verisimilitude. Because our culture is a lateral descendant of sixteenth-century Iberian culture, it not only shares the narrative history form, but also some of the underlying stories, and we are trapped into credibility by our acceptance of their plausibility. Furthermore, by merely apprehending a narrative text as such, we participate directly in the creation of its meaning (Iser 1978:107–231), and we have to learn at least how to observe our participation if we are not to fall in love with our very own version.

The Archaeological Analogy

If archaeologists and anthropologists want to make credible use of the narratives of early contact, they must first take these problems of textual analysis as seriously as they take the nearly identical problem of reconstructing culture from material remains. Because the written text is also the material evidence of the past actions of human beings, some aspects of such archaeological theory as applies to other material remains can also be seen to apply to texts. We have not noticed this, because even as social scientists we still share the Western European bias in favor of a written text as evidence for a privileged kind of past human activity, intellectual activity recording nonmaterial aspects of culture, which we as participants in a literate culture have valorized as more important than its material aspects and somehow different in kind. Yet, paradoxically, the text is just as material as the ceramic pot, just as subject to exterior cultural influence, just as constrained by its medium. In similar ways, it is "a distorted reflection of a past behavioral system" (Schiffer 1976:12), and we must find a way to stand back from it and see how it works.

I am certainly not the first to attempt an analogy between the historical text and the archaeological record; Ian Hodder discusses archaeological epistemology by analogy with the historical record under the rubric of "reading the past" (Hodder 1986), while Michel Foucault more pertinently discusses the "archaeology of knowledge" as a many-layered construct (Foucault 1972). I will not even try to go so far as either in philosophical subtlety, but rather aim for a straightforward analogy—inevitably oversimplified—that draws an archaeological parallel to the interpretive complexity that I am trying to establish for the historical text.

Text Formation Processes

The long-sustained work of Michael Schiffer on the processes by which archaeological sites and artifacts are created, altered, and recovered offers a useful common-sense frame of reference for the archaeological analogy (Schiffer 1976, 1987), although with the significant reservation that "text formation processes" can be described but would be very difficult to predict. Schiffer himself originally dodged the task of treating historical texts explicitly within his theory of cultural formation processes by situating the historical record along with contemporary analysis in the "systemic context" (1976:27–28), and he has if anything offered less comment on the historical text in his more recent work (1987:5–6), where he continues to confine his remarks on the "historical record" to historic artifacts.

But the "systemic context" is far from monolithic, and the processes that take place within it may have very different tempos, depending upon the function of the artifact involved. Schiffer's "techno-functional" artifacts are commodities that are generally consumed through use, whereas "socio-functional" and particularly "ideo-functional" items would be less likely to meet with such demise and more likely to remain in the systemic context through reuse processes, which Schiffer holds responsible for the creation of the historical record but admits are "little understood" (1987:28).

The persistence of historical texts as ideofunctional artifacts in the systemic context requires the important reminder that the systemic context itself is in fact nothing other than the ever-changing living culture, and just because an item remains within the culture does not mean that the culture itself and the item's function within it do not change over time. The historical record does not stand outside of culture, since without a cultural function it would not exist at all, but instead is shaped by the needs of culture and changes as culture changes. Just like the archaeological record, the historical record constitutes a many-layered cake of the customs of mankind, and the further the layer from the "surface" of the present, the more effort we require to understand it.

The problems introduced by this disjunction between past and present systemic contexts are enormous and have occupied a whole school of textual critics in recent years (Holub 1984). It is very unlikely that it would ever be possible for us to know fully what a sixteenth-century audience made of the histories of first contact with peoples of the New World, just as five hundred years hence it will be impossible for an audience to understand the highly topical references in protest songs of the 1960s, as teenagers today have already invested Woodstock with mythic overtones. And if this analogy seems far-fetched, consider for a moment the apparent anomaly of Garcilaso de la Vega's comparison of de Soto's burial in the Mississippi to that of Alaric the Visigoth in the diverted Busento riverbed, which lengthy description Garcilaso quotes from an Italian historian because, he says, the Spaniards are descended from the Goths. This reference becomes intelligible if we know that the Castilian kings obsessively traced their lineage to the Visigoths to stress the legitimacy of their rule and that Garcilaso was concerned to obtain favor at court. Awareness of these facts enables the reader to understand that the parallel was being drawn not to further explain or add details to the disposal of de Soto's body, but both to glorify the necessity for its secretiveness and to make events in the New World more immediate for the influential people Garcilaso hoped to reach with his arguments for the desirability of further efforts by Spain in Florida. Thus the inclusion of extraneous material in the narrative is influenced by the subplot of Garcilaso's intentions.

A second example, taken from Oviedo's retelling of Ranjel's account of the de Soto expedition, has the expedition members referring to a town where a false cacique was taken prisoner and escaped as "Mala Paz." Certainly from the Spanish point of view, this bad faith made the Spanish—Indian relations at the town a "bad peace," but the real force of the label comes from de Soto's disappointment at having been denied the right to explore and colonize Guatemala, because the "Defender of the Indians," Bartolomé de Las Casas, had claimed it to carry out his successful "Vera Paz" experiment of peaceful and voluntary conversion of the natives. This example contrasts with the preceding one, because it makes use of a phrase that was well-known to Oviedo's potential audience and thus was capable without explanation both of conjuring up the entire Vera Paz experiment and Las Casas's critique of the Spanish conquest and of implying a critique of de Soto's expedition's violent behavior toward the Indians, thereby subtly reinforcing Oviedo's overt commentary along those lines.

These examples demonstrate that sixteenth-century histories have not remained in the systemic context as fully meaningful as the day they were first written, because most of us are simply not adequately informed about the cultural context in which they were written to extract from them the full range of meaning that they had for a contemporary audience. Products of the recycling and reuse both of contemporary testimonies and of other historical texts, these texts have been recycled and reused by subsequent writers for their own purposes, but because they have not been critically analyzed, the process has allowed important elements of their meaning to be ignored and thus to drop out of the systemic context. To restore the historical text fully to the systemic context, it is necessary to "excavate" those lost elements by making explicit analysis of the text itself and its intertexts, as we have just done.

To "excavate" a historical text it is first necessary to develop a general hypothesis of the "text formation processes" that created it. Although the analogy I will be drawing is generally applicable to all sorts of documents that belong to "history," I will confine my discussion of specific examples here to secondary narrative histories and to my own research experience with the de Soto expedition narratives. It should be noted that no matter what the claims of the secondary author as to the purity of his reproduction of a primary text, alterations that favor one reading or another of the text are always introduced, even in a modern critical edition. Thus a primary aspect of the formation of these histories is their intertextuality, "a system of references to other books, other texts, other sentences . . . a node within a network" (Foucault 1972:23), where "text" refers to written or oral discourse.

This concept of intertextuality was devised to express the notion that in literate societies an enormous proportion of what is written (and thought) is the product of complex reuse processes in which the objects being reused are written and oral texts. Intertextuality is more broadly a phenomenon of all discourses in all cultures, but it is overtly acknowledged in the writing of history in general; and in the case at hand, continental European historical discourse of the Renaissance, it is a consciously exploited and often proudly proclaimed phenomenon.

According to Schiffer's terminology, the "S-S" (systemic to systemic) reuse processes are recycling, secondary use, lateral cycling, and conservation, but the creation of narrative histories from the raw materials of actual experience and intertextual relationships requires some reworking of Schiffer's "flow model" to account for several peculiarities of the textual artifact (see Figure 23–1). Clearly, the ideal raw material for history writing is the direct experience of events by individuals, but there must be an intervening "manufacturing process" to make it available for use, and that is the "narrativizing" of the events by the witnesses. As with manufacturing processes in general, this process may be additive, reductive, or both; it is never neither, since the event cannot be precisely reflected through the experience of any individual. And, of course, the individual makes this event available not for no reason at all, but because he is required to do so by being questioned or because he wishes to do so in order to gain some advantage for himself, so that the use to which the resulting eyewitness testimony is put has the power of influencing the way it is created. Finally, the eyewitness testimony may be presented orally or may be embodied in a document.

Once the testimony is available, it then becomes raw material, along with other evidence, with respect to a different manufacturing process: the writing of a history. Here the process becomes recursive, and the narrative history incorporates many types of sources, ranging from "raw" oral first-person narratives to documents to other histories. Once constructed, the narrative history enters the use stream (reading), after (or during) which it may be recycled (quoted from, plagiarized, or paraphrased), or secondarily used (as a model of good history writing or a source of comparative examples). The issue of use and lateral cycling is the complex one that is the cause of all our problems here, since al-

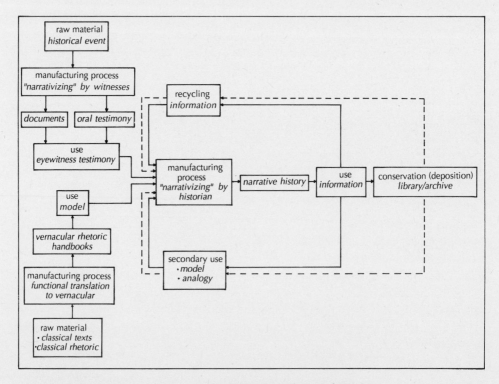

Figure 23–1. Text formation processes for the Renaissance historical text.

though the history reaches many readers without changing its form, the reader's ability to recover the intended content varies over time. The fourth reuse process, conservation, can obviously be mapped onto the preservation of the history in a library or archive for further reuse, but this form of reuse can also be akin to archaeological deposition, since a history may languish unread for centuries before being revived for one or several kinds of reuse.

To add detail to this schema, it is worthwhile to look at the various sources for the writing of history. The primary source materials used by sixteenth-century historians, the documents or oral accounts of participants (most now lost to us), are in many ways the least of the materials that went to make up a history. It is worth repeating this: What we would now consider essential primary sources were considered raw material only, not proper (interpretive) history. History was (and is) constructed according to a set of notions of what *constituted* a history—what it should contain, look like, teach, and cause. This source material, in order to become an acceptable narrative history, had to be reworked according to concepts of acceptable purpose and form and embedded in an intertextual network of references that established the learning and credibility of the author. "It was the novel contribution of the humanists," Paul Kristeller wrote, "to add the firm belief that in order to write and speak well it was necessary to study and to imitate the ancients" (1961:13).

The "ancients," along with not-so-ancient writers of the Middle Ages and the early Renaissance, came to be viewed as authorities, and they influenced Renaissance historical writing profoundly. Specific classical writers found secondary reuse to provide structural and rhetorical models, and none was so popular with the authors of the conquest as Caesar, whose *Commentaries* on the conquest of barbarian peoples were especially relevant to the stories historians of the New World enterprise had to tell (Cochrane 1981:256) and frequently provided them with materials to recycle for analogy as well as structure (Durand 1963). Most of the historians of Spanish conquest prided themselves on their Latin at least, and many commanded Italian as well, proving it by translating Italian works (e.g., Oviedo, Garcilaso). Hence there is also a broad range of Italian historians, themselves forging models based on the ancients, who had been read and were drawn upon by the historians of the New World, both for models and metaphors.

Although one of the Renaissance revolutions, reflected by most of the conquest authors, was the adoption of vernacular languages for serious writing, historians were able to take advantage of the humanists' adaptation of classical rhetorical rules to the governance of composition in the vernacular. This was a very serious source of influence on historical writers—here reflecting a primary use, since the rhetoricians wrote prescriptive, procedural texts—because classical rhetoric dictated not just the syntactic rules with which we are familiar, but also defined the kinds of figurative language, topics, and structures proper to the different genres of writing. It could demand that in a certain setting a formal speech on a certain topic was appropriate; it could demand that a description of the natural world take place in a certain order and incorporate a particular set of observations (Curtius 1963:193–202).

The conquest historians were writing about a New World, but they were nearly all doing it for an Old World audience. Hence the shaping influences of other histories seeing secondary reuse, but hence also the recycling of materials that had nothing to do with history. The tradition of medieval religious commentary had especially taught the value of analogy for the explanation of unfamiliar things, and our authors—like other Renaissance historians—drew not only upon parallels from ancient history and literature, but also upon contemporary historical writing, as we have seen above with the "Alaric the Goth" example, and even European folk traditions for explanatory analogies (see Chang-Rodriguez 1982; Lankford 1990).

Cochrane has pointed out that Renaissance history "was exclusively political history . . . concerned solely with the collective acts of a political community" (1981:9), and many historians and philosophers of history have argued more fundamentally that all narrative history is political history—that narrative is the form that political history takes and implies. Thus, although it bore a chain of alleged events at its heart and its structure was dictated by classical models, its message was articulated in terms of political and spiritual ideals particular to the culture of its author, and it was meant to be read and understood in terms of those ideals. Like narrative interpretive history of any age, Renaissance historical discourse was managed by historians using the models and rules already mentioned in such a way as to achieve the purpose. Their histories "came out" in a particular way not necessarily because that was how events transpired, but because they should have done so.

Having specified the process of formation of the Renaissance historical narrative, we arrive at the problem of determining what kind of site it looks like. I would liken it to a multicomponent site whose earlier features, as well as imported materials and curated objects, are consciously reused and carefully retailored to the purposes of a leader among its last occupants—probably a ceremonial site, where site structure has a consciously orchestrated presentational purpose. Schiffer's main concern in discussing stratified multicomponent sites is to examine how later occupations alter the archaeological record of earlier ones, and that is certainly the problem here, if we consider the first-person source as the earliest occupation. It is necessary also to recognize that the "intertextual stratigraphy" here is more of a network than a vertical sequence, and one of the tasks of textual excavation is to define how examination of the text can uncover its intertextual relationships. The historical narrative is thus a complex site of several dimensions; it is more than a simple set of superpositions. The narrative itself creates a three-dimensional "world" and characters who inhabit it. They and it "move" through the fourth dimension of time as the narrative develops. And the narrative itself has its own material situation in time and its own multiple realizations as created and as reenacted when read. But all this is so much theory without concrete methods of analysis.

Excavating the Narrative Text

The analysis of a narrative text is not conceptually different from the excavation of a site and its postexcavation analysis or from some levels of specific-feature analysis in linguistics, since it consists of the identification of elements and the definition of patterning among those elements. The first step is to establish an arbitrary grid with reference to which distributions and features can emerge. Like an archaeological grid, this one really has to do with counting things, and for this purpose the text can initially be conceived as a long thin transect whose width corresponds to a single word. Because the physical size of the text is precisely defined, it can be divided into any number of units of absolute length in words, by applying any culturally relevant partitions: halves, thirds, sevenths, and so on. Against this grid, the major "features" of the text can easily be seen: the books and chapters into which the author has divided his work and that offer an initial signal of how he means for it to be read. By comparing the author's gross structure with the absolute measurement of length granted us by the grid, we are able to discern how the author uses gross length for emphasis and as a structuring device. This is graphically illustrated in Table 23–1, where the major divisions of three narrative histories of the de Soto expedition are tallied against the topics covered in each of them.

Once the major features are discovered, they represent the grid defined by the author for the text, against which we attempt to discern variously defined "activity areas" by means of the horizontal distribution of materials. The materials that are thus distributed are of several scales and even of several fundamentally different kinds. The author's linguistic habits and indeed the tone and seriousness of his language can be perceived at the most superficial level, through an analysis of his vocabulary and its distribution and a comparison of these elements with similar such elements in comparable texts of the same period. Alone among the narrators of the de Soto expedition, Garcilaso de la Vega has received loving attention from specialists in Spanish language and literature because his style offers a model of elegant and artistically controlled Spanish prose (e.g., Stimson and Navas-Ruiz 1971:74–75).

Word distributions may also be used to establish semantic clusters, but such clusters must in turn be correlated with features discerned at an intermediate level. Semantic features longer than a word or phrase are defined as discursive units like episodes, authorial asides, analogies, and examples, and are generally found grouped in such a way as to correlate with the authorial divisions of the narrative. The distribution of such features therefore allows us to see how the author is managing his text. The length and complexity of these units account for the pacing of the text, and the author's skill in connecting them one to another accounts for its coherence.

With the horizontal features of the site thus excavated, it is necessary to proceed to the subtle analysis of artifacts and artifact distributions that reveals the traces of the site formation process. It is here that we begin to show how the narrative creates its three-dimensional extension, the mechanism through which it connects with the reader's knowledge to create meaning by articulating a nested series of worlds in which things happen, some of them implied and some more explicitly presented.

The first world to be set up is the communicative situation between a more or less well-defined reader and the narrator who is to tell him the story. We con-

Table 23–1. Distribution of Topics in Three Narratives of the de Soto Expedition

Oviedo Chapters	Elvas Chapters	Topics Covered	Garcilaso Books (Chapters)
	1	de Soto's career	
	2	Cabeza de Vaca, muster	
	3	Portuguese at muster	
21	4	Voyage to Cuba	Book I (15)
	5	Description of Cuba	
	6	Santiago to Havana	
	7	Departure to Ucita	
22	8	Exploration	
	9	Ortiz's story	Book II, 1 (30)
23	10	Camp to Paracoxi to Cale	
	11	Cale to Malapaz to Napetaca	
24	12	Napetaca to Apalache	Book II, 2 (25)
25	13	Apalache to Patofa	
	14	Patofa to Cutifachiqui	
26	15	Cutifachiqui to Chiaha	
	16	Chiaha to Coça	Book III (39)
	17	Coça to Mavilla	
	18	Mavilla	
27	19	Mavilla	
	20	Mavilla to Chicaça	
	21	Chicaca to Alimamu	
	22	Alimamu to River crossing	
	23	Aquixo to Pacaha	
28	24	Pacaha	Book IV (16)
	25	Pacaha to Tanico	
	26	Tanico to Tulla	
	27	Tulla to Autiamque	
	28	Autiamque to Guachoya	
	29	Guachoya	Book V, 1 (8)
	30	Death of de Soto	
	31	Guachoya to Aguacay	
	32	Aguacay to Naguatex	
	33	Naguatex to Nondacao	Book V, 2 (15)
	34	Nondacao to Daycao	
(29)	35	Daycao to Aminoya	
	36	Aminoya	
	37	Aminoya to Quigualtam (boats)	
	38	Quigualtam to River mouth	
	39	River mouth to sea	
	40	sea	Book VI (22)
	41	sea to Panico	
	42	Panico	
	43	Mexico, fates	
(30)	44	Geography/natural history	

struct "reader" and "narrator" as surely as we construct the people who populated a prehistoric settlement, and we do it by the same kind of implication: the evidence of their activities revealed distributed over the site. The very language of the text and the attitudes it expresses, as well as any overt addresses to the reader, define the audience to which it is addressed. Nearly all the narrative histories of early contact are dedicated to some influential patron, but internal evidence—elliptical reference to quotations not given in full, for example—demonstrates not only the educational level of the expected audience, but, because descriptions of new things are always made on the basis of how they differ from familiar things, also the audience's entire material, intellectual, and moral context.

On the other side of the communication, the historical text is by its very definition the blending of at least several "voices"; in this way, it is something like an orchestral score, and this communicative filter is what led me to propose that the historical text was like a ceremonial site: Important aspects of the textual site's structure and content are under the control of a small elite who decide what information will be dispensed through the text. The author's voice is dominant, for even if he creates a separate narrator to tell the story who comments overtly as well as represents himself overtly as arranging the narrative, it is always necessary to remember that all the words and all the arrangement are ultimately the author's, and what we have to read is his theory of what happened. Fernandez de Oviedo created a stern and censorious narrator for his history of the de Soto expedition, who regularly speaks in the first person to voice diatribes criticizing the conduct of the expedition. The rest of the account, however, is presented in a deceptively neutral third person that is clearly not the alleged informant Ranjel's voice, since it speaks objectively of Ranjel's own deeds, but rather a second, invisible narrator persona: the story telling itself.

Discerning the other voices is therefore not always easy. Often in the texts that are of interest here the author represents another as telling the story. Sometimes these voices have actual referents as claimed and sometimes not, but this cannot be confirmed without reference to information from outside the text: intersite comparisons. José Durand had recourse to external evidence when he searched local records in Spain to establish the probability that Garcilaso's alleged sources Juan Coles and Alonso de Carmona could actually have given him access to additional data (Durand 1963:600–605). The point of this concern is that sometimes overtly presented voices do not have genuine historical referents, while sometimes genuine historical referents are not presented overtly as voices in the text.

The most crucial elements to be discerned for our purposes here are the sources providing the information presented in the text—this is the primary goal of the investigation, because "genuineness" is at the heart of our valuation of the historical text. As we have seen, our historians were working with used and reused source materials of several kinds. First, there are the sets of models and rules that pertain to the presentation of the account. Second, there is additional source material, ancient as well as contemporary, for the analogical apparatus the author adopts for explanatory purposes. Third, there is the primary source material for the target "story" itself: the written or oral account or accounts by actual witnesses or participants.

The sources present in the text, like multiple cultural manifestations on a site, cannot be recognized without a thorough knowledge of the intertextual field likely to be available to the author—who would think a sherd of Ramey Incised important at Winterville without a knowledge both of the Cahokia sequence and of the possible contexts for Ramey ceramics, as well as a thorough knowledge of other contemporary sites in the Mississippi Valley? Renaissance historians were textual omnivores; as literacy and printing created a new network of communication across Europe, they read, translated, and assimilated everything they could lay hands on, and a notable fraction of that "everything" amounted to the curated heirlooms (given contemporary interpretations) of the literature of Greece and Rome, as well as commented/reworked versions of sacred texts. They were proud of this learning and sought to demonstrate it by filling their works with overt and oblique references to the intertexts that informed them. It is our ignorance of this rich intertextual field, not their sneaking plagiarism, that makes us miss these references.

But the secondary sources provide more than such recognizable materials as encapsulated metaphors or episodes. They are also responsible, in their role as models, for the extensional form of a text, and this aspect of their influence is what we can discern through a careful analysis of the distribution of elements throughout the text. Thus we are able to characterize many of the histories as "commentaries" patterned after Caesar's, and thus on a smaller scale we are able to identify the catalogues of ships and personnel seen at the beginnings of expeditions as patterned after a tradition as old as Homer.

It is through the careful delineation of textual structure that the rhetorical rules of the text are uncovered, as the various rhetorical figures proper to various forms of discourse are seen to have been applied to specific episodes. Narrative structure itself is capable of lending variable emphasis through sheer length or placement within a substructure such as a chapter just as the rhythm of spatial presentation within a ceremonial precinct is capable of emphasizing the importance of a specific structure.

Intertextual influence in the shape both of structural models and of analogical materials is demonstrated in the example of Garcilaso's description of the temple/mortuary of the Cofitachequi village of Talomeco, replete with analogies to Roman statuary and painting, and accompanied by a catalogue of armories included in the temple complex. This description occupies two and a half chapters in the middle of the longest book of the narrative (III, 15–17). It is the only such lengthy description of a building in the *Florida*, which Garcilaso justifies by claiming that his major informant made him do it. Chang-Rodriguez (1982) has argued that these classical echoes are no accident, because they reenforce the Antony/Cleopatra parallel to de Soto and the Lady of Cofitachequi drawn explicitly by Garcilaso in a paraphrase of Plutarch a few chapters earlier, the whole segment at Cofitachequi, itself of impressive length (10 chapters), being a set piece emphasizing the importance of Garcilaso's constant theme that Indians of the New World, like pagans of the Old, were ready to receive the word of God.

It is also this distributional analysis that reveals the "genuine" observational materials provided by the participants: Each event in a narrative is reported either by an ostensible eyewitness or at second hand as the narrator shows us the events. Yet, even though an omniscient narrator's point of view is often the one through which the narrative is presented, a distributional analysis can reveal that of a limited number of identifiable people who are named as having actually witnessed a given event, only one of these is present in numerous other events also detailed in the narrative, and is thus likely to represent a constituent witness (cf. Galloway 1982:34–37)—it was just this kind of analysis that targeted Gonzalo Silvestre as the main informant in Garcilaso de la Vega's *Florida*, since Silvestre is the hero of so many episodes that appear in a unique form only in this account of the expedition (Castanien 1969:64; cf. Henige 1986). Similar analysis has revealed the independent witness of an unnamed soldier in the narrative of the same events by the "Gentleman of Elvas," otherwise derivative from the Oviedo/Ranjel version (Galloway 1990).

Having carried out the excavation and the postexcavation analysis thus far—having discovered the intentional design of the site and identified the "intrusive" elements so that the "genuine" materials now lie open to view—we can finally attempt to do the last thing that has to be done before these materials can be taken as ethnohistorical evidence: get rid of the ethnocentrism. At last we have come to something we should know how to do. Having identified the sources of genuine observations and the structural and rhetorical baggage added by the author in his management of the narration, we have at our disposal vast amounts of historical documentation to define the historical circumstances of each informant and to make well-informed conjectures about his attitudes and capacity for understanding. Factoring such prejudices out and removing the historian's artistic input, we have the grail of ethnographic observation in our hands. Although it is much smaller and less impressive than we thought it would be, and almost intolerably hard-won, it is much more certainly useful as a commentary on or mutual verification of the evidence of actual excavation.

If archaeological method and theory had remained at the stage of development of the historical method now being used all too frequently to evaluate Contact period histories, archaeologists would be unable to controvert the ravings of a Von Daniken. It was this outdated concept of historical method that led to the vigorous rejection of the entire discipline by the New Archaeology, and indeed historical sources apprehended in this way continue to be worse than useless because they are being given such emphasis in determining the meaning of archaeological remains. Until the historical texts have been subjected to such an "excavation" as I have described, therefore, many of their truly valuable data will remain buried, ignored in favor of grab samples taken from congenial spots on a very disturbed and redeposited surface.

References

Baldwin, Charles Sears
  1928 *Medieval Rhetoric and Poetic*. Macmillan, New York.
Brain, Jeffrey P.
  1985 The Archaeology of the Hernando de Soto Expedition. In *Alabama and the Borderlands*, edited by R. Reid Badger and Lawrence A. Clayton, pp. 96–107. University of Alabama Press, Tuscaloosa.

Brain, Jeffrey P., Alan Toth, and Antonio Rodriguez-Buckingham
  1974 Ethnohistoric Archaeology and the De Soto Entrada into the Lower Mississippi
  Valley. *The Conference on Historic Site Archaeology Papers 1972* 7:232–289.
Castanien, Donald G.
  1969 *El Inca Garcilaso de la Vega*. Twayne, New York.
Chang-Rodriguez, Raquel
  1982 Armonía y disyunción en *La Florida del Inca*. *Revista de la Universidad Catolica*
  11–12:31–31.
Cochrane, Eric
  1981 *Historians and Historiography in the Italian Renaissance*. University of Chicago Press,
  Chicago.
Culler, Jonathan
  1975 *Structuralist Poetics: Structuralism, Linguistics, and the Study of Literature*. Routledge
  and Kegan Paul, London.
Curtius, Ernst Robert
  1963 *European Literature and the Latin Middle Ages*. Translated by Willard R. Trask.
  Harper and Row, New York.
Durand, Jose
  1963 Las enigmáticas fuentes de *La Florida del Inca*. *Cuadernos Hispanoamericanos* 168:
  597–609.
Foucault, Michel
  1972 *The Archaeology of Knowledge*. Translated by A. M. Sheridan Smith. Pantheon, New
  York.
Galloway, Patricia
  1982 Sources for the La Salle Expedition of 1682. In *La Salle and His Legacy: Frenchmen
  and Indians in the Lower Mississippi Valley*, edited by P. Galloway, pp. 11–40. University
  Press of Mississippi, Jackson.
  1990 Sources for the Soto Expedition: Intertextuality and the Elusiveness of Truth.
  Paper presented at the 1990 meeting of the Society for Spanish and Portuguese Historical Studies, New Orleans.
Henige, David
  1986 The Context, Content, and Credibility of La Florida del Ynca. *The Americas*
  43:1–23.
Henige, David, and Margarita Zamora
  1989 Text, Context, Intertext: Columbus' diario de a bordo as Palimpsest. *The Americas*
  46(1):17–40.
Hodder, Ian
  1986 *Reading the Past*. Cambridge University Press, Cambridge.
Holub, Robert C.
  1984 *Reception Theory: A Critical Introduction*. Methuen, London.
Hudson, Charles
  1987 *The Use of Evidence in Reconstructing the Route of the Hernando de Soto Expedition*. Alabama De Soto Commission Working Paper No. 1. Tuscaloosa.
Iser, Wolfgang
  1978 *The Act of Reading: A Theory of Aesthetic Response*. Johns Hopkins University Press,
  Baltimore, Md.
Kellner, Hans
  1987 Narrativity in History: Post-Structuralism and Since. *History and Theory* 26 (December 1987):1–29.
Kristeller, Paul Oskar
  1961 *Renaissance Thought: The Classic, Scholastic, and Humanist Strains*. Harper, New
  York.
Kuhn, Thomas S.
  1970 *The Structure of Scientific Revolutions*. 2d ed. University of Chicago Press, Chicago.

Lankford, George
  1990 Legends of the Adelantado. Paper presented at University of Arkansas de Soto
    expedition symnposium, Fayetteville, Ark.
Norris, Christopher
  1982 *Deconstruction: Theory and Practice.* Methuen, London.
Phillips, Philip, James A. Ford, and James B. Griffin
  1951 *Archaeological Survey in the Lower Mississippi Alluvial Valley, 1940–1947.* Peabody Mu-
    seum of Archaeology and Ethnology Papers No. 25. Harvard University, Cambridge,
    Mass.
Schiffer, Michael
  1976 *Behavioral Archaeology.* Academic Press, New York.
  1987 *Formation Processes of the Archaeological Record.* University of New Mexico Press,
    Albuquerque.
Stimson, Frederick S., and Ricardo Navas-Ruiz
  1971 *Literatura de la América Hispánica,* vol. 1. Dodd, Mead, New York.
Swanton, John R.
  1939 *Final Report of the U.S. De Soto Expedition Commission.* Government Printing Office,
    Washington, D.C.
White, Hayden
  1987 *The Content of the Form.* Johns Hopkins University Press, Baltimore, Md.

Chapter 24 ■

William R. Swagerty

Protohistoric Trade in Western North America: Archaeological and Ethnohistorical Considerations

In the fall of 1540, horse cavalry attached to a large Spanish expedition under the command of Francisco Vásquez de Coronado rode into the plaza of Pecos Pueblo. From the reports compiled later, we know that the Castilians and their Indian auxiliaries were impressed with the architecture, as well as with the level of urban activity about them. One officer wrote:

> Cicuye [Pecos] is a pueblo containing about 500 warriors. It is feared throughout that land. It is square, perched on a rock in the center of a vast patio or plaza, with its estufas [kivas]. The houses are all alike, four stories high . . . The people of this town pride themselves because no one has been able to subjugate them, while they dominate the pueblos as they wish [Castañeda in Hammond and Rey 1940:256–257].

Later in his narrative, the same chronicler explained Pecos's strategic location as a gateway community. He commented:

> The Teyas [Plains Indians] whom the army met, although they were brave, were known by the people of the towns [Pueblos] as their friends. The Teyas often go to

the latter's pueblos to spend the winter, finding shelter under the eaves, as the inhabitants do not dare to allow them inside. Evidently they do not trust them, although they accept them as friends and have dealings with them [Castañeda in Hammond and Rey 1940:258].

Almost 400 years later, Alfred Vincent Kidder unearthed the evidence of those "dealings" and documented centuries of trade at this important crossroads connecting the world of the Pueblos with that of the Plains. Among the thousands of artifacts of Pecos, Kidder found marine shells that had been carried 700 miles from their source in the Gulf of Mexico. Several stone grooved mauls, or "pemmican pounders," and other tool kits convinced him of a lively traffic with buffalo hunters, who received in turn, some of Pecos's produce, as is evident from the quantity and sizes of manos and metates unearthed (Kidder 1932).

"Medicine outfits" of adult males buried at Pecos contained a variety of exotics, including obsidian blades, quartz and gypsum crystals, hematite, copper ore, red ochre, and bunches of feathers. Most common in these graves were turquoises in a variety of art forms, and worked shell ornaments, especially *Olivella* from the Pacific Coast. The most unusual of Pecos's treasures was a chocolate-brown chert drill. Kidder described this as an "aberrant specimen . . . with a notched stem, a feature unique among Pecos drills, but found commonly enough in those of the Mississippi Valley" (Kidder 1932:28).

Although Kidder did not speculate on trade beyond the Plains into the Southeast, he was interested in long-distance exchange and was especially intrigued with G. H. Pepper's previous discovery at Pueblo Bonito of sherds from a cloisonné vessel (Pepper 1920). The notion that a pot may have traveled 1,300 miles from the Toltec region of Mexico north to Chaco Canyon prompted Kidder to write in 1924: "That anything so fragile as pottery should have been carried in aboriginal trade all the way from central Mexico to northern New Mexico is very surprising. It is also encouraging, for it gives rise to the hope that many other Mexican objects less difficult of transportation will yet be found in Southwestern sites" (Kidder 1924:351).

Since Kidder's day, we have come far in our study of the prehistoric and protohistoric trade of western North America. The purpose of this chapter is to review major conceptual approaches to trade by archaeologists and ethnohistorians since the 1930s. Methodological problems facing both types of scholars are also discussed in the context of the most important models and cartographic projections that have been published to date. These follow three lines of investigation, each complementary of the other two: "trade center" identification and analysis; sourcing and functional uses of specific commodities; and transfers of these commodities from one spatial area to another through cross-cultural trade. The essay does not treat the equally important subject of exchange mechanisms or the social and economic meaning of trade to specific cultures (e.g., Wilmsen 1972), nor is it my purpose here to catalogue earliest European material introductions (see Vol. 1 of this series). I wish to highlight the most successful approaches used to demonstrate the sophisticated spatial patterning of commodity exchanges through *trade networks* (e.g., Wood 1972) or *trade diasporas* (e.g., Cohen 1971) extant throughout the region at European contact. The combined data on each culture area in the region suggests that extensive trade networks, however changed from late prehistoric times, remained an essential part of native socioeconomic lifeways during the period of European exploration and colonization. A survey of the literature also validates both the use of ethnographic analogy from the archaeological record in reconstructing protohistoric trade systems and the use of inference from documentary sources to "upstream" back into prehistoric times.

Contexts for Prehistoric Exchange Systems

From the sixteenth century to the present, seldom have the few chroniclers who documented Native American *trade* or scholars who subsequently analyzed the written and the artifactual records defined their terms. At the broadest level and from a Eurocentric economic perspective, *trade* has been traditionally conceptualized as being synonymous with *exchange* of goods between two or more parties (Polanyi 1977:81). With the spread of European mercantilist and capitalistic systems into the Americas, ideas of Western or *formal* economies (with price structures, rates of exchange, profit motives, and marketplaces) were superimposed on non-Western economies, and trade was seen as a universal function of rational decision making employed by all societies to satisfy their material needs and wants (Herskovits 1952; Earle and Christensen 1980; Jochim 1976). This neoclassical economic view was often applied to non-Western cultures as well as to those within the European historical tradition and went unchallenged until the mid-twentieth century.

In the 1950s, the substantivist perspectives of Karl Polanyi and his followers (Dalton 1971, 1980; Polanyi et al. 1957), forced scholars to reconsider the use of neoclassical economic principles in the Americas and elsewhere. The Polanyi position emphasizes the social contexts of exchange and sees the economy as an "instituted process." At the heart of this school's belief is the assumption that economic behavior is embedded in sociopolitical and cultural institutions, not exclusively in rational, individual concern for material gain and loss, or relative scarcity of resources (Dalton 1971).

Although practitioners of both of these theoretical schools continued to champion their respective, polarized views into the 1960s (Cook 1966, 1969; Humphreys 1969; LeClair and Schneider 1968), by the 1970s many scholars considered the debate moot, while others welcomed a middle position (Dalton 1978; Hodder 1980; Sabloff and Lamberg-Karlovsky 1975). Two anthologies edited by Ericson and Earle (Earle and Ericson 1977; Ericson and Earle 1982) demonstrated the possibilities for this dual application, especially where artifacts are used to reconstruct prehistoric social organization and cultural formation (Earle 1982:2–3). Without abandoning his formalist footing, Earle offered a syncretized definition as a working concept for both theoretical camps. Throughout this paper, Earle's attempt at consensus is followed, whereby

exchange is the spatial distribution of materials from hand to hand and from social group to social group. Exchange is a transfer with strong individual and social aspects. Individuals are the hands in exchange, and they strive within the constraints of their society, ideology, and environment to survive and to prosper. And the commodities exchanged—whether food products or subsistence technology or wealth objects—are essential for their strivings. The social contexts of exchange are equally critical because they define the social needs beyond biology, and because they profoundly affect the form and possibility of individual exchange relations [Earle 1982:2].

Context of Exchange in the Early Documentary Record

The context of early documentary records cannot be established without taking into account the cultural baggage of European chroniclers. As the eminent British historian, J. H. Elliott has reflected, "The obstacles to the incorporation of the New World within Europe's intellectual horizon were formidable. They were obstacles of time and space, of inheritance, environment and language; and efforts would be required at many different levels before they were removed" (Elliot 1970:17).

To see is not to perceive; and, observation alone does not lead to comprehension. Elsewhere Elliott writes: "Even where Europeans in the New World had the desire to look, and the eyes to see, there is no guarantee that the image which presented itself to them—whether of people or places—necessarily accorded with the reality" (Elliot 1970:20).

The apparent *reality* of Indian trade economics as reported by Spanish observers placed what they saw in the context of Old World barter and marketplace economies. Estimates of the values of the goods traded between Indian groups and rates of exchange by then familiar to a monetary-based Mediterranean culture were sometimes reported, but little thought was given to the social or ideological implications of trade. However, transfers between Indian traders were understood as a *process* important to the participating cultures. For example, in the context of barter economies, Gonzálo Fernández de Oviedo, one of the earliest and more perceptive European chroniclers in the Americas, wrote of the Taino of the West Indies in 1526: "The Indians more than any people in the world are inclined to barter, sell, and trade things. Their dugouts go from one place to another, and they carry salt where it is needed and in exchange they receive gold or cloth or cotton thread, slaves, fish, or other things" (Oviedo [1526] 1959:105–106).

Marketplace economies were also understood and described in terms of early modern European conventions. During the conquest of Mexico, Bernal Díaz del Castillo, among others, saw in the Aztec economic system both a place and a process quite comfortable and familiar to all Europeans: "When we arrived at the great market place, called Tlaltelolco, we were astounded at the number of people and the quantity of merchandise that it contained, and at the good order and control that was maintained, for we had never seen such a thing before" (Díaz del Castillo 1956:215).

In 1536, another Spaniard who had lived for six years among various Indian societies shared both Oviedo's recognition of barter and Díaz's association with marketplace. However, he distinguished those items used by his native hosts for subsistence and production activities from those acquired or manufactured for ceremonial use. During a stay among Piman-speakers in present-day Sonora, Alvar Núñez and his three companions were presented "a great stock of maize and beans," as well as many deer hides, coral beads, and turquoises. One member of the group received a special gift of "five emeralds" (possibly malachite) shaped into points, "which arrows they use in their feasts and dances" (Núñez in Bandelier 1904:156–157). Elsewhere, we learn that these same Lower Pimas presented Núñez with over 600 dried deer hearts, kept in a special ceremonial temple, "of which they kept a great store for eating" (Núñez in Bandelier 1904:160).

These three Spaniards' perceptions of what they thought they saw among three different cultures illustrate the variation in contextual meaning that ethnohistorians often find in early printed or manuscript sources. When coupled with archaeological data, the context for exchanges becomes even more complex. In the remainder of this chapter I look at the contributions that scholars in the social sciences have made in working out the complex puzzle of native North American trade.

Multidisciplinary Approaches to Trade since the 1930s

From the first publication of key, eyewitness accounts such as those by Oviedo, Díaz del Castillo, and Núñez until well into the twentieth century, very few attempts were made to link historical narratives with archaeological records. The situation began to change in the 1930s when a few archaeologists, notably William Duncan Strong and Waldo Wedel, began using documents (Strong 1935; Wedel 1936, 1938), thus pioneering the "direct-historical approach" (Willey and Sabloff 1980:108). Cultural anthropologists and historians took two decades longer to organize themselves as "ethnohistorians" (Sturtevant 1966), formally convening in 1963 to promote a methodology as old as Mooney's 1896 *Calendar History of the Kiowas* (Ewers 1979) and applied most successfully in the first half of the twentieth century by Smithsonian-based ethnologist John Reed Swanton (Swanton 1911, 1939, 1946). However, not until the 1970s would a few ethnohistorians begin utilizing archaeological techniques and reports (Trigger 1982), paralleling in research techniques the ethnographic analogies of archaeologists such as Binford (Binford 1978), who had begun to champion themselves as "ethnoarchaeologists" (see Trigger 1989:370–371).

Despite these advances and the general consensus that much is to be gained from examining the continuum from prehistory into historic times (and vice versa), ethnohistorians and ethnoarchaeologists continue to tiptoe through protohistoric North American forests. We enter from opposite directions, stalk each other's progress, and selectively use the other discipline's findings without much concern for the other party's method or theory (Trigger 1986). There is, however, shared interest in a common ground dating back to the scholarship of the late 1930s.

Methodological Problems in Defining the Protohistoric West

The Protohistoric period is broadly viewed as the gap between the time when European influences and effects reached a region and the time when Europeans arrived to colonize. For the student of trade, it thus represents a critical period in both the history of the indigenous peoples of the region and in the history of the invading European cultures. Refinement of this general definition has proved difficult, largely because of problems in chronology. What historians since the 1940s have labeled post-1492 "first contacts" or "the era of discoveries" (e.g., Quinn 1977; Sauer 1971), anthropologists have thought of as the "contact period" or the "early contact phase" (e.g., Fitzhugh 1985:2; Fontana 1965; Leacock 1971:10–11). Some archaeologists continue to avoid the term entirely, preferring a clean jump from prehistory to the historic era (e.g., Cordell and Gumerman 1989:14).

Use of the term dates back to the first Pecos Conference in 1927, where "Pueblo IV or proto-Historic" was defined as the period between prehistoric Pueblo III and historic Pueblo V (Ravelsloot and Whittlesey 1987). Today, the term is frequently used, but there is little agreement as to what it means. Broad, rather than narrow usage has produced a lack of consensus. For some scholars, the period is that large window somewhere between prehistory and the ethnographic present (Wilcox and Masse 1981:1), while for others, it is the "transitional" zone between prehistoric and historic patterns (Ewers [1954] 1968:18).

A third view places it between an early sixteenth-century "disease horizon" and historical documentation of early contacts (Dobyns 1983; Ramenofsky 1987). Yet another group defines it as a space in time bracketed by precise dates. For example, Bennyhoff and Hughes have suggested A.D. 1500–1800 as a reasonable protohistoric era for trade between California and the Great Basin (Bennyhoff and Hughes 1987:161). One study of the protohistoric Southwest asks readers to accept "A.D. 1450–1700" (Wilcox and Masse 1981), while another also begins in 1450, but ends at 1650 (Riley 1987).

A protohistoric chronology for the Southwest is relatively trouble-free compared to other regions, where Euroamerican colonization did not take place until the eighteenth or nineteenth centuries. Thus, for the Northwest Coast, Plateau, California, and the Plains, a different protohistoric dateline has to be applied. In some cases, the beginning point lags two centuries or more behind a fifteenth-century or early sixteenth-century dateline in the Southwest.

This dilemma in definition is not likely to be resolved if we insist on a rigid chronology. But an alternative way of envisioning the protohistoric is possible and more practical for broad regions such as the North American West. By this definition, I would suggest that the Protohistoric is the interval between first European material, biological, or ideological introductions and subsequent permanent Euroamerican colonization within a *specific* native culture area. This definition does not resolve dating disputes among scholars of specific culture areas. It also fails to address the "indirect" influences of Indian traders and travelers who crossed cultural boundaries, taking with them ideas, material objects, and microbes of European origin prior to direct contact with Europeans.

If we accept Henry Dobyns's thesis that a major pandemic in the early six-teenth century swept northward beyond the direct line of physical contacts be-tween Spaniards and North American Indians (Dobyns 1983, and this volume; Ramenofsky, this volume) as far north as the Subarctic, we have a common be-ginning date of around A.D. 1520 for all regions north of the central valley of Mexico. Dobyns has postulated that between 1520 and 1524, smallpox spread "at least from Chile across [the] present United States, causing greater mortality than any later episode" (Dobyns 1983:Table 1, p. 15). If we use Dobyns's small-pox pandemic and allow a range of the remaining eight decades of the sixteenth century as a beginning point for the biological Protohistoric, we have a loosely bracketed period for the major culture areas under consideration here (Table 24–1).

A different set of protohistoric dates is obtained if we factor out initial probable disease transmissions and rely instead on two other lines of evidence: first docu-mented human contacts; and, the diffusion of the horse. We encounter another major problem in methodology here. What may apply to one tribe or band within a culture area, may not necessarily apply to a distant group within that same linguistic or culture area. For example, should we use the accepted geo-graphical grids for western culture areas (Sturtevant 1978), we run into the im-mediate problem of variations in chronology within a region such as the Plains, where the Wichita were first contacted by Spaniards in 1541, but the Crow to their far north did not greet white explorers until at least two centuries later, long after they had incorporated the horse and many items of European manu-facture (Ewers, personal communication, May 12, 1990). With this cautionary note, bracketed dates for the Protohistoric are thus offered in Table 24–2 as a flex-ible range for the broad chronological horizons of each area and to illustrate the problem we face in precise definition.

A third approach would be to assemble a list of all documented archaeological findings of items of European origin. These data would verify exotics in use be-fore or during first face-to-face contact with Europeans. This has not been at-tempted and would, at present, be limited to those few areas for which we can be assured of tight chronological control over objects and site-specific stratigraphy.

Table 24–1. The Protohistoric West: Disease Transmission to Colonization

Culture Area	Dobyns's Disease Horizon[a]	Permanent Colonization
Puebloan Southwest	ca. A.D. 1520–1540	ca. A.D. 1600
Alta California	ca. A.D. 1520–1600	ca. A.D. 1770
Northwest Coast	ca. A.D. 1520–1600	ca. A.D. 1790
Plains		
Southern	ca. A.D. 1520–1600	ca. A.D. 1720
Northern	ca. A.D. 1520–1600	ca. A.D. 1740
Plateau	ca. A.D. 1520–1600	ca. A.D. 1810
Great Basin	ca. A.D. 1520–1600	ca. A.D. 1825

a. Dobyns (1983).

Table 24–2. The Protohistoric West: Documented Contact and Colonization

Culture Area/Subarea	Beginning Date	Terminal Date
Puebloan Southwest	ca. 1530 (Núñez;Niza)	ca. 1600 (San Gabriel)
Upper California	ca. 1540 (Cabrillo)	ca. 1770 (San Diego)
Northwest Coast	ca. 1600 (Vizcaino)	ca. 1790 (Sitka and Santa Cruz de Nutka)
Plains		
Southern	ca. 1540 (Coronado)	ca. 1700 (French traders)
Northern	ca. 1650 (Jesuits)	ca. 1740 (French traders)
Plateau		
(a)	ca. 1700 (horse complex)	ca. 1810 (British posts)
(b)	ca. 1780 (Thompson)	ca. 1810 (British posts)
Great Basin		
(a)	ca. 1640–1710 (horse complex)	ca. 1770 (Spanish missionary-explorers and traders)
(b)	ca. 1640–1710 (horse complex)	ca. 1825 (Mexican traders; American traders and posts)

Note: Where (a) and (b) are given, these are suggested as alternatives.

Previous Scholarship on Protohistoric Trade in the West

The three major lines of investigation that have been historically employed by scholars in the study of trade may also be properly thought of as major strategies, each somewhat dependent on the others. Specific approaches examined here can be traced to the 1930s. Nearly all studies for the region since then have been concerned with the logistics of the exchange of commodities and with the organizational levels of the societies engaged in trade. Very few published works have focused on what may be distinguished as *internal exchange* within cultural boundaries or *intrasettlement exchange* within a specific settlement landscape, in contrast to *external trade* across cultural boundaries (Renfrew 1975:4). Preference has been shown specifically for the spatial extent of exchange networks, as well as for the frequency and volume of transactions in those relationships. These studies have largely been conducted within the framework of external relationships between two culture areas (such as Southwest to Plains; California to the Great Basin) or as studies of specific commodity origins, movements, and archaeological recoveries (as with obsidian and turquoise).

The "Trade Center" Approach

Early twentieth-century archaeologists were quick to recognize the importance of major settlements as collecting and redistribution points for regional and interregional trade. Following the lead of Victor Mindeleff (1891), Adolph Bandelier

(1892), and Jesse Fewkes (1896, 1919), interest in reconstructing the architectural landscape of sites coupled with analysis of the origins of exotics in artifactual assemblages led to some recognition of Native American settlements as major processing, manufacturing, and/or redistribution points. Studies here include Pepper's 1920 survey of Pueblo Bonito (1920); Kidder's work at Pecos (1924, 1932); that of Hodge at Zuñi (1937); and William Duncan Strong's report on the Dalles in Oregon (Strong et al. 1930).

None of the above went so far as to formulate the paradigm of the "trade center" in western North America. That would be left to the following generation who benefited from application of ethnohistorical methods in the 1950s. Credit is due to John C. Ewers for the first systematic statement on western trade centers. In his seminal article, "The Indian Trade of the Upper Missouri before Lewis and Clark" ([1954] 1968), Ewers went a step beyond tribal trading relationships such as that outlined by Jablow on the Cheyenne (1951; see Figure 24–1). Documentary sources from the eighteenth and nineteenth centuries convinced Ewers that surplus-abundant horticultural economies existed in several Middle Missouri River societies. Two village complexes stood out as central food providers for the entire region. These were the Arikara villages near Grand River in present-day South Dakota and the Mandan-Hidatsa villages on the Knife River in present-day North Dakota. To these village clusters, Crees and Assiniboins traveled from the north, Teton Sioux from the southeast, Crows from the west, and Cheyennes, Arapahoes, Comanches, Kiowas, and Kiowa-Apaches from the southwest (Ewers [1954] 1968:14–17).

In addition to these "primary trade centers," Ewers designated two "rendezvous" for annual seasonal trade. Siouan-speaking bands held what he labeled a "Dakota Rendezvous" each summer on the James River. A much larger, intertribal affair was hosted by the Shoshone in southwestern Wyoming and was attended by Nez Perce, Flatheads, Crows, and Utes (Ewers [1954] 1968:17).

Ewers was the first ethnologist to link trade of the Plains with the Southwest and Plateau. To him, "the distinguishing characteristic of the protohistoric or transitional trade pattern was the use of articles of European origin in intertribal trade. Through the medium of this trade, horses and objects made in Europe were diffused from the peripheral white men's trading centers by Indian intermediaries to remote tribes of the Great Plains long before some of those tribes first were met by white explorers" (Ewers [1954] 1968:23).

The trade center approach is a theoretical variant of geographer Walter Christaller's Central Place theory (1966), where the ideal "central place" is a hierarchically dominant settlement at the center of a symmetrical service area—a territory graphically represented with hexagonal outlying communities that are dependent upon a central, core settlement. Intensive review of the archaeology and ethnography of Mandan sites in the 1960s (Wood 1967) led W. Raymond Wood toward wider application of central place hierarchies beyond the Missouri River country in the 1970s. Following Ewers, in 1972, Wood relabeled the Mandan-Hidatsa and Arikara villages as vortices within the center of a "Middle Missouri System" (Wood 1972:155). Wood also defined a "Pacific-Plateau System"

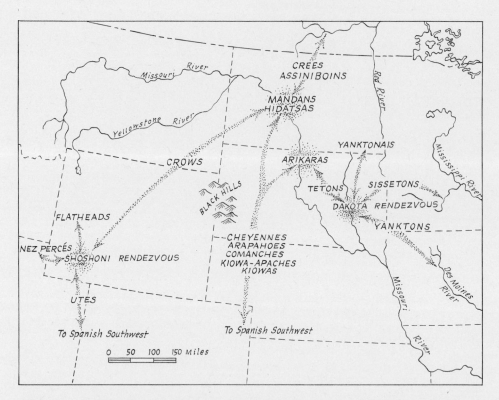

Figure 24–1. Routes and centers of intertribal trade in 1805. (Source: Ewers 1968. Reproduced courtesy of the University of Oklahoma Press)

with the Dalles as a central redistribution point and credited Spier and Sapir (1931) and Teit (Teit 1930) for the data that enabled scholars to take a systems approach in the Northwest (Wood 1972:155–156). A series of "trade nets" was outlined here and was further refined (Wood 1980). For the Pacific Plateau System, a new concept of "minor trading points" was added as a third tier of ranking smaller villages or seasonal trade fairs (Wood 1980:Figure 1).

During the 1950s and 1960s, several trade centers in the protohistoric Southwest were identified, while previously recognized sites such as Zuñi, Pecos, Hopi, and Taos were studied further within a broad range of new questions posed about previously collected data (see Schroeder 1979:12–13). The most important "new" discovery was that of the La Junta Village Complex at the junction of the Rio Grande and Conchos rivers on the Texas-Mexican border. J. Charles Kelley's thesis that the site was associated with a middleman-trading culture known from Spanish documents as the *Jumano* provided an important missing link in the trade relationships between the western limits of the Southeast and the eastern limits of the Southwest (Kelley 1949, 1955), a view that has since gained wide acceptance (Applegate and Hanselka 1974; Hickerson 1990; Riley 1987:285–310).

Early trade centers became better known during the 1970s and 1980s. Although Chaco Canyon's zenith was antecedent to the Protohistoric, its description as an "interaction sphere" increased the spatial and theoretical limits of the complexity of prehistoric trade (Altschul 1978; Noble 1984; Smith 1983) and sparked heightened interest in continuities of Mesoamerican-Southwestern exchanges after A.D. 1400.

Scholars searching for connections "across the Chichimec Sea" used trade as a major body of evidence (Hedrick et al. 1974; Riley and Hedrick 1978). Through the persistent efforts of Charles Di Peso, the trade center of Casas Grandes (Paquimé), in modern Chihuahua, emerged as the best-studied test case. His findings, summarized in 1974, provided compelling evidence for the prehistoric existence of more than a trade center: Casas Grandes housed a trading culture. According to Di Peso (1974:vol. 2), a true "mercantile" economy, complete with a central marketplace and specialty guilds could be found at this site at its peak in the thirteenth century.

The economic sophistication of Casas Grandes provided much-needed support for those seeking to connect the Southwest and Mesoamerica through a "world systems" theoretical approach (e.g., Pailes and Reff 1979, 1985), but doubt surrounds many of Di Peso's grander claims (Minnis 1989).

Less spectacular but equally important findings emerged in Carroll Riley's synthesis of trade in the Southwest. His analysis of seven "cultural provinces" skirted Casas Grandes but included the Opata and Piman trade villages in northern Mexico—a protohistoric sequel to the fallen trade center at Casas Grandes (Riley 1976, 1987). Other studies of Pecos (Kessell 1979; Riley 1978) and the Northern Panya or Haldichoma villages of the lower Colorado River (Dobyns 1984) added to our understanding of the concept of trade center.

Several locations, some corresponding to Wood's third-level "trading points" (Wood 1972, 1980), were identified within the Pacific-Plateau System by Swagerty, who described them as "tertiary trade centers usually lacking permanent resident populations." These included four seasonal trade fairs in present-day Idaho at or near the present-day locations of Moscow, Boise, Bear Lake, and southwest of Sun Valley on the Camas Prairie. Flathead Rendezvous was held in northern Montana and may have been as significant as the Shoshone Rendezvous in both the number of tribes participating and in the volume of horses and goods exchanged. In present-day Oregon, the Grande Ronde Valley was the scene of a periodic rendezvous. Okanogan Falls and Kittitas Fair served a similar function for a variety of tribes who met seasonally in present-day Washington State (Swagerty 1988:351–353; see Figure 24–2). Further research by Dobyns, who has recently completed a study of North American trade "about 1500 A.D.," promises to reenforce Riley's revised findings on the protohistoric Southwest (Riley 1987) and will improve our understanding of specific trade centers and trading relationships between the Southwest and California, and the Southwest and the Southern Plains (Dobyns 1989).

Unlike the major centers of the Southwest, the Middle Missouri System, and the Pacific-Plateau System, many of the primary and secondary centers now identified were not centrally located. Nor did they service near-symmetrical and geographically compact hinterlands beyond the main complex of permanent villages as required for the ideal, hierarchical "center" under Central Place theory

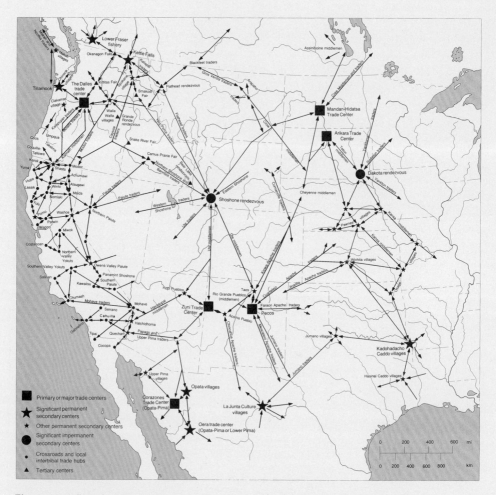

Figure 24–2. Protohistoric Indian trade networks in the trans-Mississippi. (Source: Swagerty 1988:Figure 1)

(Christaller 1966). Instead, many permanent villages such as those of the Makah on the Olympic Peninsula, Pecos and Taos pueblos in the Southwest, and the Kadohadacho villages on the Red River are better conceptualized following Burghardt as "gateway communities," passage points into and out of distinct natural or cultural regions which linked their respective regions to external trade routes and ultimately through "head-links" to central places (Burghardt 1971). Some served as "middlemen" trading points, bottlenecks for imports; redistributive points for exports in the immediate area beyond the settlement. Others serviced a much more extensive area, specializing in long-distance trade spanning ethnic, linguistic, and environmental zones. According to Kenneth Hirth, who has applied this concept to Mesoamerica (Hirth 1978), the gateway community may develop for two reasons: as a response to increased trade or to the settling of sparsely populated frontier areas: "They generally are located along natural corridors of communication and at the critical passages between areas of high mineral, agricultural, or craft productivity; dense population; high demand or supply for scarce resources; and, at the interface of different technologies or levels of sociopolitical complexity" (Hirth 1978:37; see Figure 24–3).

No one has systematically applied gateway community theory to the protohistoric West, but it is the logical step beyond the ranking of trade centers, identification of middlemen, and linkage of trading partners. Furthermore, it provides an alternative way of cartographically projecting communities along a "dendritic network," a treelike schema wherein goods are funneled into a central site and redistributed up the trunk to main collecting points along main branches, ultimately reaching the smallest of communities within the trade territory (Smith 1976). This contrasts to central places, which are ideally located in the heart of a given trade area, and which absorb and redistribute commodities from

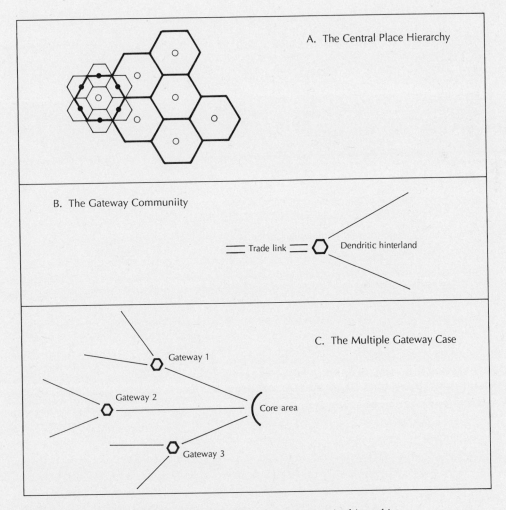

Figure 24–3. A comparison of central place and gateway community hierarchies. (Source: Hirth 1978:Figure 2, p. 39)

all directions. In theory, both systems can function simultaneously in different parts of the same region.

The "Commodity" Approach

A second strategy used by scholars to study native trade may be thought of as the *commodity approach*. This overlaps with interest in trade centers and dates back to early archaeological collecting efforts in all western culture areas. It is important to acknowledge, as Richard Ford's study of Tewa intertribal exchange reminds us, that the great majority of items that passed from one Indian's hands to another even in early historic times were locally or regionally produced items, not foreign imports from exotic lands. Most of these were perishables in the form of foodstuffs, hides, textiles, and containers made of organic material (Ford 1972).

That the Tewa and all other Indian groups within the region had access to exotics in prehistoric as well as in more recent times can be assumed and is certainly borne out in the archaeological record. But the material world of the average Native American—especially his subsistence—whether in California, on the Plains, or in the Southwest depended more on internal redistribution than on external exchanges, a point often lost in the search for long-distance relationships (Driver and Massey 1957:373–375; Ford 1983). Still, the allure of the study of trade has been the analysis of the exotic, rather than the locally produced item; interregional, rather than intraregional trade.

Unusual objects, however unique or rare, invite comparison and speculation. Kidder's brown chert drill at Pecos and Pepper's cloissoné vessel at Chaco forced new mental constructs for interregional trade, as evidenced in the discussions at the early Pecos Conferences of the late 1920s and early 1930s (Schroeder 1979). But it was not the one-of-a-kind artifact that eventually led to the systematic study of the commodities of exchange. Rather, those exotic items found in large enough numbers and in proper associations to be considered standard truck captured the attention of scholars. The provenience of the exotics, as well as the logistics of trade routes, had to be established.

Geographers combined interests with ethnologists and archaeologists to produce a few pioneering works. Carl O. Sauer's *The Road to Cíbola* (1932) firmly established through ethnographic sources and geographic correlations a "west coast corridor" from modern Guadalajara to the Corazónes of Alvar Núñez's time, and beyond to Zuñi. Elsie C. Parsons (1939:33–37) tabulated from her fieldwork in New Mexico a near-comprehensive list of trade items circulated internally in the puebloan Southwest.

Meanwhile, geographer Donald D. Brand produced a brief, but important work in the 1930s. His "Aboriginal Trade Routes for Sea Shells in the Southwest" (Brand 1938; see Figure 24–4) included a crudely drawn map to illustrate the importance of archaeological sites *and* trade vectors. To his credit, he ranked these routes in importance and provided tables with the provenience of marine shells discussed in this brief article.

Brand's map became well known in the 1940s and 1950s and was used as a departure point for several additional studies of specific commodities. Harold

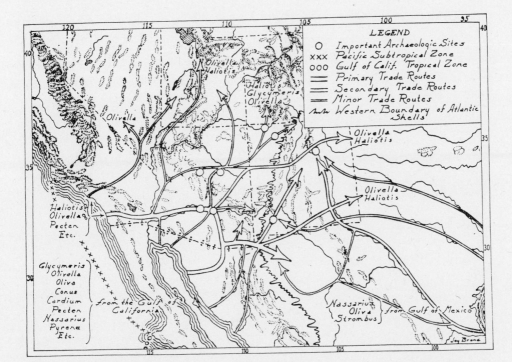

Figure 24–4. Aboriginal trade routes for sea shells in the Southwest. (Source: Brand 1938. Reproduced courtesy of the Association of Pacific Coast Geographers)

Colton redrafted it in 1941 for an article in *Scientific Monthly* in which he gave his readers a tour of "prehistoric commerce" along modern highways of the Southwest (Colton [1941] 1987). As head of the Museum of Northern Arizona, Colton was especially interested in drawing out unreported findings of exotics in sites far from their source. A specialist on pottery, he was also one of the first to recognize the importance of quantification of ceramics as an indicator of total volume of trade (Colton 1939). He wrote: "Copper bells, parrot remains, argillite and turquoise ornaments are rather rare, so rare that their contribution to commerce was rather small unless the ornaments represent a medium of exchange. However, the volume of pottery traded was enormous" (Colton [1941] 1987:316).

Despite this early pronouncement, the weight of research in the 1940s continued along the same lines of investigation initiated by Sauer and Brand. Donald Tower's "Use of Marine Mollusca and Their Value in Reconstructing Prehistoric Trade Routes in the American Southwest" (Tower 1945) built upon Brand's study and went further by providing an analysis of the actual functional and ceremonial use of each shell found up to 1945 in a prehistoric southwestern site.

A similar encyclopedic survey by Sydney Ball outlined 84 gems and ornamental stones mined by American Indians throughout the Americas before European colonization. Ball was more interested in the extraction than in the transfer of stones, but he included a section on trade acknowledging long distance treks and down-the-line transactions in obsidian, turquoise, and other commodities from east to west and north to south respectively (Ball 1941:16–17).

Since the 1950s, four categories of commodities have proven to be excellent gauges in spatial and quantitative analyses of long distance trade. For the region at large, marine shells (Lehmer 1954; Phillips and Brown 1978) and obsidian (Anderson et al. 1986; Ericson 1982; Findlow and Bolognese 1982; Hughes 1984) are markers for the outside limits of extensive trade networks stretching eastward into the heart of the Midwest. To these, turquoise and pipestone (catlinite) must be added.

Although the highly prized blue-green turquoise stone is not found throughout the entire West, we know exactly where different types of turquoise originate. For example, when turquoise from the mines at Los Cerrillos in northern New Mexico is found deep within Mexico, we do not know how many times the stone changed hands, but we can plot the exact distance and thus are assured of the range from the source. (Weigand et al. 1977). This same principle applies to New Mexican turquoise and obsidian found in protohistoric Plains village complexes in Nebraska (Wedel 1986:144), obsidian from Yellowstone Park, found as far east as Hopewellian sites in Ohio (Wedel 1961:274; Griffin 1969), and catlinite, found throughout the northern Plains and as far south as Kansas and known to be from one source in Minnesota (Wedel 1961:106, 110, 189, 198, 207).

Through chemical analysis, X-ray florescence, and mathematical modeling (Harbottle 1982), archaeologists now have the tools to correlate original source with archaeological specimens, literally "fingerprinting" a mineral object from habitation or usage area back to the quarry, but that literature has been slow in being released. What has been published is of interest. Examples here include Weigand, Harbottle, and Sayre's study of turquoise (1977:Figure 1); and, Hughes and Bennyhoff's maps for the Great Basin volume of the *Handbook of North American Indians* (1986:Figures 1–2, pp. 239–240; see Figure 24–5). Such resource-specific mapping has the potential to put flesh on the bones of more general commodity and route maps such as Ferguson and Hart's "Zuni Trade Relationships" (Ferguson and Hart 1985:Map 19, p. 52) and flow charts such as the Oregon Historical Society's schematic of the Dalles Trade Center (Zucker et al. 1983:43).

The Geographic and Cultural Region Approach

A final strategy applied to western protohistoric trade analyzes exchanges within a specific geographic region or cultural area. Focus on a specific spatial area has several advantages over studies of larger scope. The smaller aerial study necessitates precision in detail on specific commodities, trade relationships, and locations of trade centers. A narrow geographic focus should also force a better understanding of the context of exchanges by consideration of specific economic, social, and ceremonial values within well-defined cultural systems. But the advantages of accuracy and improved understanding of context can isolate the process as well as the place from external factors necessary for the system to function in the first instance. Thus, in 1954, had Ewers not boldly extended his study beyond the Plains into the Southwest and the Plateau, the central point of the extensiveness of Native American trade networks in the West before Lewis

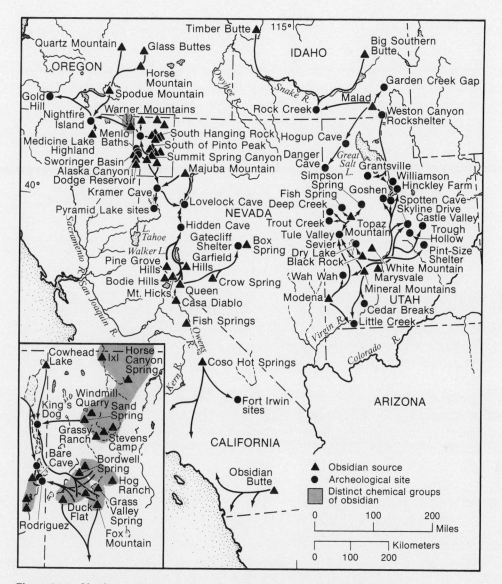

Figure 24–5. Obsidian trade routes. (Source: Hughes and Bennyhoff 1984:Figure 2)

and Clark would have been undermined by singular focus on the economies of Middle Missouri horticultural villages.

A second limitation is the lack of uniformity in applying cartographic projections from one culture area or region to those of adjacent territories. With the exception of Ewers's concept of trade centers as physical vortices of trade activity, which has been used by Wood (1972), Riley (1987), and Swagerty (1988), the same mapping techniques or conceptual principles have not been applied consistently. Thus, painting with broad strokes across the entire protohistoric West has many obstacles to overcome. It is arguable that this is unavoidable given the fundamental differences in social and economic systems of societies within the region. The Northwest Coast's "social economy" (Oberg 1973) differs markedly from that of the Plateau; cultural and economic relations on the Plateau (Ray 1939) are not the same as those of the Great Basin (Steward 1938), and so forth.

Trade in California provides a poignant example. From the 1920s on, studies of California tribes have emphasized the egalitarian nature of trading relationships within what Kroeber defined as the California cultural area (Kroeber 1925). In his summary of "Trade and Trails" for the California volume of the *Handbook of North American Indians*, Robert F. Heizer wrote:

> There is no good evidence for specialists in trade—that is, professional traders—and there is no information on the existence of regular markets. At times certain individuals or groups may have engaged more frequently in trade than others by reason of having control over a desirable and scarce resource such as a salt spring, flint exposure, or obsidian deposit, but the occupants of such villages in no recorded instance made procurement and marketing of a resource their primary activity [Heizer 1978:690].

Heizer relied heavily on James Davis's 1961 monograph in which Davis plotted aboriginal trade routes in California and tabulated more than 80 native trade items known from the ethnographic record to have been exchanged from one California tribal group to another. (Davis [1961] 1965). Davis provided trading hubs corresponding to villages or tribal locations on his map but avoided ranking or elevating them to the status of gateway communities, ports-of-trade, or trade centers. These crossroads were described as being connected by "Indian trails" and "paths" and were catalogued in similar fashion to those in William E. Myer's classic study, "Indian Trails of the Southeast" (1928).

Davis's encyclopedic lists of trails and goods and his maps have been used as the base for most studies since 1961 (e.g., Hughes and Bennyhoff 1986). The concept of egalitarian exchange networks within California still has currency (e.g., Ericson 1977), but the map is somewhat misleading. One glance at the list of goods flowing in and out of certain tribal areas indicates disequilibrium in volume, if not in access. Even Heizer acknowledges this in his statement: "Certain large villages situated at some strategic spot near a tribal boundary may have developed into 'import-export centers' where certain desirable goods were handled, but markets in the sense of places where traders regularly came with exchange goods are not known" (1978:690).

The literature on obsidian procurement, production, and distribution (Ericson 1982:146–147) indicates that quarry workshops near mines specialized in ceremonial biface blades for export, whereas more common points, blades, and scrapers were made by the users from obsidian blanks away from the mining sites. Recent analysis by Bennyhoff and Hughes of more than 7,000 marine shells traded into the western Great Basin supports the idea of "manufacturing centers in northern, central, and southern California, as well as on the Gulf of California and the Oregon-California coast" for the specialized export trade (Bennyhoff and Hughes 1987; Hughes and Bennyhoff 1986:244). "Trade feasts," best studied among the Pomo (Chagnon 1970; Vayda 1966), were held regularly among surplus-abundant tribal groups and served as a redistributive mechanism for many exotic imports as well as locally procured foods, hides, and shell-money. Procurement of luxuries as well as necessities through parallel institutions such as giveaways, potlatches, and harvest ceremonies, took place throughout western North America. While California must be regarded as different, it is not unique; nor have we all the data necessary to rule out a network system conceptually consistent with that suggested by Wood for the Pacific Plateau (Wood 1972) or Irwin-Williams for the Southwest (Irwin-Williams 1977).

With the exception of the Southwest (Ford 1983) and the Great Basin (Hughes and Bennyhoff 1986), the internal trade of other culture areas in the region awaits further synthesis. Angel Anastasio's concept of cooperative intertribal "task groups" for division of labor and services (including trade) among various societies of the Plateau (Anastasio 1975) has possible applications beyond that region. Although the Northwest Coast has one of the grander reputations for its trade, the literature on prehistoric and protohistoric trade in the culture area is just now being released in accessible formats other than graduate theses and contract reports (Isaac 1988). Of special significance is the exciting prospect of micro-level knowledge of one culture's material world from the Ozette Site, western America's Pompei, which was buried by a mudslide over 400 years ago (Daugherty 1990; Huelsbeck 1988). During excavations between 1970 and 1980, more than 50,000 artifacts, 40,000 structural remains, and 1 million faunal remains were recovered from the protohistoric levels at this Makah site (Gleeson 1980a, 1980b).

No summaries of prehistoric or protohistoric trade for the Plateau or the Plains writ large have been attempted, but some progress has been made in the study of external relations between the southern Plains and the Southwest (Lange 1979). Pottery, especially utilitarian glazeware made in New Mexico between A.D. 1200 and 1600, continues to be unearthed at sites located along major waterways in the Texas Panhandle (Spielmann 1983), thus strengthening the case for systematic, indirect trade between Caddoans of the Southeast and Southern Plains with distant Puebloans.

The Southwest remains the most fertile and ever-maturing laboratory on trade. Two principal topics continue to capture the interests of both archaeologists and ethnohistorians: the relationship between Mesoamerica and the Southwest in late prehistoric and protohistoric times (e.g., Wilcox and Masse 1981; Foster and Weigand 1985; Mathien and McGuire 1986) and the sociopolitical structure of southwestern societies on the eve of and during early contact with Europeans (Cordell and Gumerman 1989; Upham et al. 1989; Thomas 1989). The various debates over the extent of Mesoamerican-Southwestern trade networks and "interaction spheres" and the degree to which, if at all, the Southwest was "incorporated" into a Mesoamerican "World System" in prehistoric times (Hall 1989; Pailes and Reff 1979) are not likely to end in the near future. In the meantime, application of theories, models, and new methodologies in southwestern archaeology promise to build new foundations for comparative work with similar studies on successful trading cultures by Mesoamericanists, especially those focusing on the Maya (e.g., Hirth 1984; Sabloff and Rathje 1975) and the Aztec (e.g., Drennen 1984; Hassig 1985).

Conclusion

Over 450 years have passed since Coronado and his men first set eyes on Zuñi, Taos, Pecos, and other major trade centers and gateway communities in the Southwest. Very little material evidence of that first major encounter with a large European contingent has been unearthed. A few pieces of chain mail, with a sixteenth-century association, have surfaced in Kansas (Wedel 1975), the eastern limit of the Spanish expeditions. Five copper metal fragments, very similar to one artifact reported by Kidder at Pecos (1932) and thought by some to be Spanish crossbow boltheads, were unearthed at Puaray Pueblo by a School of American Research team in 1934 (Ellis 1957). More recently, one archaeologist is certain that he has located a Coronado campsite near Albuquerque (Vierra 1987). But we have yet to pull out of the ground a single, uncontroversial Coronado-era artifact in New Mexico or Arizona. Undoubtedly, as Haury (1984) has speculated, some are intact; others are in circulation among amateurs, but historical archaeology has not been as frequent a player or as successful in the Southwest as in other parts of the Spanish colonial world, especially the Southeast and the Caribbean (e.g., Deagan 1983; Milanich and Milbrath 1989; Thomas 1990).

What has been reported from the first European settlement in New Mexico (Ellis 1987, 1989) leaves one wondering how much or how *little* the European invasion of the Puebloan world affected the local inhabitants. Certainly, if Dobyns (Dobyns 1983) is correct and a 1520 disease horizon caught the Pueblos as well as many other native peoples north of the European line of colonization, the demographic profile at 1598 was quite different from the human landscape of the previous two generations. If only "thin residues" of former native communities (Dobyns, this volume) remained at 1540, it is little wonder that the volume and frequency of Mesoamerican-Southwestern trade had declined to a trickle of traffic compared with previous centuries. Even so, what Europeans saw and reported well into the seventeenth century was an economic and social world in which the Native American trader remained a prominent actor and his villages, not those of the Europeans, remained the primary locales for intertribal, interethnic exchanges.

In other culture areas, a protohistoric interval would soon follow. Whatever chronologies we choose, each of these other regions has become a more difficult academic puzzle than the sparsely documented, but very well trodden paths of the Southwest. We now have a large data base on native trade items and on trade relationships in late prehistoric and early historic times for the entire region. What is still lacking is synthesis and close collaboration between archaeologists and historians.

Sometime between his retirement from the Bureau of American Ethnology in 1944 and his death in 1958, John Reed Swanton abandoned his final scholarly project and sent several boxes to the National Anthropological Archives that were filed under the heading, "Miscellaneous, 2400 cards" (Swanton, n.d.). Appended to the first drawer is the following note, personally typed by Swanton:

Originally intended as a study in aboriginal trade routes, but was expanded to include an attempt to locate sources of raw materials, hunting and fishing grounds, and so on, but the program proved too big and the results were laid aside. It is hoped that some time it may develop into an ethnological survey and a series of accompanying maps.—J.R.S.

A half-century later, the issues are more complicated than in Swanton's time and the project has yet to be completed. The literature on western late prehistoric and protohistoric trade has matured appreciably and now the time has come to expand the theoretical as well as successfully established evidential approaches in regions beyond the Southwest. This large task challenges us in the 1990s.

References

Applegate, Howard G., and C. Wayne Hanselka
   1974 *La Junta de los Rios Del Norte y Conchos*. Texas Western Press for the University of Texas at El Paso, El Paso.
Altschul, Jeffrey H.
   1978 The Development of the Chacoan Interaction Sphere. *Journal of Anthropological Research* 34(1):109–146.
Anastasio, Angelo.
   1975 *The Southern Plateau: An Ecological Analysis of Intergroup Relations*. University of Idaho Laboratory of Anthropology, Moscow.
Anderson, Duane C., Joseph A. Tiffany, and Fred W. Nelson
   1986 Recent Research on Obsidian from Iowa Archaeological Sites. *American Antiquity* 51(4):837–852.
Ball, Sydney H.
   1941 *The Mining of Gems and Ornamental Stones by American Indians*. Bureau of American Ethnology Bulletin No. 128. Washington, D.C.
Bandelier, Adolph F.
   1892 An Outline of the Documentary History of the Zuni Tribe. *A Journal of American Ethnology and Archaeology*, vol 3. Houghton Mifflin, New York.
Bandelier, Adolph F. (editor)
   1904 *The Journey of Alvar Nuñez Cabeza de Vaca and His Companions from Florida to the Pacific, 1528–1536*. Translated by Fanny Bandelier. Allerton, New York.
Bennyhoff, James A., and Richard E. Hughes
   1987 *Shell Bead and Ornament Exchange Networks between California and the Western Great Basin*. Anthropological Papers of the American Museum of Natural History 64(2). New York.
Binford, Lewis R.
   1978 *Nunamiut Ethnoarchaeology*. Academic Press, New York.
Brand, Donald D.
   1938 Aboriginal Trade Routes for Sea Shells in the Southwest. *Yearbook of the Association of Pacific Coast Geographers* 4:3–10.
Burghardt, A. F.
   1971 A Hypothesis about Gateway Cities. *Annals, Association of American Geographers* 61:269–285.
Chagnon, Napoleon A.
   1970 Ecological and Adaptive Aspects of California Shell Money. *Annual Reports of the University of California Archaeological Survey* 12:1–25. Los Angeles.
Christaller, Walter

1966 *Central Places in Southern Germany*. Translated by C. W. Baskin. Prentice-Hall, Englewood Cliffs, N.J.

Cohen, Abner
1971 Cultural Strategies in the Organization of Trading Diasporas. In *The Development of Indigenous Trade and Markets in West Africa*, edited by Claude Meillassoux, pp. 266–281. Oxford University Press, London.

Colton, Harold S.
1939 *Prehistoric Culture Units and Their Relationships in Northern Arizona*. Bulletin No. 17. Museum of Northern Arizona, Flagstaff.
1987 Prehistoric Trade in the Southwest. In *The Prehistoric American Southwest: A Source Book: History, Chronology, Ecology, and Technology*, edited by Richard I. Ford, pp. 308–319. Garland, New York. Originally published 1941.

Cook, Scott
1966 The Obsolete "Anti-Market" Mentality: A Critique of the Substantive Approach to Economic Anthropology. *American Anthropologist* 68(2):323–345.
1969 The "Anti-Market" Mentality Re-examined: A Further Critique of the Substantive Approach to Economic Anthropology. *Southwestern Journal of Anthropology* 25(4):378–406.

Cordell, Linda S., and George J. Gumerman (editors)
1989 *Dynamics of Southwest Prehistory*. Smithsonian Institution Press, Washington, D.C.

Dalton, George (editor)
1971 *Primitive, Archaic and Modern Economics: Essays of Karl Polanyi*. Beacon Press, Boston.
1978 *Research in Economic Anthropology I*. JAI Press, Greenwich, Conn.

Daugherty, Richard
1990 People of the Salmon: The Pacific Northwest at 1492. In *America in 1492*, edited by Alvin Josephy, Jr. Alfred A. Knopf, New York, in press.

Davis, James T.
1965 Trade Routes and Economic Exchange among the Indians of California. In *Aboriginal California: Three Studies in Culture History*, pp. 1–80. University of California Archaeological Research Facility, Berkeley.

Deagan, Kathleen
1983 *Spanish St. Augustine: The Archaeology of a Colonial Creole Community*. Academic Press, New York.

Díaz del Castillo, Bernal
1956 *The Discovery and Conquest of Mexico, 1517–1521*. Translated by Irving A. Leonard. Farrar, Straus and Cudahy, New York.

Di Peso, Charles C.
1974 *Casas Grandes: A Fallen Trading Center of the Gran Chichimeca*. 3 vols. Northland Press, Flagstaff, Ariz.

Dobyns, Henry F.
1983 *Their Number Become Thinned: Native American Population Dynamics in Eastern North America*. University of Tennessee Press, Knoxville.
1984 Trade Centers: The Concept and a Rancherian Culture Area Example. *American Indian Culture and Research Journal* 8(1):23–35.
1989 A Fortune in Feathers: Native North American Trade about A.D. 1500. Ms. in possession of the author.

Drennen, Robert D.
1984 Long-Distance Movement of Goods in the Mesoamerican Formative and Classic. *American Antiquity* 49(1):27–43.

Driver, Harold E., and William C. Massey
1957 *Comparative Studies of North American Indians*. Transactions of the American Philosophical Society 47(2). Philadelphia, Pa.

Earle, Timothy K.

1982 Prehistoric Economics and the Archaeology of Exchange. In *Contexts for Prehistoric Exchange*, edited by Jonathon E. Ericson and Timothy K. Earle, pp. 1–12. Academic Press, New York.

Earle, Timothy K., and A. Christenson
1980 Modeling Change in Prehistoric Subsistence Economies. Academic Press, New York.

Earle, Timothy K., and Jonathon E. Ericson (editors)
1977 *Exchange Systems in Prehistory.* Academic Press, New York.

Elliott, J. H.
1970 *The Old World and the New, 1492–1650.* Cambridge University Press, New York.

Ellis, Bruce T.
1957 Crossbow Boltheads from Historic Pueblo Sites. *El Palacio* 64(7–8):209–214. Santa Fe, N.M.

Ellis, Florence Hawley
1987 The Long Lost "City" of San Gabriel del Yungue, Second Oldest European Settlement in the United States. In *When Cultures Meet: Remembering San Gabriel del Yunge Oweenge*, pp. 10–38. Sunstone Press, Santa Fe, N.M.
1989 *San Gabriel del Yunque as Seen by an Archaeologist.* Sunstone Press, Santa Fe, N.M.

Ericson, Jonathon E.
1977 Egalitarian Exchange Systems in California: A Preliminary View. In *Exchange Systems in Prehistory*, edited by Timothy K. Earle and Jonathon E. Ericson, pp. 109–126. Academic Press, New York.
1982 Production for Obsidian Exchange in California. In *Contexts for Prehistoric Exchange*, edited by Jonathon E. Ericson and Timothy K. Earle, pp. 129–148. Academic Press, New York.

Ericson, Jonathon E., and Timothy K. Earle (editors)
1982 *Contexts for Prehistoric Exchange.* Academic Press, New York.

Ewers, John C.
1954 The Indian Trade of the Upper Missouri before Lewis and Clark: An Interpretation. *Bulletin of the Missouri Historical Society* 10(4):429–446. St. Louis.
1968 The Indian Trade of the Upper Missouri Before Lewis and Clark: An Interpretation. In *Indian Life on the Upper Missouri*, pp. 14–33. University of Oklahoma Press, Norman. Originally published 1954.
1979 "Introduction" to James Mooney, *Calendar History of the Kiowa Indians* [1896]. Smithsonian Institution Press, Washington, D.C.

Fewkes, J. Walter
1896 Pacific Coast Shells from Prehistoric Tusayan Pueblos. *American Anthropologist* 9(11):359–367.
1919 *Prehistoric Villages, Castles, and Towns of Southwestern Colorado.* Bureau of American Ethnology Bulletin No. 70. Washington, D.C.

Ferguson, T. J., and E. Richard Hart
1985 *A Zuni Atlas.* University of Oklahoma Press, Norman.

Findlow, Frank J., and Marisa Bolognese
1982 Regional Modeling of Obsidian Procurement in the American Southwest. In *Contexts for Prehistoric Exchange*, edited by Jonathon E. Ericson and Timothy K. Earle, pp. 53–82. Academic Press, New York.

Fitzhugh, William W. (editor)
1985 *Cultures in Contact: The Impact of European Contacts on Native Americn Cultural Institutions*, A.D. 1000–1800. Smithsonian Institution Press, Washington, D.C.

Fontana, Bernard
1965 On the Meaning of Historic Sites Archaeology. *American Antiquity* 31(1):61–65.

Foster, Michael S., and Phil C. Weigand (editors)
1985 *The Archaeology of West and Northwest Mesoamerica.* Westview Press, Boulder, Colo.

Ford, Richard I.

1972 Barter, Gift, or Violence: An Analysis of Tewa Intertribal Exchange. In *Social Exchange and Interaction*, edited by Edwin N. Wilmsen, pp. 21–46. University of Michigan Anthropological Papers No. 46. Ann Arbor.

1983 Inter-Indian Exchange in the Southwest. In *Southwest*, edited by Alfonso Ortiz, pp. 711–722. Handbook of North American Indians, vol. 10, William C. Sturtevant, general editor. Smithsonian Institution, Washington, D.C.

Gleeson, Paul F.

1980a *Ozette Woodworking Technology*. Project Report No. 3. Laboratory of Archaeology and History, Washington State University, Pullman.

1980b *Ozette Archaeological Project, Interim Final Report: Phase XIII*, edited by Richard D. Daugherty. Project Report No. 97. Washington State University, Pullman.

Griffin, James B., A. A. Gordus, and G. A. Wright

1969 Identification of the Sources of Hopewellian Obsidian in the Middle West. *American Antiquity* 24(1):1–14.

Hall, Thomas D.

1989 *Social Change in the Southwest, 1350–1880*. University Press of Kansas, Lawrence.

Hammond, George P., and Agapito Rey (editors)

1940 *Narratives of the Coronado Expedition, 1540–1542*. University of New Mexico Press, Albuquerque.

Harbottle, Garman

1982 Chemical Characterization in Archaeology. In *Contexts for Prehistoric Exchange*, edited by Jonathon E. Ericson and Timothy K. Earle, pp. 13–51. Academic Press, New York.

Hassig, Ross

1985 *Trade, Tribute, and Transportation: The Sixteenth Century Political Economy of the Valley of Mexico*. University of Oklahoma Press, Norman.

Haury, Emil W.

1984 "The Search for Chichilticale." *Arizona Highways* 60(4):14–19.

Hedrick, Basil C., J. Charles Kelley, and Carroll L. Riley (editors)

1974 *The Mesoamerican Southwest: Readings in Archaeology, Ethnohistory, and Ethnology*. Southern Illinois University Press, Carbondale.

Heizer, Robert F.

1978 Trade and Trails. In *California*, edited by Robert F. Heizer, pp. 690–693. Handbook of North American Indians, vol. 8. William C. Sturtevant, general editor. Smithsonian Institution, Washington, D.C.

Herskovits, Melville J.

1952 *Economic Anthropology: The Economic Life of Primitive Peoples*. Norton, New York.

Hickerson, Nancy

1990 Jumano: The Missing Link in South Plains History. Ms. in possession of the author.

Hirth, Kenneth G.

1978 Interregional Trade and the Formation of Prehistoric Gateway Communities. *American Antiquity* 43(1):35–45.

Hirth, Kenneth G. (editor)

1984 *Trade and Exchange in Early Mesoamerica*. University of New Mexico Press, Albuquerque.

Hodder, Ian

1980 Trade and Exchange: Definitions, Identification and Function. In *Models and Methods in Regional Exchange*, edited by Robert E. Fry, pp. 151–156. Society for American Archaeology Papers, No. 1. Washington, D.C.

Hodge, Frederick Webb

1937 *History of Hawikuh, New Mexico: One of the So-called Cities of Cibola*. Publications of the Frederick Webb Hodge Anniversary Publication Fund 1. Southwest Museum, Los Angeles.

Huelsbeck, David R.
  1988 The Surplus Economy of the Central Northwest Coast. In *Prehistoric Economies of the Pacific Northwest Coast*, edited by Barry L. Isaac, pp. 149–178. Research in Economic Anthropology Supplement 3. JAI Press, Greenwich, Conn.

Hughes, Richard E., and James A. Bennyhoff
  1986 Early Trade. In *Great Basin*, edited by Warren L. d'Azevedo, pp. 238–255. Handbook of North American Indians, vol. 11, William C. Sturtevant, general editor. Smithsonian Institution, Washington, D.C.

Hughes, Richard E. (editor)
  1984 *Obsidian Studies in the Great Basin*. Contributions of the University of California Archaeology Research Facility No. 45. Department of Anthropology, University of California, Berkeley.

Humphreys, S. C.
  1969 History, Economics, and Anthropology: The Work of Karl Polanyi. *History and Theory* 8:165–212.

Irwin-Williams, Cynthia
  1977 A Network Model for the Analysis of Prehistoric Trade. In *Exchange Systems in Prehistory*, edited by Timothy K. Earle and Jonathon E. Ericson, pp. 141–152. Academic Press, New York.

Isaac, Barry L. (editor)
  1988 *Prehistoric Economies of the Pacific Northwest Coast*. Research in Economic Anthropology Supplement No. 3. JAI Press, Greenwich, Conn.

Jochim, Michael A.
  1976 *Hunter-Gatherer Subsistence and Settlement*. Academic Press, New York.

Jablow, Joseph
  1951 *The Cheyenne in Plains Indian Trade Relations, 1795–1840*. Monographs of the American Ethnological Society No. 19. New York.

Kelley, J. Charles
  1949 Archaeological Notes on Two Excavated House Structures in Western Texas. *Texas Archaeological and Paleontological Society Bulletin* 20:89–114.
  1955 Juan Sabeata and Diffusion in Aboriginal Texas. *American Anthropologist* 57(5):981–995.

Kessell, John L.
  1979 *Kiva, Cross and Crown: The Pecos Indians and New Mexico, 1540–1840*. U. S. National Park Service, Washington, D.C.

Kidder, Alfred Vincent
  1924 *An Introduction to the Study of Southwestern Archaeology*. Yale University Press, New Haven, Conn.
  1932 *The Artifacts of Pecos*. Yale University Press for the Phillips Academy, New Haven, Conn.

Kroeber, Alfred L.
  1925 *Handbook of the Indians of California*. Bureau of American Ethnology Bulletin No. 78. Washington, D.C.

Lange, Charles H.
  1979 Relations of the Southwest with the Plains and Great Basin. In *Southwest*, edited by Alfonso Ortiz, pp. 201–223. Handbook of North American Indians, vol. 9, William C. Sturtevant, general editor. Smithsonian Institution, Washington, D.C.

Leacock, Eleanor Burke
  1971 Introduction. In *North American Indians in Historical Perspective*, edited by Eleanor Burke Leacock and Nancy Lurie, pp. 3–28. Random House, New York.

LeClair, E., and H. Schneider
  1968 *Economic Anthropology*. Holt, Rinehart and Winston, New York.

Lehmer, Donald J.
  1954 *Archaeological Investigations in the Oahe Dam Area, South Dakota, 1950–1951*. Bureau

of American Ethnology Bulletin No. 158. Washington, D.C.

Mathien, Frances Joan, and Randall H. McGuire (editors)

1986 *Ripples in the Chichimec Sea: New Considerations of Southwestern-Mesoamerican Interactions*. Southern Illinois University Press, Carbondale.

Milanich, Jerald T., and Susan Milbrath (editors)

1989 *First Encounters: Spanish Explorations in the Caribbean and the United States, 1492–1570*. University of Florida Press, Gainesville.

Mindeleff, Victor

1891 A Study of Pueblo Architecture in Tusayan and Cibola. In *Eighth Annual Report of the Bureau of American Ethnology for the Years 1886–1887*, pp. 3–228. Washington, D.C.

Minnis, Paul E.

1989 The Casas Grande Polity in the International Four Corners. In *The Sociopolitical Structure of Prehistoric Southwest Societies*, edited by Steadman Upham, Kent G. Lightfoot, and Roberta A. Jewett, pp. 269–305. Westview Press, Boulder, Colo.

Myer, William E.

1928 Indian Trails of the Southeast. In *Forty-Second Annual Report of the Bureau of American Ethnology*, pp. 729–857. Washington, D.C.

Noble, David Grant (editor)

1984 *New Light on Chaco Canyon*. School of American Research Press, Santa Fe, N.M.

Oberg, Kalervo

1973 *The Social Economy of the Tlingit Indians*. University of Washington Press, Seattle.

Oviedo y Valdes, Gonzalo Fernández de

1959 *Summary of the Natural and General History of the West Indies*. Translated and edited by Sterling A. Stoudemire. Studies in the Romance Languages and Literature No. 32. University of North Carolina, Chapel Hill. Originally published 1526.

Pailes, Richard A., and Daniel T. Reff

1979 The Greater Southwest and the Mesoamerican "World System": An Exploratory Model of Frontier Relationships. In *The Frontier: Comparative Studies II*, edited by William W. Savage, Jr., and Stephen I. Thompson, pp. 105–122. University of Oklahoma Press, Norman.

1985 Colonial Exchange Systems and the Decline of Paquime. In *The Archaeology of West and Northwest Mesoamerica*, edited by M. S. Foster and P. C. Weigand, pp. 353–364. Westview Press, Boulder, Colo.

Parsons, Elsie Clews

1939 *Pueblo Indian Religion*. University of Chicago Press, Chicago.

Pepper, George H.

1920 *Pueblo Bonito*. Anthropological Papers of the American Museum of Natural History No. 27. New York.

Phillips, Philip, and James A. Brown

1978 *Pre-Columbian Shell Engravings from the Craig Mound at Spiro, Oklahoma*. 2 parts. Peabody Museum of Archaeology and Ethnology, Harvard University, Cambridge, Mass.

Polanyi, Karl, Conrad M. Arensberg, and Harry W. Pearson (editors)

1957 *Trade and Market in the Early Empires: Economies in History and Theory*. Free Press, Glencoe, Ill.

1977 Traders and Trade. In *The Livelihood of Man*, edited by Harry W. Pearson, pp. 81–96. Academic Press, New York.

Quinn, David Beers

1977 *North America from Earliest Discovery to First Settlements: The Norse Voyages to 1612*. Harper and Row, New York.

Ramenofsky, Ann F.

1987 *Vectors of Death: The Archaeology of European Contact*. University of New Mexico Press, Albuquerque.

Ravesloot, John C., and Stephanie M. Whittlesey
   1987 Inferring the Protohistoric Period in Southern Arizona. In *The Archaeology of the San Xavier Bridge Site*. Arizona State Museum Archaeological Series 171:81–98. Tucson.
Ray, Verne F.
   1939 *Cultural Relations in the Plateau of Northwestern America*. Publications of the Frederick Webb Hodge Anniversary Publication Fund No. 3. Southwest Museum, Los Angeles, Calif.
Renfrew, Colin
   1975 Trade as Action at a Distance: Questions of Integrations and Communication. In *Ancient Civilization and Trade*, edited by Jeremy A. Sabloff and C. C. Lamberg-Karlovsky, pp. 3–59. University of New Mexico Press, Albuquerque.
Riley, Carroll L.
   1976 *Sixteenth-Century Trade in the Greater Southwest*. Southern Illinois University, University Museum Mesoamerican Studies No. 10. Carbondale.
   1978 Pecos and Trade. In *Across the Chichimec Sea: Papers in Honor of J. Charles Kelley*, edited by Carroll L. Riley and Basil C. Hedrick, pp. 53–64. University of Southern Illinois Press, Carbondale.
   1987 *The Frontier People: The Greater Southwest in the Protohistoric Period*. University of New Mexico Press, Albuquerque.
Riley, Carroll L., and Basil C. Hedrick (editors)
   1978 *Across the Chichimec Sea: Papers in Honor of J. Charles Kelley*. Southern Illinois University Press, Carbondale.
Sabloff, Jeremy A., and C.C. Lamberg-Karlovsky (editors)
   1975 *Ancient Civilization and Trade*. University of New Mexico Press, Albuquerque.
Sabloff, Jeremy, and William L. Rathje
   1975 *A Study of Changing Pre-Columbian Commercial Systems: The 1972–1973 Seasons at Cozumel, Mexico*. Peabody Museum of Archaeology and Ethnology, Harvard University, Cambridge.
Sauer, Carl Ortwin
   1932 *The Road to Cíbola*. Ibero-Americana No. 3. University of California Press, Berkeley.
   1971 *Sixteenth-Century North America: The Land and the People as Seen by the Europeans*. University of California Press, Berkeley.
Schroeder, Albert H.
   1979 History of Archeological Research. In *Southwest*, edited by Alfonso Ortiz, pp. 5–13. Handbook of North American Indians, vol. 9, William C. Sturtevant, general editor, Smithsonian Institution, Washington, D.C.
Smith, Carol A.
   1976 Exchange Systems and the Spatial Distribution of Elites: The Organization of Stratification in Agrarian Societies. In *Regional Analysis*, vol. 2, *Social Systems*, edited by Carol A. Smith, pp. 309–374. Academic Press, New York.
Smith, Jack E. (compiler and editor)
   1983 *Proceedings of the Anasazi Symposium, 1981*. Mesa Verde Museum Association, Mesa Verde National Park, Colo.
Spier, Leslie, and Edward Sapir
   1931 *Wishram Ethnography*. University of Washington Publications in Anthropology No. 3. Seattle.
Spielmann, Katherine A.
   1983 Late Prehistoric Exchange between the Southwest and Southern Plains. *Plains Anthropologist* 28(102, part 1):257–272.
Steward, Julian H.
   1938 *Basin-Plateau Aboriginal Sociopolitical Groups*. Bureau of American Ethnology Bulletin No. 120. Smithsonian Institution, Washington, D.C.

Strong, William Duncan, W. Egbert Schenck, and Julian H. Stewart
   1930 *Archaeology of the Dalles-Deschutes Region.* University of California Publications in American Archaeology and Ethnology 29(1). Berkeley.
   1935 *An Introduction to Nebraska Archeology.* Smithsonian Miscellaneous Collections 93(10). Smithsonian Institution, Washington, D.C.
Sturtevant, William C.
   1966 Anthropology, History, and Ethnohistory. *Ethnohistory* 13(1–2):1–51.
Sturtevant, William C. (general editor)
   1978– *Handbook of North American Indians.* 20 vols. Smithsonian Institution, Washington, D.C.
Swagerty, William R.
   1988 Indian Trade in the Trans-Mississippi West to 1870. In *Indian–White Relations*, edited by Wilcomb E. Washburn, pp. 351–374. Handbook of North American Indians, vol. 4, William C. Sturtevant, general editor. Smithsonian Institution, Washington, D.C.
Swanton, John Reed
   1911 *Indian Tribes of the Lower Mississippi Valley and Adjacent Coast of the Gulf of Mexico.* Bureau of American Ethnology Bulletin No. 43. Smithsonian Institution, Washington, D.C.
   1939 *Final Report of the United States De Soto Expedition Commission.* U.S. House of Representatives, 76th Cong., 1st session, Doc. 71. Washington, D.C.
   1946 *The Indians of the Southeastern United States.* Bureau of American Ethnology Bulletin No. 137. Smithsonian Institution, Washington, D.C.
   n.d. "Miscellaneous" manuscripts on file, No. 4281. National Anthropological Archives, Smithsonian Institution, Washington, D.C.
Teit, James A.
   1930 The Salishan Tribes of the Western Plateaus. In *Forty-Fifth Annual Report of the Bureau of American Ethnology*, pp. 23–396. Washington, D.C.
Thomas, David Hurst (editor)
   1989 *Columbian Consequences*, vol. 1, *Archaeological and Historical Perspectives on the Spanish Borderlands West.* Smithsonian Institution Press, Washington, D.C.
   1990 *Columbian Consequences*, vol. 2, *Archaeological and Historical Perspectives on the Spanish Borderlands East.* Smithsonian Institution Press, Washington, D.C.
Tower, Donald B.
   1945 *The Use of Marine Mollusca and Their Value in Reconstructing Prehistoric Trade Routes in the American Southwest.* Papers of the Excavators' Club 2(3). Cambridge, Mass.
Trigger, Bruce G.
   1982 Ethnohistory: Problems and Prospects. *Ethnohistory* 29(1):1–19.
   1986 Ethnohistory: The Unfinished Edifice. *Ethnohistory* 33(3):253–267.
   1989 *A History of Archeological Thought.* Cambridge University Press, New York.
Upham, Steadman, Kent G. Lightfoot, and Roberta A. Jewett (editors)
   1989 *The Sociopolitical Structure of Prehistoric Southwestern Societies.* Westview Press, Boulder, Colo.
Vayda, Andrew
   1966 Pomo Trade Feasts. Humanitiés: Cahiers de l'Institut de Science Economique Appliquée. Reprinted in *Tribal and Peasant Economies*, edited by George Dalton, pp. 494–500. Natural History Press, Garden City, N.Y., 1967.
Vierra, Bradley J.
   1987 A Sixteenth-Century Spanish Campsite in the Tiguex Province: An Archaeologist's Perspective. Paper presented at the 65th annual meeting of the Southwestern Social Science Association, Dallas, Tex.
Wedel, Waldo R.
   1936 *An Introduction to Pawnee Archaeology.* Bureau of American Ethnology Bulletin No. 112. Smithsonian Institution, Washington, D.C.

1938 *The Direct-Historical Approach in Pawnee Archeology*. Smithsonian Miscellaneous Collections 97(7).

1961 *Prehistoric Man on the Great Plains*. University of Oklahoma Press, Norman.

1975 Chain Mail in Plains Archeology. *Plains Anthropologist* 20(69):187–196.

1986 *Central Plains Prehistory: Holocene Environments and Culture Change in the Republican River Basin*. University of Nebraska Press, Lincoln.

Weigand, Phil C., Garman Harbottle, and Edward V. Sayre

1972 Turquoise Sources and Source Analysis: Mesoamerica and the Southwestern U.S.A. In *Exchange Systems in Prehistory*, edited by Timothy K. Earle and Jonathon E. Ericson, pp. 15–34. Academic Press, New York.

Wilcox, David R., and W. Bruce Masse (editors)

1981 *The Protohistoric Period in the North American Southwest, A.D. 1450–1700*. Anthropological Research Papers No. 24. Arizona State University, Tempe.

Wilmsen, Edwin N. (editor)

1972 *Social Exchange and Interaction*. University of Michigan, Museum of Anthropology Anthropological Papers No. 46. Ann Arbor, Mich.

Willey, Gordon R., and Jeremy A. Sabloff

1980 *A History of American Archaeology*. 2d. ed. W. H. Freeman, San Francisco, Calif.

Wood, W. Raymond

1967 *An Interpretation of Mandan Culture History*. Inter-Agency Archeological Salvage Program River Basin Surveys Papers No. 39, edited by Robert L. Stephenson. Bureau of American Ethnology Bulletin No. 198. Washington, D.C.

1972 Contrastive Features of Native North American Trade Systems. In *For the Chief: Essays in Honor of Luther S. Cressman*, edited by Fred W. Voget and Robert L. Stephenson, pp. 153–169. University of Oregon Anthropological Papers No. 4. Eugene.

1980 Plains Trade in Prehistoric and Protohistoric Intertribal Relations. In *Anthropology on the Great Plains*, edited by W. Raymond Wood and Margot Liberty, pp. 98–109. University of Nebraska Press, Lincoln.

Zucker, Jeff, Kay Hummel, and Bob Hogfoss, with cartography by Jay Forest Penniman

1983 *Oregon Indians: Culture, History and Current Affairs*. Western Imprints for the Oregon Historical Society, Portland.

Chapter 25 ◼

Timothy K. Perttula

European Contact and Its Effects on Aboriginal Caddoan Populations between A.D. 1520 and A.D. 1680

The first European explorers of the Caddoan area were the 200 or so ragged and exhausted members of the de Soto—Moscoso entrada of 1542. In their search for treasure and great wealth, the de Soto entrada hoped to discover in La Florida native civilizations that it could exploit like those encountered in Mexico and Peru (Quinn 1979:2:93–96). One group of aboriginal societies that the Spaniards encountered lived west of the Mississippi Valley, in the direction of New Spain. Because they had much the same material culture, customs, and language, they were recognized as being different from other aborigines previously encountered by the Spanish (Swanton 1939). These people were the Caddoan-speaking groups who lived in the area between the Arkansas and Red River valleys, in what are now parts of Texas, Oklahoma, Louisiana, Arkansas, and Missouri. They were maize agriculturists and bison hunters who "were still in the full state of their indigenous developments" (Brain 1985:xlvii). The de Soto chronicles provide a great deal of information about them that has proved to be particularly valuable because these people came to play a significant role in the Euro-American settlement of the area in the eighteenth and nineteenth centuries (see Corbin 1989; Perttula 1989). This chapter investigates the immediate and long-term effects and consequences of contact and interaction between these Caddoan peoples and Europeans arising from the de Soto—Moscoso entrada.

The Question of Contact

The periods of European contact in the Caddoan area can be divided into the Protohistoric period of indirect and intermittent direct contact between Europeans and Caddoan peoples and a subsequent Historic Caddoan period of direct, sustained, and continuous contact between both populations. The Protohistoric period extends from ca. A.D. 1520 to 1680, which encompasses the latter part of the Late Caddoan period as recently defined by Story (1990:334). The period of direct contact with Europeans begins sometime after A.D. 1680 and lasts to ca. A.D. 1860 (Perttula 1989:85–125; Story 1990:334).

Steward (1954:296) has noted that "even limited contacts with Europeans . . . may affect Indian society in a very fundamental sense." While processes of indirect and intermittent direct contact are difficult to document thoroughly or explicate from an ethnohistoric or archaeological perspective, it is evident that the focus on the Protohistoric period is of singular importance in the study of "initial changes brought about by European contact" (Trigger 1985:118). However, the duration or intensity of interaction between different cultural systems is only one part of the process of episodic contacts between Europeans and Native Americans because the consequences of European contact can be initiated even while these groups are independent tribal or sociopolitical entities. Therefore, profound demographic, social, and political changes that substantially altered aboriginal Caddoan societies could have occurred prior to the onset of face-to-face European contact.

Trigger (1983:440) has commented that an "increasing number of ethnologists and ethnohistorians are beginning to recognize that only archaeological data can provide a true base line for measuring changes brought about by a European presence in North America." Before we can formulate hypotheses concerning the long-term effects and consequences of European contact on Caddoan groups, we must explore the processes and causes that were responsible for change and the cultural dynamics embedded in the archaeological record of the Late Caddoan period.

Although there is no direct evidence of the transmission of epidemic diseases during the de Soto entrada, or indeed until 1687–1691 (Table 25–1), it is probable that Caddoan groups were being affected by infectious diseases throughout this first period of contact. Smallpox, some form of tuberculosis, and certain zoonoses (typhus, plague, and malaria) could all have been introduced to the New World by de Soto or other European explorations. Thus, while the effects of indirect and intermittent contact between European and Caddoan peoples were probably not significant in terms of the European goods and products introduced to the Caddoan peoples, the biological effects of the entrada were manifold. In "virgin soil" conditions like those in North America during the Contact period, the introduction of an exotic virus such as smallpox can result in 100 percent mortality (Crosby 1986; Ramenofsky 1987b).

Table 25-1. Known Epidemics in the Caddoan Area of Texas

Date	Type of Disease
1691	? (unidentified)
1718	? (unidentified)
1731	Smallpox
1759	Measles
1777–1778	Cholera or bubonic plague, smallpox
1801–1802	Smallpox
1803	Measles
1816	Smallpox
1864[a]	Smallpox
1867[a]	Cholera
1892[a]	Measles, influenza, whooping cough

a. Recorded among the Caddoan peoples living in Indian territory, within the present boundaries of Oklahoma.
Source: Ewers (1973).

Theoretical and Methodological Concerns

As already mentioned, the Caddoan groups may have experienced many cultural changes long before the first in-depth accounts of these peoples were recorded by European explorers and settlers. That is why it is essential to study the archaeology of this period and to further integrate the Caddoan ethnographic, ethnohistoric, and archaeological records as complementary data sets (see Story 1990:322–324).

There are a number of important questions to ask of the Caddoan archaeological record for the Protohistoric period:

1. In what ways did Caddoan society and culture change or remain the same as a result of European contact and interaction?
2. What is the historical significance of European-introduced diseases in the Caddoan area, and when did they have a significant effect on population size or social structure?
3. Are there changes in settlement density, location, and the tempo of abandonment that relate to episodes of disease introduction?
4. Do the effects of European contact and the spread of European diseases engender the same types of responses by Caddoan groups living along major rivers as they do among those Caddoan groups inhabiting upland and hinterland areas?

To begin with, however, we must ask how it is possible to discuss, measure, and evaluate cultural change during the period between ca. A.D. 1520 and A.D. 1680 using the archaeological record. A key issue is the timing and magnitude of population declines in Caddoan groups caused by the introduction of European acute epidemic diseases.

Henige (1986:303–305) has thoroughly reviewed the documentary evidence used by Dobyns (1983) to argue that periodic epidemics or pandemics caused dramatic population declines among North American Indians prior to 1565 and rather convincingly refutes the value of documentary sources as a means of demonstrating population reduction during this period. Instead, Henige (1986) proposes that "arguments of silence," in this case the archaeological record of the sixteenth and seventeenth centuries, be employed to independently demonstrate the timing and magnitude of such a population decline or demographic collapse, and thereby corroborate and extend the historic record.

The effects of European-introduced diseases on aboriginal populations have increasingly come to play one of the more significant interpretive roles in the study of the impact of European contact (e.g., Dobyns 1983; Thomas 1989). Only recently, however, have archaeologists and bioarchaeologists begun to give attention to the demographic issue, and the important role both disciplines have to play in interpreting and understanding contact cultural change in the New World in light of European-introduced diseases and their diffusion (e.g., Ramenofsky 1987b, 1990; Trigger 1985).

Significant diseases introduced in the Caddoan area include smallpox, measles, plague, diphtheria, whooping cough, trachoma, and influenza, among others, none of which were present in North America before the arrival of Europeans (Crosby 1986:197–198). The introduction of infectious diseases into nonimmune or virgin soil populations could result in epidemics characterized by high mortality and morbidity rates as well as abnormal age mortality distributions.

According to Ramenofsky (1982:80), all introduced European diseases share certain characteristics affecting exposed populations:

1. Exposure and infection for most of the diseases result in permanent or long-term immunity.
2. Therefore, if populations are unfamiliar with such parasites, they have no immunity and are virgin colonizing territories for the reproduction of parasites.
3. In such populations, the parasite infestation is acute and epidemics erupt.

As the mortality from virgin soil epidemics increases among adolescents and young adults, population fertility and reproductive success decline. At the same time, episodic infectious pathogens kill off those born between epidemics who had no previous exposure or immunity.

As Table 25–1 shows, Caddoan populations of the Texas area experienced epidemics "at least once every generation from 1731 to 1877" (Ewers 1973:107). The cumulative effects of these recorded epidemics among the Texas Caddoan groups were a known 94 percent population reduction between 1690–1890 (Ewers 1973:Table 1). Taking into consideration, therefore, the possibility of even more virulent and devastating epidemics between A.D. 1520–1680 (Table 25–2; see also Dobyns 1983:14; Vehik 1989:Table 11), the combined effect on aboriginal populations was unparalleled.

One of the more important demographic issues that has been raised recently

Table 25-2. Known or Suspected Sixteenth- and Seventeenth-Century Epidemics in Florida, the Lower Mississippi Valley, and Texas

Florida (Deagan 1985)	Florida (Dobyns 1983)	Lower Mississippi (Ramenofsky 1985, 1987b)	Texas (Ewers 1973)
	1513		
	1519		
			1528
	1535–1538		
	1545–1538		
	1549		
	1550		
	1559		
1570	1564–1570		
1586	1585–1586		
1591			
	1596		
1613	1613–1617		
1617			
1649	1649		
	1653		
1659	1659		
1670			
1672–1674	1672		
	1675		1674–1675
1686			1686
			1691
		1698	

is that of disease diffusion (e.g., Dobyns 1983; Ramenofsky 1987a). Disease diffusion refers to the potential of introduced diseases to diffuse in advance of direct transmission from European settlers and explorers, and therefore explains how unrecorded disease outbreaks could be transmitted and diffused beyond points of their initial introduction.

Ramenofsky's (1987a) analyses of the diffusion potential of the different reported or inferred sixteenth- or seventeenth-century disease events used their means of transmission to estimate the probability with which they could have diffused to or within North America, and what type of spatial patterns they might have taken. She distinguished between directly transmitted pathogens (such as measles, influenza, viruses, and smallpox) and zoonoses (typhus, plague, and malaria) which are transmitted through an intermediate host or vector. Human populations are not essential for the zoonotic pathogen to survive, and proximity usually is responsible for the spread of the infection to humans (Ramenofsky 1987b). These infections have a higher diffusion potential than most of the directly transmitted diseases because the period of communicability of these latter pathogens would probably not survive European voyages across the Atlantic Ocean. Smallpox, however, is an exception, because it can remain viable in a dried state for more than a year (Ramenofsky 1987b). That being the case, it could have been transmitted from Mexico or Cuba to North America following aboriginal trails and trade routes, then could have been diffused across the continent and into the Caddoan area.

The hypothesis that a major demographic decline probably occurred among Caddoan populations before there was a documented and sustained European presence in the area has important implications for any investigation of the archaeological record during the Protohistoric period, as well as for the periods following the first detailed European accounts of Caddoan peoples. Fundamental changes in aboriginal lifeways during these periods need to be evaluated in the light of new and more reliable information on the composition and structure of sociopolitical entities described in the ethnographic record. Furthermore, these changes need to be taken into account in interpreting possible continuity or discontinuity between the archaeological and ethnological cultures.

Population Estimates

No overall estimates have yet been made of the aboriginal population in the Caddoan area in the Protohistoric period. Archaeological considerations suggest that Caddoan societies had dispersed settlement systems characterized by a relatively low regional population density when compared with the denser nucleated populations in the Mississippi Valley and parts of the interior Southeast (see Steponaitis 1986).

Estimates of Native American population sizes will vary, depending primarily on whether the impact of European diseases is taken into account (Ramenofsky 1987b:6–21). Lower population estimates, such as those in Mooney's (1928) study of the Caddoan peoples, disregard acute infectious diseases as a factor in population estimation prior to sustained European contact ca. A.D. 1690 (see also Gregory 1973). When European acute diseases are considered as a major factor affecting the size of nonimmune populations from the period of initial contact, then assumptions of population size changes, and their consequences, must be reevaluated (Perttula 1989, 1990).

Two opposing views of demographic change in the Caddoan area may be proposed on the basis of assumptions about when introduced European diseases affected Caddoan populations. The basic difference between the two demographic models is in their assumptions about when depopulation begins (Figure 25–1).

In the first view, no epidemics would have taken place among any Caddoan groups until 1687–1691, which is when the first ethnographically recorded epidemic was described by the Spanish (see Mooney 1928). The period between ca. A.D. 1520–1680 would therefore be one of continued Caddoan population growth, and the population would have reached its maximum level about A.D. 1690. Ethnographic records among Caddoan groups indicate that population sizes decreased approximately 80 percent from A.D. 1700 to 1780 (from 7,000 to 1,400 individuals) and continued to decrease until ca. 1900 (see Figure 25–2; Thornton 1987:127–131). The overall "Mooney" depopulation trend in Figure

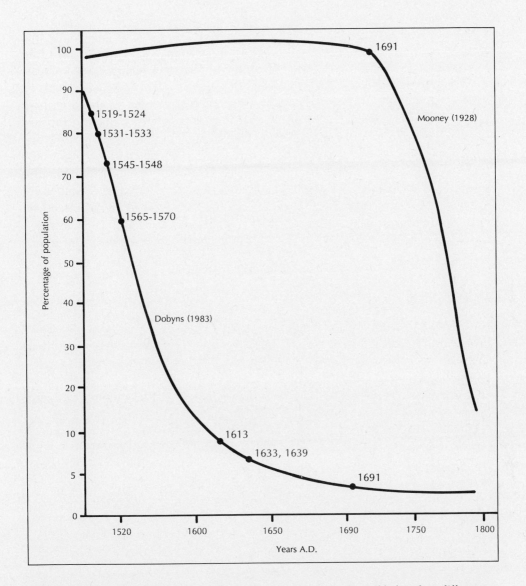

Figure 25–1. Schematic differences in depopulation trends among the Caddo based on differences in the assumed effect of European diseases, their appearances, and the period of maximum population size.

25–1 resembles a smooth monotonic decrease, although in fact it would probably take a stairstep form—that is, one reflecting some population recovery or rise between epidemics and further population decline, but the rise would not have been to precontact population levels.

The alternative depopulation trend advocated herein assumes that the aboriginal population maximum for Caddoan peoples occurred ca. A.D. 1520, just before initial European contacts and the diffusion of disease events. If a series of epidemics had been transmitted along aboriginal trading routes (depicted as points in time on the "Dobyns" depopulation trend), the population frequenting

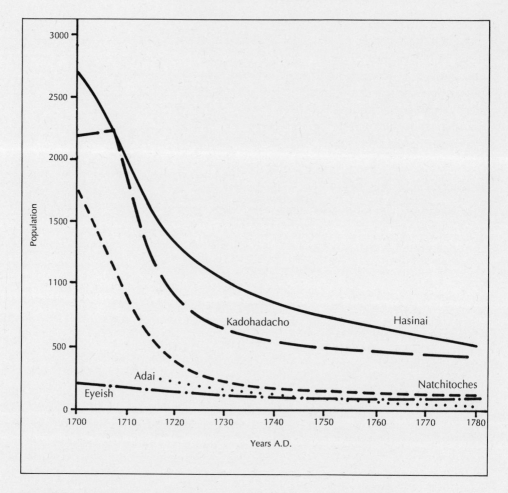

Figure 25–2. Populations of Caddoan tribes A.D. 1700–1780. (From Swanton 1942)

them would have declined precipitously between ca. A.D. 1520 and 1680. Further epidemic events after A.D. 1680 would have continued to have adverse effects on Caddoan populations that had already been subjected to episodes of high mortality, population declines, and general infertility.

A total estimated population on the order of 200,000 at ca. A.D. 1520 (e.g., Perttula 1989:61–67) and 8,500 at ca. A.D. 1680 would argue for an estimated 96 percent decline in the Caddoan population over that time. This is congruent with estimated overall demographic losses elsewhere, for example, in the Southeast, among populations that were probably episodically exposed to the same types of epidemic diseases (Dobyns 1983:288). The earlier and steeper depopulation trend in Figure 25–1 therefore takes into account the possibility that the initial epidemics of the sixteenth and seventeenth centuries were actually responsible for the greatest absolute declines in population.

Differential population densities within the Caddoan area have direct implications for the study of contact and the consequences of European epidemic diseases. Smaller, dispersed rural communities, or nomadic populations, are thought to have had an adaptive advantage over denser populated town communities in minimizing direct contact with Europeans, and in lessening the impact and the spread of epidemic diseases (e.g., Ramenofsky 1990). Therefore, while population densities in the Caddoan area were probably not as high as in nucleated settlement systems in the Mississippi Valley, the patterns of differential population density formed demographic constraints that need to be considered in evaluating the consequences and effects of European-introduced diseases.

Research Directions

The archaeological record of the Caddoan area during the Protohistoric period can provide important information that can be used to assess Caddoan—European interaction and Caddoan cultural changes following European contact (Perttula 1989:126–210). To explore these possibilities, I examined elements of social and ceremonial activities, settlement change, and regional population densities within the Western, Northern, and Central (Red, Little, and Ouachita River Basins) Caddoan areas from A.D. 1520 to 1680 (Figure 25–3).

In situations where population size is declining significantly and/or continuously due to the effects of disease, repeated population loss would exert a considerable influence on the existing scale of supracommunity organization. For instance, the loss of the support population for the elite individuals in Caddoan society would be reflected in a general decline or collapse of the civic-ceremonial system and those facilities that constitute integrative mechanisms (e.g., Knight 1986).

The elements of the archaeological record that can inform us about processes of integration in past societies are those that indicate social differentiation and complexity—in other words, that provide evidence of social ranking in economic, sociopolitical, and ceremonial spheres. There are two principal means of inferring details of social organization and complexity from the archaeological record: (1) by studying mortuary practices, and (2) by examining hierarchical organization, in this case, the hierarchy of settlements or site types within regional Caddoan settlement systems.

Thus, I examined burial assemblages from the Caddoan area dating to the period between A.D. 1520 and 1800 for systemic changes in social differentiation, especially vertical differentiation (Perttula 1989:152–164, 260–284). The factors of particular concern were the diversity of grave offerings, the spatial segregation of the individuals, the inclusion of valued symbols and trappings of authority, and differences in the treatment of the burial (i.e., mode and place of interment).

Hierarchical systems in the archaeological record of the Caddoan area are identified by the presence of civic-ceremonial centers and supralocal or multicommunity cemeteries. Both of these elements occur in the Caddoan archaeological record beginning ca. A.D. 900 (see Jeter et al. 1989; Story 1990), but it is their later manifestations that are important in the present context.

Civic-ceremonial centers are manifestations of a highly developed system of

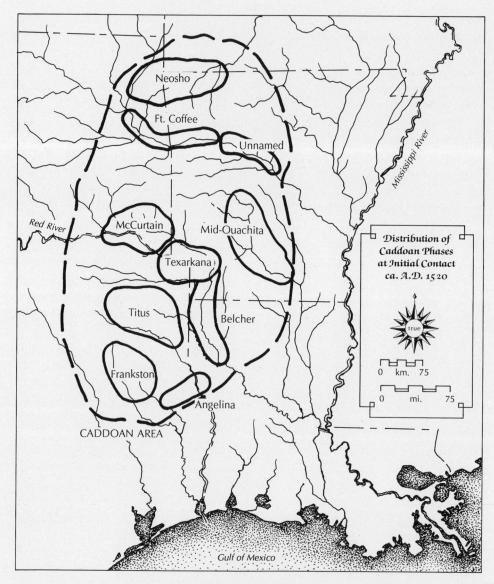

Figure 25–3. The distribution of Caddoan phases at initial contact, ca. A.D. 1520.

ceremonial activity among Caddoan peoples (Story 1990:339–342). The construction of specialized facilities such as platform mounds, public buildings, plazas, and charnel houses at civic-ceremonial centers are assumed to represent expressions of a regional and centralized sociopolitical structure, one that was maintained by an elite group of individuals to sanctify chiefly authority, political power, ritual, and supernatural prerogatives of the community (Knight 1986:681).

Supralocal or community cemeteries are a related manifestation of a specialized structural context that is based upon social differences within a population (e.g., Story 1990:339). They are recognized by type of burial interment, cemetery size (usually more than 70 individuals), diverse and elaborate grave-good associations in the case of some individuals, and isolation from habitation sites, characteristics that can be duplicated in a civic-ceremonial context. Such cemeteries were presumably used by more than one community, and may have had a longer duration of use than the family or community subgroup cemeteries.

These types of supracommunity organization would, under demographic conditions of population decline, be replaced by newer and more viable forms of political and social integration. New ascendant and functional forms of social integration that might arise from the collapse or abandonment of the civic-ceremonial system during the early phase of European contact would include confederation and annexation (Knight 1986:683).

Unfortunately, the local and regional settlement data for the Caddoan area are somewhat biased because of previous emphasis on the excavation of cemeteries and mounds to the exclusion of obtaining archaeological data from associated settlements, or of acquiring intra- and intersite information on site structure and community organization (e.g., Story 1990:346–355). Sampling problems of this nature, therefore, obviate the consideration of quantitative differences in settlement frequencies through time.

The dispersed nature of Caddoan settlement systems and the presumed short occupation of hamlets and farmsteads makes it difficult to conduct the type of demographic analyses employed in other parts of North America that have relied on quantitative differences in settlement frequencies through time (e.g., Ramenofsky 1987b; Smith 1987). Therefore, inferences about population or settlement change in the Caddoan area must be made at the regional scale.

Regional differences in population densities at initial contact are expected to be variably affected by epidemic diseases introduced by Europeans, owing to the settlement character of upland/rural communities versus major riverine town communities (Perttula 1989:67–70), as well as their location relative to communication axes (Ramenofsky 1990). The higher the relative population density at initial contact, the more rapid and pervasive the processes of depopulation, since those groups with the highest populations would be the ones most adversely affected by European diseases. Denser populations and some settlement compaction at, or near, the civic-ceremonial centers of the A.D. 1520 Caddoan town communities suggest that the most apparent effects of population decline would be concentrated there, regardless of any overall regional trends in depopulation.

Ewers (1973:109) has argued that only rarely did a Caddoan group size fall below about 150 people before it merged or coalesced with another group. This minimum group size was probably an attempt to maintain stable population levels and population fertility within the group. Once the labor and defense forces were reduced by the effects of the European diseases, amalgamation would begin to take place. As amalgamation of population groups continued, original settlement areas could be expected to be abandoned and the areas where the population remnants amalgamated might actually be represented as a local population increase, at least over the short term.

Summary of the Archaeological Record, ca. A.D. 1520–1680

The following summary of the Caddoan area archaeological record by region for the period between ca. A.D. 1520 and 1680 is derived from a recent review (Perttula 1989:126–210), as well as from pertinent sections of the U.S. Army Corps of Engineers' Southwestern Division Overview (Story et al. 1990; Jeter et al. 1989:233–239). Figure 25–3 shows the distribution of Caddoan cultural phases at ca. A.D. 1520.

In terms of broad categories of mortuary and community behavior, some similar features can be seen in the A.D. 1520–1680 archaeological record for both the East Texas and the Ouachita Mountains regions of the Western Caddoan area. For example, both mound construction and shaft burials are discontinued shortly after the middle of the sixteenth century (Figure 25–4).

There is no evidence that other forms of community sociopolitical integration evolved in the latter part of the Late Caddoan period in the Ouachita Mountains to replace the civic-ceremonial centers. Indeed, there is little in the archaeological record to indicate that the Ouachita Mountains or adjacent Coastal Plain were permanently inhabited after ca. A.D. 1600 except in widely separated locales (e.g., Burnett and Murray 1990; Early 1988). In these areas, significant changes in settlement or sociopolitical complexity seem to have been restricted primarily to the seventeenth century.

The discontinuation of mound construction in East Texas was generally contemporaneous with the formation of community cemetery centers, and with the possible short-lived utilization of deep shaft burials at nonmound centers, until ca. A.D. 1650 (Thurmond 1985, 1990). Temporal differences in mortuary behavior imply a decrease in the overall complexity of community organization, followed by the localization and persistence of rural community systems in only a few areas within East Texas.

The archaeological record for the Central Caddoan area of the Red River Basin during the period A.D. 1520–1680 was examined for evidence of civic-ceremonial and mortuary behavior, and how it changed through time. In this area, mound construction and mound shaft burial interments reflect a hierarchical sociopolitical community structure only until ca. A.D. 1650. In the McCurtain and Saratoga phases (see Figure 25–3), this hierarchical structure does not continue past A.D. 1550, and evidently went through several phases of reorganization in the Great Bend region of the Red River, and through the Belcher phase, before being discontinued.

After the last periods of mound construction, the Little River drainage was apparently abandoned. All other areas exhibit some settlement in the form of small hamlets or farmsteads, community cemeteries as intrusive burials in nonfunctioning structural mounds, and evidence that settlement was restricted to widely separated locales within what had once been continuously and densely populated regions (the Belcher, Texarkana, and McCurtain phases) (Perttula 1989:Figure 5–6). This type of regional settlement coalescence is consistent with a diminished population during this period.

In the Northern Caddoan area, post-A.D. 1520 sites are restricted to only a few

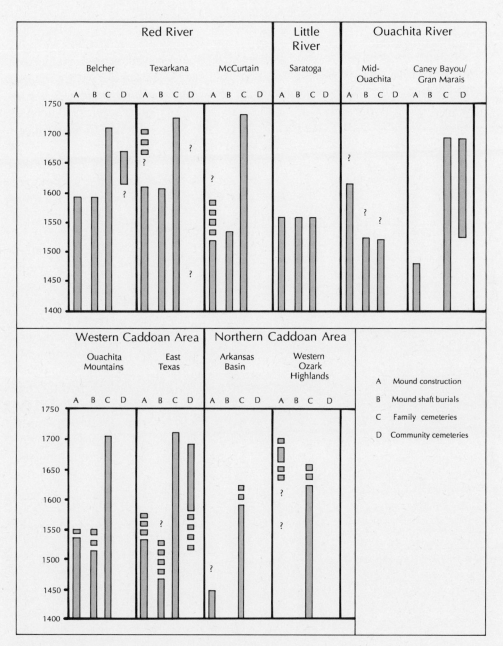

Figure 25–4. Temporal trends in the archaeological record.

locales, most notably the Arkansas Basin Fort Coffee phase in Eastern Oklahoma. Radiocarbon dates and ceramic associations from the Fort Coffee phase suggest that most of the area was abandoned shortly after A.D. 1520. Trends in seasonal settlement mobility noted in the Fort Coffee phase (Rohrbaugh 1984) prior to European contact culminated in the abandonment of the area within a hundred years of initial indirect contact.

The historic Caddoan archaeological record (A.D. 1680–1860) in the Caddoan area indicates that only certain Caddoan communities continued into the ethnographically recorded historic period (see Gregory 1973; Perttula 1989:211–327). However, these communities existed within general areas of territorial continuity carried over from the period dating between ca. A.D. 1520 and 1680. The areas of settlement were greatly contracted in space, but local amalgamation and patterns of valley abandonment initiated during earlier episodes of European contact and interaction were already more or less established by the time of direct European contact.

Summary

The period between A.D. 1520 and 1680 precedes sustained European contact with Caddoan peoples of the Trans-Mississippi South. Changes in aboriginal adaptations that occurred during this time are not mentioned in archival records or ethnographic observations, but must be documented and studied from the Caddoan archaeological record. Qualitative differences in sociopolitical and community-wide aspects of Caddoan lifeways provide a means of characterizing A.D. 1520–1680 Caddoan group or phase differences as they relate to inferred population loss from disease, settlement movements, and systemic changes in social and political organization.

By the time of sustained European contact ca. A.D. 1680, large parts of the Caddoan area had apparently been abandoned. Along the major streams such as the Arkansas, Red, and Ouachita rivers, abandonment seems to have occurred between ca. A.D. 1600 and the first substantial face-to-face European contact. This abandonment involved some movement of groups, as well as the coalescence with other Caddoan groups that lived mainly in major riverine settlements along the Red River.

In East Texas and the Ouachita Mountains, the archaeology of Caddoan rural communities is indicative of changes in sociopolitical complexity, accompanied by a localization of community systems, similar to the record in the Red River Valley. In the Ouachita Mountains, moreover, it appears that most of the mountains were not permanently inhabited after A.D. 1600.

Relatively specific changes in the nature of Caddoan community organization have been noted in the Cypress Creek/Upper Sabine archaeological records (Perttula 1989:134–164). Examples of nonmound shaft burials and isolated community cemeteries associated with distinct spatial groups (Thurmond 1985) were identified as manifestations of sociopolitical integration which replaced mound centers. Both the community cemeteries and the nonmound shaft burials are short-lived phenomena, lasting in the archaeological record until ca. A.D. 1650.

Therefore, although processes of regional abandonment and possible depopulation affected East Texas and Western Caddoan populations, the fact that community reintegration occurred suggests that initially depopulation was not as severe among rural Caddoan communities as it was along the major river valleys. That the Sabine, Neches, and Angelina River basins in East Texas appear to have had a higher density of early historic and post-A.D. 1680 settlements than was the case on the major rivers (see Story 1990:346–355) also suggests a greater depopulation in large riverine town communities than in rural Caddoan communities following European contact. Even in the areas where rural Caddoan communities predominated, the occupations are more scattered than they were ca. A.D. 1520, with many of the small river valleys unoccupied or with a smaller overall population. Even after ca. A.D. 1700, however, the Caddoan populations in East Texas were larger than were the Kadohadacho and the Natchitoches on the Red River (see Figure 25–2).

Future Directions

One promising avenue of research for archaeologists interested in Caddoan lifeways in the period after A.D. 1520 would be to examine the context of Late Caddoan period settlement-subsistence strategies for information on at least relative population sizes or settlement densities within each of the regions and river basins. Existing cultural patterns at contact would certainly provide clues to indicate how these Caddoan groups responded to new circumstances. Depending on precontact population sizes in particular regions; the size, nature, and distribution of settlement networks; communication networks; and the position of the remaining population clusters—each region within the Caddoan area would have been affected differentially by European contact, interaction, and the attendant population declines. Therefore, settlement relocation, abandonment, and aggregation may not all have taken place within each of the regions and river valleys. To ascertain why some regions were abandoned and never reoccupied, whereas others served as a focus for the coalescence and integration of disparate groups, it is essential also to know more about prehistoric settlement sizes, the minimum number of people that was necessary to maintain an integrated and coherent entity given projected subsistence strategies, and the dynamics of the agglomeration process.

It would also be important to obtain ordinal-scale measurements of Caddoan populations in particular regions and temporal intervals in the Late Caddoan and Historic Caddoan period archaeological records. Because Caddoan settlements are usually dispersed, site-survey programs (see Fish and Kowalewski 1990) should be designed specifically to locate evidence of post-A.D. 1520 Caddoan occupations. Only in this way will it be possible to obtain quantifiable estimates of site and population density within specific parameters.

A reliable, fine-scale chronological framework for post-A.D. 1520 Caddoan sites is also needed. Certainly, it would be possible to construct quite detailed chronological frameworks at some known sites, but these are typically cemetery assemblages. The existing chronological framework needs to be extended to contemporaneous habitation sites and midden mounds, particularly in the case of the Historic Caddoan archaeological record, since only a handful of habitation locales have been thoroughly examined (see Story 1990). Until we have chronological samples from a series of post-A.D. 1520 sites within different regions of the Caddoan area, we will be unable to deal with basic questions of settlement and sociopolitical change in anything less than intervals of 100 to 150 years.

Future studies also need to expand upon three different but complementary types of data: (1) Spanish, French, and American archival and documentary records; (2) the archaeological record of the fur trade; and (3) paleodemographic and bioarchaeological investigations. Taken together, these various measures would vastly improve our understanding of the relationships between the European newcomers and the Native Americans living in the Caddoan area.

Acknowledgments

I wish to thank Ann Ramenofsky, Robert Dunnell, and Ann Early for their comments on earlier versions of this essay, and Jim Bruseth for engaging discussions about the Caddoan contact archaeological record. I am also indebted to my wife, Cecile, for her assistance along the way, and to Nancy Reese for timely computer guidance.

References

Brain, J. P.
  1985 Introduction: Update of de Soto Studies since the United States De Soto Expedition Commission Report. In *Final Report of the United States De Soto Expedition Commission*, by J. R. Swanton, pp. xi—lxxii. Classics in Anthropology Series, Smithsonian Institution Press, Washington, D.C.
Burnett, B. A., and K. Murray
  1990 Biological Effects of the *Entrada* of the De Soto Expedition in Arkansas. Paper presented at the "De Soto in Caddo Country" symposium, sponsored by the University of Arkansas, University Museum, March 29–30, 1990. Fayetteville.
Corbin, J. E.
  1989 Spanish—Indian Interaction on the Eastern Frontier of Texas. In *Columbian Consequences*, vol. 1, *Archaeological and Historical Perspectives on the Spanish Borderlands West*, edited by D. H. Thomas, pp. 269–276. Smithsonian Institution Press, Washington, D.C.
Crosby, A. W.
  1986 *Ecological Imperialism: The Biological Expansion of Europe, 900–1900*. Cambridge University Press, Cambridge.
Deagan, K.
  1985 Spanish—Indian Interaction in Sixteenth-Century Florida and Hispaniola. In *Cultures in Contact: The Impact of European Contacts on Native American Cultural Institutions, A.D. 1000–1800*, edited by W. W. Fitzhugh, pp. 281–318. Smithsonian Institution Press, Washington, D.C.
Dobyns, H. F.
  1983 *Their Number Become Thinned: Native American Population Dynamics in Eastern North America*. University of Tennessee Press, Knoxville.
Early, A. M.
  1988 *Standridge: Caddoan Settlement in a Mountain Environment*. Arkansas Archeological Survey, Research Series No. 29. Fayetteville.
Ewers, J. C.
  1973 The Influence of Epidemics on the Indian Populations and Cultures of Texas. *Plains Anthropologist* 18:104–115.
Fish, S. K., and S. A. Kowalewski (editors)

1990 *The Archaeology of Regions: A Case for Full-Coverage Survey*. Smithsonian Institution Press, Washington, D.C.

Gregory, H. F.
1973 *Eighteenth Century Caddoan Archaeology: A Study in Models and Interpretation*. Ph.D. dissertation, Southern Methodist University, Dallas.

Henige, D.
1986 Primary Source by Primary Source? On the Role of Epidemics in New World Depopulation. *Ethnohistory* 33:293–312.

Jeter, M. D., J. C. Rose, G. I. Williams, and A. M. Harmon
1989 *Archeology and Bioarcheology of the Lower Mississippi Valley and Trans-Mississippi South in Arkansas and Louisiana*. Arkansas Archeological Survey, Research Series No. 37. Fayetteville.

Knight, V. J.
1986 The Institutional Organization of Mississippian Religion. *American Antiquity* 51:675–687.

Mooney, J.
1928 *The Aboriginal Population of America North of Mexico*, edited by J. R. Swanton. Smithsonian Miscellaneous Collections, Volume 80(7). Washington, D.C.

Perttula, T. K.
1989 *Contact and Interaction between Caddoan and European Peoples: The Historic Archaeological and Ethnohistorical Records*. Ph.D. dissertation, University of Washington, Seattle.
1990 The Long-term Consequences and Effects of the Entrada on Aboriginal Caddoan Populations. Paper presented at the "De Soto in Caddo Country" symposium, sponsored by the University of Arkansas, University Museum, March 29–30, 1990. Fayetteville.

Quinn, D. B. (editor)
1979 *New American World: A Documentary History of North America to 1612*, vol. 2, *Major Spanish Searches in Eastern North America: Franco-Spanish Clash in Florida. The Beginnings of Spanish Florida*, and vol. 5, *The Extension of Settlement in Florida, Virginia, and the Spanish Southwest*. Arno Press, New York.

Ramenofsky, A. F.
1982 *The Archaeology of Population Collapse: Native American Response to the Introduction of Infectious Disease*. Ph.D. dissertation, University of Washington, Seattle.
1985 The Introduction of European Disease and the Aboriginal Population Collapse. *Mississippi Archaeologist* 20:2–18.
1987a Diffusion of Disease at European Contact. Paper presented at the 52nd Annual Meeting of the Society for American Archaeology, Toronto.
1987b *Vectors of Death: The Archaeology of European Contact*. The University of New Mexico Press, Albuquerque.
1990 Loss of Innocence: Explanations of Differential Persistence in the Sixteenth-Century Southeast. In *Columbian Consequences: Archaeological and Historical Perspectives on the Spanish Borderlands East*, vol. 2, edited by D. H. Thomas, pp. 27–43. Smithsonian Institution Press, Washington, D.C.

Rohrbaugh, C. L.
1984 Arkansas Valley Caddoan: Fort Coffee Focus and Neosho Focus. In *Prehistory of Oklahoma*, edited by R. E. Bell, pp. 265–285. Academic Press, New York.

Smith, M. T.
1987 *Archaeology of Aboriginal Culture Change in the Interior Southeast: Depopulation during the Early Historic Period*. University of Florida Press, Gainesville.

Steponaitis, V. P.
1986 Prehistoric Archaeology in the Southeastern United States, 1970–1985. *Annual Reviews in Anthropology* 15:363–404.

Steward, J. H.
1954 Theory and Application in a Social Science. *Ethnohistory* 1:292–302.

Story, D. A.
   1990 Culture History of the Native Americans. In *The Archeology and Bioarcheology of the Gulf Coastal Plain*, by D. A. Story et al., pp. 163–366. Arkansas Archeological Survey, Research Series No. 38. Fayetteville.
Swanton, J. R.
   1939 Final Report of the United States De Soto Expedition Commission. 76th Congress, 1st Session, H.R. 71.
   1942 *Source Material on the History and Ethnology of the Caddo Indians*. Bureau of American Ethnology, Bulletin No. 132. Washington, D.C.
Thomas, D. H. (editor)
   1989 *Columbian Consequences*, vol. 1, *Archaeological and Historical Perspectives on the Spanish Borderlands West*. Smithsonian Institution Press, Washington, D.C.
Thornton, R.
   1987 *American Indian Holocaust and Survival: A Population History since 1492*. University of Oklahoma Press, Norman.
Thurmond, J. P.
   1985 Late Caddoan Social Group Identifications and Sociopolitical Organization in the Upper Cypress Basin and Its Vicinity, Northeastern Texas. *Bulletin of the Texas Archeological Society* 54:185–200.
   1990 Was the Cypress Cluster One of the (Many) Victims of the 1539–1543 De Soto Expedition? *Caddoan Archeology Newsletter* I(3).
Trigger, B. G.
   1983 American Archaeology as Native History: A Review Essay. *William and Mary Quarterly* 40:413–452.
   1985 *Natives and Newcomers: Canada's 'Heroic Age' Reconsidered*. McGill-Queen's University Press, Montreal.
Vehik, S. C.
   1989 Problems and Potential in Plains Indian Demography. In *Plains Indian Historical Demography and Health: Perspectives, Interpretations, and Critiques*, edited by G. R. Campbell, pp. 115–125. Plains Anthropologist 34(124), Part 2, Memoir 23. Lincoln, Nebr.

Chapter 26 ■

David E. Stannard

The Consequences of Contact: Toward an Interdisciplinary Theory of Native Responses to Biological and Cultural Invasion

While word has yet to trickle down to the authors of most history textbooks it has been at least two decades since the relevant scholarly communities recognized that the so-called New World, on the eve of Western contact in the fifteenth and sixteenth centuries, contained at least as many people as were living in Europe, including Russia, at that time. Just *how* large that New World population was remains a matter of much dispute, beyond the common acknowledgment that it was many times greater than earlier writers had believed. There is little doubt, however, that the New World's enormous population of perhaps 80 to 100 million persons—and maybe more—suffered a sudden and catastrophic collapse that began almost immediately upon European contact.

A rule of thumb, worked out in the 1960s by anthropologist Henry F. Dobyns, has held that, on average, a depopulation ratio of at least 20:1, from the time of first contact to the date of population nadir, fairly accurately describes the de-

---

Editor's Note: The Anglicized spelling of Hawaii has been used throughout this series, although the preference of individual authors may be the Hawaiian spelling: Hawai'i.

mographic fate of America's indigenous people (Dobyns 1966:415). Nadir—or, the bottoming out of the population decline trajectory—conventionally seems to have been reached a little more than a century after contact, and the ratio, of course, represents the contrast between the number of people living in a given place at the time of contact and the number surviving once nadir is reached. Thus, if Dobyns's supposition is correct, most of the Americas' native population groups—those, at least, that were not driven to extinction—suffered 95 percent or greater decline rates within five to six generations following Western contact.

When first propounded, Dobyns's overall decline ratio was greeted in many quarters with unexamined disbelief. In time, as acceptance grew, it suffered a different unexamined fate: It was used as an indiscriminate retrospective short-hand to calculate quickly the probable precontact indigenous population in a given region, regardless of local circumstances. Although in many cases a 95 percent or greater decline rate did indeed fit the available facts, most serious an-thropological and historical demographers (including Dobyns) recognized that, as with all averages, the round figure tended to conceal extremes. To begin with, decline ratios cannot be used at all when the nadir reached is zero, that is, in those circumstances when New World populations declined by 100 percent and thus became extinct. In addition, inland and coastal populations generally suf-fered drastically different proportional declines; in the Andes, for example, one researcher has calculated a 50–year decline rate of greater than 98 percent in coastal areas versus a rate of about 71 percent in the highlands (Smith 1970:459). While the "average" decline rate in the Andes thus might be put at approximately 85 percent, such a figure would totally misrepresent what actually happened to both the coastal and the highland peoples in this area. This is seen even more dramatically if the decline *ratio* is used in place of the decline *rate*, since a 98 percent decline rate equals a decline ratio of 58:1, whereas a 71 percent decline rate equals a decline ratio of less than 4:1.

Some of the most detailed recent research on Postcolumbian population de-clines suggests that similarly wide variations in depopulation rates and ratios within the boundaries of conventionally defined political and geographic locales may be more the norm than the exception. Although what might be called "Dobyns's law" of a 95 percent or greater overall decline tends to hold up well as a general *hemispheric* estimate, it is now plainly apparent that the Postcolumbian fates of *individual* native societies varied across an extremely wide spectrum and that future advancement in this field is going to require the use of more finely tuned instruments trained on a broader array of data. Dobyns himself has recognized this; hence, his research in the early 1980s turned to a detailed study of disease and depopulation in sixteenth- and seventeenth-century Florida (Dobyns 1983). But it is an undeniable paradox that at precisely the moment when scholars in this field might expect to be building, as Ann F. Ramenofsky has put it, a "theory, or system of knowledge, that unites research efforts and directs inquiry" (Ramenofsky 1990:31), they are in fact finding that even relatively low-level and long-lived hypotheses are not immune to chal-lenges that are arising from increasingly sophisticated research.

Moreover, although Ramenofsky, as an archaeologist, joins others in her discipline by noting her concurrence with a 35–year-old observation by Julian Steward that "archaeological data are the primary data for determining the nature and magnitude of Native American change in the postcontact period" (1990:44), in truth it is becoming increasingly evident that no single discipline holds the key to understanding this subject. As research efforts deepen and prior generalizations begin to unravel or to reveal hitherto unseen complexities, it is clear that scholars in this field increasingly will have to turn for assistance to specialists in other disciplines. The remainder of this essay is devoted to an assessment of some of the problems that need to be addressed by interdisciplinary scholarship on this topic in the future, an assessment that concludes with a look at recent and ongoing research in Hawaii that is of comparative cross-cultural relevance to research in the Americas.

Rates of Population Collapse

At first, the apparent dissolving of hard-earned and generally accepted hypotheses may be discouraging, at least to those archaeologists and historians in search of an overarching theory to guide analyses of Postcolumbian population decline and/or persistence, but in fact it is a sign of strength and advancement in the field. Consider as an example the well-established observation that in Mexico and Central America (and elsewhere as well) not only did coastal and lowland populations collapse earlier and more rapidly than highland populations, but that coastal and lowland populations also were the first to begin to recover (Cook and Borah 1960:53). Two assiduous studies published in recent years examine this proposition in passing. And, although their findings differ on this specific point—that is, the generalization holds in one case, but not in the other—in the process both studies greatly enlarge and deepen knowledge in the general area of inquiry, thus leading the field closer to a defined body of questions that need to be pursued before any general theory can be responsibly advanced.

Take the most recent of these studies first, a close analysis of colonial Sierra Zapoteca in southern Mexico by John K. Chance. Overall, the region appears to have suffered a 94 percent population decline between contact in 1520 and nadir about 80 years later—close to the figure that would be predicted using Dobyns's rule of thumb. (At least two dozen of the area's communities also became extinct during this time.) Throughout these years, the magnitude of decline was substantially greater in the region's lowland areas, such as Chinantec—again, as would be predicted; but in at least some of these lowland locales the decline was not arrested for nearly two centuries, whereas in the highland areas—although the steepest declines commenced there later than in the lowlands, as would be expected—recovery began earlier than in most of the lowlands, as would not be anticipated (Chance 1989:46–88).

Now, while some—those in search of a unified theory—might find this exception to the Cook-Borah hypothesis disappointing, Chance's investigation in fact furthers that quest by raising a number of questions that need to be folded into the search for a larger system of knowledge. The relationship between soil productivity and pre- and postcontact settlement patterns, for instance, appears crucial in explaining this area's intraregional differences in historical demography (1989:72), as does the connection between topography and degree of successful armed resistance to Spanish invasion (1989:16–20). Moreover, the rapidity of population decline in the years immediately following first contact, despite the small numbers of Spaniards or Africans in the region and their virtual absence from some areas that suffered drastic early declines, lends strength to the still-controversial idea that devastating diseases brought to the Americas by European explorers, adventurers, and colonists spread with great speed among their New World hosts and commonly preceded the actual European penetration of particular locales, thus laying waste to entire populations well before they were even seen by their would-be conquerors (Chance 1989:68; cf. Ramenofsky 1987).

In colonial Nicaragua, to take the second example, the so-called Mesoamerican zone suffered a depopulation rate two and a half times that of its neighboring South American zone during the first half of the sixteenth century. Conversely, during the second half of that century, the South American zone declined in population at a nearly 50 percent greater rate than did the Mesoamerican zone. By the time population nadir was reached in the seventeenth century, the overall regional decline ratio was 13.5:1, or 93 percent, with the Mesoamerican zone suffering a greater than 24:1 decline ratio (or 96 percent decline) and the South American zone a 5.6:1 decline ratio (82 percent). Why the differential? Much of the answer, as would be expected, lies in the lowland locale of the Mesoamerican zone and in the not coincidental fact that in precontact times the Mesoamerican zone was much more densely populated than the South American zone. Although this finding is hardly surprising, the explanatory details behind it suggest the complex array of interrelationships that undergird the conventional lowland/highland hypothesis and raise a host of questions that are relevant to research in other parts of the Americas as well. As Linda A. Newson points out:

> The large concentrations of Indians in the Pacific lowlands [of the Mesoamerican zone] constituted the major attraction for Spaniards. It was in this area, therefore, that towns were founded and encomiendas granted within their jurisdictions. In these areas contact between Spaniards and Indians was greatest, with the result that here the Indians suffered most from overwork and ill-treatment and their communities experienced the most profound economic and social changes. Spanish demands for tribute and labor put strains on the Indian economy, leading to food shortages and famines and increasing the susceptibility of the Indians to deadly Old World diseases. Population losses in their turn led to social disorganization, which together with the psychological impact of conquest and colonization contributed to a lowering of the fertility rate. The larger concentrations of Indians in the Mesoamerican zone also made the area the most attractive for slaving activities [Newson 1987:337].

As for the predictably more rapid rate of decline in the South American zone during the second half of the sixteenth century, Newson attributes it to "the greater intensity of contacts between the Indians and other races [Africans as well as Europeans], resulting in the widespread introduction of Old World diseases and the beginnings of profound cultural change" (1987:338). In short, in the second half of the century the South American zone experienced the shock of first contact that the Mesoamerican zone had suffered earlier, but it was shock mitigated by a lower existing population density; thus, because of its comparative scarcity of people in relation to land area, the South American zone was a far less fertile field for the spread of disease, for the exacting of tribute, and for colonial labor exploitation. Finally, unlike southern Mexico's Sierra Zapoteca, Nicaragua's lowland Mesoamerican zone—which, as already mentioned, had experienced a dramatically higher rate of depopulation than the highland South American zone during the early Colonial period—also recovered earlier and more rapidly, thereby fitting the Cook-Borah hypothesis (1987:336).

Carrying Capacity and "Standard Populations"

With just these two studies, then, it is apparent that a great many factors must be entered into any formulas for generalizing about the magnitude of the precontact population and subsequent population decline, whether under colonial rule or in the absence of political conquest. In addition to those factors just touched on—topography, soil productivity, settlement pattern, population density, and the intents and actions of the invading forces—information on the native peoples' range of food resources, mode of subsistence, labor output and caloric requirements, climate, preexisting disease load (among both invader and invaded populations), and the nature of indigenous culture and political organization make up just some of what ideally must be known if a given indigenous peoples' precontact population magnitude and their susceptibility to demographic catastrophe are to be gauged.

The matters of topography, climate, soil and other resource productivity, mode of subsistence, and labor output and caloric requirements are central to estimating thoroughly the carrying capacity of a given area––and here, although archaeology is of course essential, ethnographic and geographic research will greatly enrich our knowledge. For far too long estimates of carrying capacity have been forced to rely on relatively crude and general person-land ratios that may or may not be appropriate in specific locales, or they have had to depend on comparative data from other regions and/or early postcontact estimates of cultivated land-population ratios by missionaries or settlers (see, e.g., Feacham 1973; Street 1969; cf. Dewar 1984). In some cases, this remains the best that can be done, because of severely limited precontact data; for more than a decade, however, an alternative method of carrying-capacity analysis (the so-called standard population approach) has been available for historical demographic use.

The standard population approach goes to the heart of a key problem in carrying-capacity analysis—that is, the tendency of observed preindustrial agricultural societies to rarely attain population magnitudes or densities in excess of 50 to 60 percent of apparent carrying capacity, given available resources and level of technology. Unlike conventional carrying-capacity approaches, standard population models factor in such subjective variables as culturally preferred work-leisure ratios and surplus production for status or exchange purposes

(Bailiss-Smith 1978, 1980:esp. 70–76). This approach builds on top of a foundation of more objective data regarding soil, climate, and so on, and is, of course, inappropriate in situations of greatly limited data on ecological, cultural, and social matters. Nevertheless, there are numerous examples of historical communities that are susceptible to this approach, and in the future it should be more frequently employed in analyzing likely precontact population magnitudes and densities. Moreover, it should not be supposed that the standard population approach invariably will reduce precontact population estimates. On the contrary, despite its consideration of factors responsible for holding population levels well below carrying capacity maximums, much research in this field (which thus far is heavily concentrated on island populations) has revealed that those maximums themselves were much higher than conventionally believed.

Population Density and the Spread of Disease

Density of population, as noted earlier, has long been recognized as a fundamental element in assessing a community's vulnerability to introduced disease: Higher densities provide greater opportunity for microbes to spread from source to recipient, increasing the likelihood of epidemic infection (see Haggett 1975). This was a problem in Old World societies from the rise of proto-urban centers millennia ago down through the nineteenth century. Almost without exception, urban centers in the West during that time were so disease-ridden that they required constant in-migration from less densely populated rural areas merely to maintain their population size (McNeill 1979:96; Mols 1973:49; Stannard, 1991). Without the immunity-conferring disease history of the Old World, New World urban centers in Mexico and Peru became firestorms of disease epidemics following Western contact. However, most work in contact-era historical demography is no longer focused on those New World urban centers and it is now recognized that an elementary understanding of the density-disease phenomenon is insufficient for analyzing a variety of demographic situations.

While acknowledging, as she puts it, that "the spatial distribution of people promotes or retards the spread of pathogens," Ann Ramenofsky has constructed a more complex model that expands that truism by integrating it with two categories of settlement *type* (sedentary or mobile), two categories of settlement *form* (nucleated or dispersed), and three categories of settlement *location* (navigable drainage; secondary drainage; or removed from axis of communication) (Ramenofsky 1990:41–43). The resulting matrix is a cross-index of 12 classes of settlement description ranging in extremes from sedentary nucleated settlements located in close proximity to navigable-drainage axes of communication (highest likely disease impact) to mobile dispersed settlements that are well removed from axes of communication (lowest likely disease impact). This is an important advance because, as Ramenofsky observes:

> If the model is at all successful, we will have the beginning of a coherent body of archaeological knowledge that can explain why there was differential persistence from disease, why for instance, the Creek or Choctaw survive in a modified state,

but the Quapaw become extinct. Although this classification will not answer all questions related to demographic or cultural change during the Columbian period, it will anchor other, more sophisticated, investigations by building a description of settlement that is comparable across space. Such a description is crucial if we ever want to get beyond impressionistic statements or archaeological stories about what we think was occurring rather than what was actually occurring [1990:43].

To be sure, as Ramenofsky herself notes, there are questions internal to her model that remain unsettled. For instance, she hypothesizes that contagion risk was higher among sedentary peoples (presumably because of their predictably greater density of population) than among mobile peoples, but she acknowledges that this assumption may be compromised to a certain extent because of the countervailing factor that mobile people were more likely to come into contact with other infected populations (1990:41). Moreover, the general hypothesis, or its opposite, may hold in some situations but not in others owing to such variables as overall regional population density (and thus the prospects for intersettlement contacts), the presence or absence of nonhuman disease vectors, and the specific nature of the existing disease load. Nevertheless, Ramenofsky has opened a new approach to this aspect of population/depopulation inquiry that cannot help but refine analysis, extend knowledge, and build toward the larger theoretical framework that she seeks.

Pandemics and the Question of Migration

Part of that larger theoretical framework will have to address at least several other important controversies that show little sign of resolution in the near future. The first of these is the debate over the extent to which nearly simultaneous but isolated outbreaks of the same apparent disease among Native Americans in the sixteenth century—that is, in the Postcolumbian era, but before many tribes had direct contact with Europeans—can be taken as evidence of European-originated regional or even continent-wide pandemics. Dobyns has been most closely associated with this hypothesis, as advanced in his 1983 study, *Their Number Become Thinned*, and in more recent work as well (e.g., 1989a), but Ramenofsky (1987), Smith (1987), and others have subsequently contributed to its veracity. Still others remain adamant in their resistance—for instance, David Henige (1986, 1989) and Dean R. Snow and Kim M. Lanphear (1988, 1989).

Needless to say, the implications of this debate for assessing both precontact population levels and postcontact population decline are enormous. For the moment, the most judicious assessment is probably Ramenofsky's: There is good evidence to support the so-called sixteenth-century hypothesis in numerous locales, she notes, but "until we have descriptions of the archaeological record developed according to these guidelines [i.e., probability-based regional samples of settlements and finer-grained chronologies], the question of a sixteenth century collapse must remain open" (Ramenofsky 1987:174).

As the search for more and better archaeological evidence proceeds, however, care must be taken to ascertain, if possible, whether an apparent population decline in a given area was in fact the result of a high death rate or simply migration—migration that could be a secondary consequence of epidemic disease, of political or military depredation, or of changing climatic or other environmental circumstances. Nearly two decades ago, Nicolas Sanchez-Albornoz warned that evidence of Peruvian Indian flight to avoid the encomenderos and corregidores was possibly being confused historically with disease-induced depopulation (Sanchez-Albornoz 1974:104). More recently, Ann M. Wightman (1990) has examined and greatly extended this observation.

To further complicate matters, it must be remembered that archaeological hypotheses that mistake population movement for population decline can have the effect of underestimating as well as overestimating postcontact population collapse, since migrations obviously add population to some areas at the same time that they reduce populations in other areas. If, therefore, an area under study happened to have been the *recipient* of out-migrants from another area, the error could result in a gross *under*estimate of population loss in the host community—as we now know indeed happened in parts of Peru when "the reassessment of Indian migrants and their reincorporation into official population totals following the epidemics of 1719–21 lessened the official population loss throughout that period of dramatic demographic decline and actually increased the size of the available *tributario-mitayo* pool by the early eighteenth century" (Wightman 1990:73).

Precontact Native Diseases

In addition to taking great care in sorting out disease- and migration-induced population changes in both the precontact and postcontact eras, future scholarship in this area needs to pay close attention to delineating, as precisely as possible, the preexisting disease loads of both the intruder and native communities at the time of contact.

With the exception of syphilis, there is little debate concerning the overall suite of diseases that the European explorers and settlers brought with them to the New World. In certain cases, it also is relevant to explore the question of African diseases, since Africans sometimes accompanied the European troops and the two continents' disease histories differed greatly—thus the European characterization of colonial Africa as the "white man's grave." Indeed, as historian Kenneth F. Kiple has shown, it was the whipsaw of European *and* African diseases that was a major factor in the virtual extinction of most Caribbean island peoples (Kiple 1984:9–12). However, the most prominent controversies surround the presence or absence of specific diseases among the Precolumbian New World peoples. Although it has long been held that there was a general absence of so-called crowd type pathogens in the Americas, such as smallpox, typhoid fever, yellow fever, measles, plague, diphtheria, influenza, mumps, chicken pox, and malaria (Newman 1976), evidence does exist suggesting the presence of both nonvenereal treponemal infection (which is related to syphilis) and tuberculosis in parts of the Precolumbian Americas. Since histories of these diseases *could* have established some unspecified level of immunity among the native peoples, knowledge of whether or not they were in fact afflicted by them prior to Western contact plays a large part in estimating the potential population loss that those diseases might have caused following the European invasion.

The evidence regarding these diseases in the Precolumbian Americas is primarily osteological. And osteological analyses often are far from precise. First, skeletal damage from one pathology may mimic other pathologies. For example, both yaws and acute osteomyelitis (usually the result of severe staphylococcal infection) often leave lesions that are nearly indistinguishable from those caused by both syphilis and tuberculosis, while acute osteoarthritis can cause damage to individual bones that is very similar to damage attributable to tuberculosis (Steinbock 1976:82, 188). Thus, the mere presence or absence of apparently symptomatic osteological evidence is by itself an insufficient basis for determining the existence of a given disease at a given time. This is especially true when—as is often the case—ambiguous evidence suggestive of a highly infectious disease such as syphilis or tuberculosis is found only on a single skeleton (or, worse, a partial skeleton) in a substantial skeletal series. The evidence for tuberculosis may be particularly problematic here, especially in North America where population densities would usually not have been conducive to horizontal transfer of the disease. Indeed, although there is some postcontact evidence that tuberculosis can persist in populations the size of Amazon tribes (Black 1975; McGrath 1986), the strongest support for its existence in the Precolumbian Americas remains a single study in Peru (Allison et al. 1974).

In addition to misdiagnosis, other serious pitfalls and problems in the use of paleopathology include the possibility of misdating remains and the need to exercise great care in limiting generalizations about the presence of particular diseases to the specific locales in which evidence for them has been found. The error factor in dating skeletal series, for example, often is so wide that even properly diagnosed remains may be as likely to have derived from a postcontact as from a late precontact burial (see Dobyns 1989b). As for the matter of specific locale, although there now appears to be fairly strong evidence for the existence of a nonvenereal form of treponemal infection in parts of the New World prior to Columbus (Baker and Armelagos 1988), vast areas of the Americas show no evidence at all of such an affliction despite a good deal of paleopathological research (Williams 1988). The same is true for tuberculosis. Since both diseases have long been known to have devastated many New World peoples in postcontact times (for instance, Cook 1943; Ferguson 1955:69), it is clear that numerous societies in the Americas had not acquired immunities to them. Moreover, it is worthy of note that the best evidence for treponemal infection in the Precolumbian Americas is for *non*venereal infection. Although the matter of cross-immunity in treponemal infections is still being researched, the best data to date indicate that while *some* level of immunity to venereal syphilis may develop among peoples who have had historical experience with nonvenereal treponemal infection, any such immunity "is not complete and may be overcome by a large inoculum of treponemes" (Moodie 1986:1361–1362). Thus, even if nonvenereal treponemal infection of some sort did exist in parts of the Precolumbian Americas, that fact may have had little or no impact on those peoples' resistance to venereal syphilis and, consequently, little or no mitigating influence on depopulation resulting from epidemic syphilis infection.

Specific Disease Scenarios

Although it is well known that today between 10 and 50 percent of sexual contacts with a syphilis-infected person in the primary or secondary stages of the disease result in transmission of the infection to the uninfected partner (McFalls and McFalls 1984:320)—with the higher end of the scale reserved for male-to-female transmission—to date we have only been able to guess at possible rates of transmission or likely progress of the disease among peoples with no history of exposure to syphilis. Recent research with AIDS victims, however, may begin to offer some clues.

While far from a direct parallel, contemporary AIDS victims are the closest model we are likely to find for indigenous peoples of centuries ago who found themselves lacking immunities to ward off introduced diseases. In a sense, AIDS creates a condition of compromised immunity that New World peoples had as a natural condition of their isolation from millennia of disease evolution in Europe, Africa, and Asia. And among other diseases that attack AIDS victims with extraordinary aggression is syphilis. Although still preliminary and controversial, some research shows HIV-positive subjects to be five times more likely than others to succumb to syphilitic infection, while other research has found neurosyphilis to advance to a stage not usually reached for 5 to 12 years in as little as four *months* among HIV-infected individuals (Johns et al. 1987). It may be that research focusing on other opportunistic infections, including tuberculosis, that invade immunocompromised AIDS victims will in the future be helpful in estimating the possible damage wrought by introduced diseases among immunity-deficient historical populations.

In constructing disease and depopulation scenarios for particular peoples at particular times, it is also crucial to determine as completely as possible the makeup of the armada of new diseases that constituted the biological invasion forces. This is so not only because specific diseases have specific and more or less predictable morbidity and mortality rates (albeit usually based upon research among modern populations), but because *combinations* of diseases—and combinations of diseases with other health-related environmental factors, such as nutrition—also have roughly predictable, and much greater, morbidity and mortality consequences.

One of the better-known examples among students of disease and depopulation in the Americas of the combined effects of infection is the work of van Mazijk, Pinheiro, and Black among the Tirio Indians. In that case, a parainfluenza infection occurred at the same time that a measles vaccine program was being carried out. While parainfluenza generally causes at most a common cold in adults, and the measles vaccine only a slight fever, together they created serious and life-threatening symptoms (van Mazijk et al. 1982). There are various reasons for this, notably the fact that certain parasitic and viral diseases directly compromise the immune system, making for a devastating combined effect when they occur simultaneously with other diseases.

Variations on this phenomenon include heightened impacts of disease among peoples with a history of other specific infections and sharply increased mortality from many diseases in a population also suffering from malnutrition. One recent study, for instance, has shown that severe complications from measles follow commonly among people with a history of respiratory infections (Aaby et al. 1986), while another study in Bangladesh has demonstrated that malnutrition can easily double the expected mortality rate among individuals suffering from diarrheal diseases (Islam and Khan 1986).

In the contact-era Americas, of course, such tandem disease assaults were overwhelmingly the rule rather than the exception. Peoples with no previous exposure to venereal syphilis, gonorrhea, smallpox, plague, typhoid fever, yellow fever, diphtheria, influenza, mumps, chicken pox, and in most places, if not all, tuberculosis, were *most commonly* assaulted by several of these diseases at once. The first result, on top of the explosive impact of a singularly devastating disease among a nonimmune population, was a synergistic magnification of that explosion as each new disease fed on and compounded the debilitation caused by the others. In the wake of this carnage—which attacked everyone in the affected community at once—normal patterns of social life, including drawing water and gathering food and caring for others, hopelessly collapsed. As a result, the horrifying impact of the diseases was heightened even more by malnutrition, dehydration, and despair.

Psychological and Cultural Factors

In this tumultuous environment of agonizing mass death, despair may well have been, in the end, the most destructive force of all. That case has been well made by a number of writers, but perhaps none more tellingly than J. V. Neel, whose observations on the collapsing village life and the growth of a pervading sense of doom and helplessness among the Yanamama Indians following unprecedented sickness and death has led some to conclude that despair is the *major* cause of overall demographic disaster in such situations (Neel 1977; Neel et al. 1970). If so, more research needs to be done on the precise mechanisms by which this phenomenon would operate. Already, however, there is an enormous research literature (see, for instance, Locke and Hornig-Rohan 1983) on linkages between the nervous and immune systems—including the involvement of stress, fear, despair, depression, and bereavement in enhancing susceptibility to serious infection—that can be built upon in exploring the psychological element in contact-era Native American population collapse.

As with all the topics discussed thus far, there is a cautionary aspect to this one that needs to be kept in mind: The psychological and cultural variable is extraordinarily complicated, something that too often is ignored in scholarship on the effects of both historical and contemporary disasters. It is commonplace, for instance, for students of disaster to catalogue and analyze typical human responses to certain types of catastrophe—such as forms of "post-traumatic stress disorder" (Horowitz 1976; Raphael 1986)—without paying attention to the particular preexisting social and cultural systems of the affected people.

The need for careful specification in this area may be graphically illustrated by looking at the kinds of problems that can result from overgeneralization based on modern American Indian suicide rates. Suicide commonly is recognized as a reaction to great psychological stress, and, as is well known, American Indians as a major ethnic group have the highest suicide rate in the United States—about 30 percent higher than the overall national rate (Group for the Advancement of Psychiatry 1989:6). It would be easy to generate indiscriminate hypotheses regarding American Indian mental health and cultural vitality by focusing on this singular piece of apparently revealing data. However, within the general category of American Indians, there are huge differentials not only by gender, as among all ethnic groups, but by tribe, depending in large part on degree of integration within the dominant American culture: The greater the level of acculturation, it seems, the higher the suicide rate. Even among what to outsiders may appear a single Native American group—say, the Pueblo peoples of New Mexico—there are enormous differentials, as can be seen in Table 26–1.

To the extent that suicide rates can be separated out from other overlapping indices of stress and despair, these figures clearly would seem to indicate that those Pueblo peoples who have been able to maintain a distance from the invasive effects of modern American culture have fared better in terms of experienced stress levels than have their more acculturated Pueblo brethren. This, of course, severely compromises most generalizations that might be made about overall American Indian (or even Pueblo) culture based upon a comparison of the crude American Indian suicide rate with that of the overall American sample.

Of more direct relevance to the present discussion, there is good reason to suppose that similar differentials were operative, for a wide variety of reasons, among different groups of Native Americans during the contact and postcontact

Table 26–1. Crude Suicide Rates Per 100,000 and Level of Acculturation

Pueblo	Rate	Acculturation Level
Laguna	45.2	High
Isleta	41.3	High
Taos	35.6	Intermediate
Zuni	31.4	Intermediate
San Felipe	21.3	Low
Acoma	15.8	Low
Jemez	13.2	Low
Santo Domingo	2.4	Low

Source: Adapted from Group for the Advancement of Psychiatry (1989) summarizing Van Winkle and May (1986).

eras. For instance, while it has long been known that alcoholism and drunkenness (as partial indicators of despair and social breakdown) became serious problems in many native communities in the wake of their first contacts with Europeans, William B. Taylor has shown that at least in Central Mexico this is a generalization in need of some refinement. There, Taylor has found, the so-called plague of alcoholism was largely limited to urban areas that quickly were drawn under Spanish political and cultural control; there is comparatively little evidence that rural Indians, who were not integrated into the life of the colonial metropole, suffered the same fate (Taylor 1979:28–72).

These sorts of findings lead to larger questions on a host of subjects, questions that can result in radically different hypotheses depending on how the initial queries are answered. To take just one example, what difference might it have made to the long-term demographic fate of an invaded indigenous population whether their society at the time of contact was sharply hierarchical and politically centralized or relatively egalitarian and politically decentralized? On the one hand, since leaders in hierarchical societies often were subject to direct manipulation by the stronger military force of the invader (see for instance, the discussion in Newson 1987:340–342), the very existence of such a manipulable elite might have served as a protective buffer between the invader and the general population, not just politically and militarily, but also, by extension, culturally and psychologically. On the other hand, a steeply hierarchical polity is subject to relatively easy decapitation at the hands of a strong invasion force, whether such an invasion be military or microbial; far from being a buffer, then, the sudden absence of the elite upon which the larger population has become politically, militarily, and/or culturally dependent may spell chaos and, as a secondary consequence, result in demographic disaster.

As with Ramenofsky's problematic assumption, noted earlier, that bacterial contagion risk necessarily is higher among sedentary peoples than among mobile peoples (along with subsidiary difficulties with that assumption depending on a given peoples' precise environmental situation), generalizations regarding demographic vulnerability based upon the nature of an invaded native peoples' political system clearly are fraught with complications and potential contradictions. Nevertheless, as also with Ramenofsky's insightful effort to construct a coherent if tentative model capable of handling variables of settlement type, form, and location, some effective generalization regarding existing structures of native polity at the moment of contact and their differential relationships to demographic vulnerability needs to be developed.

Induced Infertility and Subfecundity

The preceding discussions suggest various approaches toward addressing the skepticism of some demographers who continue to write about, as S. Ryan Johansson has directly put it, "the problem of explaining how so many people could seemingly disappear so fast" (Johansson 1982:137). But at least one more area of exploration needs to be delineated before we can begin to construct an overall theory of contact era disease and population history. That is the study not only of the causes of *initial* population decline, but the examination of *continued* population decline once the first epidemic waves had passed.

The continuing downward spiral of native populations in the Americas was largely due, Dobyns has argued, to "the relatively long intervals between invasions by the same disease [that] prevented Native Americans from acquiring much immunity for well over three centuries" (Dobyns 1983:24). Thus, according to this scenario, the same diseases returned repeatedly to the afflicted peoples, killing in great numbers generation after generation. While this does indeed appear to be the case, another factor that has been insufficiently studied—but that could account for precipitous and continuing population collapse across many generations—is the induced infertility and subfecundity that was a direct consequence of the epidemic disease invasions.

The most obvious causes of low live birth rates among native peoples following Western contact would have been gonorrhea and syphilis. Gonorrhea is a principal cause of pelvic inflammatory disease (PID) in women and a single episode of PID—under contemporary medical treatment—results in tubal occlusion and sterility in almost one out of eight cases; two episodes of PID triples the risk of infertility, while three or more episodes results in sterility in up to 75 percent of cases. In the absence of medical treatment, which was the situation for all infected women in the sixteenth and seventeenth centuries, it is now believed that 60 to 70 percent of women with any episode of PID will become sterile (Bernstine 1987; Thompson and Hager 1977; Westrom 1975, 1980). Syphilis, of course, is a common companion of gonorrhea and at least 30 percent of fetuses carried by women during the primary or secondary phases of syphilis will spontaneously abort—again, under contemporary medical conditions (Barrett-Connor 1969; McFalls and McFalls 1984:336). Between them, then, gonorrhea and syphilis tend to whipsaw afflicted women and their would-be offspring between extremely high rates of sterility and miscarriage. And among many native peoples of the Americas following Western contact, venereal disease was, as Sherburne F. Cook once put it, "a totalitarian disease, universally incident" (Cook 1943:26–27).

Less well known for its effects on fertility is tuberculosis, which can attack any organ in the body that is seeded by the tuberculosis bacillus—including the genitals. In many societies in the world today where immunological defenses have been suppressed by one or another cause (such as malnutrition), genital tuberculosis is common, especially in women, and has been cited as the most important cause of subfecundity in especially low fertility regions of Africa (McFalls and McFalls 1984:91). As this leading scholarly survey on the subject flatly states: "Genital TB is a disease that almost always causes primary sterility in affected men and women" (1984:98).

Many of the other diseases known to have been introduced by Europeans to the indigenous peoples of the Americas—influenza, measles, mumps, chicken pox, and smallpox among them—also have debilitating effects on their victims' fertility and fecundity potential. This is true for males as well as females: For example, smallpox—in addition to routinely killing at least 20 to 40 percent of those afflicted with it—is known in India as the single most important cause of obstructive azoospermia (which is a direct cause of male conceptive failure), while among smallpox-infected women very few pregnancies continue to term (McFalls and McFalls 1984:532–533).

Finally, the psychological element is as important here as it was in the matters discussed earlier. Nearly half the reported infertility in industrialized societies today is attributed to stress and related emotional concerns (McGrady 1984; Seibel and Taynor 1982), and the virtual collapse of fertility among recently contacted Brazilian natives in the 1960s and 1970s has also been attributed to psychological factors resulting from social dislocation (Baruzzi et al. 1977).

In sum, contrary to conventional wisdom on this topic—as expressed in a recent study by Russell Thornton: "The American Indian decline was due to both increases in death rates and decreases in birth rates, but it is clear that the increased death rates were of primary importance" (Thornton 1987:43)—it may well be that the *principal* cause of the massive long-term population decline among most native peoples of the Americas was induced infertility, subfecundity, and high infant mortality that were secondary consequences of the new diseases that were introduced in the Columbian and Postcolumbian eras.

Comparative Cross-Cultural Analyses

This conclusion regarding the demographic impact of low live birth rates derives not only from theoretical projections based on medical literature, but from analyses of comparative data from Hawaii. Although removed from the continents of the Americas by more than 2,000 miles of open ocean, Hawaii—along with other Pacific island locales—provides a wealth of relevant comparative data for students of this subject. Most important, it provides relatively detailed written historical documentation of demographic events that occurred within decades of Western contact, documentation of the sort that generally was not created in the Americas—particularly North America—until centuries following Western contact had passed.

On the matter of low birth rates versus high death rates as the principal cause of population decline, for example, the Hawaiian data, based on missionary censuses, show the native population declining at a median annual rate of 2.6 percent during the 1830s and early 1840s, 60 to 70 years following Western contact and a time when there is no evidence of widespread epidemics in the islands. This derived from a mortality rate of about 47 per 1,000 and a birth rate of less than 20 per 1,000—a combination, if sustained, sufficient to exterminate a population in well under half a century. In Hawaii that level of death rate/birth rate differential was not sustained for half a century, but in the 40 years between 1831 and 1871 the native population did fall, again by censal count, from about 124,000 to about 50,000. That is a drop of 74,000 (or almost 60 percent) in two generations, of which only about a third can be attributed to epidemics that occurred in the late 1840s and early 1850s. The remainder of the decline was the result primarily of an exceptionally low birth rate and a very high infant and child mortality rate (Stannard 1990).

This is not to say that there was little impact from introduced disease in Hawaii. On the contrary, venereal diseases, tuberculosis, and more began ravaging the islands' populations almost immediately upon contact. With most of the native inhabitants concentrated in populous village settlements all along the approximately 800 miles of low-lying island coastlines, Hawaii was a textbook case for documenting both the Cook and Borah (1960) and Ramenofsky (1990) hypotheses discussed earlier regarding the environmental conditions that produce high susceptibility to introduced disease. In Hawaii, it now appears, the population declined by about 50 percent within 25 years following European contact and by 75 percent within half a century, a devastating situation, to be sure, but well within the range of population declines found in parallel environments in the Americas. During that time, the most momentous epidemic was what, in retrospect, appears to have been typhoid (in 1804), but—as in the Americas—other diseases such as tuberculosis, syphilis, and a number of respiratory infections, including probably diphtheria, took on epidemic and rapidly fatal characteristics in the virgin-soil environment (Stannard 1989).

Although it has traditionally been held that the population of Hawaii in 1778, at the moment of first Western contact, was perhaps 250,000 to 300,000, the evidence now suggests a figure of at least 800,000; within a little more than a century it was down to less than 40,000—roughly the same 95 percent rate of decline Dobyns and others have found common in the Americas (Stannard 1989). The decline would have been even more drastic but for the fact that Hawaii's great isolation—it is the most isolated archipelago in the world—served to prevent the importation of smallpox until 1853 when ships, by then departing from California ports, could reach Hawaii after a relatively short ocean voyage. Even then, despite emergency vaccination and quarantine campaigns, at least 1 of every 10 Hawaiians who had been alive in May of 1853 was dead before the year was out (Greer 1965). Had smallpox arrived with the earliest European explorers, as it did in the Americas, the long-term population collapse would have been incalculably worse.

Overall, then, the comparative experience of the Hawaiians lends significant support to those students of historical demography in the Americas who have advanced the argument of high Precolumbian populations and massive Postcolumbian collapse. And since almost all of the Hawaiian population collapse took place within a century of Western contact—without major warfare or enslavement efforts and with a mitigated impact from smallpox, the most lethal of the diseases introduced by Europeans to the Americas (Dobyns 1983:11–16)—the Hawaiian experience also lends credence to the so-called sixteenth-century hypothesis, discussed earlier, which contends that there were huge population declines among America's native peoples in the immediately Postcolumbian era, but before Western witnesses arrived to record the events in writing.

Additional data from Hawaii and other parts of the Pacific, including possible genetic aspects of native susceptibility to specific infections (Black 1990; Stannard 1989:71–72), may be suggestive of directions future scholarship on the Americas might take, just as past scholarship on the Americas has clearly laid the foundations for recent inquiry in the Pacific (e.g., Crosby 1986:esp. 195–268; Kirkby 1984; Stannard 1989).

Conclusion

In sum, the study of New World demographics and depopulation in the contact and postcontact eras has developed at an extraordinary pace during the past few decades. Indeed, it may be that no other subject of comparable proportions in anthropology, history, and related disciplines has generated more data and more sophisticated—and controversial—analyses than this one during that time. While that escalating pace of knowledge acquisition has driven some researchers of late to call for a theoretical system to integrate data and direct future inquiry, the state of the field remains too laden with unreconciled and insufficiently explored variables to permit the development of such a theory at this time— although most of the relevant scholarship of late does at least point in directions supportive of the so-called sixteenth century hypothesis of extremely high precontact native populations followed by devastating and almost immediate Postcolumbian population loss.

This essay has touched on only some of the issues that recently have enriched the field of inquiry at the same time, paradoxically, that they have greatly complicated the search for a unified theoretical approach to that acquired knowledge. In addition, we have here only suggested a few of the complex scenarios that emerge when several variables from among those mentioned impinge on one another. Clearly, the search for a theory of native responses to biological and cultural invasion remains in its infancy. This is as much a matter for celebration, however, as it is for disappointment, since the cause of our great distance from a theory to organize the accumulated data is a virtual embarrassment of riches. Given that situation, at least one part of our strategy for the future is abundantly evident: only a rigorous and cooperative interdisciplinary and comparative approach to this subject of such great importance—it is after all, nothing less than the study of the worst demographic disaster, the worst holocaust, in the history of the world—will advance us on the path to unified knowledge and a unified vision.

References

Aaby, Peter, Jette Bukh, Ida Maria Lisse, and Adron J. Smits
   1986 Severe Measles in Sunderland, 1885: A European-African Comparison of Causes of Severe Infection. *International Journal of Epidemiology* 15:101–107.
Allison, M. J., J. Mendoza, and A. Pezzia
   1973 Documentation of a Case of Tuberculosis in Pre-Columbian America. *American Review of Respiratory Diseases* 107:985–991.
Baillis-Smith, Tim
   1978 Maximum Populations and Standard Populations: The Carrying Capacity Question. In *Social Organisation and Settlement: Contributions from Anthropology, Archaeology, and Geography Part I*, edited by David Green, Colin Haselgrove, and Matthew Spriggs, pp. 129–151. Cambridge University Press, Cambridge.

1980 Population Pressure, Resources, and Welfare: Towards a More Realistic Measure of Carrying Capacity. In *Population-Environment Relations in Tropical Islands: The Case of Eastern Fiji*, edited by H. C. Brookfield, pp. 61–93. UNESCO, Paris.

Baker, Brenda J., and George J. Armelagos
1988 The Origin and Antiquity of Syphilis. *Current Anthropology* 29:703–720.

Barrett-Connor, E.
1969 Infections and Pregnancy. *Southern Medical Journal* 62:275.

Baruzzi, R. G., L. F. Marcopito, M. L. C. Serra, F. A. A. Souza, and C. Stabile
1977 The Kren-Akorore: A Recently Contacted Indigenous Tribe. In *Health and Disease in Tribal Societies*, Ciba Foundation Symposium No. 4, n.s., pp. 179–211. Elsevier/Excerpta Medica, Amsterdam.

Bernstine, R., W. R. Kennedy, and J. Waldron
1987 Acute Pelvic Inflammatory Disease: A Clinical Follow-Up. *International Journal of Fertility* 32:229–232.

Black, Francis L.
1975 Infectious Diseases in Primitive Societies. *Science* 187:515–518.
1990 Review of *Before the Horror: The Population of Hawaii on the Eve of Western Contact* by David E. Stannard. *Pacific Studies* 13:269–79.

Chance, John K.
1989 *Conquest of the Sierra: Spaniards and Indians in Colonial Oaxaca*. University of Oklahoma Press, Norman.

Cook, Sherburne F.
1943 *The Indian versus the Spanish Mission*. Ibero-Americana No. 21. University of California Press, Berkeley.

Cook, Sherburne F., and Woodrow Borah
1960 *The Indian Population of Central Mexico, 1531–1610*. Ibero-Americana No. 44. University of California Press, Berkeley.

Crosby, Alfred W.
1986 *Ecological Imperialism: The Biological Expansion of Europe, 900–1900*. Cambridge University Press, Cambridge.

Dewar, Robert E.
1984 Environmental Productivity, Population Regulation, and Carrying Capacity. *American Anthropologist* 86:601–614.

Dobyns, Henry F.
1966 Estimating Aboriginal American Population: An Appraisal of Techniques with a New Hemispheric Estimate. *Current Anthropology* 7:395–416.
1983 *Their Number Become Thinned: Native American Population Dynamics in Eastern North America*. University of Tennessee Press, Knoxville.
1989a More Methodological Perspectives on Historical Demography. *Ethnohistory* 36:285–299.
1989b On Issues in Treponemal Epidemiology. *Current Anthropology* 30:342–343.

Feacham, R. G. A.
1973 A Clarification of Carrying Capacity Formulae. *Australian Geographical Studies* 11:234–236.

Ferguson, R. G.
1955 *Studies in Tuberculosis*. University of Toronto Press, Toronto.

Greer, Richard A.
1965 Oahu's Ordeal—The Smallpox Epidemic of 1853. *Hawaiian Journal of History* 1:221–242.

Group for the Advancement of Psychiatry
1989 *Suicide and Ethnicity in the United States*. Brunner/Mazel, New York.

Haggett, P.
1975 Simple Epidemics in Human Populations. In *Processes in Physical and Human Geog-*

raphy, edited by R. Peel, M. Chisholm, and P. Haggett, pp. 372–391. Heinemann, London.

Henige, David
  1986 Primary Source by Primary Source? On the Role of Epidemics in New World Depopulation. *Ethnohistory* 33:293–312.
  1989 On the Current Devaluation of the Notion of Evidence: A Rejoinder to Dobyns. *Ethnohistory* 36:304–307.

Horowitz, M. J.
  1976 *Stress Response Syndromes*. Jason Aronson, New York.

Islam, S. S., and M. U. Khan
  1986 Risk Factors for Diarrhoeal Deaths: A Case-Control Study at a Diarrhoeal Disease Hospital in Bangladesh. *International Journal of Epidemiology* 15:116–121.

Johansson, S. Ryan
  1982 The Demographic History of the Native Peoples of North America: A Selective Bibliography. *Yearbook of Physical Anthropology* 25:133–152.

Johns, Donald R., Maureen Tierney, and Donna Felsenstein
  1987 Alteration in the Natural History of Neurosyphilis by Concurrent Infection with the Human Immunodeficiency Virus. *New England Journal of Medicine* 316:1569–1572.

Kiple, Kenneth F.
  1984 *The Caribbean Slave: A Biological History*. Cambridge University Press, Cambridge.

Kirkby, Dianne
  1984 Colonial Policy and Native Depopulation in California and New South Wales, 1770–1840. *Ethnohistory* 31:1–16.

Locke, Steven E., and Mady Hornig-Rohan
  1983 *Mind and Immunity: Behavioral Immunology, An Annotated Bibliography, 1976–1982*. Praeger, New York.

McFalls, J. A., and M. H. McFalls
  1984 *Disease and Fertility*. Academic Press, New York.

McGrady, A. V.
  1984 Effects of Psychological Stress on Male Reproduction. *Archives of Andrology* 13:1–7.

McGrath, J. W.
  1986 A Computer Simulation of the Occurrence of Tuberculosis in Prehistoric North America. *American Journal of Physical Anthropology* 69:238.

McNeill, William H.
  1979 Historical Patterns of Migration. *Current Anthropology* 20:95–102.

Mols, R. P. R.
  1973 Population in Europe, 1500–1700. In *The Fontana Economic History of Europe*, vol. 2, edited by C. M. Cipolla. Fontana, London.

Móodie, Peter M.
  1986 Yaws, Pinta, and Bejel. In *Infectious Diseases and Medical Microbiology*, edited by Abraham I. Braude, pp. 1361–1366. W. B. Saunders, Philadelphia.

Neel, J. V.
  1977 Health and Disease in Unacculturated Amerindian Populations. In *Health and Disease in Tribal Societies*, Ciba Foundation Symposium No. 49, n.s., pp. 155–168. Elsevier/Excerpta Medica, Amsterdam.

Neel, J. V., W. R. Centerwall, N. A. Chagnon, and H. L. Casey
  1970 Notes on the Effect of Measles and Measles Vaccine in a Virgin Soil Population of South American Indians. *American Journal of Epidemiology* 91:418–429.

Newman, Marshall T.
  1976 Aboriginal New World Epidemiology and Medical Care, and the Impact of Old World Disease Imports. *American Journal of Physical Anthropology* 45:667–672.

Newson, Linda A.
  1987 *Indian Survival in Colonial Nicaragua*. University of Oklahoma Press, Norman.

Ramenofsky, Ann F.

1987 *Vectors of Death: The Archaeology of European Contact.* University of New Mexico Press, Albuquerque.

1990 Loss of Innocence: Explanations of Differential Persistence in the Sixteenth-Century Southeast. In *Columbian Consequences,* vol. 2, *Archaeological and Historical Perspectives on the Spanish Borderlands East,* edited by David Hurst Thomas, pp. 31–48. Smithsonian Institution Press, Washington, D.C.

Raphael, Beverley

1986 *When Disaster Strikes: How Individuals and Communities Cope with Catastrophe.* Basic Books, New York.

Sanchez-Albornoz, Nicolas

1974 *The Population of Latin America: A History.* Translated by W.A.R. Richardson. University of California Press, Berkeley.

Seibel, M., and M. Taynor

1982 Emotional Aspects of Infertility. *Fertility and Sterility* 37:137–145.

Smith, C. T.

1970 Depopulation of the Central Andes in the Sixteenth Century. *Current Anthropology* 11:453–464.

Smith, M. T.

1987 *Archaeology of Aboriginal Culture Change in the Interior Southeast.* Florida State Museum, Gainesville.

Snow, Dean R., and Kim M. Lanphear

1988 European Contact and Indian Depopulation in the Northeast: The Timing of the First Epidemics. *Ethnohistory* 35:15–33.

1989 "More Methodological Perspectives": A Rejoinder to Dobyns. *Ethnohistory* 36:229–304.

Stannard, David E.

1989 *Before the Horror: The Population of Hawaii on the Eve of Western Contact.* Social Science Research Institute and University of Hawaii Press, Honolulu.

1990 Disease and Infertility: A New Look at the Demographic Collapse of Native Populations in the Wake of Western Contact. *Journal of American Studies* 24(3):1–26.

1991 Disease and Human Migration. In *The History and Geography of Human Disease,* edited by Kenneth F. Kiple. Cambridge University Press, Cambridge, in press.

Steinbock, R. Ted

1976 *Paleopathological Diagnosis and Interpretation: Bone Diseases in Ancient Human Populations.* Thomas, Springfield.

Street, J. M.

1969 An Evaluation of the Concept of Carrying Capacity. *Professional Geographer* 21:104–107.

Taylor, William B.

1979 *Drinking, Homicide, and Rebellion in Colonial Mexican Villages.* Stanford University Press, Stanford.

Thompson, S. and W. Hager

1977 Acute Pelvic Inflammatory Disease. *Sexually Transmitted Diseases* 4:105.

Thornton, Russell

1987 *American Indian Holocaust and Survival: A Population History since 1492.* University of Oklahoma Press, Norman.

van Mazijk, J., F. P. Pinheiro, and F. L. Black

1982 Measles and Measles Vaccine in Isolated Amerindian Tribes. *Tropical and Geographic Medicine* 34:3–6.

Van Winkle, N., and P. May

1986 Native American Suicide in New Mexico, 1957–1979: A Comparative Study. *Human Organization* 45:296–309.

Westrom, L.
  1975 Effect of Acute Pelvic Inflammatory Disease on Fertility. *American Journal of Obstetrics and Gynecology* 127:707.
  1980 Incidence, Prevalance, and Trends of Acute Pelvic Inflammatory Disease and Its Consequences in Industrialized Countries. *American Journal of Obstetrics and Gynecology* 138:880–886.
Wightman, Ann M.
  1990 *Indigenous Migration and Social Change: The Forasteros of Cuzco. 1570–1720.* Duke University Press, Durham.

Chapter 27 ■

Henry F. Dobyns

New Native World: Links between Demographic and Cultural Changes

An increasing number of scholars have been for some years engaged in analyzing what may be called the historic demography of peoples native to the New World. One result of these efforts has been to complicate the analytical task of archeographers "writing of contexts based on material culture" (Deetz 1988:18) in the Americas. Once upon a time, archeographers could employ an analytically simple Kroeberian two-part paradigm assuming (1) explicitly that there were few natives in 1492 and (2) implicitly that the impacts of Columbian exchange disease were insignificant. That demographic paradigm allowed archeographers and ethnologists alike to assume that past processes could be accurately reconstructed using isomorphisms (Wylie 1982:393) "observed in present-day stone-age communities" (Kuper 1983:9). Reasoning that native "culture pattern, personality type, and value system mutually reinforce one another so as to preserve . . . the essentially aboriginal way-of-life" (Steward 1955:296), archeographers assumed continuity of native culture.

An example of archeographic reasoning on these premises under the most favorable of circumstances exposes one among many limitations on it. Size of Hopi pueblo rooms, "room story location, number of wall doors, and presence or absence of doors connecting rooms" serve to identify household unit and matrilineage residence boundaries, as well as rooms used as granaries, for secular or religious storage, habitation, piki baking, and religious activities (Adams 1983:49, 59). These ethnographic data collected during the 1880s (Mindeleff 1891) and 1970s cannot be employed to interpret significant aspects of ruined former multistory pueblos. Three-fourths of ethnographic nonstorage rooms are located on a top floor, whereas but 16 percent of the storage rooms are so located. "Thus in a multistory village lying in ruins, one would expect to uncover primarily storage and granary rooms . . . population and other estimates based on floor area or number of rooms are likely to be overstated" (Adams 1983:53). Even in the semiarid Southwest, architectural ruination at most sites has destroyed the upper stories and the habitation rooms they presumably once contained. Such irreversible events happen to abandoned buildings as well as to living people. "Past actuality can never be known in its totality" (Deetz 1988:15) because archeography is inherently an historic science (Aberle 1987:556).

Deliberately collecting portable residues selectively diminishes, moreover, those available for archeographic analysis. Treasure hunters have looted many a monument of Precolumbian civilization (Hrdlicka 1971:129). At 12,000+ feet above sea level in Andean Vicos, for example, a Tiahuanacoid military post on the brink of a deep quebrada once commanded a trans-Andean trail below. *Huaqueros* long ago emptied a multistory burial edifice, strewing sherds and bones just outside the entryways so the latter disintegrated.

Interviewing a winter visitor to southern Arizona reputed locally to be knowledgeable about sites in the lower Río Santa Cruz Valley, I confirmed his reputation. He knew that by walking over the residues after every rain, he could collect red-on-buff painted ceramic sherds to make into more bolo ties for sale. I found no painted sherds on the sides he selectively gleaned.

Scientifically ignorant newcomers seeking recreation destroy evidence as effectively as huaqueros. I was able to locate one small ceramic sherd on a doubly documented Walapai occupation area. Native oral history clearly identified the zone contiguous to a major spring in the midst of relatively arid lands as having been a major band headquarters. Historic records identified the spring as the site of native habitation at the beginning of interethnic contact, and later the site where hundreds of natives were concentrated adjacent to a U.S. military reservation (Dobyns 1974:2:400). (There had been a small army contingent stationed a few miles away during World War II. The extremely bored soldiers actually enjoyed picking up every stone point and every ceramic sherd, however plain and undecorated, they could find.) Such experiences drive home the point that the physical record is "more impoverished" even than the documentary record (Deetz 1988:16), seriously handicapping "objective" archeographic interpretation.

A logical shortcoming of reconstructing past human behaviors using analogs observed in present-day "stone age communities" is that ethnographers find it extraordinarily difficult to describe and analyze much observed behavior. Basic anthropological concepts such as human familial residence patterns and rules can be defined only quantitatively using data obtained by careful and time-consuming enumeration (Allen and Richardson 1971:44–47; Bohannon 1957). It is, therefore, merely archeographic "new speak" to claim that excavatable data are relevant to most elements of past sociocultural systems (Binford 1968:22), especially ones that ethnographers discern with great difficulty even when they enumerate living populations.

Seeking relationships between "modern behavior and modern material culture" simply cannot elucidate "cultural behaviors" or epidemiological phenomena "not found in the present" (Cordell et al. 1987:568). Roman Catholic convent communities have been closing at a fast clip. Their doctrinal bases and specific rules always made them dubious analogs for Incan acllas described postconquest as "beautiful" specialists in weaving delicate fabrics, in brewing "a special rich chicha," in preparing gourmet meals for the emperor, and at times in pleasing him in bed. It is now very difficult even to identify which structure—excavatable though it is—in a ruined Incan city was its *acllahuasi* (Hemming 1982:39). So excavation can add absolutely nothing to brief native oral history of *acllas* written during early colonial times. No *aclla* exists at present.

Depopulation

Research in historic demography has revealed another major impediment to interpreting prehistoric events in terms of present-day apparent isomorphisms or analogs. Sherburne F. Cook and Woodrow Borah (1960, 1971) very effectively changed the Kroeberian paradigm by analyzing sixteenth-century Spanish colonial records. Kroeber (1939:166) estimated 3,000,000 people in Central Mexico, Guatemala, and El Salvador in 1492. On the basis of rapid depopulation reported from a large sample of native settlements, Cook and Borah calculated that 25,300,00 people inhabited Central Mexico alone in 1519. The numerical projection technique Cook and Borah used masks the magnitude of mortality during the hemisphere's first smallpox, measles, and plague pandemics reported in colonial documents (Dobyns 1963). Conservatively considering that mortality, I (Dobyns 1966:407) have calculated the Central Mexican 1519 population as 30 million people.

The new historic demography paradigm demonstrates catastrophic depopulation of the populous native civilizations from 1520 until 1650 in Mesoamerica and from 1524 until 1750 in the Andes. In colonial New Spain, fewer than 1 million natives survived by 1620 (Cook and Borah 1971). Depopulation during the initial colonial century was on the order of at least 25.3 to 30 to 1. Andean depopulation was on the same order, although colonial records have thus far not yielded enough data to calculate the 1519 population with the same precision that Cook and Borah achieved for Central Mexico (Cook 1981). However many people perished during the initial colonial century of horror for natives from 1520 to 1620, they constituted the majority of the entire hemispheric population. Native populations in South America's southern cone, in Amazonia, and north of Mesoamerica were culturally and demographically marginal to civilized Native America. Only in densely populated Mesoamerica and the central Andes did "complex, state-organized societies" emerge (Fiedel 1987:351).

Lingering uncertainty as to when and how far contagious diseases spread from civilized Native America and directly from Europe and Africa (Snow and Lanphear 1988) cannot alter the new fundamental historic demography paradigm. So many civilized Americans perished from 1520 to 1620—26 to 29 million in Central Mexico alone—that 9 million in Amazonia and 9 to 18 million north of Mesoamerica only marginally mitigate the magnitude of depopulation even if none of them died until after 1620. Demonstrably some did die before then in 1535–1536 (Dobyns 1983:302), although scant documentation leaves the scale of mortality uncertain. About 90 percent of the nuclear zone's population perished by 1568, or more than 39 million individuals if there were but 57 million in the hemisphere in 1492 (Denevan 1976; Fiedel 1987:355). Consequently, "contemporary thought" about Precolumbian American numbers and historic depopulation differs (Collingwood 1946:228; Taylor 1948:31) dramatically from discarded Kroeberian thought. Cook and Borah (1971), Crosby (1972), Denevan (1976), Dobyns (1966, 1983), N. D. Cook (1981), Thornton (1987), and others have shaped the current paradigm of American historical demography.

As European powers other than Spain colonized North America during the seventeenth century, their written records attest that Europeans, their African slaves, and their diseases were highly lethal to natives (Dobyns 1983:16–30; Hurlich 1983:151–176). *The Invasion of America*, as Jennings (1975) correctly called it, caused native depopulation that continued until approximately 1900. Some ethnic groups such as Pueblos began recovering in mid-nineteenth century (Simmons 1979). Others such as the Mescalero Apaches did not begin recovering until well into the present century (Dobyns 1977). Some, including the entire Timucuan-speaking population (Dobyns 1983:284) and many pueblos (Schroeder 1979), became extinct. Lower Mississippi River Valley statelets "disappeared without a trace" (Ramenofsky 1987:174).

Some cautious scholars think that depopulation ultimately left about 351,000 natives north of Mesoamerica in 1900 (Thornton 1987:31). A depopulation ratio of 22:1 estimates Precolumbian population as 7,898,000.

Depopulation was a huge demographic discontinuity that caused sharp discontinuities in native societies and cultures (Ramenofsky 1987:176). Conquest coupled with depopulation to alter "age-old, autochthonous, and hence most suitable ways of conducting work, worship, play, and even digestion" (Borah 1979:2). These discontinuities were so great that it is impossible to explain all past events "based upon uniformitarian principles observed to be operating in the present" (Gould 1985:638). Infectious disease mortality such as historic records describe cannot be observed at present. Archeographic inference, compared to geological inference, is fatally handicapped not only by complex human behaviors (Gould and Watson 1982:357), but also by human parasite behaviors and human biological responses during the Columbian exchange that are not now observable. Moreover, parasite attacks and human responses were imperfectly and often inaccurately and only indirectly reported by literate contemporaries. As a result, "the size and organizational complexity of populations recorded ethnographically are very poor analogs for periods earlier than about 1850" (Upham 1986:126).

The depopulation process thrust America's natives into a "world," a "physical and cultural milieu" just as new to them as the New World "place" was to invading Europeans and Africans (Merrell 1984:538). Depopulation and the Euro-African invasion of the Americas plunged surviving natives into a period of rapid cultural change paralleled only in other Neo-Europes (Crosby 1986). Residues from that period reflect native cultural adjustments to their new physical and cultural milieu at a rate without prehistoric precedent.

The new Hopi world allowed five or six family members to use two granaries, one religious and three secular storehouses, as well as a piki house per habitation around 1900 (Adams 1983:51, 54). Such spaciousness resulted, however, from using metal tools dating back at least 125 years and depopulation by epidemic smallpox most recently in 1898–1899 and 1853 (Dobyns 1983; Yount 1966:60–61). One cannot, therefore, be confident that the 1:7 habitation-to-other-room ratio existed earlier than 1850.

The new demographic paradigm recognizes that the Columbian exchange of subvisible organisms predatory on human beings fostered a rapid biological unification of *Homo sapiens* (Ladurie 1981:28). Many more predatory viruses and germs evolved in the Old World, with its numerous domestic animal reservoirs, than in the Americas. Consequently, millions of American natives died because the American population had to acquire relatively rapidly immunities gained by surviving predators' attacks that Old World peoples had acquired much more gradually.

Subvisible predators killed far more natives of the Americas than did conquistadores, forced labor in mines or on plantations, and newcomer seizure of natural resources. Indeed, once they crossed the Atlantic (or Pacific) Ocean as stowaways, subvisible predators from the Old World spread from native peoples under colonial control to still-autonomous natives beyond the colonial frontiers. This predator behavior makes studying historic epedemiology vital to improving the new paradigm's accuracy (Cook 1981: Dobyns 1983:291–295).

The purpose of this chapter is not to belabor numbers or the historic sequence of epidemics, but to point out that the new demographic paradigm poses serious interpretational problems for the archeographer. "Archaeologists have generally assumed that complex sociopolitical institutions presuppose large populations, and that the latter can only be supported by intensive agriculture" (Fiedel 1987:249). This logic is bidirectional. Large populations presuppose organization in complex sociopolitical structures as well as food production in Africa (Stevenson 1968), Polynesia (Sahlins 1958), the Southeastern (Peebles and Kus 1977:411–445; Ramenofsky 1987:42–71; Smith 1987), and Southwestern United States (Spicer 1962:39, 99), and modern nation-states (Dobyns 1966:495–496). Physical residues left by predepopulation complex sociopolitical institutions cannot be reconstructed by analogy from postdepopulation sociopolitically attenuated (Dobyns 1983:328) stone-age peoples of small social scale (Wilson and Wilson 1945). Neither can historic socioeconomic arrangements such as debt peonage, which arose in New Spain by 1567 (Borah 1951:37–42), be analogs for any native labor regimes during predepopulation times.

No more can predepopulation cultures be reconstructed by analogy from surviving natives who adapted to the new environmental world of the Columbian exchange by becoming pastoral with Old World domestic animals (outside the Andean camelid pastoral zone). A twentieth-century Navajo camp (Dobyns and Euler 1971) is neither isomorphic with nor an analog for any prepastoral settlement pattern or house-type, even of ancestral Navajos!

The new demographic paradigm makes clear that the native human muscle power available to alter the natural American landscape in 1500 was no longer available in 1550. It had further diminished in 1600, and north of Mesoamerica diminished even further until after 1800. Lacking labor, native economies retrogressed (McNeill 1976:205). Historic records make plain that psychological traumas among survivors of lethal epidemics combined with their diminished work forces to generate characteristic kinds of discontinuities and changes which differentiate the cultures of postdepopulation peoples from even those of their own predepopulation ancestors. This chapter attempts no more than to outline discontinuities.

Scanty Residues

A consequence of depopulation during what is often labeled a "Protohistoric" period (prior to the arrival of literate Euroamericans) is that settlement and artifactual remains of native peoples diminished in quantity. Declining natives "left a diverse veneer of archeological materials on an expansive landscape which had been used by Native Americans for 12,000 years or more." (Hofman 1989:99). That veneer is so thin that simply finding it is often a difficult task for the surveyor. Moreover, the same factors that led European colonists often to misinterpret native habitation on networks of "invisible" small sites (Handsman and Maymon 1987:4) makes such small residue locations difficult to find now. Indeed, some residues of depopulation events disappeared within a few years. A visitor to Black Mesa Hopis the year after smallpox decimated them in 1853 reported: "The bodies . . . had decayed where they . . . died . . . the whitened bones lay thickly strewed around" (Yount 1966:60). Similarly, condors consumed the bodies of Incas who in 1536 died defending Sacsahuaman Fort above Cuzco (Hemming 1982:77). Finding the thin residual veneer that was deposited and preserved is made additionally difficult by newcomer activities. "Many of the locations used by Protohistoric hunting and trading groups and their farming neighbors have subsequently been severely disturbed by modern land use: primarily agriculture, roads, construction, and reservoirs of various sizes" (Hofman 1989:99).

Labor Loss

Some analytical consequences of historic declines in native muscle-power are readily evident in the history of American archeography. Seventeenth- and eighteenth-century colonists could not conceive the ancestors of small remnant native groups as having been capable of constructing huge earthworks. Consequently, newcomers invented the concept of a prehistoric, distinct race of mound builders that mysteriously disappeared (Willey and Sabloff 1974:30–34; Dunnell this volume).

Erecting a mound to contain burials or as a base for a temple or ruler's dwelling is a cultural option. So is protecting a settlement with a palisade (Smith 1987:89–97). Certain other activities that require large quantities of human muscle-power are more mandatory in economic and subsistence terms for the populous, food-producing society. When native New World societies reached critical sizes, in many regions they embarked upon irrigation and runoff-control projects of varying sizes and muscle-power requirements. The labor force and the organization of it required to build mounds or irrigation systems differ fundamentally in magnitude from what is needed to scrape Australian mulgawood, a task prompting certain natives to prefer white chert scrapers (Gould 1978:829). Such large-scale "residues" require true analogical analysis, therefore, rather than a search for simple isomorphisms (Wylie 1982:394). Focusing analytical light on the people-power needs of different irrigation works illuminates two issues.

First, the human labor demands of environmentally specific projects highlight some significant aspects of declining muscle-power, despite the fact that "precision is foreign to real life" (Kuper 1983:16). Second, cross-cultural analysis of irrigation works in different environments illustrates how levels of confidence in analogical reasoning increase as various environmental constraints on human behavior are explicitly identified. On one technological level, environment links activities, materials, and social structure. Comparing Andean and Sonoran Desert irrigation systems illustrates the point.

At the upper altitude limit of central Andean horticulture, a rather small pole-and-brush structure diverts a small but steady flow of the Río Santa into an irrigation canal. Driving past that structure many times, I never saw anyone maintaining or repairing it. That vital system component requires minimal human muscle-power even though there is a pronounced precipitation difference between the central Andean wet and dry seasons.

In contrast, keeping the isomorphic technological device—pole-and-brush diversion structures—on the middle Gila River in southern Arizona demands much muscle-power. A 1915 photograph shows 50+ Pima men plus 21 four-wheeled wagons with two-horse teams repairing a diversion structure across the Gila River at the Little Gila Canal heading (Haury 1976:149). This structure was fashioned from the same kinds of materials as the one on the Río Santa, yet the different riverine environments require different amounts of human muscle-power to perform identical tasks. More people and social organization are required to replace pole-and-brush diversion structures in fluctuating than in steady-flow streams. Each modern system serves, therefore, as the better analog for Precolumbian irrigation in its own environment.

In the central Andes, much of the precipitation usable for irrigation falls on the highest peaks, where it freezes on mountain-top glaciers. The lower glacier edge at about 16,000 feet above mean sea level melts steadily through the tropical year. Morrains impound glacial lakes, but meltwater drains from them to form numerous *Cordillera Blanca* rivulets tributary to the Río Santa. During prehistoric times, natives established canals to carry water to cultivated fields. Canals are stable, requiring little year-in, year-out maintenance. Glacial meltwater begins its downslope course virtually pure, carrying no silt load to erode or to deposit even where gradient decreases. Little muscle-power is required to maintain such canals or diversion structures. Horticulture is (other factors such as plant diseases being equal) very productive per capita, leaving significant proportions of the population free to engage in labor-intensive, nonhorticultural tasks.

Andean slope productivity and that of the Altiplano enabled Incas to "mobilize vast squads of laborers" who, within the short span of eight decades, built in hundreds of cities, towns, and villages, thousands of imperial palaces, shrines, temples, festive halls, posthouses, and roads of "astonishing Inca masonry," which was "the product of innumerable man-days of patient labor" (Alcina Franch 1983:350; Hemming 1982:19, 49–50). Inca stone masonry in itself makes plausible Inca oral history related to sixteenth-century Spaniards that 30,000 men labored at a time on state structures in Cuzco alone (Hemming 1982:23) and that 8,000 attendants rotated service at a single provincial administrative center (D'Altroy 1987b:91). The Inca elite could pursue a "high-control, high extraction strategy" (D'Altroy 1987a:6) and have massive monuments built in part because the irrigation and terrace infrastructure installed earlier required minimal maintenance.

Yet, some Altiplano twentieth-century irrigation installations are not at all isomorphic with or even accurate analogs of Precolumbian works. At Accopata, in the Lake Titicaca basin, an irrigation system "improved" by professional engineers with foreign funds failed because water froze in shallow canals (Castillo A. et al. 1964). Recent experimentation has shown, in contrast, that contemporary cultivators can obtain seven times the customary yields from excavated and restored Precolumbian raised ridge plots with broad, fish-supporting canals between them (Anonymous 1990:52). These restored works and relatively small surviving *chinampa* raised fields at Xochomilco in the Valley of Mexico are pertinent ethnographic and historic analogs for Precolumbian raised fields in once-Mayan swampy lowlands (Turner and Harrison 1981) or the Bolivian Mojos (Denevan 1966).

The Río Gila's environment is quite different from that on either the steep Andean slope or nearly level Altiplano. Although the Río Gila is located well to the north of the tropics, none of the peaks that receive most of the precipitation falling on its watershed are high enough to be glaciated. Summer precipitation not absorbed on mountain slopes becomes stream flow with little delay. Winter snows accumulate on the peaks when temperatures remain low enough, resulting in spring freshets or floods when temperatures rise to the snow melts. Stream flow tends to peak during March (Baker 1987), which is spring planting time on the middle reach. Stream flow then drops to a minimum in May-June, increasing again once thunderstorms begin during July.

Pronounced seasonal fluctuations in Río Gila volume create inelastic energy and organizational requirements for irrigators. Spring freshets typically run high and fast enough to wash away the pole-and-brush diversion structures at the head of every canal along the low gradient middle reach where cultivators clustered since about the time of Christ. Horticulturists benefited from the physical failure of diversion structures. Dam failure kept canals from being choked with silt, sand, and gravel, which high-velocity flood waters transported. Deposits blocking water movement through canals had to be removed before canals could be restored to service and fields again irrigated. The muscle-power needed to remove flood deposits varied with the magnitude of run-off and silt, sand, and gravel load and the length of deposition time until the diversion structure failed, allowing flow and load to course down the channel. It is extremely difficult to identify any present-day isomorphism or analog for quantifying such variable human energy needs for keeping an irrigation system in near-constant operation during the crop season.

When floods quickly destroyed a fragile diversion structure, they carried little sand and gravel into its canal. The muscle-power required for restoring a pole-and-brush dam was less than for clearing a clogged canal. Moreover, one can identify modern analogs that make it possible to quantify those muscle-power demands. Whether a spring or a summer monsoon flood washed away a diversionary structure along the middle Río Gila, irrigators necessarily replaced it as soon as possible in order not to lose growing crops.

One significant component for interpretation is a present-day cropping pattern isomorphic with or like the earlier one in the specific riverine oasis. Food crops that historic Gila River Pimas planted in March had to be irrigated as much as possible during April in order to saturate the soil so it would contain sufficient moisture to sustain plants during dry May and June. Fiber crops, especially, needed April irrigation to build up soil moisture to carry still-small and tender plants through the dry months until summer monsoon thundershowers raised runoff with which to irrigate cotton and devil's claw until their fall maturation. When March floods washed away a Pima diversion structure, men replaced it as soon as possible after flood crests passed so as not to lose the spring season food crops and the year's fiber crops. Historic Pima muscle-power requirements constitute an accurate analog for the muscle-power requirements of prehistoric irrigators growing the same crops in the same riverine oasis environment.

The physical activities of early twentieth-century Pima irrigators are analogs for earlier irrigation on the middle Río Gila because through time this stream demanded identical physical activities most likely organized in the same or very similar ways to divert its waters into canals, using probably identical materials (Gould and Watson 1982:359). Ethnographers have, however, conducted little research into Pima historic muscle-power demands in the middle Río Gila oasis, partly because newcomers began diverting irrigation water upstream before ethnography was invented. When such research began, there was very little middle Río Gila horticulture left (Dobyns 1989:71–78). There is, fortunately, one historic 1915 photograph already mentioned (see Galloway, this volume, for analytical criteria).

The Gila River Pima work party photographed restoring the diversion structure at the Little Gila Canal heading is not isomorphic with a pre–1880 work party performing the same task at the same site. Changes in native cultures caused by depopulation are but one type. The Columbian exchange confronted natives of the Americas with many other dynamics of cultural change, including crop diversification, forced labor, and forced migration (Dobyns 1976a:19–20; Dobyns and Doughty 1976) and integration into the capitalist world market (Braudel 1982:325–327, 421–423).

In the United States, the national government reserved some lands for continued native exploitation and residence, dispatching newcomer agents to accelerate directed cultural changes (Spicer 1962:345–349). One agent at Gila River Indian Reservation in 1886 fostered change in domestic housing by giving a four-wheeled wagon to families that built homes of sun-dried earthen bricks laid up in walls with square corners (Wheeler 1886). Consequently, the 1915 photograph shows 21 wagons powered by two-horse teams deployed in the river. This photographically recorded work party is a true analog for prewagon, instream, dam-building work forces because its "difference as well as similarities" to earlier labor forces must be considered (Wylie 1982:394).

Declining Military Power and De-urbanization

As polities lost people, their military power declined and their physical and psychological ability to resist European invaders was reduced (Crosby 1972:35–63; Dobyns 1983:311; Dobyns and Doughty 1976:61–62). Cities in civilized America proved to be particularly vulnerable to depopulation and the concomitant decline of native military power plus European conquest that drastically altered Precolumbian economic structures and values. At least four regional administrative Tawantinsuyu cities—Huánuco Pampa, Tomebamba, Incallacta, and Tambo Colorado—were abandoned (Kolata 1983:347–348) as "extraneous to European survival" (Ramenofsky 1987:175). Lakeshore cities in the Valley of Mexico that held 1,500,000 people in 1520 crashed to a few tens of thousands despite the urban cultural pattern of colonial Spaniards. Mexico City did not grow to 1,500,000 until this century. Given the staggering quantity of social science research that has been carried out on modern cities and on urban-rural differences, it should be at once obvious that no postdepopulation American settlement is isomorphic with or can serve as an analog pertinent to interpreting predepopulation urban settlements. Neither are Old World cities instructive analogs because of fundamental cultural differences between Old and New World peoples, shown by the necessity of redefining "city" in cultural terms to encompass the American demographic cities (Kolata 1983:365–368).

Amalgamation

As numbers within settlements declined, survivors amalgamated, so that ethnic occupation zones altered and contracted (Cook and Borah 1960; Dobyns 1983: 302–6, 311; Smith 1987:72–75), shifting from less to more productive natural environments while abandoning "whole regions" (Ramenofsky 1987:173). Paradoxically, amalgamation could enlarge surviving native settlements (Dobyns

1976a:133) influenced by newcomer activities, attitudes, and proximity (Ramenofsky 1987:175).

Even more dramatically, survivors amalgamated not only settlements but ethnic groups, creating ethnic entities different from those extant in predepopulation times (Brain 1971:215–233; Dobyns 1983:306, 1989; Merrell 1984:539; Spicer 1962:212; White 1978;). Known amalgamation of "previously distinct cultural groups must be considered" when analyzing the "ethnic distinctiveness" of producers of physical residues (Hofman 1989:99). Demographic amalgamation did not necessarily result in rapid cultural amalgamation, so that ethnic diversity that generated factionalism in some surviving historic groups (despite dilution of initial distinctions by intermarriages and linguistic unification) cannot be considered a pertinent analog for interpreting predepopulation societies without ethnic enclaves.

Throughout the Americas, natives mingled with newcomers to create a fecund, rapidly growing (Dobyns 1976a:146–148; Dobyns and Doughty 1976: 153) "New American" population (Dobyns 1976b:46–48), in typical derogatory fashion labeled métis, mestizo, or half-breed. "By the eighteenth century central Mexico was essentially Europeanized and mixed-blood rather than Indian" (Borah 1979:11). The 1980 United States census shows the demographic importance of historic mingling. Seven times as many people claimed some Indian ancestry as identified themselves as members of a surviving native ethnic group (Snipp 1986:241). The distinctive roles "New Americans" play today are isomorphic with and analogous to no Precolumbian ones, inasmuch as no such population then existed.

Migration

Amalgamation of survivors meant human migration during the depopulation process (Smith 1987:75–83). Even when it was voluntary, that migration inevitably brought some of the lethal and cultural consequences that recent anthropological research has identified as being caused by forced migration (Scudder 1968). Differential depopulation of riverine and upland peoples historically opened highly productive riverine habitats to highlander invasion and occupation (Dobyns 1983:306–310; Morey and Morey 1973). Long-distance migration, which took survivors into environmental niches their ancestors never saw, makes postmigration cultural patterns nonisomorphic with and inappropriate analogs for ancestral adaptations.

Seminoles, for example, withstood nineteenth-century American efforts forcibly to relocate them by adapting to the Everglades environment in ways unknown to their Precolumbian ancestors. The latter lived in different environments several hundred miles to the north. Before beating a strategic retreat into the Everglades, the new Seminole ethnic group formed by amalgamation had become cattle-horse pastoralists on the plains of North Florida. Seminole pastoral culture was also not isomorphic with nor any sort of analog for that of their ancestors farther north at an earlier time.

Despecialization

Diminishing numbers meant decreasing demand and opportunity for social and economic specialization, making survivors necessarily jacks of more and masters of fewer trades than their forebears (Dobyns 1983:331). Ceramic production declined in quality among some peoples (Heisey and Witmer 1962:99–130), although others managed "a remarkable persistence of ceramic style despite social disruption and displacement" (Voss and Blitz 1988:136). One research frontier common to archeography and ethnohistory in the vast area north of Mesoamerica is detailed analysis of local instances of despecialization and its consequences. An archeographer assuming that ancient ceramic types define interaction spheres whether among Wankas (D'Altroy 1987b:85) or Pueblos (Stanislawski 1969:27–33; Upham 1982:61–69) must employ a pertinent analog.

The new historic demography paradigm emphasizes how limited prospective pertinent analogs are. Unspecialized native hunters who butcher and distribute big game animals in culturally patterned ways (Gould and Watson 1982:366–367) provide the archeographer with no analog for interpreting even societies with specialized hunters.

As native elites lost power and wealth, their demand for Precolumbian symbols of high status dissipated (Smith 1987:98–108). Those native elite lineages that preserved some power in European colonies perforce adapted European status symbols such as riding horseback, carrying a sword, and wearing European clothing. Conquest rewrote the rules for gaining access to power (D'Altroy 1987b:78). Spanish conquistadores shipped to Europe a Mesoamerican feather ceremonial coat-of-arms (coyote rampant) and a feather-on-wood circular standard (Alcina Franch 1983:Pl. 147, 150). One can see such curated art works and discern how they were made. One cannot today observe a feather worker's techniques or count man- and woman-days of highly skilled, specialized labor required to produce such art works.

Today no one can observe natives wearing feather garments. Reading colonial exploration reports, however, one learns that during the sixteenth century Pueblo peoples wore feather night-time quilts as day-time cloaks for warmth and herded flocks of domesticated turkeys (Hammond and Rey 1966:172, 177). The laconic historic texts describe the only behavioral analog available for interpreting physical residues of domestic turkey-raising at a riverine Hopi Pueblo (Senior and Pierce 1989:246–253).

Redefining Supernatural Worlds

Depopulation played a fundamental part in changing native religions. "When many of the elders succumbed at once, the deep pools of collective memory grew shallow, and some dried up altogether" (Merrell 1984:543). For example, natives of South Carolina in 1710 told newcomers that they had forgotten "most of their traditions" since Charleston was established only 40 years earlier. When newcomers invaded, natives made at least two characteristic adjustments to the loss of religious leaders and sacred tradition-keepers:

1. Interpreting adult newcomer immunity to many diseases as a result of newcomer supernatural power or access thereto, natives sought membership in newcomer congregations. "The situation was ripe for the mass conversions recorded so proudly by Christian missionaries" (McNeill 1976).

2. When psychological stress became unmanageable, native survivors participated in militant or millenarian movements that sought to end the newcomer and Old World disease onslaught and return natives and their environment to the status quo ante 1493.

Militant nativistic movements on New Spain's northern frontier (Bancroft 1886:490–515) began with the 1540 Mixton War. As New Spain expanded, other native peoples reacted to stress overloads by militant nativism. Tepehuanes in 1616–1618 (Spicer 1962:527), Pueblos in 1680 (Hackett and Shelby 1942), Lower Pimas in 1633 and 1766 (Spicer 1962:89), Northern Pimans in 1695 and 1751 (Dobyns 1972:23–26; Spicer 1962:124) fought for freedom.

These ideological mobilizations left physical traces. In 1680–1694, Tewas took refuge in mesa-top pueblos. An archeographer may be able to identify these conventionally constructed sites as special-purpose, short-term, settlements without recourse to colonial documents (Espinosa 1940). Without the contemporary records, only a miraculously informed archeographer could recognize the builders as participants in a militant nativistic movement.

Depopulation triggered millenarian movements among the Hurons during the 1630s (Ronda 1977), among California and Nevada natives in 1870 (Du Bois 1939), and among the most recently conquered natives of the western United States in 1889–1890 (Dobyns and Euler 1967; Thornton 1986). Ghost dancing in 1889–1890 created a distinctive class of historic site occupied by relatively large groups encamped for brief periods around a ritual dance area centered typically on one pole. Such a site probably can be identified only with the assistance of accurate native oral history (Dobyns 1974:2:421). Yet ghost dancing followed by loss of faith in its efficacy typically was the liminal period between traditional ethnic beliefs and conversion to some Christian denomination or the peyote way. Such conversion led to archeologically detectable changes in native peoples' ceremonial structures, forms, and materials (except among Plains peyotists conducting rites in tepees like those in which they had long resided).

Other technological changes typically accompany conversion and generate secular social change. Such cultural transformations inhibit accurate inference based upon even an ethnographic item isomorphic with one used earlier. The observations "that enable archaeological interpretation" (Gould and Watson 1982:356) cannot be made "in the present." One social anthropologist made them soon enough to record an idealogically staggering change and consequent cultural discontinuity. Missionaries rewarded compliant (or manipulative [Stoffle and Evans 1976:185]) Australian women and children by giving them steel axes. The efficient steel blade influx destroyed an older male monopoly on scarce, valuable greenstone axes Yir Yoront acquired by long-distance commodity exchange. The trading network collapsed. Two hitherto rigid ranks quickly collapsed into one. The loss of the power and prestige older Yir Yoront males had wielded for an unknown period facilitated religious discontinuity—conversion to Christianity (Sharp 1952).

The social anthropologist certainly discovered isomorphisms—what greenstone axes were and for what tasks they were used. By reporting in detail how such axes symbolically structured the native population, he made patent the historical nature of archeography. The classic study highlights the logical absurdity of pretensions that archeography can achieve "lawlike generalizations" about relationships between "material culture" and the human behavior producing excavatable residues (Gould and Watson 1982:356). A greenstone axe recovered as a material residue does not and cannot reflect the broad range of "intangible human behavior patterns" (Gould and Watson 1982:358) the social anthropologist found to be basic to Yir Yoront native society and culture (Sharp 1952). Human culture is, after all, unique. Consequently, the "uniformitarian" principle of geology does not apply to human culture as some analytically anachronistic (Gould 1965:227) archeographers claim (Binford 1978:12; Gould and Watson 1982:369).

Human cultures change; this truism requires emphasis. Disease mortalities and colonialism cause sharp cultural discontinuities. Ethnographic artifacts isomorphic with residual Precolumbian ones permit accurate identification of only a limited portion of prehistoric residues. Historic cultural changes among native peoples of the Americas make the social structure and cultural practices of postdepopulation groups nonisomorphic with and often inappropriate analogs for interpreting physical residues natives created during predepopulation times. Even when ethnographic analogs are pertinent to residues, their interpretation demands extreme caution, great skill, and meticulous analysis of environmental contexts and other intervening variables. The discontinuities characterizing historic times mean that archeographers cannot always accurately interpret residues. At such times, it is appropriate not to attempt the impossible.

References

Aberle, David F.
   1987 What Kind of Science Is Anthropology? *American Anthropologist* 89:551–566.
Adams, E. Charles
   1983 The Architectural Analogue to Hopi Social Organization and Room Use, and Implications for Prehistoric Northern Southwestern Culture. *American Antiquity* 48:44–61.
Alcina Franch, José
   1983 *Pre-Columbian Art*. Translated by I. Mark Paris. Harry N. Abrams, New York.
Allen, William L., and James B. Richardson III
   1971 The Reconstruction of Kinship from Archaeological Data: The Concepts, the Methods, and the Feasibility. *American Antiquity* 36:41–53.
Anonymous
   1990 Lost Empire of the Americas. *U.S. News and World Report* 108:46–54.
Baker, Malchus B., Jr.
   1987 The Diversity in Streamflow Response from Upland Basins in Arizona. In *Management of Subalpine Forests: Building on 50 Years of Research*, pp. 211–215. USDA Rocky

Mountain Forest and Range Experiment Station, General Technical Report RM–149. Fort Collins.

Bancroft, Hubert H.
1886 *History of Mexico*, vol. 2, *1521–1600*. History Co., San Francisco.

Binford, Lewis R.
1968 Archaeological Perspectives. In *New Perspectives in Archaeology*, edited by Sally R. and Lewis R. Binford, pp. 5–32. Aldine, Chicago.
1978 *Nunamiut Ethnoarchaeology*. Academic Press, New York.

Bohannon, Paul
1957 An Alternate Residence Classification. *American Anthropologist* 59:126–131.

Borah, Woodrow
1951 *New Spain's Century of Depression*. Ibero-Americana No. 35. University of California Press, Berkeley.
1979 Discontinuity and Continuity in Mexican History. *Pacific Historical Review* 48:1–25.

Brain, Jeffrey P.
1971 The Natchez "Paradox." *Ethnology* 10:215–233.

Braudel, Fernand
1982 *The Wheels of Commerce. Civilization & Capitalism, 15th–18th Century*, vol. 2. Translated by Sian Reynolds. Harper and Row, New York.

Castillo Ardiles, Hernán, Teresa Egoávil de Castillo, and Arcenio Revilla
1964 *Accopata*. Translated by Eileen A. Maynard. Cornell University Department of Anthropology, Ithaca, N.Y.

Collingwood, R. G.
1946 *The Idea of History*. Clarendon Press, Oxford.

Cook, Noble David
1981 *Demographic Collapse: Indian Peru, 1520–1620*. Cambridge University Press, Cambridge.

Cook, Sherburne F., and Woodrow Borah
1960 *The Indian Population of Central Mexico, 1531–1610*. Ibero-Americana No. 31. University of California Press, Berkeley.
1971 *Essays in Population History: Mexico and the Caribbean*. University of California Press, Berkeley.

Cordell, Linda S., Steadman Upham, and Sharon L. Brock
1987 Obscuring Cultural Patterns in the Archaeological Record: A Discussion from Southwestern Archaeology. *American Antiquity* 52:565–577.

Crosby, Alfred W., Jr.
1972 *The Columbian Exchange: Biological and Cultural Consequences of 1492*. Greenwood Press, Westport, Conn.
1986 *Ecological Imperialism: The Biological Expansion of Europe, 900–1900*. Cambridge University Press, Cambridge.

D'Altroy, Terence N.
1987a Introduction: Inka Ethnohistory. *Ethnohistory* 34:1–13.
1987b Transitions in Power: Centralization of Wanka Political Organization under Inka Rule. *Ethnohistory* 34:78–102.

Deetz, James
1988 History and Archaeological Theory: Walter Taylor Revisited. *American Antiquity* 53:13–22.

Denevan, William M.
1966 *The Aboriginal Cultural Geography of the Llanos de Mojos of Bolivia*. Ibero-Americana No. 48. University of California Press, Berkeley.
1976 *The Population of the Americas in 1492*. University of Wisconsin Press, Madison.

Dobyns, Henry F.
1963 An Outline of Andean Epidemics to 1720. *Bulletin of the History of Medicine* 37:493–515.

1966 Estimating Aboriginal American Population: An Appraisal of Techniques with a New Hemispheric Estimate. *Current Anthropology* 7:395–416.

1972 *The Papago People*. Indian Tribal Series, Phoenix.

1974 *Prehistoric Occupation within the Eastern Area of the Yuman Complex: A Study in Applied Archaeology*. 3 vols. In *Hualapai Indians*, edited by David A. Horr. Garland, New York.

1976a *Spanish Colonial Tucson: A Demographic History*. University of Arizona Press, Tucson.

1976b *Native American Historical Demography*. Indiana University Press, Bloomington.

1977 The Decline of Mescalero Apache Indian Population from 1873 to 1913. In *Essays in Honor of Morris E. Opler*, edited by Gerry C. Williams and Carolyn Pool. University of Oklahoma *Papers in Anthropology* 18:61–69.

1983 *Their Number Become Thinned: Native American Population Dynamics in Eastern North America*. University of Tennessee Press, Knoxville.

1989 *The Pima-Maricopa*. Chelsea House, New York.

Dobyns, Henry F., and Paul L. Doughty
1976 *Peru, A Cultural History*. Oxford University Press, New York.

Dobyns, Henry F., and Robert C. Euler
1967 *The Ghost Dance of 1889 among the Pai Indians of Northwestern Arizona*. Prescott College Press, Prescott.

1971 *The Navajo People*. Indian Tribal Series, Phoenix.

Du Bois, Cora
1939 *The Ghost Dance of 1870*. University of California Anthropological Records 3:1, Berkeley.

Espinosa, J. Manuel
1940 *First Expedition of Vargas into New Mexico*. University of New Mexico Press, Albuquerque.

Fiedel, Stuart J.
1987 *Prehistory of the Americas*. Cambridge University Press, Cambridge.

Gould, Richard A.
1978 The Anthropology of Human Residues. *American Anthropologist* 80:815–835.

1985 The Empiricist Strikes Back: Reply to Binford. *American Antiquity* 50:638–644.

Gould, Richard A., and Patty Jo Watson
1982 A Dialogue on the Meaning and Use of Analogy in Ethnoarchaeological Reasoning. *Journal of Anthropological Archaeology* 1:355–381.

Gould, Stephen J.
1965 Is Uniformitarianism Necessary? *American Journal of Science* 263:223–228.

Hackett, Charles W., and Charmion C. Shelby
1942 *Revolt of the Pueblo Indians of New Mexico and Otermin's Attempted Reconquest, 1680–1682*. University of New Mexico Press, Albuquerque.

Hammond, George P., and Agapito Rey
1966 *The Rediscovery of New Mexico, 1580–1594*. University of New Mexico Press, Albuquerque.

Handsman, Russell G., and Jeffrey H. Maymon
1987 The Weantinoge Site and an Archaeology of Ten Centuries of Native History. *Artifacts* 15:4–11.

Haury, Emil W.
1976 *The Hohokam: Desert Farmers & Craftsmen*. University of Arizona Press, Tucson.

Heisey, Henry W., and J. Paul Witmer
1962 On Historic Susquehanna Cemeteries. *Pennsylvania Archaeologist* 32:99–130.

Hemming, John
1982 *Monuments of the Incas*. Little, Brown, Boston.

Hofman, Jack L.
1989 Protohistoric Culture History on the Southern Great Plains. In *From Clovis to*

Comanchero: Archeological Overview of the Southern Great Plains, by Jack L. Hofman, Robert L. Books, Joe S. Hays, Douglas W. Owsley, Richard L. Jantz, Murray K. Marks and Mary H. Manhein, pp. 91–100. Arkansas Archeological Survey Research Series No. 35, Fayetteville.

Hrdlicka, Ales
1971 The Region of the Ancient Chichimecs, with Notes on the Tepecanos and the Ruin of La Quemada, Mexico. In *The North Mexican Frontier*, edited by B. C. Hedrick, J. C. Kelly, and C. L. Riley, pp. 79–129. Southern Illinois University Press, Carbondale and Edwardsville.

Hurlich, Marshall G.
1983 Historical and Recent Demography of the Algonkians of Northern Ontario. In *Boreal Forest Adaptations: The Northern Algonkians*, edited by A. Theodore Steegman, Jr., pp. 143–200. Plenum Press, New York.

Jennings, Francis
1975 *The Invasion of America: Indians, Colonialism, and the Cant of Conquest.* University of North Carolina Press, Chapel Hill.

Kolata, Alan L.
1983 Chan Chan and Cuzco: On the Nature of the Ancient Andean City. In *Civilization in the Ancient Americas: Essays in Honor of Gordon R. Willey*, edited by Richard M. Leventhal and Alan L. Kolata, pp. 345–371. University of New Mexico Press, Albuquerque.

Kroeber, A. L.
1939 *Cultural and Natural Areas of Native North America.* University of California Press, Berkeley.

Kuper, Adam
1983 *Anthropology and Anthropologists: The Modern British School.* Rev. ed. Routledge & Kegan Paul, London.

Ladurie, Emmanuel Le Roy
1981 *The Mind and Method of the Historian.* Translated by Sian and Ben Reynolds. University of Chicago Press, Chicago.

McNeill, William H.
1976 *Plagues and Peoples.* Anchor Press/Doubleday, Garden City, N.Y.

Merrell, James H.
1984 The Indians' "New World": The Catawba Experience. *William and Mary Quarterly*, 3d Ser., 41:537–564.

Mindeleff, Victor
1891 A Study of Pueblo Architecture: Tusayan and Cibola. *Eighth Annual Report of the Bureau of American Ethnology*. Government Printing Office, Washington, D.C.

Morey, Nancy C., and Robert V. Morey
1973 Foragers and Farmers: Differential Consequences of Spanish Contact. *Ethnohistory* 20:229–246.

Peebles, Christopher S., and Susan M. Kus
1977 Some Archaeological Correlates of Ranked Societies. *American Antiquity* 42: 421–428.

Ramenofsky, Ann F.
1987 *Vectors of Death: The Archaeology of European Contact.* University of New Mexico Press, Albuquerque.

Ronda, James
1977 "We Are Well As We Are": An Indian Critique of Seventeenth-Century Christian Missions. *William and Mary Quarterly*, 3d Ser., 34:66–82.

Sahlins, Marshall
1958 *Social Stratification in Polynesia.* University of Washington Press, Seattle.

Schroeder, Albert H.
1979 Pueblos Abandoned in Historic Times. In *Southwest*, edited by Alfonso Ortiz, pp.

236–254. Handbook of North American Indians, vol. 9, William C. Sturtevant, general editor. Smithsonian Institution, Washington, D.C.

Scudder, Thayer
  1968 Social Anthropology, Man-Made Lakes and Population Relocation in Africa. *Anthropological Quarterly* 41:168–176.
Senior, Louise M., and Linda J. Pierce
  1989 Turkeys and Domestication in the Southwest: Implications from Homol'ovi. *The Kiva* 54:245–260.
Sharp, Lauriston
  1952 Steel Axes for Stone-Age Australians. In *Human Problems in Technological Change*, edited by Edward H. Spicer, pp. 69–90. Russell Sage Foundation, New York.
Simmons, Marc
  1979 History of the Pueblos Since 1821. In *Southwest*, edited by Alfonso Ortiz, pp. 206–223. Handbook of North American Indians, vol. 9, William C. Sturtevant, general editor. Smithsonian Institution, Washington, D.C.
Smith, Marvin T.
  1987 *Archaeology of Aboriginal Culture Change in the Interior Southeast*. Bullen Monograph in Anthropology and History No. 6. University Presses of Florida, Gainesville.
Snipp, C. Matthew
  1986 Who Are American Indians? *Population Research and Policy Review* 5:237–252.
Snow, Dean R., and Kim M. Lanphear
  1988 European Contact and Indian Depopulation in the Northeast: The Timing of the First Epidemics. *Ethnohistory* 35:15–33.
Spicer, Edward H.
  1962 *Cycles of Conquest*. University of Arizona Press, Tucson.
Stanislawski, M. B.
  1969 The Ethno-archaeology of Hopi Pottery Making. *Plateau* 42:27–33.
Stevenson, Robert F.
  1968 *Population and Political Systems in Tropical Africa*. Columbia University Press, New York.
Steward, Julian H.
  1955 Theory and Application in a Social Science. *Ethnohistory* 2:292–302.
Stoffle, Richard W., and Michael J. Evans
  1976 Resource Competition and Population Change: A Kaibab Paiute Ethnohistorical Case. *Ethnohistory* 23:173–197.
Taylor, Walter
  1948 *A Study of Archeology*. American Anthropological Association, Memoir 69.
Thornton, Russell
  1986 *We Shall Live Again: The 1870 and 1890 Ghost Dance Movements as Demographic Revitalization*. Cambridge University Press, Cambridge.
  1987 *American Indian Holocaust and Survival: A Population History since 1492*. University of Oklahoma Press, Norman.
Turner, B. L. II, and P. D. Harrison
  1981 Prehistoric Raised-Field Agriculture in the Maya Lowlands. *Science* 213:399–405.
Upham, Steadman
  1982 *Politics and Power*. Academic Press, New York.
  1986 Smallpox and Climate in the American Southwest. *American Anthropologist* 88:115–128.
Voss, Jerome A., and John H. Blitz
  1988 Archaeological Investigations in the Choctaw Homeland. *American Antiquity* 53:125–145.
Wheeler, Roswell G.
  1886 Pima, Maricopa, and Papago Agency, Arizona. In *Report of the Secretary of the Inte-*

rior, vol. 1, pp. 256–257. House Ex. Doc. 1, Part 5; 49th Congr., 2d Sess. Government Printing Office, Washington, D.C.

White, Marian E.
1978 Neutral and Wenroe. In *Northeast*, edited by Bruce G. Trigger. Handbook of North American Indians, vol. 15, William C. Sturtevant, general editor. Smithsonian Institution, Washington, D.C.

Willey, Gordon R., and Jerome A. Sabloff
1974 *A History of American Archaeology*. Thames and Hudson, London.

Wilson, Godfrey, and Monica Hunter Wilson
1945 *The Analysis of Social Change*. Cambridge University Press, Cambridge.

Wylie, Alison
1982 An Analogy by Another Name Is Just as Analogical. *Journal of Anthropological Archaeology* 1:382–401.

Yount, George C.
1966 *George C. Yount and His Chronicles of the West*, edited by Charles L. Camp. Old West Publishing, Denver.

Chapter 28 ■

Robert C. Dunnell

Methodological Impacts of Catastrophic Depopulation on American Archaeology and Ethnology

The idea that American populations suffered a precipitous and catastrophic decline in direct consequence of contact with Europeans, particularly the epidemic diseases associated with those populations, is currently treated in some quarters (e.g., Roberts 1989) as if it were news. It also seems to have become an "in" topic in the profession. While this general attention may only be recent, the idea itself has been vigorously argued literally for decades (Ramenofsky 1987:1–5). No less scholars than Dobyns (e.g., 1963, 1966, 1983) and Cook (e.g., 1937, 1978; Borah and Cook 1963) contended that, given the nature of the epidemic diseases, their etiology, and the virgin condition of New World populations, such diseases must have swept the New World with rapid and devastating effect. Secondary sociocultural effects of population loss (e.g., Keen 1971:353) also must have played a significant role in further losses.

That such arguments did not obtain a decisive consensus is evident from the recent "rediscovery" of the issue. Critics (e.g., Bernal 1966; Blaski 1966; Denevan 1966; Driver 1966; Keyfitz and Carnaganani 1966; Kunstadter 1966; Trigger 1966) of Dobyns's 1966 paper, the piece that forcibly brought the issue to the general attention of anthropology, supply a cross section of reaction to the thesis. In general, the position taken by Dobyns was condemned with faint praise: a noteworthy contribution with a long bibliography, but. . . The exceptions ranged from nit-picking with the means of calculating the "depopulation ratio" and the "unreliability" of the nonanthropological authors of the historical records to decrying Dobyns's failure to take up related issues (e.g., regional variability of disease impact). The modal reaction was, however, to propose various compromises (a curious, unscientific way to treat disagreement) between the traditional estimates (e.g., Kroeber 1939; Mooney 1928) and Dobyns's estimate. This kind of response effectively transformed a major intellectual issue into a squabble over the size of American populations that ignored or denied the radical thesis upon which Dobyns's estimate of New World population size rested. The logic of the population collapse argument was not challenged; the emphasis was subtly redirected from the argument to the evidence of population size. This redirection continues to be a frequent response to the idea of catastrophic population decline (e.g., Milner 1980; Roberts 1989; Sempowski et al. 1990). Thus, a fundamentally new way of viewing aboriginal history is suborned into just another academic squabble over a more or less trivial detail. The main contention of this paper is that the collapse argument has large methodological implications regardless of the evidence for a catastrophic population decline in any particular area.

The failure of the collapse notion to have a large impact in either archaeology or anthropology once raised seems to be at least partly in consequence of active suppression. The implications of such an event were much broader than the event itself. The eastern United States, where most archaeologists live and play, presents now, as it did in the 1960s, abundant evidence of a major population decline. At the most general level, there is a stark contrast between the number of Indians present in the East now, or in colonial times, and the richness of the Late Prehistoric archaeological record. The same is true of many regional sequences. Driver's (1961) compendium on North American Indians shows the Ohio Valley, most of Ohio, West Virginia, and Kentucky, as vacant at the time of contact with Europeans. This gap apparently confirms the "dark and bloody ground" thesis of regional historians who contended aboriginal use was limited to hunting and warfare in this vast tract. Yet the Late Prehistoric record (Fort Ancient, Monongahela, etc.) is well known and abundant, suggesting very large populations up to the time of contact. One might blame poor integration of archaeology and ethnography, but historical records, the same used by ethnographers, were employed routinely by archaeologists to interpret the archaeological record (Callander 1979; Griffin 1946, 1964; Phillips et al. 1951). These records often told the same story of population decline or abandonment. For example, consider the contrast between the Mississippi Valley teeming with people when encountered by de Soto but virtually empty when described by the French a century later (Hodge and Lewis 1907:127–272; Phillips et al. 1951:394–397; Shea 1903). Biological historians (e.g., Crosby 1972, 1986:215) also argued from their perspective that such a decline might well be expected. So the failure of American archaeologists and ethnologists to reckon with catastrophic population decline cannot be construed simply as an oversight.

Dobyns and Cook were certainly cognizant of this professional reluctance to accept the idea of population collapse (Cook 1966; Dobyns 1966). In fact, Bennett (1966:426) even made an effort to analyze the causes of anthropological reticence, but his analysis is largely within the traditional context. Undoubtedly, as was quickly appreciated by the so-called critical theorists (cf. Trigger 1986), there are, as Schwartz (1968) and Silverberg (1969) argued, plausible sociopolitical reasons to deny population collapse (e.g., denigrating an enemy, justifying western expansion). It is difficult to regard such rationalizations as causative, however, in light of other more immediate, substantial factors. In retrospect, the population collapse argument seems to have had little impact because of two unrelated elements: (1) the almost unfathomable, if wholly unexplored, implications for archaeological and ethnological methodologies; and, (2) a methodological error in the catastrophic decline argument itself.

On the first account, acceptance of catastrophic population decline implied a disjunction, not only between archaeological and ethnographic records, but between the "pristine" conditions of an "ethnographic present" that had been the focus of American anthropology and the ethnographic and ethnohistoric sources from which it was constructed. Both archaeological interpretation and ethnographic reconstruction depended on continuity; anything that threatened the implied continuity threatened both the substance and the fabric of American archaeology and anthropology. On the second score, the population collapse hypothesis called for the destruction of most populations in advance of the physical presence of Europeans to record the decimation, and thus the decline was historically invisible. The question of a disease-induced population collapse is fundamentally an archaeological problem (Ramenofsky 1987:3; Trigger 1985a). Until quite recently, however, the debate was conducted largely by ethnographers and ethnohistorians concerned about the veracity of documentary evidence (Denevan 1976:8–11) that was, in the last analysis, irrelevant to the issue of disease-induced collapse. As long as the debate was confined to the ethnographic and historical context, it could rage forever without conclusion.

As the priority of archaeological evidence in this debate now seems at least on its way to being established (Roberts 1989), I address only the methodological implications of the collapse argument, most particularly those implications that affect archaeology. Two related consequences of the depopulation thesis are pertinent in this context: (1) the nature of the implied discontinuity introduced by population collapse at contact; and (2) the founder's effect that must necessarily accompany a major loss of population. Each has important implications for how the archaeological record is related to historic and ethnographic observations, how those observations may be used by archaeologists, if at all, and what kind of meaning might be attributed to ethnographic accounts themselves. These issues have political impacts for contemporary society, some of which are briefly mentioned to introduce this aspect of the depopulation argument.

Recent literature does depart in tone from the earlier phase of the depopulation debate. While archaeologists and anthropologists may be prepared to quibble indefinitely over whether depopulation occurred in "their area" or was of thus and such magnitude, scholars appear to agree that catastrophic population loss could have occurred at contact and probably did occur in at least some places. This change in attitude is probably the most important consequence of the context of the debate shifting from sterile arguments over irrelevant historical estimates to examining the archaeological record. It means the default position has changed as well. No longer can it be assumed, barring specific evidence, that there is continuity between archaeological and historical records; rather, now one must assume that a catastrophic decline did take place unless there is specific countervailing evidence. As the onus of "proof" shifts to the other side of the debate, the larger implications of depopulation, which could have been easily ignored without justification in earlier scholarship, now must be considered.

Continuity

Background

The relationship between archaeological and ethnographic/historical records has been the subject of controversy since Europeans arrived in North America. Indeed, the relationship played an important role in one of the first "great debates" (Silverberg 1969:97–165) that shaped American archaeology, the so-called Moundbuilder question (DePratter 1986; Hinsley 1981:22–23; Willey and Sabloff 1980:40–41). One school of thought held that much of the archaeological record, the mounds and earthworks in particular, had not been produced by American Indians; the attribution of authorship varied from mythical races and various Old World groups to simply other American groups (e.g., the Toltecs) no longer resident in North America. The other school saw the archaeological and historic records as different aspects of a continuum and attributed all archaeological remains to American Indians. Today the received view is that the Moundbuilder hypothesis dominated American thought until overthrown by the "correct" view in the late nineteenth century (Silverberg 1969:58; Trigger 1985b:16; Willey and Sabloff 1980:40–41). This is a decidedly inaccurate picture (cf. Williams 1988).

Although it is not easy to distinguish "academic" or "scientific" and lay communities until the closing years of the nineteenth century, it nonetheless seems to be the case that both views were widely held irrespective of a particular writer's claims or pretentions to science until about 1840–1850. Writers such as Atwater (1820), Barton (1787), Brackenridge (1818), Clinton (1820), Fiske (1820), Gallatin (1836), Harris (1805), Harrison (1839), and Priest (1833) all argued for a separate Moundbuilder race to one degree or another, though none very adamantly. Indeed, some, such as Barton (1797, 1799) and Gallatin (1845), shifted sides of the debate while others (e.g., Bartram 1791; Stoddard 1812) were always equivocal. Favoring an Indian origin of the archaeological record were people like Cass (1826, cited in Carr [1883:4]), Haywood (1823), Jefferson (1801), Madison (1803), McCulloh (1829), Morton (1839, 1842), and Webster (1788). After 1840, with a few notable exceptions (Squier and Davis 1848; Wilson 1876), the Moundbuilder hypothesis was limited to popular accounts (e.g., Baldwin 1874; Bancroft 1882; Nadaillac 1884; cf. Abbott 1860:154). The general concept continues to the present day in some lay quarters (e.g., von Daniken 1974). Foster (1869, 1874), whose 1874 *Prehistoric Races of the United States of America* bears the brunt of Silverberg's (1969:157–161) critique, is difficult to place because, although Foster was an emminent nineteenth century academician, he was a lawyer and physical geographer and not particularly well versed in archeological or ethnological matters. The bulk of scholarly writers, that is, those writing for institutionally sponsored publications or those whose work is cited in such journals, (e.g., Brinton 1859; Carr 1883; Carr and Shaler 1876; Force 1873; Haven 1856; Jones 1874; Lapham 1855; Schoolcraft 1851) were clearly on the side of Indian origins, although it was not until the late nineteenth century that such advocacy became adamant (e.g., Powell 1885). Even Squier (1850) changed his views, at least in respect to earthworks in New York State.

The nature of the eighteenth- and nineteenth-century arguments for and against the Indian origin of the archaeological record are particularly germane and generally omitted from historical treatments of the period (e.g., Silverberg 1969; Willey and Sabloff 1980). The early proponents of the Moundbuilder thesis raised three points commonly. First, and most important, both in terms of the weight given it and its frequency, was the observation that there were far too few Indians to account for the abundant mounds and earthworks. Sometimes this was simply a comparison of numbers; occasionally it was expanded to include a consideration of the labor requirements for the mounds. Second, a subsidiary argument treated the so-called cultural level or stage of Indian culture and that implied by the archaeological remains. Cultural level was variously identified but commonly reduced to a list of things known or believed to be part of the Moundbuilder repetoire but believed absent in American Indians—the use of metal, the use of cloth, the presence of agriculture. Some authors, of course, contrasted the savage mentality of the Indians with inferred barbaric mentality of the earthwork authors. Third, and much less important than either of the first two, was the notion that since Indians were not known to build mounds historically they did not do so in the past. This argument, even though incorrect, has received the most attention from modern reviewers (Silverberg 1969:7; Willey and Sabloff 1980:21). For nineteenth-century writers, however, it was the absence of Indian claims of authorship and the presence of myths linking them to other authors (Mathews 1839; Whittlesey 1875) rather than the lack of historical observations of Indian mound building that seems to have been the key. In fact, some proponents of the Moundbuilder view also admitted that Indians made and/or used mounds (e.g., Stoddard 1812); consequently, it is not surprising that the ambiguous drawing so frequently cited from Du Pratz (1758, vol. 3, facing 55) was accorded no significance.

The counter argument—that the Moundbuilders and Indians were the same people at different times—has two elements, one physical and one cultural. The physical component, that the Moundbuilders were a distinct biological race, genetically unrelated to the historical inhabitants of North America, was demolished by Morton's cranial studies (1839, 1842), although some hypothetical origins had been disposed of earlier (e.g., Fiske's [1820] argument as to why the mounds could not be the product of Welsh immigrants). Morton's studies

(1839:260, 1842:192–194) led him to conclude that all American crania, whether North American or South American, ancient or recent, were of a kind; any distinctions that could be drawn were mental and cultural, not physical. With the exception of Foster's (1874:275–309) attempt to revive a physical basis for a distinction (curiously not pursued in his earlier [1869:416–421] discussion of the question), Morton's work effectively killed the Moundbuilders as a distinct physical type in scholarly circles. To appreciate fully the impact of Morton's arguments, one must remember the strongly polygenic character of developing physical anthropology in the nineteenth century and the correlative tendency to taxonomic splitting (e.g., Stanton 1960). His conclusions were, of course, still compatible with migrations from (and to) other parts of the New World; Mexico continued to be a popular source as well as final home for the Moundbuilders (Baldwin 1874; Wilson 1876).

The difference in cultural level portion of the argument died somewhat more slowly. Interestingly, it was not an increase in knowledge about the archaeological record, but about American Indians, that played the key role. What was required was an appreciation that many of the features attributed to Indians—a nonsedentary, nonagricultural mode of life and the absence of particular technologies such as the weaving of cloth and the use of metals—were inaccurate characterizations brought about by the disruption of aboriginal life by the Europeans themselves. Once these differences were eliminated, the basis for the cultural level argument disappeared. In short there was no reason not to suppose Indians had been the authors of all of the American archaeological record.

While it is commonly held today that Smithsonian scholars, especially Thomas's (1894) monumental study of the mounds of eastern North America, established, once and for all, the continuity of archaeological and historical records (e.g., Silverberg 1969:173; Trigger 1985b:16; Willey and Sabloff 1980:41;) this review makes it clear that by that time the Moundbuilder thesis had not been respectable in academic quarters for nearly half a century. The unanimity and adamancy of the Smithsonian scholars on this issue may have been a reflection of the strong views of the Bureau of Ethnology's Director, J. W. Powell (e.g., Powell 1885; cf. Hinsley 1981:265; Silverberg 1969:174–175), as much as it was any of the evidence amassed by Thomas. Certainly much of the data adduced to support the Smithsonian view were at least as contrived (cf. Willey and Sabloff 1980:43 on Thomas's "errors"; Powell 1885) as the evidence they were intended to discredit. This is not a particular indictment of Thomas or the Smithsonian anthropologists. In the absence of explicit guiding theory beyond "common sense" and lacking any general consensus on epistemological standards, it was almost inevitable that the new view came to dominate for sociological and political reasons, not because of new or better evidence. As Gould (1981) argues, although overzealously (Michael 1988), this kind of inadvertent penetration of natural science by societal values, made possible by a lack of theory, is common in the nineteenth century.

Much has been made of the conjectured influence of nineteenth-century (and earlier) Euroamerican attitudes toward Indians on the Moundbuilder/cultural continuity issues (e.g., Hinsley 1981:10–22; Silverberg 1969; Trigger 1985b:16,

1986:188–195). The general argument is that Europeans found it salubrious to view Indians, active enemies at the time, as savages, even as savages that had destroyed the earlier, more civilized occupants of the continent. This view serves thus to rationalize the extermination of American Indians and the territorial ambitions of the Euroamericans (e.g., Schwartz 1968; Silverberg 1969:159; Trigger 1985b:15–16). Perhaps there is a grain of truth in such arguments, although ascertaining the motives of nineteenth-century scholars is more than a little risky. It is, however, just as clear that men like Atwater, even Foster—the arch devil in Silverberg's eyes—especially given the short chronology then current, reached their conclusions in large measure from what they correctly perceived as a vast discrepancy between the numbers of American Indians and their apparent "cultural level" as known historically and the abundance and sophistication of the Moundbuilder remains coming to light with western expansion. The discrepancy in numbers particularly, and also the presence of such things as the geometric earthworks, the sheer volume of earth moved, and the ubiquity of metal artifacts in the archaeological record were facts to be explained. It is difficult to see how, given what they knew about the archaeological record and the American Indians, they could have reached any other conclusion, dark motives notwithstanding.

Methodological Implications

The American Indian as the author of the North American archaeological record, however flimsy in its foundation, did quickly become the received wisdom of the early twentieth century. The most far-reaching, but subtle, consequence of the acceptance of Indian authorship for the archaeological record was a general change in attitude about the context of the remains themselves. Relics, once natural curiosities, now were evidence of, reflections of, "people" or cultures (cf. Gruber 1986). Now, instead of the object of inductive speculation of various sorts, the remains were deductively preexplained simply by reference to their authorship. The historical record, one particular kind of data, thus came to usurp the role played by theory in modern physical science (i.e., principles of explanation for . . .).

The most important specific methodological consequence was the rise of "ethnographic analogy" as the explicit basis for archaeological interpretation (e.g., Holmes 1903). The liabilities of the methodology were immediately apparent: "Wherein does the power of our science lie if we must interpret through a comparison with specimens in use in historic times amongst modern tribes? We are not true students of 'pre-history' if we depend upon things purely historic" (Moorehead 1900:iv). But such critiques were ignored then as they are now, at least in part because of the institutionalization of archaeology as a part of anthropology in the United States and because no other interpretive alternatives presented themselves immediately.

The advent of a methodology for chronological measurement in the 1915–1935 period (Dunnell 1986) shifted almost all archaeological attention to the construction of time-space schemata and ushered in the culture historical paradigm (ca.

1930–1965). The principal consequence of this shift in interest relevant here was the relegation of ethnographic analogy to a relatively minor and inconspicuous role, a role that did not invite analysis or methodological development. Even so, culture historical use of ethnographic analogy deserves close inspection.

Although the implicit, uncritical use of ethnographic analogy to interpret archaeological materials is the dominant culture historical usage, the "direct historical approach" (Steward 1942; Strong 1940), which had its explicit beginnings in the early part of the twentieth century (e.g., Dixon 1913) did see elaboration during this period. To use the direct historical approach, one began with the historic period ethnohistorical descriptions and worked backward in time to increasingly ancient material, using the historic descriptions as a guide to interpreting the prehistoric material. This amounts to controlling the source of analogs (cf. Binford 1967) in an effort to improve the plausibility, not the accuracy, of the inferences. The same approach is taken by Ascher (1961) in his post-Taylor (1948) analysis of the role of analogic reasoning in culture history. He distinguishes "specific" analogies, those drawn between homologous groups (ancestor-descendant) as envisioned in the direct historical approach, and "general" analogies, those drawn between groups of similar cultural level in similar environments (analogously related groups) (cf. Binford 1967). Although some scholars (e.g., MacWhite 1956; Slotkin 1952) continued to question the methodology as a whole in the tradition of Moorehead, to the extent that anyone paid attention to the use of analogy, most archaeologists were committed to its improvement, not its replacement. The key point to note, however, is that the use of ethnohistorical and ethnographic descriptions to interpret the archaeological record, regardless of the culture historical "improvements," depends upon continuity between the archaeological and Historic period records.

Just as characteristic of culture historical use of ethnographic analogy, and far more important methodologically, is the fact that the analogies employed were "simple" or "formal" analogy (Wylie 1985). The features or traits used to establish an ethnographic and an archaeological occurrence as analogs were just a set of traits. One trait bore no necessary relation to any other trait used; neither did they bear any necessary relation to the inferred property (cf. Binford 1967; Wylie 1982, 1985). Thus a simple pattern or configuration of similarities served to unite the two occurrences as analogs. That the culture historians embraced such a primitive kind of analogic argument is by no means accidental. American cultural anthropology embraced just such an approach up through World War II as well (cf. Harris 1968:328–334). As I have argued elsewhere (Dunnell 1986), this predilection arose from the peculiar historical circumstances surrounding the development of American anthropology. The Boasian view that dominated in the first half of the twentieth century eschewed the study of contemporary Native Americans in their own right (e.g., Trigger 1985b:20) in favor of an "ethnographic present," the pristine state of precontact Americans. This "salvage" view compelled ethnologists to manufacture reconstructions using isolated "facts" remembered by people no longer participating in the same cultural context as the remembered fact. Thus the reconstructions, the fictive cultures of the ethnographic present, were themselves patterns or configurations of traits, things that were for all intents and purposes archaeological constructions (i.e., analogous to a focus or phase) built without the benefit of the archaeological record. Not surprisingly, there was a strong connection between culture history and cultural anthropology.

Sociocultural anthropology of a modern sort began to emerge in the 1940s under the influence of the strongly functional British social anthropology. The new emphasis on functional systems, rather than formal patterns, created a methodological gap between archaeology and anthropology that stimulated critiques of archaeology (e.g., Taylor 1948) and ultimately spawned a "new archaeology" heavily committed to a systemic view of culture and the explanation of analogous (in the biological sense) similarities (Dunnell 1986). Since the primary culture historical use of analogy had been to attribute function to objects and larger constructs, this shift, coupled with an explicit emphasis on method (Binford 1968; Watson et al. 1971, 1984), served to make ethnographic analogy a focal point of the emerging methodology. The new found prominence of ethnographic analogy prompted critical reexamination of the concept (e.g., Binford 1967). Although some people continued to question the use of analogy on logical or other grounds (Dunnell 1978; Freeman 1968; Gould 1980), the thrust of the new effort was again to find ways to improve analogic argument. The strength of the argument depends upon the accuracy of the ethnographic description (Sabloff et al. 1973). One means, therefore, of improving ethnographic analogy, particularly since ethnographers were often interested in different things, was to improve the quality and detail of ethnographic description. The effort became "ethnoarchaeology." The impact of this attempt was obviously less in North America, which lacked "pristine" aborigines, than elsewhere, but the new archaeology's emphasis on analogous similarities also tended to highlight Ascher's "general" analogy. The major change in the use of analogy, however, was to shift from the pattern or formal analogy to the functional or relational analogy (Wylie 1985). This change is consonant with the overall shift in orientation of the new archaeology from patterns to systems.

Even though analogy was recognized as having serious, even fatal, flaws for the methodological role in which it had been cast (e.g., Longacre 1970), the apparent lack of alternatives, coupled with a commitment to a behavioral language of discourse (Dunnell 1990), compelled archaeologists to continue to use ethnographic analogy. Indeed, most archaeologists are adamant on the necessity of ethnographic analogy (Watson et al. 1984:259; Willey and Sabloff 1980:205).

Even though ethnographic analogy may be flawed as a means of inference, there can be no doubt about its central role in contemporary archaeological methodologies nor its dependence on an assumption of continuity between ethnographic/historical records and archaeological materials. Setting aside concerns over analogy as a form of inference, accepting the possiblity of catastrophic population collapse undermines the substantive basis of its application in the New World (and anywhere that contact produced similar responses). Defenders of analogy and "new archaeology" will predictably contend that regardless of catastrophic population loss, the American archaeological record is the product of American Indians and analogic inference thereby justified. To contest such sophistry is, of course, to fly in the face of "reality" (cf. Osgood 1951:205). And certainly, the political attitudes of academic, white America toward American Indians have come about-face in the last hundred years.

A second line of defense might be drawn around salvaging "general" analogy as unaffected by the discontinuity. The general "laws" on which analogies depend, however, are plainly empirical generalizations (Sabloff et al. 1973) and, to the extent that any particular generalization is based upon the reconstructed ethnographies of the Americas, just as liable to err. General analogies, furthermore, have even less to recommend them as interpretive tools than do specific analogies (Dunnell 1982).

The assertion that the archaeolgical record is a product of American Indians is a trivial assertion. There are clearly some senses in which it is true and others in which it is not. It is, for example, largely true in the genetic sense. Apart from recognizing admixture with the invading populations, Morton's 150-year old contention remains true: American Indians are descended from some of the people responsible for the archaeological record.

It is, however, important to recognize that catastrophic population loss does have profound implications for the genealogy of American Indians in relation to the archaeological record through the agency of the founder effect thus implied. The founder effect or founder principle (Dobzhansky 1970:249–257; Dobzhansky and Pavlovsky 1957; Mayr 1942:237, 1963:211–212, 529–535; Stebbins 1982:72), is a special case of genetic drift or random drift (Wright 1977:444). As Mayr (1942:237), who coined the term "founder effect," argued, the founder effect is a mechanical consequence of the simple observation that a small number of gametes cannot contain the total range of variation in any ordinary population. Thus a new population founded by a small number of individuals necessarily represents a fraction of the diversity of the original population. The principal role accorded founder effects in evolution has been in the consideration of migration and colonization and their role in speciation. There is some debate about the frequency with which founder effects have played important roles in this context (e.g., MacArthur 1967:154–157), mainly because of the difficulty of maintaining isolation between the parent and daughter populations; however, a temporal bottleneck of the sort posed by a population collapse completely precludes any supplemental communication. Founder effects are thus both a necessary and highly effective consequence of mass losses of population.

Thus the physical and genetic diversity of seventeenth-century, eighteenth-century, or modern American Indians has been limited by a random demographic event. Contemporary American Indians, as much as those of the Colonial period, are descended from only a tiny fraction of American Indians living in the early sixteenth century. Most of the people who were responsible for the archaeological record, given catastrophic population loss, do not have living descendants now or in the post-contact past. Simply to assert that the archaeological record is the product of American Indians ignores the magnitude of the catastrophy and glosses over its necessary consequences for the transmission of cultural and genetic variation.

Cultural continuity is a separate issue and the one that underlies the use of ethnographic analogy and the construction of the ethnographic present. As noted earlier, most American ethnography does not consist of descriptions of ongoing systems as observed or participated in by an anthropological witness. The focus on the "pristine" conditions of the Precolumbian era meant that cultural anthropologists had to resort to two kinds of indirect observation: the accounts of early travelers, and the memories of individuals presumed to have descended from the subject population. Traveler accounts were faulted by anthropologists themselves because of the untutored, biased character of the nonanthropological observer. In addition, a major implication of the population collapse thesis is that the conditions being observed by all but a handful of the very earliest explorers were already of dubious and unknown relevance to the "pristine" state. The memories of even the oldest individuals are likewise suspect when those memories are generations removed from the Precolumbian era and pertain to extinct practice. Trigger (1966:439–440) noted long ago that epidemic disease typically kills disproportionate numbers of the very young and very old and that this selective loss of older individuals would also affect the repositories of "lore" that they represent disproportionately. So the small number of potential informants, further reduced by the effects of disease, constitutes a second, cultural level on which founder's effects must be present. The founder's effect must have reduced cultural variability even more drastically than genetic variability. Much of the content of Indian cultures must have been lost before it was described or remembered.

But what of the traits that have been recorded and that constitute the substance of ethnographic descriptions? Again it is true, but trivially so, that they must bear some relation to past practice. There is no way, however, to determine precisely what that relation might have been. This problem is partly obscured by the ethnocentrism of the observer. Routinely, anthropologists seem to assume that the modest rate of convergence toward Euroamerican culture and values means that Indian cultures have changed less and thus are more "traditional," more like the past. Clearly underlying this position is a unilinear, progressive notion of cultural change that has the Euroamerican system at its apex (cf. Trigger 1985b:15). That Indian and Euroamerican cultures may have simply followed different trajectories does not seem to have been considered in constructing the ethnographic present or in ethnographic analogy.

Far more important than the verity of particular traits is the fact that their context has changed. Unlike traits, cultural systems as a whole cannot be collected from memories; the remembered traits are not part of ongoing, functional wholes. Trait continuity, even in cases where a critical warrant for assuming such might be supposed to exist, does not, in any fashion, guarantee systemic continuity. Both archaeologists and anthropologists have been aware of particular instances of this problem. The so-called Natchez paradox, a class system that would within a few generations cease to exist because of faulty recruitment rules, makes little sense as a component of a "pristine" system (Swanton 1911; cf. Brain 1971; Fischer 1964; Hart 1943; Josselin de Jong 1928; Tooker 1963). It is, however, readily understandable as an adaptation to conditions presented by depopulation and societal collapse (Quimby 1946), especially when it is realized that the system did not have to work; the Natchez did not persist as an independent, functioning cultural system. Cases like the Natchez paradox are easily dismissed as aberrant simply because we usually lack the means with which to assess the validity of any particular descriptive assertion.

Where opportunities to test do occur, as in cases in which physical-chemical constraints provide a guide for the evaluation of "remembered" practice, the results are not very encouraging. Holmes, for example, makes heavy use of historical and ethnographic information in his classic *Aboriginal Pottery of the Eastern United States* (1903). In this work, Holmes discussed the veracity of nineteenth-century Pamunkey "traditional" pottery-making technology (1903:152–153). Clay is obtained from a particular source at a particular time of year. It is cleaned, kneaded, and worked to a particular consistency. Shell is burned, crushed, and added to the paste as temper. The paste is then formed into vessels that are first dried before a fire before finally being fired briefly. This is a perfectly plausible scenario save that the vessels thus produced will not function as vessels. Further, as Holmes notes to his dismay, even though not subjected to centuries or millenia in the ground, these vessels fall apart in only a few years on the shelves of the Smithsonian. Since pottery does survive from ancient times and must be assumed to have been functional at one point, the "traditional" Pamunkey pottery technology must be reckoned to be a modern confection. The pots so produced no longer function to cook or store food but to generate cash income from curiosity seekers (Holmes 1903:152). It is very likely that many, if not most, of the elements of pottery manufacture were remembered, but they were not integrated into a system, leading to "errors." The products no longer functioned in a larger system in the same fashion, leading to still more "errors." The spontaneous self-destruction of the pottery suggests strongly that one "error" lay in the treatment of the temper. Although shell was undoubtedly used as temper prehistorically and there is every reason to suppose that it was burned, burning the shell to such a temperature as to convert the shell, $CaCO_3$, to CaO will cause pots to self-destruct. The hydroscopic CaO rehydrates and expands after cooling to ambient temperatures (Bronitsky and Hamer 1986; Dunnell and Feathers 1986; Feathers 1989). The fact remains, however, that for most memories, we lack any means to judge their veracity.

Conclusions

The dramatic loss of population in the New World in consequence of contact with Europeans is not just another fact to be discussed, modified, and integrated in the existing anthropological lore of the Americas. That huge losses did occur seems now firmly established, although the precise magnitude, regional variability, and exact timing has yet to be worked out in detail. As a consequence, the general assumption of continuity between ethnographic/historical accounts of native Americans and the people responsible for the archaeolgoical record is no longer valid. A collapse must be assumed to have taken place unless it can be explained how and why particular areas escaped the devastation of epidemic disease.

Apparent continuity in the form of traits does not, in and of itself, necessitate systemic continuity. In fact, because of the loss of context and the inability to test the validity of attributing any particular trait to a "pristine" ethnographic present, even trait continuity is probably grossly overestimated. Furthermore, founder's effects, both in respect to biological populations and cultural lineages, are a predictable, unavoidable consequence of large population losses. Only a fraction of sixteenth-century variation has served to generate subsequent populations and cultural developments. About the only inference that can be drawn with certainty is that the founder's effects are more pronounced the more complex the society involved. Where age and sex are the primary determinants of knowledge and roles, a better representation will occur at a given level of population loss than where a society's technology, for example, is parceled over a variety of specialists and whole segments lost by accident.

The loss of variability through founder's effects and the destruction of cultural systems independently of cultural traits not only makes North American ethnography a wholly inadequate basis on which to found other interpretations, but it also calls into question the value of those reconstructions as ethnographic documents. The realization that estimating Precolumbian population size is an archaeological problem is thus just the tip of the iceberg; understanding all aspects of Native American cultural systems at the time of contact is also an archaeological problem, one in which the traditional ethnographic and historical records can only play a supplemental role (e.g., Trigger 1985b:27–29; Wilcox and Masse 1981:11–130). Archaeology is the only direct evidence about the condition, size, and distribution of aboriginal populations at contact. At least insofar as American ethnology is concerned, archaeology is not a "tail on an ethnological kite," as Steward (1942:341) so quaintly phrased it.

Both systemic discontinuity and founder's effects on surviving traits compel the view that contemporary American Indians' claims to the archaeological record are generic at best (cf. Rosen 1980:18–19). Modern Indians, both biologically and culturally, are very much a phenomenon of contact and derive from only a small fraction of peoples and cultural variability of the early sixteenth century. In some important respects, our eighteenth- and nineteenth-century predecessors got it right; they even got it right for the right reasons, although the terminology is not exactly modern. The people responsible for the archaeological record were, just as they supposed, a far more numerous, culturally different group of people than were known in historic times. The entire relation between past and present, between history and archaeology must be rethought (Trigger 1985b:32–34; Wilcox and Masse 1981:11–13). Most of the consequences are likely to prove troubling simply because the assumption of cultural continuity has been so dominant for so long.

There is a timely lesson to be learned in the age of critical theory. It is easy to impugn the motives of our predecessors. A plausible just-so story about why Indians were rejected as the authors of the archaeological record has been spun by twentieth-century scholars: It is a story of deep penetration of a budding archaeology by the social and political attitudes of nineteenth-century American society. Closer inspection does not suggest such penetration was a strong force in nineteenth-century scholarship at all, but rather that it may well have played a critical role in the twentieth-century story about the eighteenth- and nineteenth-century scholars. Until such time as archaeologists adopt an empirical epistemological standard, stories will please the mind and become part of archaeology for a variety of reasons, not too many of which will prove praiseworthy in subsequent generations.

Acknowledgments

This paper has benefited from the comments of J. Buikstra, A. F. Ramenofsky, J. A. Sabloff, and D. H. Thomas. Their generosity is much appreciated. M. D. Dunnell provided important editorial assistance.

References

Abbott, J.
 1860 *American History*, vol. 1, *Aboriginal America*. Sheldon, New York.
Ascher, R.
 1961 Analogy in Archaeological Interpretation. *Southwestern Journal of Anthropology* 17:317–325.
Atwater, C.
 1820 Description of the Antiquities Discovered in the State of Ohio and Other Western States. *Archaeologia Americana, Collections and Transactions* 1:105–267.
Baldwin, J. D.
 1874 Ancient America. In *Notes on American Archaeology*. Harper and Brothers, New York.
Bancroft, H. H.
 1882 *Native Races*. H. H. Bancroft, New York.
Barton, B. S.
 1787 *Observations on Some Parts of Natural History*. London.
 1797 *New Views on the Origin of the Tribes and Nations of America*. John Bioren, Philadelphia.
 1799 *Fragments of the Natural History of Pennsylvania, Part I*. John Bioren, Philadelphia.
Bartram, W.
 1791 *Travels through North and South Carolina, Georgia, East and West Florida, the Cherokee Country, the Extensive Territories of the Muscogulges or Creek Confederacy, and the Country of the Chactaws*. James and Johnson, Philadelphia.
Bennett, J. W.
 1966 Comments on Estimating Aboriginal American Population (Dobyns and Thompson). *Current Anthropology* 7:425–426.
Bernal, I.
 1966 Comments on Estimating Aboriginal American Population (Dobyns and Thompson). *Current Anthropology* 7:426.
Binford, L. R.
 1968 Archeological Perspectives. In *New Perspectives in Archeology*, edited by S. R. Binford and L. R. Binford, pp. 5–32. Aldine, Chicago.
Binford, L. R.
 1967 Smudge Pits and Hide Smoking: The Use of Analogy in Archaeological Reasoning. *American Antiquity* 32:1–12.
Blaski, O.

1966 Comments on Estimating Aboriginal American Population (Dobyns and Thompson). *Current Anthropology* 7:426–427.

Borah, W. W., and S. F. Cook
1963 *The Aboriginal Population of Central Mexico on the Eve of the Spanish Conquest.* Ibero-Americana No. 45. Berkeley.

Brackenridge, H. M.
1818 *On the Population and Tumuli of the Aborigines of North America.* Transactions of the American Philosophical Society, n.s., 1:115–159.

Brain, Jeffrey P.
1971 The Natchez Paradox. *Ethnology* 10:215–222.

Brinton, D. G.
1859 *Notes on the Floridian Peninsula, Its Literary History, Indian Tribes and Antiquities.* Joseph Sabin, Philadelphia. (Reprinted, Paladin Press, New York, 1969)

Bronitsky, G., and R. Hamer
1986 Experiments in Ceramic Technology: The Effect of Various Tempering Materials on Impact and Thermal Shock Resistance. *American Antiquity* 51:89–101.

Callander, C.
1979 Hopewell Archaeology and American Ethnology. In *Hopewell Archaeology, The Chillocothe Conference*, edited by D. S. Brose and N. Greber, pp. 254–257. MCJA Special Publication, No. 3. Kent State University Press, Kent, Ohio.

Carr, L.
1883 *The Mounds of the Misssissippi Valley Historically Considered.* Kentucky Geological Survey, Memoir, 2d ser., No. 2. Frankfort.

Carr, L., and N. S. Shaler
1876 *On the Prehistoric Remains of Kentucky.* Kentucky Geological Survey, Memoir, 2d ser., No. 1(4). Frankfort.

Clinton, D. W.
1820 *A Memoir on the Antiquities of the Western Part of the State of New York.* E. and E. Hosford, Albany.

Cook, S. F.
1937 *The Extent and Significance of Disease among the Indians of Baja California, 1697–1773.* Ibero-Americana No. 12. Berkeley.
1966 Comment on Estimating Aboriginal American Population (Dobyns and Thompson). *Current Anthropology* 7:427–429.
1978 Historical Demography. In *California*, edited by R. F. Heizer, pp. 91–98. Handbook of North American Indians, vol. 8, W. C. Sturtevant, general editor. Smithsonian Institution, Washington, D.C.

Crosby, A. W.
1972 *The Columbian Exchange: Biocultural Consequences of 1492.* Greenwood Press, Westport, Conn.
1986 *Ecological Imperialism. The Biological Expansion of Europe, 900–1900.* Cambridge University Press, Cambridge.

Denevan, W. M.
1966 Comments on Estimating Aboriginal American Population (Dobyns and Thompson). *Current Anthropology* 7:429.
1976 Introduction. In *The Native Population of the Americas in 1492*, edited by W. M. Denevan, pp. 1–12. University of Wisconsin Press, Madison.

DePratter, C. B.
1986 Introduction. In *The Late Prehistoric Southeast. A Source Book*, edited by C. B. DePratter, pp.xiii—lxxiii. Garland Press, New York.

Dixon, R. B.
1913 Some Aspects of North American Archaeology. *American Anthropologist* 15:549–577.

Dobyns, H. F.

1963 An Outline of Andian Epidemic History to 1720. *Bulletin of the History of Medicine* 37:493–515.

1966 An Appraisal of Techniques for Estimating Aboriginal Population with a New Hemispheric Estimate. *Current Anthropology* 7:395–416.

1983 *Their Number Become Thinned.* University of Tennessee Press, Knoxville.

Dobzhansky, T. G.

1970 *Genetics of the Evolutionary Process.* Columbia University Press, New York.

Dobzhansky, T. G., and O. Pavlovsky

1957 An Experimental Study of Interaction between Genetic Drift and Natural Selection. *Evolution* 7:198–210.

Driver, H. E.

1961 *Indians of North America.* University of Chicago Press, Chicago.

1966 Comments on Estimating Aboriginal American Population (Dobyns and Thompson). *Current Anthropology* 7:430.

Dunnell, R. C.

1978 Archaeological Potential of Anthropological and Scientific Models of Function. In *Archaeological Essays in Honor of Irving B. Rouse,* edited by R. C. Dunnell and E. S. Hall, Jr., pp. 41–73. Mouton, The Hague.

1982 Science, Social Science, and Common Sense: The Agonizing Dilemma of Modern Archaeology. *Journal of Anthropological Research* 38:1–25.

1986 Five Decades of American Archaeology. In *American Archaeology, Past and Future,* edited by D. J. Meltzer, D. D. Fowler, and J. A. Sabloff, pp. 23–49. Smithsonian Institution Press, Washington.

1990 Archaeology and Evolutionary Science. Paper presented at the conference "The Future of the Past: American Archaeology A. D. 2001," 4–5 May, Carbondale, Ill.

Dunnell, R. C., and J. K. Feathers

1986 Later Woodland Manifestations of the Malden Plain, Southeast Missouri. Paper presented at the 1986 Southeastern Archaeological Conference, Nashville.

Du Pratz, L. P.

1758 *Historie de la Louisiane.* 3 volumes. Paris.

Feathers, J. K.

1989 Effects of Temper on Strength of Ceramics: Response to Bronitsky and Hamer. *American Antiquity* 54:579–588.

Fischer, J. L.

1964 Solution for the Natchez Paradox. *Ethnology* 3:53–65.

Fiske, M.

1820 *Conjectures Respecting the Ancient Inhabitants of North America.* Archaeologia Americana, Collections and Transactions 1:300–307.

Force, M. F.

1873 *Some Considerations on the Mound Builders.* Robert Clarke, Cincinnati.

Foster, J. W.

1869 *The Mississippi Valley: Its Physical Geography, Including Sketches of the Topography, Botany, Climate, and Mineral Resources; and of the Progress of Development in Population and Material Wealth.* S. C. Grigg, Chicago.

1874 *Prehistoric Races of the United States of America.* 3d ed. S. C. Grigg, Chicago.

Freeman, L. G.

1968 A Theoretical Framework for Interpreting Archaeological Materials. In *Man the Hunter,* edited by R. B. Lee and I. DeVore, pp. 262–267. Aldine, Chicago.

Gallatin, A.

1836 *A Synopsis of the Indian Tribes within the United States East of the Rocky Mountains, in the British and Russian Possessions in North America.* Archaeolgia Americana, Collections and Transactions 2:1–422. Cambridge.

1845 *Origin of American Civilization.* Transactions of the American Ethnological Society 1:194–214.

Gould, R. A.
1980 *Living Archaeology*. Cambridge University Press, Cambridge.
Gould, S. J.
1981 *The Mismeasure of Man*. Norton, New York.
Griffin, J. B.
1946 *The Fort Ancient Aspect, Its Cultural and Chronological Position in Mississippi Valley Archaeology*. University of Michigan Press, Ann Arbor.
1964 The Northeast Woodlands Area. In *Prehistoric Man in the New World*, edited by J. D. Jennings and E. Norbeck, pp. 223–258. University of Chicago Press, Chicago.
Gruber, J. W.
1986 Archaeology, History, and Culture. In *American Archaeology, Past and Future*, edited by D. J. Meltzer, D. D. Fowler, and J. A. Sabloff, pp. 163–186. Smithsonian Institution Press, Washington, D.C.
Harris, M.
1968 *The Rise of Anthropological Theory*. T. Y. Crowell, New York.
Harris, T. M.
1805 The Journal of a Tour in the Territory Northwest of the Alleghany Mountains; Made in the Spring of the Year 1803. In *Early Western Travels, 1748–1846*, edited by T. G. Thwaites, (1903), vol. 3, pp. 307–382.
Harrison, W. H.
1839 *A Discourse on the Aborigines of the Ohio Valley*. Transaction of the Historical and Philosophical Society of Ohio 1(2):3–96.
Hart, C. W. M.
1943 A Reconsideration of Natchez Social Structure. *American Anthropologist* 45:379–386.
Haven, S. F.
1856 *Archaeology of the United States*. Smithsonian Contributions to Knowledge 8(2). Washington, D.C.
Haywood, J.
1823 *The Natural and Aboriginal History of Tennessee, Up to the First Settlements Therein by the White People, in the Year 1768*. Nashville. (Reprinted McCowat-Mercer Press, 1959, Jackson, Tenn.).
Hinsley, C. M., Jr.
1981 *Scientist and Savages: The Smithsonian Institution and the Development of American Anthropology, 1846–1910*. Smithsonian Institution Press, Washington, D.C.
Hodge, F. W., and T. H. Lewis (editors)
1907 *Spanish Explorers in the Southern United States, 1528–1543*. Charles Scribner's Sons, New York.
Holmes, W. H.
1903 *Aboriginal Pottery of the Eastern United States*. Bureau of American Ethnology, 20th Annual Report. Washington, D.C.
Jefferson, T.
1801 *Notes on the State of Virginia*. R. T. Rawle, Philadelphia.
Jones, C. C.
1874 Art. III, Antiquity of the North American Indians. *The North American Review* 65:70–87.
Josselin de Jong, J. P. B.
1928 The Natchez Social System. *Proceedings of the 23rd International Congress of Americanists*, pp. 553–562. Talleres Graficos de la Nacion, Mexico.
Keen, B.
1971 The White Legend Revisted: A Reply to Professor Hanke's 'Modest Proposal.' *Hispanic American Historical Review* 49:703–719.
Keyfitz, N., and A. Carmagnani
1966 Comments on Estimating Aboriginal American Population (Dobyns and Thompson). *Current Anthropology* 7:435–436.

Kroeber, A. L.
  1939 *Cultural and Natural Areas of Native North America*. University of California Publications in American Archaeology and Ethnology No. 38. Berkeley.
Kunstadter, P.
  1966 Comments on Estimating Aboriginal American Population (Dobyns and Thompson). *Current Anthropology* 7:436–437.
Longacre, W. A.
  1970 Current Thinking in American Archaeology. In *Current Directions in Anthropology*, edited by N. S. F. Woodbury, pp. 126–138. American Anthropological Association Bulletin 3(3), Part 2. Washington, D.C.
Lapham, I. A.
  1855 *The Antiquities of Wisconsin*. Smithsonian Contributions to Knowledge 7(4). Washington, D.C.
MacArthur, R. H.
  1967 *Theory of Island Biogeography*. Princeton University Press, Princeton, N.J.
McCullough, J. H.
  1829 *Researches Philosophical and Antiquarian Concerning the Aboriginal History of America*. Fielding Lucas, Baltimore, Md.
MacWhite, E.
  1956 On the Interpretation of Archaeological Evidence in Historical and Sociological Terms. *American Anthropologist* 58:3–25.
Madison, J.
  1803 *A Letter on the Supposed Fortifications of the Western Country from Bishop Madison to Dr. Barton*. Transactions of the American Philosophical Society 6:132–142.
Mathews, C.
  1839 *Behemoth: A Legend of the Mound-Builders*. Weeks, Jordan, Boston.
Mayr, E.
  1942 *Systematics and the Origin of Species*. Columbia University Press, New York.
  1963 *Animal Species and Evolution*. Harvard University Press, Cambridge, Mass.
Michael, J. S.
  1988 A New Look at Morton's Craniological Research. *Current Anthropology* 29:349–354.
Milner, G. R.
  1980 Epidemic Disease in the Post-Contact Southeast: A Reappraisal. *Midcontinental Journal of Archaeology* 5:39–56.
Mooney, J.
  1928 *The Aboriginal Population of America North of Mexico*. Smithsonian Miscellaneous Collections 80(7). Washington, D.C.
Moorehead, W. K.
  1900 *Prehistoric Implements*. Robert Clarke, Cincinnati, Ohio.
Morton, S. G.
  1839 *Crania Americana*. John Pennington, Philadelphia.
  1842 An Inquiry into the Distinctive Characteristics of the Aboriginal Race of America. *Boston Journal of Natural History* 4:190–223.
Nadaillac, Marquis de
  1884 *Pre-Historic America*. G. P. Putnam's Sons, New York.
Osgood, C.
  1951 Culture: Its Empirical and Non-Empirical Character. *Southwestern Journal of Anthropology* 7:202–214.
Phillips, P., J. A. Ford, and J. B. Griffin
  1951 *Archaeological Survey in the Lower Mississippi Alluvial Valley, 1940–1947*. Peabody Museum of Archaeology and Ethnology, Papers, 25. Harvard University, Cambridge, Mass.

Powell, J. W.
　1885 The Indians Are the Moundbuilders. *Science* 5:267.
Priest, J.
　1833 *American Antiquities and Discoveries in the West.* 3d ed. Hoffman and White, Albany, N.Y.
Quimby, G. I.
　1946 Natchez Social Structure as an Instrument of Assimilation. *American Anthropologist* 48:134–137.
Ramenofsky, A. F.
　1987 *Vectors of Death: The Archaeology of European Contact.* University of New Mexico Press, Albuquerque.
Roberts, L.
　1989 Large Numbers, Big Assumptions. *Science* 246:1245–1247.
Rosen, L.
　1980 The Excavation of American Indian Burial Sites: A Problem in Law and Professional Responsibility. *American Anthropologist* 82:5–27.
Sabloff, J. A., T. W. Beale, and A. M. Kurland, Jr.
　1973 Recent Developments in Archaeology. *Annals of the American Academy of Political and Social Science* 408:103–118.
Schoolcraft, H. R.
　1851 *Information Respecting the History, Condition and Prospects of the Indian Tribes of the United States,* vol. 1, *Historical and Statistical Information Respecting the History, Condition and Prospects of the Indian Tribes of the United States.* Lippincott, Grambo, Philadelphia.
Schwartz, D. W.
　1968 North American Archaeology in Historical Perspective. In *Actes du XIe Congres International du Historie de Sciences,* vol. 2, pp. 311–315. Warsaw and Cracow.
Sempowski, M. L., L. P. Saunders, and J. W. Bradley
　1990 New World Epidemics. Letter to the Editor. *Science* 247:788–789.
Shea, J. G.
　1903 *Discovery and Exploration of the Mississippi Valley.* 2d ed. Joseph McDonaugh, Albany, N.Y.
Silverberg, R.
　1969 *Mound Builders of Ancient America: The Archaeology of a Myth.* New York Graphic Society, Greenwich, Conn.
Slotkin, J. S.
　1952 Some Basic Problems in Prehistory. *Southwestern Journal of Anthropology* 8:442–443.
Squier, E. G.
　1850 *Aboriginal Monuments of the State of New York.* Smithsonian Contributions to Knowledge 2. Washington, D.C.
Squier, E. G., and E. H. Davis
　1848 *Ancient Monuments of the Mississippi Valley.* Smithsonian Contributions to Knowledge 1. Washington, D.C.
Stanton, W.
　1960 *The Leopard's Spots: Scientific Attitudes toward Race in America 1815–1859.* University of Chicago Press, Chicago.
Stebbins, G. L.
　1982 *Darwin to DNA, Molecules to Humanity.* W. H. Freeman, San Francisco.
Steward, J. H.
　1942 The Direct Historical Approach. *American Antiquity* 7:337–343.
Stoddard, A.
　1812 *Sketches, Historical and Descriptive of Louisiana.* M. Carey, Philadelphia. (Reprinted, AMS Press, New York, 1973)
Strong, W. D.

1940 *From History to Prehistory in the Northern Great Plains*. Smithsonian Miscellaneous Collections 100:353–394. Washington, D.C.

Swanton, J. R.

1911 *Indian Tribes of the Lower Mississippi Valley*. Bureau of American Ethnology, Bulletin No. 43. Washington, D.C.

Taylor, W. W.

1848 *A Study of Archaeology*. American Anthropological Association, Memoir 69. Menasha, Wis.

Thomas, C.

1894 *Report on the Mound Explorations of the Bureau of Ethnology*. Twelfth Annual Report of the Bureau of Ethnology, 1890–1891, pp. 3–742. Washington, D.C.

Tooker, E.

1963 Natchez Social Organization, Fact or Anthropological Folklore. *Ethnohistory* 10: 358–372.

Trigger, B. G.

1966 Comments on Estimating Aboriginal American Population (Dobyns and Thompson). *Current Anthropology* 7:439–440.

1985a *Natives and Newcomers*. McGill-Queen's University Press, Kingston.

1985b The Past as Power. Anthropology and the North American Indian. In *Who Owns the Past?* edited by I. McBryde, pp. 11–40. Oxford University Press, Oxford.

1986 Prehistoric Archaeology and American Society. In *American Archaeology, Past and Future*, edited by D. J. Meltzer, D. D. Fowler, and J. A. Sabloff, pp. 187–215. Smithsonian Institution Press, Washington, D.C.

Von Daniken, E.

1974 *The Gold of the Gods*. Bantam Books, Toronto.

Watson, P. J., S. A. LeBlanc, and C. L. Redman

1971 *Explanation in Archeology*. Columbia University Press, New York.

1984 *Archeological Explanation*. Columbia University Press, New York.

Webster, N.

1788 Letter to the Rev. Dr. Stiles, President of Yale College, on the Remains of Fortifications in the Western Country. *American Magazine* February:146–156.

Whittlesey, C.

1875 The Great Mound on the Etawah River near Cartersville, Georgia. *American Naturalist* 5:42–44.

Wilcox, D. R., and W. B. Masse

1981 A History of Protohistoric Studies in the North American Southwest. In *The Protohistoric Period in the North American Southwest*, A.D. 1450–1700, edited by D. R. Wilcox and W. B. Masse, pp. 1–27. Arizona State University, Anthropological Research Papers, No. 24. Tempe.

Willey, G. R., and J. A. Sabloff

1980 *A History of American Archaeology*. W. H. Freeman, San Francisco.

Williams, S.

1988 Time and Stratigraphy: The Eternal Search in the Southeast. Plenary address to the 50th Southeastern Archaeological Conference, New Orleans.

Wilson, D.

1876 *Prehistoric Man*. 2 vols. 3d ed. Macmillan, London.

Wright, S.

1977 *Evolution and the Genetics of Populations*, vol. 3, *Experimental Results and Evolutionary Deductions*. University of Chicago Press, Chicago.

Wylie, A. M.

1982 An Analogy by Another Name Is Just as Analogical: A Commentary on the Gould-Watson Dialogue. *Journal of Anthropological Archaeology* 1:382–401.

1985 The Reaction against Analogy. *Advances in Archaeological Method and Theory* 8:63–111.

Chapter 29 ■

Marvin Harris

Depopulation and Cultural Evolution: A Cultural Materialist Perspective

Among the points of contrast between cultural materialism and classical Marxism (and various so-called structural neo-Marxisms as well), is the cultural materialist specification of the mode of reproduction as a universal infrastructural component of sociocultural systems. In direct opposition to Marx, cultural materialists consider the processes of biocultural reproduction to be as important as the processes of production (Harris 1979a:66; Harris and Ross 1987:5). True, most cultural materialists have emphasized the evolutionary consequences of "population pressure" and population growth (e.g., Johnson and Earle 1987; Keely 1988; Sanders and Price 1968; Sanders, et al. 1979). But this emphasis corresponds to the predominant macroevolutionary trend of world population, despite long periods of stasis, minor fluctuations, and regional variations. (After all, efforts to avert population decline are not high on the agenda of contemporary political ecology.) It is clear, however, that the cultural materialist principle of infrastructural determinism applies as forcefully to population crashes as to population booms (just as it applies as readily to falling as to rising rates of production). Whether population is expanding or contracting, cultural materialism predicts that (probabilistically) determined effects will appear in the rest of the infrastructural conjunction, and that these will cause concomitant changes in the structural and superstructural sectors.

Although the effects of population growth rather than decline has been a major focus of cultural materialist theory, interest in population decline ante-dates the growing acceptance of Dobyns's account of the first-contact epidemic-induced Native American population crash. Harris's (1971:250) introductory text-book, for example, from the first edition and thereafter, attributes destructive Kwakiutl potlatches to increased competition among Kwakiutl chiefs for the alle-giance of workers and warriors whose numbers had been cut by two-thirds dur-ing smallpox epidemics early in the nineteenth century. Depopulation of the Upper Orinoco mainstream also figures in cultural materialist explanations of the surge in population growth and warfare among the Yanomami (Ferguson 1989; Harris 1979b:129). It has also been proposed (with no claim to originality) that the great plagues of fourteenth-century Europe and the ensuing population crash triggered various peasant uprisings, messianic movements, crusades against heretics, and the founding of the Inquisition (Harris 1974, 1977:172).

Given the paradigmatic emphasis on demographic processes in cultural ma-terialism, and the existence of theories that link both population increase and decrease to important changes in structure and superstructure, it is difficult to understand why some contributors to this volume believe that "The entire rela-tion between past and present, between history and archaeology must be re-thought" (see Dunnell, this volume), or why the "uniformitarian principle" must forthwith be abandoned (see Dobyns, this volume). Much the opposite sort of conclusion would seem to be warranted—namely, that recognition of the pro-found effects of Postcolumbian depopulation on various components of Native American sociocultural systems, including reversions to lower levels of hierar-chy and complexity, clears the way for the explanation of archaeological and eth-nographic "anomalies" that have hitherto been used to discredit nomothetic processual approaches in general, and cultural materialism in particular (Harris 1990). Dunnell himself provides a prime example in the form of the Natchez sys-tem of class exogamy, which becomes intelligible "as an adaptation" to "depopu-lation and societal collapse." And Dobyns (1983:302–311) himself has suggested that the phenomenon of nonstate, nonchiefdom confederacies, which has misled and baffled evolutionist models since the time of Lewis Henry Morgan, is related (at least in the Southeast) to the need to develop new forms of political organiza-tion to cope with the Postcolumbian population crash. As Smith (1987) has shown, remnants of the population base of Mississippian chiefdoms formed the Creek confederacy as a means of regaining some of the advantages of political centralization.

The same disjunction between, on the one hand, an assertion that there is no theoretical framework that can handle the startling new facts about the pace of early contact depopulation and cultural change and, on the other, the presen-tation of clear, testable, essentially cultural materialist hypotheses for explaining this phenomenon and its local variations, figures prominently in the contribu-tions of Ramenofsky and Stannard.

Ramenofsky laments the absence of a "theory or system of knowledge" without which the "why questions" about the nature, magnitude, and the direction of change that occurred during the Contact period cannot be answered. Yet Ramenofsky herself (1987) has elsewhere reviewed a number of theories that explain the differential impact of introduced pathogens in terms of such factors as the size and density of precontact settlements.

At the end of his essay, Stannard alludes to the "great distance" that separates us from "a theory to organize the accumulated data." Yet the essay itself provides an excellent overview of a corpus of interrelated and essentially cultural materialist theories that go a long way toward explaining the variations as well as the uniformities in the depopulation process.[1] For example, Stannard notes that Cook and Borah's theory that highland populations collapsed later and recovered earlier than lowland populations is contradicted by the case of Sierra Zapoteca, where the highlands recovered earlier than the lowlands. To understand this exception, Stannard (following Chance 1989), suggests that particular factors of soil productivity, settlement pattern, and militarily significant aspects of topography in this case overrode the logic of Cook and Borah's theory. Citing Newson (1987), Stanning invokes another set of what appear to be etic behavioral and infrastructural factors to explain the contrasting depopulation rates of two regions of colonial Nicaragua: labor regimens (town versus other forms of encomiendas), opportunities for slave capture, and population density in relation to introduced diseases. Stannard's final list of factors to be considered includes carrying capacity,[2] range of native food resources, labor output, caloric requirements, climate, preexisting disease loads, indigenous political organization, and indigenous "culture." With the exception of the last item, which I take to mean ideology, this is a list of infrastructural and structural variables that would form the initial starting point for a cultural materialist analysis.

The analytic problems raised by massive Postcolumbian depopulations are formidable but not quite as draconian and certainly not as novel as Dobyns and Dunnell claim. As Ramenofsky points out, attempts to identify the effects of Western contact on native peoples have been the subject of debate since the beginning of modern archaeology and sociocultural anthropology. A classic instance is Elman Service's (1962) contention that all precontact bands had been patrilineal and that bilateral and matrilineal bands owed their existence to the disruptions of the Contact period. Another classic case is the demonstration by Leacock (1954) that individually owned Algonkian trapping territories were, contra Speck (1915), not indigenous but a consequence of trade with the Hudson Bay Company. More recently, Wolf's (1983) ambitious attempt to document the global impact of early European capitalism on native cultures in effect denies that we can safely rely on any purely ethnographic sources as descriptions of the social life of any world area prior to 1500.

It does not follow from the vast changes brought about by the European expansion that we must abandon the attempt to depict the nature of human social life in precontact times; nor that ethnographic and historical documents have suddenly become worthless; nor that the gap between archaeology and ethnohistory has suddenly become unbridgeable. What does follow is that we need to be skeptical about any one kind of knowledge—be it historical document, ethnographic monograph, or archaeological site report; that as much as ever, we need all three kinds of studies; and perhaps most important, that we need theories about the probable trajectories of sociocultural evolution that conform to a consistent nomothetic explanatory paradigm.[3]

The challenge that the great Native American population crash presents to anthropology is not in principle any different from the challenge that all singular historical events pose to any nomothetic science. Those of us who regard anthropology as a nomothetic discipline are well aware that the principles that govern selection for and selection against sociocultural innovations do not result in global parallel or convergent transformations. Divergences, especially in fine-grained perspective, are also the normal consequence of sociocultural selection. Divergences occur because sociocultural selection acts on historically given, and hence diverse, initial conditions. Yet such divergences do not constitute a refutation of the existence of general principles of sociocultural selection any more than the divergences of species constitute a refutation of the principle of reproductive success in evolutionary biology. Moreover, to push the analogy between the epistemological foundations of sociocultural and biological science one step further, the certainty of discovering unlimited degrees of sociocultural differences at the most microscopic level of description in no way precludes the possibility of discovering scientifically legitimate similarities at more macroscopic levels. At the level of the base pairs of DNA, no two individual *Hemo sapiens* are likely to be identical. This does not render the species concept any less indispensable for the conduct of biological research. Similarly, classification and categorization of varieties of sociocultural systems will always be the indispensable precondition for generalizing about the processes of sociocultural selection—in this case, the processes that account for differential resistance to pathogens, differential rates of population decline, and differential structural and ideological adaptations to depopulation.

Notes

1. I feel compelled however, to distance myself from the last few lines of Stannard's chapter in which the Native American population crash is said to be "the worst holocaust in the history of the world." In recent useage, the word "holocaust" has become widely associated with the deliberately planned extinction of the Jews of Europe by the Nazi regime. It is both ethically and theoretically important to stress that the numerically greater decline in population among postcontact Native Americans was largely an unintended consequence of the policies of the Iberian invaders. Indeed, the Spanish Crown identified its interests as much with the preservation and increase as with the exploitation of Native American peoples. Moreover, one can scarcely blame the earliest Spanish explorers of the Southeast for the firestorm of pathogens that spread in advance of their actual contact with native peoples. And finally, we do not know the proportionate contributions made by increased mortality rates versus decreased fertility rates. These are not equivalently calamitous processes.

2. Stannard uses the concept of "standard population" to explain why preindustrial populations rarely increase to more than 50 or 60 percent of apparent carrying capacity. Standard population explains nothing, however, since it posits unexplained cultural values that set acceptable limits of production and reproduction below the point at which

irreversible depletions occur. A more satisfactory solution is readily available: Human population growth is normally checked not at the limit of carrying capacity, but at the point of diminishing returns for productive and reproductive costs (see Harris 1990).

3. Galloway's failure to discuss the effect of paradigmatic principles on the distillation of reliable information from historical documents should be noted. Textual analysis is never carried out in a theoretical vacuum.

References

Chance, John
  1989 *The Conquest of the Sierra: Spaniards and Indians in Colonial Oaxaca*. University of Oklahoma Press, Norman.
Dobyns, Henry
  1983 Their Number Become Thinned: Native American Population Dynamics in Eastern North America. University of Tennessee Press, Knoxville.
Ferguson, Brian
  1989 Game Wars? Ecology and Conflict in Amazonia. *Journal of Anthropological Research* 45:179–206.
Harris, Marvin
  1971 *Culture, Man, and Nature: An Introduction to General Anthropology*. Thomas Y. Crowell, New York.
  1974 *Cows, Pigs, Wars and Witches*. Random House, New York.
  1977 *Cannibals and Kings: The Origins of Cultures*. Random House, New York.
  1979a *Cultural Materialism: The Struggle for a Science of Culture*. Random House, New York.
  1979b The Yanomamo and the Causes of War in Band and Village Societies. In *Brazil in Anthropological Perspective*, edited by M. Margolis and W. Carter, pp. 121–132. Columbia University Press, New York.
  1990 Anthropology: Ships That Crash in the Night. In *Perspectives in Social Science: The Colorado Lectures*, edited by Richard Jessor, Westview Press, Boulder, Colo., in press.
Harris, Marvin, and Eric Ross
  1987 *Death, Sex, and Fertility: Population Regulation in Pre-Industrial Societies*. Columbia University Press, New York.
Johnson, Allen, and Timothy Earle
  1987 *The Evolution of Human Society: From Foraging Group to Primitive State*. University of Stanford Press, Stanford.
Keeley, Lawrence
  1988 Hunter-gatherer Economic Complexity and "Population Pressure": A Cross Cultural Analysis. *Journal of Anthropological Archaeology* 7:373–411.
Leacock, Eleanor
  1954 *The Montagnais Hunting Territory and the Fur Trade*. American Anthropological Association, Memoir 78.
Newson, Linda
  1987 *Indian Survival in Colonial Nicaragua*. University of Oklahoma Press, Norman.
Ramenofsky, Ann
  1987 *Vectors of Death: The Archaeology of European Contact*. University of New Mexico Press, Albuquerque.
Sanders, William, and Barbara Price
  1968 *Meso-America: The Evolution of a Civilization*. Random House, New York.
Sanders, William, R. Santley, and J. Parsons
  1979 *The Basin of Mexico: Ecological Processes in the Evolution of a Civilization*. Academic Press, New York.

Service, Ellman
    1962 *Primitive Social Organization*. Random House, New York.
Smith, Marvin
    1987 *Archeology of Aboriginal Culture Change in the Interior Southeast: Depopulation during the Early Historic Period*. The University of Florida Press, Gainesville.
Speck, F. G.
    1915 The Family Hunting Band as the Basis of Algonkian Social Organization. *American Anthropologist* 13:289–305.
Wolf, Eric
    1983 *Europe and the People without History*. Viking, New York.

Contributors

Anthony P. Andrews, professor of anthropology and chair of the division of social sciences at the New College of the University of South Florida, is a Maya archaeologist with extensive field experience in the coastal archaeology of the Yucatán Peninsula. He is author of *Maya Salt Production and Trade*, coauthor of *The Ruins of Xcaret, Quintana Roo, Mexico*, and *Ecab: Poblado y Provincia del Siglo XVI en Yucatán*, and author of *Arquelogía Histórica en el Area Maya*, and *Excavaciones Arqueológicas en El Meco, Quintana Roo*.

Nancy J. Black recently completed her doctoral degree in anthropology at the State University of New York, Albany, and is an academic adviser at the University of Minnesota and adjunct assistant professor at Hamline University, St. Paul, Minnesota. Her current research interests include traditional religious beliefs and practices, and the effects of missionization on indigenous peoples of colonial and contemporary America.

Robert M. Carmack is professor of anthropology at the State University of New York, Albany, and is the current director of its Institute for Mesoamerican Studies. He has carried out over 40 months of field and archival research in Guatemala, and more recently one year of research in both Chiapas, Mexico, and Costa Rico. Among his books are *Quichean Civilization* and *The Quiché-Mayas of Utatlán*. He also served as editor for the *Har-*

vest of Violence and is currently serving as editor for a volume on the prehispanic period as part of a regional history of Central America (sponsored by FLACSO).

Dora P. Crouch is a professor emeritus, School of Architecture, Rensselaer Polytechnic Institute. She wrote *History of Architecture: Stonehenge to Skyscrapers* (1984) and is the senior author of *Spanish City Planning in North America* (1982). She is currently completing a study on ancient Greek water management and urbanization.

William Van Davidson is associate professsor of geography and anthropology at Louisiana State University, Baton Rouge, and research associate of the Instituto Hondureño de Antropología e Historia in Tegucigalpa, Honduras. He is author of *Historical Geography of the Bay Islands, Honduras* (1974) and editor of *Historical Geography of Latin America: Papers in Honor of Robert C. West* (1980). For the last two decades his research has focused on the minority populations of eastern Central America, and at the present he is in Honduras as a Fulbright scholar to study the historical ethnogeography of the country.

Henry F. Dobyns is an Americanist who has conducted research in Bolivia, Peru, Ecuador, Colombia, and Mexico as well as among various ethnic groups in the United States. His experience ranges from archeography (*Prehistoric Indian Occupation within the Eastern Area of the Yuman Complex*, 1974) to ethnohistory (*The Pima-Maricopa*, 1989), historical demography (*Spanish Colonial Tucson*, 1976), and applied policy science (*Comunidades Campesinas del Peru*, 1970; *Peasants, Power, and Applied Social Change*, edited with P. L. Doughty and H. D. Laswell, 1971).

Robert C. Dunnell is currently professor of anthropology at the University of Washington, Seattle. He has done fieldwork in many parts of the continental United States, but his principal areal interests lie in the eastern United States, particularly the Ohio and Mississippi valleys. He is the author and editor of many books and monographs and has written articles on a wide range of topics in archaeology, many emphasizing theoretical aspects.

Raymond D. Fogelson is a professor of anthropology at the University of Chicago. A specialist in social and psychological anthropology, he has conducted research on primitivism, religion, tourism, and North American Indians.

Catherine S. Fowler is professor of anthropology at the University of Nevada, Reno, and research associate in anthropology at the Smithsonian Institution. She is a specialist in hunter-gatherer studies, the ethnography and ethnobiology of the native peoples of the Desert West, and in material cultural studies and museology. She is the author of numerous papers and monographs on these topics, most recently *Tule Technology*, is associate editor of the Great Basin volume of the Smithsonian's *Handbook of North American Indians*, and is secretary-treasurer of the Society of Ethnobiology.

Don D. Fowler is Mamie Kleberg Professor of Anthropology and Historic Preservation at the University of Nevada, Reno, a research associate in anthropology at the Smithsonian Institution, and a past president of the Society for American Archaeology. He is a specialist in Great Basin archaeology, the history of anthropology, and the history of western exploration and photography. He is the author of several books and numerous monographs and articles on these topics, most recently *The Western Photographs of John K. Hillers*.

William R. Fowler, Jr., is assistant professor of anthropology and Latin American studies at Vanderbilt University. He specializes in the archaeology and ethnohistory of the late prehistoric and early colonial periods of southern Mesoamerica and lower Central America. His current research focuses on the dynamics of Spanish colonial domination of the indigenous Pipil population of western El Salvador. He is author of the book *The Cultural Evolution of Ancient Nahua Civilizations: The Pipil-Nicarao of Central America* and coeditor of the journal *Ancient Mesoamerica*.

Patricia Galloway is special projects officer at the Mississippi Department of Archives and History. Her research interests include the ethnohistory of the western Muskogean tribes, colonial French Louisiana history, and ethnohistorical epistemology, and she is working on a book on the ethnogenesis of the Choctaw Indians. The current editor of *Mississippi Archaeology* and the *MDAH Archaeological Reports* series, she has also edited *La Salle and His Legacy, Mississippi Provincial Archives: French Dominion*, vols. IV and V, and *Southeastern Ceremonial Complex: Artifacts and Analysis*.

Janine Gasco is director of research for the Institute for Mesoamerican Studies, SUNY-Albany. Her research interests include the effects of the Spanish conquest and colonization process on the Indian populations of Spanish America, particularly southern Mesoamerica. She has conducted archaeological excavations at a Colonial period town site in the Soconusco region of Chiapas, and has worked in Spanish, Guatemalan, and Mexican archives.

Elizabeth Graham is assistant professor (Canada Research Fellow) in the department of anthropology, York University (Canada), and a Research Associate at the Royal Ontario Museum. She has specialized in the Maya archaeology of Belize since 1973 and at present is directing, along with David Pendergast, archaeological excavations at the site of Marco Gonzalez, Ambergris Cay, Belize.

Marvin Harris is graduate research professor of anthropology at the University of Florida, Gainesville. He has written extensively on anthropological theory, ecology, demography, and food and culture in India, the United States, Brazil, and Mozambique. He is widely known for his book *Cultural Materialism*, which has been published in Spanish, Italian, Japanese, and Chinese. His most recent book, *Our Kind*, is being reprinted in German, Spanish, and Italian. Other recent works include *Death, Sex, and Fertility* and *Food and Evolution*.

Mary W. Helms is professor of anthropology at the University of North Carolina at Greensboro. She has authored several books and numerous journal articles on the culture history and culture patterns of the indigenous peoples of Lower Central America, most notably the Miskito of Eastern Nicargara, as discussed in *Asang: Adaptations to Culture Contact in a Miskito Community* and the Precolumbian chiefdoms of Panama on the eve of the Spanish conquest as recounted in *Ancient Panama: Chiefs in Search of Power*. Her most recent book, *Ulysses' Sail: An Ethnographic Odyssey of Power, Knowledge, and Geographical Distance*, presents an aspect of her current research, which focuses on the ideological and political significance in traditional societies of knowledge of and contact with geographical distance.

Robert M. Hill II is currently associate professor of anthropology at the University of Texas at San Antonio. He has conducted ethnographic and archaeological research among the highland Maya, in addition to his ethnohistorical work. He is currently engaged in a long-term study of the Cakchiquel Maya of Guatemala.

Ira Jacknis is a curatorial consultant for the department of African, Oceanic, and New World Art at The Brooklyn Museum. He is the author of *The Storage Box of Tradition: Museums, Anthropologists, and Kwakiutl Art, 1881–1981* (Smithsonian Institution Press) and co-author of *Objects of Myth and Memory*, an exhibition catalogue on Stewart Culins's American Indian collections at The Brooklyn Museum. His research interests include art and aesthetics, museums, the history of anthropology, visual anthropology, and American Indian (especially Northwest Coast) cultures.

Grant D. Jones is professor of anthropology and chair of the Department of Anthropology and Sociology at Davidson College. He holds research associateships at the American Museum of Natural History and the Royal Ontario Museum. He has carried out ethnographic and documentary research on the Mayas of Yucatán, Belize, and Guatemala, for which he has received fellowships from ACLA and NEH. His writings include *Anthropology and History in Yucatán* (editor, 1977), *Maya Resistance to Spanish Rule: Time and History on a Colonial Frontier* (1989), and numerous articles on Maya culture and history. He has also written on the ethnohistory of St. Catherines Island (Georgia).

Wendy Kramer, a Canadian citizen, began several years of anthropological fieldwork and archival research in Cakchiquel towns near Antigua (Guatemala) and in the national archive in Guatemala City in the late 1970s. In 1981 she moved to Seville to undertake five years of research at the Archivo General de Indias, focusing on early sixteenth-century Guatemala. In 1986, she began graduate studies in Latin American history at the University of Warwick (Great Britian), completing her doctoral dissertation, *The Politics of Encomienda Distribution in Early Spanish Guatemala, 1524–1544*, in March 1990. She now lives in London and is collaborating with W. George Lovell and Christopher H. Lutz on a guide to the historical geography of sixteenth-century Guatemala.

W. George Lovell, a native of Glasgow, Scotland, is associate professor of geography at Queen's University in Kingston, Canada. He is the author of two books, *Conquest and Survival in Colonial Guatemala* (1985) and *Conquista y cambio cultural* (1990). A volume coedited with Noble David Cook, *The Secret Judgments of God: Native Peoples and Old World Disease in Colonial Spanish America*, will be published later this year by the University of Oklahoma Press. At present he is engaged, with Christopher H. Lutz and Wendy Kramer, in the preparation of a guide to the historical geography of early colonial Guatemala.

Christopher H. Lutz is among the founders of CIRMA (Centro de Investigaciones Reginales de Mesoamérica), a social science research center located in Antigua (Guatemala) with a U.S. branch, Plumsock Mesoamerican Studies, in South Woodstock, Vermont. He is the author of *Historia sociodemográfica de Santiago de Guatemala, 1541–1773* (1982) and coeditor with Robert M. Carmack and John D. Early of *The Historical Demography of Highland Guatemala* (1982). Since 1981 he has served as editor of CIRMA's Spanish language journal, *Mesoamérica*, and is currently working, with W. George Lovell and Wendy Kramer, on a guide to the historical geography of sixteenth-century Guatemala.

Murdo J. MacLeod is Graduate Research Professor of History at the University of Florida in Gainesville. He has written extensively on colonial Central America, and on other aspects of Latin American history. Currently, he is President of the Conference on Latin American History, and Associate Editor of the *Hispanic American Historical Review*. His present research is on Indian colonial revolts in Chiapas.

David M. Pendergast is curator in charge of the department of New World Archaeology at the Royal Ontario Museum, Toronto. A Mayanist with near 30 years' experience in Belize, he has directed long-term excavations at Altun Ha and Lamanai, and is currently codirector of work at the Marco Gonzalez site on Ambergris Cay, on the country's great coral reef. His scholarly publications on the Maya now number over 125.

Timothy K. Perttula is an archaeologist with the Texas Historical Commission, Archeological Planning and Review Department, Austin. Specializing in Caddoan archaeology and ethnohistory, his research interests also include the evolution of agricultural societies in eastern North America. He has conducted excavations in northeast Texas, Oklahoma, Missouri, and the upper Midwest.

Gloria Lara Pinto is the chairperson of the Department of Historical Investigations at the Honduran Institute of Anthropology and History (IHAH), Tegucigalpa. She is author of *Beitrage zur Indianischen Ethnographie von Honduras in der 1. Halfte de 16. Jahrhunderts, unter Besonderer Berucksichtigung der Historischen Demographie* (An attempt to reconstruct the indigenous settlement pattern in the province of Honduras based upon historical sources, sixteenth century). At present she is coediting (with Kenneth Hirth of the University of Kentucky and George Hasemann of the IHAH) the results of a five-year archaeological salvage and investigation project recently completed in the El Cajon Reservoir of central Honduras. Her current interests (which were supported by a Fulbright research grant in 1987–1988) include the development of a bicultural/bilingual program for public education among the indigenous minorities in that country.

Ann F. Ramenofsky is an associate professor of archaeology at the University of New Mexico. As suggested by her recent book, *Vectors of Death: The Archaeology of European Contact*, she is interested in demography, epidemiology, archaeological method, and theory of the Contact period. Her recent fieldwork has centered on the late prehistory of Louisiana.

David E. Stannard is professor of American studies at the University of Hawai'i. A cultural and intellectual historian who has recently turned his attention to the demographic histories of indigenous peoples, his published books include *Death in America* (an edited collection of essays); *The Puritan Way of Death: A Study in Religion, Culture and Social Change; Shrinking History: On Freud and the Failure of Psychohistory;* and *Before the Horror: The Population of Hawai'i on the Eve of Western Contact.* His next book, *Many Millions Gone: Native Peoples and the Legacy of 1492,* is scheduled for publication in 1992.

William R. Swagerty, an associate professor of history at the University of Idaho, is former associate director of the D'Arcy McNickle Center for the History of the American Indian at the Newberry Library. A specialist on sixteenth-century North America, he edited *Scholars and the Indian Experience* and is a contributor to the *Handbook of North American Indians* (Smithsonian Institution) and the *Cambridge History of the Native Peoples of the Americas.*

David Hurst Thomas, a member of the National Academy of Sciences, is curator of anthropology at the American Museum of Natural History (New York). He has specialized in North American archaeology, conducting extensive research in the Great Basin and the American Southeast, including the discovery and 10-year excavation of sixteenth- and seventeenth-century Mission Santa Catalina de Guale (St. Catherines Island, Georgia). He has published four archaeology textbooks, written several dozen monographs and scientific articles dealing with archaeological method and theory, and served as general editor for *The North American Indian* (21 volumes) and *The Spanish Borderlands Sourcebooks* (30 volumes). He is a founding trustee of the Smithsonian Institution's newest museum, the National Museum of the American Indian.

David J. Weber, Robert and Nancy Dedman Professor of History at Southern Methodist University, is author or editor of 14 books, including: *The Taos Trappers: The Fur Trade in the Far Southwest, 1540–1846, Foreigners in their Native Land: Historical Roots of the Mexican Americans, New Spain's Far Northern Frontier . . . 1540–1821, The Mexican Frontier, 1821– 1846: The American Southwest under Mexico, Richard H. Kern: Expeditionary Artist in the Far Southwest, 1948–1853,* and *Myth and History of the Hispanic Southwest.* He is currently working on a history of the borderlands, "The Spanish Frontier in North America, 1513–1821."

John M. Weeks is associate librarian at the Humanities/Social Sciences Libraries and adjunct faculty member in the Department of Anthropology and Latin American studies program at the University of Minnesota. His research interests include the late prehistory and ethnohistory of southern Mesoamerica.